Christian leaders of Japan need to read Heisswolf's formative cultural analysis of contemporary culture. He makes overt religious beliefs that are typically hidden but become operational during times of illness and death. This book could reframe Christian proclamation and ministry and revitalize the church to disarm the principalities and powers.

Dr Gailyn Van Rheenen, PhD
Former Executive Director, Mission Alive
Author of *Communicating Christ in Animistic Contexts*

A virtual encyclopedia on animism and its impact on the everyday worldview and religious thinking of the Japanese. A valuable resource to be set alongside Nakamura's *Ways of Thinking of Eastern Peoples*, consulted by anyone who desires a nuanced understanding of how to bring the gospel to Japan.

Randal Gilmore, D.R.S.
Director, Word of Life, Japan
Regional Director, Word of Life, Pacific Rim

Japanese Understanding of Salvation

Langham
ACADEMIC

Japanese Understanding of Salvation

Soteriology in the Context of Japanese Animism

Martin Heißwolf

© 2018 by Martin Heißwolf

Published 2018 by Langham Academic
An imprint of Langham Publishing
www.langhampublishing.org

Langham Publishing and its imprints are a ministry of Langham Partnership

Langham Partnership
PO Box 296, Carlisle, Cumbria CA3 9WZ, UK
www.langham.org

ISBNs:
978-1-78368-370-3 Print
978-1-78368-371-0 ePub
978-1-78368-373-4 PDF

Martin Heißwolf has asserted his right under the Copyright, Designs and Patents Act, 1988 to be identified as the Author of this work.

All rights reserved. No part of this publication may be reproduced, stored in a retrieval system or transmitted, in any form or by any means, electronic, mechanical, photocopying, recording or otherwise, without the prior written permission of the publisher or the Copyright Licensing Agency.

All Scripture quotations, unless otherwise indicated, are taken from the Holy Bible, New International Version®, NIV®. Copyright ©1973, 1978, 1984, 2011 by Biblica, Inc.™ Used by permission of Zondervan.

Translated from German into English by Martin Heißwolf. All quotations from the original German edition of this book are translated into English by the author.

British Library Cataloguing in Publication Data
A catalogue record for this book is available from the British Library

ISBN: 978-1-78368-370-3

Cover & Book Design: projectluz.com

Langham Partnership actively supports theological dialogue and an author's right to publish but does not necessarily endorse the views and opinions set forth here or in works referenced within this publication, nor can we guarantee technical and grammatical correctness. Langham Partnership does not accept any responsibility or liability to persons or property as a consequence of the reading, use or interpretation of its published content.

Dedication

For my wife, Andrea

CONTENTS

List of Tables and Figures xiii

Abstract xv

Transcription and Pronunciation of Japanese Words xvii

List of Abbreviations xxi

Introduction 1

Part I: The Context of Salvation 5
1   What Is Animism? 7
    1.1 What Is a Worldview? 9
    1.2 Working Definition: Animism 10
        1.2.1 Various Characteristics of Animistic Worldviews 11
        1.2.2 Terminological Clarifications 13
    1.3 Christian Faith and Animism 15
        1.3.1 Bruce Bradshaw's *Bridging the Gap* 15
        1.3.2 Caution When Dealing with Occult Practices 19

2   Japanese Animism 21
    2.1 Japan and Animism? 21
        2.1.1 The Unanimous Judgment of Many Japanologists 22
        2.1.2 Various Other Findings Pointing towards Animism as a Basic Japanese Worldview 26
        2.1.3 Shintoism "Even Today"? 30
    2.2 The Japanese *Mana*-Concept *Ki* (気) 34
        2.2.1 Theory 34
        2.2.2 Christian Belief and the *Mana*-Concept of Japanese Animism . . 49
    2.3 The Japanese God-Concept *Kami* (神) 54
        2.3.1 Preliminary Considerations 55
        2.3.2 The Semantic Field of *Kami* (神), "god" 59
        2.3.3 Positive Encounter with the God-Concept of Japanese Animism 70
        2.3.4 Critical Encounter with the God-Concept of Japanese Animism 79
    2.4 The Japanese Soul-Concept 111
        2.4.1 Preliminary Considerations 111

2.4.2 The Model..114
2.4.3 The Word-Field *Tamashii* (魂 or 魄) (Soul)..............115
2.4.4 The Word-Field *Rei* (霊) (Spirit) / *Sudama* (魅) (Ghost).....121
2.4.5 The Word-Field *Kokoro* (心) (Heart)......................128
2.4.6 The Word-Field *Kami* (神) (god)...........................135
2.4.7 The Word-Field *Ki* (気) (Energy)..........................135
2.4.8 Comparison with the Soul-Concept of the Old Testament....139
2.4.9 Positive Encounter with the Japanese Soul-Concept.........144
2.4.10 Negative Encounter with the Japanese Soul-Concept.......149
2.5 Sociology in the Context of Japanese Animism.................151
2.5.1 Japan as Group Culture.....................................153
2.5.2 The Relationship with the *Living Dead*....................180
2.5.3 Evaluation of Some Aspects of Japanese Sociology..........190
"Ancestor Rituals" for Deceased Children..............................219

Part II: Peace as a Central Concept of Soteriology.................247

3 The Japanese Peace-Concept *Wa* (和)..............................249
3.1 Word-Field Study of *Wa* (和)...................................249
3.1.1 *Wa* (和) as Sum..252
3.1.2 *Wa* (和) as Harmony.......................................253
3.1.3 *Wa* (和) as "Non-War".....................................261
3.1.4 *Wa* (和) as Japan..262

4 The Biblical Peace-Concept..267
4.1 The Hebrew *Shalom*-Concept...................................267
4.2 The Christian Peace-Concept...................................271

Part III: Four Aspects of Salvation in the Context of Japanese Animism..275

5 The Theological Aspect of Salvation................................277
5.1 Preliminaries..279
5.2 The Experience of *Unheil* under the Theological Aspect..........280
5.2.1 The Theological Locus of Hamartiology......................281
5.2.2 "Original Sin"...282
5.2.3 "Original Sin" and the Sin of "Pre-existence of Souls".......284
5.2.4 Causes of Sin..287
5.2.5 The Nature of Sin...288
5.3 The Experience of *Heil* under the Theological Aspect............289

6 The Cosmological Aspect of Salvation..............................291
6.1 The Cosmological Aspect of Salvation in Japanese Animism.......291

	6.1.1 The Experience of *Unheil* under the Cosmological Aspect 291
	6.1.2 The Experience of *Heil* under the Cosmological Aspect 297
	6.2 Discussion with Biblical Concepts 319
	6.2.1 At the Mercy of God 319
	6.2.2 *Kingdom-Theology* and *Power Encounter* 321
	6.2.3 Divination and the Bible 325
	6.2.4 Shamanism and Church Leadership 327
	6.2.5 Apotropaic Magic and Allegiance to God 330

7 The Sociological Aspect of Salvation 331
   7.1 The Sociological Aspect of Salvation in the Context
      of Japanese Animism 331
      7.1.1 The Experience of *Unheil* under the Sociological Aspect 331
      7.1.2 The Experience of *Heil* under the Sociological Aspect 342
   7.2 Discussion with Christian approaches 344
      7.2.1 The Experience of *Unheil* under the Sociological Aspect 344
      7.2.2 The Experience of *Heil* under the Sociological Aspect 347

8 The Anthropological Aspect of Salvation 355
   8.1 The Anthropological Aspect of Salvation in the Context
      of Japanese Animism 355
      8.1.1 The Experience of *Unheil* as Impurity 356
      8.1.2 The Experience of *Heil* under the Anthropological Aspect 365
   8.2 Discussion with Christian Concepts 380
      8.2.1 The Experience of *Unheil* under the Anthropological Aspect . . 380
      8.2.2 The Experience of *Heil* under the Anthropological Aspect 382

Part IV: The Dimensions of Salvation 385

9 The Animistic Focus on Salvation in this World 387
   9.1 An Outline of *Gense Riyaku* (現世利益),
      "This-Worldly Benefits" 388
      9.1.1 Definition 388
      9.1.2 History 389
   9.2 The "Seven Auspicious Deities" *Shichifukujin* (七福神) 393
      9.2.1 *Ebisu* (恵比寿) 396
      9.2.2 *Daikokuten* (大黒天) 398
      9.2.3 *Benzaiten* (弁財天) 400
      9.2.4 *Bishamonten* (毘沙門天) 401
      9.2.5 *Juroujin* (寿老人) 404
      9.2.6 *Fukurokuju* (福禄寿) 405
      9.2.7 *Hotei Oshou* (布袋和尚) 406
      9.2.8 Summary 409

| 10 | Discussion with Christian Concepts | 411 |

    10.1 Salvation and Suffering..412
        10.1.1 Kazou Kitamori (北森嘉蔵) (1916–1998) 412
        10.1.2 Georg Friedrich Vicedom (1903–1974)................415
        10.1.3 Reflection 417
    10.2 Between "This" World and "Yonder" World 420
        10.2.1 Tokutarou Takakura (高倉徳太郎) (1885–1934)........422
        10.2.2 Masao Takenaka (竹中正夫) (1925–2006)..............424
        10.2.3 Aloysius Pieris (1934–) 425
        10.2.4 Collectivistic Concepts...........................427
        10.2.5 My Own (Preliminary) Opinion....................432
    10.3 Between "This" World and the "Coming" World 437
        10.3.1 *Aum-Shinrikyou* (オウム真理教) 439
        10.3.2 Between Eschatology as Principle and Eschatology
             as History 445
        10.3.3 Between World and Heaven.......................463
        10.3.4 My Own (Preliminary) Opinion....................468
    10.4 Between Redemption and Emancipation 471
        10.4.1 The Hubris of Feuerbach..........................472
        10.4.2 Anthropocentrism 472
        10.4.3 Horizontalism 475
        10.4.4 My Own (Preliminary) Opinion 480

| 11 | Epilogue..483 |

    11.1 Summary 483
    11.2 Critique...484
    11.3 Horizon..485

Appendix 1: Incantations for *reiki* initiation-rites 491

Appendix 2: Japanese Bible Translations and Key-References of Wolff's *Anthropologie des Alten Testaments*............................495

Appendix 3: The Incantation of the "Great Purification"...............515

Appendix 4: The "Blessings" of the *Shichifukujin* (七福神) 522

Bibliography...525

Person Index 615

Subject Index..619

Scripture Index..653

Japanese Words Index..659

List of Tables and Figures

Table 1.1 Dualistic versus Holistic Worldviews 15
Table 1.2 Draft of a "Biblical Worldview" 17
Table 2.1 Comparison of Crim's *Ramat* and Käser's Soul-Concept 30
Table 2.2 Two Radicals of the Chinese Character 神 58
Table 2.3 Word-field Study of the Japanese Soul-concept 113
Table 2.4 Division of the Meanings of Kokoro (心) 129
Table 2.5 Relationship between Collectivism and Individualism 204
Table 2.6 Rituals 235
Table 6.1 Unlucky Ages 305
Table 8.1 Sin and Defilement and Its Remedies 356
Table 8.2 Spatial Categories 380
Table 9.1 The "Seven Auspicious Deities" Grouped by
    Religious-Historical Background 394
Table 9.2 The "Seven Auspicious Deities" Grouped by
    Countries of Origin 395

Figure 1.1 Cultural Layers 9
Figure 1.2 The Modern Worldview 16
Figure 2.1 *Ki* (気) as Energy and Substance 37
Figure 2.2 Correlation of the Main Synonyms for *Kami* (神) 56
Figure 2.3 Graph of Word-field Study of the Japanese Soul-concept 114
Figure 2.4 Outline of a "Biblical" Worldview 148
Figure 2.5 Group Structure System 157
Figure 2.6 Aspects of Ancestor Veneration 181
Figure 2.7 Aspects of Ancestor Veneration
    (theology replacing worldview) 215

Figure 3.1 The Four Basic Meanings of *Wa* (和) 252
Figure 4.1 The Eschatological Dimensions of "Positive Peace" 270
Figure 8.1 Japanese Terms for "Impurity" 360
Figure 8.2 Impurity 361
Figure 8.3 Japanese Cosmological Terms Correlated to
  Greek Cosmological Terms 366
Figure 8.4 Japanese Terms for "Purification" 367

Abstract

Cosmology and sociology show that animism is the predominant worldview of Japan. Concepts of God, the issue of controlling *mana*-power, implications of the Japanese soul-concept, the orientation of the conscience, and ancestor veneration are critically discussed in relation to Christian beliefs.

When compared to the biblical concept of peace, the Japanese concept of peace shows an aesthetic bias that has to be overcome by adding the concept of justice.

Japanese soteriology has no reference to God the Creator, whose proclamation is the basis of understanding human misfortune as rebellion against God and their salvation as reconciliation with him.

Cosmologically speaking, human beings experience misfortune as fear of superhuman powers. Salvation is sought through defensive magic and fortunetelling. Christianity acknowledges security as a basic human need but seeks protection and guidance from God.

The main focus of Japanese soteriology is in the field of sociology, which in Japan also includes the relationship with the *living dead*. Misfortune is mainly experienced as shame and ostracism, salvation as rehabilitation.

Defilement of naturally good humans is a central theme in Japan's understanding of human misfortune. The Christian concept of sin, on the contrary, has a theological and an ontological dimension as well.

In Japan salvation is understood solely as this-worldly, with benefits such as health, happiness, prosperity, fertility, and longevity. But in Christianity suffering is a central theme of salvation.

An overly strong orientation on "this world" can lead to ethical shallowness, overemphasizing the "coming world" can lead to a dangerous ethical relativism. Christian soteriology must keep the tension between these two extremes.

The hope of the coming world must neither be robbed of its historical truth by its transformation into a principle, nor must it be historically ineffective.

As for humans' relationship with God, people are solely the object of God's salvation. But as for Christian acts, humans are called to act "in the Lord."

Keywords: Japan, animism, Shintoism, soteriology, peace, eudaimonia, cosmology, sociology, anthropology, eschatology

見えない幕の向こうに
　だれかが
　　微笑んでいる。

星野富弘

Mienai maku-no mukou-ni
　　dare ka-ga
　　　hohoende iru.

Behind the invisible curtain,
　　over there,
　　　somebody is smiling.
Tomihiro Hoshino (星野富弘)

Transcription and Pronunciation of Japanese Words

Transcription

The Romanization of Japanese words follows with a few exceptions the widely used Hepburn System.[1] It focuses rather on easy usability for linguistically less-educated readers than on linguistic consistency. The following tables follow the fifty-syllable system of the Japanese language.

a	ka	sa	ta	na	ha	ma	ya	ra	wa	
i	ki	shi	chi	ni	hi	mi		ri	(i)	
u	ku	su	tsu	nu	fu	mu	yu	ru		
e	ke	se	te	ne	he	me		re	(e)	
o	ko	so	to	no	ho	mo	yo	ro	-o	n

(according to Coulmas 1999, 201)

This table has to be supplemented by the following tables which show the voiced pronunciation of syllables and diphthongs as used in this book.

ga	za	da	ba
gi	ji	ji	bi
gu	zu	zu	bu
ge	ze	de	be
go	zo	do	bo

kya	sha	tya	nya	hya	mya	rya
kyu	shu	chu	nyu		myu	ryu
kyo	sho	cho	nyo	hyo	myo	ryo

gya	ja	ja	bya
gyu	ju	ju	byu
gyo	jo	jo	byo

---

1. James Curtis Hepburn (1815–1911) was an American missionary to Japan, who developed this system for his renowned Japanese-English Dictionary (Coulmas 1999, 201).

Vowels with length are transcribed as follows: a by *aa*, i by *ii*, u by *uu*, e by *ei*, the o lengthened with u by *ou*, the o lengthened with o by *oo*.

Consonants with length are transcribed as follows: k by *kk*, s by *ss*, t by *tt*, ch by *tch*, n by *nn*, m by *nm*.

Pronunciation

The consonants *k*, *s*, *sh*, *ch*, *ts*, *n*, and *m* are not voiced and not aspirated. The consonants *g*, *j*, *z*, and *b* are voiced. The following need to be mentioned:

sh in shi	strongly frontated
f in fu	not a dental-labial fricative; lips are formed as if whistling
r	as the "r" in the German Bavarian dialect, but with only one flip of the tongue (there is no good English equivalent, but the closest would be a voiceless, unaspirated "d")
w	as "w" in "water"

Vowels:

a	as "a" in "under"
i	as "i" in "in"
u	strongly frontated as the "u" in the German Saxon dialect; between "u" in "you" and the German "ü"
e	as "a" in "and" (AE)
o	Between "o" in "online" and "o" in the German "oben"
n	"n," forming the end of (English) syllables, is rendered a vowel in Japanese and has thus syllable length

The lengthened vowels *kk*, *ss*, *tt*, *tch*, *nn* and *nm* are lengthened by keeping the consonant closure until reaching double length before releasing into the following vowel, as "tt" in the Italian "spaghetti."

Timetable

The following timetable is by no means complete. It is adopted from Ehmcke and Reese (2000, 173) and extended. The division into ages follows Kimura (木村直司) (2003, 46–47). The eras referred to in this book are listed completely.

The Nonliterate, Prehistoric Age		
縄文時代	*Joumon*-Era	2500–280 BC
弥生時代	*Yayoi*-Era	300 BC–300 AC
古墳時代	*Kofun*-Era	3rd–7th century
The Age of Imperial Court Culture[2]		
奈良時代	*Nara*-Era	710–784
Age of Nobility		
平安時代	*Heian*-Era	794–1185
Middle Ages: The Warring Age		
延喜時代	*Engi*-Era	901–923
鎌倉時代	*Kamakura*-Era	1185–1333
南北朝時代	*Nanbokuchou*-Era	1336–1392
室町時代・足利時代	*Muromachi*-Era; *Ashikaga*-Era	1392–1573
安土桃山時代	*Azuchi-Momoyama*-Era	1573–1603
Age of Bourgeoisie		
江戸時代 徳川時代	*Edo*-Era *Tokugawa*-Era	1603–1867
寛文時代	*Kanbun*-Era	1661–1671
Prewar-Japan: Japan's Road to Modernity		
明治時代	*Meiji*-Era	1868–1912
大正時代	*Taishou*-Era	1912–1926
昭和時代	*Shouwa*-Era (pre-war)	1926–1945
Postwar-Japan: Democratization of Japan		
昭和時代	*Shouwa*-Era (post-war)	1945–1988
平成時代	*Heisei*-Era	from 1989

---

2. This age can be divided in its early stage (646–709), also referred to as the *Asuka*-Era (飛鳥時代) (538–710), and its later stage (710–793).

List of Abbreviations

AEM	Arbeitskreis Evangelikaler Missionen
AEPM	Allgemeiner Evangelisch-Protestantischer Missionsverein
AERA	*Asahi Shinbun* Extra Research and Analysis (Magazine)
AFEM	Arbeitskreis für evangelikale Missiologie e.V.
ARD	Arbeitsgemeinschaft der öffentlich-rechtlichen Rundfunkanstalten der Bundesrepublik Deutschland
ATD	Altes Testament Deutsch
CBS	Columbia Biblical Seminary
CCA	Christian Conferences of Asia
CPI	Church Planting Institute
DOMEI	Abbreviation of *Nihon Doumei Kirisuto Kyoudan* (日本同盟基督教団); Japanese Alliance-Christian Denomination
EKK	Evangelisch-katholischer Kommentar zum Neuen Testament
EMM	Evangelisches Missionsmagazin
FHM	Freie Hochschule für Mission (Akademie für Weltmission)
IBC	Intercultural Book Company (publisher)
IMC	International Missionary Council
JEMA	Japan Evangelical Missionary Alliance
LDP	Liberal Democratic Party (of Japan)
MBB	Muslim Background Believer
NHK	*Nippon Housou Kyoku* (日本放送局); Japanese Broadcasting Station
OAG	Ostasien Gesellschaft
ÖRK	Ökumenischer Rat der Kirchen
PHP	Peace and Happiness through Prosperity (Institute)
RGG	Religion in Geschichte und Gegenwart
STM	Systematisch-theologische Monographien
TEAM	The Evangelical Alliance Mission (Wheaton, Illinois)
TRE	Theologische Realenzyklopädie

Introduction

1.1 Purpose of this book

The first purpose of this book is to show that the dominating worldview of Japan is animistic. The Japanese *mana*-concept *ki* (気), the Japanese concept for God/god(s), *kami* (神), as well as the animistic influence on Japanese society, are the proof. These findings will be critically discussed in the light of Christian core beliefs.

The second purpose of this book is to relate these findings with the Christian and animism-influenced Shintoist core values – "salvation" and "peace" – in a missiologically adequate and praxis-oriented way and further discuss them critically.

1.2 Necessity of this book

Many reasons have been given to explain the fact that "Christianity has largely been rejected in Japan" (Mullins 1998, 167): (1) the Japanese are too nationalistic (Lea in IFon 1993, 120),[1] (2) they think too abstractly and have no use for the practical teachings of Christianity (Ishizaka 2009, 24), (3) they recognize Christianity as a religion prohibiting loyalty and piety (Ishizaka 2009, 25; Cary 1995, 162;[2] Lea in Ion 1993, 120), and (4) they have a deeply rooted dislike for organized religion (Lee 1995, 109). I believe the main reason is found in Japan's this-worldly orientation as a distinctive feature of Animism. As early as 1905, Arthur Lea wrote: "For the first time in history a nation educated according to naturalistic principles is asked to accept Christianity with its doctrine of the supernatural" (Lea in Ion 1993, 120). Similarly, pastors in an 1882 questionnaire named "the supernatural elements in Christianity" as an obstacle for its acceptance in Japan (Cary 1995, 161). This "this-worldly" orientation is particularly apparent in the Japanese understanding of salvation.

---

1. Lea said, Christianity "does not amalgamate with the spirit of Japanese nationalism" (*kokutai-ni awanai,* 国体に合わない).

2. Quoting the responses of ten Japanese pastors in a 1882 questionnaire.

As old as this knowledge is – at least among Japanese scholars – it has been rarely recognized in missiology and missionary praxis. Instead, Christianity has been promoted in dialogue with Buddhism. Buddhism however has largely the function of a nominal high-religion in present-day Japan.[3] A Christianity promoting itself in dialogue with, and as a potential substitute for, Buddhism faces the danger of being recognized as a high-religion itself, never reaching down into the deep layers of (animistic) folk religion and becoming a "split-level Christianity" (Jaime Bulatao).

Accepting animism as Japan's ruling worldview framework of understanding, and using the new interpretation in a (hopefully) more competent communication of the Christian message, is long overdue.

1.3 Current state of research

Even though the majority of Japanologists implicitly describe animistic elements in the Japanese wordview, and even though mainly native Japanese scholars explicitly refer to Japan's traditional worldview as "animistic" or "animatistic," there are to my knowledge no publications which:

- explicitly and consequently explain and outline other topics than the traditional religiosity by using animistic paradigms;
- relate their findings with research done in other animistic cultures;
- seriously discuss the Christian message in dialogue with Japanese animism, engage in encounter with it, humbly learn from it, and objectively and in a fair way contradict it.

1.4 Methodology

The subject of research fashions the method of research – *Der Stoff macht die Methode*. In Japan this implies two things:

First, the subject of research is mainly nonliterate folklore. Thus the appropriate method of obtaining data is listening. I have been living in Japan since 1991, spending about two decades listening. By "listening" I mean:

---

3. The "osmotic" Japanization of Buddhism together with the "Buddhification" of the native Shintoism (Küng and Bowden 2006, 150) is according to my observations more and more merely a matter of formality.

- listening without (conscious) evaluation or judging;
- "*be-greifen*" (understanding, grasping) with Japanese "*Begrifflichkeit*" (terminology);
- verifying the data obtained by listening by confirming discussion with others.

Nonliteracy does not mean speechlessness. The Japanese worldview has fashioned and influenced the Japanese language. I therefore frequently use the method of word-field study.

Second, secondary literature has to be included in the research. Secondary literature means old literature – historiography, legal documents, edicts, prayers, mythology, poetry, and fairytales. Secondary literature also means modern literature – psychological literature, Japanese research on mythology, as well as the ever growing genre of self-describing Japanism. There is no nation that writes more about itself than Japan. The best-known representatives are Doi (土居健郎) and Nakane (中根千枝).

I have always pursued the strategy of combining both methods; I have sought to verify my findings from discussions with the research of others; and I have sought to bring back what I have read in literature to discussion with my friends who helped me to verify and meaningfully relate my findings.

Part I

The Context of Salvation

The worldview of Japan is predominantly influenced by Shintoism[1] and is animistic (Shimazono 1999, 89; Makimoto 2006, 71). Käser (2004, 22) and Dülfer and Jöstingmeier (2008, 312) also connect Shintoism and Animism. Pieris (55) explicitly calls the religion of the *kami* (神), the Japanese gods, that is Shintoism, a "cosmic religion." Pieris uses "cosmic" as a substitute term for "animistic." And by calling the "spiritual connectedness" of all people and things an element of the Shintoist faith, De Mente does the same. He refers to *musubi* (結び, 掬び) as the Japanese special term which describes the undifferentiated co-existence of humans, nature and gods (De Mente 1994, 33).

---

1. "Shintoism" is the term for the traditional religiosity of Japan. It is very complex. Tsuda divides as follows: (1) folk customs of Japan, handed down from old ages as religious (and magical) beliefs; (2) authority, power, deeds of a deity, its rank as deity, or the deity itself; (3) ideas enriched with mythological material, ideas or teachings with a theological approach; (4) the particular non-theological teachings of each shrine, which form its core and determines its propagation; this group is the same as group "3" but the teachings came into being in connection with the particular shrine; (5) Shintoism as "way of the gods" meaning the model typical for Japan's politics and morals; a term created to describe the way of the Confucian saints, and the way of the holy rulers; this kind of Shintoism was most frequent among the scholars of the Tokogawa-Era; one example is the *sumekami-no michi* (皇神の道), "the way of the divine emperor"; (6) sect-*Shintou* (Mitsuhashi 2007, 19–20). Pye opposes the term "Shintoism," because the suffix "ism" suggests an ideology. He suggests using *Shintou* (神道) instead (Pye 2001, 4). I use "Shintoism" because it is widely acknowledged and used.

1

What Is Animism?

Summary: In this book animism is used as a term which describes a worldview, that is, a framework which helps to understand this world. In the wordview of animism there exists a world, unseen to the human eye, which exists next to and together with the visible world.

Typical characteristics of animistic worldviews are the coexistence of material and immaterial things and beings, holism, as well as the tendency to explain "natural" events "spiritually."

When it comes to the understanding of reality, animistic wordviews are closer to the Bible than secular Christian worldviews. They need to be substituted with the teaching of God as the Creator, who is not part of this world.

Apart from wildly populist notions – Bloch for instance equates animism with "belief in ghosts" (1982, 802) – the term "animism" is even used in a rather diverse scientific way and therefore prone to misunderstandings.[1]

---

1. Harvey gives a good introduction into the history of the term "animism," taking up the contributions of Stahl (vitalism), Hume (sentiments), Frazer (*The Golden Bough*), Tylor (development of religions), Huxley (antagonism against Stahl's vitalism), Marett (impersonal powers), Freud (projections), Durkheim and Lévy-Strauss (totemism), Mauss (gift-exchanging among the Maori), Piaget (development, animism in early childhood), Guthrie (anthropomorphism), de Quincey (philosophical panpsychism), Hallowell (other-than-human persons of the Ojibwe), Kohák (personalism of the Ojibwe), Goodhall (culture among animals), Garuba (animistic realism in African, South-American, and Indian literature), Quinn ("leavers"), Bird-David, Abram, Plumwood and others (*Environmentalists' Participation*) (Harvey 2005, 3–29).

The term "animism" was coined by Edward Burnett Tylor (1832–1917)[2] who speculated that the human race in its earliest stage interpreted the pictures they saw in their dream as impressions of a "soul," *anima* (therefore "animism"), wandering about;[3] that not only humans but animals and things had such an *anima* as well; that these "soul-concepts" were developed into concepts of spirits, gods, and eventually the idea of one God (Priest 2000, 63; Käser 2004, 21–22).

Today the term animism is considered obsolete in religious science. As a classificatory term, it was, under the influence of Tylor, Frazer, and others (Hiebert et al. 1999, 28), exchanged for the term "primitive religiosity."[4] I do not favor this term because it suggests that this kind of religiosity is the root of all religions. Others call animism an early yet not original form of religiosity.[5] Pieris therefore speaks in favor of using "cosmic religion" rather than using "animism" (Pieris 1988, 71).

As a descriptive term, "animism" was replaced by terms such as "folk religion," "spiritism," "tribal religions" (Hesselgrave 1978, 148),[6] and in Africa by "traditional religion" (Greschat 1992, 23). In this book, the term "animism" is not used as a term of religion science, but drawing on Käser, as a term that describes worldviews (Käser 2004, 27).

---

2. On the evolutionary approach of Tylor, presently discussed controversially, see Saler (1997).

3. The term "double" is better that the term "soul" because it neutrally describes what various cultures express in ways which are at times rather confusing for outsiders. Examples: The "double" of the Algonkins, the Tasmans and the Quiche is called "shadow of the human"; the Californian Indians call it "breath" (Hiebert et al. 1999, 59); the Ainu, Japan's indigenous people call it *ramat* (Crim 1981, 17). The term "double" also suggests that there is a certain familiarity between the visible body and the invisible "double." The Hurons (Wyandot People) in America, the indigenous people of British-Columbia, the Ainu and many peoples in Africa depict the "double" as a miniature of the human (Gilmore 1919, ch. 3). Thurn postulates that in animism, "that all tangible objects, animate . . . and inanimate alike, consist each of two separable parts – a body and a spirit; and that these are not only always readily separable involuntarily, as in death, and daily in sleep, but are also, in certain individuals, always voluntarily separable" (Thurn in Gilmore 1919, ch. 1).

4. "Primitive" does not in this case mean "inferior" or "base." Sometimes animism is rated that way (Taber 1981, 37). The contrary is true. Greschat wrote about African animism: "That African religion should be 'primitive' is only a prejudice. In reality African religion presents a mature and well-balanced belief system, which earns the respect of all" (Greschat 1992, 23). "Primitive" as it is used here means "original."

5. According to them, before "animism" there was "naturism" and "dynamism" (Gilmore 1919, ch. 1). Together with Hiebert, Shaw, and Tiénou (1999, 76), Huber (1992, 670), Käser (2004, 22), and Schreiter (2004b, 49) I reject this notion of animism.

6. Animistic worldviews cannot be limited to "tribal cultures." Hesselgrave admits that this kind of worldview is present in Japan, however only in the "traditional" Japan (1978, 150, 154).

1.1 What Is a Worldview?

A worldview is a model or a matrix that determines how people think rather than what people think. "Religion," on the other hand, is a term that describes the content of worldviews. Hiebert (2002) distinguished worldview from religion by using his layer-model. Similarly Hisakazu Inagaki (稲垣久和) described culture as an onion, the skin being the upper layers of Hiebert's model, and the core being the worldview (Inagaki 1990, 8).[7] Systems of thought and belief define what people think and believe. Worldviews define how or in which way people think (Hiebert 2000). Worldviews are, so to speak, "glasses" (Nash 1992, 19, 24)[8] through which people perceive and interpret the world (Hiebert 2002).

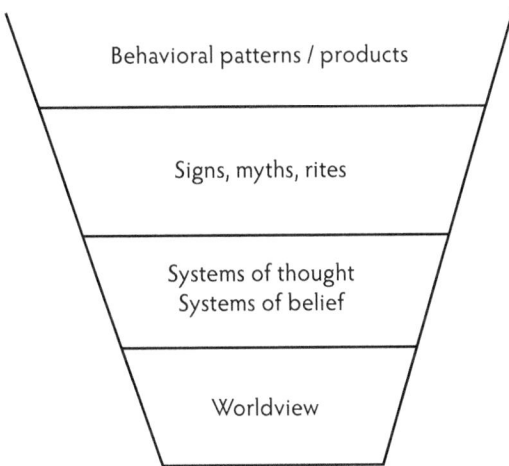

Figure 1.1 Cultural Layers (according to Hiebert, 2002)

---

7. Similar to Hiebert, Kraft also calls the worldview the core of a certain culture (Nishioka 1998, 459).

8. According to Nash, Schreiter explained that as people do not recognize they are wearing good glasses, people are also not aware of their own worldview. According to Lévy-Strauss, indigenous people are not able at all to understand their own culture (Schreiter 2004a, 41). According to Hiebert, the basic presuppositions of a worldview are taken for granted and never questioned (Nishioka 1998, 459).

Inagaki defined the term "worldview" thus:

> We start from the position that "neutral facts" do not exist. That is, the phenomena that occur in the real world are recognized by the observer as "facts" only when the conceptual schemes giving them meaning are in place. Observations, far from being an exact duplicate of neutral facts, actively construct facts according to conceptual scheme.[9] If the observation itself is part of a specific theoretical mold, it is impossible to use neutral observation to prove the theory or basic outlook. Within the system itself statements or facts can be verified using the logic within the conceptual scheme. When the conceptual theme includes the three basic relations of god, humans, and nature then it is called a worldview. Since a worldview includes a relationship to God (or a god), it is essentially religious rather than theoretical. (Inagaki 1990, 8–9)

Thus Inagaki has also explained why it is so difficult to distinguish worldviews from religions. The kind of religiosity which shows the background of animism most clearly is the religiosity of folk religions. Together with Katsumoto (勝本正實) (1992, 36) I distinguish these folk religions from the (falsely) so-called "high-religions."

1.2 Working Definition: Animism

In this book "animism" is used to describe a worldview that understands this world as a fabric of visible and invisible things and beings. Käser states five characteristics of animistic worldviews:[10]

- Material things and beings exist.
- Immaterial (spirit-like) things and beings exist.

---

9. Inagaki heavily leans on the Sapir-Whorf-hypothesis. "Language shows how people view reality. Nobody encounters reality ... objectively. Everybody perceives reality with his own understanding of reality, shaped by his own culture" (Figel 1994, 7).

10. At first sight this definition has nothing in common with what Inagaki named as crucial characteristics of a worldview, because Käser does not mention "God" or "gods." But the contradiction is only outward. Käser uses "immaterial beings" instead of "God" or "gods." His terminology is wider and less determining. Also Käser does not use the term "religion," whereas Inagaki states that worldviews are basically religious. But Inagaki uses the term "religious" not as the opposite of "profane" but as the opposite of "theoretical." And finally, animistic worldviews do not distinguish between the profane and the religious (Hiebert and Meneses 1995, 62; Pachuau 2006, 42).

- Material and immaterial things and beings co-exist in time and space.[11]
- Material and immaterial things and beings interact.
- "In a world thus fashioned a principle called *mana* exists that can exert extraordinary effects" (Käser 2004, 65).[12]

1.2.1 Various Characteristics of Animistic Worldviews

1.2.1.1 Co-existence of material and immaterial things and beings

Material and immaterial things and beings co-exist in time and space. They can exist independently,[13] or they can be connected. This is particularly true for the (soul-) double. The so-called "pan-animation of nature"[14] assigns to all purely material things "spirit-like doubles." The material part and the immaterial part belong closely together, but can at the same time be separated as well. When for example, material things lose their immaterial double, they can more easily be broken or they are ineffective. Also the immaterial double of a human can be far away during dreams or when a shaman sends one of his souls away for investigation. However, if the double does not find its way back, the human is in grave danger. Shamans have several doubles and can therefore afford to send one away (Käser 1995). Depending on the culture, other humans can also have several doubles (Gilmore 1919, ch. 3).[15]

---

11. "Animism is the belief in spirit-like beings" states Vivelo (259) briefly and concisely, but his definition lacks comprehensiveness. From African cosmologies can be learned that the whole cosmos is divided into "two inter-penetrating and inseparable, yet distinguishable, parts" (Okorocha in Larbi 2002, 89).

12. These characteristics are defined very broadly, paying tribute to the vast plurality of animistic worldviews. Käser even talks about "animism-complexes" (2004, 7.13).

13. Spirits may in a previous stage of the existence have been humans (Eberhard 1983, 103–104), they may even now and then manifest materially (Klaes 2000, 546) and influence the material world, yet they exist independently from material things.

14. "*Allbeseelung der Natur*."

15. Steyne called animism "spiritual" (63–64), yet "spiritual" does not mean "belonging to another world." Warneck (1913, 135), defying this misunderstanding, classified the "*Seelenstoff*," the "stuff," from which the immaterial double is made as "material." This is yet another example of the uselessness of Western terminology when describing animism.

The German "*Seele*" and the English "soul" have their pre-Christian history in the old German word *sé(u)la*, which means "those belonging to the lake." The old Germanic tribes envisioned the souls of the unborn children as living in the "lake" (German *See*) (Wernhart 2002, 46). Others thought that the "lake" was the dwelling place of the souls of the dead (Klein 2002, 27).

1.2.1.2 Holism

Another characteristic of animistic worldviews is that they do not distinguish between "this world" and "yonder world" and thus do not distinguish between the religious and the profane. Rohrbach calls this a "peculiar being interwoven" (39, 41). Even back in 1891 Chamberlain (143) judged, "Not religion only, but every art here is or has been esoteric – poetry, music, porcelain-making, fencing, even bone-setting, and cookery itself." Steyne (62) explained this holistic unity as follows: "The animist does not distinguish between the holy and the profane, between the secular and the religious, between his vocation and his responsibility toward society. They all belong to an 'interconnected entity.'"[16] This "being interwoven," this "whole," can be seen in various areas:

- Unity of the "secular" and the "sacral":

    The worldview of tribal cultures often (not always) transcends the border between secular and sacral, which is an important part of Western thinking. This unity is mainly occupied with gods, spirits and ghosts, but is also substantially anthropocentric (and ethnocentric).[17] It brings together the nature and supernatural in a peculiar mixture. It brings together space and time in an inseparable mixture, cementing this world and the other into one system (according to Hesselgrave 1978, 149).

    In most societies religion is not just one part but all areas of life have a religious dimension (Bock 1979, 231). "In secluded cultures … the term 'religion' is not necessary, if these cultures are based on a universal worldview. The term 'religion' is only necessary when secular trends occur" (Lanczowski in a discussion documented by Koslowski 1985, 243).[18]

---

16. Weiming (5) judges similarly when he states that traditional Chinese and Asian worldviews do not distinguish between religion and philosophy.

17. Therefore, Käser recommends to start with the concept of humankind when studying animistic worldviews (2004, 37–38).

18. Langczkowski in the discussion following Mtumba Tshiamalenga's lecture *Mythos und Religion in Afrika heute.*

- Unity of science and faith: Distinguishing between science and faith is a Western phenomenon,[19] which is absent from all other cultures (Hiebert et al. 1999, 35).
- Unity of the world of the living and the world of the *living dead*: Likewise the world of the living and the dead belong together inseparably. Therefore the community with the deceased, the *living dead*, is of crucial importance (Steyne 1993, 64–65).

1.2.1.3 "Spiritual" explanation for "natural" events

The third characteristic is that within an animistic worldview people always seek "spiritual" explanations for "natural" events (Steyne 1993, 41–42), because immaterial things and beings influence material things and beings. In a mythical worldview, "there is no event in the world" not caused by some kind of action in the spiritual world (Klein 2002, 29). This kind of "heteronomy" can go so far that the individual has almost no "free will" left (van Rheenen 1996, 98). But not only immaterial things and beings influence the material world, the opposite is also true. Many practices of folk religions influenced by animisms are occupied with finding and controlling the powers of the immaterial world (Steyne 1993, 39–40, 63–64). Specialists are mostly shamans who find it easier than other people to access the immaterial world, because they have two or more "spiritual doubles."[20]

1.2.2 Terminological Clarifications

Because the term "animism" is broadly used and also has a long history many wrong conceptions have been associated with it. It is therefore important to differentiate:

- When we call the immaterial world "supernatural" (Steyne 1993, 63–64), it only means that it can neither be described nor controlled by means of the material or "natural" world. Contrasting "natural" and "supernatural" is rejected by Käser for anthropological reasons (Käser 1995; 2004, 72), and by Noble for theological reasons (Noble

---

19. "The Western civilization is the *only* one which is explicitly *non-religious*, or post-religious. This is the basic difference between the West and other civilizations" (Kurth in Jost 2004, 9).

20. While shamans want to use their skills mostly for the good of others there are also others who use their knowledge for example in witchcraft to harm others. Therefore people always consider the influence of witchcraft in cases of suspicious deaths and all sickness (Käser 1995).

1996, 189). When I use the term "supernatural," nevertheless, I write it with inverted commas.

- The fact is that among the "spirit-like" beings and things in animism (Grunlan and Mayers 1981, 240) not only impersonal powers (Steyne 1993, 38) and spirits and ancestors exist, but also "various gods" (Gates 1979, 6) and even a High-God (Steyne 1993, 38) which can be very confusing. These beings have nothing in common with the "God" of the Bible. Gods and spirits of animistic worldviews do not belong to another world. They are an "interwoven and essential part of this world" (Hoffmann 2007, 74). The God of the Bible on the contrary is not part of this world, not even part of its "immaterial" or invisible part.

- Often animism is considered the "occult" (Käser 2004, 28–30). "Occult" means "hidden" (Rohrbach 1985, 93; Wright 1974, 18). Practitioners of occult practices try to access the "supernatural" world and gain control over it (Moreau 2000, 702). Technically speaking, it is therefore correct to call animism part of the occult. It is concerned about things and beings that are not accessible by means of the material world. In this sense Fasching contrasts our Western "scientific worldview" with "occult realities,"[21] which as "special paradigms" are "cultural-historically interesting" (Fasching 2000, 10). Likewise Susumu Shimazono (1999, 108) (島薗進) claims that there is a close connection between occultism and animism. However, since the term "occultism" also carries a strongly devaluating tone (Hasenfratz 1992, 479) it can only be used with caution. The judgment of Warneck (1913, 124–125), who equated

---

21. Fasching uses the term "reality" ("*Wirklichkeit*") developed in *Das Kaleidoskop der Wirklichkeiten* (1999). He defines: "'Oneself' never belongs to reality, always stands outside. One stands outside and has command over a more or less wide range of different panorama-like realities, in which one can find orientation and help for living. Each one of the realities one belongs to shows a particular part of the Source of Being, of Existence itself. Realities are always something which came into being later; they constitute a paradigm, a specific construct" (Fasching 2000, 5). Using the so-called "scientific" worldview, Fasching shows how such paradigms come into being: "By systematically cutting out large portions of this reality of life, natural science turns to a narrowed horizon, in a specific way takes up only certain elements of experience, and using a specific method structures them into the reality of natural science" (6). The variety of paradigmatical construct, lined up side by side without any priority can be advantageous, because different realities offer instructions for goal-oriented action. Different ways offer alternatives which are valuable in times when realities used until then are not helpful anymore. As an example Fasching mentions "realities of traditional medicine" (8).

"occult" with "diabolic,"[22] conveys a distorted understanding of animism (Käser 2004, 24–26).

1.3 Christian Faith and Animism
1.3.1 Bruce Bradshaw's Bridging the Gap

Bradshaw's *Bridging the Gap: Evangelism, Development and Shalom, Innovations in Missions* (1996), based on Hiebert's model for distinguishing different worldviews can be very helpful here:[23]

Table 1.1 Dualistic versus Holistic Worldviews (according to Bradshaw 1996, 26)

Dualistic Worldviews	Holistic Worldviews
God angels, gods, demons	The Highest Being
	spirits, ancestors, powers
nature, matter, humans	humans
	nature, matter

According to Hiebert, the Western worldview in the sixteenth century was fashioned after Cartesian dualism. Dualistic worldviews have two separate, diametrically opposed realms. The upper realm is usually called "transcendence," the lower "immanence." The classification into a spiritual sphere (God, angels, demons) and a physical sphere (humans, matter) is also widely used (Bradshaw 1996, 25). It can be traced back as far as Thomas Aquinas (Van Rheenen 2003a).

Holistic worldviews do not separate the "one world." They only classify various yet connected spheres or "stories" (Bradshaw 1996, 25). The middle

---

22. In criticizing animism Warneck repeatedly overreaches in a rather offensive way. However his work *Lebenskräfte des Evangeliums: Missionserfahrungen innerhalb des animistischen Heidentums* offers rich material.

23. Later Hiebert developed his analysis of worldviews considerably introducing the distinction between "organic" and "mechanical" concepts. The analytical methods developed in *Understanding Folk Religion* (Hiebert et al. 1999, from page 45) can be used not only for animistic worldviews but for others as well. However, for comparing animistic, Western, and biblical worldviews the basic model is more helpful.

part of these worldviews is not found in dualistic worldviews. Hiebert therefore calls it the "excluded middle."[24]

> Belief in the middle level – in this-worldly spirits, magic, witchcraft, and evil eye – began to die out in the nineteenth century with the spread of Enlightenment thinking based on Platonic dualism and science based on materialistic naturalism. The result was the secularization of science and the mystification of religion. Science dealt with the empirical world … Religion was brought in to deal with miracles and exceptions to the natural order. (Hiebert et al. 1999, 89; similarly, Rohrbach 1985, 34)

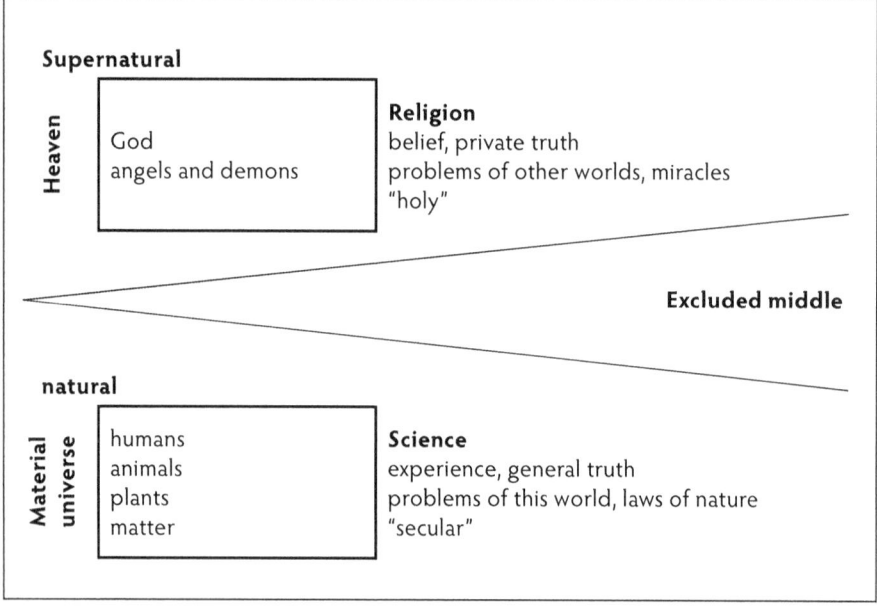

Figure 1.2 The Modern Worldview (according to Hiebert 2000)

---

24. Hiebert coined this term in *The Flaw of the Excluded Middle* (1982): "I had excluded the middle level of supernatural, both this-worldly beings and forces, from my own world view. As a scientist I had been trained to deal with the empirical world in naturalistic terms. As a theologian, I was taught to answer ultimate questions in theistic terms. For me the middle zone did not really exist." Hiebert concluded this was why he did not have answers for the Indian villagers (1982, 43).

In the present, the "worldview of the West," widely and without deeper reflection accepted as "biblical worldview," exists almost only in the form of secularism. Schaeffer says this is due to the separation of "nature" and "grace": "Nature, having been made autonomous, has eaten up both grace and freedom. An autonomous lower story will always eat up the upper" (Schaeffer 2006, 16). The upper realm of dualistic worldviews has been separated, its result being "materialistic monism" (Hiebert et al. 1999, 89). Subsequently secularism has to interpret things which cannot be explained by means of natural science as "para-psychological." "Today we know that dualism is based on projecting the two poles of the psyche, I and Self. Mysterious contents appear as transcendent, the obvious finds its place in the immanent" (Kaufmann 2006, 26). The so-called parapsychology is but a "story" added on top of secularism.[25]

This trend has influenced the so-called "Christian worldview" as well, one result being the fact that many Christians cannot understand the existence of demons on one side nor the miracles reported in the New Testament on the other. One part of western Christianity can be classified as secularist. The other adheres to dualistic thinking. According to Bradshaw's judgment, "dualistic theism" separates creation into a "physical" and a "spiritual" sphere (1996, 27).

On the other hand, dualistic worldviews cannot be called "biblical" either. God does not, along with "angels, gods, and demons," belong to the invisible world (Deppe and Deppe 2002, 191). According to the Bible, they belong to creation whereas God is the Creator (Hiebert et al. 1999, 35).

Table 1.2 Draft of a "Biblical Worldview"

God

gods, angels, demons, spirits, ancestors, powers
humans, nature, matter

The Bible has both elements, that of modern theistic dualism, and that of holism. It can therefore "bridge the gap" between them (Bradshaw 1996, 32). The Hebrew-holistic worldview distinguishes between God Creator on one side and the creation with angels, demons, humans, animals, plants, and matter on the other (34). Judging from the separation into two realms, the biblical worldview bears a formal resemblance to dualistic worldviews. The resemblance however is only formal, because in the Bible the border runs somewhere else. It does not separate the "visible" from the "invisible" world,

---

25. For the connection between occultism and parapsychology see Hasenfratz (1992, 479).

nor the "physical" from the "spiritual" sphere. It draws the line between the Creator and creation. That means that according to the Christian faith God and world are categorically different. "The Christian faith considers God and world as distinct entities. They are different not quantitatively nor qualitatively but categorically" (Härle 1995, 411–413). The Bible offers a third worldview, neither secular nor animistic. Christians take the biblical reference concerning God, angels, Satan, and demons very seriously. Yet they focus their theology not on their needs and desires (as secularism and animism do) but on God and his deeds (Sharrock 2007, 303).

Jorissen claims that the opposites – "immanence" and "transcendence" – only make sense if we think of them as separate realms.

> Creation (as act) constitutes the world as the non-Divine per se, and as the non-Divine infinitely different from God … because there is nothing between "created" and "uncreated." Here only pure disjunction rules. The transcendence of God means God's absolute superiority over the world, his infinite difference in essence. (Jorissen 1992, 679)

Thus the biblical worldview is unique. It stands in stark contrast to the holistic worldview. God and world are categorically different. But at the same time, it stands in stark contrast to the dualistic worldview of the "Christian" West. The biblical classification of the different realms of creation resembles that of holistic worldviews. I am even convinced that holistic worldviews – and that means animistic worldviews – are much closer to the Bible in their interpretation of creation than dualistic worldviews.

Here I wish to distance myself from Wellhausen's assumptions – he wants to see signs of animism in the earliest stages of Hebrew religion (Harrison 1969, 353). The worldview of the Bible is closer to animism than to the Western worldview. However, that does not mean that animism, interpreted by Wellhausen as a religion (rudiments of Arab heathen paganism), constitutes the origin of Old Testament religion. Harrison gives a good introduction into Wellhausen and his successors' theory (Harrison 1969, 353–361), and in his critique traces his theory back to the evolutionism of his days (381).[26] He also proves that Wellhausen's choice of archeological material was not careful.

---

26. Peters (1972, 107) mentions David Humes and his premise that the perfect is always developed from the imperfect. He judges that this premise is not valid for the Bible which starts and ends with monotheism. According to Whiteman (2003, 400), anthropology recovered from this evolutionistic obsession at the beginning of the twentieth century.

According to Harrison, animism as a religion had vanished centuries before the biblical patriarchs came onto the stage of history (383).

1.3.2 Caution When Dealing with Occult Practices

Just as close as the animist interpretation of creation may be to the "biblical" worldview, so stark is the contrast when it comes to evaluating occult practices. There are two reasons why, from a Christian viewpoint, occult practices are to be avoided:

- Because "Good and Evil" can hardly be distinguished in animism (Käser 1995). Good and evil influences from the "unseen world" cannot be distinguished either. Therefore it is better to avoid occult practices for safety's sake. I certainly do not concur with Fasching when he almost forcefully demands the "plurality of paradigmatic constructs being unbiasedly on equal footing" (Fasching 2000, 8). Fasching is right when with regard to the Western "scientific" worldviews he warns against the "absolutizing" of a single reality (10). That cannot mean however that Christians must refrain from any kind of critique. The protection of "operational leeway for alternative action" (10) must not blindly throw the gates wide open for evil.
- On the other hand, as important as caution is, it must never lead to fear of evil powers. There is also danger in a negative involvement with evil powers. Exploring, explaining, exposing, and judging evil can easily become sensationalist fascination with evil. Evil powers, however powerful they may be, have only delegated authority and can only act within the will of God, under his permission (God "gave them up"; Rom 1:24) or under his direct command (e.g. 1 Kgs 22:22–23; 2 Chr 18:21–22). The One who truly is to be feared is the living God, because he alone holds all power in his hands.

The decisive rejection of all occult practices and even questionable things related must not lead to a Christian witness that has nothing to say about the "excluded middle." Christians must have answers in the field of occult practices, parapsychological phenomena, ancestor veneration, fear of powers, and the fear of the future. Otherwise these subjects go underground and Christianity becomes "Christianized paganism,"[27] invisible to the public eye under the guise of orthodoxy (Hiebert et al. 1999, 13, 19). The surrender to God in all areas of life becomes impossible[28] and Father Jaime Bulatao's "split-level Christianity" (1966) is furthered.[29]

---

27. Friedrich Pfister talks about a "religion of the deep" (Langczkowski in a discussion documented by Koslowski 1985, 244).

28. Schiller (2007) gave a good example from an African country: Christians went to the hospital for the treatment of symptoms and afterwards to the traditional expert for clarification of the spiritual reasons of their disease.

29. According to Dijkstra, the phenomenon of "split-level Christianity" is much older than Christianity. The average Jew was probably not as pious as one might think while reading the Old Testament. Outside the official cult worshipping, lower deities and ancestors and the belief in good and evil demons may have also been important in the familial cult (Dijkstra 2001, 167). The *Teraphim* (as in Jacob's family) come to mind, which Albertz understands as familial patron deities or "lower deities" (Albertz 1992, 64–65). Albertz et al. talk about "unconscious syncretism": "On the familial level the practical henolatry lacks any demarcation and exclusiveness. The concept of god is functional. That means the divine functions remain constant even if the gods change. When choosing their gods the family adapts to their religious and cultic context . . . It was not before the end of the monarchial era that Jahwe became a natural familial deity; until then it was no problem that families worshipped other gods (Jer 2:27). It didn't pose a problem to the practitioners" (Albertz et al. 2003, 363).

2

Japanese Animism

Summary: Käser's general characteristics of animistic worldviews are valid for the worldview of Japanese animism even in today's Japan. This is especially true for the Japanese *mana*-concept *ki* (気), the Japanese god-concept *kami* (神), the Japanese soul-concept, as well as for the animistic influence on the sociology of Japan.

2.1 Japan and Animism?

Summary: Counter to common ideas, the Japanese worldview is, according to many Japanologists, animistic. Singular observations such as the "spiritual" explanation of "natural" events, notions of a world seen as formed of many layers and the soul-double are proof of that. Japan's technological advancements are not detrimental to this fact.

Japan is hardly ever connected with animism. One reason is that animism is wrongly understood as religion. Japan however is often considered a-religious (Watanabe 2002, 10). Another reason is that the highly idealized perception of Japan is very limited and one-sided. Japan stands for the "purest" of all Buddhist forms, *Zen* (禅) (Lutherjohann 1998, 119),[1] whereas animism is –

---

1. *Zen* (禅) is but one form of Japanese Buddhism, but it is the only form that is an amalgamation of Japanese religiosity and Buddhism. *Zen* (禅) is the Japanese term for meditation and contemplation, and represents a tradition of Mahayana-Buddhism. The central religious practice is *zazen* (座禅), the "sitting contemplation." The characteristics of *Zen* (禅) can be summarized as follows: *Zen* (禅) understands itself a special tradition outside the Buddhist orthodoxy. Independence from holy scriptures, the communication of its teachings from heart to heart and *satori* (悟り), the "awakening," are important teachings. *Zen* (禅) values the personal

according to the judgment of many – "only" an "Indian's religion." The IMC Jerusalem Conference in 1925 named only "Islam, Buddhism, Hinduism, and Confucianism" as counterparts for Christianity (Bosch 1991, 480). There are three examples of this one-sidedness:

- The *Allgemeine Evangelisch-Protestantische Missionsverein* (AEPM), founded in 1884 for India, China and Japan considered Shintoism as animistic "witchcraft" and therefore not a "competitor in the struggle for the salvation of souls" (Wippich 2001, 54).
- Griffiths (20) dismisses the idea of the spirits of the dead as obsolete, animistic fear, and devotes his book on Japan solely to Buddhism as *the* religion of Japan.
- In his chapter on Asian theology in *Learning about Theology from the Third World* (1990), Dyrness almost only focuses on Hinduism and Buddhism. But then he opens his chapter on Japan with Beavers's words: "None of the generalities of Asia apply to Japan" (Beavers in Dyrness 1990, 141), while his chapter on African theology offers many parallels to Japanese religiosity.

Just how important is Buddhism in Japan? Wendt judges:

> The fact that in the field of religious science hardly anybody has given much thought or time to the study of Shamanistic-Shintoist religions is probably due to their premature dismissal as "superstition." The studies of Buddhism, on the other hand, are extensive, which is the opposite of its distribution in Japan. *Zen* for example, frequently referred to in the West, has from the beginning only been a religion of few. (Wendt 1970, 182)

2.1.1 The Unanimous Judgment of Many Japanologists

This kind of underestimation of animist Shintoism as a worldview framework of Japan stands in contrast to the judgment of many Japanologists. I want to start with a longer quote by Abe (阿部正路):

> 古来、神は聖人であるとか、人の心であるとか...人の霊あるいは祖先の霊であるとか、さまざまに解釈されてき

---

awakening more highly than the intellectual encounter with Buddhist teachings or elaborate ritualism. *Zen* (禅) reinterprets the understanding of the ritual: Commonplace actions are performed with this new kind of awareness and become a daily ritual (Beyreuther 2000, 31).

ました。このように、神の観念や起源は、複雑で内容の深いものですが、人間は、死や夢、幻覚などの現象を通して、肉体と霊魂という二元の上に存在するのです。そして、霊魂が人間以外のもの、すなわち、山川、草木、無生物などに宿るもの、それが精霊なのです。こうした霊的存在に対する信仰が、やがて神に至るのです。こうした霊魂観念が発達するより前に、直接的な情緒的激動に接し、かつてない異常なものに出会ったときの驚きと怖れの心、あるいはその対象となっているものを、すべて神秘的あるいは超自然的な力としてとらえ、そのものを神の具現として信仰しつづけてきました。超人的、超自然な力のあるものこそ神的な存在あるという信仰の基礎となっているのです

Korai, kami-wa seijin de aru toka, hito-no kokoro de aru toka . . . hito-no rei arui-wa sosen-no rei de aru toka, samazama-ni kaishaku sarete kimashita. Kono you-ni, kami-no kannen-ya kigen-wa, fukuzatsu de, naiyou-no fukai mono desu-ga, ningen-wa, shi-ya yume, genkaku nado-no gensho-o tooshite, nikutai-to reikon-to iu ningen-no ue-ni sonzai suru-no desu. Soshite, reikon-ga ningenigai-no mono, sunawachi, yamakawa, souboku, museibutsu nado-ni yadoru mono, sore-ga seirei-nano desu. Koushita reiteki sonzai-ni taisuru shinkou-ga, yagate kami-ni itaru-no desu. Koushita reikonkannen-ga hattatsu suru yori mae-ni, chokusetsuteki-na jouchoteki gekidou-ni sesshi, katsutenai ijou-na mono-ni deatta toki-no odoroki-to osore-no kokoro, arui-wa sono taishou-to natte iru mono-o, subete shimpiteki arui-wa choushizenteki-na chikara toshite torae, sono mono-o kami-no gugen-to shite shinkou shitsuzukete kimashita. Choujinteki, choushizen-na chikara-no aru mono koso shinteki-na sonzai aru-to iu shinkou-no kiso-to natte iru-no desu.

From ancient times "god" was interpreted in various ways: by saints, as the human heart . . . the human spirit or the spirit of the ancestors. Therefore, the concept and the origin of "god" are complicated and deep content-wise, but humans transcend the two-dimensionality of body and soul by means of phenomena such as death or dreams and hallucinations. And the soul, which dwells outside humans, dwells in mountains and rivers, grasses and trees, in inanimate nature, and is the mana-force. Belief in such spirit-like existences were gradually developed into [the conception of] "god." Before the development of soul-concepts of that kind, the encounter with the immediate atmospheric panic, with the panic when encountering the extraordinary, with the fearful heart, respectively with all things which induced this fear, was considered mystic or in possession of supernatural power. Ever since, these things have been believed to be a manifestation of "god." And it was exactly these things which became the basic of the faith in a divine existence (Abe 2004, 25–26).

Further testimonies:

- First a very old testimony, that of the distinguished William Elliot Griffis. After discussing the Japanese "high-religions" he derogatively (an attitude I do not share) refers to animism as the "dead level of paganism" and states:

  > It is not with any or all of these . . . religions that the Christian missionary comes first, oftenest or longest in contact. In ancient, in mediaeval, and in modern times the student notices a great undergrowth of superstition clinging parasitically to all religions, though formally recognized by none. Whether we call it fetichism, shamanism, nature worship or heathenism in its myriad forms, it is there in awful reality. It is as omnipresent, as persistent, as hard to kill as the scrub bamboo which both efficiently and sufficiently takes the place of thorns and thistles as the curse of Japanese ground. . . . Such prevalence of mental and spiritual disease is the sad fact that confronts every lover of his fellow-men. This paganism is more ancient and universal than any one of the religions founded on writing or teachers of name and fame. . . . Out of the soil of diseased imagination has sprung up a growth as terrible as the drunkard's phantasies. … The Ainos of Yezo may be called Shamanists or Animists; that is, their minds are cramped and confused by their belief in a multitude of inferior spirits. (Griffis 1895, ch. 1)

- Shintoism is the leading indigenous religion of Japan (Pye 1996, 1).
- Shintoism is the "real religion of the Japanese people" (Oguro 1982, 95). Ono (小野泰博) et al. (605) use *minzoku-no shuukyou*

(民俗の宗教) and equate both using furigana-transcribing:[2] 民俗 transcribed with フォーク (folk). Takenaka uses "civil religion" for *folk religion* (1972, 83).

- Shintoism is the only original religion of Japan (Aoki 1994, 202; Solheim 1984, 213).
- Shintoism is a "shamanistic popular religion" (Takenaka 1972, 83).
- "Animism is the basic element of Shintoism" (Iga 1986, 119).
- Shintoism is "the religion of the folk belief formed around a nature deity"[3] (Mitsuhashi 2007, 13).
- Shintoism is the "foundation" (Freed 2000, 17).
- "The original Shintoism is that religion, which encompasses the entirety of the religious, worldview, and moral concepts and customs, which were present in Japan before the introduction of the Chinese and Korean high culture, and particularly before the introduction of Confucian and Taoist literature, that is before about the 3rd and 4th century" (Numazawa 1970, 193).
- Shintoism is the "characteristic Japanese life-style" (Kreiner 1992, 607).
- Shintoism is the *seikatsu-no michi* (生活の道), the *way of life* of the Japanese (Mitsuhashi 2007, 18).[4]
- Shintoism is the will which forms the foundation of Japanese culture (Hori in Kuroda 1981, 2).
- Shintoism is rooted together with the life of the Japanese even though it is not propagated as Buddhism or Christianity (Mitsuhashi 2007, 11).
- Shintoism is the basic belief of the Japanese people which includes its folk morals (Miyata 1984, 49).

---

2. Furigana (振り仮名) are small letters of the Japanese writing system written above Chinese characters. They are used when the character's reading is difficult or irregular. フォーク as used above is the Japanese transliteration of *folk*.

3. *Shizenshin* (自然神).

4. The Japanese word for religion *shuukyou* (宗教), a compound of *shuu* (宗), sect or denomination, and *kyou* (教), teaching, means "teaching of a school or a confession." "Very often even the members of a sect are not familiar with the teachings and doctrines of the various religious schools." According to Reader, Japanese religiosity is "rather focused on demands of society, social contexts, religious acts, practices and rites, shared habits, and etiquette than on teachings." Japanese religiosity is much more an "everyday spirituality" (Hildebrandt 1996, 136).

- Shintoism is "the value orientation as basis of the Japanese people," "the synergism of religious convictions and cultural attitudes" (Kitagawa and Ludwig 1984, 1633).
- Shintoism (*shintou*, 神道) goes back to the Old-Japanese *kannagara-no michi* (神ながらの道) or *kamunagara-no michi* (随神ノ道). According to Inoue, author of the official commentary to the *Imperial Rescript on Education* (Bellah 1965, 576) this is "the ultimate, primordial basis of Japan, untouched by any Confucian-Buddhist influence." It is present in all aspects of Japanese national identity as their most important element (Nawrocki 1998, 210–211).[5]

However, Nishida's (西田幾多郎) assumption that Shintoism should be as old as Japan herself can be dismissed as an ideological overstatement. Many present-day scholars voice considerable doubt (Asoya 1994, 26).[6] To start with, the term Shintoism is comparatively new. It was not coined until 730 AC in an encounter with Buddhism and Confucianism (Ono et al. 1985, 55; Mitsuhashi 2007, 12, 21–22). Pye talks about the "retrospective invention" of Shintoism (2001, 3). Furthermore, Shintoism does not originally come from Japan but from Northeast Asia (Tsunoda et al. 1964, I, 21; Mitsuhashi 1995, 10). Mitsuhashi (三橋健) and Zukeran even called Shintoism a "worldwide phenomenon" (Mitsuhashi 2007, 11; Zukeran 2002, 1).

2.1.2 Various Other Findings Pointing towards Animism as a Basic Japanese Worldview

2.1.2.1 "Spiritual" interpretation for "natural" things

Mullins (130) said that, according to the Japanese folk religion, each state of being in which a person found themself in this world was causally determined by the spiritual world. The basic Japanese interpretation of this world is that causes may not only be sought in the physical realm but also in the psychological and spiritual realm (Reader and Tanabe 1998, 109). Weggel (39) talks about an "analogy in the psychological, social, cosmic, and spiritual realm." This is

---

5. Nawrocki quotes Inoue: "Our Japan carries out the Way from its earliest epoch until today... In a narrow sense the meaning of this Way is consistent with *Shintou* (神道). However, when comparing *Shintou* (神道) and *kannagara-no michi* (神ながらの道), the *kannagara-no michi* (神ながらの道) is the far wider concept... It is a pure Way... The term 'Japan, the country of the Way' is by no means an empty name. It accurately depicts the specific cultural identity of our nation" (Nawrocki 1998, 211–212).

6. Kuroda (黒田俊雄) gives an exhaustive overview of the historical development of the term in *Shinto in the History of Japanese Religion* (1981).

particularly true for Shintoism, the worship of the nature force influencing the entire human life (Solheim 1984, 214). This cross-linking and influencing is depicted in the Japanese myth of the Sun Goddess weaving a divine garment in the "heavenly weaving mill." Nelly Naumann interprets the "heavenly weaving mill" as an archetype of the cosmos:

> The Universe is like fabric, the manifestation of a final, absolute reality, being reigned by mysterious powers and forces (*mana*). All phenomena own a soul, which depending on the circumstances is revealed either as *aramitama* (荒御魂) (wild soul) or as *nigimitama* (和御魂) (mild soul).[7] Man stands in this macro-cosmos as a micro-cosmos and thus in the center of this fabric of forces, influences its course.[8] In principle there is meaning ruling everything. It is the task of man to recognize this meaning and influence the processes of life in way that cosmos springs from chaos, in a way that the wild soul may change to the mild soul. (Naumann in Immoos 1991, 18)

2.1.2.2 Ordering the world in stories

The ordering of the world in stories, which is typical for animist worldviews, is also present in Japanese thought (Sakamaki 1987, 24; Tsunoda et al. 1964, II, 17).[9] However, as Blacker stated, in Japan there is no clear distinction, as in

---

7. This is by no means a dualism of good and evil. "What is revealed as 'evil' is but the expression of one of these souls in the wrong place" (Adami 1991, 22–23). I think the interpretation of Fairchild who understands *aramitama* (荒御魂) as the soul of the living and *nigimitama* (和御魂) as the soul of the dead is wrong. Numazawa (沼澤喜) interprets as follows: "According to the Japanese sources, we can see that a human does not have only one soul but two or even more. Every human has at least two souls, a *aramitama* (荒御魂), that is, a 'wild or coarse spirit,' and a *nigimitama* (和御魂), that is, a 'gentle spirit' . . . If one of the spirits is particularly vigorous it leaves the body and works various miracles" (Numazawa 1970, 203).

8. Based on this Katsumoto shows how the micro-cosmos of the ritual year (seasonal festivals) corresponds with the macro-cosmos of the human life (the journey from birth to death) (Katsumoto 1992, 58).

9. The Aztecs understood "sky and underworld . . . as two pyramids, one with nine stages, one with 13, joined together at their base . . . The place where the bases met formed the earth's disc . . . While the stages of the skies were thought to be the residence of . . . gods, the nine underworlds were depicted as one worse than the other (Borengässer 1992, 301). A similar ordering of the "underworld" is found with the Brazilian Yanomam (Käser 2004, 64). In Old Mesopotamia, sky and earth were ordered in different spheres. The lowest sphere of earth was the underworld, which again held seven different stories (Parusel 1992, 688). In a similar way, the Iraya envision the sky (Käser 2004, 63). The Central African Bayaka-Pygmies distinguish between "earth," "world," and "sky" (Käser 2004, 61).

other cultures. She equates the "other world" with shot silk, ever changing its color depending on the onlooker's viewpoint:

> But in Japan the vision of the other world is riddled with ambivalence, like a piece of shot silk. Move it ever so slightly and what we thought to be red is now blue; another tremor and both colors flash out simultaneously. It is the same with the other world. No sooner do we see it across the sea, removed horizontally in space, then it dives down beneath the waves or beneath the earth. No sooner are we shown an eerie and verminous waste land, where prisoners are immured in chambers of centipedes and snakes, then again the shape shifts and we are dazzled by a magical palace under the sea, shimmering with pillars of jade and gates of pearl, and where carpets of sealskin and silk are laid out for the guest. And again, no sooner have we caught sight of the *kami* (神), the "gods" there, in their own world, then they are here, in ours, hidden invisibly within certain suggestive shapes. (Blacker 1999, 49–50)

Today the terminology of the various "worlds" or "stories" is influenced by Buddhism. But this must not hide the fact that the ordering in stories is a genuine animist characteristic. The traditional, pre-Buddhist Shintoism knows three "stories":

tenjou-no takamagahara (天上の高天原), the "Plain of the Highest Sky above the Skies" (*Kogugo Jiten* Dictionary) or *takamagahara* (高天原), the "Plain of the Highest Sky" (Abe 2004, 37–38; Hall 1968, 32)
ashiwara-no nakatsu kuni (葦原の中つ国), the "Plain of Reeds of the Middle Lands" (Orloff-Matsunaga 1966, 203) or *toyoashihara-no mizuho-no kuni* (豊葦原の瑞穂の国), the "Land of the Rice Sheaves of the Abundant Plain of Reeds (Abe 2004, 39), *nakatsukuni* (中律国), the "Land of the Middle Law" (Abe 2004, 37–38)
yomi-no kuni (黄泉の国), the "Land of the Yellow Fount(s)" (*Kokugo Jiten* Dictionary) or *yomi-no kuni* (夜見の国), the "Land of the Night View" (Abe 2004, 37–38) or *toyoko-no kuni* (常世の国), the "Land of Perpetual Youth," the "Never-Land" or *ne-no kuni* (根国), the "Land of Roots" (Akima 1982, 488).

The plane of the skies is – as the residence of the Sun Goddess – the land of light. In contrast, the *yomi-no kuni* (夜見の国) is the habitat of the "abominable gods of the underworld" (*seishitsu-no susamajii yomotsukami*, 性質のすさまじい黄泉神), who – as evil spirits (*akuryou*, 悪霊) – disturb peace on earth (Abe 2004, 37–38). The "Land of Roots" is situated above the sea. Gods and other mythological characters travel by boat over the *unasaka* (海境 or 海坂 or 海界) to the meeting place of the "800 strong salt-water currents"[10] in "Nether-Land." Because of this myth there used to be burial rituals in Old Japan where coffins were placed in a boat which was then pulled away from land (Akima 1982, 488).

According to Japanese Buddhism, a "soul" is reborn into one of the Ten Worlds (*jikkai*, 十界): Hell (*jigoku*, 地獄);[11] the World of the Famined Ghosts or Hungry Ghosts (*gaki*, 餓鬼); the World of Animals; the World of Demons (*ashura*, 阿修羅);[12] the World of Humans (*ningen*, 人間); sky (*tenjou*, 天上); the World of Buddhist Disciples (*shoumon*, 唱門 or 唱聞); The World of the Buddhas who Reached Enlightenment by Themselves (*engaku*, 縁覚); the World of the Buddhas to Be (*bosatsu*, 菩薩); the World of Buddhas (*butsu*, 仏) (Takemura and Tamura 1984a, 1589).[13] It is very important that these "worlds" are not detached from earth. They are connected to earth (Miyata 1984, 49). Correspondingly the fairytale *Yamasachiko and Umisachiko* (山幸彦と海幸彦) plays in an age "when demigods still walked earth, when they still

---

10. A term from the *ooharae-no norito* (大祓祝詞), the incantation of the "Great Purification Ritual."

11. The Japanese popular religion located *jigoku* (地獄) in the volcanic mountains (Mace 1993, 274).

12. *Ashura* (阿修羅) and *gaki* (餓鬼) are of different origin but are today subsumed under *jigoku* (地獄). *Gaki* (餓鬼) are the condemned. They "populate a lower realm of reincarnation . . . They are not able to still their insatiable appetite, because everything they eat turns into fire, and because their throat is too tight for food" (Pye et al. 2007, 237). "These beings – some of whom are visible to humans, some of whom are not – are depicted iconographically with huge, distended bellies and emaciated limbs. Their throats are said to be size of the eye of a needle, rendering them constantly hungry and thirsty and forcing them to search constantly for food and drink" (Lopez 2007, 13). Those who are consumed by their desire even after death become *ashura* (阿修羅). Because of their love for the world they cannot depart from it and wreak havoc at cursed places (Mace 1993, 274). Others call them a "race of Titans" (Pflugfelder 1999, 67), "mean-spirited lesser deities" or "demigods" that can cause harm to humans (Lopez 2007, 13), yet others like Yonemura understand them as dead who cannot become ancestors because they don't have descendants (Yonemura 1976, 178).

13. Others classify in a Buddhist way according to which people have to walk one of the six ways depending on their deeds: the "Way of the Sky" (*tentou*, 天道), the "Way of the Humans" (*ningendou*, 人間道), the "Way of Bloodshed" (*shuuratou*, 修羅道), the "Way of the Beasts" (*chikushoudou*, 畜生道), the "Way of the Famined Ghosts" (*gakidou*, 餓鬼道), or the "Way of Hell" (*jigokudou*, 地獄道) (Makimoto 2006, 70).

were able to wander from sky to earth as they pleased (Hammitzsch 1969, 5). The Ainu fairytale of *The Man Who Went to Search for His Lost Wife* narrates how the man Penri rode a golden horse to a city "on the highest place of the sky, up there where it is deep blue" and where "the sky-people" live (Nauwald 2012, 68–70).

2.1.2.3 Conceptions of the "spiritual double"

The widespread conception of animistic cultures according to which the reflection in a mirror shows a real person living in the mirror is evident in the Japanese fairytale *Matsuyama Mirror* (松山鏡) where a mother believed that the reflection she saw in a mirror was her double. So before she died she gave the mirror to her daughter and comforted her that she could always see her in the mirror (Kusuyama; James 2014, no page information). The comparison of Käser's general definition and Crim's (1981, 17) definition of *ramat*, the "spirit-like double" of the Ainu, speaks for itself:

Table 2.1 Comparison of Crim's *Ramat* and Käser's Soul-Concept

Ramat according to Crim	"Spirit-like things" according to Käser
cannot be destroyed	"imperishable and indelible" (2004, 108)
penetrates everything	"can penetrate human bodies" (2004, 102)
can freely move from one place to another	"not limited to space or time"; can move "from one place to another at any time" (2004, 102)
the "total *ramat*" can never decrease	

2.1.3 Shintoism "Even Today"?

I quite often hear the skeptical question: Is Shintoism relevant "even today" in "modern" Japan? As an answer Kahlert observes that even though "Japan is generally considered a strongly secularized country, this view of Japan clouds the vision of the superficial observer on a living Japanese encounter with religion" (44).[14] There are four reasons that speak in favor that Shintoism and particularly animism is the central worldview of Japan "even today":

---

14. Quite differently, Araki (荒木美智雄) argues that with the "Enlightenment" of the *Meiji*-Era "religion vanished from the general public" and "religion became a private affair within the framework of a secular, modern state" (Araki 2003, 200).

First the testimony of Shintoist leaders is important. According to a Shintoist leader,[15] Shintoism is not a dead religion. Even though the Emperor had to renounce his deity after the war, even though Shintoist education vanished from schools, the Japanese mentality does not allow for a radical shift away from traditional values. Today the slogan "To neglect Shintoism is suicide for the Japanese" brings the issue of Shintoism back to national awareness (Norton 1993, 16).[16]

Second, so-called Modernity never has been a part of the Japanese mentality. "Modernity" and "Post-Modernity" are Western concepts (Gigliardi 2003, 1) which do not apply to Japan. What could and can be found as Japanese Modernity is, as Nemeto put it, mere "fiction." "Japan lived Modernity as fiction." If Japan seems to be post-modern today it is because it never departed from the place to which the West now returns (Nemeto 2002, 51). If one wants to describe Japan with Western terminology it is "post-modern, modern, and pre-modern at the same time" (Gigliardi 2003, 2):

> Upper story[17] modern rationalism is a transplant from the West, not native to the thought of non-Western cultures, including Japan. Japan has always had a rather irrational emotional thinking pattern which forms the core of its traditional folk culture. (Inagaki 1990, 8)[18]

Third, "Modernity" did not force out traditional ideas even when it was able to gain a foothold in Japan. Masatoshi Doi (土居真俊) observed the following tendency in the 1970s:

> Following the rapid advance of science and technology today, the Western notion which envisions nature as something that has to be conquered by reason penetrates into the heads of young people who enjoyed new science education. Step by step nature

---

15. Unfortunately, Norton does not give his name.

16. Nelson in his article *Warden + Virtuoso + Salary man = Priest: Paradigms within Japanese Shinto for Religious Specialists and Institutions* (1997) gives a good assessment of the social position of Shintoism in present-day Japan.

17. Inagaki draws upon F. Schaeffer's diagram which calls rational thinking the "upper story" and irrational thinking the "lower story."

18. In a similar way Weiming criticizes the Enlightenment from an Asian viewpoint: "Nevertheless the Enlightenment mentality has serious defects as well. Based on anthropocentrism, ruled by an instrumentalist rationality, and driven by an aggressive individualism, it is a kind of secularism which suffers from disregard of religion and destruction of nature. Unless Enlightenment undergoes a radical restructuring of its worldview, it cannot provide guidance for the survival of humanity, let alone guidance for its welfare" (Weiming 2006, 3).

has been deprived of its religious veil and its deeper dimension. (M. Doi 1979, 79)

Nevertheless, traditional perceptions prevail. Some examples for the co-existence of modern and traditional elements are:

- In the essay, *Das Phänomen der Geburt in der japanischen Kultur,* Shimada (島田真吾), taking the example of traditional animistic birth preparation practices prevailing against most modern medicine, shows that the "sphere" of "ritualistic-magical perceptions" cannot be separated from the "sphere" of the "modern context." In fact they can be integrated with each other without problems. When the physician brings a magical protective sash[19] from the temple and hands it over to his pregnant patient on the "Day of the Dog,"[20] it is "pointless to argue whether he acts as a representative of modern medical knowledge or as a traditional 'medicine man.'" The distinction between "modern" and "traditional" is not permissible in Japan (Shimada 1993, 23). A similar example from more recent times is a report from the Hokkaido Tunnel (1983), with which Hielscher opens his article on "superstition" in his Japan Handbook:

   > The very same building authorities that created this technical construction of the century using most modern technology would not allow a woman access to the building site: They were afraid that the intruding of a woman could kindle the jealousy of the Mountain Goddess and thus conjure up calamity. (Hielscher 1995, 9)

- A glimpse into contemporary literature also shows that alongside and opposed to modern views traditional animistic conceptions still remain. In Furui's (古井由吉) novel *Tani* (峪, Ravine) (1980),[21] an autobiographic reflection concerning the death of a friend, deliberately leaves open whether the return of the dead actually occurs or whether it is just a psychological projection. In Kuroi's (黒井千次) *Die Finger* (1990),[22] fingers haunt a living room. Not even

---

19. The *haraobi* (腹帯), a protective sash around the belly, put on the *inu-no hi* (戌の日), on the Day of the Dog upon entering the fifth month of pregnancy (Kobayashi 2004, 54).

20. This patron deity is said to protect the unborn.

21. English translation contributed by Meredith McKinney (Rimer and Gessel 2007, 528–541).

22. To my knowledge there is no English translation available.

once is there any remark that this is something extraordinary. In Murakami's (村上春樹) *Zou-no shoumetsu* (象の消滅, *The Elephant Vanishes*) (1990)[23] an entire elephant dematerializes. Tsushima's (津島佑子) strongly autobiographical *Yokushitsu* (浴室, *The Bath*) (1990)[24] describes the "partition" between this world and the world of the dead with the metaphor of the translucent glass screen in the bath. Through this screen humans can see the dead who want to return to this world in a shadowy way. In Hoshi's (星新一) *Der Mann im Park* (1990), a man without any attributes appears out of nothing. He then takes over the body and identity of a man who has just died in an accident.

- The following column of the German ARD is supposed to be funny. However, it depicts a phenomenon becoming more and more popular:

> In the Japanese capital Tokyo people make a pilgrimage to the Kanda-Myoujin-Shrine, conveniently located right next to perpetually flashing amusement quarter Akihabara, Mecca, for all fans of the latest entertainment electronics. The priests of the 17th century Shinto-Shrine promise divine help with computer problems. Centuries-old ceremonies evoke the gods' help for vulnerable hardware, says a spokesman of the shrine . . . After several companies in the IT sector asked for visits the priests go directly to the companies . . . Even with problems with mobile phones the Shintoist priests offer help. A student asks for divine help because she was bothered by unwanted SMS messages. (ARD, Tagesschau 2008/9/8)

Fourth, the modernization of Japan did not lead to secularization but to the formation of the so-called "New Religions" (Schreiter 2004b, 11). According to Ogata, Japan is in the midst of a religious boom. "Since the dawn of the so-called 'spirituality age' the Japanese became very open for the New Religions [of Japan] as well as for the New Age Movement." What Ogata then describes as the religious sentiment is congruent with animism: Young people "don't understand science as almighty but as something that needs to be integrated

---

23. Information on the Japanese book (2005) as well as the English translation of this work and others (1994) are in the bibliography.
24. Information on the English translation (1993) is in the bibliography.

into everyday life. There is even a movement which connects science with religion." People with a stronger individualistic inclination become adherents of the New Age Movement, those with a stronger group orientation become members of the New Religions.[25] There they seek a fully animistic-oriented, "mystical experience, not in the yonder world but in this world" (Ogata 1993, 8). The so-called New Religions are nothing else than another remake of the old religiosity (Beardsley 1965, 341–342; similarly, Schreiter 2004b, 76).

In a lecture on Japanese religiosity and Spiritism, Richard Fox Young said that modernization and the tendency towards spiritism develop simultaneously (1990, 35):

> Rather than an archaic cognitive anomaly, contemporary spirit-belief might better be understood as an expanded rationality with its own modality of logic. Spiritism is not only compatible with modernity but is also capable of enhancing the meaning of life in Japan's highly urbanized and industrialized society where a sense of disconnectedness often prevails that no dose of scientific reasoning appears able to cure. (Fox Young 1990, 31)

2.2 The Japanese *Mana*-Concept *Ki* (気)

> **Summary:** The Japanese *mana*-concept *ki* (気) does not describe a supernatural but a cosmic energy or power. This energy or power is at times physically sensible, at times not, exists at times within humans, at times not. *Mana* must, being as part of creation, not be "demonized," but its uncritical facilitation is also dangerous.

2.2.1 Theory

The Japanese term for *mana* is *ki* (気),[26] which in the interest of simplification can be translated as "energy."[27] "Philosophically speaking, *ki* (気) means a material-spiritual cosmic energy which forms the primary matter and the

---

   25. The *Aum*-Sect seems to be the only exemption. According to Repp, it pointedly criticizes the secularization of religion (1997, 81–83).
   26. Thus Hosaka (保坂幸博) (2003, 232–233), McVeigh (1992, 55–56), Wallace (2006, 64), *The Backgrounder* (2005, 1), Muirhead (2005, 4), and Leonard (1999).
   27. On the connection between Western and Buddhist (Eastern) energy concepts (2006).

primary form of the world" (Yamaguchi 1997, 82). According to Yamaguchi (山口一郎) *ki* (気), is "cosmic" and therefore explicitly not "supernatural"!

> There is an extremely widespread notion that *ki* (気) is a basic constituent of the psychological, natural, and spiritual worlds. This is reflected in the hundreds of books about *ki* that can be bought in almost any bookstore in Japan. The subject matter varies, from how to increase one's mental abilities, physical strength, or supernatural powers, to how to master one's own *ki* (気) for use in the martial arts, calligraphy, and the tea ceremony. (McVeigh 1992, 55)

Just how much the Japanese *ki* (気) is congruent with the animistic *mana*-concept, can be seen in the following quote:

> The rationale of *ki* (気) . . . springs from the experience of immediate co-existence with nature . . . It supposes that there is a universal primary element at work . . . in the dynamic transformation of nature with its various phenomena. The word [itself] is hard to translate. It roughly corresponds with the Greek "*pneuma*" . . . and means "vapor, spirit, subtle influence," "breath of life,"[28] aerial expansion," "ether." (Yamaguchi 1997, 45–46)

2.2.1.1 *Ki* (気) and the originally Japanese *ke* (気)

The originally Japanese term for *mana* before the introduction of the Chinese *ki* (気) was *mono-no ke* (物の気), the "*ke* (気) of things."

> Before the introduction of the term *ki* (気) from China there was the word *ke* (気), which was used in an animistic way to express the psychic[29] influence of all beings, the *mono-no ke* (物の気) (psychic energy of things). With this understanding, the Japanese picked up the Chinese-philosophical term *ki* (気). (Yamaguchi 1997, 58)

Ki and *ke* are written with the same Chinese character (気). When pronounced *ke* the original animistic meaning is expressed more clearly. "Present-day Japanese generally don't have this specific perception of an indwelling spirit in all things (Oguro talks about *ki/ke*, 気), but the influence

---

28. Hiebert similarly translates with "life-giving cosmic breath" (Hiebert et al. 1999, 139).
29. *Seelisch*.

[of this thinking] is still present" (Oguro 1982, 26). Today many associate *mono-no ke* (物の気) with ghosts. The fact that *ke* is written with the same Chinese character as *ki* (気) is frequently unknown, even to highly educated and well-read people.

Before the encounter with Buddhism there were no images in Shinto shrines (Rotermund 1993, 275), because the Japanese originally sought something far more primal, that is this very *ke* (気). It was only when Shintoism entered into competition with Buddhism that images were used (Hosaka 2003, 232).

The *Kokugo Dai Jiten Dictionary* defines *ke* (気) as follows:

1. the hot air emanating from things, or the force things possess
2. emotions, *kokochi* (心地), the "texture of the heart," will-power
3. the feeling one gets from the condition of humans and things, evidence, called *kehai* (気配), the subject which emits *ke* (気).

The reason why the Chinese *ki* (気) was introduced for the originally Japanese *ke* (気) is that both terms are almost identical. In the following word-field study they are dealt with together.

2.2.1.2 The word-field of *ki* (気)

McVeigh warned about the formidability of a word-field study on *ki* (気): "In ordinary Japanese *ki* (気) possesses such a wide range of meanings that even a brief sketch becomes a formidable task" (56). The following study can therefore only be a brief outline. McVeigh structures *ki* (気) in accordance with Yamaguchi's definition as follows:

- "the quintessential substance or stuff out of which the cosmos is made";
- "the vital power or force that sustains all life" (57).

Halpern (1479) also acknowledges this double character when he specifies two basic meanings for *ki* (気): "gas" and "spirit." The term "spirit" has to be used with caution because in Western thinking "spirit" carries a "supernatural" notion, totally alien to *ki* (気). Leaning on McVeigh, I am going to specify two areas, "energy" and "substance":

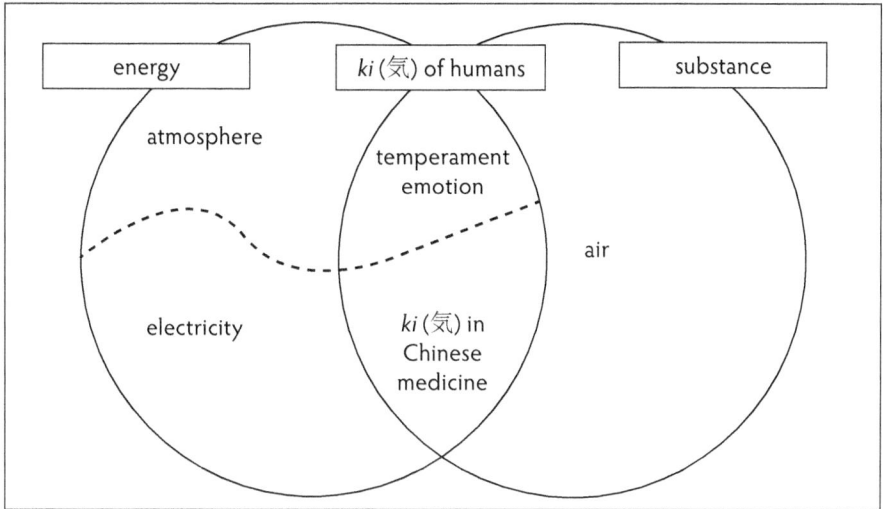

Figure 2.1 *Ki* (気) **as Energy and Substance**

Three preliminary remarks:

- When *ki* (気) means pure substance, Japanese exclusively think of gas, mainly the air. But when *ki* (気) means energy they distinguish. This is why the graph shows a dividing line in the energy circle. The line is curved and dashed because any "clear-cut" terminology would not do justice to the matter at hand. The upper area ("atmosphere") can be described as scientifically intangible, yet psychologically or intuitively accessible by experience. The lower area ("electricity") can be described as scientifically measurable, maybe only empirically accessible by experience. This virtually incomprehensible ambiguity is particularly apparent with the *ki* (気) of humans.
- The *ki* (気) of humans is part of both circles, "substance" and "energy." The *ki* (気) of humans is part of both areas, "substance" and "energy." That *ki* (気) can be understood as substance is particularly apparent in Chinese medicine which hardly ever distinguishes between energy and substance.
- Halpern (1479) holds that "air" is the original meaning of *ki* (気). Judging from the vast majority of terms denoting *mana* ("atmosphere," "temperament, emotion"), I would differ. The original meaning of *ki* (気) is *mana*.

As a term for "substance," *ki* (気) is used in meteorology, in pneumatics, and in medicine. As a term for "energy" it is used in electrical engineering and in magnetism. As *mana*-energy *ki* (気) exists outside humans as well as *mana*-energy of humans. *Ki* (気) also means "soul, sentiments,[30] and emotions" (Yamaguchi 1997, 58). However, *ki* (気) as "soul" will be covered under the Japanese soul-concept.

Ki (気) as substance

Ki (気) can be interpreted as "formless, yet formable primal substance" (Yamaguchi 1997, 46), as well as "fluidum" (82). In this sense *ki* (気) is used as a term for "air," that is *kuuki* (空気) (the "*ki* of the sky"). The great *ki* (気), *taiki* (大気) is the atmosphere (in the sense of air layer). *Ki* (気) itself can also be used as "air," *umi-no ki* (海の気); the *ki* (気) of the sea is the sea air, *yama-no ki* (山の気); the *ki* (気) of the mountains the mountain air; and *yaki* (夜気), the *ki* (気) of the night, the night air. The *ki* (気)-ball, *kikyuu* (気球), is a balloon; *ki* (気)-tight, *kimitsu* (気密), means air-tight. The temperature of *ki* (気), *kion* (気温), is the air temperature. The exchange of *ki* (気), *kanki* (換気), means ventilation. Other gaseous things can be called *ki* (気): *hoke* (火気), the *ki* (気) of fire, means smoke; *suijouki* (水蒸気), the *ki* (気) of *suijou* (水蒸), vapor.

In the sense of air, *ki* (気) is used in various technical terms:

Meteorology:
- *tenki* (天気), the *ki* (気) of the sky is the general term for weather
- *kishou* (気象) are atmospheric phenomena (象)
- *kikou* (気候) is the climate
- *kiatsu* (気圧) is the atmospheric pressure, the pressure of *ki* (気)
- *kanki* (寒気) a cold air mass
- *shoki* (暑気) on the other hand "hot *ki* (気)," the summer heat
- *shikke* or *shikki* (湿気) means humidity
- *kiryuu* (気流) is the airflow
- in antiquity the year was divided according to the weather into twenty-four *ki* (気) (*nijuushiki*, 二十四気 or 二十四季); that is there were twenty-four seasons.

Pneumatics:
- *kigaku* (気学) or *kuukirikigaku* (空気力学) means pneumatics, the "science of *ki* (気)" or the "air dynamics"

---

30. *Gemüt*.

- *kisoukan* (気送管) are the pipes of a pneumatic system, through which *ki* (気) is sent (送)
- *kika* (気化) is vaporization (*ka* (化) means "change into")
- *kikaki* (気化器) is the carburetor
- *haiki* (排気), exhaust-*ki* (気), is the exhaust
- *kitai* (気体) is a gaseous body (体)
- *kihou* (気泡) is an air bubble.

Medicine:
- *kidou* (気道) means the respiratory tract, the "ways of *ki* (気)"
- *kikan* (気管) is the trachea, the "pipe" of *ki* (気) (as in windpipe)
- *kisoku* (気息) is a general term for respiration
- *ikki* (一気) one (一) *ki* (気), means "in one gulp"
- *kikou* (気孔), is the *ki* (気)-hole, the pore
- *koukiseiseibutsu* (好気性生物) are aerobic bacteria and *kenkiseiseibutsu* (嫌気性生物) anaerobic bacteria, literally organisms "loving" *ki* (気) and organisms "hating" it. In this case *ki* (気) means oxygen.

Ki (気) as *mana*-energy of humans outside of humans

By defining the *ki* (気)-category "cosmological principle" as a "transferable, transferring, controllable, controlling spiritual energy, vitality, or essence that exists in, among, and between people and things, animating the cosmos," (Mc Veigh 1992, 57), he is clearly speakings about *ki* (気) as *mana*-energy. It is very difficult to distinguish between *mana* inside the human and *mana* outside the human because according to my knowledge there is little linguistic data available on this subject.

What first comes to mind is the term *seiki* (生気), the "life"-*ki* (気), which stands for "life" or "vitality." The term *seiki* (精気) also has this notion. *Sei* (精) in itself means life-force and is connected with *banbutsu-no reiki* (万物の霊気), the "*ki* (気)-spirit of the entire world." It is also called the "root of all life-force." If a person regains his *seiki* (精気), he becomes alive again. The *Houki Hongi* (宝基本紀) (*Yamato-hime-no Mikoto Seiki,* 倭姫命世記, and *Gochinza Denki,* 御鎮座伝記)[31] reports the oracle *Koutaijin Takusen* (皇太神託宣) of the Sun Goddess *Amaterasu-Ookami* (天照大神), sent to Princess *Yamato-hime* (倭姫). It warns against the damaging and obfuscating of the mind-god (*shinshin,* 心神) by dualistic thinking, lest it crumbles and the body decays.

---

31. Shintoist texts dating back to the middle of the 13th century (Itou 2003, 105).

Humans have to protect *reiki* (霊気), the spiritual substance of heaven and earth (Teeuwen 1993, 227–228).

Another important related term is *funiki* (雰囲気), the atmosphere in the sense of surroundings or mood outside yet around a person. *Fun* (雰) means fog, *i* (囲) "to enclose." *Funiki* (雰囲気) therefore is the *ki* (気) enclosing everything with a thick fog. One can speak about an "educated" or "religious" *funiki* (雰囲気), meaning an environment. One can speak about the family-*funiki* (雰囲気), meaning the warm feeling of being at home. A person with a special air about herself, effusing a special atmosphere, is called a person with *funiki* (雰囲気). Similarly a cozy restaurant is a called a "restaurant with *funiki* (雰囲気)." This is also true for negative atmospheres such as the threatening atmosphere of imminent violence, called *sakki* (殺気), the "murder-*ki* (気)."

Yet another important term is *kehai* (気配), meaning sense, instinct, or omen. The term literally says that a person distributes (配) *ke* (気) which other persons in turn can perceive. The phrase *rinshitsu-ni hito-ga iru kehai-ga shita* (隣室に人のいる気配がした) literally says that such *kehai* (気配) is at work that indicates the presence of a person in the next room. This means that one can "feel" the presence of the other person without seeing him. Not only persons but other things can "distribute" *ke* (気) in this way: *yoru-no kehai* (夜の気配) is the evening-atmosphere, *aki-no kehai* (秋の気配) the fall-atmosphere.

Other terms are *ninki* (人気), literally "people-*ki* (気)." *Ninki* (人気) is the *ki* (気) a gathering of people sends out. It means "popularity" or "business conditions." In the same sense the word *kiun* (気運) is the "*ki* (気) moved by others," meaning "trend."

Ki (気) in the Japanese view of nature

As an introduction, it is interesting how Kurita (栗田勇) distinguishes between animism and animatism.[32] According to the Western understanding of animism, "each object – whether it is a rock, a tree, or water – is home to its own peculiar spirit that makes the object what it is" (Kurita 2005).

> In the Japanese view, however, at the root of these myriad manifestations (*anima*) exists one invisible, underlying, and uniform sacred entity, the one life-giving force. This sacred entity exists in all objects as life itself. This is why the Japanese

---

32. The term "animatism" is considered obsolete. For further discussion see Käser (2004, 20).

believe that nature is in close relationship with the sacred – a view somewhat akin to animatism. (Kurita 2005, under "Elements")[33]

The Western animism Kurita refers to is that kind of animism focusing on the "spirit-like" double. What he calls the "Japanese view on nature" is not unknown to Western animism research. In Western research that "life-giving force" is called *mana*. Kurita might distinguish "Western animism" from "Japanese animatism" because in Japanese *ki*, respectively *ke* (気), means both the *mana*-concept as well as the soul-concept.

On the other hand, Kurita is aware of the fact that his observations of the *mana*-concept are universal:

> What Japan has done is merely to assimilate and continue to believe in, ancient spiritual elements that at one time, long before the days of Greek civilization, were actually global viewpoints. (Kurita 2005, under "Introduction")

At this point it is beneficial to take up the three terms, which Kurita calls the basic terms of the Japanese understanding of nature. The modern word for "nature", *shizen* (自然), is relatively new. It was introduced by Amane Nishi (西周) for the Latin *natura* in the *Meiji*-Era.[34] Before that the Japanese understanding of nature was expressed by the term *zouka* (造化), a compound of the Chinese characters for "create" (造) and "change" (化). However, even this term is not an original Japanese term. It can be traced back to Chinese Taoism (Kurita 2005). Before that two terms were used: *sansen soumoku* (山川草木), "mountains and rivers, grass and trees," expressing the "plurality of deities" and *kachou fuugetsu* (花鳥風月), "flowers and birds, wind and moon," expressing the beauty of nature (Morita 2001, 251).

According to Kurita, the original Japanese term for nature has much in common with the original Greek term φύσις, which means "generation" (in the sense of genesis) or "birth," or, according to Menge (1981, 739), "creative power of nature."[35] This term is congruent with the Old-Japanese *musubi* or

---

33. Holtom (1940b, 398) holds that this thinking is akin to Buddhism, rather than to Shintoism.

34. Before that this term was known as *jinen* (自然) in classical literature. "The word *jinen* (自然) was not used as a noun for all creatures in heaven and on earth, but it stands for status quo where all things are left in their original state" (Morita 2001, 251).

35. Bloch claims that the original meaning of φύσις is "not-aging" and "holding together" (1982, 983).

musuhi (産霊), which means "birthing spirit" (Kurita 2005).[36] Even though the character for "spirit" is used (霊), it is clear that the meaning is *ki* (気). The *Kogo Daijiten* Dictionary (Vol. 5, 574)[37] defines *ki* (気) accordingly as *reiryoku* (霊力), "spirit-power."[38] This birthing natural power can also be personified.

According to Atsutane Hirata (平田篤胤) (1776–1843), who was influenced by Christianity, the nature deities *Takami-musubi-no-kami* (高皇産霊神) and *Kami-musubi-no-kami* (神皇産霊神) emanated from the "first ancestral deity" (*taigen kousoshin,* 大元高祖神) *Ame-no Minakanu-Nushi-no Mikami* (天之御中主神), the Absolute God, the Great Life of the Universe (Devine 1981, 42). *Takami-musubi-no-kami* (高皇産霊神) is "the spiritual power that expresses masculine and positive expansion." *Kami-musubi-no-kami* (神皇産霊神) is "the spiritual power that expresses feminine and negative concentration. Expansion is positive manifestation; concentration is returning to origin" (Holtom 1941, 378).[39]

Ki (気) in traditional medicine

The example of *reiki* (霊気)[40] shows how *ki* (気) works. "*Reiki* is neither a religion nor a cult, but a natural healing method, which helps by activation the self-healing powers of the body through the universal life-energy, in literature also called universal light-energy" (Nickel 2002). The sources of the healing method of *ki* (気) are in China. *Reiki* is a compound of *rei* (霊) (spirit) and *ki* (気) (power).

---

36. This term must not be confused with the homonymic *musubi* (結び, 掬び) as a sociological term. De Mente defines *musubi* (結び, 掬び) as "undifferentiated co-existence of humans, nature, and gods" (33).

37. A dictionary for Old-Japanese.

38. The terms *rei* (霊) and *ki* (気) are hardly distinguishable. Kubota (41) defines *rei* (霊) as the basic power dwelling in all life-forms as well as in all things and nature phenomena (43). Sears claims that *rei* (霊) is the "universal energy," and *ki* (気) "the internal earth-energy" (Sears, n.d.: 1). I cannot agree.

39. These deities belong to the group of the Eight *Kami* (神), the *hasshinden* (八神殿), who protect the emperor:
 Kami-Musubi-no-Kami (神皇産霊神), Sacred-Creator-*Kami* (神)
 Takami-Musubi-no-Kami (高皇産霊神), High-August-Creator-*Kami* (神)
 Tama-Tsume-Musubi-no-Kami (魂留産霊), Soul-Detaining-Creator-*Kami* (神)
 Iku-Musubi-no-Kami (生産霊), Life-Giving-Creator-*Kami* (神)
 Taru-Musubi-no-Kami (足産霊), Health-Giving-Creator-*Kami* (神)
 Oomiya-Me-no-Kami (大宮売神), Great-Shrine-Female-*Kami* (神)
 Miketsu-no-Kami (御膳神), August-Food-*Kami* (神)
 Koto-Shiro-Nushi-no-Kami (事代主神), Thing-Rule-Master-*Kami* (神) (Holtom 1941, 388).

40. Nickel (2002) gives a short introduction into the history of *reiki*. On the history of *reiki* also see Deppe and Deppe (135–136).

On one side *ki* (気) is understood as power outside the human. Kindler writes about the "treatment":

> If somebody says that he "gets *reiki*," he means that he undergoes a *reiki*-treatment . . . Such a treatment usually takes 60 to 90 minutes . . . The practitioner lays his hands on various body parts of the patient . . . As the intuition of the practitioner deepens he himself focuses on parts where he feels a surplus or a lack of energy . . . Through the dedication [into *reiki*] the practitioner is connected to *reiki*. When laying on hands, it is not his energy but *reiki*-energy that flows. The practitioner is not drained of energy during the treatment. He can even experience healing himself. (Kindler 2003)

At the same time *ki* (気) is also part of the practitioner. The dedication ceremony is a ritual, during which the novice undergoes a cultic act with closed eyes. It is typical for the interpretation of *ki* (気) that the explanations of what happens during the dedication ceremony are contradictory and inconsistent. Some claim that the novice "becomes miraculously connected with *reiki* as if a *reiki*-channel would be opened."[41] But other masters claim that the novice is "reminded of the *reiki*-power dormant in himself" (Kindler 2003).

Ki (気) is no "supernatural" power, yet at the same time owns "spirit-like" qualities. This is specifically apparent in Chinese medicine. "All functions of the human body are caused by the fluidum [which is *ki* (気)]. Because of that, people with a strong fluidum do not become sick" (Yamaguchi 1997, 82). Less *ki* (気) on the other hand leads to fatigue (Yaegashi 2002, 91) or emaciation (Kawakami 2002, 122). When the *ki* (気) of a person lessens, she loses consciousness. In Japanese this is called *kizetsu* (気絶) literally the cessation of *ki* (気). People can also have dispensable *ki* (気) (Iimura 1997, 1).

> Above all *ki* (気) owns the motion helping the physical and psychological development that furthers the activity of the organs, that serves as the heat source warming the body, that strengthens the body's defense or immune system, and that wards off diseases. (Miura 2005, 85)

---

41. Dalberg (169) talks about a "cleansing of the aura-channels," which helps the *reiki* to flow undisturbed. "To practice *reiki* means . . . nothing else than to be a channel for the life-force, which lies in ourselves and which surrounds us . . . Once initiated correctly into the first *reiki*-grade the *reiki*-power keeps flowing the whole life. It will never dry up again – provided of course that one regularly uses this channel, that is, practices *reiki*" (140).

By contrasting *ki* (気) and blood, Miura (三浦於菟) shows how closely spirit-like things and material things are interconnected: "The 'blood' cannot move by itself. The *ki* (気) moves through the whole body, transporting the 'blood,' receiving nutrients from the blood, and at the same time sustaining its activity" (85).

> Chinese medicine imagines that the three elements, *ki* (気), blood, and water, circulate in the body, [thus] sustaining its functions . . . The perception is that blood and water constitute the liquid fraction as blood serum, secretions and the like, whereas *ki* (気) constitutes gas as the life-possessing energy of psychic disposition, e.g. *kiryoku* (気力) (*ki* [気]-power) or *konki* (根気) (root-*ki*, 気), *genki* (元気) (original *ki*, 気). (Satou 2002, 19)[42]

According to Matsumoto, the element of *ki* (気) of Chinese medicine corresponds with the psychoneurotic system of Western medicine; the element of "blood" corresponds with the immune system; and the element of "water" with the endocrine organs (Matsumoto in Matsuda 2002, 330).

Here the connection with the Japanese *kokoro* (心), the heart, as the location of ethical decision making is of interest. "If the heart is not light[43] the fluidum strays off its path and starts moving around arbitrarily. If the fluidum moves around in confusion it loses control over strength and decisiveness" (Yamaguchi 1997, 82–83). In this sense the heart (*kokoro*, 心) and the "fluidum" (*ki*, 気) form a unity (82). The *ki* (気) forms a unity with the material blood as well as with the spirit-like heart.

Ki (気) in Japanese art

If something is of extraordinary brilliance or beauty, it is called *eiki* (英気). *Ei*, also read *hanabusa* (英), means the corolla and stands for beauty. *Mana* seems to possess beauty in a special way. Similarly things (品) with *ki* (気) are called *kihin* (気品) which means "cultivated" or "elegant."

In order to understand the connection between the Japanese *mana*-concept and Japanese art, three terms must be considered: (1) *mono-no aware* (ものの哀れ), (2) *mono-no ke* (ものの気), and (3) *mono-no kokoro* (ものの心). *Mono-no aware* (ものの哀れ) is the central term. Preliminary translations are:

---

42. Others hold that in Chinese medicine *ki* (気) is the basis of energy (Kawakami 2002, 122).

43. *Klar.*

mono-no aware (もののあわれ) – awareness of the things; *mono-no ke* (ものの気) – "energy" of the things; *mono-no kokoro* (ものの心) – mood of the things.

According to Park, *mono* (もの) simply means "thing." It is the Japanese term for physical reality. "The implication is that *mono* (もの) is an animistic spiritual substance, uncanny and strange, which can threaten people. This feeling for the strange and mysterious is very important in Japanese religion and popular beliefs" (Nesbitt 2007, 26). By means of the "things," humans recognize the life-energy *ke* (気), because the "things" "exude the *ke* (気)." This is the explanation behind the term *mono-no ke* (もの の 気), the "*ke* (気) of things." The *torii* (鳥居) located in front of Shinto shrines "were meant to have a vital energy and therefore served as a sacred place with cosmic charisma" (Park o. J., 4). Kamata (鎌田東二) expresses it like this:

> Shintoism holds the understanding that nature is spirit-like.[44] Furthermore it does not really distinguish man and god. Not humans but nature gives the shrine its dimension[45] and makes it a holy place.[46] The trees owning eternal life[47] and surrounding the shrine reach up to the sky with their branches and create a divine atmosphere of the holistic divinity[48] which denies the division between the human and the divine. (Kamata 2000, 58)

> Shintoism strives to capture "the mood of things" (*mono-no kokoro,* ものの心) or to feel the tangible world, thereby realizing a profound sympathetic resonance with one's environment. To be affectively and cognitively attuned to the things around us is the most intimate form of knowledge – that is, to know the heart-mind (*kokoro,* 心) of a thing (*mono,* もの). (Park n.d., 4)

The central term *mono-no aware* (もののあわれ) goes back to Noringa Motoori (本居宣長) (Hooker 1996). He postulated this term in order to "define an essential ingredient of Japanese culture . . . [It] meant to characterize both a certain aesthetic and a capacity to understand the world directly, immediately, and sympathetically" (Masahide in Woolfolk 2002, 23). The Japanese want to

---

44. *Reisei* (霊性). Literally "spirit-character."
45. *Kakudai suru* (拡大する), "enlarge."
46. *Seidou* (聖堂). Literally "Holy Halls."
47. The term *tokoshieteki seimei* (永久的な生命) has nothing in common with the Christian notion of "eternal life." Here "eternal" means the "time" of matter, which is without beginning or ending.
48. *Zentaiteki shinsei-no shinseiteki funiki-o kamoshidasu* (全体的神性の神性的雰囲気を醸し出す).

be at one with nature; and they work toward this objective through the creation of works of beauty . . . When a Japanese artist draws a landscape painting, for example, the overriding purpose is not so much to describe a particular or isolated scene, but rather to suggest a universal idea underlying the overall composition. (Kurita 2005, under "Truth")

The literal translation of *mono-no aware* (ものの哀れ) is, according to Kurita, "pathos of things" (Kurita 2005). However, the original meaning of *aware* (哀れ) is "wretchedness." *Mono-no aware* (ものの哀れ) therefore also means "wretchedness of things" or "pity of things." The reason for this ambivalence of terminology lies in the holistic thinking of the Japanese which oftentimes does not distinguish between subject and object. Hooker defines the linguistic usage of *aware* (哀れ) in the *Heian*-Era as "awareness" or "sadness" (Kurita 2005). Others claim that in the *Heian*-Era *aware* (哀れ) used to be a rather shallow word similar to the English "Wow," a term expressing a strong emotional participation. In the *Heian*-Era a lover was called an *aware-to omou hito* (哀れと思う人), a person thinking "with emotions" (Kondou 1995, 240).

Today *mono-no aware* (ものの哀れ) is a negative term with a melancholic undertone (Odin 2001, 259; Ginsberg 2008, 132; Carter 2008, 82). How did the meaning of this term change in this way when Japan is so profoundly life-affirming? This is the influence of Buddhism which shaped the concept of *mono-no aware* (ものの哀れ) of Japan irreversibly. With the introduction of Buddhism, the world was explicitly perceived as transient. The Japanese poet Mansei (満誓) (about 720 AD) wrote a poem which beautifully expresses this sentiment:[49]

世の中を何に譬へむ朝びらき
　(*yo-no naka-o nani-ni tatoemu asabiraki*)
漕ぎいにし船の跡無きごとし
　(*kogii-ni shi fune-no atonashiki-gotoshi*)
To what shall I compare
This world?
To the white wake behind

---

49. Japanese Buddhist proverbs carry the same sentiment: *Au-wa wakare-no hajime* (会うは別れの始め), literally "meeting is the beginning of parting." Hearn explains, "Regret and desire are equally vain in this world of impermanency"; *Banji-wa yume* (万事は夢), "all is a dream"; *Goshou-wa daiji* (後生は大事), "what is important is the life hereafter" (Hearn 2015, Japanese Buddhist Proverbs).

A ship that was rowed away
At dawn! (Keene in Corwin 1978, 298)[50]

The Buddhist technical term for this transience is *mujou* (無常) literally meaning "without constancy" (Park, n.d., 4).

> Japanese art owes its specific humanity to the Japanese' keen intuition of the transience and their almost fatalistic yet always readily enjoying expectation of the inevitable, associated with a distinctive sense for the extraordinary of the seasons. (Pörtner 2002, 12)

In the Japanese martial arts, *ki* (気) plays a special role. The Japanese *dou* (道), "way," found in the name of virtually all Japanese martial arts is derived from the Chinese Tao, in Japanese called *doukyou* (道教), "religion of the way."

> The notion of Tao expresses the essential unity of man and nature, and Taoism has long been concerned with techniques aimed at bringing heaven and earth together, blending the sacred powers of the heavens with ritual practice in the mundane world so that human beings can harmonize their life energies with the Tao, or universal spirit. (Davies and Ikeno 2002, 72)

In Japan the goal of all education, particularly in martial arts, is that the "contradiction between Self and world cannot be found anymore" (Yamaguchi 1997, 73–74). It is interesting just how Yamaguchi describes this state: He calls it "body-soul-unity" (74). Yamaguchi herewith follows the (wrong) equation of *mana* and the (universal) soul. Using anthropological terminology Yamaguchi talks about the body-*mana*-unity.

Even though respiration and *ki* (気) are not identical, respiration is important. Respiration can be understood as "main entrance into the *ki* (気)-exercise" (Yamaguchi 1997, 82), by which one can "tap into" *ki* (気) (De Castro et al., n.d., 3). Yamaguchi quotes a report of a Western disciple of Japanese martial arts:

> Through respiration you not only discover the fountainhead of spiritual power, but you also achieve its continuing and rich flow . . . I learned to unconcernedly get lost in respiration that at times I got the impression, that not I breathed but that I was breathed. (Herrigel in Yamaguchi 1997, 76)

---

50. Japanese source: http://home.earthlink.net/~khaitani1/mysx3.htm (downloaded 13 Oct 2012).

In *kendou* (剣道), the Japanese martial art of fencing, the unity of *ki* (気) and man is described by the term *kikentaiitchi* (気剣体一致), the "*ki* (気)-sword-body-unity." This unity goes so far that *ki* (気) and human cannot be distinguished anymore. In a similar context Csiksentmihalyi talks about "integration of spirit and body" or "transcending of ego-boundaries" (Csiksentmihalyi in Yamaguchi 1997, 87). "In this case *ki* (気) means attention and will as well as the dynamic sensing of the whole movement, one's own and that of the other person" (Yamaguchi 1997, 77–79). In *kendou* (剣道) the term *kiai* (気合), "unified *ki* (気)" is used. *Kiai* (気合) is the unification of *ki* (気) and *ki* (気). It means that in the struggle of *seishin* with *seishin* (精神), the struggle of "spirit" with "spirit," or "mind" with "mind," the *ki* (気) can be overcome by identifying oneself with *ki* (気) (Saimura in Yoshiyama 2003, 82).

> The flow of *ch'i* is the basis of the flowing motions of *Taichi-ch'uan*, the "Dance of Taoist warriors." All martial arts use the same principle . . . Like all martial arts *Tai-chi-ch'uan* is not a fighting technique but the cultivation of *ch'i* in the body and its projection towards the opponent. It again becomes apparent that control over the mind, respiration and the flow of *ch'i* is the basic prerequisite of martial arts. (Page in Deppe and Deppe 2002, 128–129)

Ki (気) is perceived as the energy or substance that connects everything, even the most distant point that "merges every corner of the cosmos into one organic unity." He who therefore "masters" *ki* (気), "masters" the universe (Holcombe in de Castro et al., n.d., 3).

The unity with the universe goes so far that Self as independent entity ceases to exist. This then is called "Self-lessness," "Not-heart-spirit" (*mushin*, 無心) (Yamaguchi 1997, 85). "This *mushin* (無心) attitude leads to an acceptance of the world as it is, which is the core of learning in any kind of *dou* (道) practice (Davies and Ikeno 2002, 76).

> Man in the connections with his environment relevant for his life . . . is not seen as an independent being taking possession of the world on his own accord. Rather, an "affected object"[51] of processes. In the Japanese worldview these processes appear to be the fundamental element of all events. (Hartmann in Yamaguchi 1997, 88)

---

51. *Affiziertes Objekt*.

2.2.2 Christian Belief and the Mana-Concept of Japanese Animism

The sweeping judgment that "cosmic powers" are merely the product of "superstition" (Rohrbach 1985, 167) is not sufficient, nor is it true in my conviction. Also arguments such as "Christians worship the one God who created the universe and therefore do not believe in [the existence of] the universal, *ch'i*-power" (Hanegraaff 1991, 1), categorically defying this power, is much too shallow.[52] Judgments like this do not stem from the Christian faith anyway, but from the unteachable spirit of Enlightenment, which does not allow anything that cannot be explained in materialistic categories. When Schopenhauer, in opposition against Mesmer's universal Ether, trenchantly claimed that "that agent was nothing else than the will of magnetizing person" (1854, 92) he wanted to defy Mesmer. Yet according to Schopenhauer himself, the "will" is "the thing [!] itself, the inner substance, the essence of the world" (1859, 324), thus defining what the East has always called *ki* (気). The attitude that wants to explain everything in the spirit of "scientific Enlightenment" is by no means "Christian." The following telling quote is taken from Bloch's *Das Prinzip Hoffnung*,[53] which surely is not a Christian manifesto:

> Immortal were especially those "cosmic universal powers," ever discovered afresh, ever re-named anew. The "fluidum" of the old Mesmer was revived anyhow, when it took on the scientific term "electricity" of the nineteenth century. And the transition to the present-day, the even more lively "radiation-magnetism" was introduced by an otherwise sound scientist with but a sound madness, the chemist Reichenbach ... All this ... belongs in its petty bourgeois humbug guise of today still to the technical dreamland; this accounts for its old magical rudiments, even if they are grotesquely degenerated. (Bloch 1982, 738–739)[54]

---

52. Mechanical studies on techniques of *aikidou* (合気道), the "way of harmony with *ki* (気)" (de Castro et al., n.d., 5; Lindblad 2000), show that much has just not been researched yet. The so far "mystical" processes of *aikidou* (合気道)-techniques can definitely be explained by Western "science." As an example see Singh's *Compliance Analysis of a Fundamental Aikido Technique* (2005). *Ki* (気) is not (!) "supernatural."

53. *The Principle of Hope*.

54. Elsewhere Bloch takes a much more conciliatory, and above all humbler, tone especially concerning Asian *ki* (気)-techniques: "Also our knowledge of *real broadening* of trained will-force is not sufficient; our knowledge might possibly be on the same level as the Greek knowledge on electrical engineering, who only knew electrified amber" (1982, 791).

What materialists and materialistic Christians can or cannot imagine cannot be the benchmark for God's creation of spiritual or "spirit-like" things. Turaki demands "Christianity must recognize and study the theological basis of the traditional African belief in the existence of mystical and mysterious forces" (Turaki 2000, under "Belief in Impersonal"). This is also true for the debate with Asian traditions.

Bloch's biting satire and Turaki's demand bring up the question whether *ki* (気) exists at all. I can only put up my own opinion for discussion: (1) I have no reason to doubt the existence of *ki* (気). (2) The evidence for the existence of *ki* (気) is convincing. (3) I want to draw attention to the fact that *mana* must have been known in the West as well, which is amply proven by both the English and German languages.[55]

2.2.2.1 "Testing the spirits"

> Dear friends, do not believe every spirit, but test the spirits to see whether they are from God, because many false prophets have gone out into the world. (1 John 4:1 NIV)

Even though the quote from 1 John 4:1 uses "spirits" in the sense of "spiritual beings," I use "spirit" here in the sense of attitude. Especially with regard to *mana*, the question is not so much whether "mystical and mysterious powers and forces" exist, but what are the underlying "religious core values" that make people want to control and use them. How do we apply the Bible and the gospel of Christ to the nature of this belief and to the nature of its impact or influence upon man? The "how" people believe in these powers is crucial. This kind of "trying the spirits" is important, especially when Christians talk about "the power of the blood of Christ; the power of Christ; the power of the Holy Spirit; the power of God; the power of prayer in the name of Jesus" (Turaki 2000, under "Belief in Impersonal").

---

55. In Japanese, weather phenomena or the change of the seasons are connected with *ki* (気). English and German also have phrases that point in that direction: <u>it</u> is raining, <u>it</u> is stormy, <u>es</u> *regent* (it rains), <u>es</u> *blitzt* (there is lightning), <u>es</u> *stürmt* (it is stormy); also, <u>it</u> is summer, <u>it</u> is cold or warm, <u>es</u> *wird Frühling* (spring has come), <u>es</u> *ist kalt* (it is cold), <u>es</u> *ist warm* (its warm). In Japanese emotional states are expressed with the interpersonal *ki* (気), so also German has phrases such as: <u>es</u> *freut mich* (I am pleased), <u>es</u> *ärgert mich* (I am angry), <u>es</u> *reut mich* (I feel remorse), <u>es</u> *interessiert mich* (I am interested). And as in Chinese medicine *ki* (気) is responsible for the physical condition of the body, there are German phrases like: <u>es</u> *geht mir gut* (I am fine), <u>es</u> *geht mir schlecht* (I am not feeling well), <u>es</u> *ist mir kalt* (I am cold), <u>es</u> *ist mir übel* (I am feeling sick), <u>es</u> *ist mir schwindelig* (I feeling dizzy). In English, the well-known Old-English phrase, "<u>it</u> is well with my soul" comes to mind, too.

On one side Christians have to demonstrate a positive attitude and thankful appreciation. Energy – no matter what kind of energy – is part of creation and thus a gift of God (Deppe and Deppe 2002, 126), yet not "God" as the New Age Movement claims (Pontifical Council for Culture 2005, 13). It is the very freedom from the deification of nature which frees Christians to fully "investigate all the potentials of creation" (Sears, n.d., 5). "To be grounded in Jesus . . . is not to ignore those created energies" (8). Whether visible or invisible powers are "used" it is in both cases God who is the "ultimate healer" (6).[56]

On the other side, caution should be exercised. Sears also warned that *reiki*, the satori of its founder Mikao Usui (臼井甕男), was not a Christian enlightenment but a Buddhist one (Sears, n.d., 3; Hauth 2008, 76–80). The Christianization of *reiki* was probably invented retroactively in order to further the acceptance of *reiki* in America during World War II with its hostility towards Japan. Usui probably has never been to the States, nor has he ever earned a doctoral degree (Hauth 2008, 92).

The paper by Robert Sears, *Discernment of Energy Healing* (n.d.), gives important criteria for discernment. I want to outline it also adding some other points:

Does the therapy glorify God and bring us closer to God?

The motives of the therapist should be investigated (see Acts 8:9–13). Also the patient needs to be asked, "Does the form of therapy draw the recipient closer to God?" "Does he/she feel a deeper desire to read Scripture, attend church services, read devotional literature, fellowship with other Christians, etc.?" (Sears, n.d., 9). "What is the fruit of their work?" (Matt 7:16) (Sears, n.d., 10). When the glory of God is at stake, the motives of the practitioner need to be examined. Any arbitrariness which understands itself as subject or agent of the healing process is opposed to God's glory. Christian healing knows that God alone is the agent.[57]

---

56. This statement also strongly opposes the praxis of "Christian" prayers with self-effective magical powers. "Christian prayers are the same. Prayers can kill bacteria. Prayers can be similar to *ki* (気)." (Foreman in an interview with Iimura 1997, 2). I do not dispute that *ki* (気)-healing and prayers can work the same way. But I strongly hold that such "prayers" cannot be called Christian. They are not prayers in the Christian sense but rather incantations.

57. This is strictly opposed to positions like that of Prentice Mulford (*Your Forces and How to Use Them*). Bloch derides positions like that: "This is a solely capitalistic paternoster, nay, even an engineering-pantheistic one: a man, when his engine slows down, throws the will of his prayer like a transmission belt around the ultimate dynamo God" (1982, 795–796). Here God is misused as the means to the end of human (all) empowering.

The symbols drawn during *reiki*-initiation rituals are by no means value free. They have a deep, religious meaning, dominated by Buddhism:[58]

- *Chokurei* (直霊) is the symbol of Daiseishi Bosatsu (大勢至菩薩), the "Buddha who powerfully strides ahead, who owns the power and the wisdom to awaken . . . the Buddha-nature in a person and to lead him on the path towards enlightenment" (Hauth 2008, 95).
- *Seiheiki* (青碧) points to Amida Nyorai (阿弥陀如来), the main deity of the "*Sect of the Pure Land.*" It is the Buddha of the Endless Light. "The mantra *Seiheiki* is supposed to call forth the 'heavenly light-energy'" (95).
- The *Hon Sha Ze Sho Nen* is often thought to be associated with the Avalokiteshvara, the "sound enlightening the world," a bodhisattva of mercy, in Japan called *Kannon* (観音) (95).
- The *Dai Komio* can be found on the walls of the temple on *Mt Kuruma* (車山). It embodies the main deity of the *Shingon* sect (真言宗), *Danichi Nyorai* (大日如来), the "Great and Shining Buddha" (95).

The incantations chanted while tracing the respective symbols during *reiki*-initiation also speak for themselves. It is irresponsible to overlook the religious aspect of the worldview backdrop (maybe even deliberately). Dalberg addresses the issue of the religious character of the *reiki*-initiations: "Such an initiation can be . . . some kind of '*religio*,' a re-connecting to God or some higher power" (175).

Why do Dalberg (and others) talk about "God"? According to Dalberg, "humans have been taken out of the unity and will return to it." Meanwhile they live a "life of polarity," marked by the sentiment of "being separated." "Humans experience themselves as separated from other humans, as separated from the Higher Self, and as separated from God" (51).

One of the basic principles of *reiki* is the "principle of energy":

> Everything that is, is energy! . . . The energies of the polarized world arise from one single primal-energy. This primal-energy represents unity and therefore is of divine origin. A part of this primal-energy manifests itself as life-force. This is the Holy Spirit, the life-force, the *reiki*-energy, or love.

---

58. For the symbols, their meaning, and the initiation prayers see Appendix 1.

If then everything is energy, everything is connected, and everything influences everything. (Dalberg 1997, 68–69).

As the religious character of *reiki* and other methods to control *ki* (気) are undeniable, the critical question arises whether one has to surrender to some kind of power in order to gain control over *ki* (気). Turaki points out that there is always an "act of self-giving or the giving of oneself to the authorities or entities that lie behind these powers" (Turaki 2000, under "Means of Exercising"). Dalberg admits that during the initiation even the master must be aware of merely "being an instrument," so he can "surrender completely" (173). One of the rituals in *kyuudou* (弓道), the Japanese art of archery, is the *shinpai* (神拝; worship of god) before practice. In this ritual one "turns towards the deity" and "unifies one's heart with it." The bowing during this rite is called *kutsukarada* (屈体) which means "humbling expressed by the posture" (Takayanagi 2001, 10). Hanegraaff (1) might think of such kinds of rituals when he writes that Christians should learn Asian martial arts only under masters that distinguish between technique and this worldview. Especially *reiki*-healers place themselves "under the leadership of controlling spirits" (Ankerberg and Weldon 2001, 67). The *reiki*-initiation has something to do with "surrender" and "connection to the demonic world" (Deppe and Deppe 2002, 137). Deppe and Deppe warn that "Treatment success is always ascribed to an improvable cosmic energy, which the Bible traces back to unseen powers 'in the air' (Eph 2:2), which in turn are defined as part of the Satanic kingdom" (151). Accordingly, Ankerberg and Weldon hold the sweeping judgment, that "in animism every supernatural power one contacts comes from the realm of the spirit world" (35–36). The agents are thought to be spiritual persons. This sweeping judgment is based on the premise that everything that cannot be explained by means of Western science must be of satanic origin. I do not approve of this premise. However, the verification on whether surrender to alien powers is involved is of crucial importance.

"Discernment is individual and relates to one's stage of development"
Both the practitioner of spiritual healing as well as the one who is opposed to spiritual healing need to be respected and loved as people who are on different stages of development (Sears, n.d., 9).

Discernment presupposes a "positive God-image"
"A hidden fear of an accusing God or a rejection of the goodness of creation is not a reliable guide to discernment" (Sears, n.d., 9).

The central criterion: Is Jesus present?

The central criterion is:

> Is Jesus present in the beginning, middle and end of our involvement with any method, theory or philosophy? Did we ask Jesus whether we should start? Do we discern the ongoing effects on ourselves and others of our involvement? Is involvement leading me more deeply into faith in Jesus and harmony with the Scripture? It is not just unfamiliar methods like energy healing that must be evaluated by this criterion, but ordinary medical methods. Do they increase my faith in Jesus or lessen it? (Sears, n.d., 9–10)

Regarding the accusations of syncretism made against Hyun Kyung Chung's presentation delivered in Canberra (1991), the delegates dedicated considerable attention to the subject of discernment. They realized that the "Holy Spirit" needs to be distinguished from other "spirits," no matter whether they are benevolent or demonic. One of their decisive criteria was the christological criteria. "The Holy Spirit points to the Cross and the Resurrection. He gives witness to the Rule of Christ" (Kim 2004, 358).

Ecclesiological discernment

A further criterion is: "How open is the method to all and to be critiqued by others? . . . Does the therapist welcome 'external verification' of a cure or healing?" (Sears, n.d., 10).

2.3 The Japanese God-Concept *Kami* (神)

> **Summary:** The concept and view of God is crucial for the communication of the gospel.[59] Today the Christian churches in Japan all use *kami* (神) when referring to the God of the Bible. However, according to Endou (遠藤周作),[60] the essentials of the Christian concept of God

---

59. "Japanese have difficulty perceiving God as personal, loving, and involved in human life. This inability to comprehend the personal Creator God partially explains the resistance of the Japanese people to the Gospel" (Van Rheenen 1993, 171).

60. "Shuusaku Endou (遠藤周作) was born in 1923 in Tokyo. He became acquainted with Christianity in his childhood when he was baptized with his divorced single mother. After the war he studied French literature at the *Keiou*-University. He was especially interested in French writers like J. Maritain, F. Mauriac, and G. Bernanos. He then studied for several years in Lyon. While staying in France he discovered the problems, which later were to become the main

are lost by using this term.⁶¹ The Japanese god-concept describes immanent beings, things and phenomena, which stand out because of special characteristics and are thus awe-inspiring.

Since the usage of *kami* (神) for the God of the Bible is a choice of the Japanese church that cannot be undone, it is important not only to learn from Japanese god-concepts, but also, where necessary, to take a stand against them. God is "wholly other by category." Can anything at all be known about him? The discussion between "natural theology" and revelation theology is important, especially if the discussion is to be led with people who think animisticly.

2.3.1 Preliminary Considerations

2.3.1.1 Preliminary considerations concerning terminology

I want to briefly explain why I mainly dwell on the Japanese term *kami* (神), even though it has various synonyms. The major synonyms correlate in the following way:

---

themes of his literary activity: the radical differences between Japanese and European culture and the difficulties for Japanese people to become Christians" (Miyata 1984, 174).

61. In a very moving and rigorously self-critical dialogue between the old missionary Ferreira, who had renounced his faith under torture (Miyata 1984, 175), and Rodrigo, the main character of his novel *Silence* (*chinmoku*, ちんもく), Shuusaku Endou lets Ferreira criticize the missionaries' focus on the impressive outwardness of the number of the Japanese converts, while they never ponder about the "kernel" of Christianity. They should not be proud of the outward success. They could only be proud if the Japanese had truly become believers of the Christian God. But, in the words of Ferreira, "the Japanese were not praying to the Christian God. They twisted God to their own way of thinking in a way we can never imagine . . . It is like a butterfly caught in a spider's web. At first it is certainly a butterfly, but the next day only the externals, the wings and the trunk, are those of a butterfly; it has lost its true reality and has become a skeleton" (Mase-Hasegawa 2008, 182).

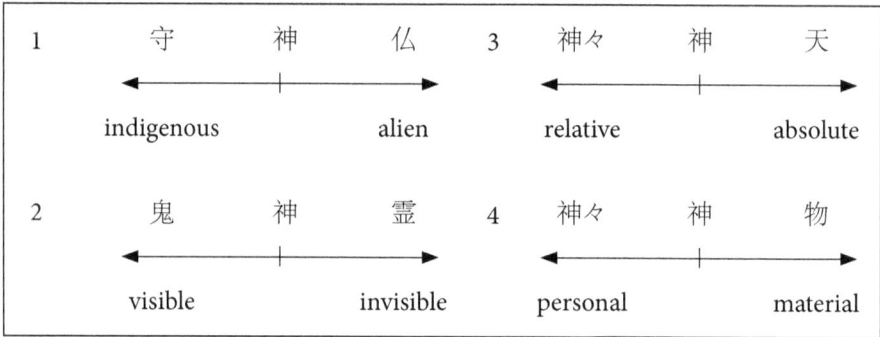

Figure 2.2 Correlation of the Main Synonyms for *Kami* (神)

In the first continuum "indigenous–alien," the typically Japanese *kami* (守), and the clearly alien *hotoke* (仏), pose as extreme opposites. *Kami* (守), usually read *mamori*, means protection, safeguard, amulet. This might even be the most intimate "god-concept" of the Japanese. Quite often amulets are called *expressis verbis kamisama* (神様), "honorable deity." *Hotoke* (仏) is the Japanese name for Buddha. Buddhism is not an original Japanese religion. Even though it has a long history of syncretistic indigenization, it is nevertheless labeled alien with the marker *kyou* (教), "teaching," as in the Japanese word for Buddhism *bukkyou* (仏教). Christianity, Hinduism, and Islam alike are written with the same marker *kyou* (教) and thus rendered alien. In the center of this continuum there is *kami* (here it is written 神). As homophone to *kami* (守) it is connected with *kami* (守), while at the same time, due to many deliberately ambiguous words and phrases, it is also connected with *hotoke* (仏).

In the second continuum "visible–invisible" *oni* (鬼), demon, and *tama* (霊), spirit, pose as extreme opposites. Demons, unlike in the Western-Christian context, are not "fallen angels" but monsters, ogres, goblins, and ruffians, powerful and scary, yet at the same time stupid, repelling, and gluttonous. The term *tama* (霊), usually meaning *rei* (spirit), but here in its animistic meaning meaning *tama* (soul), stresses the invisibility of the gods, with their power present yet not visible. Ayabe (97) equates *tama* (霊) and *kami* (神). Words such as *kijin* or *onigami* (鬼神), demon-god, show how close *kami* (神) and *oni* (鬼) are.

In the third continuum, "relative–absolute," the quasi-plural *kamigami* (神々), gods, and the originally Chinese *ten* (天), "heaven," pose as extreme opposites. The Japanese language does not have plural forms,[62] but the redoubled *kamigami* (神々) often means the countless gods of the Japanese pantheon as opposed to a "one and only God" or "God" as philosophical idea. This resembles the difference between *gods* and *God* in English. The "gods" are, according to the Japanese animistic worldview, part of the one and only world (holism), where there is no difference between immanence and transcendence.[63] They are explicitly not absolute beings. *Ten* (天), "heaven," is the complete opposite. In Confucianism *ten* (天) is the "primary"; in Chinese Taoism it is equated with the "highest and ultimate world principle" (Störig 1976, 94; Abegg 1970, 90). There are many gods, yet only one "heaven," *ten* (天). "All human goodness comes from the "heaven." "It is all-embracingly wide" (Douglas 1895, 71–72), the "governor of fate," and "Creator of all things" (77). In Japan this notion is found in the Shintoist *Tenrikyou* (天理教), one of the cults of the "new religious movement." It was influenced by Buddhism and Christianity and worships *Tenriou-no Mikoto* (天理王の尊), the "Honorable King of the Heavenly Rule," as its supreme deity. According to the teaching of *Tenrikyou* (天理教), this deity was revealed first as Shintoist *kamigami* (神々), then as *tsuki-hi* (月日), "Moon and Sun Deity," then as *oya-gami* (親神), "parental deity" (Thomsen 1963, 49). *Oya-gami* (親神), "parental deity" is an absolute concept *per se*. *Kami* (神) is found in the center, because on one side it is the singular of *kamigami* (神々), and because on the other side there are various proverbs which equate *kami* (神) and *ten* (天).[64]

In the fourth continuum "personal–material" *kamigami* (神々) and *mono* (物) pose as extreme opposites. While the gods of the Japanese pantheon can be understood as culture heroes (Käser 2004, 169) and thus have some kind

---

62. Japanese has the suffix *-ra* (ら), which serves as a plural marker of quasi personal pronouns: *warera* (我ら), "we" as opposed to *ware* (我), "I," *karera* or *kanojora* (彼ら or 彼女ら), "they" as opposed to *kare* or *kanojo* (彼 or 彼女), "she" or "he." Also Japanese has the redoubling of words as an equivalent of the Western plural, commonly accompanied with a sound shift: *kami* (神) redoubled to *kamigami* (神神 or with the redoubling shorthand character 神々), "god" and "gods," *hito* (人) redoubled to *hitobito* (人人, 人々), "human" and "people," *iro* (色) redoubled to *iroiro* (色色, 色々), "color" and "various." I call these forms quasi plurals because they are not the same as the plural of Western languages.

63. For more detailed studies see Hesselgrave (1978, 149) and Gerlitz (1977, 16).

64. "The voice of the people is the voice of God" (*vox populi vox dei*) (*tami-no koe-wa kami-no koe*, 民の声は神の声) is synonymously used with the saying, "The heaven, having no mouth, can only talk through people" (*ten-ni-wa kuchi-nashi, hito-o motte iwashimu*, 天に口なし、人を以って言わしむ). "Demanding of god in hard times" ("*Not lehrt Beten*," "in our hour of need we all turn to God") (*kurushii toki-no kamidanomi*, 苦しいときの神頼み) is used synonymously with "When man suffers he calls heaven" (*hito kyuusureba ten-o yobu*, 人窮すれば天を呼ぶ).

58 Japanese Understanding of Salvation

of personality, *mono* (物), literally "thing," is the Japanese term which comes closest to the pantheistic "All-One."

2.3.1.2 Preliminary considerations concerning linguistics

The Japanese god-concept can only be written in Japanese. The reading *kami* for 神 stands only for a very small part of the wide word-field of 神. Since reducing 神 to *kami* would mislead the research I shall use the character 神.

The term 神 is going to be used over and over again. Therefore it seems to be helpful to list its various readings: Chinese readings (*on-yomi*, 音読み) are *shin* and *jin*, Japanese readings (*kun-yomi*, 訓読み) *kami, kan, kou, gou,* and *ka*.[65]

The Chinese character 神 is composed of two radicals:

Table 2.2 Two Radicals of the Chinese Character 神

Figure 1   Figure 2

The radical in Figure 1 (left), derived from the character in Figure 1 (right) means "to reveal"; the radical in Figure 2 (left) and its corresponding character mean "to honorably speak," "to proclaim," "to announce." Christian researchers always wanted to interpret this character as a testimony of God's existence in the meaning of primeval monotheism. They interpreted the character 神 as "the God who speaks" (Kang and Nelson 1998, 49). Others interpret the right radical of 神 as hands reaching down from above, as shown in Figure 2 (right) and interpret this character as a testimony for the knowledge of a God who

---

65. The problem of the amalgamation of written Japanese and Chinese cannot be dealt with in this book. Vance explains the origin of the confusion as stemming from the *Nara*-Era with its highly proliferated phonetical annotation (Vance 1984). In her paper *Sprache und Nation: Zur aktuellen Diskussion um die sozialen Funktionen des Japanischen* Hijiya-Kirschnereit discusses Takao Suzuki's (鈴木孝夫) contribution to the writing system of Japanese (1988, 62–95). In the given context, pages 72–80 are particularly helpful. Also helpful are: In Suzuki's work *Eine verschlossene Sprache: Die Welt des Japanischen* the article *Die Beziehung zwischen Schrift und Sprache* (Suzuki 1990, 52–65); in Miller's *Die Japanische Sprache: Geschichte und Struktur* the third chapter *Schriftsysteme* (Miller 1993, 95–146); in Dettmer's *Einführung in das Studium der japanischen Geschichte* the paragraph *Sprachkenntnisse* (Dettmer 1987, 3); in Bowring's article about the Japanese language the paragraph *Kanji* (1993, 118–120); and in *Japanese Religions: Past and Present* Lande's paper *The Japanese Language* (1993).

created mankind. However, pictographic interpretations of Chinese characters are not relevant for semantic studies of the usage in the Japanese language. Also, phonetically deriving *kami* from *kagami* (mirror), from *kakurimi* (hidden body), from the Ainu-word for "god" *kamui* (Naumann et al. 1984, 1583; Ölschleger 1993, 147) or from *kamu* in original Japanese is not helpful. A comprehensive word-field study is necessary.

2.3.2 The Semantic Field of Kami *(神), "god"*[66]

The term *kami* (神) has basically two meanings that are important for its religious usage, and two meanings that are important for its secular usage.

The two secular meanings are "above" or "top,"[67] and "supreme" or "excellent,"[68] even though phonetic etymology rejects this connection (Naumann 1984b, 1583; Vance 1983, 277–278). Semantically speaking there can be no doubt about it (Sakamaki 1987, 24; Schinzinger 1983, 10; Rochedieu 1973, 69). This is also true for the sociology, influenced by workplace conditions and geography. Here "above" (*kami*, here not written 神, but 上, "above") and "below" (*shimo*, 下) are quite important (Bairy 1969, 43–47).

The meanings of the religious usage are "holy," "extraordinary," "awe," "fear," and "reverence." These meanings are attested for by the famous *Shintou*-expert Norinaga Motoori (本居宣長)[69] (Rosenkranz 1962, 11). When using *kami* (神) together with the adjective marker *teki* (的) the derived adjective *kamiteki* (神的) means "holy" (Holtom 1949b, 409). When redoubling *kami* (神) and adding another adjective marker the derived *kougoushii* (神々しい) means

---

66. As thoroughly as I have conducted the semantic field study, I am still aware of the fact that it can be by no means comprehensive. The renowned *Shintou*-theologian Norinaga Motoori (本居宣長) (1730–1801) confessed that he had not understood yet what *kami* (神) meant, and his contemporary Hisaoyu Arakida (荒木田久老) said, "There are all sorts of interpretations of the word *kami* (神), and all of them are wrong" (Holtom 1940a, 2).

67. In the world of business, managers are sometimes called *kami* (上) (Miller 1993, 246). In early or old Japanese *kami* (神), or *kamu* (神) also meant a "high-ranking person" (194). In this sense the German loan-word *ouben* (オーベン), used in hospitals for superiors and derived from the German *oben* (above), is used. In place names, areas or towns closer to the capital are marked with the marker *kami* (上) (56). However, there is also justified doubt that the 神 and 上 were originally pronounced the same way (Vance 2010).

68. Sugimoto (256) defined *kami* (神) as anything that distinguishes itself through deeds, no matter whether they are good or evil. For example one Japanese word for supernatural is *shingi* (神技), literally "divine skill," another *nyuushin* (入神), which states that in a piece of art or the like "god" has "entered," thus making it a "work of god" a *kamiwaza* (神業).

69. 1730–1801. Motoori (本居宣長) is one of the fathers of the *Shintou*-Renaissance (Rosenkranz 1962, 10).

"awe-inspiring" or "solemn." The following interpretations possibly point into the same direction:

- *kagayakimiru*, according to Holtom (1940a, 5), the oldest interpretation of Inbe-no Masamichi (忌部正通) (14th century), and its synonym *shouran* (照覽), mean "to see in brilliant light."
- *kami* (神) as derived from *akami* (明見), "glorious beholding," "glorious appearing."
- *kami* (神) as derived from *kashikomu* (畏),[70] "feel awe," and
- *kami* (神) as derived from *kabi* (彼靈), "that mystery" (1940a, 7).[71]

2.3.2.1 The secular usage of *kami* (神)

In secular usage there are two meanings of *kami* (神): (1) heart, with two sub-meanings – mind and psyche; and (2) nerves or consciousness. In Japanese thinking this is no contradiction because "god" and "man" pose no categorical opposites. For the same reason the line between *kokoro* (心), heart,[72] and *kami* (神), "god," is very blurry. This can be shown with the following words. In all of them the character for *kami* (神) (god) and the character for *kokoro* (心) (heart) can be used interchangeably without any change of meaning:

- *anshin* (安心 or 安神) (relief)
- *shisshin* (失心 or 失神) (unconsciousness)
- *soushin* (送心 or 送神) (absence of mind)
- *shinkon* (心魂 or 神魂) (heart, soul)
- *kyuushin* (休心 or 休神) (the "resting heart")
- *shinki* (心気 or 神気) (psychic power).

Furthermore, there are many character compounds in which the character 神 is combined with characters that have something to do with the Japanese soul-concept:

---

70. According to Harada, awe can be expressed by many characters: (1) 威: power (*ikioi*), valiant (*takeshi*), impressive, majestic (*ogosoka*); (2) 慄: to tremble (*wananaku* and *ononoku*); (3) 賢: to excel (*suguru* and *masaru*), majestic, solemn (*kashikoki*); (4) 懼: to tremble (*ononoku*); (5) 貴: precious, exalted (*toutoshi*), to revere, to worship (*uyamau*) (6) 惶: to fear (*osoru*); (7) 恐: terrible, fearful (*osoroshii*), majestic, solemn (*kashikoshi*), to fear (*osoru*). Furthermore, all these characters have the reading *osore*, to fear (Holtom 1940b, 406–407).

71. According to my knowledge, Holtom's *The Meaning of Kami*, chapter I, *Japanese Derivations* (1940a) offers the most comprehensive collection of interpretations of the word *kami* (神).

72. *Kokoro* (心), heart, is one of the terms that belong to the Japanese soul-concept.

- when the characters for *kokoro* (心), heart, and *kami* (神) are combined, the compound reads *shinshin* (心神) which means "mind";[73] losing one's mind is called "losing one's *shinshin* (心神)";
- the "soul" or quintessence of something can be called *shinzui* (真髄 or 神髄), literally "the true marrow" (真髄) or the "god-marrow" (神髄);
- when literally translating *shinshoku* (神色) with "divine color" or "god-color" this word does not make any sense; but when the character for *kami* (神) (in this compound read *shin*) is understood as psyche, the meaning is clear: it means "heart and countenance"; *shinshoku jijaku* (神色自若), the "control of heart and countenance" stands for a perfect attitude with total readiness of mind;
- *shinsoku* (神速) is not the "speed of the gods," but here again 神 needs to be interpreted as mind; then the meaning is quick-wittedness; the *Kokugo Dai Jiten Dictionary* explains in a different way when it explains *shinsoku* (神速) as something that happens "so fast that it has to be a divine miracle";
- *shinkei* (神経) is not the "way of god" but the nerves; the nervous system *shinkeikei* (神経系) is the system that directs and transports the thoughts of the mind;
- *shinki* (神気) is not the "power of god" but the psychological strength of a human.

2.3.2.2 The absolute as *kami* (神)

In this semantic group *kami* (神) is interpreted as *oomoto* (大元), the "Great Origin" (Iwagou 2010).[74] This interpretation is surely not originally Japanese but rather a philosophical abstraction, introduced into Japanese thought by Confucian and Buddhist thinkers, which Japanese scholars always opposed (Fessler 1996, 1). The first attempt to form an absolute god-concept goes back to the thirteenth century when

> the *Watarai-Shintou* (度会神道) observed the Great Nature-*Kami* (神) which, in fact, is nothing else then the formless "chaos" or the

---

73. Teeuwen (227) translates literally with "mind-god."
74. Rumi Iwagou (岩合流美) was an *ama* (尼) or *nisou* (尼僧), a Buddhist nun, for 20 years, as oracle and fortune teller mainly involved in counseling, before she converted to Shintoism. Today she works as a cult dancer in a shrine and extra-professional in counseling. On 10 September 2010 I had a long conversation with her.

"non-existence" as the primal matter, existing in the universe, in things as well as in living beings. (Rochedieu 1973, 79)

In the fifteenth century the *Yoshida-Shintou* (吉田神道) interpreted *kami* (神) as "the unfathomable, supernatural,[75] and spiritual absolute . . . existing out of itself." Other names for *kami* (神) were: "divine void," the one "glorified above all," and the "fount of truth" (Rochedieu 1973, 79–80). According to Geldsetzer (1), the unifying element between this "nihilistic-metaphysical faith in *kami* (神) as 'nothingness'" and the animistic understanding of *kami* (神) is the Shintoist fundamental philosophy that "beyond the divinized reality 'nothing' can be constituted anymore."

Another approach can be found in Holtom's article "Kami Considered as Mana" (1941). Summarizing his findings on *kami* (神) he says that "we are . . . prepared to look for a primitive psychological matrix in reactions of awe and mystery in the presence of the unknown and uncontrolled." He wants to "look for an original complex of experience beneath the *kami* (神)-idea, or the *kami* (神)-emotion, that is broader and more fundamental than the idea of god." He equates this "idea" as *mana* (Holtom 1941, 351–352).

> The objects that induce the *mana*-feeling may seem strangely diverse and uncorrelated when approached from the point of view of the categories of modern thought, but they are all, nevertheless, intimately bound together in the possession of a power to strike sharply into the human heart. The original events are all extraordinary, new, mysterious, uncanny, terrifying, "lovely," majestic, overwhelming, full of power, or of unusual significance; that is, not controllable within the range of the technique of the ordinary folkways. The unique object of experience, whether thunder, lightning, storm, miraculous sword, stone of odd shape, uncanny animal, efficacious medicine, healer of sickness, worker of witchcraft, . . . great chief, or mighty sovereign – whatever it might be – emanates a strange power and induces an unusual emotional response. This response is the "religious thrill." The attention is thrown into a special activity; a "watch-out" attitude is induced which perhaps originally had its vocal registration merely in an exclamation or cry. The emotion is found to repeat itself in contact with a multitude of different objects or events that externally appear to have no connection whatsoever. Nevertheless

---

75. *Übersinnlich*.

the uniformity of the emotion becomes the ground on which a belief is reached of the existence of a mysterious agency operating as an outgoing power in all the various objects that have stimulated the emotion itself. This is *mana*, or, to use the Japanese term for the same thing, it is *kami* (神). (Holtom 1941, 356)

2.3.2.3 Humans as *kami* (神)

In animism, humans, in the widest sense, can be counted among the *kami* (神) already in their lifetime.[76] This has something to do with the fact that all Japanese, not just the emperor, understand themselves as physical offspring of the first deities (Schinzinger 1983, 13). Chikafusa Kitabatake (北畠親房)[77] said: "Our great Nippon is the Divine nation. Our Divine ancestors have founded her. The Sun-Deity allowed her descendants to reign for a long time. This makes our nation unique" (Nakamura 167, 153).

At times *kami* (神) and "human" are interchangeable, as the following proverb and its variations suggest. The context of when they are used shows that they do not necessarily talk about *kami* (神) but often about humans:

- "Where there is a forsaking god there is also a helping god" (*suteru kami areba tasukeru kami aru,* 捨てる神あれば助ける神あり);
- "Where there is a killing god there is also a helping god" (*korosu kami areba tasukeru kami aru,* 殺す神あれば助ける神あり);
- "Where there is a throwing down god there is also a lifting up god" (*taosu kami areba okosu kami aru,* 倒す神あれば起こす神あり);
- "Where there is a putting to the (sick) bed god there is also a lifting up god (*neseru kami areba okosu kami aru,* 寝せる神あれば起こす神ある).

Also the proverb "Better than the Buddha/god you don't know is the demon you are familiar with" (*shiranu hotoke/kami yori najimi-no oni,* 知らぬ仏・神より馴染みの鬼) does not mean Buddhas or demons, but humans.

In a special sense, powerful rulers,[78] sages, heroes, charismatic maidens who produce divine offspring through a mystical consummation with a deity

---

76. Even though man and god cannot be clearly distinguished they cannot be equated either. Between man and god exists not a categorical but a gradual difference (Berentsen 1985a, 96).

77. Shintoist author (1293–1354).

78. On the island *Ukamijima* (御神島) in the *Ryuukyuu*-Archipelago (琉球列島) lived the so called *kaminchu* (神人), literally translated the "*kami*-men." Using their spiritual power, they ruled the island (Shirohara 2000).

(Okano 1976, 98–99), and sect leaders are considered as *kami* (神). They are called *arahitogami* (現人神), "revelation of gods in human form," *ikigami* (生神), "living gods" or "incarnate gods" (Klaes 2000, 546), or *hitogami* (人神), "human deities" (Hori 1987, 202), as opposed to the *takagami* (高神), the "high gods." Not only god people but also evil people such as thieves can be called *kami* (神), as long as they "are superior to other thieves by virtue of [extraordinary, my comment] good or evil attributes" (Rosenkranz 1962, 11).

When heroes are worshipped as *kami* (神), people are not worshipping them as humans but worshipping the god or the divine "revealed in human form" (Rochedieu 1973, 81). In the Japanese thinking it is no contradiction that on one side humans become *kami* (神) and on the other divine *kami* (神) reveal themselves in human form.

All humans become *kami* (神) after their death at the latest. Then they are invoked as such through priests (Schinzinger 1983, 13).[79]

In the Taoist-philosophical way, humans can also be understood as "god," as the following Japanese proverb shows: "*Kami* (神) as well as Buddha are both the heart" (*kami-mo hotoke-mo mina kokoro,* 神も仏も皆心). This is especially expressed in *Zen* Buddhism. Daisetsu Teitaro Suzuki (鈴木大拙貞太郎) (1870–1966) teaches that there is no difference between Buddha and humans (Suzuki 1973, 17).

2.3.2.4 Spirits as *kami* (神)

Generally speaking all humans are "sublimated" to the spirit of the dead and then become *kami* (神). In this sense it is true that all national deities once were humans (Eberhard 1983, 103–104). According to Ichirou Hori (堀一郎), this kind of *kami* (神) originally belonged to the *ujigami* (氏神)-system, in which the dead, having assumed a position as "tribal elders" (Hall 1968, 34), were venerated as family patron deities (Hori 1987, 202). The *uji* (氏) in *ujigami* (氏神) means "family."[80] Whether *ujigami* (氏神) are gods with an intimate relationship to the family, or whether they are *sosengami* (祖先神), ancestral deities, or *oyagami* and *soshin* (祖神), parental deities of the clan, is not distinguished.

---

79. See under "Spirits as *kami* (神)."

80. Similar to patron deities for clans, patron deities for households (*yashiki ujigami,* 屋敷氏神) and villages (*mura ujigami,* 村氏神). Depending on the area they were called *ubusuna kami* (産土神 or 生土神 or 産社神) (Hall 1968, 35), birth-place god, *chinju kami* (鎮守神), patron, or *inari kami* (稲荷神), harvest-deity or fox-deity (Fairchild 1962, 31).

Most scientists agree that the early *Yamato*-kingdom[81] was not more than a federation of powerful and autonomous *uji* (氏) (lineage-groups, usually translated by "clans"). Each *uji* (氏) had its consanguine members (*ujibito,* 氏人), various related groups not related by blood, but with hereditary memberships, working as professionals for the *uji* (氏) (*be* (邊 or 部)[82] or *tomo,* 友), as well as servants and slaves (*nuhi,* 奴婢), all being reigned over by the head man of the *uji* (氏), the *uji-no kami* (氏の神). Each *uji* (氏) was a social, economic-political, and often military unit. At the same time it is often a religious unit, a religious solidarity, grouped around its progenitor, its *ujigami* (氏神), the patron-*kami* (神). (Kitagawa 1987, 50)

2.3.2.5 Gods as *kami* (神)

Kami (神) in the sense of "god" have two characteristics:

- They are always immanent beings (Okano 1976, 71), populating the classically animistic three-storied world (firmament, surface of the earth, world of the shadows) (Sakamaki 1987, 24).
- They are not preexistent, not beings that created the world and thus stand above it. Rather they have emanated from the core of the world, and are to be understood as the powers through which life is generated and through which it grows. Both nature and man, stemming from the same deity, partake in its divine power (Kitagawa and Ludwig 1984, 1640).

According to Japanese thinking, there are eight million (*yaoyorozu ookami,* 八百万大神) or even ten million (*chiyorozu-no kami,* 千万の神) gods (Mitsuhashi 2007, 73). These figures stand for an infinite number, because one of the characteristics of Shintoism is "unlimited multiplication of gods" (Rochedieu 1973, 69). In Japan this specific way of expressing infinity was also used in Buddhism, as the proverb "Thousand Buddhas, thousand [Shinto, my comment] *kami* (神)" (*hotoke sennin, kami sennin,* 仏千人、神千人) shows.

According to Kimura, there are different classes of gods: (1) nature-gods rooted in the native soil, based on the belief in natural forces, as well as on fertility cults (phallus worship); (2) patron deities of tribes and clans; (3) deified

---

81. *Yamato* (大和) is an old word for Japan.
82. Even today the common family names Abe (安部 or 阿部) or Watanabe (渡部 or 渡邊) are derived from these professions.

souls of the dead; (4) naturalized Buddhist gods; (5) the gods of the Japanese mythology[83] (Kimura 2003, 69).

Gods are not always good but can very well be demonic (Okano 1976, 71). According to Motoori, it takes only the induced fear or terror for something to become "god" (Sakamaki 1987, 25). "Eminence does not here refer to the superiority of nobility, goodness, or meritorious deeds. Evil and mysterious things, if they are extraordinary and dreadful, are called *kami* (神)" (Motoori in Holtom 1941, 390). Therefore, when for instance Bachelor in his research of the Ainu-pantheon clearly distinguishes between "good gods" and "evil demons" (Ölschleger 1993, 147), he introduces Western categories of thought which blocks the understanding of the Japanese reality.

Here are some examples of "evil gods":

- The Kojiki (古事記) names the two chief malicious Mysterious-Kami-of-Eighty-Evils (*Yaso-Maga-tsu-Bi-no-Kami*, 八十禍津日神 or 八十枉津日神) and Mysterious-Kami-of-Great-Evils (*Oo-Maga-tsu-Bi-no-Kami*, 大禍津日神 or 大枉津日神). They inflict sickness and were born from the filth Izanagi (伊邪那美命, 伊弉諾神 or 伊邪那岐命 or 伊耶那岐命) washed off after his journey through the underworld (Holtom 1941, 390–391).
- The god *Konjin* (金神) loves bloodshed.
- As the obsolete word *kamikakushi* (神隠し) shows, gods (神) or demons can let children disappear (隠す) without trace.[84]
- The *shinigami* (死神), "death-god," who escorts people to their death, is a harbinger of death.
- Demons are also called demon-神 (*kijin* or *onigami*, 鬼神). "The Nihongi (日本記) in its chronicles for the year AD 110 says that the mountains of the 'eastern savages' are inhabited by 'malignant *kami* (神),' and couples them with malicious demons that beset the highways and bar the roads. In immediate connection the same evil powers are called 'violent *kami* (神)'" (Holtom 1941, 391). The present-day proverb "appear as a god – disappear as a demon" (*shinshutsu kibotsu*, 神出鬼没), used for criminals that

---

83. The folk deities of the Japanese mythology, called *shinwa* (神話), "stories of the gods," are divided into the "gods of the heavenly rule" (*amatsugami*, 天津神) and the "gods of the earthly rule" (*kunitsugami*, 国津神) (Klaes 2000, 545). A similar division is found in the term "god of heaven, god of earth" (*tenjin chigi*, 天神地祇). *Chigi* (地祇) is a synonym for *kunitsukami* (国津神).

84. The phrase "Swallowed up by the earth" comes close.

strike unexpectedly and disappear without trace, shows that there is no categorical difference between god and demon. The difference between "god" and" "demon" is deliberately ambiguous. Bachelor's clear-cut distinction between "good gods" and "evil gods" of the Ainu-pantheon (Ölschleger 1993, 147) follows western thinking categories and rather falsifies Japanese realities.

"Gods" of this semantic group have two characteristics:

(1) They are always immanent beings (Okano 1976, 71), populating the three-story world (firmament, surface of the earth, world of shadows) of classic animism (Sakamaki 1987, 24).

(2) They are not pre-existing in a way that they have created the world and stand above it. They rather generated from the nucleus of the world and are to be understood as the powers that bring forth and grow life. Both nature and man as descendants of the gods thus share in the same divine power (Kitagawa und Ludwig 1984, 1640).

2.3.2.6 Animals as *kami* (神)

Akinari Ueda (上田秋成) (1734–1809), contemporary of Motoori, was not only a writer but also a *kokugaku*(国学)-scholar,[85] and therefore also one of the scholars who dealt with the *kami*(神)-concept. However, as for his interpretation of *kami* (神), he was an academic outsider. For him *kami* (神) were rather "animal spirits, foxes, badgers and the like, animals that are attributed in Japanese folklore with supernatural powers" (Fessler 1969, 1), one of them being the ability to speak (Hastings 2003, 238). Their common attribute is, according to Ueda, "an inability to conceive of a moral right and wrong" (Fessler 1996, 1).

> By nature, such [fox] spirits do not distinguish between good and bad, or right or wrong. They protect what is good for them and curse what is bad … The *kami* (神) are believed to be the same … They bless their faithful with happiness and curse the unfaithful … The *kami* (神) love well the man who serves them well. If someone scorns them, they punish him. Foxes and badgers seem to be the same as the *kami* (神). (Ueda in Fessler 1996, 2)

---

85. *Kokugaku* (国学), literally "science of the country."

Generally speaking, various kinds of white animals can be considered "supernatural portents, good omens, or as messengers of the gods, and are sometimes called *kami* (神)." The reason for the divinization is the extraordinary "feelings of weirdness and awe" (Holtom 1941, 357). Furthermore, Hastings classifies *kami* (神) as animals as follows:

- Reptiles: In this group the snake or serpent plays a central role, be it as river-god, mountain-god, virgin-devouring monster, or omen. It is used in purification rituals and ordeals.[86]
- Birds: Divine birds mainly occur as messengers of gods.
- Quadrupeds: Here especially the bear, the wild boar, monkeys, and the wolf can be mentioned.[87]

Fish and insects have their place in mythologies and are thus revered, but they are not considered divine (Hastings 2003, 238–239).

Among the god-animals, the "four incarnations of the spirits that misrule the world," mythological animals, play an important role. They are:

- the *Kirin* (麒麟) which "has the body of a deer, the tail of an ox, and a single, soft horn. As messenger of mercy and benevolence";
- the *Feng-hwang* (鳳凰) or Phoenix is "the second of the incarnations of the spirits, is of wondrous form and mystic nature. The rare advent of this bird upon the earth is, like that of the kirin or unicorn, a presage of the advent of virtuous rulers and good government. It has the head of a pheasant, the beak of a swallow, the neck of a tortoise, and the features of the dragon and fish";

---

86. One example is the *Yatsu-no Kami* (谷津の神), the "*kami* (神) of dales" (Holtom 1941, 374). Another writing is for *Yatsu-no Kami*, 夜刀神, literally the "god of the night-sword."

87. In Japanese the wolf is called *ookami* (狼), literally the "great god." The fact that the Chinese character is different today (狼) cannot obscure the original meaning was "great god" (大神) (Holtom 1941, 373–374). "The Nihongi (日本記) in its early record for the year AD 539 mentions two mountain wolves that were called 'Awesome *Kami* (神)' (*kashikoki kami*, 賢き神)." In the Manyoushuu (万葉集) the wolf is called "Great-Mouthed-True-*Kami* (*ooguchi-magami*, 大口真神)," the "*kami* (神) with the wide open mouth." "The messenger of the mountain shrine of Mimine (三峰神社) in Musashino (武蔵野) is a wolf" (374). Other quadrupeds being considered as *kami* (神) are the tiger (Holtom 1941, 374), and the hare (*usagi-kami*, 兎神) (376).

- the *Kwei* or tortoise "is not the actual horny reptile known to naturalists and to common experience, but a spirit, an animated creature that ages ago rose up out of the Yellow River";
- the *Lung*, the chief and leader of the four divinely constituted beasts, the dragon, "which has the power of transformation and of making itself visible or invisible. At will it reduces itself to the size of a silkworm, or is swollen until it fills the space of heaven and earth" (Griffis 1895, ch.1 – Primitive Faith: Religion before Books).

2.3.2.7 Things as *kami* (神)

This semantic field can be subdivided into three groups:

- *Kami* (神) can be used to signify natural phenomena which are powerful, scary, or awe-inspiring, such as the thunder, in Japanese called *kaminari*, today written 雷, but as the reading reveals, originally understood as the *kami* (神)-sound. Sometimes the "thunder god" was called *Takatsu Kami* (高津神), the "god of the high rule." "The most well-known designation for the thunder god is *Take-Maka-Zuchi-no-Oo-no-kami* (建御雷之男神), which probably means Fierce-Awful-Hammer-Male-*Kami* (神)" (Holtom 1941, 377). "The wind that blows from the sacred shrine of Watarai (Great Shrine of Ise) is *kamu-kaze* or *kan-kaze* (神風) (378).
- *Kami* (神) can be used to signify extraordinary things (Schinzinger 1983, 10). If something changes in an extraordinary or strange way, the word *shinpenka* (神変化) is used which means "divine change." The concept is ambiguous: sometimes things are worshipped as divine, sometimes it is only the "soul" (*tama*, 魂) of the *kami* (神) which makes a thing a *kami* (神)-body (*shintai*, 神体)[88] (Ayabe 1992, 98–99; Hall 1968, 38), or a symbol of the deity (Naumann 1984b, 1583).
- Also various representatives of the divine nature – according to Bak, nature and gods are "almost identical" (Bak 2008, 1) – can by themselves already be the object of veneration. Geldsetzer names the following:

---

88. These things became *kami* (神)-bodies "because they were filled with *mana*" (Holtom 1941, 379). "The early and purely Japanese designation for such an object is *kami-sane* or *kami-zane* (神さね or 神ざね), '*kami* (神)-seed,' or '*kami* (神)-kernel'" (378).

In addition to the cult in special shrines the popular nature cult is reflected in the veneration of some distinguished localities (such as *Mt Fuji*)[89] as well as in various folk customs such as *hanami* (花見) (flower viewing in spring, mainly the viewing of cherry blossoms), *bonsai* (盆栽) (cultivating of miniature plants), *ikebana* (生花) (flower arrangement), *cha-no yu* (茶の湯) (tea ceremony),[90] the *geisha* (芸者)-cult (the cult of femininity),[91] *bushidou* (武士道) ("way of the warrior," the cult of masculinity), ancestor veneration, the *Yamato*(大和)-cult (the cult of the Japanese islands as divine land), the *Tennou* (天皇)-cult (Emperor-veneration as cult of the sun-deity *Amaterasu* (天照) and her imperial progeny). (Geldsetzer 1996/1997, 2)

2.3.3 Positive Encounter with the God-Concept of Japanese Animism

Summary: When present-day Japanese hear the word *kami* (神) they think about the animistic soul-concept *tama* (魂) (Ayabe 1992, 102) or about one of the many gods of the Japanese pantheon. Judging from this influenced terminology the word *kami* (神) cannot be used for the proclamation of the Christian message. Nevertheless it is important to engage in an encounter with the content of the Japanese god-concept. Content aspects such as God's affection, his way of forgiving, God's

---

89. The Manyoushuu (万葉集) quotes a poem that sings of the divinity of *Mt Fuji*:
    Ayashiku mo imasu kami ka mo
    あやしくもいます神かも
    Yamato no kuni no shizume to mo imasu kami ka mo
    大和の国の鎮めともいます神かも
    Taka to nareru yama ka mo
    宝ともなれる山かも
   Holtom translates:
    Oh mountain that sittest an awe inspiring *kami*
    Oh thou *kami* that sittest as the guardian of the Yamato land
    Oh precious mountain, thou (Holtom 1941, 377).
90. *Chanoyu* (茶の湯), literally the "warm tea-water."
91. *Geisha* (芸者) simply means "artist."

"motherly aspects," and the "pain of God" can be accepted positively in this discussion.

2.3.3.1 The Christian history of the term *kami* (神)

When Francis Xavier came to Japan in 1549, he was so impressed by the Japanese culture that he choose as his missiological approach the idea of accommodating "to the local culture as far as possible" (Wetzel 1995, 206) over the until then common approach of the *tabula rasa*. His first contextualization attempt, equating the God of the Bible with *Dainichi* (大日) (Great Sun-Deity), was a failure because he was considered a preacher of the Buddhist *Shingon* sect (*shingonshuu,* 真言宗) who used that term as well (Ayabe 1992, 100–101; Endou 1970, 238–239; Whelan 1996, 4).[92] He then used a loan-word from Taoism, combining the Chinese character for "heaven" (天) in the Taoist sense and "lord" (主). In order to avoid repeated misunderstandings, he then changed the original reading, in Japanese *tenshu* (天主), to the Latin *deos* (Ayabe 1992, 100–101). The form *deusu-sama* (天主様) with the honorific suffix *sama* (様) was also used (Endou 1970, 95).[93]

In retrospect this might have been the best contextualization of the Western concept of "God." Long after the Protestant churches attempts, among various others,[94] there eventually followed the translation of James Curtis Hepburn (1815–1911) who started using *kami* (神) for the God of the Bible (Ayabe 1992, 100–101). The Catholic Church used the Taoist loan-word. It was only after 1945 that the Catholic Church in Japan used the term *kami* (神) for the God of the Bible (Waldenfels 1995, 132).

Since the Japanese god-concept is closely related to Shintoism,[95] a short look into the common history of the Shintoist and the Christian term is of interest. Even though religious freedom has been guaranteed since 1889, this freedom was only of theoretical value during the epoch of hegemonic struggles. Between 1889 and 1945 Shintoism was divided into State-Shinto

---

92. In a similar way the translation attempts of the Jesuits translating into Guarani failed (Whiteman 2003, 406–407).

93. However, the introduction of the Latin *Deus* proved to be difficult as well. The Japanese pronunciation *de-usu* is similar to the pronunciation of *dai uso* (大うそ) in Southern dialects. It means "big lie." It has been reported that the Japanese therefore responded with derision when they first heard this name of God (Skoglund 1975, 461).

94. Heaven (*ten,* 天), highest "*tennou*" (*joutei,* 上帝), Honorable of the Way of Heaven (personified sun) (*otentousama,* お天道様) (Ayabe 1992, 100–101).

95. The *shin* (神) in *shintou* (神道) means *kami* (神), "god."

(*kokkashintou,* 国家神道,[96] from 1945 on called Shrine-Shinto, *jinjashintou,* 神社神道), and Sect-Shinto (*shuuhashintou,* 宗派神道) (Rochedieu 1973, 59–61). Different from Sect-Shinto, State-Shinto was not considered religious but was interpreted as "a civil expression of respect for the Emperor and His ancestors [and therefore] as the duty of subjects" (Rosenkranz 1962, 10). No matter to what religion they adhered, all Japanese had to partake in the rituals of State-Shinto (Klaes 2000, 545). Seiran Oouchi (大内青巒)[97] wrote at the dawn of the twentieth century:

> Christianity and our imperial house can never coexist, for it is impossible to truly revere the imperial house while believing in Christianity . . . Christianity is a heresy which endangers our imperial house and destroys the foundation of our country . . . Therefore we all have to join forces to stop this heresy from spreading in our country. (Seiran Oouchi in Victoria 1999, 87)

In 1996 the Christian churches allowed their adherents to partake in the rituals of State-Shinto, giving way to the political pressure (Rosenkranz 1962, 11).

The Japanese consider themselves Shintoists by birth (Rosenkranz 1962, 11–12) and according to Genchi Katou, a Japanese never ceases to be a Shintoist even as an adherent of another religion (Rosenkranz 1959, 30; Kitagawa and Ludwig 1984, 1633). Shintoism regulates not only religious affairs but all of society: "Whether consciously or unconsciously Shintoism has remained the foundation of the general behavior of the Japanese nation. It is more than just a religious belief" (Hammitzsch 1984, 1517/1518). Schreiter (2004a, 148) rightfully asks whether one can be a Japanese without being a Shintoist as well.

In this context, at the end of the nineteenth century the liberal[98] theologian Danjou Ebina (海老名弾正) attempted to develop a Christian spirituality

---

96. Even though the Japanese government over and over stressed that the State-Shinto had no "religious value" at all, and the duty to partake in its rites would not violate religious freedom, many Japanese clearly sensed that those laws were designed as religious laws (Grayson 2001, 289). Between 1890 and 1930 the Protestant churches as well as the Roman Catholic church repeatedly declared that the rites of State-Shinto were of religious nature. However, in 1936 they gave way to the political pressure of the national-socialist government and endorsed the official interpretation of State-Shinto as "patriotism" (292–293). Kleine has rightfully compared this with the attitude of the *Deutsche Christen* (Kleine 2002).

97. Seiran Oouchi (1845–1919) was a priest of *Zen*-Buddhism. He became famous for the reviving of *Zen*-Buddhist *Soutou* (曹洞)-School (Dumoulin 2005, 413).

98. Ebina renounced the divine sonship of Jesus Christ as well as the authority of the Bible (Schwade 1984, 1573).

which was to inherit and develop the best of Shintoism (Thelle 1987, 175). He desired the "happy (re-)union of Christianity and Shintoism (231) and called himself a "Shinto-Christian," "because he was convinced that Christianity would inherit and fulfill the ideals of Shintoism" (242). He demanded:

> We ought to believe in Christianity as Japanese . . . We ought to hold up Christianity with our right hand while reaching down to our forty million [Japanese] brothers, taking hold of them. (Ebina in Thelle 1987, 175)

2.3.3.2 Formal aspects

Ayabe wants to see a certain contiguousness of the Japanese *kami*(神)-term to the biblical God-concept. He gives five reasons (Ayabe 1992, 102), which I would like to challenge critically:

- By choosing the term *kami* (神) for the God of the Bible the existence of a spiritual world is acknowledged. I would argue against this reason because even though *kami* (神) are spiritual beings they are in an animistic sense not transcendent and not personal beings (Rochedieu 1973, 227).
- *Kami* (神) are stronger than humans. I would argue against this that the power of the *kami* (神) is relative. They are not almighty as Rochedieu (1973, 228) wrongly claimed. As Tetsurou Watsuji (和辻哲郎) showed the Japanese value system and Japanese society are organized hierarchically. According to Hori, this is also true of the world of the gods. In the Japanese hierarchical pantheon there is no place for an almighty God, but each and every *kami* (神) is responsible to others (Hori 1987, 203). Their unique abilities make them only more powerful than humans (Naumann 1984b, 1583).
- Humans can communicate with *kami* (神) in one way or another. However, the way of communication between *kami* (神) and humans in Japanese animism has next to nothing in common with the biblical dialogue between God and man. According to Japanese understanding, humans live immersed in the spiritual world. They can be permeated by the divine, obsessed as mediums (Rochedieu 1973, 227–228). These shamanic concepts have nothing in common with the fellowship of Christians with God through the ministry of the Holy Spirit.

- Humans can benefit from worshipping *kami* (神). In my opinion this motivation cannot be juxtaposed with Christian prayer.

2.3.3.3 Aspects of content

A positive encounter in search of a "link" for the proclamation of the Christian message has to reach much deeper than Ayabe's formal and highly questionable similarities. Loewen demanded "that we as missionaries from the West need to be a lot more critical of the shortcomings in our God concept" (Loewen 1986, 18). The following Japanese god-concepts could be understood as a positive challenge to Western theology:

The mercy of God and motherly tenderness

What remained under all superficial and temporary concepts of a father-God, even after centuries of Christianization, was, according to Shuusaku Endou, that "which corresponds with the truest essence of Japanese religion: the longing for mother" (Endou in Kohler 1976, 55). The reason why Christianization in Japan has been a failure is that this motherly element of the Japanese god-concept has never been utilized in missions, says Yoshizawa (1996, 185). Communicators of the Christian message should part from the unbalanced traditional teaching of a harsh, Western father-god and find in the Bible those elements which speak of a God of "tenderness," a predicate in the West attributed to women. Demanding this does not compromise God's revelation in the Bible. It challenges and criticizes the unbalance of Western theology, which perceives God as a strict and punishing medieval father. The approach of the Jesuit father Hermann Heuvers (1890–1977) could point into the right direction. He translated the German "*der liebe Gott*" with *natsukashii kami* (なつかしい神). The closest translation is "intimate God," but the Japanese have a much deeper and richer meaning. According to Doi (土居健郎), Heuvers' translation echoed deeply in the Japanese' hearts (1997, 124–125).

The Hebrew thinking which describes God's love with the most basic word for motherly tenderness could help to (re)discover character traits of God in the West traditionally attributed to women. The Hebrew word for "love" or "mercy," רַחֲמִים, is a derivative of the Hebrew word for womb, רחם. The writers of the Bible used this word without hesitation when talking about God's love. Only seven of the forty references using רַחֲמִים talk about the love and mercy of humans.

Repentance and forgiveness – or forgiveness and repentance?

Judging from these motherly attributes of God the (Western) praxis of evangelism seems to be in need of reconsideration. Is it really necessary to shame and accuse the sinner until he, in agonizing remorse, pleads for mercy before he may hear the liberating message of grace? This approach to evangelism is based upon the perception of a harsh and strict father-god. In a culture which understands tearful remorse as unaesthetic and therefore ethically suspicious (Abegg 1970, 97) the understanding of God as a loving mother who forgives and through forgiveness leads into even deeper remorse and repentance seems to be much more helpful.

A glimpse into Japanese psychology can be helpful. The mother-son relationship is in Japan not described with the Oedipus-complex as in the West, but with the Ajase-complex.[99] Ajase was an Indian prince. His mother had learned from a diviner that she was to wait three more years for her long-awaited male descendant because a certain hermit had not yet died. Fearing that until then she might lose the favor of her husband, she killed the monk. While she was pregnant, she felt the grudge of the hermit inside her and tried to kill Ajase even while giving birth to him. When Ajase learned about this he was so disappointed in his mother that he sought to kill her. Holding this kind of grudge brought a severe sickness upon him. Festering ulcers kept him from partaking in social life and only his mother would sacrificially nurse him. "The mother forgave Ajase who had tried to kill her, and he in turn conceived her agony and forgave her" (Okonogi 1990, 35). According to Okonogi (小此木啓吾) (37–38), the feelings of guilt only reached their full depth through forgiveness, through the sacrificial love of the mother. This kind of consciousness of guilt is on a higher level than that which is generated by fear of punishment. Contrary to the Western paternal principle, "the uniqueness of Japanese religion which warmheartedly embraces and forgives all human weaknesses and failures clearly can be seen" (Miyata 1984, 180). Okonogi illustrates this Japanese, motherly way of forgiving:

> In all this[100] the following words of one of the released hostages, a Japanese Lady in her fifties, moved me most: "I also felt some pity for these children . . . Aren't they pitiful? Always on the run,

---

99. This observation is by no means new. Even at the dawn of the 20th century the Japanese psychologist Heisaku Kozawa (小沢平作) sought to convince Sigmund Freud, that the overwhelming superego was not the father, but the mother. Freud showed great interest in Kozawa but in Japan his work went unrecognized for centuries (Christopher 1983, 73).

100. Okonogi is talking about the hijacking of Dacca in September 1977.

no place to call home. And then I suddenly thought: Wouldn't it be possible to just forgive them?" (Okonogi 1990, 39)

Repentance and forgiveness – or forgiveness and repentance? Weber's commentary on the forgiveness of sins as confessed in the Apostles' Creed is quite interesting: "It is not insignificant that in the Apostles' Creed sin occurs only in the confession of its forgiveness" (Weber 1955, 641). The praxis of Jesus also shows that he first lovingly received people before talking with them about their sin. The command not to sin anymore was preceded by the unconditional healing of a certain blind man (John 5:14). In the case of the "adulteress," the admonition not to sin anymore was preceded by the full acquittal (John 8:11). Jesus forgave the lame man without first asking for his confession of sins solely on the basis of his and his friends' faith (Matt 9:2; Mark 2:7). The father embraces the Prodigal Son before he can stammer his confession (Luke 15:20–21) and by doing so leads him to an even deeper repentance. The rehearsed apodosis "make me like one of your hired men" (Luke 15:19) became impossible. The Good Shepherd seeks the lost sheep – and by doing so lays down his life (John 10:11, 15) – even before the sheep can comprehend that it is lost (Luke 15:4–7). Also Paul points out the fact that humans cannot earn God's kindness, but that in turn God's kindness leads to repentance (Rom 2:4).

The theological encounter with motherly god concepts and their implications will be taken up in connection with Japanese sociology and the *amae*(甘え)-concept under 2.5.3.4.

God's provision and eco-feminism

There are only a few biblical references that show God's "motherly" provision. Psalm 104:27 and Psalm 131 are two of them. These references show that God not only has a fatherly side but by his provision through nature shows also a motherly, providing side.

According to M. Doi, Western theologies never developed an "adequate understanding of nature." He therefore calls for the development of a "well-balanced theology of nature" as an urgent task for Christians in the East (1979, 79–80).[101] Such a theology should apprehend humans and nature not as opposites, but rather with a "sense of identity and kinship" (1979, 80). "Most Japanese do not draw a clear boundary between humans and nature, while

---

101. As an Asian theologian, Ok takes a similar approach when emphasizing nature in the context of theology much more than Western theologies do (Ok 2004, 5).

Westerners discuss nature in the context of its relationship to humans" (Aoyagi-Usui et al. 2003, 24).[102]

> Christian theology in Japan has two tasks: On one side it has, on the basis of the teaching of creation, to liberate man from the spell of nature's magic power. On the other side it has to correct the materialistic interpretation of nature by emphasizing the solidarity between man and nature . . . On the basis of their belief in creation, Japanese Christians need to have a deep understanding in and due respect for the inner *telos* (purpose) of all existing things. This is nothing else than what the ancestors intuitively apprehended and naively expressed through friendliness and awe towards nature and things. (M. Doi 1979, 88)

As an example for such a theology Takenaka's *God Is Rice* (1986) can be mentioned. He talks about "atmosphere" or "air" as a metaphor of the Japanese *mana*-concept *ki* (気). "Air" is given, not made, a gift of nature. Takenaka (1986, 13) sees humans as called to live as companions of nature. Mountains and rivers, sun and moon, trees and flowers are all gifts of God who permeates the world with his spirit.

"God is rice." For Takenaka this means:

- "When we say that God is rice . . . we take rice as the symbol of God's gift of life." Takenaka does not want this sentence to be understood as an affront to his "radical monotheism" (1986, 21).
- Recognizing God as rice and nature as our companion, which ought not to be exploited nor to be conquered, leads to a change in the attitude towards ecological subjects (1986, 21–22).
- We live in harmony with nature (1986, 24).

The call for a "balanced theology of nature" was also made in the West. Yet it was often not heard in the Christian churches. On the contrary, "Our present-day understanding of nature was mainly formed by Christianity and then, with the beginning of modern times, got its particular character through the philosophy of Descartes" (Sachsse 1976, 28). "It is the well-ordered world . . . from which the Christian faith liberates." 1 Corinthians 10:23 put the world "totally at man's disposal" (Gogarten in Sachsse 1976, 28).

---

102. In the East, humans are submitted to nature. This can clearly be seen in Eastern nature drawings where humans are painted infinitesimally small, vanishing in a vast natural landscape (Corwin 1978, 300).

Descartes understands nature as "composition of mechanical parts," animals as "automatic machines," and nature as "matter of man as its constructor." In his understanding, humans are "masters and owners of nature." This approach led to a paradoxical relationship with nature in the West: Even though through the sciences humans know more and more about nature, the "understanding of nature is more and more lost . . . The concept of mastering nature has led us into a blind alley" (Sachsse 1976, 27).

> Man has started a fight with nature, a fight we cannot sustain. We have to revise our natural philosophical basic concept if we want to be able to get along with our world, if we want to be able to feel at home in it again. (Sachsse 1976, 53)

For Sachsse (29), "revision" has to do with the question "whether nature is animated,"[103] whether nature is self-conscious, which is how he understands "animated." The self-consciousness of nature has three implications, among others:

- "Humans are far too dependent on nature to see it merely as counterpart" (48).
- "The idea of an animated nature[104] creates a certain respect for nature, creates a relationship . . . based on partnership" (48).
- "The thesis of an animated nature directs man to its lawful place in nature thus teaching him to be humble" (49–50).

The "pain" of God and suffering in Asian feminist theologies

Another keyword of Asian feminist theology is the "pain and suffering" of Asian women. In the context of Japanese theologies this points towards a "female aspect of God's character." According to Kitamori (北森嘉蔵),[105] "the theological plan of the church is pressed into the pain of God. This is true not only for the New Testament but also for the Old Testament" (Kitamori 1968, 113–114).[106] The central biblical reference of his *Theology of the Pain of God* is Jeremiah 31:20 (Terazono 1987, 186): ". . . therefore my heart breaks, so that I must have mercy upon him (רִחֵם אֲרַחֲמֶנּוּ[!]), says the Lord." According to Kitamori, God's ability to suffer is not seen in the West due to

---

103. *Beseelt*.
104. Sachsse talks about the *Beseeltheit der Natur*, which literally implies that nature has a soul.
105. Kitamori's theology will be discussed in more detail under 10.1.1.
106. Kitamori justifies this with references such as Gen 6:6; Isa 63:9.

Greek influence during early theological formation. Hebrew thinking does not know about "God's inability to suffer" (Kitamori 1968, 115; Moltmann 1987, 255).[107] Kitamori called his *Theology of the Pain of God* "a specific Japanese contribution to the history of the Gospel" (Ratschow in his foreword to the German edition *Theologie des Schmerzes Gottes*, 1972, 5–6). In a similar way, Asian female theologians attach great importance to pain and suffering in feminist theologies. Kitamori influenced C. S. Song ("God's gravitating love pulls him into the life of humans") and Shuusaku Endou (遠藤周作) (Jesus as the "eternal companion always suffering with humanity"). In approaches like these the aspect of Christ's vicarious suffering is replaced by his identification with human suffering. According to Levison and Pope-Levison (1994, 7–8), this particular emphasis originated from the Buddhist basic view that suffering is inevitable. This influence has led to a certain degree to a nihilistic apathy.

2.3.4 Critical Encounter with the God-Concept of Japanese Animism

> **Summary:** It is only natural that the Japanese god-concept as part of the worldview of Japanese animism is not exclusive but syncretistic. This needs to be acknowledged. However, acknowledgment must never mean concealment of the explicit differences of the Christian God-concept, of which Japanese scholars are very well aware. Contrary to the Japanese god-concept, the Christian understanding of God sees God as (a) "categorically" other, and (b) not as available to humans, but on the contrary, being the one to whom humans are responsible.
>
> The prerogative of Christian thinking is the existence of God, which can and must be known through God's revelation in creation. This statement kindles the argument between "natural theology" and revelation

---

107. The first Christian encounter with the Greek concept of *apathia* is found in Lactantius' *De ira Dei*, in which he opposed Epicureans and Stoics talking about God's passion. In Asia the "Stoic notion" is found particularly in Buddhism (Koyama 1968, 50–51). "Classical theism and Christian orthodoxy have long held that God cannot suffer. The conviction arises out of the Greek notion that, by definition, perfection excludes the possibility of suffering and change. Relying in particular on Plato and Aristotle, early Christians concluded that God is, therefore, both impassable (unable to suffer) and immutable (unchanging)" (Park 2000, 83). "From the viewpoint of the implications of Divine suffering, it is actually correct to talk about a paradigm shift of theological orientation" (Nnamani 1995, 393).

theology, which cannot be solved by an either-or solution, but only by an as-well-as solution.

2.3.4.1 *Kami* (神) is a syncretistic term

It is not by chance that *kami* (神) is a syncretistic term. On the contrary this choice is deliberate (Rochedieu 1973, 226). The plurality of religions in Japan has always been characterized by a "strong syncretism" (Triplett 2006a, 117). As Abegg (148) observed, Japanese have a strong dislike for any kind of absolutism.[108] The political scientist and theologian Mitsuo Miyata (宮田光雄) links this to the fact that "the number of adherents of religions is bigger than the total population of Japan." He calls this phenomenon "multiple faith" (1984, 17), combined of Shintoism, Buddhism, and Christianity which after 1900 took the third rank from Confucianism" (1984, 46).

> This kind of religiosity seems to be hard to understand for Europeans, because they understand faith as an act of trusting in and deciding on an absolute or transcendent person . . . The tendency to let heterogeneous religions coexist is a specific feature of Shintoism. This feature is due to Shintoism's lack of personal inwardness and religious fidelity. (Miyata 1984, 47–48)

Schreiter (2004b, 63) pointed out that syncretism only has a poor image in Christianity, while in the social sciences it is used neutrally for the formation of new identities from different cultural elements. From a Japanese point of view "this syncretism is not . . . something negative." It is an essential characteristic not only of Japanese religiosity but also of the Japanese culture in general. "Japan has, ever since becoming a nation, had the tendency to accept alien things, assimilate them and even mold them into their own" (Hammitzsch 1984, 1515/1516).[109] In all affairs Japan shows tolerance and harmony, co-

---

108. Even though Lily Abegg (1901–1974) has made more striking observations like this, the fact that she is best classified as a travel author must not be forgotten. Her judgment of Asian cultures and particularly the Japanese culture are considered stereotype today (Kim 2001). Kim examined travelogues of the 1930s and 1940s with research methods of stereotype science. According to Erlinghagen (early 1980s[?], 78), this is also true today. "The Japanese are extremely adaptable and in the process of adapting to foreign cultures they form a lifestyle which they deem fitting for the living conditions of a certain time. This attitude, flexible and at times elusive, shows also in their rejection of distinguishing between good and evil in everyday life (Matsuoka 1971, 375).

109. Schreiter calls this process "incorporative" (2004a, 71). However, it must not be overlooked that the Japanese themselves do at times evaluate this process rather negatively. The Japanese political scientist Masao Maruyama (丸山眞男) (1914–1996) called the Japanese tradition of syncretism "spiritual promiscuity" (Miyata 1984, 185).

existence, even interwovenness, an "as-well-as." According to Lundell, the integrating framework is *nihonkyou* (日本教), the "teaching of Japan," or the "Japan-religion," or *nihonjinron* (日本人論), the "theory of the Japanese people," or the "science of Japanese people" (Lundell 1995, 403).[110]

> This attitude . . . has soon led the Japanese not to consider one religion as "universally valid." For the Japanese, religion is mainly a matter of different "ways" . . . they walk to find self and one's own position in the world. (Hammitzsch 1984, 1515/1516)

As one practical example for Japanese syncretism Schinzinger's observation on the Middle Ages serves well:[111]

> In a Buddhist temple there used to be a small *Shintou*-shrine for the local deity. At times the temple considered the *kami* (神) as low-ranking Buddhist deities. And at times Buddhist deities were accepted as *kami* (神) by the shrines. (Schinzinger 1983, 12)[112]

Sometimes *Shintou*-deities were interpreted as *bodhisattvas* (Köpping 1974, 35) or as devas waiting for their *bodhisattvas* or Buddhas to redeem them (Klaes 2000, 548). The following proverbs, phrases, and observations show that *kami* (神) and Buddhas are essentially one:

- The sayings *kami-to hotoke-wa suiha-no hedate* (神と仏は水波の隔て), "[*Shintou*]-god and Buddha – wave crest and wave trough," shows that making a difference between *kami* (神) and Buddhas is as meaningless as distinguishing between wave crest and wave trough.
- The saying *butsujin-wa suiha-no hedate* (仏神は水波の隔て) means the same as the previous.
- The phrase *honji suijaku* (本地垂迹) means that a "basic essence" (*honji*, 本地) such as a Buddha leaves a "trail," an "impression" (*suijaku*, 垂迹) in form of a *kami* (神). The reason is that the

---

110. "*Nihonjinron* (日本人論) (literally, 'the discussions of the Japanese') is a genre of writing on Japanese society that focuses on the uniqueness of the Japanese. Other terms associated with this genre of writing include, but are not limited to, '*nihon bunkaron* (日本文化論) [the discussion of Japanese culture];' 'the group model,' and 'the consensus model' of Japanese society." According to Sugimoto and Mourer (1989), these terms designate a "fairly coherent image of Japanese society" (Gudykunst and San Anonio 1993, 24). Lundell traces the ideological roots of *nihonkyou* (日本教) (and *nihonjinron*, 日本人論) back to three dominant *Shintou*-scientists of the 19th century: Mabuchi Kamono (賀茂真淵) (1697–1769), Norinaga Motoori (本居宣長) (1730–1801), and Atsutane Hirata (平田篤胤) (1776–1843) (Lundell 1995, 406).

111. According to my own observations, this is still true for present-day Japan.

112. An example is the composition of the Seven Auspicious Deities (see 9.2).

actual presence of a Buddha could be too overwhelming, but the more approachable form of a *kami* (神) helps the believer to reach enlightenment.

- "Sometimes the combination of Buddhist and Shintoist deities leads to something called *shinbutsu shuugou* (神仏集合), a fusion of these deities, because they are both considered parts of the same essence" (Triplett 2006b, 181). "This is actually about the assimilation or harmonization of *Shintou* and Buddhism" (117).[113] Küng and Bowden (2006, 150) talk about an "osmotic" Japanization of Buddhism with a simultaneous "Buddhification" of the native *Shintou*.
- According to Schinzinger (11), the fact that the Japanese language does not distinguish between singular and plural also has implications for the Japanese god-concept. Even on the level of language "God" as singular, as One, is hardly perceivable.

2.3.4.2 Broken and unbroken relationship between God and people

In animism the relationship between (the) god(s) and people usually is understood as an unbroken relationship. This does not mean that there is a close relationship between deities and humans. Rather there is no difference between them and humans in principle. Japan does not know a god "as an absolutely separate being" (Nakane 1970, 139–140). All Japanese are considered descendants of the *kami* (神) (Kitagawa and Ludwig 1984, 1640). And after their death they naturally become *kami* (神). Humans, living in this visible world, can be *kami* (神)-manifestations in human form.[114] In contrast to this understanding, the God of the Bible is "categorically different" (Härle 1995, 411–413). The early Karl Barth even talked about God being *totaliter aliter*. God is in fact far beyond what humans can imagine. This has to be stated clearly when engaging in dialogue with Japanese animism with its highly imaginative ideas about the *kami* (神). However, if God was so different that there would

---

113. These theoretical harmonization attempts of Japanese theologians must not obscure the fact that there are also tensions between Buddhism and Shintoism. The hostile encounters between Buddhism and Shintoism must not be forgotten. At the beginning of the *Meiji*-Restoration, a law for separation of Buddhism and the state (*shinbutsu bunri-no rei*, 神仏分離の令) lead to the closing of 40,000 Buddhist temples and a subsequent reduction of their priests to the rank of laity (Victoria 1999, 22–23). The fairytale about a giant-ape deity in the country of *Hida* who was offered a girl for appeasement (Kikuchi-Brinkley) tells, with biting irony, the story of a Buddhist monk who freed the natives of *Hida* (飛騨, also called *Hinshuu*, 飛州) from their traditional idol worship (Hammitzsch 1969, 49ff).

114. The *ikigami* (生神), "incarnate gods" (Klaes 2000, 546) or *hitogami* (人神), human-gods (Hori 1987, 202) own mystical powers while living on earth (Berentsen 1985a, 96).

be no connection to human conception, talking about him would be totally meaningless. Just how is God *totaliter aliter*? This is the basic question of this section.

The context in and to which Barth talked about God being *totaliter aliter* is important.

> His theology was . . . partly a response to some of the anti-theological challenges presented by modern thought. Instead of beginning with humanity, he argues, theology begins with *God* . . . Liberalism, according to Barth, spoke about God by speaking about human religious experience; in his dialectical phase, Barth spoke about God by opposing God to human religious experience as the *totaliter aliter* who condemns human religiosity. (Badcock 1997, 172)

If this was everything that could be said about God, humans could as well not talk about him at all. Nay, they must not talk about him at all. In his first study of Anselm (1931), Barth made a new departure, which is speaking about God "on the basis of revelation." "The order of theological method involves revelation, faith, and only then knowledge" (Badcock 1997, 172). It is not that humans cannot know about God in principle, but they have to submit knowledge to revelation.

> In Barth's mature theology, however, this principle is combined with an enormous emphasis on Jesus Christ as the ground and content of all thought about God. God becomes in this way not so much the *totaliter aliter* of Barth's early dialectical phase as the Immanuel, the God who is with us, of the Bible. (Badcock 1997, 172)

It is bitterly ironic that Barth's God *totaliter aliter* was, under the code "Immanuel," quite differently interpreted in the context of Japanese thought. Katsumi Takizawa (滝沢克己) (1909–1984) studied Buddhist philosophy under Nishida[115] who commended studying under Barth (Y. Furuya 1996,

---

115. It was only since the 17th century that Japan took notice of Western thinking and adapted those idealistic-pantheistic trends that were compatible to the native Shintoist-Buddhist thinking (Kant, German Idealism, Phenomenology, Heidegger). Only then did genuine Japanese philosophical systems (Nishida) emerge in the late 19th and early 20th century, which in turn represent the modern Japanese thinking as "Japanese classics" (Geldsetzer 1996/1997, 1). Nishida is the founder of the Kyoto School of Philosophy (Buri 1997, 37).

117–119).[116] With reference to Barth,[117] Takizawa detached the *Urfaktum Immanuel* from the historical person of Jesus.

> As far as he "discovers" this *Urfaktum Immanuel*, believes in and abides by it, Karl Barth is by virtue of light and love of the same *Urfaktum Immanuel* completely free from all fetters of historical[118] form, including the Bible and Jesus of Nazareth. As he purposefully said to me on occasion of his last visit: I know nothing of the historical Jesus. (Takizawa 1988, 303)

Based on his Buddhist presupposition about the absolute (Hennecke and Venemans 2015, 23), Takizawa talked about the first *Urfaktum*, "eternal Jesus" or "pre-exting logos" (24), of which Jesus as the second *Urfaktum* was only some kind of "prototype." "According to Takizawa, God's primary contact with creation existed even before the appearance of the historical Jesus. Therefore, the event of Jesus alone should not be regarded as the exclusive ground for the salvific relationship between God and human beings" (Chung 2010, 121). If *Urfaktum* I and *Urfaktum* II are not distinguished, one "still dreams up in the darkest places of one's heart a humanity isolated from the almighty Creator God" (Takizawa in Hennecke and Venemans 2015, 26). In *Buddhism and Christianity* (1964) Takizawa, drawing on Barth, said that "the basic

---

116. Even though Nishida was closer to Heidegger (Hennecke and Venemans 2015, 17), he advised him: "Nowadays rather study under theologians than under philosophers, because theologians are much more interesting than philosophers. Even Heidegger still lacks what is absolutely necessary – God. The best for you is to go to Karl Barth, who also is the firmest among the theologians" (Nishida in Furuya 1996, 59). Nishida's advice might have been based on the *Shintou*-theologian Atsutane Hirata (平田篤胤) (1776–1843), who was influenced by Christianity and who, similar to Barth's distinction, distinguished between the *arahanigoto* (as he called it) (顕明事), the "Here and Now" reigned by the emperor (here called *Sumemima-no Mikoto*, 皇美麻命) and the categorical eschatologically interpreted *kamigoto* (幽冥事) (Devine 1981, 43). In Shintoism *kamigoto* (幽冥) means the world after death which in Buddhism, however, is called *yuumeikai* (幽冥界), the world in which gods and Buddhas live. As Barth turned historical eschatology into an ahistorical eschatology (see under 10.3.2.1 Jürgen Moltmann's understanding of eschatology), Hirata distinguished between historical and ahistorical reality. According to Barth, eschatology is an expression of quality, of the quality of the eternal, the quality of God himself (Maier 1981, 551–552). In a similar way Hirata used the 幽 in *kamigoto* (幽冥事) in the term *kakure-no kami* (幽神) as a synonym to *ten-shu* or *t'ien chu* (天主), the contemporary Christian word for the God of the Bible (Devine 1981, 44). The reading *kakure-no kami* which he preferred to the more common reading *yuushin* means "hidden" or "concealed." Both, Barth (Maier 1981, 551–552) and Hirata think platonically.

117. Takizawa chose Barth's "infinite qualitative difference" between eternity and time, between God and man as point of departure of his Barth-interpretation (Hennecke and Venemans 2015, 15).

118. *Innergeschichtlich-historisch.*

mode of being was Immanuel." "The *Urfaktum* of human beings and creation corresponds to the universal *Sunyata* of *Zen* Buddhism. This *Urfaktum* means the true I-self of *Zen* Buddhism that already existed from the foundation of the world" (Chung 2010, 121). Takizawa associates Barth's *totaliter aliter* with "Nishida's Self-Identity of Absolute Contradiction" (Y. Furuya 1996, 117–119).

In answer to Takizawa's Barth-reception two things can be said:

First, according to Thielicke (1978, 543), the fundamental error of this thought starts with the detaching of the christological basis from all interpretation. The point where the total reversal started is Barth's critique of Christianity as religion. "Immanuel is the *Urfaktum* pre-existent to all man-made distinctions, between God and Man, belief and unbelief, Christian or non-Christian" (Y. Furuya 1996, 117–119). Hans Urs von Balthasar criticized Barth and the basic approach of his dialectical theology by saying that it criticizes what it is itself in essence. He concluded, "There is no congenial method to prove the 'infinite qualitative distinction,' not even a negative congenial method. Dialectic can never substitute theology (von Balthasar 1962, 92). Holding fast to dialectical formulation of all statements about God in early-Barthian manner, eventually leads to Takizawa's "theology."

Second, Barth's rejection of what he called "Jesus-cult" was a decided setting of course towards Takizawa's theology.

> God is by no means object, not a man, not flesh, but unrescindably subject, unrestrictedly God, completely spirit, . . . not only as the Father and the Holy Spirit but also as the Son, as the Word. (Barth 1982, 364)

If the historical Jesus is turned into a principle *Urfaktum Immanuel*, it opens the door for any theological indistinctiveness, even for Takizawa's absolute indistinctiveness and therefore meaninglessness.

God is *totaliter aliter*. This needs to be emphasized, especially in the dialogue with Japanese animism which in endless repetition talks about the gods in a way comprehensible for human reason. But Barth's "totally different God" is in final analysis nothing more than a philosophical construct. And as a construct of little help. Kreck questions its practical relevance: "When the word of God is thus circumscribed . . . in its paradox reality, one may rightfully question its perceptibility" (Kreck 1978, 89). What kind of message is that which, instead of "clearly portraying Jesus Christ before their eyes" (Gal 3:1), only "says" about God what in reality "cannot be said." We must be humble and modest and never dare to take possession of God, not even the incarnate

God. Yet this humility must not lead us into a predicament where we cannot say anything about God anymore.

What then is the essence of God being *totaliter aliter*? Not that God cannot be known at all. "Since the creation of the world God's invisible qualities – his eternal power and divine nature – have been clearly seen, being understood from what has been made" (Rom 1:20). The difference between God and man, which always needs to be emphasized in the dialogue with Japanese animism, is the categorical difference between Creator and creature. The sin of man can be overcome and he can live in perfect harmony with God and share in his glory. Yet man's createdness will never be rescinded (Berentsen 1985b, 271).

Contrary to the "vast abyss between the human and the divine" in the West (Benedict 1986, 127), Japan stands for a relationship between *kami* (神) and humans which can be best described as *oyakokankei* (親子関係), as "parent-child-relationship" (Matsumoto 1972, 14). Even though the Bible also talks about God's fatherhood and humans as being created in God's image, but humans are, as children of God, never beings "identical with God in the deepest sense" (Weber (opposing Augustine) 1955, 583), but,

> God's fatherhood ... cannot be understood as a relation of origin in the meaning of "emanation." The eternal origin ... would not be the Creator, but the kernel of the world, and the relationship with him not that of a child, but that of the deducted to the origin. (Weber 1955, 530–531)

In Christian theology the fact that humans are God's image is not a statement about any human quality, but first and foremost a statement about God (Westermann 1985, 83) and about the relationship between God and humans (Weber 1955, 618). "The *imago-Dei* is ... not a concept of being or a concept of quality, but a concept of relation" (Faix 2004, 262).

Japanese scholars are well aware of this difference. Ben-Dasan[119] called attention to the fundamental difference between the relationship between the Jews and their God who adopted them by means of the covenant (135) and the relationship between the Japanese and their gods (137, 140). Keil on Hosea 11:1 talked about adoption and said that "Israel was the son of Jehovah, by virtue of its election to be Jehovah's peculiar people" (136–137). Ono et al. (191) claim that, contrary to the Christian understanding of "created children," humans are, according to the Japanese worldview, *kami-no umi-no ko* (神の生みの子), "children born of *kami* (神)", and that *kami* (神) and humans

---

119. Ben-Dasan is the pen name of Shichihei Yamamotos (山本七平) (Lundell 1995, 407).

are *ketsuen-no oyako* (血縁の親子), "parent and child related by blood."[120] Miyata (1984, 49) calls this "theogonic continuity." In Shintoist terminology this is called *shinjin gouitsu* (神人合一) (Nawrocki 1998, 208) which means that *kami* (神) and humans (人) are unified (合) into a single entity (一). In Buddhist terminology this is expressed in the notion that the inner Buddha-nature of humans, *busshou* (仏性), will do *joubutsu* (成仏) after death, that is, that humans become (成) what they always have been (仏), Buddha (Nesbitt 2007, 90).

2.3.4.3 God disposable versus human responsible

In animism the disposability of spiritual energy is very important. Naming is considered as ruling. In Japan craftsmen would name their tools, which due to this identification were then considered "animate" (Kitano 2007, 2). He who knows someone's name can control that person. Concerning the "practice of religion and magic in all cultures" Kraus wrote that deities can be magically invoked by those who call out their correct names (Kraus 1987, 24; also Bloch 1982, 1315–1316). The name of the deity and the deity are mysteriously connected and therefore must not be changed phonetically. "Power is inherent to a name in itself, as to a magic formula, or a magical sign; he who knows the name has the power at his command" (Anrich 1990, 96; also Grundmann 1981, 198).[121] In the Jewish Halakah the magician using the name of God can even be identified with God himself (Veltri 1997, 88).

The Bible vigorously opposes all attempts to control God. On one side, in the world of the Old and New Testament the name of a person is much more important than in modern times in the West. It is an expression of the being of

---

120. This idea is also known by the natives of Japan, the Ainu. The fairytale *The Louse and the Flea* (Hammitzsch 1969, 293–295) plays in an age where there have "been no humans." A witch had two daughters. One of them she gave to a god in marriage. Their offspring are, according to the fairytale, the Ainu.

121. This thinking still exists. "In the USA, 'handle' has long been a slang term for 'name.' Knowing a person's name gives us a 'handle' in addressing him" (Clowney 1994, 138). In Hayao Miyazaki's (宮崎駿) (Bak calls him a "passionate Shintoist" [Bak 2008, 2]) *Sen-to Chihiro-no kamikakushi* (千と千尋の神隠し) (English: *Spirited Away*) the witch Yubaba (ゆばば), the "bathhouse Aunty," takes off one Chinese character from Chihiro's (千尋) name, who is then called *Sen* (千), and thus gains control over her (Knörer 2001). In the same way she betrays the Spirit of the "Amber-River," Nigihayami Kohaku Nushi (饒速水琥珀主) by leaving only *Kohaku* (琥珀) as his name forgetting the rest (Bak 2008, 5). Ogihara-Schuck (2014) gives an excellent discussion of Miyazaki's work, its Western reception, and its encounter of animism and monotheism.

a person to the degree that the person is present in his name.¹²² On the other side, the formula "I will have compassion on whom I will have compassion" (Exod 33:19) "resounds the sovereign freedom of Jahweh who, particularly when he reveals his name, let no one get hold of himself, let no one control him" (Zimmerli 1982, 14). When Moses was called, he asked for God's name, and God told him, "I am the one working all – and I am here, here for you!"¹²³ In the first place this is a clear rejection of all attempts to control God. But then this revelation is also the comforting promise of God's Omnipotence and his presence. There are two safeguards to protect God's name from misuse:

- "The prohibition of any imagery of God seems to have its real purpose in keeping humans from influencing God in any way by means of magic" (Hennig 1982, 80).
- God's freedom is also safeguarded by the third commandment (Exod 3:7). Hennig (1982, 102) refers to Martin Luther's Small Catechism: "We should fear and love God that we may not curse, swear, use witchcraft, lie, or deceive by His name, but call upon it in every trouble, pray, praise, and give thanks" (Evangelical Lutheran Synod of Missouri, Ohio, and Other States 1912). According to Hennig, "using witchcraft by his name" means "forcing God to help in a way only a learned conjurer can do, and in a way that is different from common prayer" (Hennig 1982, 109).

In the Bible the relationship between God and humans is not one where humans create God and thus able to control him, but that God is the Creator of humans and therefore also their lord. God is not the one to answer humans using magic, but humans must answer God. Humans are "responsible." God demands of humans (Mic 6:8). And God demands accountability.

> When God addresses humans in a human way, his purpose is not so much the communication of mere facts – even though this is not precluded – but his purpose is that man may know him . . . Knowing God ultimately means acknowledging him as sovereign lord . . . The purpose of God's words and acts is man's faith, his personal attachment to God. The personal nature of God therefore means that God faces man as "I" talking to a "You" . . . God and man have a relationship as persons. Consequently man

---

122. So Proksch (1933, 102, 113). "The 'name' of God is the Holy God himself" (Barth 1985, 567).

123. In a similar way Vicedom (1965, 43) interprets Exod 3:14.

as historical person is accountable to God for deeds and acts, as well as in his talking. Man's responsibility to God's word and will is a given from the first page of the Old Testament which talks about God as the Creator and man as being created in his image. (Zobel 1993, 8)

In his treatise *Verantwortung: Vom Sein und Ethos der Person* (1948) Alfred Schüler inseparably tied together humanity and responsibility:

Man is ... in his very essence, in his humanity as creature, directly addressed by God, and therefore in principle responsible to him ... Man is responsible because there is somebody who demands it of him ... because he is only as much human as he lives responsibly. (Schüler 1948, 105)

2.3.4.4 Dissonance in the harmonic orchestra of religions

I would not be honest, if I didn't address what is considered the tiresome annoyance of the Christian message, what in the age of "tolerance," seems to be shrill dissonance in the harmonic orchestra of religions – the Christian claim to absoluteness. God is not "a kind of god." The gods of various religions and cultures can be compared to each other as of "their kind." God is the only one and besides him there is none other. The approach of comparative religious studies is therefore wrong from the very outset – as irreplaceable as the term "god-concept"[124] as it is misleading. It suggests that what the Bible says about God is one "God-concept" among equal others, equally faulty and equally wanting. This term is irreplaceable because humans can always and only think in pictures or concepts. This is also true for the writers of the biblical texts. But to postulate that there is no connection between these pictures and concepts and the reality they speak of, renders all reasoning impossible and inevitably leads to stupidity (Rom 1:21–22).[125] The Bible does not add yet another "god-concept" to the many others. It is not a question about how the Hebrews thought their God to be. Of course they thought about him, and of course they had their concepts and "pictures," their metaphors. But this is not all they had to say. Their "seeing," "envisioning," "thinking" was preceded

---

124. *Gottesbild*.

125. I use "stupidity" as Paul uses "folly" in a polemic, but neutrally descriptive, way as the Latin *stupiditas*, dullness, senselessness. So does Schlatter: "Paul explains the impoverishment (*Verarmung*) and enfeeblement (*Verblödung*) of the human inner being. Man became so empty because he refused to honor and thank God" (1952, 62).

by God's self-revelation. God reveals himself indisputably through creation (Rom 1:20), unarguably through his word (Mic 6:8), unignorably through his Son (Heb 1:2).

God reveals himself as the one and only God (Deut 6:4). This forbids all comparison, forbids the usage of the word "God" for any other but himself. And yet we cannot but talk about the "gods." God forbids making "images" of him (Exod 20:4) which includes "god-concepts." And yet we cannot but think of him in pictures, images, or concepts. This is our human dilemma. The way out of the dilemma is not equating the "existence of God" with his "non-existence," or talking about the "great void." The way out of the dilemma is that God addresses us and that we obey him. Therefore the Jewish Credo does not start with "See, o Israel!" but with "Hear, o Israel!" which also means "Obey, o Israel!"

But what about the "gods" of which the Old Testament also talks? The polemic of the prophets is no carte blanche for denying the existence of the "gods" in a haughty Enlightenment manner. They "exist" and none other than the Apostle Paul speaks of them with words that show respect (Rom 8:38; Col 1:16). It is alone "before God" that they are "no gods." And for those who followed the call to be his – and in Christ all are called – they are not vis-à-vis anymore, which is what Exodus 20:3 literally means: "לֹא יִהְיֶה־לְךָ אֱלֹהִים אֲחֵרִים עַל־פָּנָי‎." The fact that in Jeremiah 10:3 they are called חֻקּוֹת, "customs" (NIV) does not deny them their existence.[126] However, they are הֶבֶל, a "vapor,"[127] that is corruptible as everything else that belongs to creation. They "exist" alone before God, they are לֹא־אֵל, "non-God" (Deut 32:21).

It seems at times that questions of that kind are only a problem for Christian theologians craving recognition. Their hasty and zealous readiness to deny God is by no means new and reminds one of Bible references such as Ezekiel 16 and Jeremiah 2:20 and 13:27. Against this attitude I want to say two things:

First, Japanese and other Asian scientists name clearly what certain Christian theologians dare not say:

> On one side the religious beliefs of the West are formed thus that God is the ruling element.[128] The relationship between the one and

---

126. Luther, taking into account the context, masterly translates with "gods" (*Götter*).

127. Deut 32:21; 1 Kgs 16:26; 2 Kgs 17:15; Ps 31:7; Jer 2:5; 8:19; 10:3, 10:8–14; 14:22; 16:19; 51:17–18; Jonah 2:9.

128. The corresponding Japanese terms are probably neologisms of Watanabe. They can only be circumscribed. Watanabe talks about *shinshudougata* (神主導型). *Shin* (神) means God (神), *shudou* (主導) means "to assume leadership," and *kata* (型) means "form."

only God, as he is understood in Christianity and Judaism (as well as in Islam), and Self is thus formed that the first is the purpose and the second the means, because the first is the Ruler and the second servant ... On the other side the form of the religions of the Japanese is formed thus that Self is the ruling element.[129] Because the Buddhas of Buddhism are there to open the way to enlightenment for Self, the relationship between Buddha and Self is thus formed that Self is the purpose and Buddha the means. And because the gods of Shintoism are used by Self, the relationship between the gods and Self is thus formed that Self is the purpose and the gods are the means. Because gods and Buddhas of the Japanese religions are all means to an end, one "prays to god in hard times,"[130] the religious heart is awakened in times of need and grows weak when there is no need. (Watanabe 2002, 24)

In this sense Takeshi Mitsuhashi (三橋健) explains why there are so many gods in Japan. "The deities of Shintoism are not unique, not absolute, not omniscient, not all wise, as the high god Allah, but each of them is assigned to a certain task" (2007, 74).

Lee claimed that the main reason why it is so hard for Japan to accept Christianity is the Christian teaching of God's transcendence:

> There is no philosophical basis in the Japanese system of thought for the idea of the transcendence of God. The Christian God, an uncreated God who stands above and beyond human activity, differs from the Japanese *kami* (神)[131] who are various, immanent, and human. (Lee 1995, 109)

Second, Japanese non-Christians think it rather strange and repelling when Christians indifferently declare all religious concepts as basically the same. Many non-Christians naturally distinguish between Buddha or the gods of the Japanese pantheon and the "God who created heaven and earth." I cannot share the concerns of the Vietnamese-American theologian Peter C. Phan who renders the "question of religious pluralism" in Asia as "literally a matter of life and death" and who worries that "the future of Asian Christianity hangs

---

129. Correspondingly Watanabe uses *jikoshudougata* (自己主導型) here. *Jiko* (自己) means "Self."

130. *Kurushii toki-no kamidanomi,* (苦しいときの神頼み).

131. The *maki* used in Lee's book must be a misprint. There is no term significant to the given subject as *maki*.

in balance depending on how religious pluralism is understood and lived out (Tan 2004, 69). The "dissonance" which certain Christian theologians attempt to avoid is for many of my Japanese friends but a temporary "combination of tones contextually considered to suggest unrelieved tension and require resolution" (The Free Dictionary by Farlex).[132] They seek God and will find him (Deut 4:29; Isa 65:1; Matt 7:7).

2.3.4.5 Predisposition: God is

The question whether God is or not must be the starting point of all Christian missionary communication, especially in the context of Japanese animism. In his foreword to his Genesis Commentary (1523) Melanchthon asked *Kardinalfrage*: "The question of all questions is: Is God? Is this world created by a Divine power? Is it ruled by a Divine being?" (Melanchthon in Engelland 1961, 59). Japanese religiosity has clearly answered this question. It does not know of a transcendent God (Schründer-Lenzen 1996, 11; Itou 1996, 34; Yoshizawa 1996, 185). In this sense the internationally renowned *Zen*-teacher, Daisetsu Teitarou Suzuki, sharply denied the existence of God as well as any notion of transcendence. "*Zen* has no God to worship and no future in a yonder world" (1973, 50). This means that Japanese religiosity is technically speaking atheistic.

Faith is more than a mere believing in the truth of certain facts. It is a trusting relationship with God. But the naked belief that God is is still the basis of any relationship with God. "Anyone who comes to him must believe that he is (Heb 11:6). Mulligan (1857, 78) holds that the verb "to be" means simply "exist." He speaks against understanding "to be" as a mere copula (79). Especially in Hebrews 11:6, he wants to interpret it as the main verb (82). "There can be no dealings with the invisible God unless there is absolute faith in His existence. We must believe in His reality even though He is unseen" (Evans 2014, 110). This is true not only for sciences concerning philosophy or religion, but also in the natural sciences. In all areas of learning certain fundamental facts need to be accepted before learning can be successful in any way. Reason needs faith to work properly. God does not confront humans with proof of his existence but with an all-encompassing statement that he already existed at the beginning of this world. This is the absolute truth that has to be accepted and believed (Lightner 1998, 48).

---

132. http://www.thefreedictionary.com.

The existence of God is "first truth, and must logically precede and condition all observation and reasoning" (Wiley 1940, I.217). As a predisposition it cannot and it must not be proven. It "cannot" be proven, because the God of the Bible is not part of this world. Proving his existence would make God the object of reason and thus part of this world. Weber rightly calls the proofs of the existence of God "secularization of God" (156). And it "must not" be proven, because any attempt to do so would necessarily be methodologically faulty. Natural theology's predisposed concept of God (Creator) cannot be verified or proven by natural theology. Especially if the methodology is that of "cause and effect," predisposed in itself (Petit 1993, 4). The crucial thing is not whether humans can prove God – they cannot – but whether they choose to come to him.[133] The starting point of faith is not the proof for the thinkable, but the acceptance of the unthinkable.

For the dialogue with Japanese interested in the Christian faith I suggest using two semantic concepts. I strive not to use the Japanese word for "faith," *shinkou* (信仰), because it's meaning is much too broad to be precise. *Shinkou* (信仰) comprises "belief," "faith," and "trust." For belief in facts I use the verb *mitomeru* (認める), "accept" for trust *shinrai* (信頼).[134] *Mitomeru* (認める) is used in various Japanese translations of Romans 1:28 – because "humans didn't even attempt to accept (*mitomeru*, 認める) God,"[135] because they "didn't think it right to accept (*mitomeru*, 認める) God,"[136] because they "rejected and didn't even attempt to accept (*mitomeru*, 認める) God,"[137] he gave them over. "The primary barrier to faith is not lack of evidence . . . The real problem is an unwillingness to believe, regardless of the evidence. This is because man is a sinner and doesn't want to believe" (Cox 1998a, 5). The reference to Romans 1 leads to the question of "natural theology" and "natural knowledge of God."

2.3.4.6 "Natural theology" or revelation theology

Pannenberg (1993, 87) talks about the "hopeless confusion" caused by the term "natural theology." First of all, there is the metaphysical, classic "natural theology" going back to Panaitios:

---

133. Martin Luther translated "*wer zu Gott kommen will*" ("he who wants to come to God") which is not a literal translation but a translation which masterly underlines the decisional character of Heb 11:6.
134. For *shinkou* (信仰) meaning belief system I use *oshie* (教え), "teaching," or *kyouten* (教典), "dogma."
135. *Shin Kyoudouyaku* (新共同訳).
136. *Kougoyaku* (口語訳).
137. *Ribingu Baiburu* (リビングバイブル).

> Panaitios called the philosophical teaching about god "natural theology" as opposed to the "mythical theology" of the poets, and as opposed to the "political theology" of the state-supported cults . . . In this sense "natural theology" means the teaching about god which corresponds to nature, the essence of the divine itself, unadultered by political interests and also free of falsifications stemming from the poetic phantasies, the "lies" of the poets. (Pannenberg 1993, 87)

The first context of "natural theology" was the encounter with "mythical theology" and "political theology." In a very different way the "natural theology" occurring in the Bible (e.g. Rom 1) was formulated in the context of the encounter with "revelation theology," that is, God's revelation through the Old Testament (Klumbies 1992, 182). One reason for this confusion is that the philosophical and the biblical concept are taken out of their original context and discussed vis-à-vis.

Another reason for this confusion is that the purpose of theologizing is not taken into consideration. In philosophy "natural theology" is a "method of reasoning with the purpose of reaching the knowledge of god through nature (the world), and rationally proving his existence explicitly" (Petit 1994, 4). For Paul "the knowing of God through nature was not a basically theological problem, but a practical problem of missions. He was confronted with the question how to communicate with the Gentiles" (Stuhlmacher 1989, 43).

What Barth and others after him so radically rejected is not evidence of God in nature (Rom 1), but seeking to prove God through nature (Pöhlmann 1980, 108). He fought against a knowledge of God as something at human disposal (Pannenberg 1993, 86). Dialectical theologians have in common "a zealous protest against any human attempt to have God at man's disposal" (Kreck 1978, 9). Therefore neither extreme is correct; neither total disregard of nature nor overvaluation of nature to a source of theology; neither total incapacity to know about God at all, nor seizing God by means of human reason. The right path is the middle way between these extremes.

The *cognitio naturalis* and *cognitio supernaturalis* of Thomas Aquinas must not be understood as mutually excluding opposites. They have to be related with each other. Thus is the relation, that without *cognitio supernaturalis* there can be no *cognitio naturalis*; and that through *cognitio supernaturalis* there must necessarily be *cognitio naturalis*. This dethrones human reason as ruler seizing God. And it unmasks and destroys materialistic ignorance as a bulwark of Atheism.[138]

Without *cognitio supernaturalis* there is no *cognitio naturalis*

There can be no doubt that "the invisible things of him from the creation of the world are clearly seen, being understood by the things that are made, even his eternal power and Godhead" (Rom 1:20). It must be rejected that humans can know God without his Divine help.[139]

Before all others Luther fought against the Roman Catholic progressive principle of knowing God through nature (deducted from evidence) and supernatural knowledge of God (mediated through authority),[140] leaning on Thomas Aquinas' *cognitio naturalis* and *cognitio supernaturalis* (Harbeck-Pingel and Roth 1977, 1). The fight was also against his own Melanchthon who with reference to Romans 1–2 considered the natural knowledge of God as a "starting point of appropriation of salvation" (Lau and Bizer 1969, 69). According to Melanchthon, natural knowledge has its own "power of persuasion" because man's spirit and God's spirit are kindred spirits (Fraenkel 1961, 39). According to Engelland, the basic difference between Catholic and Reformed theology lies in the interpretation of the relationship between God and fallen man. The "Catholic primary principle" (Przywara), derived from the Plato's *analogia entis*, holds that this relationship is one of "analogy of being." This Catholic principle on one side guards the alikeness of God and man, on the other the categorical and therefore unbridgeable difference between God and man (Engelland 1961, 56). The early Melanchthon rejected this principle clearly. "Man cannot fathom

---

138. In a similar way Torrance suggests not to understand natural theology and revealed theology as mutually excluding opposites, but rather place natural theology into the framework of revealed theology, in a way, which places natural theology under revelation (McGrath 2004, 86–87).

139. Paul's contemporaries argued that way. According to Jewish wisdom literature (see Barr 1993, 68ff.), God through his creating word, here equated with wisdom, implanted in man "a sense for God and his will" (Stuhlmacher 1989, 43).

140. U. Barth describes this approach as follows: Between the two dimensions, nature and super-nature, "Thomas does not perceive any real opposition, but rather a teleological relationship. Because nature as a whole is destined to be perfected by grace, so man's reason is destined to be perfected by means of the supernatural habitus of the infused grace . . . Faith and rationality permeate and revive each other" (2005, 84). However, the Roman-Catholic interpretation is not only based on Thomas, but also borrows from Panaitios. "Within the Catholic thinking it is not uncommon to identify philosophical theology with natural theology" (Schüßler 1993, 17).

creation nor the governance[141] of the world; yet he fantasizes[142] that things happen, come into being, cease to be and come back again by mere chance" (Melanchthon in Engelland 1961, 59). According to Engelland (62–63), it is a tragedy that Melanchthon did not hold fast to this position. He later talked about the "natural light" in humans, giving "natural knowledge of God," by virtue of which humans can not only anticipate God's existence but also gain positive knowledge about his character. Thus Melanchthon returned to the Roman Catholic principle of *analogia entis* (69). Luther replaced the absolute opposition of natural and supernatural knowledge of God by the absolute opposition of faith and sin.[143] According to Luther, human reason is not intrinsically bad,[144] but it is corrupted by sin,[145] seeks what is sinful, and needs to be born again to become a tool of the Holy Spirit (Harbeck-Pingel and Roth 1977, 1).[146] Reason over and over again misuses the natural knowledge of God for the heightening of its own glory (Zur Mühlen 1995, 159), over and over again shows the tendency towards haughty arbitration rebelling against God and therefore has its hand in every sinful deed (Lohse 1995, 218). According to Luther, natural knowledge of God is,

> not a coherently proper basic stage upon which is built by revelation. It is rather knowledge of God perverted already, *falsa opinio de Deo*, idolatry, enmity to God, flight from God. (Ebeling 1982, 420–421)

It is in this sense that Barth understood his theology as "radicalizing of the reformatory approach" (Veldhuis and Drewes-Siebel 1994, 12).[147] His theology

---

141. *Leitung*.

142. *Meint*.

143. For Luther "the fact of sin was also defining for the interpretation of rational knowledge of God" (Ebeling 1982, 416).

144. Luther also knew about the "light of God" which gives man a certain idea about rules and commandments, but which does not lead him into a right knowing of God but into idolatry. "It lets man know that he has to worship God, but it only leads into all kinds of cults through which he tries to please God" (Olsson, n.d.: 59).

145. In his *Table Talk,* Luther called reason the "devil's whore" (Luther 1983, 41). This stands in stark opposition to Dydimos the Blind who called reason the maidservant of theology (Bienert 1972, 157).

146. Olsson rejects that Luther believed man was able to explore God before the Fall. "According to Luther, God was unexplorable (*unerforschlich*) and hidden to man even in his original, untainted state of creation. God's concealment is therefore part of the conditioning of creation" (Olsson, n.d.: 52).

147. This claim did not go unchallenged. Barr (9) called it, as well as Barth's radical one-sidedness, "ridiculous."

can be seen as an attempt to theologically challenge the atheist reason of late modernity (Harbeck-Pingel and Roth 1977, 3). "If revelation is nothing more than just man's best thoughts about religion, nothing more than just his best insights on morals and ethics, why then should revelation be called divine revelation? (Ramm 1976, 36). According to Schleiermacher, Barth's new theological start with its dominant theme of revelation consisted in making a "given word" the basis of theology again (Ramm 1976, 37).

Radicalizing Luther's "knowledge of God perverted already" Barth even considered any turning to God on the basis of natural evidence for the existence of God idolatry. The only legitimate basis is, according to Barth, faith (Connell 2000, 160). Opposing the Roma-Catholic *analogia entis*[148] Barth rejected any knowledge about God outside the "given word":

> Natural theology . . . needs to be avoided like an abyss into which, lest one wants to fall into it, one should not draw close. Only by ignoring it altogether one can with terror and indignation turn one's back on her as the great temptation and source of error. (Barth in Thielicke 1981, 48)

On the other side, the early Barth wrote in Romans 1:20 "that man – not by virtue of his own reasoning, but empowered by God's revelation – very well knows God and that he owes himself to him" (1970, 335). The keyword is "empowered by God's revelation." Paul Tillich, even though his standpoint on "natural theology" is completely different from Barth's (Schüßler 1993, 15), agrees with Barth on this. "We can know about God only through God himself, that is through [the ministry of] his Spirit who is in us yet not from us . . . God can only be known through God, that is through revelation" (Tillich 1959, 50; Barth 1970, 205). In my opinion the position of the early Barth – natural revelation embedded in supernatural revelation – seems to be the better position.

Because of *cognitio supernaturalis* without fail *cognitio naturalis* as well

Adolf Schlatter coherently connects supernatural and natural revelation. For Schlatter the first and fundamental act of all science – including theological

---

148. According to Veldhuis and Drewes-Siebel, Barth held "that the theological conflict between Rome and the Reformation consisted in the following two mutually excluding concepts of nature and grace: according to Catholic theology, man through the Fall has lost the supernatural gifts, but his natural capacities such as free will and reason were not affected by sin. The Protestants hold that sin affected all of human nature, and that there is no natural basis left which could serve as a link for special revelation" (Veldhuis and Drewes-Siebel 1994, 12).

science – is perception, followed by the conceptual condensation of the knowledge. While doing so man follows "a principle we have to follow as God's gracious will." Schlatter holds that the perception of God is not only possible, it is even inevitable (Maier 1990, 312–313). Schlatter argues that through the "things invisible" for man, man gains assurance, knows that the "visible did not come into being through perceivable causes, but through the word of God"; and that this discovery has to lead man, "that he cannot remain with the visible," but that he – "having perceived the world with the very first act of knowing as something created[149] – must reach out[150] for the invisible" (Schlatter 1905, 531). Schlatter goes as far as to deal with special theology (revelation) within the context of anthropology (the teaching of perceiving man) (Maier 1990, 313). However, this does not mean that Schlatter thinks God can be known without God's revelation. Weber emphasized that his theology was "truly theocentric" (Weber in von Bülow 1999, 49).

> Even the very first knowledge which sees the world as God's creation is possible only through faith. It is only possible because the invisible bears witness to itself in us, because it convicts us of its reality, and because it turns our desire towards itself, as it is revealed as the uniquely reliable *bonum*. Without this actual connection with things Divine[151] which we consciously and personally have to safeguard within us, our thinking remains a prisoner of the visible and can never embrace God's word as the reason of [all] things in a way which leads to clear and certain knowledge. (Schlatter 1905, 531)

"Without revelation unable to know" – "with revelation unable not to know." In his commentary on Romans, Schlatter binds both together: "Nothing can be known of God save what he shows us; and all he shows us is known by us" (1952, 55). Michel (99) agrees: Romans 1:19b "emphasizes that the knowability of God is not by chance nor to be taken for granted, but caused by himself."

Von Bülow (49) sees in Schlatter's approval of a natural theology a "two-stage model of a natural theology," similar to Thomas Aquinas's model of *cognitio supernaturalis* and *cognitio naturalis*. As described before, the problem with this model lies not in the justification of both forms of revelation, but

---

149. *Geworden.*
150. *Ergreifen.*
151. *Realverband mit den göttlichen Dingen.*

in how these two forms are correlated. Bancroft gives the following three foundations for theology: First, it is based upon the existence of God who maintains a relationship with the universe (Bancroft 1976, 14). Second, it is based upon the capacity of the human spirit to know God and some of these relationships (15). Third, it is based upon the means which actually bring God in contact with the spirit, in other words, upon the provision of revelation of God himself and some of these relations (16).

Limits of the *cognitio naturalis*

This section would not be complete with only establishing the necessity of a "natural theology" and defining its place in the context of "revelation theology." It is also necessary to show the limits of *cognito naturalis*.

Luther relocated the knowing God and separated it from "pure reason." The subject knowing God is not the philosopher but the "everyday man." And the agent of knowing God is not his theoretical reasoning but his stricken conscience by the Law (Ebeling 1982, 416). Or with Luther's own words:

> Man can have no reliable foundation except wrapping and enclosing his heart in the words of the Scripture. Then the Scripture gently and step by step leads to Christ, first to Christ as a man, then to him as a lord of all creatures, then to him as lord over all things, then to him as God . . . And since the philosophers want to start from the top they became fools. Man needs to start from the bottom. (Luther 1891, 587)[152]

That means that for Luther the question of God the Creator, that is the theology of the first article, can only then be understood correctly, if the connection "between protology and soteriology, and that means [the connection] with Christology and eschatology" is not severed (Ebeling 1982, 424).

Especially in the dialogue with other religions and various missiological approaches it cannot be emphasized enough that there is no salvific power in "natural knowledge of God" alone. According to Luther, reason can know that God is, but not who he is (zur Mühlen 1995, 159). The "natural man without faith" knows God,

---

152. *Darum kan man kainen gewissen grundt haben, dann das man das hertze wickel und schliess in die sprüch der schrifft, dann die schrifft hebt fein sanfft an und füret uns zu Christo, wie zu einem menschen und darnach zu einem herren uber alle creatur, darnach zu einem herren uber alle ding, darnach zu einem got . . . Nun die Philosophi wöllen oben anheben, da sein sie zu narren geworden, man muss von unten anheben.*

> only as the one who causes everything, and this almighty work he experiences as the wrath of God. Because man by virtue of his reasoning powers owns a rudimentary knowledge of God, and also knows the natural law which demands the worship of God, man perceives God as the one who punishes him for his violation of the law. It is only through revelation that man can know God as the one who has mercy upon violators of the law. (Rohls 2002, 277)

"Unspeakably great things are thus said about man, that he can see the works of God. Yet this knowledge is not the power that can save him" (Schlatter 1952, 59). Therefore, man without special revelation, man left alone with general revelation is faced with an "epistemological-soteriological dilemma: he knows enough of God to be condemned, yet not enough to be saved" (Pienisch 2000). Nature does not prove God but it points towards him. God cannot be truly known but only anticipated (Pöhlmann 1980, 108). The connection to Romans 1 is of crucial importance. "Natural knowledge of God achieves only the wrath of God (Rom 1:18ff), not his grace, not his essence, only the veil by which he conceals it" (Pöhlmann 1980, 108).[153] Klumbies formulates:

> As Paul presented it, the attempts of a direct knowing of God through the works of creation do not lead to access to God. As Paul learned from experience a salvific relationship with God cannot be accomplished that way. The knowledge of the ἀόρατα in the works of creation accessible to reason has not led to a salvific relationship with God, but to the opposite (Rom 1:20). Instead of offering God honor and thanksgiving, mankind made God into the likeness of things[154] (Rom 1:23). (Klumbies 1992, 182)

According to Barth, the whole world is the footprint of God. But as humans preferred the scandal to faith, the footprint of the world's great riddle is the footprint of his wrath (Barth in Connell 2000, 160). Paul does not state "natural knowledge of God" as an argument, but he talks about an "erring knowledge of God" (Schroeter 2006, 41).

---

153. E. Brunner's concept of the "natural understanding of good" (*Das Gebot und die Ordnungen*) does not deal with the salvation of man, but with the preservation of the world (Harbeck-Pingel and Roth 1977, 8).

154. *Haben die Menschen ihn vergegenständlicht.*

Limits of the *cognitio supernaturalis*

Does revelation theology also have its limits? Yes, not concerning its content, but concerning its primacy, which Barth attributed to it. God certainly reveals himself to us as the merciful God always and only for the sake of Christ. In this sense Barth rightfully deals with the first article of the Apostles' Creed after its second. But (deliberately) masking out certain biblical basic truths for the sake of systematic theology has also its dangers. Wingren points at them:

The work of God in the death and resurrection of Christ is new as opposed to an old work [also] coming from God. This old work comes to us in the simple fact that we as humans live together in this world. In theology this kind of newness cannot be clearly apprehended if God's universal reign over all the world through his decrees is clearly apprehended. And again God's reign over all the world cannot be clearly distinguished as long as the first article of creation is outshone, classed second after the second article, and as long as the New Testament is the exclusive basis of theology. If the first article and the Old Testament narrative of origins principally comes second and third this is a sign that our way to intelligibleness, and not God's work itself, determined the structure of theology. The rightful question is how all this [as seen] in present-day theology can ever be healed. It is obvious that a discussion on the operating principles and the methodology of theology cannot be avoided (Wingren 1962, 108–109).

McGrath (2006, 224) divided the role and significance of the teaching of creation within the Old Testament into three areas according to the main parts of the Old Testament. I am going to use this structure for an outline of the importance of a theology based on creation, particularly important in Japan.

First, McGrath talks about the significance of the doctrine of creation in the historical writings, where it plays a role combating the Canaanite nature religions. Especially in dialogue with people in Japan who are thinking in animistic ("nature-religious") concepts, and for whom the theological systematics of Western theology is scarcely relevant, it over and again proves helpful not to start with the second but with the first article. As Allen and Springstedt pointed out, Western theologians are not aware of the fact that creation is the basis of all Christian theology. "The Genesis stories of creation make it clear that the world has a beginning. Because it has a beginning, it is not eternal. This means that it is not ultimate. God, its Maker, who is without beginning or end, is ultimate" (Allen and Springstedt 2007, XV). In the following part I am going to discuss Ralph Cox's approach which substantiates this impressively. Ralph Cox worked as a missionary to Japan for many decades.

Second, McGrath talks about the significance of the doctrine of creation in the prophetical writings: [It] "is used to affirm the universal sovereignty of the God of Israel. The gods of Babylon were merely local creations, lacking the power and authority of the God of Israel. The doctrine of creation thus became the foundation of the hope of liberation" (2006, 224). It is obvious that this thought is very important for dialogue with people in other countries, especially if they, as in Japan, believe in an animistic concept of geographically limited local deities. Particularly people suffering under the seemingly inevitable dictate of Japanese society, people who have painfully experienced the enchaining power of their local deities, they will find hope in the message of liberation.

Third, McGrath talks about the significance of the doctrine of creation in the poetic writings, mainly Job and Proverbs, where it is "linked to the acquisition of wisdom" (2006, 224). Christians with a different worldview need the doctrine of creation as the basis of a new moral system.

Ralph Cox's approach for the Japanese context

Ralph Cox first came to Japan in 1954 where he started more than eighty churches in a period of over fifty years, and where he died in 2008. The book *God Is, God Spoke, God Came,* published in 1998, was forged through decades of communicating the gospel in the Japanese context. The Japanese translation *Nihonjin-to kami, seisho, Kirisuto* (日本人と神、聖書、キリスト; Japanese, God, the Bible, and Christ)[155] was published in late 1998. As the English title suggests, the book is divided into three sections, the "three main pillars of the Christian faith," as Cox calls them (1998a, V). Cox deals with the evidence for the existence of God as the first and most important part, then God's revelation through the Bible, and last his revelation through Jesus Christ.

Methodology

> Faith leading to a knowledge of fact and truth must be based on evidence, objective and provable. It is precisely at this point that Christian faith makes its departure from the other belief systems of the world and lays its claim to being unique. The key word in comparing the different faiths of the world is *evidence*,[156] just

---

155. The structure of the Japanese translation partly differs from that of the English original. Another difference is that the Japanese edition uses many graphs for visualization.

156. In the Japanese translation Cox uses *shouko* (証拠), "evidence."

as evidence is the key word in separating scientific truth from superstition. (Cox 1998a, V)

The equation of Christian faith and scientific truth hinted at in the foreword is elaborated further in chapter 3 of his book. In the Japanese translation, chapter 3 has the telling headline *kagakuteki shinkou* (科学的信仰), "scientific faith" (Cox 1998b, 25). This comparatively short chapter is important for the definition of Cox's faith concept. "True science starts with a set of assumptions that cannot be proven but appear to be true." These assumptions are that the world surrounding humans is real, that humans have only their reasoning power to lead them to fact and truth, and that the laws of nature are "not capricious" (1998a, 19). Departing from these assumptions, Cox's scientific work is guided by the following principles:

- Separation from subjectivity (separation from feelings, biases, prejudices, etc.)
- Adherence to objectivity (seeing what really is – reality, fact)
  - Gathering of evidence[157]
  - Comparing evidence with evidence
  - Drawing conclusions based on this objective evidence
  - Obtaining verification[158] by unbiased third parties (1998a, 19–20).

This is where Cox introduces his faith concept. He equates it with "drawing conclusions." "What they [the scientists] are really saying is, 'based on the evidence, we believe (conclude) certain things are true'" (1998a, 20). "We must draw conclusions from the known, as scientists have already done. To do otherwise is to revert to pure speculation. That is not science" (1998a, 36). "Comparing evidence with evidence" is also important for Cox's faith concept. "Only through the process of *comparing* evidence with evidence and then *believing* what the evidence indicates has science progressed" (1998a, 23).[159]

---

157. In the Japanese translation Cox constantly uses *shouko* (証拠), "evidence" (1998b, 26).

158. In the Japanese translation Cox uses *shoumei* (証明), "proof" (1998b, 26).

159. This purely immanent way of arguing reminds us of Thomas Aquinas. "According to Thomas Aquinas, man can reach knowledge about God and knowledge of God only through experience of this present world, at least in this present life . . . in this worldly life man reaches it [knowledge of God] only by way of knowing the material world, by way of experiencing sensually perceptible things. This conception was a consequence from Aristotelian empiricism" (Pannenberg 1993, 94).

Course of development of thought

God is – creation

Cox's point of departure is a "riddle" borrowed from Newton:[160]

> Let's suppose that all of us were born in your house and lived together until the present. Let's suppose that your house doesn't have (never has had) any doors or windows. In other words, the inside of your house is all that we know or ever have known. We cannot see outside, and nothing from outside ever penetrates your house. (Cox 1998a, 9)

All talk about outside the house would be mere speculation. Then Cox continues:

> Is there any possible way that we could know that someone besides us exists? . . . There is only one way that we can really know that anyone else exists. We can argue among ourselves, guess and speculate, but that will never result in sure knowledge. The only way we can know for certain that a person or persons besides us must exist is to look at the abundant evidence that surrounds us. (Cox 1998a, 10)[161]

In the second chapter Cox lays out the following train of logic thought, based on Romans 1:20:

- We live in a world that is wonderfully prepared for us.
- The one who prepared this world for us is not visible or evident.
- He has, however, left proof of his existence through all the things that he has made – things so superior to anything humans can make that there is no comparison.
    - These intricate systems are seen in the cosmos, in inorganic minerals, in all plants, animals, and humans, and are evident to all.
    - Each of the hundreds of complete systems (a bird, a bee, a tree, a man, an atom, an amoeba, etc.) is composed of hundreds of other unbelievably intricate, minute systems.

---

160. "Newton perceived the whole universe and all in it as *riddle*, a mystery, which could be read by using pure reason on certain evidence, on certain mystical hints scattered by God to enable us to go on a philosophical treasure hunt . . . The universe is a cryptogram encoded by the Almighty" (Keynes in Stark 2003, 172).

161. Cox introduces the term "system" which is of importance later (1998a, 10).

- We can, then, conclude not only that he exists but also that:
  - He is living;
  - He is extremely intelligent;
  - He has great power; and
  - He cares for us because he provides for our needs.
- Anyone who denies the bountiful evidence of an intelligent being behind these intricate systems condemns himself[162] because
  - the totality of human experience proves that only intelligent beings can produce systems;
  - systems never come into being by themselves (Cox 1998a, 12–14).

The two last points are then discussed in detail in the following chapters. In chapter 4 Cox shows that first, every system made by humans is preceded by an idea of an intelligent being; that second, this being finds a way to realize the idea envisioned by his spirit; that third, the thus created system independently fulfills what it has been created for (1998a, 27–28). Then Cox asks, "How can so many of them [the scientists] conclude that there is no intelligent being behind the universe" (30)? According to Cox, the answer is the theory of evolution which is believed to explain everything. But those who honestly search for evidence for the existence of God must critically question the claims of the theory of evolution (31). According to Cox, Darwin's theory of evolution, also called "macro-evolution" is not based "on proof but on faith" (32). Cox does not want to critique the theory of evolution but "to eliminate it as a barrier to faith" (31). Cox understands "evolution" as a derivative of "evolve" and writes:

> We need to emphasize that evolution, even if true, explains only the *process* that produced all living things. We, however, are not discussing the process but the source. Evolution does not answer the question, "What caused the process?" Therefore, whether true or false, evolution is unrelated to the question of God's existence. (32)

In chapter 5 Cox returns to the term "system." It is the common experience of all humans that all systems we can trace back to their origin have been invented and created by intelligent beings. On this basis Christians "believe" that this must also be true for the highly intricate systems of nature. Atheists on the other hand believe against this evidence that these systems came into being

---

162. The English "condemn" sounds too harsh in the Japanese context. In his Japanese translation Cox therefore uses *hinan suru* (非難する), "criticize," "blame."

without being invented or created by an intelligent being. Cox summarizes his experience gained from discussions with thousands of atheists (36):

> I have never met an atheist who has been able to answer this logic. Once the unrelated discussion of the *process* is removed, the poverty of this position is exposed and he has nowhere to flee.
> This . . . is the argument of Romans 1:20. (40)

Chapter 6 (42–49) is dedicated to practical questions. Cox outlines the various objections of atheists which can be responded to. The overarching theme of these objections is the so-called evidence that "atheists present to try to bolster their position" (42). Cox shows how these positions can be refuted. At no point does he calls this refutation "proof for God's existence." He only exposes the atheists' "proofs" for God's non-existence.

Cox's following two chapters are dedicated to the creation report. Chapter 7 (50–58) is a collection of various interpretations of the creation report, given with the intention of providing "information that will help a seeking evolutionist see that Genesis need not be a barrier to faith in God, the Bible, and Jesus Christ" (51). Chapter 8 (60–67) further develops one of these interpretations.

The title of chapter 9 (68–76) is "The Christian and Scientific Thought." It is Cox's advice that Christians should not fear scientific investigation but face the encounter with science. Evolutionists on the other hand also should not be evasive and talk about "inevitable laws of nature" (73) which then cannot be questioned.[163]

God spoke – the Bible

Introducing the second part of his book Cox revisits the riddle used at the beginning. While the house only leads to the conclusion "that at least one other person" exists "who prepared the house for us," there is only one way that we could know anything about the wonderful world outside the house: "There is only <u>one</u> way, and that is if the person who furnished our home and prepared it for us informed us about the outside world." This brings Cox to the next question: Could we trust the transmission of the message not being able to verify its truth? If the message only talks about the realm outside the

---

163. Chapters 6 to 9 need not be further discussed here because they are not relevant for the subject at hand. However, it is important to mention that Cox attaches great importance to creation. It is also my experience that the subject of creation and evolution plays an important role when communicating the Christian message to people with an animistic worldview.

house, we cannot verify its truth. This is only possible if it also talks about the inside of the house. If the information about the inside of the house is true we can conclude that we can also trust the information about the outside (1998a, 78–80).

In chapter 11 (86–98) Cox elaborates what he explained by his parable in chapter 10. He distinguishes between religions given information about verifiable, "objective evidence" in this world, and religions given little or no information about this world (88). According to Cox, "revelations" without information about our world lead to a "blind, superstitious faith based on little or no objective evidence" (86).[164] In comparison to the Holy Scriptures of other religions the Bible says much about things of our world.[165] They can all be verified, and many of them have been found true. Cox concludes:

> Scientifically speaking, based on the evidence of accuracy in the realm that we can test, we have grounds to "conclude" that the Bible (God's revelation to man) is trustworthy in the realm that we cannot test. This is the basis of Christian faith. This is the step of faith that the Bible asks followers to take. This is the same methodology that scientists through the ages have applied as they have investigated the unknown. (94)

Because the Bible is trustworthy "it tells us":

> Who God is, why God made us, where we are going, how we can live with God forever, the history of believers from the beginning, about life after death, about the spiritual realm, where evil came from, the ultimate eradication of evil, [and] the end of all things. (96–97)

God came – Jesus Christ

Cox starts this part of the book with an extensive explanation on the Trinity. He uses the analogy of water: it has indispensable elements, an analogy for God the Father, God the Son, and God the Spirit; and it has three physical states

---

164. These religions demand faith on the basis of miracles such as healings, answered prayer, prophetic utterances and more. However, these "are of little help in distinguishing which religion is speaking the truth" (1998a, 89–90).

165. Cox talks about some 70% (1998a, 92).

(Jesus as spirit, as heavenly body, as physical body).[166] The main outcome of this explanation is that Jesus Christ is no one else than God himself. "Christianity starts with God and ends with God. The God who created is the same God who spoke (the Bible) and is the same God who came (1998a, 105).

This has missiological consequences:

> In our witnessing, we are not attempting to convince people to follow a different religion or a different religious leader. We are just trying to persuade them to do what they were created for – *walk with the god who is*. This is the duty of all mankind because GOD IS and he created us for this purpose. (106, emphasis original)

Again Cox uses the argument of evidence. He believes in God and in the Bible because:

- Conclusive evidence supports the existence of God.
- If we want to know spiritual truth, *revelation* is absolutely necessary.
- The Bible claims to be this revelation and there is abundant evidence verifying this claim (113).
- The logic of "the Bible's principal teaching" is "that God who created us will also redeem us . . . Since the existence of God is proven, this makes sense to me" (113–114).
- More than one hundred prophecies in the Old Testament foretold the coming of Jesus hundreds of years before.
- There are numerous claims of Jesus to deity.
- These claims are amply proven by his life and deeds – recorded by eye-witnesses.
- The bodily resurrection and ascension into heaven are certainly believable of one who *came* from heaven.
- All New Testament writers give consistent testimony to the deity of Christ and to his resurrection.
- The church fathers of the second and third centuries show the same consistent testimony.
- The preponderance of solid manuscriptural, historical, and archeological evidence from the first through the third centuries (1998a, 114).

---

166. Cox admits that this interpretation is not perfect (1998a, 105). How could it possibly be?

Evaluation of Ralph Cox's approach

"Natural religion" as basis?

The title of the book and the short outline above leave no doubt as to how Cox argues: the credibility of the Bible is based upon the basis of a "natural theology," proving the existence of God by means of evidence; the credibility of Jesus in turn is based upon the credibility of God and the Bible. This poses several questions: Does Cox build his approach on the proofs for God's existence?[167] Does his approach lean on Thomas Aquinas and is it therefore "Catholic"? Is God's special revelation therefore rendered unnecessary?

Yes, Cox builds his approach upon the cosmological argument for the existence of God. But that does not mean that he also stands for a "natural theology" according to Thomas Aquinas or even a Roman Catholic soteriology. It is necessary to distinguish between the purposes of the various approaches. Cox strictly derives his approach from Romans 1:20 (1998a, 12). As Stuhlmacher showed, Paul's purpose was missiological-practical (Stuhlmacher 1989, 43). Michel even calls Romans 1:18–32 "a model of a missionary sermon . . . as delivered many times to Gentile listeners" (Michel 1978, 96). This is also Cox's purpose. Neither Paul nor Cox design systematic theology. Paul is sometimes accused of having been a "missionary" rather than a "theologian." Of all theologians it is Barth to speak against this accusation. In his paper *Paulus als Missionar und Theologe* (1991), Barrett called attention to Barth who called the proclamation of the message the third way of theological thinking which to him was, together with exposition and ethical critique, "necessary for the perfection of the process" (Barrett 1991, 1). The work towards a proclamation that is to arouse faith is also theological work. Barrett also speaks against the accusation against Paul, but then he admits that even though Paul did not write a "systematic textbook" he still was a "systematic theologian" (2). Barrett defines "systematic theology" thus: "One has to be able to work with the Christian tradition in a way that one is able to express the Christian truth with relevance in the context of contemporary philosophy" (3). He then concludes:

> Paul was a pioneer, not only as missionary but also as theologian . . . Of course he does not offer us a systematic theology for our age. This is impossible even for an apostle, because a systematic

---

167. "If knowledge of God is a matter of 'natural theology' in the sense that it has to be gained by means of reflection and arguments, then it ultimately rests on the proofs for the existence of God . . . In modern times the duty of man to worship God and connected subjects were also considered part of natural theology" (Pannenberg 1993, 93).

theology of our age needs to be relevant for the spiritual world of today. (Barrett 1991, 3)

In this sense Paul and Cox were both "systematic theologians" – each of them for his missionary context. Both of them were systematic theologians, yet in a different way than Karl Barth was a systematic theologian. Their philosophical context was neither the encounter with a Roman Catholic understanding of salvation nor a "natural theology" substantially formed and ghettoized by the Enlightenment. The context of Paul's proclamation was the context of Judaism (Barrett 1991, 3). Neither of them rejects "natural theology" as categorically as Barth did. But that does not mean that they are in favor of it. They did not reject "natural theology" because they did not have to deal with it since it was not part of their "contemporary philosophy."

Cox does not oppose the basic teaching that people need God's special revelation if they ever want to know God. Using the riddle of the house, Cox says:

> We could speculate about the unknown, but "Is there any possible way that we can learn about the wonderful world existing outside our home?" . . . There is only *one* way, and that is if the person who furnished our home and prepared it for us informed us about the outside world. (Cox 1998a, 79)

Cox also says that atheists need to have "open hearts" (41) in order to understand his "scientific" argument. He wants to help them overcome "stumbling blocks" on their way to faith. The critical work is still, and will always be, that of the Holy Spirit (5).

Faith as a noetic act?

Cox's book leaves the impression that his concept of faith is solely noetic. But this is not the case.[168] Caution is necessary. Knowing God is not a matter of reason but of will, because in Hebrew thinking knowledge is not a matter of knowing but of love, because God is not a thing or a concept but a person. The "existence of God itself" or a certain "God-concept" may be an object of knowing reason; however, the person of God can only be the object of knowing love, the object of the will to fellowship.

---

168. I can say that because I had the privilege of personally knowing Cox for almost two decades. He was a great role model for me, not only as a colleague, but because of his fervent faith and integrity also as a Christian.

2.4 The Japanese Soul-Concept

Summary: In general the soul-concept is central for the understanding of animism. This is also true for Japanese animism: *hito* (人), "man," is per etymological definition *to*, "the place," where *hi*, the "soul" lives (Numazawa 1970, 202). The Japanese soul-concept is comprised of *tamashii* (魂, 魄) (soul), *rei* (霊) (spirit)/*sudama* (魅) (ghost), *kokoro* (心) (heart, mind) and *ki* (気) (energy). As the discussion with the anthropology of the Old Testament (Wolff) shows, animistic ideas are not necessarily congruent with biblical ideas. The one thing most alien to Japanese animism is the reference to God as the key-terms of the Old Testament soul-concept show.

2.4.1 Preliminary Considerations

As important as the Japanese soul-concept is, it is just as difficult to grasp for non-Japanese. It is even hard to describe for the Japanese. When discussing the Japanese soul-concept with native Japanese I often see them struggling for words. Besides a growing secularization, particularly among young people, this can have two reasons.

One reason has to do with the content:

> Even working with terms can already mean that I am dealing with the matter in a European way which may lead to the impossibility to describe the actual proprium. Because I would have to capture conceptually[169] things of culture which hardly know about capturing things conceptually. (Mijima in Schründer-Lenzen 1996, 11)

The actual matter is not accessible for the European striving for conceptual unambiguity.

The other reason is a formal reason: the Japanese always think in two language systems. On one hand, they think in Chinese characters which stand for relatively unambiguous, singular contents. When the Japanese associate language with concepts, they usually associate language not with pictures of everyday life, but with Chinese characters (e.g. if they hear the word *kuruma*

---

169. *Auf-den-Begriff-Bringen.*

they don't envision a car but the Chinese character for car: 車). On the other hand, they most naturally use the Japanese which was spoken before the Chinese characters were introduced. This language system was originally not connected with Chinese characters and is even today associated with pictures of everyday life. When the Chinese characters were introduced, the at times rather complicated process of associating Japanese concepts with Chinese characters ("pictures") took place.

A word-field study has therefore always considered both language systems. Because of the usage of pictographic characters Schreiter calls Japan, together with China, a "high-context culture." A high-context culture is a culture in which communication depends less on the explicit content of communication text and more on the implicit content of its context (Schreiter 2004b, 37).[170]

Therefore a word-field study of the Japanese soul-concept needs to be conducted carefully and thoroughly.[171] Thomas Aquinas said that we do not name "things as they are in themselves but as they are to our minds" (Aquinas in Hesselgrave 1978, 41). This is particularly true for the Japanese soul-concept. The Japanese language knows many different words which translated into English all mean "soul." According to my research, the following words need to be considered:

---

170. Spoken Japanese has nothing in common with Chinese (Phillipps 2004, 9). However, this is not true for written Japanese. Edward Twitchell Hall "distinguishes cultures according to the degree of context in their communication systems. In high-context communication, most of the information is part of the context or internalized in the person; very little is made explicit. The information in a low-context message is carried on the explicit code of the message. In general, high-context communication is economical, fast, and efficient. However, time must be devoted to programming. If this programming does not take place, the communication is incomplete. To an observer, an unknown high-context culture can be completely mystifying, because symbols that are not known to the observer play such an important role. Thus, high-context communication can also be defined as inaccessible to the outsider. Low-context cultures are characterized by explicit verbal messages. Effective verbal communication is expected to be direct and unambiguous. Low-context cultures demonstrate high value and positive attitudes toward words. The Western world has had a long tradition of rhetoric, a tradition that places central importance on the delivery of verbal messages. . . . Hofstede suggested a correlation between collectivism and high context in cultures. In collectivistic cultures, information flows more easily between members of the group, and there is less need for explicit communication than in individualistic cultures" (De Mooij 2013, 85).

171. Any other methodology would be a falsifying shortcut. On this problem in the context with the soul-concept see Käser (2004, 52–56).

Table 2.3 Word-field Study of the Japanese Soul-concept

魂　玉　球	魄
Graph 1	Graph 2
魅　鬼	霊
Graph 3	Graph 4
心　精神　清心	気
Graph 5	Graph 6

Graph 1 (魂): Even though this first term (graph 1, left) has associations that rather forbid the equation with the Western soul-concept (Adami 1991, 22)[172] it usually is translated "soul." It can be read *tamashii* or *tama*. *Tama* basically means "bowl" in the traditional language system. A "soul" is commonly thought of as a flying or hovering fireball. This connection is concealed by the fact that in the language system using Chinese characters "soul"-*tama* (魂) and "bowl"-*tama* (玉 or 球) are written with different characters. 玉 rather means natural things such as gems or the eyeball, while 球 rather means manmade things such as balls.

Graph 2 (魄): The second term, pronounced *tama*, *tamashii*, or *haku*, also means "soul" and often is used as a synonym to the first term. It stresses more the aspect of limited visibility and thus slips into the concept of souls of the dead.

Graph 3, left (魅): The third term means a phantom, ghost, or specter misleading humans. In the traditional language system, it is pronounced *sudama*.[173] The pronunciation is similar to *tama*, but I have added it to this list because the Chinese characters show an interesting connection: all terms so far have a common root element which used as an independent character means *oni* (demon, devil, goblin) (graph 3, right). I shall explore the connection later on.

Graph 4 (霊): The fourth term means "spirit." Judging from the form of the Chinese character it does not seem to have any connections. Also the Chinese pronunciation *rei* seems to remove this term from the others. But the pronunciation of this character in the traditional language system is also *tama* or *sudama*.

Graph 5 (心): The fifth term means "heart." *Seishin* (精神 or 清心) is used as a synonym. Judging from the appearance of the Chinese character it has no connection with the soul-concept, but as it is used as a synonym to *tamashii* I have added it to this list.

Graph 6 (気): In the center of all these terms there is the term of *ki* (気). As the others *ki* (気) can also be translated with "soul" (Yamaguchi 1997, 82). It is of central importance in the Chinese as well as the Japanese worldviews.

---

172. When Schründer-Lenzen (11) writes that any "soul-concept" and any "transcendence" is alien to the Japanese culture. She wants to fight off this European misunderstanding.

173. In Japanese *bakasu* means "to mislead." It is written with 化かす or with the same character as *sudama* (魅),魅かす). *Sudama* can also be written 魑魅.

2.4.2 The Model

All these terms are connected. However, just how they are connected cannot be defined (1) with lexical accuracy, (2) by the Western way of antithetical approximation, not applicable in the East, or (3) by clearly cut and written dogmatical definitions, absent from any folk religions (Hiebert et al. 1999, 77). Therefore the following graph can only be a tentative model.

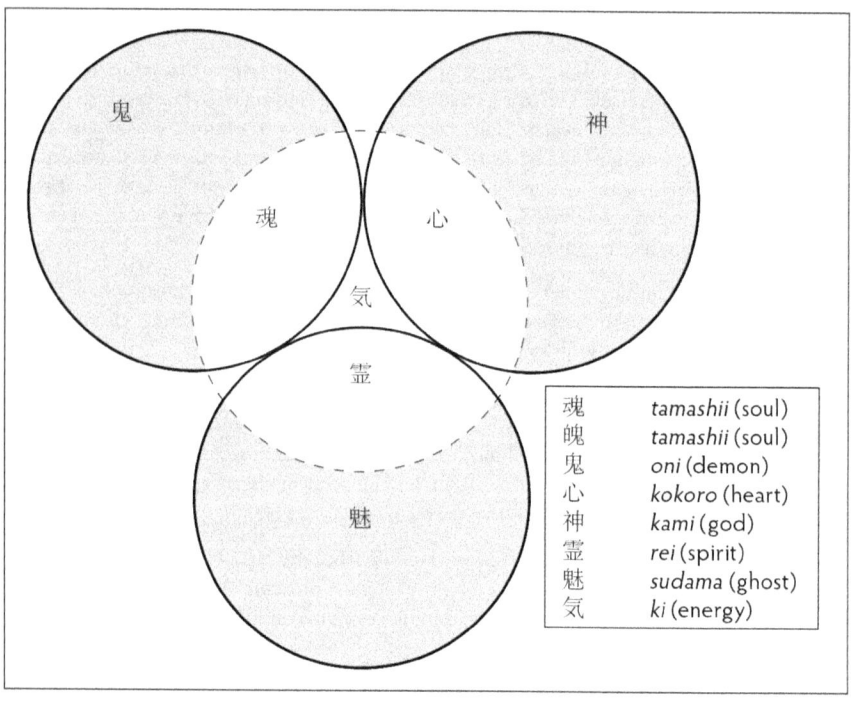

Figure 2.3 Graph of Word-field Study of the Japanese Soul-concept

To gain a better understanding I decided on one English translation for one Chinese character, knowing of course that any classification is a falsifying generalization. Words need to have a certain terminological clarity to be useful at all.[174] I am also aware of the fact that the external specification (English) is not entirely congruent with the internal meaning (Japanese). Cultural outsiders are never capable of such a thing as "purely objective" apprehension, because

---

174. I speak against the post-modern deconstruction of language (Jaichandran and Madhav 2003, 46).

"the mind of the commentator consciously or unconsciously distinguishes, chooses, and judges" (von Brandt 2007, 62). On the other hand, does "the idea a culture could only be understood from the inside, by means of its own terminology, lead nowhere, because it, a priori, defies the possibility of a real understanding gained from the outside" (Coulmas 2005, 16)?

The three central terms in the white circle – *tamashii* (魂), *kokoro* (心), and *rei* (霊) – describe the non-material aspects of man. At times they are clearly distinguishable, at other times they become blurred. For this reason I used a dotted line for the inner circle. Each one of these three circles has an area close to the other circles (white area), and an area totally different (grey area). The white areas stand for a living person, the grey areas for a dead person. Within one circle the transition from white to grey can also be blurred. *Tamashii*-terms (魂, 魄) and *oni* (鬼), demon; *kokoro* (心), heart and *kami* (神), god; and *rei* (霊), spirit and *sudama* (魅), ghost, respectively belong together closely.

2.4.3 The Word-Field *Tamashii* (魂 or 魄) (Soul)

2.4.3.1 Introduction

The meaning of the characters 魂 and 魄 can hardly be distinguished. Their compound reads *konpaku* or *konbaku* (魂魄). This also means "soul." The *Kokugo Dai Jiten* Dictionary explains the difference thus that the first (魂) means *kokoro* (心), heart, the second (魄) that which gives power to the heart. As the second character (魄) also means the invisible part of the waning moon, 魂 can be equated with the consciousness, 魄 respectively with the sub-consciousness.

According to leading dictionaries, *tamashii* (soul) has two basic meanings:

(1) that which controls *seishin* (精神) (psyche, heart, mind); *sudama* (魅) (where emotions are based); that which controls the *nikutai* (肉体) (body) of a human; that which depart from the body after death; in the sense of *reikon* (霊魂) or *hakurei* (魄霊) (soul) the opposite of *nikutai* (肉体) (body) (*Kango Hayashi* Dictionary); "blurry and formless something which is the basis of life" (*Gakken* Chinese-Japanese Dictionary).

(2) *kokoro* (心) (heart); *omoi* (思い) (thoughts, thoughtfulness, memory) (*Kango Hayashi* Dictionary); psyche of a human, heart (*Gakken* Chinese-Japanese Dictionary).

I extend this outline and organize the data as follows:

soul as that which moves a living human . . .	
	. . . that which moves him intellectually-consciously (above under (1))
	. . . that which moves him emotionally-unconsciously (above under (2))
soul as that which can depart from a human even during his lifetime ("dream-ego," "excursion soul" or "detachable soul" [Illius 2002, 97])[175]	
soul as a dead human	

The general term combining (1) and (2) is *seikon* (精魂), best translated with "psyche." The first Chinese character of this word originally meant "heart," *kokoro* (心) or the "*ke* (気) of things," *mono-no ke* (物の気). It is widely used in various technical terms of psychology.

2.4.3.2 *Tamashii* (魂) (soul) and body belong together

Body and *tamashii* (魂), soul, belong closely together. The proverb "The pain of the *tamashii* (魂) dries out the bones" (*tamashii-no urei-wa hone-o karasu*, 魂の憂いは骨を枯らす) describes psychosomatic connections.

2.4.3.3 *Tamashii* (魂) (soul) is the power that moves a human

Tamashii (魂), soul, means the power which moves humans and all other living creatures. *Hakuryoku* (魄力), also *kihaku* (気魄), literally the "soul-*ki* (気)," means psychic power or will-power. In the case of humans *tama* (魂) is the "spiritual or psychic power" (Naumann 1996, 125).

From ages past, Shintoism knew the ceremony of *tamashizume-no matsuri* (魂鎮めの祭), the "ceremony for the appeasement of the soul." It was originally held for the emperors in times of their physical ailment. "It was believed that the soul of the sick Emperor could be appeased by this ceremony and that he would gain life-force and *mana* befitting his standing and dignity." With time this ceremony became an annual occasion and was extended to crown princes and empresses, later even to commoners. According to A. Saki, this ceremony

---

175. In the Japanese context this meaning has only a few references not yet unknown. "Man's *tama* (魂) can function independently of his body, and assist in the achievements of his work" (Nakamura and Wiener 1964, 361).

was connected to Japanese shamanism, as it was accompanied with clapping of hands and music. "It was assumed that the souls of nature and man could be strengthened by shaking and exciting [the body]. Also, it was assumed that the soul departed from the body could be called back, appeased and detained. It was believed that the detention of the soul in the body protected man from death" as death occurred when the soul was separated from the body (Numazawa 1970, 202–203).

Sasaki (佐々木宏幹) (1980, 64) reports a ritual which is still practiced in Okinawa. If a toddler cries at night, if he faints, or suffers from an epileptic seizure, his *tamashii* (魂), departs from the body.[176] Whether the case at hand is really a *mabuiotoshi* (マブイ落とし), a "loss of the soul" is then determined by experts – in Okinawa the *yuta*[177] or *kankakariya*. To do so, sand and three stones wrapped in cloth are placed upon the chest of the child. This ritual is called *mabuigume* (マブイ籠め), "recovering of the soul." It brings back the soul and the child has then recovered. According to my understanding, these perceptions of *tamashii* (魂) are congruent with what Käser calls the "spirit-like double" (2004, 102–108).

2.4.3.4 *Tamashii* (魂) (soul) moves a human intellectually and emotionally

Humans experience *tamashii* (魂), the power that moves them, in different ways – conscious ways (intellectual) and unconscious ways (emotional). According to Hiebert et al. (61), many cultures have different terminology for these two ways, but in Japan, there is only one term. This categorizes Japan as a "primitive culture" where "sensing and feeling" and "thinking, desiring, wisdom" are "generally" subsumed under one term (Resch 1992, 597).

The proverb that says that "the *tamashii* (the soul) of a three-year-old (remains) until one hundred" (*mitsugo-no tamashii hyaku made*, 三つ子の魂百まで), means basically the same as "You can't teach an old dog new tricks," or "A tree must be bent while it is young." In this case *tamashii* (soul) explicitly means knowledge and thinking. The term *kontan* (魂胆) also shows that *tamashii* (魂) can mean "thoughts." *Kontan* (魂胆) is the ulterior motive, that which is hidden in the heart. If somebody is very skillful he is referred

---

176. In Okinawa, the *tamashii* (魂), soul, of a living human (Uchima 2006, 255) is called *mabui* (Tanigawa 1999, 33).

177. According to Uchima (内間直仁) (2006, 293), *yuta* are still part of everyday life. In an interview conducted by Murakami (村上春樹) with people involved in the sarin gas attack in Tokyo (1995/3/20), Akio Namimura reports about the practical help he got from a *yuta* on Okinawa who counseled him (Murakami 2002, 197–198). Sered (194–198) studied the equation of *yuta* and "shaman" and reports about their changing role today.

to as *tama ari* (魂あり), as somebody who "has soul." In this case, *tamashii* (魂) means conscious reception and understanding. The eager attitude of a businessman is called *shoukon* (商魂), literally the "trading-soul." Also the term *tamagaeri* (魂帰り), the "return of the *tamashii* (魂)" can be used as an equivalent to *kokorogawari* (心変わり), which means "change of mind." The term *kokoro* (心) will be dealt with later. In this context I want to point out that *tamashii* and *kokoro* (心), heart, are closely related. The *Kokugo Daijiten* Dictionary even equates both terms. In this case *kokoro* (心), heart, means thinking and attitude. However, more commonly it means the place of emotions.

In Japanese, the English phrase "one heart and soul" is expressed with *jikkon* or *nyuukon* (入魂), which means that one enters into the soul of the friend. If somebody works "with all his heart" he is referred to as one who "puts in his *tamashii* as he works" (*kare-wa tamashii-o irete shigoto-o suru*, 彼は魂を入れて仕事をする). However, someone who does not show the same eagerness is admonished: "Put in (literally 'drive in') more *tamashii* (魂), more soul, when working!" (*motto tamashii-o uchikonde shigoto-o shinasai*, もっと魂を打ち込んで仕事とをしなさい). When an artist pours out his everything into a piece of art, this is called *nyuukon* (入魂), the "putting in of the *tamashii* (魂), the soul." The above referred to *shoukon* (商魂) can also mean that a businessman goes about his business "with all his heart." The term *toukon* (闘魂) is also interpreted in this way. In means "untamable fighting spirit." Also the term *tsuradamashii* (面魂), the wild, challenging look, points in this direction. It literally means: the *tamashii*, the soul, (魂) in the countenance (面).

The most common object of a Japanese wholehearted effort is Japan. *Nippondamashii* (日本魂), *yamatodamashii* (大和魂)[178] – according to Hearn, synonym to *yamatogokoro* (大和心) (Hearn 1971, 159) – designate the sacrificial love for Japan, the power, the "spirit," the "national soul" of Japan. It is a nationalistic term. This can be seen from a report from the beginning of the *Meiji*-Era – the term "Soul of Japan" was used to fanaticize young men to lay down their lives on the battlefield (Reischauer 1984, 130). Ejima also called attention to the connection between the celebration of death on the battlefield (*Todeskult*) and *yamatodamashii* (大和魂) (Ejima 1996, 97). In the 1930s the term "Soul of Japan" was used in the propaganda of Nazi-Japan

---

178. The difference between *Nippon* and *Yamato* is the same as the difference between *Deutschland* and *Germania*, the second having a distinctive nationalistic ring.

(Reischauer 1984, 174; Taya-Cook and Cook 1992, 339; Kawai 1990, 129). The report of a female worker in the military industry during World War II illustrates this vividly:

> We were absolutely determined to attack them [the Americans] with our bamboo spears[179] when they would land in Japan . . . We had our spears always ready to hand. "Each and every one! Each and every one stabs one! Without fail!" they said to us and we answered with one voice: "Yes!" Our spears were about one and half meters long, with a sharp point carved diagonally on the end. We would train every morning. "Push! Push! Push!" I actually thought that I could stab one . . . "Americans are tall, well built," they told us, "so you have to aim for the throat. And from there into the head! Don't look into the face! Stab without looking!" We actually thought we could do it. Isn't that scary? We would call that *yamato-damashii*, the "Spirit of Japan"! Then we would wrap the bandana with the "Rising Sun" around our heads and bow towards the Imperial Palace before exercising with our bamboo spears. Then we would start working. But I liked it. It was for Japan, to support and protect our country. (Shigeko 1992, 324–325)

Even today the concept of *yamatodamashii* (大和魂) is alive. Yoshikazu Takiya holds that it was not replaced when the Japanese emperor renounced his divinity (Takiya 1992, 71). The combination of the "Japanese Spirit" and Chinese knowledge is called *wakonkansai* (和魂漢才), that with Western knowledge *wakonyousai* (和魂洋才).

2.4.3.5 *Tamashii* (魂), soul postmortem

According to traditional Japanese understanding, there is no basic change when a person dies. "One's *tama* (魂) is supposed to remain in this world and continue functioning after one's death, and essentially no distinction is drawn between the state of one's *tama* (魂) before and after death" (Nakamura and Wiener 1964, 361). The only thing that changes is that the *tamashii* (魂) departs from its "host" (Blacker 1993, 154) and lives on without a body. The *tama-no o* (玉の緒 or 魂の緒) the cord of life, is severed and the biological

---

179. Ejima (96) also reported about the idea that the American bombers of World War II could be attacked with bamboo spears, provided one had the spiritual strength and the will to prevail over the enemies. The Japanese thought that the Americans "would fear for their lives and soon surrender, due to lack of *yamatodamashii* (大和魂) (Horio 1995, 307).

life comes to an end (Naumann 1996, 125). The severing, however, takes time and is considered complete only after the first festival of the dead (Turnbull 1998, 197). The *tamashii* (魂) itself lives on and is called a *reikon fumetsu* (霊魂不滅), an "incorruptible soul." The dead live on as the *living dead* and all functions of the *tamashii* (魂), the soul, the intellect, and the emotion, are preserved. Character traits also remain.

2.4.3.6 *Tamashii* (魂) (soul) and *oni* (鬼) (demon)

The above model for the Japanese soul-concept shows a certain closeness between *tamashii* (魂), soul, and *oni* (鬼), demon. This is a puzzling fact because originally *oni* (鬼) was not connected with the Japanese soul-concept.

What the Japanese *oni* (鬼) are and do can best be studied in Japanese fairytales.[180] *Oni* (鬼) are malicious,[181] abduct people, steal (Sakade 1971, 10, 70), and destroy fields (97–98). *Oni* (鬼) are stupid (Tadokoro 1976, 29; Obara 1976, 40–41; Ouhira 1976, 45), gullible (Sakade 1971, 73), kill and devour humans (Tanno 1976, 28; Yamashita 1976, 38–39; Sakade 1971, 98; Hammitzsch 1969, 91–92, 200; Ozaki 1970, 25, 46), and have an overwhelming hunger (Tadokoro 1976, 29).

Some spirits (Hammitzsch 1969, 200) such as the *kappa* (河童), the water goblins, half monkey-half tortoise, live at rivers and ponds. They love blood (Storm 2000, 204) and seize children bathing in the rivers (Griffis 1895, ch. 1). According to some tales, *oni* (鬼) are interested in the souls of humans (Storm 2000, 220). They have supernatural skills. Some use objects with magical power (Sakade 1971, 73). Usually they are invisible (Storm 2000, 238), but they can change into almost any natural phenomena: into things (Yamashita 1976, 38–39; Takariki 1976, 45), into humans and animals (Tanno 1976, 28; Irie 1976, 50–51; Hammitzsch 1969, 130, 133, 141–142, 191), and even into ghosts (Ogasawara 1976, 62).

In some tales they have a material body (Tadokoro 1976, 29; Ozaki 1970, 140) with blood (Ebina 1976, 37). When they become visible they are often seen as huge red, blue, or black demons (Sakade 1971, 15). Some of them, the *tengu* (天狗), have long noses which they can extend to a length of several

---

180. Of course fairytales reflect ideals and they only "pinpoint" the "stupid devil" (Bloch 1982, 411). When talking with Japanese about demons I carefully avoid the term *oni* (鬼). For the spiritual beings the Bible calls "demons," I use *akuryou* (悪霊) or *ikiryou* (生霊) instead, which mean as much as "evil spirits."

181. Malice is their main character trait. They are the prime example of malice. When something is most sad, the proverb *oni-no me-ni-mo namida* (鬼の目にも涙) (Joseph 1982, 68) is used, which means, that the matter is so sad, that there is a tear even in the eye of an *oni* (鬼).

kilometers (29). *Oni* (鬼) can have human character traits, can be envious or comical (Sakade 1971, 33–34; Käser 2005, 103). If outwitted they can be killed. The "best" way seems to be by pouring boiling water over them (Tadokoro 1976, 29; Ebina 1976, 37).[182] Fire kills them as well (Obara 1976, 40–41).

How are these *oni* (鬼) connected with the Japanese soul-concept? Katsumoto proved that originally *oni* (鬼) meant nothing else than "soul of a dead":

> Even though *oni* (鬼) [demons] were ancestral deities for ages, protecting their families, they gradually became *yakubyouki* (疫病鬼), [*oni* (鬼) bringing calamity]. As *shinrei* (神霊) [divine spirits] and ancestral deities, the *oni* (鬼) [demons] of Japans had immense power, were associated with Buddhist *oni* (鬼) [demons], and became grotesque beings with horns growing from their heads. (Katsumoto 1992, 93–94)

Katsumoto rightly talks about a change due to "Buddhist influence." Others overlooked this fact and wrongly judged that the *oni* (鬼) "came to Japan together with Buddhism" (Storm 2000, 220; similarly Chamberlain 1990, 121). Fazzioli (32) called attention to the fact that in China the meaning of demon for the character 鬼 is a recent development, and that originally it had a positive meaning.

Old tales report that demons originated from women who had been "overly jealous" in their lifetime (Storm 2000, 220). These tales are evidence for the connection between the spirit of the dead and demons.[183]

2.4.4 The Word-Field Rei (霊) (Spirit) / Sudama (魅) (Ghost)

2.4.4.1 Introduction

The term *rei* (霊) is closely related to the term *tamashii* (魂) which can be seen from the fact that the Chinese characters 霊 and 魂 often have the same reading. The Chinese reading is always *rei*, but in the classical Japanese reading 霊 is often read *tama* and *tamashii*. This is yet another example for the fact that the Chinese meaning of a character is not enough for understanding Japanese word-fields.

---

182. This method also helps against witches, as the farytale *Der Ochsentreiber und die Hexe* shows (Hammitzsch 1969, 81–83).

183. Bolt (78–79) proved that for the Greek classicism as well.

2.4.4.2 Closeness to *rei* (霊) (spirit) and *tamashii* (魂) (soul)

In the following examples, 魂, 玉 and/or 霊 can be used interchangably. The meaning and reading remains the same:

- the welcoming of the souls of the dead *tamamukae* (魂迎 or 霊迎 or 玉迎) and their seeing off *tamaokuri* (魂送 or 霊送 or 玉送) on the occasion of the festival for the dead, the *tamamatsuri* (魂祭 or 霊祭 or 玉祭)
- the morgue *tamaya* (魂屋 or 霊室 or 玉屋)
- the "soul of words" *kotodama* (言霊 or 言魂) (McVeigh 1992, 62)
- the "exhaustion of the soul" *tamakiharu* (魂極る or 霊極る or 玉極る)
- the echo *kodama* (木魂 or 木霊 or 木玉)
- the soul of a ship *funadama* (船魂 or 船霊 or 船玉)
- a rice sapling *inadama* (稲魂 or 稲霊 or 稲玉) (Komatsu 1999, 43)
- the soul of numbers *kazudama* (数魂 or 数霊 or 数玉)
- the soul of colors *irodama* (色魂 or 色霊)
- the soul of sounds *otodama* (音魂 or 音霊 or 音玉) (McVeigh 1992, 61)
- the honorable deified soul of the dead *mitama* (御魂 or 御霊 or 御玉) or *oomitama* (大御魂 or 大御霊 or 大御玉)

But it is not just the reading that shows a close relation. The content is also closely related:

- the compound of the characters 霊 and 魂, *reikon* (霊魂), simply means "soul"
- the "miraculous power" of the "soul" is called *reiryoku* (霊力)
- the place where the "soul" lives, the heart, is also called *reifu* (霊府), the tabernacle of the 霊, or *reidai* (霊台), the "stand" of the 霊
- the "soul" of the dead is also called *seirei* (精霊), *yuurei* (幽霊) or *bourei* (亡霊)
- the ritual bringing comfort to the "souls" of the dead is called *irei* (慰霊)
- the ritual leading to *joubutsu* (成仏), the becoming (成) a Buddha (仏) of the "soul" of a dead, is called *jorei* (除霊)[184]
- the cleansing of a "soul" is called *jourei* (浄霊) (Makimoto 2006, 69).

---

184. The belief that deceased humans become "gods" existed in the thought of other nations around Israel and Egypt. According to a ritual text of the 13th centrury BC, the phrase "becoming a god" was used for the burial of the Hittite Great King (Müller-Karpe 2009, 126).

2.4.4.3 Demarcation of the world-field *rei* (霊) (spirit)

When defining a world-field, sometimes the best place to start is with its demarcation. *Rei* (霊) in the widest sense means the opposite of matter. The antonym of "material" is *reiteki* (霊的), spirit-like. According to Kubota (10), it was a general concept of the Japanese natives, that *rei* (霊) "come and go between this and yonder world and make humans possessed with *kami* (神)." The spiritual life is called *reisei* (霊生) and the general term for spirituality is *reisei* (霊性) (Gebhardt 2001, 25). The spiritual world is called *reikai* (霊界),[185] parapsychological activities *reidou* (霊動). *Rei* (霊) is also used as an antonym of the secular. Songs with spiritual content are generally called *reika* (霊歌).

The second opposite of *rei* (霊) is "flesh" in the sense of "body." This is evident in the term *reiniku* (霊肉) which means "spirit and body." In Christian terminology *reiteki* (霊的) stands for "spiritual" as opposed to "carnal" (*nikuteki,* 肉的).

2.4.4.4 Definition of *rei* (霊) (spirit): the extraordinary

The next step in defining the world-field of *rei* (霊) is the defining of its content. In the widest sense *rei* (霊) means the extraordinary, the prominent, and the special. The concept of the special is then developed into the concept of the segregated or the consecrated, the holy. The concept of the prominent developed into the concept of the outstanding, the excellent. In animism extraordinary things are generally considered bearers of extraordinary power (Käser 2004, 91–94) and are often used for divination.

Examples for *rei* (霊) as the "extraordinary"

- *reimyou* (霊妙) means the miraculous and the marvelous, even the odd; synonyms are *reii* (霊異), *reikai* (霊怪) and *reika* (霊化), "suspicious," "strange"
- a flute with an extraordinary sound is called *reiteki* (霊笛), literally a "spirit-flute"
- incense with an extraordinary fragrance is called *reikyou* (霊香)
- an extraordinary bird is a *reikin* (霊禽)
- an extraordinary beast is a *reijuu* (霊獣)

---

185. Komatsu (1999, 41) understands *reikai* (霊界) not as "spiritual world" but as the world of the *reikon* (霊魂), of the spirits of the dead.

Examples for *rei* (霊) as the "holy"
- holy places are called *reikyou* (霊境), *reiiki* (霊域), *reichi* (霊地), and *reijou* (霊場)
- holy mountains are called *reihou* (霊峰) and *reizan* (霊山)[186]
- holy herbs are called *reisou* (霊草)
- holy trees are called *reiboku* (霊木)[187]
- holy stones are called *reiseki* (霊石)
- holy birds are called *reichou* (霊鳥)

Examples for *rei* (霊) as the "miraculous"
- a rainfall evoked miraculously is called *reiu* (霊雨)
- wonder-working medicine is called *reiyaku* (霊薬)
- an effective elixir is called *reieki* (霊液)
- a thermal spring with healing power is called *reisen* (霊泉)

Examples for *rei* (霊) as the "excellent"
- the biological technical term for "primate" is *reichourui* (霊長類), literally the "class of those who by the virtue of *rei* (霊), the special power of *rei* (霊), also called *reiryoku* (霊力) or *ryouge* (霊気), qualify as rulers (長) of the world"
- in the same sense leadership personalities are called *reichou* (霊長)
- people with outstanding intellectual capacity have *reichi* (霊知 or 霊智)
- people who distinguish themselves by extraordinary ethical integrity have *reitoku* (霊徳)
- a treasure of extraordinary value is called *reihou* (霊宝)
- a temple distinguished by particularly appropriate and meaningful oracles is called *reisatsu* (霊刹) or *reiji* (霊寺)
- an excellent sword is called *reiken* (霊剣)

Examples for *rei* (霊) as the designator of means of oracles
- oracles foretelling fortune are called *reizui* (霊瑞)
- turtles used for divination are called *reiki* (霊亀)[188]
- oracle water is called *reisui* (霊水)

---

186. Ono et al. (4–5) list the holy mountains of Japan.

187. In Shintoism such trees are the embodiment of maternity, affluence, hope, and revitalization (Bak 2008, 3).

188. Also called *kiboku* (亀卜), turtle-divination. It was prevalent at the Imperial court until the 10th century (Pye et al. 2007, 248).

- clouds that serve as oracles by virtue of their extraordinary shape are called *reiun* (霊雲)

The following three sections deal with special usages of *rei* (霊): *rei* (霊) as the spirits of the dead, *rei* (霊) as spirits, and *rei* (霊) as "god."

2.4.4.5 *Rei* (霊) (spirit) as spirits of the dead

The spirits of the dead can be written with compounds using the character *rei* (霊): *shirei* (死霊), the *rei* (霊) of the dead (死); *bourei* (亡霊), the *rei* (霊) of the deceased (亡); and *yuurei* (幽霊), the dark or quiet (幽) spirits (霊). These terms have been explained above. In the widest sense the spirits of the dead are called *reibutsu* (霊物), "*rei* (霊)-things," or *shouryou* (精霊), the "refined" *rei* (霊). Those who won great fame are called *eirei* (英霊). Ancestors are generally called *sorei* (祖霊), ancestral *rei* (霊), the spirit of a dead emperor is called *kourei* (皇霊). Other combinations are:

- diseases caused by evil spirits of the dead are called *ryoubyou* (霊病), literally "*rei* (霊)-diseases"
- the graveyard is called *reien* (霊園), "*rei* (霊)-park"
- the mausoleum is called *reibyou* (霊廟), *tamaya* (霊室) (written with 霊!), and *reiden* (霊殿)
- the resting place of the *tamashii* (魂) is called *reiza* (霊座)
- the morgue is called *reianshitsu* (霊安室), the "room where the *rei* (霊) rests (安)"
- the coffin is called *reikyuu* (霊柩)
- the hearse is called *reikyuusha* (霊柩車) or *reisha* (霊車)
- memorial services are called *reishi* (霊祀) or *irei* (慰霊)
- the place where memorial services are held is called *reisha* (霊舎 or 霊社)
- rituals where prayer for the welfare of dead spirits is offered are called *reihai* (霊牌)
- Buddhist memorial tablets are called *reii* (霊位), *ryoubo* (霊簿), or *reidai* (霊代) (also read *tamashiro*)
- the offerings for the dead are called *ryougu* (霊供)
- fellowship with the dead is called *reikou* (霊交), spiritism respectively *reikoujutsu* (霊交術), *koureijutsu* (交霊術 or 降霊術) or *reibaijutsu* (霊媒術 or 冷媒術)
- the art of mediums establishing contact with the dead is called *reibai* (霊媒 or 冷媒)

2.4.4.6 Rei (霊) (spirit) as spirits

This semantic field can hardly be distinguished from the previous. This can be exemplified with the term *yuurei* (幽霊), generally meaning evil spirits of the dead. In this case it is rather uncertain whether an evil spirit of a dead person or an evil spirit in general is meant. A vengeful spirit, *onryou* (怨霊), can also be the spirit of a dead person or an evil spirit in general.

In the case of *akuryou* (悪霊), literally the "evil spirit," its origin designates it clearly as a general spirit. It is never a spirit of a dead person. An *ikiryou* (生霊) is also, as the characters already suggest, the soul of a living (生) person which he or she can send out to harm others. Apparently, this kind of *ikiryou* (生霊) are the most dreaded spirits.[189]

2.4.4.7 Rei (霊) (spirit) as "god"

The key term of this semantic field is *shinrei* (神霊), composed of *kami* (神) and *rei* (霊). Synonyms are *mitama* (御霊), the "honorable (御) spirit (霊)," and *reibutsu* (霊物) mentioned above. There are a number of words where *rei* (霊) means God or gods:

- the "spirit-nature," *reisei* (霊性), can also be translated as "divine nature"
- a *reizou* (霊像) is an image, *zou* (像), of a god; if it works miracles it is said to have *reigen* (霊験), "spirit-omen," or *reiou* (霊応), "spirit-response"; the miraculous light emitted by a *reizou* (霊像) is called *reikou* (霊光) or *reii* (霊威)
- people appearing before the gods or their images come into *reizen* (霊前), into the presence of the *rei* (霊)[190]
- the candelabras for Shinto-gods and Buddhas are called *reitou* (霊灯)
- the altar where miraculous rain, *reiu* (霊雨), is prayed for is called *reidan* (霊壇), the offerings offered there *ryougu* (霊供)
- the respective temples are called *reisatsu* (霊刹), shrines and temples *reidou* (霊堂), shrines *reisha* (霊社)
- the after-effects of a divine miracle are called the "footprints of the *rei* (霊)," *reiseki* (霊跡 or 霊迹)
- the amulets through which gods work miracles are called *reifu* (霊符)

---

189. The Lacandon people in Mexico distinguish much clearer between souls of living people, never scary, and the *kisin* (*kisin* of the feet and *kisin* of the hands), which have a certain resemblance with the pulse and who, as spirits of the dead, scare people (Ma'ax and Rätsch 1984, 202–205).

190. *Reizen* (霊前) can also mean the coming before the spirits of the dead in worship.

- mountains where gods are worshipped are called *reizan* (霊山) or *reihou* (霊峰)
- ponds where gods live are called *reichi* (霊池)
- *reichigaku* (霊智学) is theopathy
- the penetrating aspect of the gods is called *reiken* (霊見)
- the messages from the gods are called *reikoku* (霊告) or *reitaku* (霊託), sometimes conveyed through "divine dreams," *reimu* (霊夢), or through *reikan* (霊感), "inspiration" in the literal sense; *shinrai* (神来), the "coming of a *kami* (神)" is a synonym for *reikan* (霊感)
- the above mentioned *koureijutsu* (降霊術) for "spiritism" is used as a synonym for *koushin* (降神), literally the "calling down of a *kami* (神), also meaning spiritism; in the above *koureijutsu* (降霊術) the *rei* (霊) is called down, here the *kami* (神)
- the Christian churches use *mitama* (御霊) or *seirei* (聖霊) for the Holy Spirit; here, too, *rei* (霊) means "God"

2.4.4.8 *Rei* (霊) (spirit) and *sudama* (魅) (ghost)

Sudama (魅), ghost, also belongs to the word-field of *rei* (霊), spirit. Both words can be pronounced the same way. Both are connected in the cases where *rei* (霊) means (evil) spirits.

Sudama (魅), also called *chimi* (魑魅), *mouryou* (魍魎), or *chimimouryou* (魑魅魍魎)[191] are *bakemono* (化け物), literally "changing things," ghosts evolving from the "spirit of nature." They can take on any desired, mostly mysterious, form. Some dictionaries equate *sudama* (魅) with *tamashii* (魂), soul.

There are also interpretations portraying *sudama* (魅) as evil spirits: the term *miiru* (魅入る) for spirit-possession literally says that an (evil) *sudama* (魅) enters a person. Words formed with the character 魅 show what ghosts can do:

- *bakasu* (化かす or 魅かす),[192] "bewitch," "seduce," "ensnare" the human heart that it has no reasoning power anymore
- *misuru* (魅する) or *misu* (魅す), "enchant"
- *misaseru* (魅させる) or *miryousuru* (魅了する), "fascinate"
- *miwakusuru* (魅惑する), "confuse"

---

191. Ghosts living mainly in woods and rivers.

192. The first writing is the common one. The original meaning of 化 is "to change." The second (carrying the same meaning) shows the connection to "ghost."

- a person possessing *miryoku* (魅力), the "power (力) of a *sudama* (魅)," is "fascinating"; *miryoku* (魅力) shows a certain closeness to *rei* (霊) which denotes the extraordinary; a person owning *miryoku* (魅力) owns an extraordinary power and distinguishes herself

2.4.5 The Word-Field *Kokoro* (心) (Heart)

2.4.5.1 Introduction: the connection with *tamashii* (魂) (soul)

When asked for the meaning of *tamashii* (魂) many Japanese spontaneously point to their chest and say *kokoro* (心). But just how are they both connected? In this section I set forth why *kokoro* (心) belongs to the Japanese soul-concept, and how it is connected with *tamashii* (魂). There is a connection in form and a connection in content.

The formal connection can be seen from the many words in which *tamashii* (魂) and *kokoro* (心) can be used interchangeably:

- *tamagaeri* (魂帰り) as well as *kokorogaeri* (心帰り), *tama-o irekaeru* (魂を入れ替える) as well as *kokoro-o irikaeru* (心を入れ替える) mean the same: change of heart
- the adverbial phrases *kokoro-o tsukushite* (心を尽くして) and *kokoro-o komete* (心をもめて), meaning "with all one's heart" are used as synonyms of *seikon-o katabukeru*, (精魂を傾ける), to "focus one's psyche on something"
- the phrase *tamashii-o kesu* (魂を消す), "extinguish the soul," can be used as a synonym of the phrase "have a sad *kokoro* (心)"
- the phrase *kokoro-o hiyasu* (心を冷やす), "cool down the heart," can be used as a synonym of the phrase *tamashii-o kesu* (魂を消す), "extinguish the soul"
- *kokochi* (心地) (sentiment, mood), composed of "heart" (心) and "texture" (地), is a synonym of *tamashii* (魂)
- the compound of *kokoro* (心), "heart," and *tamashii* (魂), "soul," *shinkon* (心魂), shows how close they both are related; they are used in phrases such as *shigoto-ni shinkon-o itadakeru* (仕事に心魂を頂ける), "focus one's *shinkon* (心魂) on one's work"; the same compound can also be read *kokorodamashii* (心魂) and then means the psyche
- the term *kokorodama* (心魂 or 心玉), "heart-soul," "heart-bowl," simply means the "true heart" or *tamashii* (魂)
- the term *shinshin* (心身), "body and soul," composed of *kokoro* (心) (heart) and "Self," is a synonym of *shinkon* (身魂), "Self" (身) and *tamashii* (魂) (soul)

- *kokorogimo* (心肝 or 心胆), "heart-liver" and "heart-gall" means the innermost of the heart and is a synonym of *tamashii* (魂) (soul)
- *kyakkon* (客魂), the "*tamashii* (魂) (soul) of a guest (客)" is a synonym of the "*kokoro* (心) (heart) of a traveler"
- *boushin* (亡心), the "heart of a dead," can be used as a synonym of *bourei* (亡霊) and *boukon* (亡魂), "spirit of the dead," "soul of the dead"

As for the content connection, a mere glance into dictionaries shows just how wide the word-field *kokoro* (心) is. It is difficult to determine which meaning is original. I surmise that "inner" is the most basic and original meaning. The literal meaning of the organ "heart" (*cor*) is derived from this basic meaning, depicting the heart as the innermost organ. In classical Japanese the Chinese character 心 can be read in many ways. One of them is *ura* (心) which means what is not visible and "at the back." If, for example, something is without *ura* (心) it is without *Hintergedanke*, without a "hidden agenda." Another example is *uranaki* (心泣き), the "secret weeping" which does not publicly show grief.

The figurative sense of *kokoro* (心), as "true nature," is also derived from the original meaning. The term *busshin* (物心), composed of "things" (物) and "heart" (心) is a general term including the material and the spiritual. Also that which is "at the heart of a matter," which is truly "inside," can be called *kokoro* (心): the *utagokoro* (歌心), literally the "heart of a song," means the meaning of the song "in" the words of its lyrics, as opposed to the exterior and therefore visible "parts" of a human *kokoro* (心) which means what is "interior" and therefore invisible. These things are called *shinteki* (心的), "concerning the heart," psychological processes.

For the sake of simplification of matters I want to divide the meanings of *kokoro* (心) as follows:

Table 2.4 Division of the Meanings of Kokoro (心)

Inside				
organ heart (*cor*)	meaning	psychological processes		
		knowledge mind thinking	will	consciousness	emotions knowledge

This shows that the world-field of *kokoro* (心) (heart) is almost congruent with the word-field of *tamashii* (魂) (soul) where it describes the inner life of a living person. Where *tamashii* (魂) (soul) also describes the dead, the word-field of *kokoro* (心) (heart) connects to the word-field of *kami* (神) (god).

2.4.5.2 *Kokoro* (心) as knowledge, mind, thinking

Like *tamashii* (魂) (soul), *kokoro* (心) can also mean thinking. However, this meaning is expressed stronger in the world-field of *kokoro* (心).

In many phrases the connection between thinking and *kokoro* (心) is apparent:

- thoughts can simply be called *shinji* (神事), "matters of the heart"; they can sprout like grass and are then called the *kokoro-no kusa* (心の草), "grass of the heart"
- an idea, a thought, is called *kokoroatari* (心当たり), that which "hits" the heart
- worries are called *shinpai* or *kokorokubari* (心配), a term which depicts a state of heart where the "thoughts are sent here and there"
- the point in child development when a child starts to intellectually perceive his environment is called the point when *kokoro-ga tsuku* (心がつく), when his "heart is turned on"; he then gets *monogokoro* (物心), the heart that perceives the things, and becomes a knowing person
- a person who can comprehend things can see with *shingan* (心眼), with "the heart-eyes"; she then has a mental image, called *shinzou* (心像), the "heart-image"
- if something is engraved in the heart, it is firmly fixed upon memory
- if something is preserved in the heart, it will not be forgotten
- if someone understands something about a certain matter, he "has acquired heart," called *kokoroeru* (心得る)
- *kokoro-no kate* (心の糧), the "food for the heart" means "food for the mind"
- *kanshin* (関心), the state of heart where "heart is connected" means interest
- a sudden loss of mind is called *kokorowasure* (心忘れ), literally the state where the heart forgets or is forgotten
- if somebody is lost in thought or absent-minded he has sent off (放, 送) his *kokoro* (心), his "heart"; this is then called *houshin* (放心) or *soushin* (送心)

- *shinsei* (心性), the "kind of heart," means "mentality"
- people spiritually akin are said to experience *kokoro-ga kayoiatteiru* (心が通い通い合っている), that "their hearts commute," "associate"

2.4.5.3 *Kokoro* (心) as will

Kokoro (心) has, along with *tamashii* (魂), the connotation of "will." *Tamashii* (魂) rather means the unreflected, impulsive, and animalistic "will," whereas *kokoro* (心) means the well-considered and reflected "will." The Buddhist *kokoro-no uma* (心の馬), literally the "horse of the heart," seems to be an exception. It is used in the proverb *iba shinen* (意馬心猿) which means "will-horse or heart-monkey." It admonishes people not to let their desires go wild as horses and monkeys, but rather control them.

Again there are a number of phrases and words giving evidence of this meaning:

- *shini* (心意), the compound of *kokoro* (心) and will (意), simply means "will"
- *kokorozashi* (志 or 心指し) also means "will," that on which "the heart points"; a person who *kororosasu* (志す or 心指す), "sets goals"
- a person who gains "*kokorozashi* (志 or 心指し)" reaches these goals
- *mikokoro* (御心), literally the "honorable heart" means the will or the desire of the other person; in the Christian churches it means the "will of God"
- the phrase "as the heart" means "as you wish"
- he who comes to a decision "decides (決) in the heart," does *kesshin* (決心)
- he who makes a life-altering decision "exchanges his heart"
- *kokoromochi* (心持), literally "carrying heart," means "willingly"
- that which "hangs on the heart," the *kokorogake* (心掛け or 心懸), is the intention; the opposite is *kokoronarazu* (心ならず), that which is "without heart"; it means "hesitant"
- if somebody does *kokorodate* (心立て), if he literally "erects his heart," he makes up his mind, or he stubbornly insists on something
- if a person is "strong at heart" he does not falter
- the *tesshin* (鉄心), the "iron-heart," and the *tessekishin* (鉄石心), the "iron-stone-heart" is used for people with an iron will

- the opposite is the *koushin* (降心), the "heart stepped down"; it is an expression for humbleness, for the ability to suppress the heart's deepest desires

2.4.5.4 *Kokoro* (心) as consciousness

This meaning of *kokoro* (心) is also present in *tamashii* (魂) (soul), but there it is hardly developed. *Bewußtsein* and *Wissen*, awareness of Self and awareness of things, are closely connected. Many words and phrases using *kokoro* (心) in the sense of consciousness or awareness are also used as synonyms of knowledge.

The adverbs *kokoro-to-mo naku* (心ともなく) and *kokoro-ni-mo arazu* (心にもあらず) express that one does not put her heart into something, that one acts without thinking or being aware of it. The "getting of *monogokoro* (物心)" as well as the related *kokochi* (心地) (both mentioned above) don't mean the knowing grasping of the world but rather the consolidation of the consciousness on the route towards adolescence. *Kokoro-o itasu* (心を致す), when the "heart is set on something," means that the awareness is focused on the matter at hand. "Unconsciousness" is called *shisshin* (失心), literally the "lost heart." When the heart "awakes" a person comes back to consciousness.

A special form of consciousness is the state of absolute presence of mind, also referred to as enlightenment. Before one reaches enlightenment, or *satori* (悟り), his heart is "clouded" – it is in a state of illusion, a state of *kokoromayoi* (心迷い), literally the state of the "straying heart." By means of *kokorojitaku* (心支度 or 心仕度), *youjin* (用心), and *kokoroyoui* (心用意), all meaning the "preparation of heart," a person reaches the state of full consciousness. His heart then is "prepared" (*kokorogamae,* 心構え), or "composed" (*kokorogumi,* 心組み). A person thus prepared is cautious. In Japanese he "makes heart." The enlightened hears with the *shinji* (心耳), the "ears of the heart." He can hear the famous "sound of one clapping hand" of the Zen-Buddhist *koan* (Suzuki 1986, 146).

2.4.5.5 *Kokoro* (心) as emotions

The fervent feeling Japanese used to foster for Japan (and more and more foster again), the *yamatodamashii* (大和魂), the "soul of Japan," can also called *yamatogokoro* (大和心), the "heart of Japan." Generally *kokoro* (心) or *kokoroari* (心あり), "with heart," can mean the warm feeling of love and sympathy for other people. In this sense the English "heart" is also used as loan-word: *haato* (ハート), "heart" as emotions, *haato-uoomingu* (ハートウォーミング), "heartwarming," *haatobureeku* (ハートブレーク), "heartbreak," *haatofuru* (ハートフル), "heartwarming," "uplifting." The opposite is the *ebisugokokoro* (夷心), the gruel and unpitying heart of barbarian warriors.

Kokoro (心) as emotions can be grouped in three groups:

Neutral emotions: The word *shinjou* (心情) is used to generally talk about emotions. A "moved heart" is a heart with thoughts in turmoil, a heart feeling pity for others.

Positive emotions: If someone likes something, it "goes into his heart." Adorable things "move the heart" and lead to *kanshin* (感心), to a "feeling heart." If someone has a "firm heart" she is emotionally stable. If the "heart cannot be turned on," one cannot feel positive emotions.

Negative emotions: Phrases and words as *shintsuu* (心痛), "heart-ache," *mune-ga itamu* (胸が痛む), the "chest hurts," and *kokoro-ga uzuku* (心が疼く), "the heart throbs," express emotional suffering. A "burning heart" is an expression for a state of mind that is unendurable. A *kyuushin* (休心), a resting (休) *kokoro* (心), rests from disquieting thoughts. The above discussed *kokochi* (心地) can also express negative emotions. If something is *kokoronikui* (心憎い), "wholeheartedly loathsome," it provokes emotions of fear and insecurity. In the context of negative feelings, the subject of conscience needs to be dealt with. "Conscience" is generally called *ryoushin* (良心) or *zenshin* (善心), literally the "good heart." Other words are *doutokushin* (道徳心), the "moral-heart," and *jiseishin* (自制心), the "heart controlling oneself." For the heart knowing good there are terms as *akaki kokoro* (明き心), the "bright heart," *kiyoki kokoro* (清き心), the "pure heart,"[193] *tadashiki kokoro* (正しき心), the "right heart," and *naoki kokoro* (直き心), the "upright heart," *magokoro* (真心), the "true heart" or "heart open for truth" (Okano 2002, 23). Kreiner explains *magokoro* (真心): "Man is basically good and feels without [the help of] a moral codex what is right" (1992, 610).

The good decisions made in accord with good conscience are *haji-nai* (恥じない), "without shame." If a person performs "shaming" acts his conscience becomes "bad," felt by intense shame. Then the heart becomes *kokorogurushii* (心苦しい), it is full of "pain," tortured by a *kokoro-no oni* (心の鬼), a "demon of the heart," it has a "painful point." These negative feelings, called *haji* (恥), "shame," are, according to Benedict, the "root of virtue" (Benedict 1993, 29).

---

193. Also called *seishin* (清心) (Okano 2002, 24).

Käser's *SEIC*

In order to conceptually distinguish "soul" as "spirit-like double" and "soul" as "emotion," Käser created the neologism *SEIC*. It is an acronym standing for *Sitz der Emotionen, des Intellekts und Charakters*, the "center of emotions, the intellect, and the character." With *SEIC* he means the "physical organ or the place in the body," where "emotions and expressions of will are perceived, intellectual processes take place and come to awareness, and which are identified with character and personal characteristics" (Käser 2004, 181). As shown above *kokoro* (心) can be called the *SEIC* of Japanese anthropology.

Käser demands that the *SEIC* and "soul" as "spirit-like double" must be distinguishable. As mentioned previously, when asked about the meaning of *tamashii* (魂) many Japanese spontaneously point to their chest and answer with *kokoro* (心). They understand *tamashii* (魂) as the *SEIC* and therefore as synonym for *kokoro* (心). As both terms are used as synonyms it is very difficult to distinguish them. When asked the same question others point to the abdomen. Nitobe (新渡戸稲造) explained *seppuku* (切腹) or *harakiri* (腹切り), the "abdomen-cutting" during the ritual suicide of samurai, that the *reikon* (霊魂) (2007, 65), the "soul" (2001, 118–120) and therefore the center of will (Juniper 2003, 43) was located in the abdomen. Sometimes the abdomen is referred to as the opposite of "head." Yamaori (山折哲雄) (19), for example, said that religious teachings are only "understood up in the head," but that they are never "grasped nor believed" *hara-no soko-kara* (腹の底から) "from the bottom of the abdomen" because they never "fall" into the abdomen.[194]

There are a considerable number of phrases which classify the abdomen as *SEIC*:

- *hara-o yomu* (腹を読む), to "read the abdomen" to "read the mind"
- somebody who is a good person *hara-no naka* (腹の中), "in his abdomen," is a kind-hearted person
- somebody who inwardly grins, grins *hara-no naka* (腹の中), "in his abdomen"
- he who lets shine through his *hara-no naka* (腹の中), the "inside of his abdomen," gives his intention away; the same can be expressed with the phrase that he lets shine through his *honshin* (本心), his "true heart"

---

194. Some people suppose the *tamashii* (魂) to be located in the forehead or the temples.

Kokoro (心) and *hara* (腹) as the *SEIC* can probably hardly be distinguished, partly also because of their physical closeness in the body.

2.4.6 The Word-Field Kami (神) (god)

The *kami* (神)-concept has been the subject of detailed examination above. It is only for the sake of completeness that I mention it here in the context of the Japanese soul-concept. Even though the term *kami* (神) does not seem to be connected with the soul-concept according to Western understanding, it has much more to do with it than the terms dealt with so far. *Kokoro* (心) and *kami* (神) are much closer connected than *rei* (霊) and *sudama* (魅), *tamashii* (魂) and *oni* (鬼). This can be seen from the following words which can be written interchangeably either with 心, "heart" or 神, "god" without any change of meaning:

- *shisshin* (失心 or 失神), "faint"
- *soushin* (送心 or 送神), "absent-mindedness"
- *shinkon* (心魂, or 神魂), "heart," "soul"
- *kyuushin* (休心 or 休神), "resting heart"
- *shinki* (心気 or 神気), "psychic power"

2.4.7 The Word-Field Ki (気) (Energy)

The word-field *ki* (気) has also been explored in detail above. Here only the elements of *ki* (気) connected with humans shall be dealt with.

2.4.7.1 Ki (気) as elan vital

Kiryoku (気力), *ki* (気)-power generally means life-energy, *elan vital*. In a psychological context it also means courage and "guts." A person with *kisei* (気勢), with the "strength" (勢) of *ki* (気), is ardent, passionate, and enthusiastic. A person having *kakki* (活気), a "lively *ki* (気)," is full of life-energy.

If a person has her "original" (元) *ki* (気), if she is *genki* (元気), she is healthy and spry. If, on the other hand, her *ki* (気) is "sick" (病), she herself is *byouki* (病気), "sick." Accordingly, recovery is called *kaiki* (快気), the "restored *ki* (気)."

2.4.7.2 Ki (気) as reason

Reason, psychological health of consciousness, are called *seiki* (正気), "right" (正) *ki* (気). A talented person has *saiki* (才気), "talented (才)" *ki* (気), or he is *saikikappatsu* (才気活発), "talented," "brilliant," and "very smart." *Kanki* (勘気), literally the "calculating (勘) *ki* (気)," means disfavor or disinheritance.

2.4.7.3 *Ki* (気) as emotion

The two key words are *kibun* (気分) and *kimochi* (気持). *Kibun* (気分) literally means the "portion" (分) one possesses of *ki* (気). *Kimochi* (気持) literally means the *ki* (気) one "carries" (持). Both words mean "emotion," "mood," "sentiment." *Kibun* (気分) is less tangible and means the "sentiment," or the "mood," whereas *kimochi* (気持) is more physical and therefore more tangible. Even though *ki* (気) as emotion usually describes psychological processes, there are also phrases that describe physical processes: if the *kimochi* (気持) becomes "bad," one is nauseous. Nausea is simply called *hakige* (吐き気), the "vomit-*ki* (気)."

2.4.7.4 *Ki* (気) as temperament

A person's temperament, disposition, or nature in the sense of characteristic features is called *kishitsu* (気質) or *kishou* (気性). *Shitsu* (質) and *shou* (性) mean "nature," *shitsu* (質) more quality characteristics, *shou* (性) more biological differences, mainly gender differences. The "nature" of *ki* (気) therefore determines the character of a person.

2.4.7.5 *Ki* (気) as will

"Will" is called *ishi* (意志). Both Chinese characters mean "will," *i* (意) more the emotional side, *shi* (志) more the determined, resolute side. Both Chinese characters can be used together with *ki* (気): *iki* (意気) and *shiki* (志気), both meaning "will."[195] The phrase *ki-ga kawaru* (気が変わる), literally "the *ki* (気) changes," means "to change ones intention." The phrase *nanige-naku* (何気なく), literally "without any *ki* (気)," means "unintentionally."

2.4.7.6 *Ki* (気) as interpersonal factor

In Yamaguchi's study on the Japanese linguistic usage of *ki* (気) it becomes apparent that *ki* (気) can be part of the human, that is his emotions, and at the same time *ki* (気) can be independent from the human yet "something" that is somehow connected with him (*mana*). This becomes mainly apparent in phrases for psychological processes which in English take the person as their

---

195. The borders between the *ki* (気) of a human and the *ki* (気) as *mana* are flowing. Kawasaki (川崎ゆふじ) (177) associates *ki* (気) with *nenriki* (念力), the will-power used in psychokinesis.

subject, which in Japanese, however, are expressed with *ki* (気) as the "subject of the sentence" together with a "transitive verb" (Yamaguchi 1997, 58). What is understood as the function of a person in the West is in Japanese often expressed as a function of *ki* (気). Yamaguchi lists the following examples, grouped in three groups:

(1) *Ki* (気) in sentences, which describe a momentary action expressed with an intransitive verb:

Japanese		Direct Translation	Meaning
ki-ga hareru	気が晴れる	*ki* clears	somebody becomes cheerful
ki-ga shizumu	気が沈む	*ki* sinks	somebody becomes depressed
ki-ga muku	気が向く	*ki* turns	somebody gets the desire to do something
ki-ga tsuku	きがつく	*ki* sticks	somebody remembers somebody awakes (from a faint)
ki-ga suru	気がする	*ki* does	somebody senses that ...
ki-ga au	気が合う	*ki* matches	somebody is like-minded

and others

(2) *Ki* (気) used with the particle *ni* (に), which means "towards" and "in," therefore indicating a certain orientation, as expressed with the dative case:

Japanese		Direct Translation	Meaning
ki-ni iru	気に入る	enter into *ki*	something pleases somebody
ki-ni kakaru	気に掛かる	be attached to *ki*	something cannot be forgotten
ki-ni sawaru	気に触る	touch *ki*	something hurts somebody
ki-ni naru	気になる	become *ki*	to cause somebody to be worried
ki-ni suru	気にする	to turn into *ki*	to be concerned about something

and others

(3) *Ki* (気) used for a feature which, upon regular recurrence, has become a habit, expressed with the perspective adjective:

Japanese		Direct Translation	Meaning
ki-ga oukii	気が大きい	*ki* is big	somebody is generous
ki-ga chiisai	気が小さい	*ki* is small	somebody is timid
ki-ga oui	気が多い	*ki* is much	somebody is adventuresome
ki-ga nagai	気が長い	*ki* is long	somebody is longsuffering
ki-ga mijikai	気が短い	*ki* is short	somebody is impatient, short-tempered
ki-ga tsuyoi	気が強い	*ki* is strong	somebody is strong-willed
ki-ga yowai	気が弱い	*ki* is weak	somebody is weak-willed

and others (Yamaguchi 1997, 59).

Yamaguchi summarizes:

> If one analyzes this word [*ki* (気)] one can detect a very important characteristic. First of all this is the non-individualistic, interpersonal character. That means: the usage of the word *ki* (気) shows that the locality of *ki* (気) is not inside the individual, or inside a certain subject, but that it generates between humans. (Yamaguchi 1997, 58)

Ki (気) can simply not be totally detached from the individual, as the closeness to *kokoro* (心), "heart" in the following synonym phrases shows. Yamaguchi distinguishes them like this:

- *kigi* (気々) and *kokorogokoro* (心心) both mean "each person has his or her own emotions"
- *shinpai* (心配), "to set the heart on something," and *kikubari* (気配り), "set the *ki* (気) on something," both mean "worries"
- if a person knows somebody else through and through, that person is a *kigokoro-no shireta yuujin* (気心の知れた友人), a "friend whose *ki* (気) and *kokoro* (心), 'heart,' one knows"

Yamaguchi distinguishes *ki* (気) and *kokoro* (心) thus:

> *Ki* (気) [is] mobile, light, refined, vague, agile outwardly, functional, and cosmic. *Kokoro* (心), on the contrary, [is] firm, weighty, relatively distinct, internalized, substantial, and

individual. Further, *ki* (気) rather means "consciousness," whereas *kokoro* (心) rather means "soul." (Yamaguchi 1997, 61)

2.4.8 Comparison with the Soul-Concept of the Old Testament

The awareness of different worldviews of other cultures must lead to a conceptual encounter with the worldview of that respective culture, with the worldview of the Bible, and, last but not least, with the worldview of one's own culture. The goal of these comparative studies is the ability to clearly distinguish the respective worldviews, and subsequently, the ability to unambiguously use the respective terminology in the communication of the gospel. In the context of animism, the soul-concept and the god-concept have to be dealt with with great caution. Translating mere words lexically or directly, sometimes even without even consulting the biblical texts in their languages, often leads to a misunderstanding of the Christian faith.

In this section, I mainly refer to Hans Walter Wolff's *Anthropologie des Alten Testaments* (1973), which I am going to compare with the key words of the Japanese soul-concept. Like Beck (1862) I am going to take into consideration the following Hebrew terms relevant for the soul-concept: *nefesh* (נֶפֶשׁ), *ruach* (רוּחַ), and *lebab* or *leb* (לֵבָב/לֵב). I do not consider technical terms of Western languages because this would not be helpful. Neither do I consider Greek technical terms in this study because the soul-concepts of profane Greek are also misleading. Dihle (630) compared the Greek ψυχή with the Hebrew רוּחַ and judged that "soul" as an "immaterial yet invisible human kernel, conceivably separated from man" was "innately alien to the Old Testament." The technical terms of biblical Greek are conceptually specified by the Greek of the Septuagint and the respective Hebrew terminology.

The following study is concerned with various aspects of the Hebrew concept of man, so it is important to never forget the inseparable entity of man.

> The biblical writings have no formal descriptions of human nature. Theologians may synthesize an analysis of humanness from the narratives and writings, but this, though accurate in quotation, may yet be unfaithful to the Scriptures, because the image of humans in the Bible is a dynamic image-in-action, selfhood-in-relation, and person-in-community that resists a systematic construction. The central element of the Hebrew of humans is a fundamental sense of unity in the person. No dualism exists between nature and spirit, mind and body, or other part processes. The human is

a unitary organism. It is the total person who acts, thinks, feels, relates, chooses, sins, and repents. (Augsburger 1995, 106)

2.4.8.1 "Soul," (נֶפֶשׁ) in the Old Testament

In his introduction to the chapter on נֶפֶשׁ, Wolff states that "only in very few texts 'soul' is a fitting translation" of נֶפֶשׁ (Wolff 1984: 25).

In his groundbreaking study, Wolff turns against the common understanding of נֶפֶשׁ which supposes "breath" to be the basic meaning (as Gesenius) and then equates נֶפֶשׁ with Tylor's soul-concept of the classical animism (as Gilmore 1919, ch. 3). In his *Umriß einer biblischen Seelenlehre*, Beck defines in entirely animistic terminology: "The soul is a being which always and peculiarly unifies general, special, and individual classifications" (Beck 1862, 3). Gesenius defines נֶפֶשׁ as a "term for that which makes a physical being (animal . . . and human alike) an animate being, the soul (ψυχή, *anima*), of which the blood is considered to be the carrier" (514). In the blood the "invisible breath of life" is "wedded" with the "subtlest physical substance or matter (with the fluid plasma)" (Beck 1862, 5). Along the same line, Friedrich August Carus formulates in his *Psychologie der Hebräer* (1809) that נֶפֶשׁ "corresponded" with ψυχή, *anima* (Carus 1809, 38; similar Beck 1862, 5). Jacob objects: "One should not . . . conclude that the נֶפֶשׁ is considered an immaterial principle which can have an independent existent, separated from its material base" (615).

The criticism of an unreflected equation with Western terminology also touches upon the Christian usage of *tamashii* (魂) (soul) in Japan. *Tama* (魂) "is usually translated with 'soul,' but at least for the Old-Japanese era this translation is misleading" (Naumann 1996, 40).

Wolff divides the word-field of נֶפֶשׁ as follows:[196]

- throat, gullet, pharynx, mouth, muzzle (*Kehle, Schlund, Rachen, Maul*)
- neck (*Hals, Nacken*)
- desire, yearn, striving, longing, craving (*Begehren, Verlangen, Trachten, Sehnen*)

---

196. It is interesting how Carus divides the same word-field: (1) the breathing wind (*der hauchende Wind*), (2) the breath of an animal or human body alive by means of blood (*der Atem eines durch das Blut lebenden tierischen, menschlichen Körpers*), (3) the visible body of a living human or animal (*der sichtbare Körper eines lebenden Menschen oder Tieres*), (4) person, individual, (5) personal pronoun, (6) animalistic instinct (*tierischer Instinkt*), hunger, (7) voracity and craving (*Gier und Sehnsucht*), (8) disposition, heart, emotion, affection, anger, impatience (*Gemüt, Herz, Gefühl, Affekt, Zorn, Ungeduld*), (9) reason (*Verstand*) (Carus 1809, 38–42).

- also organ and act of other "psychological sensations and emotional states (*seelischer Empfindungen und Gemütszustände*)"
- life (*Leben*)
- person, individual, being (*Person, Individuum, Wesen*)
- personal pronoun

The meaning of *tamashii* (魂) as "soul of the dead" is not present in the biblical usage of נֶפֶשׁ. However, after the "biblical age" this meaning is documented. From the later usage of נֶפֶשׁ as "tomb" Jacob concludes "that the individual is in some way present even after death,[197] but he also states that the נֶפֶשׁ "does not exist outside the individual which possesses it, or better, which *is* it" (617–618). Wolff also defies the "supernatural nature of the soul."[198]

2.4.8.2 "Spirit," רוּחַ in the Old Testament

What Wolff observes by means of a lexical study in the introduction to this chapter is, even though not new (Beck 1862, 28), very interesting in connection with the Japanese soul-concept: "To a significant extent רוּחַ describes a natural force, the wind" (Wolff 1984, 56). "It needs to be recorded that רוּחַ means twice as much the wind and God's life-force than the breath, disposition, or will of man" (67). This shows the closeness of רוּחַ not only to the Japanese *rei* (霊) (spirit), but also to the Japanese *ki* (気) (energy)! However, in his Japanese translation of Wolff's *Anthropologie des Alten Testaments,* Oogushi (大串元亮) very cautiously chose the literal translation of Wolff's *Naturkraft, shizenryoku* (自然力) over *ki* (気) and *rei* (霊) (1983, 80).

Wolff divides the word-field of רוּחַ as follows:[199]

- wind
- breath, which is the "wind" of man
- creative life-force (*schöpferische Lebenskraft*)

---

197. Harder (1115) points out to this usage in late Judaism, especially among the Essene and in the Maccabees books.

198. "The human soul is originally and essentially neither a transcendental spirit-being (*überirdisches Geistwesen*) nor a immanent sensual being (*irdisches Sinnenwesen*), but created by the supernatural breathing in of the Divine breath of life (*überirdisches Einwehen des göttlichen Lebensgeistes*) into the physical matter, a double life, transcendent, spiritual life force in sensual life form and efficacy (*ein Doppelleben, überirdisch geistige Lebenskraft in sinnlicher Lebensform und Wirksamkeit*) is unified (Beck 1862, 8).

199. Carus divides similarly: (1) wind, (2) breath, (3) the inner life of man, (4) disposition, sentiment, attitude (*Gesinnung*), (5) the pondering and inquiring spirit (*der sinnende, nachforschende Geist*) (Carus 1809, 37–38).

- רוּחַ as invisible, independent being, "not necessarily thought to be Jahwe's רוּחַ, yet being totally under his command and to his disposal" (Wolff 1984, 62)
- movement of the disposition (*Bewegung des Gemüts*)
- will

2.4.8.3 "Heart," לֵבָב/לֵב in the Old Testament

Almost all references for לֵבָב/לֵב relate to man. לֵבָב/לֵב can therefore be considered the central technical term for the Old Testament anthropology (Wolff 1984, 68). Carus called לֵבָב/לֵב the term to "describe the soul, man as is, that is his greatest power," and concluded that this term was "much more a psychological emblem" than רוּחַ and נֶפֶשׁ (Carus 1809, 43). Jacob as well understood לֵבָב/לֵב as a central term of Old Testament anthropology (Jacob 1990, 623).

Wolff divides the word-field of לֵבָב/לֵב as follows:[200]

- the organ heart (*cor*): Wolff (1984, 70–71) considers this the basic meaning and justifies this judgment with observations on the locality of לֵבָב/לֵב in specifications of the symptoms of heart diseases. Because the heart is "inside" the body, לֵבָב/לֵב can also mean "inside" and "hidden" (72–73). As shown above the Japanese *kokoro* (心), "heart," has a similar figurative meaning.
- emotion (*Gefühl*): Wolff (1984, 74) considers "emotion and disposition," the "irrational stratums" of the human, as the predominant "acts of the heart." This shows a certain similarity of the Buddhist usage of *kokoro* (心), "heart," in *kokoro-no uma* (心の馬), the "heart-horse." However, the general meaning of *kokoro* (心), "heart" as well-considered and reflected will differs from that. Oogushi, however, discerns a connection to the Japanese *ki* (気), "energy," as he translates Wolff's "disposition and mood of the heart (*Gemütsverfassung und Stimmung des Herzens*)" (1984, 74) with *kibun* (気分), "sentiment," "mood," and *funiki* (雰囲気), "atmosphere" (1983, 103), both terms using *ki* (気), "energy."

---

200. Carus distinguishes between the physical and the "non-physical" heart which he then classifies as follows: (1) emotion (*Gefühl*), (2) affection, lively emotion (*Affekt, lebhaftes Gefühl*), (3) craving, lust (*Begierde*), (4) attitude, disposition, conviction (*Gesinnung*), (5) idea, I, Self (*Idee, Ich, Selbst*), (6) imagination (*Einbildungskraft, Phantasie*), (7) memory (*Gedächtnis*), (8) conscience (*Gewissen*), (9) attention (*Aufmerksamkeit*), (10) power of judgment (*Urteilskraft*), (11) reason (*Verstand*), (12) locality of consciousness (*Sitz des Bewußtseins*) (Carus 1809, 43ff).

- craving, desire (*Verlangen*), craving, lust (*Begehren*): Contrary to נֶפֶשׁ, לְבָב/לֵב has the undercurrent of "hidden craving" (Wolff 1984, 76). Wolff's judgment is similar to Yamaguchi's distinction of *ki* (気), "energy," and *kokoro* (心), "heart." In fact, Oogushi translates Wolff's "yearning heart (*sehnsüchtiges Herz*)" (1984, 76) with "overly tense *ki* (気) (1983, 105). Sometimes *kokoro* (心), "heart," is understood as akin to *nasake* (情け), "sympathy, pity," and thus related to the *jou* (情) in *ninjou* (人情), "human sentiment." It then carries the undertone of "desire" and "attachment." However, in religious language *kokoro* (心), "heart" is mostly related to purity (Heine 1994, 374–375).
- cognitive faculty (*Erkenntnisvermögen*), reason (*Vernunft*), understanding (*Verstehen*), insight, discernment (*Einsicht*), consciousness (*Bewußtsein*), memory (*Gedächtnis*), knowledge (*Wissen*), pondering (*Nachdenken*), judgment (*Urteilen*), orientation (*Orientierung*), intellect (*Verstand*) (Wolff 1984, 84): "In most cases by far, the heart is said to be the organ of intellectual and rational functions, which is exactly that which we attribute to the head, or, more precisely, to the brain" (1984, 77). For לְבָב/לֵב in this sense Wolff suggests the translation of "mind" (*Geist*) (1984, 78). Sadly Oogushi, without any further reflection and therefore falsely, translates with *rei* (霊), "spirit" (Wolff 1983, 107). What Wolff means with *Geist* has absolutely nothing in common with the Japanese *rei* (霊), "spirit." He sharply criticizes an unreflected "literal translation": "The wrong impression is to be fought off, according to which the biblical man is determined more by emotion than by reason. This anthropological misconception is easily based in an undifferentiated translation of לְבָב/לֵב" (Wolff 1984, 78). This usage of לְבָב/לֵב is completely congruent with *kokoro* (心) as "mind," even though *kokoro* (心), "heart," is more often used in connection with emotions and emotion-controlled thoughts. The Japanese *shinji* (心耳), the "heart-ears" of the enlightened man at least formally resembles the connection between לְבָב/לֵב and "ears" in Hebrew thinking. Wolff brings up the example of Solomon whose "high wisdom" was his request for a "hearing heart" (1984, 79). Also the phrase עָלָה עַל־לֵב, "ascending into the heart," which Wolff interprets as "to become aware of" (1984, 81), is congruent with the Japanese *kokoro-ni ukabu* (心に浮かぶ), "to surface in the heart." Oogushi's

translation with "switch on *ki* (気)" totally overlooks this connection (Wolff 1983, 111).
- intention (*Absicht*), location of will, planning, conscience (*Ort des Willens, Planens, Gewissens*), location where decisions are made: "The transition in the usage of לֵבָב/לֵב from the faculty of reason to the act of will is flowing." Wolff ascribes this to the absent distinction between "theory and praxis." "Thus the heart is the organ of understanding and will at the same time" (Wolff 1984, 84). In a similar way the Japanese *kokorozashi* (志し or 心指し) describes the planning heart. In this context it is interesting how Wolff connects the heart and the conscience. "Because in the heart the criteria for planning and acting are to be considered, לֵבָב/לֵב takes on the meaning of conscience" (1984, 85). He categorically states that the "biblical word" for conscience is לֵבָב/לֵב and interprets the references that talk about the "conscience-stricken" heart not as emotional but as rational anxiety. He explains 1 Samuel 24:6 as follows: "not the beating heart in a physical sense, nor an emotion is meant here, but the reaction to an ethical judgment of the conscience" (85). In Japanese there is also a connection between heart and conscience. However, in Japanese it is not the thinking but the feeling *kokoro* (心), "heart." In the Old Testament לֵבָב/לֵב is called conscience not because it can feel right or wrong in itself, but because it is a "hearing organ" (85). On the other side, the "heart of stone" is not the Japanese *tessekishin* (鉄石心), the "will hard as steel and stone," but the "dead heart" because it cannot hear anymore (89).
- the "heart of God": "Most of the references that speak of the heart of God mean the organ of God's clear will, which sets the standard for humans" (Wolff 1984, 90). As Genesis 8:21 shows, the "heart of God" can also mean that he makes decisions (92–93). This usage is congruent with the usage in the Japanese Christian church: *mikokoro* (御心), the "honorable heart" means the "will of God."

2.4.9 Positive Encounter with the Japanese Soul-Concept

The outline of the Japanese soul-concept and its comparison with Wolff's *Anthropologie des Alten Testaments* (1973) showed that it is important to be well versed in both thought systems, the biblical one as well as the one of the respective host culture. Direct translations, even paired with lexical rigidity, are as useless and dangerous as a secluding intercultural speechlessness.

2.4.9.1 Japanese Bible translations and Wolff

I limit the following to biblical key references of Wolff's *Anthropologie des Alten Testaments* (1973) and compare their German translation, Wolff's explanations and Oogushi's Japanese translation with different Japanese Bible translations which represent various denominational backgrounds, stylistic styles, and translation principles.[201]

As for the translation of נֶפֶשׁ translators are pleasantly flexible. Only in rare cases they choose the direct translation with *tamashii* (魂). Usually their translation coincides with Wolff's interpretation. However, there are two exceptions: (1) Where Wolff decides for the anatomical, physical meaning (e.g. נֶפֶשׁ as throat, neck, or sense of taste), Japanese translators also consider the emotional aspect (Isa 5:14). (2) Oogushi pointedly translates with *tamashii* (魂), "soul," even where Wolff rejects the meaning "soul" for נֶפֶשׁ. The translators follow Wolff's caution and use *tamashii* (魂), "soul" rather scarcely. The translators of the *Shinkaiyaku Seisho* (新改訳聖書) very cautiously write *tamashii* with the writing system for syllables (たましい). This is read *tamashii* as well, but the omission of the Chinese character 魂 expresses a stark skepticism and cautions against the connection between the biblical and the Japanese soul-concept (Job 30:25; Prov 3:22).

The translation of רוּחַ does not reflect the flexibility seen in the translation of נֶפֶשׁ. Where Wolff suggests the translation "faculty of vigorous actions of will" (1984, 65–66) for רוּחַ Japanese translators pleasantly translate with *kokoro* (心), "heart" (Ezra 1:5) . At the same time translators drop their caution they showed when rather not translating נֶפֶשׁ with *tamashii* (魂), "soul"; they unbiasedly use *rei* (霊), "spirit," for רוּחַ. When *rei* (霊), "spirit," means a special talent of people (Gen 41:38; Isaiah:11:2) this choice is indicated, but overall the translation with *rei* (霊), "spirit," is rather undifferentiated. As shown above, רוּחַ is to a certain extent related to the Japanese *mana*-concept *ki* (気). Concerning this relation, Oogushi and other translators are reticent and overcautious. They rather translate with *rei* (霊), "spirit." Only when *ki* (気), "energy," refers to humans they translate רוּחַ with *ki* (気), "energy" (Prov 14:29; Eccl 7:8). Here one particular translation is interesting: Oogushi translated "windpipe" in Jeremiah 4:10 not with the generally used *kikan* (気管) "*ki* (気)-pipe," but he

---

201. See Appendix 2.

used the traditional *nodobue* (喉笛), literally "throat-recorder" (Wolff 1983, 41) thus avoiding the usage of *ki* (気) in *kikan* (気管).

לֵב/לְבָב and *kokoro* (心), "heart" have two shared basic meanings: "inside" and "locality of emotions." The Japanese translators are aware of that. Avoiding *tamashii* (魂), "soul" as a translation for נֶפֶשׁ as much as possible, they use *kokoro* (心), "heart," rather freely. As *kokoro* (心) has a very broad meaning it is in many cases correct to directly translate לֵב/לְבָב and *kokoro* (心) as "heart" (Prov 14:30; Ps 21:3; Job 31:7). On the other hand, Oogushi almost mechanically translates with *shinzou* (心臓) which means the organ heart (*cor*), probably because *kokoro* (心), "heart," seems to have too broad a meaning in order to be precise.

Bible translation is theology. It is preceded by theological work and it is always expositional and contextual. Hill drew the following conclusion from her extended studies on indigenous terms in the Adjukru (Ivory Coast) translation of the Bible:

> Translation has significant theological implications. The terms that are used affect the way people perceive of both their traditional world as well as the relationship of Christianity to it, and this has a significant effect on local theology and the growth of the church. Scripture translation can affect worldview change. (Hill 2007, 333)

Missionaries are foreigners engaged in contextualization and therefore have to honor the theological work of native Japanese Bible translators. That means that they heed warnings implemented in their choice of terms. This is especially true in two cases:

- Japanese translators are very cautious when using *ki* (気), "energy."[202] Even though there is a certain consistency between the biblical and Japanese worldviews and conceptions of man, the inconsistency cannot be overlooked. In conversation they can be addressed and errors eradicated. In written text, however, ambiguous choices of terms can be dangerous and should be avoided.
- Japanese translators are also cautious when using *tamashii* (魂), "soul." The reason probably is that *tamashii* (魂), "soul," (meaning

---

202. In the same way "some Africans object to using terms from their traditional religions on the grounds that they are dirty and will pollute the Bible." Hill dismisses this caution: "This view betrays a misconception of the incarnational nature of Christianity. In the same way that Jesus purified the unclean rather than becoming polluted by it, using traditional categories in Scripture purifies and transforms the categories (Hill 2007, 332). I prefer to submit to the judgment of native Christians.

of "soul of the dead") is too predominant, a concept which is rather alien to the biblical worldview. It is advisable not to use terms that have such a close connection to the concept of the "soul of the dead."

2.4.9.2 The *mana*-concept *ki* (氣), רוּחַ: revisiting Bradshaw

As Wolff (1984, 67) showed, רוּחַ has connotations that are close to the Japanese *mana*-concept *ki* (氣). The caution of Japanese Bible translators suggests that the term *ki* (氣), "energy," should not be used when conveying the biblical worldview. On the other hand, there are undeniable parallels. I am inclined to equate רוּחַ as nature force and *ki* (氣) as *mana*. I leave it for discussion whether both terms could mean the same.[203]

This question is of great theological importance. If the parallel is denied, *mana* can only be demonized, as Deppe and Deppe suggested (2002, 151). The resulting dualism, however, which ascribes "scientifically verifiable" things to the realm of God, and "scientifically not verifiable" things to the realm of Satan, is not biblical. Such dualism seems to be the mirrored image of the Enlightenment, which ascribed "scientifically not verifiable" things to the "spiritual world" and "scientifically verifiable" things to the material, the "real" world. However, Genesis 1:1 explicitly includes "heavens and the earth." Noble (1996, 193) concludes that the invisible world is also included. Especially in the New Testament, "heavens and earth" is used parallel to "visible and invisible," and both realms are ascribed to Christ's rule (Col 1:16–17). The New Testament conceives even the ἐξουσίαι, which according to Deppe and Deppe (151) also control invisible energies, "definitely not dualistically." "As the invisible principalities are subdued to Christ they are under and within his rule, as long as they submit to him without attempting to become independent from their place of service to him" (Cullman 1991, 198). Cullmann here uses the illustration of the "long leash." All powers and principalities are under the rule of Christ. However, sometimes they seem to be independent. Within their assigned positions they have a certain freedom (1991, 199).

---

203. This though is by no means new. "In the original organisation of this earthy life in this world (Gen 1:3) the spirit becomes the general nature force, as it has the breath of God that weaves over (German: *überweben*) the earthly basic element, the water (2 Pet 3:5), from which evolve light (fire) and air (wind) as central forces of life; in this embodiment as breath the spirit on and on causes to be the cumulative and individual life in the realm of the world of [physical] bodies, from the lowest to the highest level . . . As the spirit produces all moving and breathing things in this entire world-system, the air, the all-embracing (*allgemeine*) element of life, and the breezes, the first and last stirring of life, it also appears in the nature-life as the in-itself-living and the life-giving, as *life and principle of life* (John 6:63). *It is the general, independent life force and fount of life* (Jas 2:26; Rev 11:1; Ezek 1:20)" (Beck 1862, 29).

The dualistic demonization of *mana* is to be rejected. The other extreme, held by those who demand that Christians should have the freedom to use *ki* (気), is to postulate for *mana* a neutral independency from "good and evil." This extreme is also to be questioned. *Ki* (気) may be considered independent, but רוּחַ certainly is not. "We must hold that רוּחַ especially as wind ... stands for a powerful phenomenon under God's control and in his service" (Wolff 1984, 58). The life-force רוּחַ of a human always belongs to God. He can demand it back any time. Even when רוּחַ is considered a being independent from God, it still is "totally under his control and in his service" (1994, 62).

On one side is *mana*, *ki* (気), that has nothing to do with God, on the other side רוּחַ, is totally under God's control and in his service. One could be inclined to understand them as completely different things if there were not obvious parallels. The question is how the "gap can be bridged." Revisiting Bradshaw's *Bridging the Gap* (1996) seems to be helpful. In his discussion of holistic and dualistic worldviews, Bradshaw speaks in favor of holism, while at the same time speaking against the monistic tendency of holism and adding to a holistic understanding the belief in a Creator God, who is not part of the one world of holism. This way of "bridging the gap" can be used here as well:

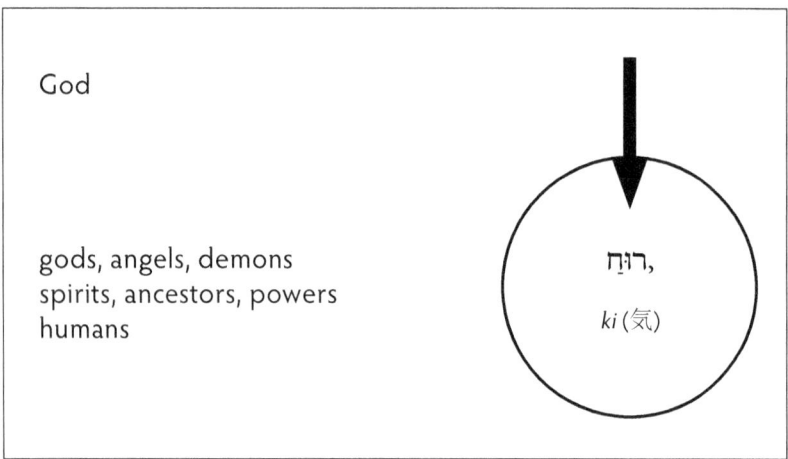

Figure 2.4 Outline of a "Biblical" Worldview

On one side רוּחַ and *ki* (気) as *mana* can be equated. Both describe phenomena which connect the visible and invisible parts of the world. But what the Old Testament says about רוּחַ cannot be disregarded either. The force that keeps alive all living beings is neither God – for he is not part of creation

– nor is it totally independent from God. What Asian cultures have to say about *ki* (気) as immanent power can be appreciated. Yet, this says nothing about God. It must be clear that *ki* (気) is neither "divine" nor independent from God. Also *mana* must never be equated with the Holy Spirit (Sears, n.d., 1). Sears is probably influenced by the Greek πνεῦμα-concept or even by ideas of the New Age Movement where *mana* is sometimes called "spirit of God" (Pontifical Council for Culture 2005, 12). The Japanese *mana*-concept is absolutely immanent and does not have personality features. Contrary to that, the Holy Spirit is a person of the transcendent God. And he is not a power but instead a powerful person of the Divine Trinity.

2.4.10 Negative Encounter with the Japanese Soul-Concept

2.4.10.1 Against human immortality

From a scientific viewpoint, the coexistence of various anthropological concepts is desirable and necessary. Problems arise when different thought systems define the boundaries of anthropology in different ways. As the study on the Japanese soul-concept showed, Japanese anthropology also includes the man in his afterlife. In Christian theology, however, life beyond the border of death does not belong to the field of anthropology, but the field of Christology and soteriology. Therefore, Christian theology does not talk about "human immortality," but about "eternal life" as a gift of God through Jesus Christ. Also Christian theology not only talks about "life after death" but differentiates between eternal life and eternal death.

It is impossible to deal with the subject of life after death in this book. I only want to show one example: the custom of *mabiki* (間引き), practiced in feudal times (before 1868).[204] *Mabiki* (間引き) is a technical term from the field of agriculture. It means the thinning of seedlings. Allegedly, in hard times farmers would kill children up to the age of seven in order to secure the survival of the other family members.[205] According to their understanding, the soul of a child was not completely connected with this world.[206] They concluded that if a child was killed before the age of seven, his or her soul would immediately be reborn

---

204. In his article *Infanticide in Early Modern Japan? Demography, Culture, and Population Growth* (1996), Cornell (46) gives an exhaustive report on the infanticide between 1600 and 1870. He concludes that the term *infant homicide* would be more appropriate.

205. Latest research shows that the purpose of *mabiki* (間引き) absolutely was safeguarding prosperity (Formanek 2008, 63-64).

206. A testimony of this thinking is the saying *nanatsu mae-wa kami-no ko* (七つ前は神の子), "before seven they are children of the gods."

in a better place (Itou 1996, 35–36). This thought which relativized death and therefore led to an impenitent killing of children has relevance for the present. Ejima (江島正子) (98–102) shows the connection between an almost impenitent abortion praxis and the *mabiki* (間引き) in feudal times, increasing more and more *ijime* (苛め), "bullying," and then suicide[207] as last resort.

2.4.10.2 Eternal life through the personal union with Jesus Christ versus immortality of the soul

I want to outline and leave for further discussion what I consider the biblical alternative to Japan's animistic concept of the *reikon fumetsu* (霊魂不滅), the concept of the incorruptibility of the soul.

In Psalm 145:12 and other references, humans are called אָדָם. בֶּן־אָדָם is derived from אֲדָמָה and therefore means "earthling." Psalm 146:4 explains: When the spirit departs אָדָם returns to אֲדָמָה, the "earthling" to "earth." For the time of his earthly life the "spirit" – it has always been and will always be the "spirit of God" – lives in the one taken from אֲדָמָה and makes him a "living soul" (Gen 2:7). In the great prayer of Moses it says, "You turn men back to dust, saying, 'Return to dust, O sons of אָדָם'" (Ps 90:3)!

The teaching of the immortality of the soul, present in all cultures, is an outcry of protest. Humans want to be eternal because God has "placed eternity into his heart" (Eccl 3:11). But they are not eternal. Humans want to be "like God" because they have been created as children of God. But they are not divine. Adam is not only the "earthling" but also the "son of God" (Luke 3:33). But he lost the "right to be called a child of God" (John 1:12). Psalm 90:7–9 says that humans perish because God holds them responsible for his iniquities.

The Bible by no means teaches that humans have an immortal part. This is true for both Testaments. There is no fundamental change in New Testament anthropology. 2 Corinthians 4:7 resounds with Genesis 2:7: "We have this treasure in jars of clay [in 'earthen vessels'] to show that this all-surpassing power is from God and not from us." The power – this is the New Testament equivalent of what was called "spirit" in the Old Testament – belongs to God.

But what is new in the New Testament is the "second Adam." God himself became "Adam," an "earthling." Of him it was said that the "Spirit of the Lord"

---

207. "Few religious prohibitions exist in Japan against suicide, and it has long been seen as a way to escape failure or to save loved ones from embarrassment. Moreover, in Japan, where honor is an ultimate virtue, many people have long regarded suicide as an 'honorable' death, rather than an act of shame and cowardice. Suicide remains almost a taboo subject in Japan. The public awareness about the problem remains low, and individuals experiencing suicidal ideation are unlikely to seek help from psychology professionals" (Shiraev and Levy 2015, 231).

"rested" upon him (Isa 11:2). The Spirit persistently remained with him. God told John the Baptist that Jesus would be the one upon whom the Spirit would "remain" (John 1:33). In the New Testament there is no change in anthropology. But God creates a new reality. It is not that humans get an immortal soul, but that the immortal God becomes an "earthling" with the Spirit of God persistently abiding in him. And this "second Adam," Jesus Christ, invites people to be eternally associated with him through faith and baptism. "He who believes in me will live, even though he dies" (John 11:25b). Christian faith is not faith in the immortality of humans but faith in the eternal and immortal God who is faithful to humans, even beyond his death. Christian faith is not faith in an endless rebirth of an immortal "soul," but faith in something entirely new, to be received in this mortal life, to be fulfilled in God's new creation.

2.5 Sociology in the Context of Japanese Animism

> **Summary:** Sociology is of greatest importance; particularly for missiology and particularly for soteriology. The Japanese society is a group-society which includes the *living dead*. Ancestor veneration has a meaningful impact on sociology, psychology and worldview.
>
> The discussion with Christian approaches shows that collectivism and individualism must not exclude each other as opposites, that a Christian answer to ancestor veneration is crucial, and that the Japanese *amae* (甘え)-mentality needs to be overcome.

A traditional culture defines the identity of an individual with the following ontological formula: *Cognatus ergo sum*: I belong therefore I am. Belonging means partaking in and contributing to the life and the welfare of the family. This is contrary to Descartes's dictum: *Cogito ergo sum*: I think therefore I am. The primary source of identity formation of an individual is not his ability to think, but rather his ability to belong, to partake, and to share. Sharing one's life with others leads to wholeness and guarantees health. (Ma Mpolo 1986, 16)[208]

---

208. Augsburger expands: Since Descartes, Westerners say, "I think therefore I am." The Africans say, "I partake therefore I am." The Orientals say, "I belong therefore I am." The Palestine villager says, "I live in the village therefore I am" (Augsburger 1995, 82).

The Japanese people's primary value is, according to Hall, their need to "integrate themselves in their home and its social structure" (1968, 37). In Shuusaku Endou's late work, *The Samurai* (1997), the Catholic missionary Valente presents a report to the conference of bishops. The historical novel takes place in the seventeenth century, but whatever father Valente says is as relevant today as it was in the past. I want to quote a longer passage in order to show just how important sociology is for missions:

> Valente: "The Japanese basically lack a sensitivity to anything that is absolute, to anything that transcends the human level, to the existence of anything beyond the realm of Nature – what we would call the supernatural. I finally realized that after thirty years there as a missionary... They abhor the idea of making a clear distinction between man and God. To them, even if there should be something greater than man, it is something which man himself can one day become. Their Buddha, for instance, is a being which man can become once he abandons his illusions. Even Nature, which for us is something totally detached from man, to them is an entity which envelopes mankind.... We failed in our attempt to rectify these attitudes of theirs... Their sensibilities are firmly grounded within the sphere of Nature and never take flight to a higher realm. Within the realm of Nature their sensibilities are remarkably delicate and subtle, but those sensibilities are unable to grasp anything on a higher plane. That is why the Japanese cannot conceive of our God, who dwells on a separate realm from man."

> When asked what had happened to some 400,000 Japanese Christians, Valente answered that half of them had "disappeared like a mist" when the King banned Christianity.

> "Disappeared?"

> Valente: "Yes. A seemingly endless stream of Japanese we considered among the best of believers renounced their faith the moment the persecution began. When a feudal lord abjured Christianity, his entire family and his knights followed suit, and when a village chief apostatized, nearly all the villagers also left the church. And to our astonishment, from their faces one could not tell that anything at all had happened."

> One of the bishops: "They felt no pangs of remorse for having abandoned God?"

Valente: "When I used to look at the map . . . the shape of Japan sometimes reminded me of a lizard. Much later it occurred to me that the true Nature of the Japanese was much the same. We missionaries were like children who delight in cutting off the lizard's tail. The lizard went on living even without its tail, and finally its tail grew back as it had been originally. Despite sixty years of proselytizing by our Society, the Japanese did not change at all. They returned to the way they originally were."

"The way they originally were . . .? Explain what you mean, Father Valente."

Valente: "The Japanese never live their lives as individuals. We European missionaries were not aware of that fact. Suppose we have a single Japanese here. We try to convert him. But there was never a single individual we could call 'him' in Japan. He has a village behind him. A family. And more. There are also his dead parents and ancestors. That village, that family, those parents and ancestors are bound to him tightly, as though they were living beings. That is why he is not an isolated human being. He is an aggregate who must shoulder the burden of village, family, parents, ancestors. When I say that he went back to the way he originally was, I mean that he returned to that world to which he is so firmly bound . . . When the first missionary to Japan, Francisco Xavier, began his labors in the southern provinces, this was the most formidable obstacle he encountered. The Japanese said, 'I believe the Christian teachings are good. But I would be betraying my ancestors if I went to a Paradise where they cannot dwell. Our ties to our parents and ancestors are very firm.' Let me point out that this is not a simple matter of ancestor worship. It is a compelling faith. Sixty years were not sufficient for us to obliterate this faith." (Endou 1997, 163–164)

2.5.1 Japan as Group Culture

As an introduction, consider these two Japanese textbooks for social studies: The *Toukyou Shoseki* (東京書籍), the most common high school textbook for social studies in Japan (44.9% in 1990) formulates: "To freely live does not . . . mean to live *jibun-no sukikatte-ni* (自分の好き勝手に), to be able to live according one's own liking and selfishly" (Ölschleger et al. 1994, 183). And the *Nihon Shoseki* (日本書籍), the most common textbook in social studies in the Tokyo metropolitan area teaches:

> Group cohesion, wherein each individual can unfold and develop, generates from the very acknowledgement of the many different characters of the others. However, if one is only concerned with his own interests, this is selfishness and leads to the destruction of the group cohesion. (Ölschleger et al. 1994, 183)

In her unpublished MA thesis, "Human Relations and Leadership in the Japanese Protestant Congregation," Dufty writes:

> In contemporary analyses of Japanese culture, most observers have focused on groupism as the most important key to understanding Japanese social organization. By groupism is meant that groups rather than individuals are the basic building blocks of society and the individual's identity is largely conceived of in terms of their membership in various groups. This is extremely important for this study as the nature of Japanese groups determines the role that leaders are expected to play. (Dufty 1995, ch. 1)[209]

To begin with a few mechanisms of Japanese groupism:

- linguistic uniformity: A main reason for the strong emphasis on groupism is the long era of *sakoku* (鎖国), the "secluded country" (1633–1842), during which Japan was almost completely secluded. In that era the high linguistic uniformity, so typical for Japan, came into being. It gives "all Japanese a strong feeling of belonging." (Morsbach 1983, 52)[210]
- honor of the group: "The group . . . is more important than the individual and demands loyalty and conformity because each member's behavior reflects upon the group." (Freed 2000, 15)[211]
- hierarchical structures of the groups[212]
- *ishin denshin* (以心伝心),[213] the transmitting of ideas from mind to mind

---

209. I have only an electronic copy of her unpublished work. There are no page numbers.
210. Language plays an important role in the development of a sense of unity (Illius 2002, 97).
211. Freed studies groups of Japanese expatriots in America.
212. This and the following points are taken from a study by Rupert A. Cox conducted in *Zen*(禅)-Art Schools.
213. Literally: "Similar hearts – communicating hearts."

- *amae* (甘え), intimacy and dependence
- *ma* (間), "pre-sensing through spatial/temporal absences"
- *haragei* (腹芸),[214] the "unspoken way" (Cox 2003, 139)

In the following I am going to outline and discuss the thoughts of three Japanese scientists: the work of sociologist Chie Nakane (中根千枝) as the main representative of the idea that the Japanese society is vertically structured; the work of psychiatrist Takeo Doi (土居健郎), the father of the anthropological *amae*(甘え)-concept; and the work of socio-legal scientist Takeyoshi Kawashima (川島武宜) and his essay *Die familiale Struktur der japanischen Gesellschaft* (1946).[215]

2.5.1.1 Chie Nakane (中根千枝): "vertical society *tateshakai* (タテ社会) as sociological key term

Summary: Nakane develops a vision of the Japanese society as a single "super-organism" similar with state-forming insects. According to Nakane, it is for Japanese not only undesirable but outright impossible to understand oneself as individuals.

Chie Nakane (born in 1926) worked as an anthropologist in India, Tibet, and Japan. She has been president of *Tokyo Jogakkan College* (東京女学館大学) since 2002.[216] In this short outline I want to focus mainly on *Japanese Society* (1970, Japanese original 1967). Its theoretical basis was developed in *Kinship and Economic Organization in Rural Japan* (1970) (Nakane 1970, viii), as well as in the article *Nihonteki Shakai-kouzou-no hakken* (日本的社会構造の発見; Discovery of a specific Japanese structure of society) (1964) (Nakane 1970, x).

---

214. Literally: "abdomen-art."

215. It is impossible to fully describe their ideas in this book. I am going to outline only what seems to be relevant for the subject of this book.

216. Publications: 1959, *Mikai-no Kao – Bunmei-no Kao* (未開の顔・文明の顔, Primitive Face – Civilized Face); 1967, *Tateshakai-no Ningenkankei: Tanritsushakai-no Riron* (タテ社会の人間関係：単一社会の理論, Interpersonal Relationships in Vertical Societies: A Simplified Social Theory); 1967, *Kinship and Economic Organization in Rural Japan*; 1970, *Japanese Society*, translation of *Tateshakai-no Ningenkankei: Tanritsu-shakai-no Riron* (タテ社会の人間関係：単一社会の理論); 1972, *Human Relations in Japan: Summary Translation of "Tateshakai-no ningen kankei"* (Personal Relations in Vertical Societies); 1978, *Tateshakai-no Rikigaku* (タテ社会の力学, Dynamics of Vertical Societies); 1987, *Shakaijinruigaku: Ajia Shoshakai-no Kousatsu* (社会人類学：アジア諸社会の考察, Anthropology of Society: Examination of Asian Societies).

Nakane's (1970, 1) basic principle is the differentiation between "frame" and "attribute."[217] She defines "frame" as a "locality, an institution or a particular relationship which binds a set of individuals into one group" (1970, 1). The classic form of such a "group" is *ie* (家), "house" or "family," which she considers a synonym for *shuudan* (集団), "group" (1978, 19). Contrary to other sociologists, Nakane understands *ie* (家) not as the classic family,[218] but as a "corporate residential group and, in the case of agriculture[219] or other similar enterprises" as "managing body" (1970, 4). The most important criteria is that "the human relationships within this household group are thought of as more important than all other human relationships" (1970, 5). In Japan the principle of group formation on the basis of "frame" is much more important than the principle of group formation on the basis of "attribute." Even if groups are formed on the basis of shared interests or shared activities, the internal organization of the group is fashioned according to principles of "frame." Only this leads to a strong and stable feeling of belonging (1970, 9). The power and influence of the group thus intrudes "on those human relations which belong to the completely private and personal sphere," even altering "ideas and ways of thinking." However, most Japanese experience this not as an "encroachment on their dignity" but as safety (1970, 10). In *Tateshakai-no Rikigaku* (タテ社会の力学, Dynamics of Vertical Societies) (1978) Nakane reports about comparative studies carried out in India and Japan: In India *kojin-wa saibunka sareru* (個人は細分化される), "the individual can be fragmented," and therefore groups as well (1978, 16–17). But in Japan there is *ittaika-no kyouchou* (一体化の強調), "the emphasis lies on group formation," literally, the "changing into single

---

217. In the Japanese original Nakane distinguishes between *ba* (場), "place" and *joretsu* (序列), "rank." In China there is a similar concept. It is not who one is that is important, but to which group one belongs (Augsburger 1995, 83). In Japan this can have very dramatic implications: the loss of importance in the company can lead people to think that they are without any value as individuals. When, for example, the employee Jiro Matsumoto in Takashi Atoda's (阿刀田高) novel *Tod eines Angestellten* learns that he is considered failure in his company, he sees suicide as the only escape (Atoda 1990a, 15–17).

218. Nakane (1970, 6) even claims that kinship terminology is less important in Japan than in Europe or America. In modern society family is not understood as independent *ie* (家), but as part of the company, the *ie* (家) of the husband and father (8).

219. Agricultural cultures specialized on rice growing require the economic use of water and thus "the cooperation of all men and women fit for work." "All have to work together in a precisely synchronized way." Therefore, rice growing hamlets form "closer communities of fate than settlements of hunters" (Dambmann 1989, 69). Graves (690) reported similar observations made in a village of fishermen on a very small Japanese island. In rural areas morals are closely connected with economy. Individuals can act according to their own liking as long as they do not jeopardize public safety (Ōe Kannzaburô in Melanowicz 1981, 93).

entities, and such a kind of group is then a *fukabun-no tan-i* (不可分の単位), "an inextricable unit" (1978, 17–18). Contrary to the Japanese system, where it is considered insolent even to mention something against the group-leader's opinion, India enjoys freedom of speech (1970, 12–13).

Groups formed on the basis of "frame" unify people with different "attributes" vertically, whereas groups formed according to "attribute" show a horizontal structure (1970, 23–24). Almost all groups in Japan are structured vertically.[220]

"Because of the overwhelming ascendancy of the vertical orientation, even a set of individuals sharing identical qualifications tend to create a *difference* among themselves. As this is reinforced, an amazingly delicate and intricate system of *ranking* takes shape" (1970, 25).[221]

Nakane illustrates this ranking system as follows:

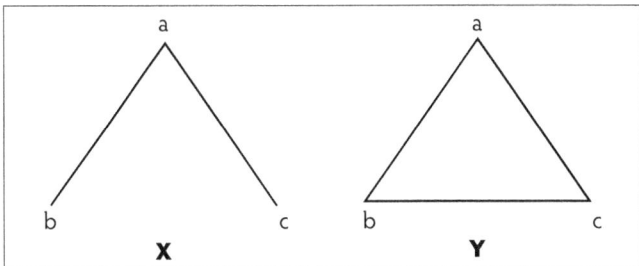

Figure 2.5 Group Structure System (according to Nakane 1970, 41)

---

220. Nakane gives a practical illustration: A university professor has closer relationships with his assistant professors and students than with his faculty colleagues (Nakane 1970, 38). Chaudhuri and Fadil discuss the difference between frame and attribute in the context of workplace ethics. "One's behavior is determined, contingent on and to a large extent organized by what the actor perceives to be the thoughts, feelings, and actions of others in the relationship" (Markus and Kitayama in Chaudhuri and Fadil 2001, 265). Japanese "have to be committed in order to maintain harmony within the group and to maintain consistency to the interdependent construal of self" (Chaudhuri and Fadil 2011, 265). However, there seems to be a shift in this orientation towards prioritizing "attribute." "Instability of organizational life and uncertainties and dissatisfactions associated with the working environment could shift individuals' commitment from organization to his/her occupation or career" (Chaudhuri and Fadil 2011, 264).

221. Using the Japanese system of addressing language, Nakane shows that this ranking system, once established, cannot be changed afterwards (1970, 27). Contrary to the so-called *Itaria-shiki* (イタリア式), the "Italian method" (which is not only valid for Italy but also for Korea and the Philippines) where the ranking of group members can change according to varying tasks of the group, in Japan the ranking once established will never be changed. In a discussion with the Japanese biologist and behaviorist Hida, Nakane and Hida agreed that this kind of sociological structures resembled that of mouse populations and craw populations (1978, 178–182).

X shows a vertical group structure, and Y shows a horizontal group structure. In vertical group structures, there is no relationship between the group members "b" and "c" on the same hierarchical level. It is only through their vertical relationship with "a" that they are members of the group. In horizontal group structures, all members, "a," "b," and "c," have relationships with each other. Vertically structured groups are expanded simply by hierarchically adding new members under "b" or "c."[222] No matter how large the group grows the basic structure will not change. This is the reason why Japanese groups are comparatively stable.[223] In horizontally structured groups, where "a," "b," and "c" have independent relationships with each other, any addition influences the group structure and is a potential threat to the structural balance of the group. This is the reason why horizontally structured groups are comparatively vulnerable (Nakane 1970, 40–41).[224]

The above model suggests that in Japan there are many groups structured like this. But this is not what Nakane thinks. According to her all groups will eventually merge into one mega-group (1978, 182). The whole nation is one single group. This is manifested in the nationwide simultaneous high school exams. All examinees are numbered according to their achievements in one single nationwide numbering system (1978, 178). According to Nakane, Japan

---

222. In Japan relationships of that kind are called *oyabun-kobun*-relationships (Nakane 1970, 42–43). *Oyabun* (親分) means "parental part," *kobun* (子分) "filial part." According to Kawashima, all relationships in Japan, even relationships outside the family, are fashioned according to this structure. "In the outside world of 'disorder'" Japanese experience themselves "as isolated, left-alone beings," always "somehow dependent on the protection of others." They "necessarily form permanent personal relationships. But people who form relationships like this cannot imagine different relationships, yes, they cannot imagine any other relationships than those inside the family" (Kawashima 1988, 72). "Therefore so-called *oyabun-kobun*-relationships evolve by transferring the relationship between parent and child. In the cold formalities of politeness outside the family, the Japanese feel lonely. This is why they transform their friendships into 'fraternal relationships, which allow an unconstrained, confidential intercourse . . . This is how fictitious parent-child-relationships evolve" (Kawashima 1988, 72–73).

223. Of course vertically structured groups have their dangers as well: (1) As it is the role of "a" to compensate frictions between "a" and "b," vertically structured groups often disintegrate when "a" is absent (Nakane 1970, 45). (2) Due to the vertical structure it is virtually impossible that two vertically structured groups sharing a common goal work together (1970, 54–55; 58–60). Nakane openly addresses the weaknesses of Japanese groups. It is not appropriate to accuse her of blind utopianism, as Hata and Smith do (Dufty 1995, ch. 1). Of course Nakane passionately stands for her view of things, but she also has, at times, a terrifyingly keen awareness of the problems of vertically structured groups.

224. This is one of the reasons why Japanese churches during leadership change are in great danger of disintegration. Nakane formulates: "It is the general pattern that such enterprises lose some of their vitality under a succeeding leader" (1970, 46). On the other side, this explains the great success of the *Cell-Group-Church* in Japan.

is the only number-society on that scale. The top of this society is the Emperor as the absolute "Number One" (1978, 182–183).

Collectivism and individualism in the Japanese context

The Japanese individualism suddenly evolved in the late *Meiji*-Era[225] and fully flourished in the *Taishou*-Era. The rulers of the *Meiji*-Era simultaneously engaged in a powerful propaganda for collectivism. This double orientation dominated the intellectual climate and caused much confusion. Protagonists of individualism were the naturalist literary critics Hougetsu Shimamura (島村抱月) (1871–1918) and Houmei Iwano (岩野泡鳴) (1873–1920), the feminist founder of the *Seitou-sha* (青鞜社), the *Bluestocking Society*, Raichou Hiratsuka (平塚雷鳥), the pragmatic philosopher Oudou Tanaka (田中王堂) (1867–1932), and the liberal political scientist Tanzan Ishibashi (石橋湛山) (1884–1969) (Nolte-Hamilton 1984, 667).[226] Nolte-Hamilton shows that Japanese individualism was by no means a homogenous movement. She roughly distinguishes three groups:

- individual character and individual talents should be cultivated in order to strengthen the state and foster an active involvement in state politics;
- personal autonomy and self-expression were legitimate in a limited "private sphere," which always was in tension with the dominant "public" sphere;
- the development of free and autonomous individuals was the most basic value for the evaluation of state and society (Nolte-Hamilton 1984, 670).

Watanabe deduces collectivism and individualism from their underlying values:

> The collectivism of the Japanese society as well as the oppositional individualism of Western societies can be explained from their respective underlying values. It is widely accepted that Japan is a collective society and Western societies are individualistic. We try to explain this conclusion from the fact that people in the West have purpose-oriented values, while Japanese have means-oriented

---

225. The dates and the Japanese writing of the Japanese eras are listed in the timetable at the beginning of the book.

226. In her paper, *Individualism in Taishou-Japan* (1984), Nolte Hamilton gives a deep insight into the individualistic movements of that era.

values. On one side individualism is one of the conclusions from purpose-oriented values, because the purpose of the individual can be given the highest priority and made the ultimate purpose. Individualism is "the way of thinking which places the highest importance on the individual and understands the nation only as a means to fulfil the purpose of the individual" (*Nihongo Daijiten,* 日本語大辞典; Koudansha, 講談社). It is therefore proper to make the individual the highest priority and the ultimate purpose. If purpose-oriented values are developed on a personal level, this is the inevitable outcome. Clearly individualism has evolved from purpose-oriented values. Collectivism, on the other hand, is the conclusion from means-oriented values, because the highest priority and ultimate purpose can be given to the group as means. (Watanabe 2002, 51)

In Japanese, collectivism is called *shuudanshugi* (集団主義). *Shugi* (主義) is the equivalent of the suffix "ism." *Shuudan* (集団) simply means "group." It is a compound of *shuu* (集), "to collect," and *dan* (団), "a mass of people." The definition given by the *Kokugojiten* (国語辞典) is very interesting: It defines *dan* (団) as *atsumatta hito-no hitokatamari* (集まった人のひとかたまり), as the "agglutination" of gathered people. *Katamari* (かたまり, 塊, 固まり) is used in various combinations:

- *tsuchi-no katamari* (土の塊) is a clod of earth
- *hitokatamari-no kumo* (一塊の雲) is a mass of clouds
- *pan-no katamari* (パンの塊) is a lump of bread

All these examples show a shared feature: they cannot be disintegrated. This illustrates Nakane's (1978, 17) statement that Japanese groups are not "divisible."

Individualism, on the other hand, is called *kojinshugi* (個人主義) in Japanese. *Kojin* (個人) stands for the individual. It is a compound of *ko* (個), "single," "lone," and *jin* (人), "person," "human." In its original meaning *ko* (個) serves as counter for small, indivisible things such as eggs, apples, pieces of soap or pieces of chocolate.

Although in India groups are not only divisible to the level of individuals but individuals themselves can be divided (Nakane 1978, 17), in Japan society as well as the individual are indivisible. Leaning on Lebra-Sugiyama, Morisaki (守﨑誠一) and Gudykunst argue that the individual first is understood as entity that derives its identity from its *bun* (分), that is, from its place allotted by society. All members of society are expected to be *bun* (分)-holders. The more an individual derives its identity from its *bun* (分), the less it is considered an individual part, the more it is counted a part of the whole. As parts of the whole, all *bun* (分)-holders are dependent on each other (Morisaki and Gudykunst 1994, 76). "The Japanese language with it characteristic absence of personal pronouns tends to immerse the individual in the environment" (Corwin 1978, 301). The Japanese phrase *messhi houkou* (滅私奉公) accurately describes this. It means that Self (私) drowns and perishes (滅) in the service (奉) for the general public (公) (Fukada 1965, 177).

This thinking which totally negates the private will was strongly propagated especially during World War II. In the *Shinmin-no Michi* (臣民の道),[227] the ideological manifesto of World War II which Japan was issued by the Ministry of Education, it says:

> One must not act arbitrarily by keeping one's own private life as unrelated to the nation and as something to one's own free disposal. Even a bowl of food or a single suit do not belong to myself alone; without being related to the state is not even possible to play or sleep just for oneself in a break. Everything is related with the state. (Miyata 1984, 54)

> Even what is commonly called private life is nothing other than exercise of one's duty as a subject, nothing else than work offered to the throne, of public significance . . . We therefore must not be oblivious of the fact that even in our private life we belong to the *Tennou* (天皇) and serve this state. (Maruyama 1988, 43)

Nakane called attention to the fact that the Japanese language has yet another term for "individual": *kotai* (個体) (1978, 15–16). In this case *tai* (体) stands for a physical body. The *Kokugojiten* (国語辞典) names two contexts where *kotai* (個体) is used:

- In philosophy *kotai* (個体) means *hitotsu hitotsu-ni wakaretemo jiko-no tokushitsu toka sonzai-o ushinau koto-no nai touitsutai* (一つ一つに分かれても自己の特質とか存在を失うことのない統一体), a "unified whole which does not lose its characteristics nor its characteristic existence when divided into its parts."
- In biology *kotai* (個体) means *guntai* (群体), the faunal and floral colonies which *ikko-no seibutsu toshite seizon suru-noni hitsuyou-na kinou-to kouzou-o sonaeta seibutsutai* (一個の生物として生存す

---

227. *Shinmin-no Michi* (臣民の道) literally means "The Way of the Subjects."

るのに必要な機能と構造を備えた生物体), as "as biomass gives function and structure to a self-existent living being."

Especially in the context of animism, which is often associated with connectedness to nature, the conceptual connection to a biological concept is interesting. In order to explain the Japanese self-conception, Nakane explicitly refers to colonial insects such as ants, termites, or bees. They can be recognized as individual living beings but are not capable of surviving without their group. The existence of the individual is totally determined by the value of the whole group (Nakane 1978, 15–16). The group members[228] are descendants of the very same parents, interchangeable. Judging from the viewpoint of colonial insects as well as from the viewpoint of humans, says Nakane, the separation into individuals is impossible (1978, 16).

As much as I support and share Nakane's critique of the Western contempt for collectivism,[229] often based on an evolutionist worldview, I also see the dangers of a naturalist sociology. If individuals cannot be distinguished anymore, a society is in danger of what Künneth called *Vermassung*.[230]

2.5.1.2 Takeo Doi (土居健郎): *Amae* (甘え) (dependence) as psychological key term

> **Summary:** Animistic worldview is rooted deeply in the experience of infants, possibly even deeply in pre-birth experience. The key relationship for understanding the world is the relationship with one's mother. The Japanese *amae* (甘え) describes this relationship with its genuine ambiguity as it comes into consciousness when endangered.

Takeo Doi (1920–2009) studied medicine and practiced and taught psychiatry, first at the University of Tokyo (東京大学, *Toukyou Daigaku*), then from 1971

---

228. Nakane uses the loan-word *guruupumenbaa* (グループメンバー), "group member."
229. Lately Hölldobler and Wilson (Hölldobler 2010, 102) revived the old term *superorganism*, coined in 1911 by William Morton Wheeler. Wheeler's work was influenced by holism (Hölldobler and Wilson 1990, 358). While sociologists at times tend to understand collectivism as "primitive" and individualism as "progressive," Hölldobler supports the very opposite. Judging from a biological-evolutionist viewpoint, societies of primates are, according to Hölldobler, primitive, while colonial insects form highly complex societies. From a biological viewpoint the individualism of societies of primates harm the whole group, because division of labor and mass communication are not optimized (Hölldobler 2010, 105).
230. *Vermassung* literally means "massification," in the sense that societies become an anonymous and impersonal mass.

to 1980 at the International Christian University (国際基督教大学, *Kokusai Kirisutokyou Daigaku*).

The selection of Doi's publications shows[231] that *amae* (甘え)[232] is the central theme of his work. *Amae* (甘え) is the feeling "first experienced by a nursling towards his mother" (Doi 1982, 27). *Amae* (甘え) also is a key term to describe other private, close relationships. *Amae* (甘え) is the attempt to "convey emotions to others without using words." In private life, this is allowed, but in public life, with more verbal communication, emotions "should not be overly expressed" (Kitayama 2005, 39). When outlining Japanese sociology Doi's *amae* (甘え)-concept cannot be avoided. Doi called it a "key concept . . . for the understanding of the structure of Japanese society as a whole" (1982, 36). As the following quote shows the feeling of *amae* (甘え) is the base for the connectedness not only with the mother and with society, but also with nature. *Amae* (甘え) is the base of an animistic awareness of life.

> Winnicott has said that there is no such thing as a baby; a baby is always a part of someone – the mother. His words remind us of the way the Japanese people feel deep at heart. Specifically, there is no such thing as a man, as he always a part of someone or something, be it his mother, his family, his motherland, or nature and the universe. (Goss and Klass 2005, 29)

The fact that *amae* (甘え) is a Japanese term may lead to the misconception that *amae* (甘え) is a solely Japanese concept. In this sense Stucki judged that Doi understood *amae* (甘え) as a "Japanese particularity" (Stucki 1978, 63).[233] But this is not the case. Doi himself wrote that *amae* (甘え) was a specific Japanese term, but that this term described a psychological phenomenon applicable for all humanity (Doi 1982, 36). However, the Japanese, more than others, are aware of the existence of *amae* (甘え) because they have a term for

---

231. His publications with a bearing on the subject at hand: 1973, *"Amae"-no Kouzou* (「甘え」の構造, Structure of *"Amae"*); 1973, *The Anatomy of Dependence*, translation of *"Amae"-no Kouzou* (「甘え」の構造, Structure of *"Amae"*); 1987, *"Amae"-no Shuuhen* (「甘え」の周辺, The Vicinity of *"Amae"*); 1989, *"Amae" Samazama* (「甘え」さまざま, All Kinds of *"Amae"*); 1997, *Seisho-to "Amae"* (聖書と「甘え」, The Bible and *"Amae"*) ; 2001, *Tsuzuki: "Amae"-no Kouzou* (続「甘え」の構造, Sequel: Structure of *"Amae"*); 2004, *"Amae"-to Nihonjin* (「甘え」と日本人, *"Amae"* and the Japanese); 2005, *Amae-to kyouiku-to Nihon-Bunka: Youji, Shotoukyouiku-no Shourai* (甘えと教育と日本文化: 幼児・初等教育の将来, Amae, Parenting, Japanese Culture: The Future of Early Childhood Parenting and Elementary Education).

232. I limit this short outline to this concept, central to Doi's work.

233. Stucki refers to the English translation of Doi's *"Amae"-no kouzou* (「甘え」の構造, Structure of *"Amae"*), first published in 1973.

it (Doi 1982, 89; 1994, 156–157). The advantage of the Japanese *amae* (甘え)-concept is that it is not only applicable to the relationship between mother and child but also to other relationships.[234] Many other relationships are fashioned as the mother-child relationship, a fact which goes unnoticed in other cultures because their languages use different words (Doi 1994, 158).

In the chapter "Language and Psychology" (Doi 1973, 65–71), Doi shows closeness to Whorf's linguistic relativity principle (linguistic determinism). Its key phrase of the "new relativity principle" is: "not all observers of the same physical reality are led to the same worldview" (Whorf 1965, 12).

> The proposition, "The worlds in which different societies live are distinct worlds," is often taken as a confession to linguistic "determinism." We do not have to follow up on the question whether … Whorf … believed that our categorization of the world is completely dependent from the structure of our mother tongue. It is generally agreed that any linguistic determinism of that rigidity is an unsustainable hypothesis. But as we earlier made confession to the fact that certain languages in their vocabulary reflect culturally significant differences of their respective societies, we have to, to a certain degree, accept linguistic and cultural "relativity." (Lyons 1971, 443)

The word-field amae (甘え)

Amae (甘え) is derived from the adjective *amai* (甘い) (Doi 1986, 121) which has the following meanings:

	positive notion	negative notion
literal meaning	1) sweet, tasting like sugar 2) sweet for sweet fragrance 3) sweet for sweet musical tones	4) mild, with little salt 5) loose, not tightly connected (as loose knots) 6) dull (of a knife) 7) sluggish (of the stock market)

---

234. In his novel *Unter der vollen Blüte im Kirschbaumwald* (Japanese title: *Sakura-no mori-no mankai-no shita*, 桜の森の満開の下, English translation: *Under the Full Bloom of the Sakura Woods* [1997]) Ango Sakaguchi (坂口安吾) gives a good illustration how a woman can make a man do anything by persistent whining and crying (1990, 139–161; 142; 145–146; 155).

figurative sense	8) sweet for sweet words[235] 9) for the infatuation of lovers 10) for the good things in life[236]	11) not strict, but lenient, mild, liberal, indulgent 12) shallow, unsubstantiatedly optimistic

For Doi's *amae* (甘え) mainly the figurative sense with its negative notion is important.[237]

If a person is considered *amai* (甘い) she is "not strict." An *amai* (甘い) mother, for example, is a lenient mother. If a parent is *amai* (甘い) for children, the children are spoiled, they become *amaenbou* (甘えん坊), literally "sweet-babies," or spoiled children. In this context the following phrases are also interesting:

- *amai* (甘い) lifestyle: shallow lifestyle[238]
- to be *amai* (甘い) for women: to have a soft spot for women
- "Life is not that *amai* (甘い)!": "You take life too easy!"
- an *amai* (甘い) attitude towards life: an attitude towards life which is too optimistic
- a *amai* (甘い) viewpoint: a shallow and thus false viewpoint
- to see *amaku* (甘く):[239] underestimate

There are quite a few verbs derived from the adjective *amai* (甘い):

- **Amaeru** (甘える): In its intransitive usage *amaeru* (甘える) as well as *amattareru* (甘ったれる) mean "to behave like a pampered, spoiled child" or "to demand attention." The transitive usage means, according to Doi, "to flatter somebody" or "surely trust in the parental indulgence and act childishly" (1982, 25).

---

235. In this sense *amai* (甘い) is used for flattery, then meaning "sentimental" or "schmaltzy." The compound *kangen* (甘言), the "sweet words" also means flattery.

236. The phrase "to slurp the *amai* (甘い) soup" means as much as "to get on the gravy train." The terms *kansan* (甘酸) and *kanku* (甘苦), both meaning "sweet things and sour things" describe life with its good and bad sides.

237. This does not mean that *amae* (甘え) is bad by definition. Doi admits that *amaeru* (甘える) (the derived verb) at times is used to describe undesirable conditions, but "it would be wrong to understand it as something bad from the start (1994, 155).

238. Doi explains the connection between *amai* (甘い) as lenient and *amai* (甘い) as shallow or superficial thus: "Such a wrong misjudgment generates when somebody allows wishful thinking (a form of self-indulgence), thus clouding one's judgment" (1982, 37).

239. *Amaku* (甘く) is the adverb of *amai* (甘い).

Amaeta (甘えた)[240] behavior is coquettish behavior. Krause (1985) translates *amaeru* (甘える) as follows: "to be pampered, to act like a pampered child," "to coax, to wheedle, to talk in a flattering way," "coquettish," and "take advantage of." From here the term is then further developed towards the notion of "to place oneself in a situation of dependence," or "to rely on." He who *amaeru*(s) (甘える), trusting the others' indulgence, bets on their kindness and deliberately becomes dependent.[241] However, dependency is not only sought by the beneficiary. Rather a co-dependence is created. This is expressed in the phrase *okotoba-ni amaete* (おことばに甘えて), "*amaeru*(ed) by your words," which is used when one accepts a (repeated) offer from another person, the offer that allows one to *amaeru* (甘える). In this phrase, however, the subject of *amaeru* (甘える) clearly is the inviting word of the giving person. This phrase is also used as an apology for lenient behavior.

- *Amattareru* (甘ったれる) or *amatareru* (甘たれる) mean "to lean on somebody," "to be dependent," "to show, to demonstrate extremely blatant confidentiality."
- *Amayakasu* (甘やかす): Contrary to the previous verbs, *amayakasu* (甘やかす) has a clearly negative notion of "leniently leaving a child to his own devices" thus spoiling him. This is expressed in the negative translations collected by Wierzbicka: "to take advantage of somebody," "to act like a pampered child," "to be coquettish," "to overly avail oneself of something," "to wheedle somebody out of something" (1996, 238).
- *Amanjiru* (甘んじる) or *amanzuru* (甘んずる): At first glance both terms seem to have nothing in common with the previous ones. They mean "to be content with something," to be "reconciled" with one's fate, "to accept something." *Kanju suru* (甘受する), literally "accepting" or "receiving" sweetness is a synonym and means "to accept" or "to put up with." However, according to Doi, this term has a deep and meaningful relation with the *amae* (甘え)-concept:

    > The term *amanzuru* (甘んずる) . . . can certainly also be interpreted that somebody imagines he would be self-

---

240. *Amaeta* (甘えた) is the past participle of *amaeru* (甘える).

241. This is why the title of the English translation of Doi's *Amae-no kouzou* (甘えの構造) reads *The Anatomy of Dependence*.

indulgent, while in reality he is not ... In short: It would be ideal to be able to yield to the desire for *amae* (甘え). But as this is not possible one manages with *amanzuru* (甘んずる). (Doi 1982, 37)

Definition of *amae* (甘え)

After the first publication of *Amae-no kouzou* (甘えの構造) in 1971 the term *amae* (甘え) has, as Doi phrased it, "almost become a common place" (Doi and Okonogi 1990, 80), and there are many ideas associated with it. In the sequel of *Amae-no kouzou* (甘えの構造), published in 2001, Doi even bemoaned the fact that for many *amae* (甘え) had become an exclusive term to label anything "Japanese" without further thinking (Doi 2001, 4). Therefore, the term *amae* (甘え) requires a clear definition. In his Japanese glossary (甘え) Jens Heise formulates: "Desire for dependence; in Doi's cultural anthropology a psychological form characterized by strong emotional ties and obligating co-dependence" (1990, 148). Heise is a very competent Japanologist and his definition is unambiguously clear and correct. And just because it is unambiguously clear it is not appropriate. With the unambiguous clarity of Western definitions it necessarily catches only certain aspects of a concept which is – in its wholeness – rather diffuse. Unambiguous definitions of ambiguous phenomena must yield results only partly correct – results therefore totally wrong. This Doi calls a "semantic problem" (Doi and Okonogi 1990, 83).

The appropriate way to describe diffuse phenomena is not to positively "get to the heart of them," but to negatively "outline" them; not to understand them "from the heart," but from the demarcations; not to "de-scribe" them, but rather "circum-scribe" them; not to say what they are, but what they are not; not to "grasp" them, but to "behold" them. Western scientists must never forget this if they want to draw anywhere near to Asian phenomena.

The following is an attempt to antithetically approach *amae* (甘え) by means of four paradoxes:

Paradox 1: *Amae* (甘え) is need <u>and</u> emotion. The nominal *amae* (甘え) combines two grammatical forms: the verb *amaeru* (甘える), "to depend on," "to lean on," describes an emotion;[242] the adjective *amaetai* (甘えたい) describes the intention or the desire to *amaeru* (甘える), the desire "to depend

---

242. In order to express himself unambiguously Doi used the English *sentiment*, even though the discussion was held in Japanese.

on," "to lean on" which generates when the emotion *amaeru* (甘える) becomes a demanding need.[243]

> Between emotion and need there exists a specific relation: the emotion *amaeru* (甘える) is a rather pleasant state. However, in the case of *amaetai* (甘えたい) . . . it becomes a need. In Japanese one talks even then about *amae* (甘え) when the *emotion* is not actually experienced, but also when this need or desire to experience this emotion exists. (Doi and Okonogi 1990, 83; similarly Doi 1994, 157)

The second paradox is similar:

Paradox 2: *Amae* (甘え) can be defined positively <u>and</u> negatively. On one hand *amae* (甘え) is the "desire [of the nursling, MH] to be emotionally one with the one who provides for him (Doi 1994, 157). This defines *amae* (甘え) negatively.

> It is interesting that nobody says of a newborn baby that he *amaeru*(es) (甘える). It is only in the second half of the first year, when the baby starts recognizing his environment[244] and seeking for his mother that he is said to *amaeru* (甘える) . . . In other words: Before a nursling starts *amaeru*(ing) (甘える), his life is, in a certain way, the continuation of his state in the womb, when mother and child were not separated yet. However, in the course of his psychological development he learns that he himself and his mother are separated beings; he now experiences that he does without the mother; it is the then developing desire for close contact with her . . . that constitutes *amae* (甘え). (Doi 1982, 88–89)

At the very same time – and Doi actually joins both definition in one single sentence – *amae* (甘え) also is the "enjoyment of [this] emotion of one-ness" (1994, 157), because *amae* (甘え) is not only experienced as an absent-yet-desired state. "On the contrary, the mother-child-relationship is not possible without *amae* (甘え)" (1982, 90). In this sense Doi can define *amae* (甘え)

---

243. Here Doi used the English *desire*.
244. The translation conceals an interesting connection. In another book Doi referred to this point of time as the point when the *monogokoro-ga tsuku* (物心が付く) takes place, when "the heart is switched on for the things," in other words, to the point when a person learns to distinguish between subject and object (1994, 157).

very positively as a medium which enables the mother to understand the soul of the nursling and respond to his needs. Thus mother and child participate in an emotion of merging and shared identity (1994, 89).

Paradox 3: *Amae* (甘え) is a technical term for the mother-child relationship and for many other relationships with people of all age groups (Doi 1994, 158). The emotion of *amae* (甘え) as well as the derived behavioral patterns date from earliest childhood, but they do not end. They continue into adulthood and determine basically all interpersonal relationships as I am going to show later. Doi calls attention to an interesting fact quoting a definition of the *Daigenkai*-dictionary: "to depend on the goodwill of another person." This is not only an age-neutral definition but the sample sentences quoted by the *Daigenkai*-dictionary relate to adults without exception. Doi concludes:

> This [quote] may be a hint that it is relatively recently that we started understanding *amae* (甘え) as something which is essentially infantine, and that this connection has been paid no attention to at all. (Doi 1982, 86)

Why then is it that *amae* (甘え) is considered an originally infantine emotion? Doi shows that *amashi* (甘し), "sweet," the etymological root of *amai* (甘い), "sweet," and *umashi* (美味し also written 甘し(!)), "be of good taste," have the same meaning. Therefore, Doi sees a connection between *ama* (あま) and *uma* (うま), both words of Japanese Motherese. A Japanese nursling expresses his hunger for the breast or for food with the words *uma-uma* (うまうま) (Doi 1982, 86–87). "If one wants to define this emotion precisely, I think that it likely correlates with the emotion of yearning, the desire for the breast (1982, 87).[245]

Paradox 4: *Amae* (甘え) has become a firmly established technical term in sociology and at the same time is still used in spoken Japanese and therefore ever changing in its meaning. Even Stucki (63) reported how the Japanese reacted when they realized that something as trivial as *amae* (甘え) was used as a highly scientific term. For the Japanese this word is most ordinary and only scientists from abroad discover a sophisticated "structure" behind it.[246]

Analyzing the latest Japanese dictionaries Doi shows how much the term *amae* (甘え) is subject to change:

---

245. See also Doi's exposition on Ps 27.

246. The last sentence can be understood as criticism against Doi himself that he speaks as a scientist from abroad. Doi admits that he did discover *amae* (甘え) only because he is an outsider among the Japanese psychiatrists (Doi and Okonogi 1990, 82–83).

> These days the appreciation of *amae* (甘え) is not deep. "Don't *amaeru* (甘える)" or "It's no good to always *amaeru* (甘える)!" are oft-heard phrases. The question, "Who *amaeru*(ed) (甘える) this?" reveals almost solely criticism . . . When one opens the latest dictionaries under "*amaeru* (甘える)" they simply say: "to be familiar with somebody and selfishly demand something." (Doi 2001, 9)

Some dictionaries even equate *amaeru* (甘える) with the English *to spoil*[247] (Doi 2001, 9).

In the following I am going to show that *amae* (甘え) is the key term for the understanding of familial social structures in animistic societies. "The home is the core and the shelter, the innermost 'circle' of intimacy, the realm of *amae* (甘え), where one is allowed to let oneself go" (Stucki 1978, 157). It is therefore important to look into the structure of the Japanese family.

2.5.1.3 Takeyoshi Kawashima (川島武宜): The family structures of the Japanese

> **Summary:** Besides the family structure of the samurai nobility, influenced by Confucianism and usually rendered the typical Japanese family structure, the family structure of the farmers was much more common. The family structure of farmers in which *amae* (甘え) prevailed, is more and more becoming the basic structure of today's families and non-family family-like groups.

When the Japanese government discussed the new constitution demanded by General McArthur, Takeyoshi Kawashima (1909–1992), who was the leading legal scholar of post-war Japan, wrote the outstanding article *Nihon shakai-no kazokuteki kousei* (日本社会の家族的構成, The Familial Structure of the Japanese Society) (1946).[248] The choice of the subject is especially outstanding, because from Japan's modernization the Japanese dispute about collectivism and individualism was held on the field of family law. Kawashima carves out the difference between the Confucian family ideal, which stands for most conceptions on "the Japanese family," and the family structures of peasant families, which was prevalent in Japan before the "universalization of the elite ethics" of the samurai, for which the *Imperial Rescript on Education* of the

---

247. Here *to spoil* is used as a loan-word.
248. It was first published as a book in 1950 (Schwentker 1998, 247). I refer to the German translation *Die familiale Struktur der japanischen Gesellschaft*.

Meiji-Reform (1890) was instrumental (Fridell 1970, 824). There is a profound and dramatic difference between the two:

> Of course the fathers of Civil Code were aware of [the familial structures of peasant families], but they considered the familial institutions "of that peculiar existence of the lower class, which didn't even know the social distinction between man and woman" irrelevant for the drafting of new laws. To the present day these familial institutions have been vaguely treated as if they were consistent with the ruling family system [of the Confucian family ideals]. The differences have never been clearly carved out. (Kawashima 1988, 62–63)

The Confucian family constitution of the samurai nobility

Even though the familial ideal of the samurai nobility is mainly considered representative for Japan, it was – according to Kawashima – only the ideal for a very small elite. "In those groups the social relationships are controlled by authority and voluntary surrender."[249] Everything nonconformist to the firm and disciplined rules created the impression of "licentiousness and confusion." Power representatives are the family head, the father, and the husband. "They all have authority over the family, the children, and the wife." "This 'authority' must not be equated with or limited to physical force. It rather focuses on the spirit of the subdued." The more the subdued are aware that they cannot resist the authority, "the more readily they submit to it" (Kawashima 1988, 64). In these systems "wives and children perceive themselves not as subject, but as . . . objects of authority to which they submit."[250]

When modernizing the Japanese law according to Western models, the legal scholars "had the difficult task to translate terms [of the individual rights]

---

249. Mae and Schmitz (51–52) judged in a similar way when they called the *ie* (家)-system of the *Meiji*-Era an "ideological construct," while "the family structure of the social reality was more and more equivalent to the modern nuclear family." A consistent family law did not exist, "but the family-concept of the late warrior nobility, shaped by Confucianism, had become the model for all social classes." Mae and Schmitz thus compared (rightly indeed) the family structure of the peasants with that of the modern nuclear family.

250. This ideal is still alive in the small subculture of the tightly organized, paramilitary *yakuza* (やくざ), the Japanese Mafia. "The *yakuza* (やくざ)-family follows the tradition of the feudal . . . ideal of *oyabun-kobun* (親分子分). *Oyabun* (親分) means both father and ruler, *kobun* (子分) both child and servant." The bosses of the *yakuza* (やくざ)-gangs invariably call their subordinates their "young" or "their children." The boss "demands unconditional obedience," but in return he "promises life-long protection and safety within the gang" (Hermann and Venzago 1992, 40–41).

into Japanese, even though they were unknown in their own culture" (Andou 2001, 45). They had to express concepts the Confucian family constitution of the samurai nobility was not even aware of. One of the biggest challenges was the coinage of a word for "subjective rights." Leaning on Vissering's[251] lecture on international law (Andou 2001, 47), Tsuda, a Japanese lawyer, introduced the word *kenri* (権利) in 1868. *Ken* (権) means "power," "authority"[252] and *ri* (利) "interests." *Kenri* (権利) is the "power to enforce one's [personal] interests." The Japanese leadership who were deeply influenced by the Confucian family constitution of the samurai nobility had great difficulties accepting this concept:

> Until the late 19th century, merely imagining that one person could exercise such power against another, even perhaps in the family, triggered off great horror among conservative Japanese. A Japanese civil servant said, "When I learned that according the new . . . Civil Code, a wife could stand up against her husband, or a child sue his parent, I was utterly shocked. I then asked the Minister of Justice whether this was really true. He said that this was inevitable, because the Western powers would not approve the abolition of the extraterritoriality if we didn't adopt a Western-styled Civil Code." One can scarcely imagine what fundamental change in awareness was necessary for the introduction of European law, and how fast it would take place in the forty-four years of the *Meiji*-Era (until 1912). (Schröder and Morinaga 2005, 45)

At the end of the nineteenth century the passages of the new Civil Code, which were concerned with family law, were attacked by conservatives and Common Law representatives. Thus debate is referred to as *hoten ronsou* (法典論争), "codification debate," or as *minpouten ronsou* (民法典論争) (Röhl 2005, 176). The main target criticism was Boissonades's cautious attempt "to modernize . . . the traditional Japanese familial constitution by means of the French law. His system was concerned rather with the content than with the form. He assimilated the familial rights into the individual rights. This was a fundamental discontinuity in opposition to the Japanese tradition"

---

251. Samuel Vissering taught Nishi and Tsuda who had been sent to the Netherlands by the Shogunate. He also introduced freemasonry to them (Johnston 1999). Vissering himself probably loaned the term *kenri* (権利) from William Martin's Chinese translation of Henry Weaton's *Elements of International Law* (Andou 2001, 47).

252. The original meaning of *ken* (権) is "scale," that is a device for determining weight. From that the meaning "weight" was derived and eventually the figurative meaning of spiritual or political "weight" in the sense of "authority" or "power" (Andou 2001, 47).

(Schenck 1997, 305). Lawyers discussed the question "to what extent Japan's legislation ... should be oriented on European laws." Target of their criticism was the "incompatibility of European laws with Japanese consuetudinary law," mainly attacking the Civil Code of 1896. The individual rights of the Civil Code were considered a "murder weapon against the nation" as it attempted "to undermine the tradition of the Japanese family and ancestor veneration by means of individualism" (Kliesow 2001, 10).[253] The layers that took action against Boissonade were not concerned with the strengthening of individual rights, but with the very fact that the relationship between parents or that between fathers and children should be thought of in juridical categories. This seemed to pose a threat. According to Hozumi, the familial relationships were a sphere, "which law should not be able to reach, in which only piety and morality rule" based upon *sosenkyou* (祖先教), upon "ancestor religion" (Mae and Schmitz 2007, 53).

The familial structures of the peasant families

In the family structures formed by the samurai nobility there was hardly room for *amae* (甘え),[254] but the familial structures of the "lower class" surely was the place of which Stucki (157) said that it was "the area of *amae* (甘え)," where "one is allowed to let oneself go."

In the families of broad sections of population, mainly in peasant families, "all family members – including women and children of all age groups – had to contribute to the agricultural work according to their respective capacity."[255] Therefore nobody is totally dependent on the family head who, in turn, does not have the same authority as a family head of a samurai family. "In a family structure like this, absolute authority and submissiveness are not controlling, but the principles of living together are, even though they are only atmospherically existent." Different from the vertically structured families

---

253. The same tension is seen in the ambivalent attitude towards the *saisei bunri* (祭政分離), the separation of religion (in this case *sai* [祭] means the Shintoist festival) and government, forced upon Japan by the American occupying forces. "In almost half a century after the regaining of sovereignty after World War II the principle of *saisei bunri* (祭政分離) was often questioned and doubted (Nawrocki 2001, 208). In his public statements Hori (1910–1974), "the leading religious scholar and Shintou-expert of post-war Japan, ... often expressed his conviction that even after long years of separation of religion and politics, Shintou would lose none of its political vitality and its original character of a national ideology ... As early as the end of the 1950s he voiced the opinion that in the long run a separation of religion and politics would be unsustainable for Japan" (208).

254. The time until the weaning of a child seemed to be an exception in most cases.

255. In families of merchants and peasants "the work force of women was crucial," which led to a "certain social respect [of women]" (Phillipps 2004, 104).

of the samurai nobility, "horizontally [structured families] are founded on unifying relationships[256] of trusting goodwill" (Kawashima 1988, 68). "Here prevails an uninhibited and intimate atmosphere" in which genuine human emotions are most important (1988, 69–70). At the beginning of the last century the Japanese philosopher and cultural historicist Tetsurou Watsuji (3) wrote that the "relationships in the family were characterized by a totally openhearted unity aimed at heartily affection."

These family relationships are horizontally structured but that does not mean that they are liberal and democratic. Forged by a longstanding tradition this system "rules over its members with absolute authority." The family order is not established from inside (e.g. from an authoritarian household head), but from outside. Kawashima talks about "blind obedience to customs and traditions" (1988, 70).[257] As the bearers of authority do not hold the authority themselves, they are only representatives of the authority based upon tradition, this authority "is exercised in a very humane way and never with brute force." This is why the force of authority never "appears as force."

Family structures today

Since the end of World War II, extended families of the traditional *ie*(家)-system have disintegrated more and more, giving way first to the modern nuclear family, and now more and more to non-marital or pre-marital partnerships,[258] a development that used to be lamented as the classical example of Yasujirou Ozu's (小津安二郎) (1903–1963) film *Toukyou Monogatari* (東京物語) (1953) (Tokyo Story) shows.

Toukyou Monogatari (東京物語)

Ozu never was married and died only a few years after his mother, with whom he lived together for almost all his life. He had "no interest in romantic love." "His only interest in the various forms of love is in those which exist between

---

256. *Gemeinschaftsbeziehungen*.

257. Hasenhüttl discussed a similar contrast. The contrast between family structures of the Japanese samurai nobility with their obligation towards living rulers and family structures of the broad sections of the population with their obligation towards the ancestors as guardians of traditional customs (Kawashima 1988, 70) is similar to the contrast between modern dictatorial societies and traditional forms of society and their obligation to the ancestors. Hasenhüttl said that community and fellowship give way to power and dominion. "Such a change of consciousness questions a whole worldview (*Gedankenwelt*). The living and the dead are separated which leads to a dualistic thinking . . . It is not [anymore] the ancestor who connects the present back to tradition, but the present potentate is the true origin . . . Ancestor veneration eventually loses its meaning" (Hasenhüttl 1991, 53–54).

258. For detailed information see Kruth (2007).

members of a family, and he is successful with [portraying, MH] romantic love only when it finds an outlet in the form of family love, as between man and wife" (Anderson and Richie 1982, 360). The strong influence of family love on his life is crucial for understanding his films (Ozu and Noda 2003, 16). The film *Toukyou Monogatari* (東京物語) shows "the breakup of the traditional Japanese family" (Desser 1997, 4). A short outline:

> An aging couple, Hirayama Shuukichi (平山周吉) and his wife Tomi (とみ), living in retirement in the port city of Onomichi (尾道), prepare for a train trip to Tokyo to visit their children. A stopover to see a son in Osaka is to be followed by a stay with their eldest son, Kouichi (幸一), a doctor. Their quiet preparation and gentle banter set a tone of contemplation and nostalgia. Once in Tokyo, however, they realize that Kouichi, living in a poor suburb and with a small pediatric practice, is hardly the success they thought he was and seems barely to have time for them. Their daughter, Shige (志げ), owner of a beauty salon, seems even less interested in their company; indeed, she appears to be outright resentful of their presence.
>
> Kouichi and Shige send their parents to Atami, a hot springs resort highly unsuitable for this elderly couple. When they return early to Tokyo, neither Kouichi nor Shige is willing to take them in. Only their daughter-in-law, Noriko (平山紀子), a war widow, seems genuinely loving and kind to them; she invites Tomi to stay at her small apartment, while Shuukichi must stay at an old friend's. When a drunken Shuukichi and his friend are brought to Shige's home by the police, the anger and disappointment the parents feel toward their children and the children toward their parents send the old Hirayamas back home.
>
> On the way home, Tomi is taken ill. A stopover in Osaka to recover for the moment finds the couple reflecting on their lives with a mixture of bitterness and resignation. When the Hirayamas return home, Tomi gets worse. Their youngest daughter, Kyouko (京子), still living at home, sends for her brothers, sister, and sister-in-law. Shortly after their arrival in Onomichi, Tomi dies. Only Kyouko and Noriko seem genuinely saddened. As Noriko prepares to return to Tokyo, the widowed Shuukichi extends his gratitude to her for love and kindness and urges her to remarry.

Noriko's contemplative journey back to home ends the film. (Desser 1997, 1–2)

In this as "in every Ozu film the whole world exists in one family. The ends of the earth are no more distant than outside of the house. The people are members of a family rather than members of society" (Anderson and Richie 1982, 359). Iles associates the film with social change "from rural to urban, from close family ties to isolation and alienation" (Iles 2007, 191). It is this change that Ozu criticizes. "To Ozu the evil side of human nature was merely the criminal act against parents or father figures" (Barrett 1989, 212). He specifically criticizes society and not the children. The children are depicted as people who are not even able to take their parents in, because their apartments are too small. The son practices in his apartment and the daughter and her husband live in an apartment behind her salon. In themselves the children are good. It is the circumstances, which they cannot control, that changed them. They are not like the children in their parents' memory, but totally self-absorbed in their struggle of survival (Carr 2002, 287). The figure of Noriko, the daughter-in-law, poses a single element of constructive criticism. The film ends with the vague hope, not founded on family but on the personal decision of the daughter-in-law (Iles 2007, 191). The ideal of family may be destroyed. Its values, though, live on. Below I am going to discuss several of those values and characteristics in quasi-familial structures of Japanese society.

According to my observations, the ideals of the families of samurai nobility are not relevant anymore in present-day Japan. Families rather resemble those families that Kawashima called the families of the "lower class."

No autonomy of individuals

"There are substantial differences" between medieval peasant families and the "modern family." One reason is that "humane . . . emotions in the community of peasant families was not ruled by rational, independent considerations, but by blind obedience to overcome customs and traditions." In this context, Kawashima wrote that "in this kind of atmosphere . . . everything was 'somehow' realized as people talked themselves into believing." Logical argument considering pros and cons was prohibited. A member of a peasant family could not act as an individual person, nor was he even able to conceive of himself as an independent individual (1988, 70–71).

Even the "familiar [*amae* (甘え)]-relations are . . . not borne by independent individuals. They rather exist in a totalitarian atmosphere which categorically rules out the existence of autonomous personalities" (1988, 70–71). He continues:

> There, every member of the family is constantly enclosed by the atmosphere of the community framework and its rules, and must therefore be aware that he is only an object of the prevalent social norm. If he set his own awareness or his own acts against this communal climate, his attitude would destroy the idyllic peace. (Kawashima 1988, 70)

These characteristics of Japanese society can be observed even today, even though they are not as extreme as in medieval Japan. According to Kawashima, not even the medieval head of the house or parents "had an independent self-awareness, nor were they able to act independently." Modern families on the other hand have "morals" to lead them and the "rational-autonomic behavior is not ruled by regulations 'from outside,' but by self-discipline 'from inside'" (Kawashima 1988, 70).

Absent sense of responsibility

As one result of this all-embracing and all-surrounding "atmosphere of life," Kawashima names the absence of a sense of responsibility. According to my own observations, this is a prevalent characteristic of present-day Japan.

> As long as there is no space[259] for an individual self-awareness or independent behavior, the awareness of personal responsibility cannot develop. The familial climate is the foundation of all awareness and behavior. Nobody is responsible. The [familial] atmosphere is responsible for everything. (Kawashima 1988, 71)

Holism

The following structures can be observed in Japanese families:

- an atmosphere determined by mutual trust and co-dependence which creates the context for *amae* (甘え);
- mainly horizontal structures under the authority of an external custom, also called "family constitution" (Yamamori 1974, 16–17);
- unconditional submission under this authority (Kawashima 1988, 74);

---

259. *Freiraum.*

- highest priority is given to placing the whole and the family above the individual, thus preserving the familial harmony;
- missing sense of responsibility[260] due to submission of the individual with a subsequently almost absolute absence of individuation.[261]

All these characteristics show a strong tendency towards holism which is typical for animistic worldviews. Inagaki explicitly linked the missing individuation to animism:

> In Japan where there is no concept of man created by God it is only natural that there is no tension between "subject" and "object," and no establishment of the "individual" or "self." Rather there is an illogical intuition, a kind of "pure experience which results in a no-self-awareness. In Japanism with its animism, people are not personal beings in fellowship with each other. They are seen only in a dependent relationship. (Inagaki 1990, 10)

Familial structures of social groups

"Humans form families, and families form the state" (Kawashima 1988, 74). Kawashima concludes: "Therefore, the basic patterns of family life are reflected in external relationships and penetrate them into even the furthest corners" (1988, 74). This is clearly illustrated by the understanding of the Constitution of the *Meiji*-Restoration: "Our subjects have always been of one mind in steadfast faithfulness towards the Sovereign and in filial love for the parents . . . This is the noble blossom of Our state, and at the same time the fountainhead from which Our education springs" (Terazono and Hamer 1988, 33). The structure of social groups is fashioned according to the familial structure, ultimately according to the mother-child structure or parent-child structure. The reason for this is that,

> in the economic and social relationships of our country, which never knew any form of typical capitalism, people always feel

---

260. Kawashima does not think that this deficiency is value-free: "As long as life proceeds in repetitive cycles, never changing, always monotonous, this behavioral pattern may create peace and stability. If however something new happens, if unexpected problems arise, this principle of life may harbor serious dangers, because all involved let themselves be carried on by the subjectless atmosphere, and nobody is aware of his or her personal responsibility, and nobody acts responsibly" (Kawashima 1988, 75).

261. Everything else would endanger peace. "In such societies it is not allowed – in fact, it is impossible – to develop one's own individuality. Rather those are honored as 'developed personalities,' who strive to wear down their 'corners and edges,' who strive to suppress their personality and go with the flow of the group's atmosphere" (Kawashima 1988, 75–76).

somehow dependent on the protection of others.[262] They are not connected simply on the basis of the exchange of goods, but necessarily enter permanent and personal relationships. But those who enter such relationships only know the social relationships of the familial community, they cannot even imagine [different] ... relationships. (Kawashima 1988, 72)

According to Kawashima, Japanese feel lonely "in the cold formalities of politeness outside the family ... This is why they transform their friendships into 'fraternal relationships,' which allow an unconstrained, confidential intercourse ... This is how fictitious parent-child relationships evolve" (Kawashima 1988, 73). This can be clearly seen in the structure of Japanese companies. Basu and Miroshnik (74) call them a "family unit." A Japanese company is not merely a place of employment, but it is considered "my society" or "our society, one's prior community, the most important in life" (Nakane 1984, 173). "As the modern patriarchy the company takes over the role of the extended family" (Dambmann 1989, 223) which is a common feature shared by collectivistic societies (Hofstede 2013, 81). Companies have (among others) the following familial structures:

- new colleagues are welcomed with the same enthusiasm as a newborn family member (Nakane 1984, 180);
- cooperation is more important than open conflict and competition (Morean 1986, 64), "individual ambition, and selfish mindlessness" (Dambmann 1989, 232); the seniority principle[263] prevents competition (234–235);[264]
- below the leadership level all are of equal rank;[265]
- the emotional ties are strong (Nakane 1984, 173);

---

262. Similarly, Yamamori: "In order to exist, the whole family – young and old, male and female – contributed their labor towards the family business. The need of the family took precedence over that of the individual" (1974, 16).

263. "Seniority principle" is a promotion system based on age in service rather than on achievements. However, under the pressure of the world economic crisis and since the burst of the bubble-economy this principle is up for discussion (Ziesemer 1995, 116). Even though the seniority principle is still important there is a trend towards remuneration according to achievement (Rothlauf 2009, 502).

264. "Japanese don't work more, but they work together" (McDowell 1974, 333).

265. Only when all are the same an equal mutual co-dependence guarantees stable social conditions (Minamoto 1986, 59). During the application process all applicants wear exactly the same thing in order not to be apparent. The main criterion of selection is the ability to fit into a team (Dambmann 1989, 218–219).

- peers that joined the company in the same year will always form sub-groups as the common socialization into the company leads to strong emotional bonds (Linhart 1984a, 538);
- the company is the sole basis of existence and controls all other spheres of life (Nakane 1984, 173);
- the leader is a father-figure, rewarding faithfulness and dedication with loving kindness (Morean 1986, 68), protection and loyalty. Even weak performance is now reason for dismissal; a child cannot be fired (Hofstede 2013, 81) (paternal principle);
- leaders create spontaneous feelings of guilt and appeal to that feeling, which is the Japanese way of controlling (Okonogi 1990, 64–65) (maternal principle); "in companies, decisions develop from bottom to top" (Dambmann 1989, 233), subordinates are thus involved as children are in the co-dependent mother-child relationship;[266]
- some control mechanisms use feelings of shame;[267]
- seniority principle, a principle prevalent all over Asia; "hardly any company is willing to let a promising youth embark on a meteoric career and make him superior to a considerably older colleague" (Dambmann 1989, 235);
- the relationship between younger and older siblings is mirrored in the "affectionate" relationship between experienced colleagues and newcomers (Linhart 1984a, 538).

2.5.2 The Relationship with the Living Dead

2.5.2.1 The unity in the extended family

In his philosophy of religion, strongly leaning on Herbert Spencer (Yusa 1996, 311), Hearn considers ancestor veneration the most basic form of all religious phenomena (Hearn 1971, 21, 24).[268] The rituals of "ancestor worship"

---

266. Another reason that decisions need to be unanimous. Majority decisions are avoided because they violate the postulate of harmony (Koschnick 1998, 375).

267. In the morning our employees "flip over their name-tag on the indicator board.... During the day their name is shown in black, flipped back after end of work, red. Any employee absent from work... sticks out in red (Crome 1985, 83).

268. Mullins agrees (1998, 130). Reischauer, on the other hand, considers ancestor veneration a tradition developed much later under the influence of China (Reischauer 1984, 12). I think Reischauer's position is unsustainable, as Japan had a rich tradition of ancestor veneration even before the 6th century (Durant 1985, 192). Also Campbell (I, 380–381) gives examples for the even older ancestor-concepts of the Ainu. Of course, these traditions were later deeply changed and reshaped by Buddhist influence.

are considered important for the social life of the Japanese even today (Shibata 1985, 250). It is historically, religiously, and sociologically integrated into the life of the Japanese nation (Berentsen 1985b, 263).

Tsan (1997, 199–202) showed that "the ancestor veneration" is not a single-layered phenomenon, but that it had a theological and a cultural aspect. I use Tsan's model and add yet another aspect: The relationship with the *living dead* or the ancestors have to be discussed under the interconnected psychological, sociological, and worldview aspects:

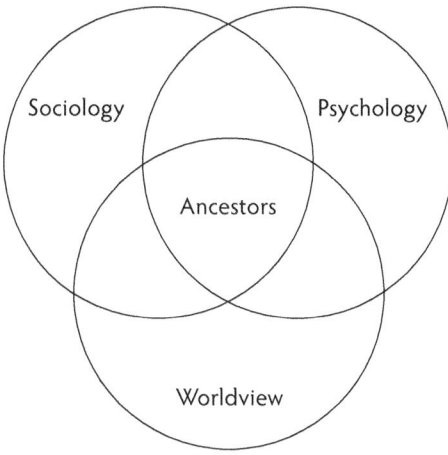

Figure 2.6 Aspects of Ancestor Veneration (according to Tsan 1997)

The psychological aspect

As the *Tokyo Shoseki* (東京書籍) shows, feelings of belonging to a group are not only applied to the living members of the group but also to the dead members: "We live connected in communion with other people: with those who lived before, and with those who live now" (Ölschleger et al. 1994, 192). The psychological aspect of togetherness is closely related with *amae* (甘え), "dependency." Relying on the work of Raphael, Goss and Klass show people that experienced strong dependency on deceased others show pathologically amplified grief. Then they continue and quote Doi: "In Japan, dependence, not autonomy, is more valued" (Goss and Klass 2005, 29). "The bonds individuals feel with ancestors are within this sense of dependence. The individual is a person as a member. The ancestors remain members, too" (30). Therefore, ancestor veneration is deeply rooted in the emotional life of the Japanese.

"Visiting graves and ancestor worship form the breeding ground in which the Japanese culture grows" (Shibata 1985, 248–249). For most people "ancestor worship" is beyond religion, the bond that ties religions together (250).

The sociological aspect

Living together with the dead give Japanese a feeling of closeness, togetherness, and continuation.[269] The *ie* (家), the "house" or the "family" is represented by the head of the house, but,

> it is the family as a whole that gives the head of the house his authority. It is not the case that the house is brought into existence at the whim of its head. The house is given a substantial and distinctive character by the fact that its unity is understood in historical terms. The family of the present shoulders the burden of this historical house and undertakes a liability for its unity from the past down into the future . . . The household member is not merely parent or child, husband or wife. He is also descendant of his ancestors and an ancestor to those who are to come. (Watsuji 1988, 3)[270]

Ancestor veneration is the Japanese way of fighting transience (Berentsen 1985b, 266). Through ancestor veneration the whole family is enveloped in its divine character and destiny. As for their origin, families perceive themselves as descendants of the *kami* (神), of the gods. *Kami* (神) in its original sense means the origin of the family. As for their destiny, deceased family members become ancestors, and as ancestor *kami* (神), gods. This defines the destiny of the family as divine (Berentsen 1985b, 268).[271] The connection between ancestors and descendants is not only understood as a linear relationship. There are families who believe that their ancestors are reborn as their children. The belief that the souls of deceased children return is also widespread. Therefore, children used to be buried in the home (Naumann 1984b, 1630). In his foreword to

---

269. Traditions that keep alive the memory of and the fellowship with the dead also keep together the living. During his field work in five Japanese villages in Morimachi (森町) (Shizuoka-Prefecture), Steffánsson (2002) observed that in addition to Buddhist and folk-religious ritual dimensions there is also a "collective dimension," that shows the communal importance of the rites for the dead.

270. In Africa the ancestor worship is also linked to the context of family (Hasenhüttl 1991, 50).

271. In Buddhist terminology this is called "becoming *hotoke* (仏)," Buddha (Berentsen 1985b, 268; 1985a, 76).

Ryuuji Tanabe's (田部隆次) (1914) biography of Lafcadio Hearn, Kitarou Nishida wrote:

> Hearn was a writer possessing a kind of mysticism that enabled him to see the working of the spirit behind everything. He not only felt the pulsation of several thousand years of ancestral heritage in simple sensation and emotion, but he also saw the activities of past generations of our ancestors' spirits revealed in our simple bodily expressions. According to Hearn, we as persons are not limited to one generation. Each of us is a composite of multiple persons coming down through the generations. Waves of life inherited from our ancestors surge up through our bodies, each body being a segment of the endless pillar of the spirit extending from the distant past to the present. Thus the physical body is the material manifestation of a host of spirits. (Nishida in Yusa 1996, 313)[272]

The worldview aspect

The connection of the ancestors with the divine shows the connection to the third, very important, aspect of ancestor veneration – the worldview aspect. Ancestor veneration as a bridge between the human and the divine is a phenomenon not only known in Japan. Goss and Klass write that "in many cultures, the lines between the deceased, the saints, the gods, and, in monotheism, God, are blurred," because "the dead link the worlds of the seen and the unseen, the worlds of the sacred and the profane" (Goss and Klass 2005, 9). According to Kunio Yanagida (柳田國男), the origin of Japanese ancestor veneration is not Buddhist, but Shintoist (Shibata 1985, 250). When interpreting the rituals of ancestor veneration in the context of animism[273] it becomes apparent that the continuity between the human and the divine is of greatest importance. The human becoming divine is not a partial aspect of ancestor veneration but one of its "pillars" (Berentsen 1985b, 268–269). Man, as part of the "spiritual-material cosmos," is himself also characterized by a "spiritual dimension." "The godhead is immanent in man, and man immanent in the godhead, and between them there is no essential difference." In this kami(神)-faith … the Japanese ancestor veneration is rooted (Hildebrandt 1996, 140).

---

272. Yusa (315) said that Hearn's thinking showed a "closeness to animism."
273. Lwamba suggests that animism is "based on ancestor veneration" (Lwamba 2013, "Animism and the Spirit World in Africa: The Akamb Experience").

The ancestors constitute intermediate beings[274] between gods and men. On one side they have something in common with the pure[275] gods and at the same time something in common with pure humans. The last of the pure gods . . . were the ancestors of humankind, while the first humans were the ancestral deities. Therefore, man has something in common with ancestors and deities. (Numazawa 1970, 199)

2.5.2.2 The family-concept or house-concept *ie* (家)

Ancestor veneration inseparably belongs together with the *ie* (家)-concept, the "house-concept." According to Berentsen, it is characterized by the "four P's" – the *ie* (家) is patriarchal, patrilinear, primogenitual, patrilocal. It is (1) patriarchal because it is grouped around the *kachou* (家長), the "head of the house" with his *kachouken* (家長権), his "authority as head of the house"; (2) it is patrilinear because the wife has to give birth to a male heir and raise him according to the *kafuu* (家風), the "way of the house"; (3) it is primogenitual because the *chounan* (長男), the "oldest son" is sole heir.[276] The other children marry into other families or they found *bunke* (分家), branch families. The ancestor altar remains with the *honke* (本家), the "main family" (Berentsen 1985a, 55). In this way families are grouped into clusters and form the *douzoku* (同族)-system, the system of the "same families" (Yonemura 1976, 186); and finally, the *ie* (家)-concept is (4) patrilocal because the oldest son stays in the house of the parents (Berentsen 1985a, 56). Here are the testimonies of three Japanologists:

> The "house," namely, is an everlasting entity transcending any actual generation and member of it. It is an entity in continuity from the past into the future including both the dead, the living, and the not-yet-born. In the *ie* (家) these groups are all united in an interdependent unity which transcends life and death. This ultimate reality of the *ie* (家) is symbolized in the family grave and the family altar. (Berentsen 1985b, 264–265)

---

274. *Mittelwesen*.

275. *Rein* in the sense of "outright," "exclusively."

276. His prominent position is also expressed in the common habit of younger siblings calling him *oyakata* (親方), literally "parental person" (Yonemura 1976, 182).

> Above all, it is an expression of the solidarity of the family, a solidarity that runs vertically through the generations as well as horizontally among the living family members. (Dale 1998, 278)

> [The family includes] all ancestors from the distant past and all descendants to the distant future. A man's duty includes obligations to descendants as well as to ancestors. He is merely one tiny link between the dead and those yet to be born – a bud on an enormous tree. (Gulick 1964, 83)

In the Japanese *ie* (家), the Japanese "house," as well as in a clan or a lineage, the living are only the smaller part of the whole. "The most important part lives in the yonder world" (Thiel 1983, 83). Nakagawa links this understanding of family explicitly to the Japanese collectivism in which any Self is dissolved. Where Nakane used an illustration from the field of biology, he uses one from the field of the inanimate nature: Individual members of the family are like the water of a stream eternally flowing on and on, while the stream itself is the same forever (Nakagawa in Gulick 1964, 83).

Ancestor veneration as a way of coping with death, which in the past was institutionalized in the Buddhist communities (Rowe 2011, 3) is very much dependent on strong family ties. After World War II[277] ancestor veneration degenerated to a mere cultural form due to the reduction of extended families to nuclear families (Berentsen 1985b, 265). "In Japan's post-industrial society, patterns of social relations within families and communities, on which the deceased's security rests, have changed greatly" (Kawano 2010, 1). "The declining birth rate, postponed marriages, and childlessness have diminished the pool of future family grave caretakers" (12). The new reality of death in isolation from the family community can be clearly seen from the following numbers: In 1947, 90.8 percent died at home. 1977 the rate of hospital deaths (50.6%) was for the first time higher than home deaths (49.4%). By 1990, 75.1 percent, in the case of cancer patients even 93.3 percent, died in hospital (Suzuki 2003, 662).

---

277. With the new postwar constitution, the position of the "house" and the ancestor worship was reinterpreted and its importance and authority weakened. The new Civil Code of 1948 "provides, in most respects, for a very different kind of family structure. The household is no longer a legal entity and its head is stripped of its powers. Legally Japan turned away from the old *ie* (家)-structure to that of the Western nuclear family. To be noted is that the genealogical records, rite utensils, tombs and burial grounds are inherited by the person who is the "president" in the worship of the memory of the ancestors (Berentsen in Nesbitt 2007, 32).

Ancestor veneration is still practiced today on a limited scale. "From the viewpoint of statistics only a certain percentage of families have mortuary tablets . . . but the ancestor altar and its mortuary tablets are widely considered a family's most valued property." Most families that actually have mortuary tablets are actively involved in cultic ceremonies. The ancestors belong to everyday life, "whether gifts are first offered before the altar, whether the ancestors are informed about all family matters, whether they are besought for protection, whether thanksgiving is offered or – in case of failure – their forgivingness is sought." Anything good is "credited to their providence, while bad luck is due to one's own failure, accompanied with the unendurable feeling of bringing shame to the ancestors (Naumann 1984a, 1543). New cabinet members are expected to report their electoral success to the ancestors as soon as possible (Shibata 1985, 248).

2.5.2.3 The *living dead* and ethical values

It is particularly true for patrinlinear and patriarchal societies that the living and the dead belong together (Yonemura 1976, 177) and are dependent on each other (Goss and Klass 2005, 30).

The dead are dependent on the living

The dead can make progress in the realm of the dead only if the living observe the *tsuizenkuyou* (追善供養), the "mediatory rituals," as well as the *houji* (法事)-ceremonies, the Buddhist "memorial ceremonies." Their development or growth from *shirei* (死霊), "spirit of the dead," to *sorei* (祖霊), "ancestral spirit" does not "happen" automatically, but only if supported by the care of the living.[278] Without their care the dead cannot reach postmortem salvation, but become *meikon* (迷魂), "souls going astray," or *mouja* (亡者). *Mouja* (亡者) simply means "lost persons" or "deceased." However, as this word can also be used for living people unable to fulfill their desires,[279] referring to the dead as *mouja* (亡者) takes on the meaning of spirits of the dead, that are not able to do *joubutsu* (成仏), that are not able to move on and "become Buddhas." Shoukou Watanabe (渡辺照宏) explains the Buddhist context:

---

278. However, Doerner furnished evidence that this automatism works in Shintoism (Berentsen 1985a, 77).

279. A *kane-no mouja* (金の亡者), a money-*mouja* (亡者) is a person with a strong addiction for money. Likewise, a *garigari mouja* (我利我利亡者) is a person that is excessively concerned with his personal advantage. *Gari* (我利) means personal (我) benefit (利).

> For the *bourei* (亡霊) or *shirei* (死霊), to become a *sorei* (祖霊), however, it is not only a problem of time. It presupposes the diligent performance of the rites by the bereaved ... If these are neglected, the *bourei* (亡霊) will not become *sorei* (祖霊); it will only fall into a miserable existence itself, but bring about all kinds of harms to the living. (Watanabe in Berentsen 1985a, 78)

In a similar way, Ivy writes:

> In conventional Buddhist thought in Japan, a distinction is made between the "newly" dead and the "settled" dead. The newly dead are those that have died, usually, within the last forty-nine days and thus are not yet settled. There are many other kinds of unsettled dead, but in all cases, memorial services are intended to settle them. That is the primary goal of many Buddhist rites (e.g. *segakie,* 施餓鬼会[280]) and the domestic household rites connected with so-called ancestor worship. Memorialization is really the remembering of the dead in order to settle them. When correct memorialization occurs, the unsettled newly dead (*shirei*, 死霊) can become settled "ancestral dead" (*sorei*, 祖霊), and as ancestors (*senzo*, 先祖) can benefit and protect the living. Those that are not remembered – or have not been remembered adequately – remain unsettled and are thus on the loose, dangerous: if the living forget or neglect the dead, then the dead can haunt them as ghosts. Ghosts indicate that the structure of remembering through memorialization is not completely efficacious, that the line between life and death that the remembering the dead institutes is not secure. (Ivy 1995, 149–150)

If the *shirei* (死霊), the "spirits of the dead," don't reach their goal but fall into misfortune,[281] they punish the living with *tatari* (祟り), with "curses"

---

280. Hungry Spirits (*gaki*, 餓鬼, and *ashura*, 阿修羅) are "potentially dangerous entities" and must be pacified and assisted every year at temple ceremonies" called *segakie* (施餓鬼会) (Rowe 2011, 46), "meetings" (会) that "aid" (施) or "feed," as Williams (2007, 199) puts it, the "Hungry Spirits" (餓鬼).

281. The Buddhist "All-Souls-Day," a festival for the ancestors in August, was named after one of the fates of dead spirits. The respective Sanskrit term is *ullam-bana*, in Japanese *urabon* (盂蘭盆). It originally means the torture of those "hanged at their ankles." This can become the fate of those souls of the dead that are not redeemed (Takemura and Tamura 1984b, 1611).

(Berentsen 1985a, 85), thus controlling the living.[282] The unity between the living and the dead is safeguarded with benevolent protection and punishing warnings (1985b, 267).[283] Therefore those who died in a particularly unfortunate way have to be "appeased and reconciled" (Okano 1976, 98–99). Victims of violent death become ancestral spirits of the highest rank, so-called *goryou* (御霊), because they need to be appeased more than others. The respective ritual is called *chinkonsai* (鎮魂際),[284] "festival for the appeasement of souls" (Naumann 1984b, 1631).[285]

All scholars of Japanese animism agree that the main function of the Japanese shamans is the communication and mediation between the living and the dead. Therefore, there has always been a connection between Japanese shamanism and ancestral rituals. Today the role of shamans (in Japan mainly female shamans) is not as important as in the past, but they are still active as mediums. Through the medium, the bereaved learn what the dead demand. Then they can act respectively. This is an essential part of the *kuyou* (供養),[286] the salvic rites for the dead (Berentsen 1985a, 86).

The living are dependent on the dead

On the other hand, the living owe everything to their forebears. Using the example of the sect *Gedatsukai* (解脱会), literally the "society of liberation," Sugiyama-Lebra shows that "one's own achievements are owed to countless benefactors, no matter whether they are known or unknown, living or dead." She concludes, "Each individual is born with an overwhelming obligation towards his or her forebears . . . Japanese feelings of guilt are founded in awareness of obligation." In this context, *kansha* (感謝), "thankfulness," is equated with *zange* (懺悔), "remorse" (Sugiyama-Lebra 1982, 274). The main element of this kind of piety is thankfulness, which in turn is a main motive of

---

282. One of the motives for suicide is to become a powerful revengeful spirit and take revenge on the living (Gundert 1874, 4).

283. Today the fear of the curses of the dead plays only a subordinate role (Berentsen 1985a, 85). Many seek to contact the dead for the sake of communion and other benefits (86). Others oppose Berentsen and claim that fear is still a prominent sentiment (Goss and Klass 2005, 30).

284. As the term *chinkonkishin* (鎮魂帰神) shows, *chinkon* (鎮魂) can also mean the appeasement of the soul of a living person. *Chinkonkishin* (鎮魂帰神) means "return (帰) to the divine (神) through spiritual (魂) quietude (鎮)."

285. In the Japanese sect *Gedatsukai* (解脱会), misfortune is generally attributed to a lack of thankfulness, *kansha* (感謝), and a lack of *zange* (懺悔), "remorse" (Sugiyama Lebra 1982, 274).

286. *Kuyou* (供養) is a kind of Japanese requiem mass. The term consists of "offer" (供) and "provision" (養).

ancestor veneration. Children feel an unlimited burden of *on* (恩), "obligation", towards their parents. But this obligation binds them not only to their parents, but also to their parents' parents, the ancestors. Each individual understands himself as the recipient of unlimited benefits and knows that he has to pay it back (Berentsen 1985a, 67).

In this way ancestors and descendants are interconnected by obligation (Berentsen 1985a, 67). Particularly the living experience this obligation is a heavy and conflicting burden:

> Recalling his or her relationship with the deceased, the survivor feels all kinds of regret . . . Part of the feeling is a kind of guilt, but it is more complex, in that the person is also regretting being obliged to feel that sense of guilt. Although the feeling is self-reproach, it is in some way also resentment toward the deceased or fate . . . In short, the survivor experienced some kind of conflict with the deceased during his lifetime, but managed not to become obsessive (*ki-ga sumanai*, 気がすまない) . . . Once the other person is dead, however, it is no longer possible to dispose of his feelings (*ki-o sumasu*, 気をすます). However "vexed" (*kuyashii*, 悔しい) the survivor feels at not having done some particular thing while the other was still alive, it is now too late. The result is that the survivor surrenders to the emotions of *kuyami* (悔やみ) (regret at having allowed the obligation to continue in such a way that it is now impossible to satisfy) . . . The survivor ends up with a feeling of sadness, which is not just sadness at being left, but it's the sadness of self-blame, that the relationship that was full of ambivalence did not get solved so the survivor remains in the deceased's debt. (Goss and Klass 2005, 40)

Another connection between the living and the *living dead* is that the dead return the favors of the living by protecting them as *ujigami* (氏神), "family patron deities" (Hori 1987, 202). The host of ancestral souls is guardian of "weal and woe of the family" (Naumann 1984b, 1631). This puts them on the same level as the gods and object of *suuhai* (崇拝), "veneration" (Berentsen 1985a, 88).

In summary, the Japanese ancestor veneration has two ethical functions:[287]

---

[287]. It is not just in Japan that the ancestors are considered the guardians of morals. The ancestors of the Igala people in Nigeria (Oyibo 2004, 115), the Nyakyusa people in East Africa (Hartung 2005, 279), and the Koreans (Kranewitter 2005, 45) have similar functions.

(1) One function is concerned with its content: Through veneration for the ancestors, ethical values are passed on. In the past, the hamlet communities were mainly held together by the adherents to common ancestors. "Nothing was more effective to rural Japanese than the appeal of common ancestry to cement the hamlet-collectivity" (Yamamori 1974, 21). The living family members carried out the hereditary will of the ancestors (Berentsen 1985a, 66). Even today the will of the ancestors is very important. If one family member dishonors the ancestors this can lead to the father's resignation from the company or even his suicide (Kitamura 1985, 53–54).

> Since the ancestors are regarded as "living" members of the family, the decisive point in this connection is that the individual and the family at any time should know themselves to be in harmony with the will of the forebears. That will be the ultimate one, and with ultimate will is ultimate authority. (Berentsen 1985b, 265)

(2) The other function is concerned with its form: Ancestor veneration not only determines ethical values but also formal criteria of ethical behavior:

> Within the primary social nexus of the family no one plays his or her own game. The prosperity, unity, harmony, and honor of the house is considered the *summum bonum*. The ultimate ethical criterion, therefore, is neither to be found in universal standards transcending the social group, nor in individual happiness and edification. Whether the interests of the family – including living and dead – are served or not, is ultimately the standard applied for a proper distinction between moral and immoral conduct. (Berentsen 1985b, 265)

2.5.3 Evaluation of Some Aspects of Japanese Sociology

2.5.3.1 Individualism and collectivism

The question whether the Bible favors individualism or collectivism is of great importance, and Christian scholars discuss it with great diversity. This question also has a significant bearing on soteriology, because the answers to it determine the very meaning of salvation. In his speech "Proclaiming the Kingdom of God among Animists and Secularists" presented at the symposium "Distinctively Christian, Distinctly Mongolian" in Ulaanbaatar, Mongolia, in 2003, Van Rheenen approached the subject starting out from sociology. Individualism as "intense" as in the West is "foreign to most animistic peoples." This observation is very important for Van Rheenen because the individualistic approach of evangelism which aims for an "individual conversion" with its emphasis on "the human response to God . . . rather than the sovereign working of God in the world" can hardly be acceptable in animistic societies. The approach of individual conversion is correct, yet at the same time incomplete. Western missionaries are well aware of this narrow understanding of conversion. But "unfortunately Westerners have tended to separate the reign of God from personal salvation." This is unfortunate because "while individualists believe they can chart their own courses, animists believe that they are living in an interconnected world." They cannot imagine a life "separate and apart from his extended family, spiritual powers, nature, or thoughts of other human beings. Animists live in an interconnected universe" (Van Rheenen 2003b).

Worldviews are like eyeglasses. Western worldviews with their emphasis on individualism are not more or less correct than animistic worldviews with their emphasis on the connectedness of the individual with the world around them. Problems only arise when adherents of either worldview are not willing to learn from each other. There is nothing wrong with Western individualists learning from animists that there are other things more important than Self. And animists can learn new strategies from individualists that can be helpful and liberating in predicaments their own worldview cannot solve.

Künneth connected "original sin" and "historic-political" "original guilt." His observation has a bearing on the subject at hand:

> Every historic-political life is a product and an execution of an original guilt. Therefore, every political existence partakes in that original guilt of humanity, which is identical with the theological term original sin. Original sin is the trans-subjective reality of all history as the proceeding *urgrund* [primal cause] from which all political life springs and which determines all political action . . . In this sense the term collective guilt can be used. Collective guilt, however, is not a collective indebtedness of a nation or a group of people, but an expression of the guilt of humanity, substantiated in the interlacement of guilt of all nations. (Künneth 1954, 431)

In addition, this question is of ethical importance. Drawing on MacIntyre, Kaminsky writes, "This fundamental shift of focus toward the rights of the individual that occurred during the Enlightenment is the direct cause of the current crisis in moral theory" (Kaminsky 1995, 180). The reason for this crisis is the "disparagement of other societies, be they earlier or contemporary, that focus less on the rights of the individual and more on the individual's responsibilities to society" (Kaminsky 1995, 179–180).

To engage in dialogue with these positions I am going to outline the two controversial positions before attempting the draft of a possible synthesis.

The preference for individualism

"The biblical faith starts with this historically unprecedented charter of autonomous and free individuals" (Mendenhall and Herion 2001, 58). The "individualism in Western culture" is "primarily a fruit of the Christian mission" (Bosch 1993, 416). Thomas Aquinas argues that authentic evangelism has a "personal dimension," because the gospel is "the announcement of a personal encounter, mediated by the Holy Spirit, with the living Christ, receiving his forgiveness and making a personal acceptance of the call to discipleship" (Thomas in Bosch 1993, 416). As German and North American representatives of individualism argue differently I am going to outline their arguments separately:

German individualism

The Wellhausen-disciple, Smend, called Wellhausen an "individualist of the highest order"[288] (Smend in Wellhausen VIII [Foreword]). Wellhausen (371) perceived the gospel as "noblest individualism." He interpreted Ezekiel 33:10–11 thus:[289]

> Here he uses "individualism as a basis of consolation" . . . Against the despair fearing to mire in the sinful context of the whole, he emphasizes the option of conversion. The oral freedom places a heavy responsibility on the individual, but it also grants him the consolation that he can break away from causality, that he can be converted and live. (Wellhausen 2004, 146)

Calling the "gospel" the "noblest individualism" clearly shows that Wellhausen presupposed the evolution of individualism through the age of the Old Testament. Wellhausen's disciple argued that this development took place mainly in the age of the prophets, sparked off by Isaiah's talk of the "holy

---

288. *Einen Individualisten reinsten Wassers.*

289. In the given context of soteriology this quote is particularly interesting because individualism is made a basic prerequisite for receiving salvation. In this sense Gese wrote, "The question for the meaning of life first presupposes individualism, then a highly developed ego-feeling and self-awareness, which can desist from the embedding of the Self in the collective, in extended family, clan, and tribe, which considers life solely under the individual aspect" (Gese 1991, 170).

remnant" (Smend 2002, 68). In the same way Gunkel stood for an evolution of individualism. According to him, "the Old Testament yielded the ultimate good . . . of the orient – human personality leading its own life." According to Gunkel, the "birth of individualism" sprang solely from the religion of Israel and was perfected in the New Testament (Oden 1999, 31). As Smend he also understood the prophetic message as the crucial contribution toward the development of individualism:

> The most important influence of the prophets was . . . that the psalmists learned from their lofty examples to despise formal worship. Because of that the poetry of the Psalms gathered decisive momentum. Originally stemming from the cult and most intimately connected with the same the poetry of the Psalms now turned its back on it. The pious souls had learned to sing songs desisting from all outward actions, not determined by the public worship anymore. And at the same time the immense individualism of the prophets returns: the soul steps into the presence of its God. (Gunkel 1985, 30)

North American individualism

North American biblicism has its roots mainly in religious voluntarism, individualism, Bible production, and the belief in a central role of Christianity. Voluntarism and individualism belong together because in the West religion is a matter of free, individual choice. The religious entity is the individual. And individuals are religious if and when they chose to be religious (Malley 2004, 156).

According to Malley (156), this is the reason for the strong emphasis on personal salvation and personal faith.[290] As Marsden shows, North American biblicism and American individualism are closely related:

> The individual stood alone before God; his choices were decisive. The church, while important as a supportive community, was made up of free individuals. The Bible, moreover, was a great

---

290. Malley has a keen awareness of the problems of this thinking: The precedence of voluntarism forces churches to compete over individual's loyalty. As evangelicalism is not a trademark of certain churches, not even certain denominations, individuals easily move on to other churches if they get the impression that the individual needs are not met in a certain church. In such a context evangelical biblicism somehow "has to" work for individuals, meet their needs, and enhance their individual experience (Malley 2004, 156).

equalizer. With Bible in hand, the common man or woman could challenge the highest temporal authority. (Marsden 2006, 224)

Claiming the authority of the Bible as the bedrock of the North American evangelical individualism may prompt the idea that the Reformation was the true source of individualism. "The Medieval Church's top-down collectivism gave way to a new vision of Christianity that more closely paralleled the Renaissance's botton-up image of individualism" (McFaul 2006, 52).

> The individual and not the Church, became the source of authority for determining the nature of truth. For many writers, embracing the new individualism did not result in rejecting Christianity. They merely maintained that any view of the truth, including the Church's, had to be inherently persuasive to human reason and not imposed by some external authority that possessed the power to do so. (McFaul 2006, 52)

A thus interpreted Christianity understands individualism as "something eternal, something absolute," and it envisions the process of the universe as "wrestling for the salvation of the individual soul, which, depraved and degenerated, needs a mediator" (Patočka and Hagedorn 2005, 366).

The possibly most prominent representative of North American individualism is the Boston Personalism, founded by Bordon Parker Bowne (Deats 1986, 2) and from 1911 carried on by Albert Cornelius Knudson (Schilling 1986, 82). "Personalism is a philosophical perspective for which the person is the ontological ultimate and for which personality is the fundamental explanatory principle" (Deats 1986, 2).

The preference for collectivism

On the other side of the spectrum are those that cannot find anything like "our modern notion" of individualism, according to which "we are free to do whatever we please as long as we do not impose on the freedom of others" (Sleeper 1992, 150).

Collectivism in the Old Testament

Albertz claims without any discrimination that "no individualism in the modern sense has ever existed in the Bible at any point in its history" (Albertz in Schaack 1998, 312).

> A person was embedded[291] in his respective personal context, in the collective of the extended family or the tribal community to an extent we can hardly imagine today. One's subjectivity, that is, the individual's awareness as an acting and thinking person, was based in the familial community,[292] in the all-embracing and all-determining tribal community. The integration into the group is so strong that one can say that it is primarily the collective that lives; it is only through the collective that the individual lives. (Lee 2001, 121)

In a similar way Eichrodt judged that the Old Testament "never, at no situation and in no period, knew anything of religious individualism ... which gives a man a private relationship with God without connection to the community (Eichrodt 1967, 265). There are two reasons: First, proponents of Old Testament individualism consider the post-exilic period the heyday of individualism. Yet Walton et al. hold that the genealogies are evidence of the importance of family lineage, because it was citizenship in Israel that was the token for participation in God's covenant.

> Often in the ancient world, genealogies served sociological rather than historical functions. Instead of offering a strictly sequential report of the order of generations, they were designed to use continuity with the past as an explanation of the current structure and condition of society. Continuity with the past would give meaning to their current theological situation. Individuals in the ancient world found their identity not in their individualism but in their solidarity with the group. This included not only those that made up their contemporary kinship but extended throughout the generations. The genealogies were their way of fitting themselves into this pan-generational solidarity. (Walton et al. 2000, 413)

The second reason belongs to the area of collective penal law. Kaminsky explains the collective punishment of old Israel within the context of the "fundamentally corporate" notions of the covenant-concept of the Old Testament,[293] which "utilize earlier theological notions such as wrath, holiness, and bloodguilt" (Kaminsky 1995, 116). With many Bible references Kaminsky

---

291. *Geborgen.*
292. *Lebensgemeinschaft.*
293. Accordingly, A. Merx understands the collective of the nation the covenant partner of Jahwe, while others (M. Weber, M. Löhr and H. Gunkel) point to the individual (Otto 2002, 102).

shows "that God punished the whole group, because (1) one individual, (2) several individuals within the group, (3) the ruler of the group, or (4) earlier leaders or ancestors, erred. Further a nation as a whole group executed "corporal punishment" against a particular group, and rulers eliminated rivals in a corporative style, following sometimes a divine oracle (30).

Collectivism in the New Testament

The French linguist E. Benveniste stated that all of Homer's moral vocabulary was full of a power which is "not personal but relational." In Homeric thought humans have rights "not just because they are humans, but through defined relationships" (Adkins in Goldhill 1986, 81). In Homer's writing this becomes particularly obvious in the usage of the verbs φιλεῖν and αἰδεῖσθαι. The noun αἴδος is usually translated with "respect," "disgrace," or "esteem," and "particularly is used for the appropriate attitude toward members of one's own family or group" (Goldhill 1986, 80).

What is true for the Old Testament is in principle true for the New Testament. This has to be considered particularly when discussing overall concepts of theology. In his book, *Paul and the Salvation of the Individual*, Burnett wrote on Romans 1:16–17: "In Old Testament thinking . . . righteousness (Hebrew root צדק) is a much more rational concept, where people are judged righteous in terms of fulfilling the demands of a relationship" (118).

According to Reinhardt, New Testament ecclesiology strongly emphasizes "being-together" (ἐπὶ τὸ αὐτὸ), connected with a "relevance of perseverance" (προσκαρτερεῖν). This "becomes apparent in the church's fundamental way of life, in common prayer, in expectant reading of the Scriptures, in sharing of experiences with God, in worship services characterized by joy and God's holiness" (349). Bonhoeffer established the necessity of the Christian community, the necessity of the church-collective, by referring to the "alien righteousness of the reformers." That means "that a Christian is dependent on the word of God, spoken to him" by and through other Christians. Because the Christian desires the righteousness of God "he desires the liberating word again and again."

> It can come only from the outside . . . But this word God has put into the mouth of humans, so that it may be shared among humans. Whenever one is confronted by the word, he shares this very word with others. It is the will of God that we may seek and find his word in the testimony of the brother, in the mouth of

humans. Therefore, the Christian needs the Christian who shares God's word with him. (Bonhoeffer 1985, 14)

According to Bonhoeffer, the fellowship of the church is an eternal fellowship (1985, 15–16), an ideal entity, but a "pneumatic reality" (1985, 18). "Self" blocks the entrance into this fellowship, because without Christ, who is "our peace" (Eph 2:14) "we would not know . . . the brother and could never come to him" (1985, 15).

But not only inside the church but also outside, that is in relationship to the state, collectivism determined the political moral of the New Testament. "Even though Christ Pantocrator[294] is immeasurably superior to all principalities, and even though earthly principalities are used as tools of the demonic, the Christian's duty of obedience [to secular power] is beside every discussion" (Künneth 1954, 53).

> The civic obligations result . . . from Rome's fundamental constitutional law. Not only are Christians not allowed to evade them, they are even obliged to fulfill them in an exemplary manner, because they have deeper and true insight in the origin and purpose of earthly authorities' empowerment. (Künneth 1954, 37)

This "submission to governing authorities," however, must be clearly demarcated from the so-called *Kadavergehorsam*, from brutishly blind obedience. *Kadavergehorsam* means, "that the obedient subject . . . is not a responsible person anymore, but degraded to a will-less and sub-human thing" (Künneth 1954, 384). According to Künneth, there are several demarcations between *Kadavergehorsam* and obedience:

- a religious demarcation: "We must obey God rather than men!" (Acts 5:29; 4:19). This demarcation is applicable for the Christian self-propagation, for the faith, and for acts of Christian love. If these basic religious rights are infringed, disobedience to the state's authority becomes a Christian duty;
- an ethical demarcation: whenever a Christian is forced to "carry out actions or take part in any such things that are in conflict with God's commands" (Künneth 1954, 385) he must choose disobedience;

---

294. *Christus als Weltenherr.*

- a demarcation of human rights: whenever a Christian is forced to take actions that depreciate or annihilate humanity (Künneth 1954, 386) he must choose disobedience.

The socio-anthropological background

In his inaugural lecture as Mitchell's successor, Knudson most clearly expressed the concept of development from collectivism to individualism:

> The Old Testament is the connecting link between "heathenism" and Christianity, and . . . Christianity is the consummate religion of rational personality. To study the Old Testament . . . is to trace the process in and beyond Hebrew religion "from superstition to rationality, from sorcery and divination to rational faith, from particularism to universalism, and from nationalism to individualism. The Bible is a narrative of progressing enlightenment. (Dorrien 2003, 291)[295]

Kaiser named the "bias for collectivism" among the "magical elements" of the Israelite religion. H. Wheeler Robinson used the term *corporate personality* even back in 1911, and as his studies showed, this concept was influenced by Durkheim and Lévy-Bruehl. Their concepts of "totemistic" and "pre-logic" psychology were most influential on Robinson. Even though he "never understood the Israelite religion as totemistic, he understood the ancient Israelites in the same way as anthropologists understand "primitive peoples" (Kaminsky 1995, 17).

The development from "pre-logic to logic mentality" and from collectivism to individualism has been questioned per se (Schäfer-Lichtenberger 1983, 4) and in new independent studies which show that the development from individualism to collectivism can also be observed (in the proverbs) (Hausmann 1995, 103). Scharbert wrote on Exodus 34:6, "that the history of the formula does not show us a development from collectivism to individualism." It is rather evidence for "a general theological clarifying and unfolding of a thought that was there from the beginning" (Scharbert in Kaminsky 1995, 117). And Pohlmann and Rudnig (2001, 263) write against the presumption that Ezekiel 18:2 is a testimony for Old Testament individualism.

I am convinced that "evolutionist" approaches are, particularly when maintained in the context of dialogue with other cultures, ugly evidence of

---

295. The common ground with Wellhausen's evolutionism (Harrison 1969, 381) cannot be overlooked.

a totally inappropriate Western presumptuousness. Western scholars and communicators have to hear how pointedly Nakane, as a protagonist of Japanese collectivism, opposes Western thinking that considers collectivism a "primitive" form, and individualism the most advanced (Nakane 1978, 12). Evolutionist approaches presuppose "advanced" and "primitive" states. Such categories are rather offending for people whose ways of thinking are implicitly or explicitly called "primitive." Such judgment tells little about the other person, but reveals all the more the intellectual poverty of one's own ethnocentrism. In Japan collectivism is – and will be – very much alive (Coll et al. 1998, 137). But that does not mean that Japan is "primitive."

Towards a meaningful synthesis

As much as Bosch spoke in favor of an individualistic interpretation of the gospel, just as resolutely did he oppose "modern" individualism: "Even so, the Gospel is not individualistic. Modern individualism is, to a large extent, a perversion of the Christian faith's understanding of the centrality and responsibility of the individual" (Bosch 1993, 416). In post-modernism individualism is central, together with relativism, materialism, and hedonism. If there is no base for judgment and if all ethical decisions are equally valid, then only ego-centered benefit is important. In individualism self-indulgence is the highest priority. Relative morality and relative truth are necessities to maintain this self-indulgence. Such individualism necessarily fosters the arrogance of narcissism. Materialism fills the thoughts, the emotions, and the identity of those narcissists as they strive to provide for their desires (Lightner 1998, 199). This is the "perversion" of modern individualism.

Speaking against the dichotomy between collectivism and individualism

Under the headline, "The Individual and the Community in the Old Testament God-Man Relationship," Eichrodt laments the "reproaches frequently leveled at the Old Testament," that it "never overcomes its fixation on the collective" especially if contrasted with "an assessment of the New Testament as the realization of a God-Man relationship that is supposedly purely individualistic." Clarification is difficult, because of "the ill-defined and inadequate delimitation of the concepts 'individualism' and 'collectivism'":

> For the most part, collectivism is understood as an impersonal attitude to the holy, guided by mass-instincts or sacred tradition, and ruling out any individual shaping of thought and action. By contrast, individualism is defined as that spiritual state which

affirms its own existence without regard for any collective ties of nation or cult community, and seeks to develop its own attitude to God and the world. (Eichrodt 1967, 231–232)

This distinction as a product of "philosophical idealism" cannot be transferred "to the condition of ancient society" (Eichrodt 1967, 232) which is also true for present-day Japan. In Japan there is no rigid either-or and the fact that the individual is not as important as the community does not mean that the community totally neglects the individual. To thus interpret Japanese collectivism would do injustice to sociological material (Berentsen 1985a, 67).

Collectivism and individualism belong together as living unity. They cannot be juxtaposed in an either-or pattern but belong together in an as-well-as pattern, because individuals need the collective: (1) They are dependent in a physical and economical way:

> The clan as a closely integrated unit not only determines the external structure of society, but ensures that the common life of the member of the clan is founded on a spiritual and physical unity in which each individual is a representative of the whole, and in turn has his entire private attitude to life shaped by the whole. This distinctive sense of belonging is rooted in the structure of patriarchal society, where the father of the tribe[296] molds the life

---

296. At first sight it seems strange to compare modern Japan with nomadic clan-societies, but a deeper comparison with what Hiebert and Meneses call "tribal societies" shows an overwhelming congruence. They rightly claim that defining an ethnic group "with a language, a culture, and a land breaks down as societies become more complex" (85). The mere size of the Japanese population and the unconscious equation of "complex" with "advanced" leads to the assumption that Japan must be a complex society. But nothing could be further from the truth as the following features of tribal societies, drawn from Hiebert and Meneses (85–97) show: common ethnic origin, common language, "strong pattern of interaction based on intermarriage or presumed kinship," common territory, common culture, "the group, not the individual, is the primary building block of tribal societies," "kinship ties remain the center of life and are used to perform the major functions of social life," "life in tribes . . . is based on families and local communities," "families and communities are linked together in higher-level social systems that can include millions of people and cover large territories. A tribe can be seen as a family of families of families," "two factors influence the passing of blood from generation to generation: marriage and descent," while in loose organizations of band societies, a high value is placed on compatibility and companionship in marriage, in the more structured tribal societies, marriage serves other important social functions, such as providing the offspring that perpetuate the extended family, lineage, and tribe," highly differentiated sex-roles, strong patriarchs, "men do not spend much time at home, may live and even sleep in the men's house," family life centers on the mother-child bond, "the children's primary ties are to their mother," "a person's identity and significance . . . depends on his or her membership in a particular lineage or clan, rather than on his personal uniqueness and skills," "kinship ties extend beyond the living" and "to the unborn." All these characteristics apply to the Japanese society.

of his great family both externally and internally, and occupies the place of decisive importance for the tribal destiny. By descent from him the members of the tribe are incorporated as kinsmen in a family community, and welded into a social unit outside which there can be no meaningful life for the individual, since he would be abandoned to every kind of danger without the protection of law ... It is a legacy from the father of the tribe that the tribal order is unassailable and binding on every member; but at the same time it also bestows wellbeing and peace on all who belong to the community. (Eichrodt 1967, 233)[297]

(2) They are dependent in a psychological way. The group provides a way of "sensing and conceiving ourselves, which in turn gives us the ground for a more effective, more integrated experience of living and working with others." The me-boundary does not separate the individual from the collective but "defines me and at the same time integrates me in a livable way into a shared world." Psychological dependence is defined not only by self-demarcation but also provides the content of one's own self, which is "inter-subjective in that it constructs its own process out of a field which includes the inner worlds of other[s]" (Goodman in Wheeler 2000, 109).[298] (3) They are dependent in a religious way. Despite the "hyper-individualism" of "contemporary Protestantism" there are "voices in both Protestantism and the Bible" that "reject the flight to individualism" and rather speak for

> an understanding of redemption as corporate, political, and communal, while at the same time deeply personal. Redemptive grace operates in community, through community, and for community. Each person's redemption is inextricably linked with the redemption and redemptive activity of the community. (Snyder 2000, 64)

This is illustrated in Abraham's petition for Sodom and Gomorrah. Abraham is not concerned with "liberating the innocent from the city," but he struggles with the question, "What determines God's verdict over Sodom? – The iniquity of the many or the innocence of the few?" This narration is not concerned with a controversial discussion of collectivism and individualism, but with a new

---

297. This quote shows the parallels between biblical collectivism and Japanese collectivism. It also connects collectivism to two key-elements of the biblical salvation-concept: protection and peace.

298. Wheeler quotes from Paul Goodman's *Novelty, Excitement and Growth* (1951).

type of collectivism in which a minority may make God "offer a reprieve for the collective" (von Rad 1987, 167).

Speaking for the co-existence of collectivism and individualism

Goffman studied strongly collectivistic social groups such as institutions. He found that even in a strongly collectivistic context, Self does not disappear completely no matter how much it is adapted to the group. There is always something left, something that lets the human be "Self." Goffman called this "Self" "inner self" or "naked self" (Goffman in Burnett 2001, 25). Collectivism and individualism can very well co-exist, even under extreme circumstances. This is also true for Japan as Kitayama (北山修) claims:

> It has been pointed out that there exists an other-centered tendency in the East, in which people pay much attention to the position of others and the relationship between self and others, and that there is a self-centered tendency in which people put priority on the individual in the West. The difference, however, is superficial, and it is quite possible that there is self-centered tendency behind the outward other-centered tendency. (Kitayama 2005, 42)

The dynamics of a society are driven by individuals as well as by collective and structural elements. This basic rule is also true for the Old Testament and Hellenistic Judaism which show that "Judaism had a rich heritage of emphasis on the individual and his responsibility to God, alongside a fundamental focus on community (Burnett 2001, 87). Eichrodt explains this coexistence as follows:

> The religious faith of the Old Testament helped religious individuality come to life in a context of strong collective ties, because it understood God's demands to the nation as at the same time a call to the individual, imposing upon him an obligation of unconditioned loyalty even when the call ran counter to the natural bonds of community. (Eichrodt 1967, 265)

Lennan described the coexistence between the individual and the collective in the church as founded on giving and taking. On one hand, all the members of the church are edified by the individual's unique experience of Jesus. On the other, the church unites the individual with an experience of Jesus which expands over ages and cultures, an experience an individual could never make in his or her lifespan. Being thus dependent on the church, the individual is liberated from the limitations of individualism (Lennan 1998, 21).

In his *Die christliche Ethik,* Schlatter even goes beyond that when he explicitly calls the collective of the Christian church to its responsibility to create and preserve *Freiraum*, literally "space of freedom," for the individual. It is the church's "right and duty" to "proclaim the word to each [member] in a way that he is personally moved." This responsibility is fulfilled only then, when "the individual has received the connection with God in his own acts of life" (Schlatter 1961a, 196).

> Thus the Christian community creates our independence, provides us with an inner property exclusively ours, and bestows on every [individual] solitariness and uniqueness, which the community not only tolerates or allows, but which is expected from all of the community as their duty, because this duty guides all to personally stand before God. (Schlatter 1961a, 132)

A model

"Human beings are personal yet communal" (Augsburger 1995, 107). Just how, then, do collectivism and individualism belong together? When discussing this question it is important in which context it is discussed, lest it yields apparently contradicting results.

The discussion in the philosophical context

If the subject of collectivism and individualism is discussed in the philosophical context, there are Christian theologians that conclude that God created humans as individuals responsible to him. Christianity stresses "personal responsibility and personal decision" (Bosch 1993, 416). As a conclusion drawn in the context of philosophical discussion I share this stance.

Buddhist philosophers or Christian theologians influenced by Buddhism come to a different conclusion. They hold that man is one part of the great whole. According to Nishida (1870–1945), "individuals are unified ... with Absolute, so that the Individual and the Absolute form a unity." Since 1927 Nishida called this "oneness" *basho* (場所)[299] (Yagi 2002, 33; Buri 1997, 41).

According to Nishida's disciple Keiji Nishitani (西谷啓治) (1900–1990), *basho* (場所) or *topos* is the sphere of the transcendent-immanent power. The individuals in this "sphere" are fashioned thus that they infinitely permeate each other. This "sphere" is a genuine Buddhist term, the Japanese for *śunyatā*,

---

299. Nakane discusses collectivism and individualism in the sociological context. She carefully avoids the theologically defined term *basho* (場所) and uses *ba* (場) instead. Linguistically both terms mean the same, "place."

which is "emptiness." Buri talks about "the sphere of Nothingness around which Buddhist thought has ever revolved" (1997, 41). In this thought system individuals do not resemble the atom in its original sense of the word, but they have their identity in their mutual relationships (Yagi 2002, 34). As a pioneer of the Christian-Buddhist dialogue in Japan, Takizawa[300] attempted to amalgamate the two positions by interpreting Christianity in a Buddhist way. His elementary thesis is that "no matter what a man is or what he is not, regardless of whether he has a religion, and if, no matter what religion he has, [he has] an elementary foundation as a basis of his self-being." Leaning on Barth, Takizawa called this primordial fact "Immanuel." "This primordial fact presupposes that mankind is in God." Takizawa called this primordial fact "unity of God mankind," "Christ," and "God's first contact with mankind." However, not every human being is aware of this primordial fact. Religious life with awareness generates only if awakened. In contrast to the "primordial fact" of "God's first contact with mankind," Takizawa called this awakening "God's second contact with mankind (Yagi 2002, 36; Miyahira 2008, 124).

Martin Buber opposes this Buddhist doctrine of "not-self":

> God embraces the universe, yet he is not the universe. In the same way, he embraces my own self, yet he is not my own self. There is "I and You," there is dialogue, there are language and spirit, whose first act is language. And there is in eternity the word. (Buber in Geering 2015, 167)

Takeo Doi, strongly influenced by Christianity, demanded that the Zen-Buddhist undifferentiated unification of subject and object be overcome. According to him it is important to "transcend" *amae* (甘え), "interdependence," through the discovery of subject and object. "If we are graced to live, breathe, think, and act as free humans, responsible to ourselves, this is solely and exclusively the influence of the Christian teaching of the freedom of each human." This freedom goes, says Doi, with the "personal faith in a transcendent God" (Miyata 1984, 185–186). The catechism of the *Yukinoshita-Church* (雪ノ下教会) in Kamakura is a testimony of this knowledge. In this catechism the joy of being a child of God is explained with the fact that man, being created in the image of God, finds his "true self" in the encounter with God himself (Katou 2005, 26).

---

300. On his theology see Ihsen (2000, 1347–1358).

The discussion in the sociological context

If the subject of collectivism and individualism is discussed in the context of sociology the results are different. God not only created humans as individuals, he also ordained that they would receive life through their parents, that they would be born into families, and that they would be socialized into societies. The relationship between collectivism and individualism can be visualized as follows:

Table 2.5 Relationship between Collectivism and Individualism

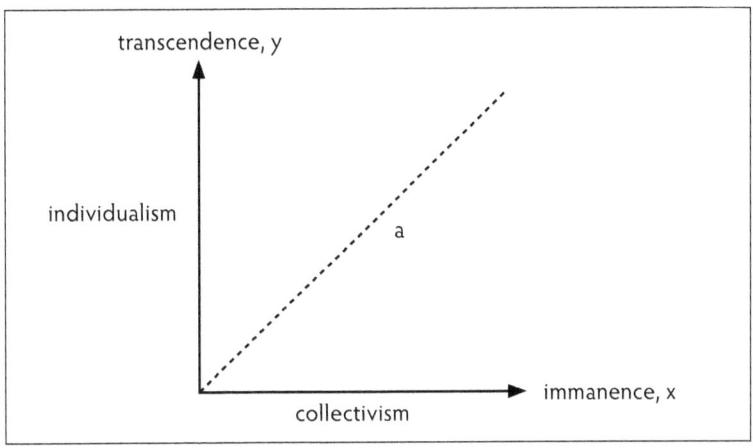

The x-axis stands for the immanent orientation, usually correlated with a focus on the collective. The y-axis stands for the transcendent orientation. The immanent x-axis gives priority to collectivism, the transcendent y-axis to individualism. The ideal balance between individualism and collectivism is depicted with the straight line "a." Both extremes, the exclusively transcendent-individualistic orientation (no matter how many "Christian" arguments it lines up), and the exclusively immanent-collectivistic orientation, are equally dangerous, as they destroy both the collective and the individual. This can be seen in their extreme protagonists Japan and the United States of America.

Japan as an example for extreme collectivism

The phrase *sekensama* (世間様) portrays the ethical orientation of an extremely collectivistic-oriented society in an almost iron way. *Seken* (世間) or *sekentai* (世間体) (Lundell 1995, 405) stand for "society." They are compounds formed of the Chinese characters for "world" (世), "between" (間), and "body" or "entity" (体). To *seken* (世間) then the honorific *sama* (様) is added. This ironically alludes to *kamisama* (神様), the common Japanese word for "god" or "God." Ethical positions are not adopted according to the will of *kamisama* (神様), particularly not according to the will of a transcendent God, but with regard to *sekensama* (世間様), to society (Yasuda 2004, 31).

> The width of one's community *seken* (世間) depends on one's way of life. For the farmer cultivating his land in a little farm village, *seken* (世間) is only his regional society and its inhabitants. However, for Prime Minister Koizumi [*seken* (世間)] is all Japan. Sometimes Japanese behave more unabashedly and more shamelessly abroad than in Japan. The reason is that the community for which he feels shame is restricted to his home country. When travelling, particularly abroad, he doesn't have to be ashamed. (Yasuda 2004, 31)

Dietrich and Luz ask why the Bible is read more among Japanese intellectuals than among Western intellectuals. They find that this is due to their cultural crisis. This crisis generates from the fact that in Japan the individual is second not just to the collective, but that also in the realm of religion the individual has to understand himself as being in relation to a trans-individual *urgrund* (primal cause). In this crisis it is important for Japanese to find their own identity to which end they turn to the Bible as a source of Western individualism – and as a heritage of the whole world (Dietrich and Luz 2002, ix).

The crisis Dietrich and Luz speak of is by no means new. As Künneth's mass-concept shows this crisis harbors great dangers:

> "Mass," . . . a new form of existence of man, co-determining body and mind, means enforced conformity of the soul and the spiritual life, of will and feeling direction, of the goal of life and way of life. A nation subject to the process of massification becomes an amorphous, inorganic entity, devalued to a mere conglomeration of humans. (Künneth 1954, 217)

Künneth names five things that lead to this conglomeration of humans: (1) urban centers with their anonymity and atomization of historically grown structures of society, typically observed in urban centers worldwide; (2) long-term dependence on an hyper-individual economic power; (3) mass-media as the technical means for manipulation of the masses, leading to serfdom under the public opinion; (4) the individual "growing into the mass" the more he submits to its authority;[301] and (5) the formation of mass-organizations (Künneth 1954, 218).

> The inner precondition for massification is religious rootlessness. It leads to the loss of the center of life and the principle doubt of the foundation of life. Relinquishing the relationship with God as supporting and binding power leads to the loss of structure, to the disintegration of framework of meaning. (Künneth 1954, 219)

Le Bon (*Psychologie der Massen*, 1895/1935) names four things that lead to massification. They are particularly interesting because they are applicable to the Japanese society:

- "Extraordinary experience of value": "Through belonging to the masses the individual experiences the feeling of safety, the feeling of being protected and carried." This gives a sense of power and superiority to the individual. "Thus man is given the highest satisfaction of his self-awareness and craving for recognition."
- "The reduction of the rational awareness and perception" as well as the "steep decrease of previous intellectual capacities" is characteristic. "The common consciousness is forced out by the unleashing of blind instincts, the clarity of reason by the heightening of affects and emotions."
- "Irresponsibility" becomes the decisive "ethical-religious factor,"[302] through immersion into the masses and into anonymity. "The masses totally equalize the individual, so that the individual is not recognizable as a person anymore." "Abandoning responsibility, however, leads to the abandoning of personality and consequently rejection of the ethos. As the masses paralyze the function of the conscience, the metaphysical contact is interrupted as well. The mass person is a person without responsibility – and without conscience.

---

301. *Man*-Hörigkeit. The Japanese equivalent is *sekensama* (世間様) discussed above.

302. It is quite telling that there is no Japanese equivalent for the English "responsibility" or the German *Verantwortung*. The dictionaries usually give *sekinin* (責任), which instead means *nin* (任), the task, duty, obligation, or jurisdiction, one can be *semeru*(ed) (責める), "sued" or "prosecuted," if found with fault. "In legal right this word means . . . liability" (Yasuda 2004, 32–33). According to my knowledge, there is no Japanese equivalent for the English "responsibility" in the sense of "duty to answer." When talking about human responsibility toward God I therefore don't use the term *sekinin* (責任), but I explain with other words, that man has to answer to God's questions about his life.

Ultimately, the mass person is the man without God." This leads to ethical disinhibition.
- The masses are easily influenced and lead. Le Bon talks about "suggestibility" (Künneth 1954, 220–221).

The United States of America as an example of extreme individualism

I chose the United States of America as an example of extreme individualism, because they have been pioneering Western thought for decades. On one side, legal scholars presuppose the guiding principle of the "free self"[303] according to which society consists of individuals who "regularize their relationships by means of contracts" (Rawls). This radical orientation on the transcendent and on individualism has led to a dangerous value loss.[304] On the other side, the Communitarian Platform (founded 1991) argues, that the American society is "sick" and "can only recover, if citizens care more for each other and form communities." Amitai Etzioni, one of the founders of the Communitarian Platform, aimed at "the strengthening of the moral foundation of society, the revival of values and primary virtues through the founding of communities that know each other and stand for shared moral positions." A society needs to be a "community of communities" (Nelle-Rublack 1999, 64–65). According to the Communitarian Platform, the United States of America has to move in the direction of collectivism. The political scientist M. Sandel (Harvard) claimed that "a society needs shared values and goals, as well as a consensus on what is to be considered good and what evil" (Nelle-Rublack 1999, 65).

2.5.3.2 Ancestor veneration and the Bible

I want to start this passage with three examples: one from the age of Japan's Christianization, one of the Japanese "church struggle (*Kirchenkampf*)," and one from the present. They all show the great importance of ancestor veneration, especially in dialogue with Christianity:

---

303. *Ungebundenes Selbst*.

304. The Muslim theologian, Hamayun A. Mughal, compared Japan and America from this point of view: "The individualism of Japan is an individualism without God. The concept of 'God and I' is unknown in Japan. The Japanese do *gasshou* (合掌) [Mughal refers to the putting together of both palms in order to show reverence; Japanese for the Sanskrit *Añjali Mudrā* or *praṇāmāsana*] when they come in contact with something mysterious or from nature. This mentality has enriched the heart of the Japanese nation . . . The 'God and I'-individualism of the American Christian mentality starts decaying and causes many different problems in America. The 'God and I'-individualism leads to the assumption of 'God on our side,' and that leads to war. Whoever believes in 'God on our side' is able to recklessly murder" (Mughal 2001, 106). Mughal admits that this is also true for Islam.

- Francis Xavier was once asked, "If one cannot be saved unless one believes in Christ and receives God's baptism, what happens with our ancestors?" "Even if they are ancestors, they went straight to hell," Xavier answered. This greatly grieved the Japanese and they started crying. And because they cried so hard, Xavier had to cry with them (Doi 1997, 106–107).
- In 1938 the Japanese government questioned Japanese pastors concerning their attitude towards the state ideology. Two of the nine questions of the survey dealt with the ancestors. These two questions were "What do you think about the ancestors and visiting the shrines?" And "What do you think about the ancestors of the Emperor?" (Videcom 1963, 24).
- In 1972 the Agency of Cultural Affairs published *Japanese Religion*. Concerning the small number of Japanese Christians they wrote that one of the reasons for the reluctant acceptance of Christianity was the Japanese religious orientation. Two points were mentioned: (1) Japan's focus on family and its preference for family-religion; and (2) Japan's almost instinctive inclination for the acceptance of an essential continuum between the Divine and the human. This religious orientation makes them feel uncomfortable about Christianity (Berentsen 1985a, 119).

Hwang harshly criticized missionaries,

> who still hold that ancestor cult is absolutely incompatible with the Christian faith and can in no way be tolerated as practice within the Church. These missionaries of goodwill seem hardly aware that this attitude results in new converts either leaving the Christian community or continuing to practice the cult in a secretive manner. It can also raise an unnecessary obstacle for many non-Christians, hindering them from experiencing explicitly the saving power of Christ. (Hwang 1977, 340)

A religion without any kind of ancestor veneration is practically not acceptable in Japan. Matteo Ricci claimed that Christianity would grow roots in a culture only when it was able to offer a Christian ancestor veneration (Shibata 1985, 250–251). Ancestor veneration is an "invariable of East-Asian religious history." There is an overall consensus that "human relationships are severed by death and therefore need to be preserved in the spirit of piety" (Malek 1992, 17). Ishizaka (石坂正信) saw the incompatible difference between

Western and Japanese attitudes toward ancestor veneration as an obstacle for the Christianization of Japan in the nineteenth century (Ishizaka 2009, 25). "Ancestor worship constitutes the very core of Japanese religiosity, and on the other side forms a basic cultural form for the Japanese" (Yewangoe 1987, 156).[305] "In respect to religion and society the life of the Japanese family is founded upon ancestor veneration" (Takeda 1976a, 119). According to Sugimoto (杉本良夫), Kunio Yanagita (柳田國男) (1875–1962), the father of indigenous Japanese ethnology, held that "faith in the ancestors was the key . . . to unhide the inner life of 'the Japanese' in its entireness" (Sugimoto in Lutum 2005, 234).[306] Ancestor veneration[307] "integrates" all religious systems (Turnbull 1998, 196), even though the term itself is more associated with Buddhism (Knecht 1986, 123).

Therefore the study of ancestor veneration is of highest missiological importance (Berentsen 1985b, 270). "Ancestor worship is undoubtedly a central element of Japanese native religiosity. In other words, the ancestors form an important part of 'the sacred' in Japan as well as in China and Korea, so that real enculturation cannot bypass that element" (Van Bragt 1992, 70). "Maintaining bonds with the dead has played a central role in the formation and transmission of religious traditions" (Goss and Klass 2005, 8). In negative terms, failure of integrating ancestor veneration has been the main obstacle for the Christianization of Japan (Ro in his foreword to Shibata's paper 1985, 247). If there is no enculturation in respect to ancestor veneration, the church remains "a colony of individuals uprooted from their homes because of their faith" (Yamamori 1974, 80). Dale claims that Japanese are simply afraid that a Christian funeral may separate them from their family (Dale 1998, 277).

The 1965 consultation of the Christian Conference of Asia (CCA) confessed that "the Asian Churches, so far, and in large measure, have not taken their

---

305. This is true not only for families but also for the thinking of the whole nation. "If the ancestors of a family have to be venerated how much more the founders of the nation? The position of the family head is that of the authority of the ancestors; the Throne is [the] place of the Sun-Deity. Father and mother are ancestors living in the present; the Emperor is the Sun-Deity living in the present. One is in filial piety devoted to one's parents and to the Throne for the very same reason; and the national doctrine combining both is that of ancestor veneration" (Hozumi in Aoki 2001, 145). Yatsuka Hozumi is the older brother of legal scholar Nobushige Hozumi quoted below.

306. The original text of Sugimoto has only "entireness" and not "inner life": *Sono soreishinkou-ga "nihonjin"-no subete-o tokiakasu kagi-ni naru* (その祖霊信仰が「日本人」の全てを解き明かす鍵になる), "This ancestor-faith becomes the key to clearly explain the entireness of 'the Japanese.'"

307. *Sosensuuhai* (祖先崇拝).

theological task seriously enough, for they have been largely content to accept the ready-made answers of Western theology or confessions." Van Bragt adds, "Fortunately, this is not the whole picture. There are in Japan, at the same time, people – philosophers rather than theologians, lay people rather than clerics[308] – who try to do theology, rethink their faith in the light of their Japanese inheritance" (Van Bragt 1992, 70–71).

Ancestor veneration in South Korea

In this context a comparison to the neighboring South Korea is interesting, not least because Christianity plays an important role there.[309] Is there a significant correlation between the fast growth of South Korea's Christianity and its attitude toward ancestor veneration?[310]

The Catholic Church at first rejected the Korean ancestor cult. Even though that led to persecution, it experienced strong growth (Wippermann 2000, 99). When "the Pope, solicited by missionaries to China, officially allowed the participation in the ancestor cult in 1929," this became a "turning point for the Catholic Church in Korea and its relationship to Korea's cultural tradition" (12,

---

308. This allegedly happens in encounters with Buddhism at the *Kyoto School of Philosophy*.

309. Underwood (1994) gives a short, well-done overview over the South Korean church history.

310. Cho names other reasons for the strong growth of the South Korean church: (1) syncretism between traditional shamanism and the charismatic movement of Christianity; (2) piety of the Korean Christian's religious life with their "hot passion of dawn prayer meetings"; (3) the adoption of the Nevius method or three-self plan with its emphasis on Bible study; (4) the turning away from the old Korean religions, Buddhism, Confucianism, and folk religion and turning to Christianity during the Japanese reign of terror; (5) separation of politics and religion in the light of the threat of the instrumentalization of Christianity by a stronger and stronger nationalism; (6) the turning away from sin in the 1907 revival (Cho 1998, 290–296). Young Kim-Sawa, the first Korean female pastor of a Japanese church, names five reasons: (1) Korean Christians are very sincere in their worship; (2) they pray very much; (3) they are very generous in donating offerings; (4) the Korean church is a church that has been committed to mission from the very beginning; (5) Korea suffered much from the neighboring super-powers, China and Japan, and can therefore identify with the Exodus-story; "the Korean people awaited the Messiah . . . I think that is why Koreans could easily accept Christianity" (Kim-Sawa 1987, 353). Besides the three-selves, that put heavy emphasis on each person sharing his or her faith, Underwood names the "spiritual vacuum with approximately 50 percent of the population claiming no religious affiliation" which let the church appear as "associated with modernism and nationalism, with education, and . . . with the improvement of the lot of women," as well as the fact that Korea is a person-oriented culture "where people are keenly aware of who is related to whom" and where "people . . . learn of religious affiliation of their friends, neighbors, and colleagues, making it easy to know whom to approach" concerning Christianity (Underwood 1994, 68–69).

99, 190).³¹¹ The Catholic Church imposed several conditions under which the participation was allowed, which served as demarcation against Confucianism: there must be no name tags or pictures representing the dead at the board set for the ancestors; ancestor rituals must not be interpreted as religious rituals, but must be considered as "cultural traditions" (190). In addition, the Catholic Church "consciously accommodated elements of the cultural tradition and gave those rituals a Christian interpretation" (116). The following testimony of a Korean woman, which shows a certain closeness to the Catholic concept of saints, illustrates:

> One day when I was six years old, one of my friends told me something she had learned in Sunday school: "You will go to hell if you continue to worship your ancestors!" This was a real shock to me, because I wanted to go to heaven. Soon, at the next ancestor worship, I asked my mother about the relationship between the Christian God and my ancestors. My mother answered that my ancestors were secretaries of Jesus Christ, who was a god to my mother. "Because Jesus Christ is so busy in heaven," she said, "he can't take care of every detail of our lives. That's why Jesus uses our ancestors as his secretaries to get things done." My mother's answer relieved me of the fear of going to hell. (Chung 1988, 64)

The protestant churches in South Korea do not have unitary regulations on ancestor veneration. At the beginning of their mission work in Korea protestant missionaries rejected ancestor veneration at large, following their praxis in China and Japan. "Anyone who wanted to become a Christian was required to renounce ancestor veneration" (Kranewitter 2005, 346). Some churches leave the decision whether to take part in ancestor veneration or not to their members. Other more conservative churches – and that is the majority of South Korean churches (Wippermann 2000, 17) – reject it. The reasons are partly of theological nature, mostly, however, of strategical nature, enforced to strengthen the seclusion and a stable group feeling within the church (191).

---

311. In a panel discussion on ancestor veneration in Africa the Roman-Catholic theologian Spaemann posed the following rhetorical question: "Is it not a great advantage of the Roman Catholic version of Christianity that the cult of the dead is given a legitimate place, in the veneration of the saints as well as in its relationship to the 'poor souls'" (Spaemann in a discussion documented by Koslowski 1985, 245). Of course this "advantage" can be interpreted in a negative way as the following remark on the Roman Catholic missionary work in the Philippines shows: "The mission work made great progress because the fathers tolerated the animism and the ancestor cults of the heathens (Koch 1984, 301).

Disambiguation

Before venturing into the dialogue between Japanese ancestor veneration and the Bible, terms and concepts of the Japanese context and of the biblical archeology need to be clarified.

Japanese terms and concepts

The most common Japanese term is *sosensuuhai* (祖先崇拝), "ancestor worship." As is often the case the most common terms are the least useful. Goss and Klass (20) call it "misleading" and lament the fact that there are no real alternatives. Japanese scholars like Takeda reject it at large because it was introduced only as an equivalent of the Western concept of "ancestor worship" (Nesbitt 2007, 64). *Suuhai* (崇拝) can mean "admiration," "adoration," "reverence," or "worship" (Goss and Klass 2005, 20). When the Catholic Church announced the Episcopal Commission in 1985, the term *sosensuuhai* (祖先崇拝) caused much confusion and anxiety. Many felt betrayed because they were anxious that the Catholic Church would want to return to what Christianity had just escaped from. They feared the church would abandon long-treasured values. Non-Christians as well as Protestants feared the revival of State-Shintoism (Knecht 1986, 138). The Protestant study group in the late 1950s, led by the liberal (Yagi and Swidler 1990, 50) theologian Masatoshi Doi studied the subject of ancestor veneration in a more differentiated way.[312] The survey forms clearly distinguished between *keii* (敬意), "respect," and *ogamu* (拝む), "to worship," or *kigan suru* (祈願する), "make a petition." There were 57.8 percent who considered their participation in ancestor rituals as *keii* (敬意), "respect," whereas only 3.3 percent said that this was *suuhai* (崇拝), "worship." The study group commented that the sentiment toward "ancestor worship" remained "rather strong" when Japanese become Christians. "However, through the instruction of the church, worship (*suuhai,* 崇拝) is consciously changed to respect (*keii,* 敬意)" (Berentsen 1985a, 138). In addition to *sosensuuhai* (祖先崇拝), "ancestor worship," the term *senzoreihai* (先祖礼拝), "worship service for the ancestors" is also used (Nakajou 1999, 119). Today, anthropologists prefer *sosen girei* (祖先儀礼), "ancestor etiquette," or *sosen saishi* (祖先祭祀), "ancestral rites" (Nesbitt 2007, 64).

According to the *Ruigojiten* (類語辞典),[313] the Japanese categorically distinguish between *keii suru* (敬意する), "pay respect," and *uyamau* (敬う)

---

312. In this survey 200 questionnaires were sent to churches of the United Church of Christ in Japan (UCCJ).

313. Dictionary for synonyms.

or *agameru* (崇める).³¹⁴ Contrary to *keii suru* (敬意する), *uyamau* (敬う) and *agameru* (崇める) can be used with gods and ancestors as objects.³¹⁵ *Toutobu suru* (尊ぶする), "adore," "cherish," which is hardly used anymore, can be used for humans and gods.³¹⁶ Depending on whether the ancestors are seen as humans or gods, different words are used. Thus the phrase *sosen-o uyamau* (祖先を敬う), "to venerate the ancestors (as gods)" (Watanabe 2005, 139; Yamashita 2003, 192), as well as the (rather rare) phrase *sosen-o agameru* (祖先を崇める), "worship the ancestors" (Takemitsu 2006, 83; Moriguchi 2005, 78), and the phrase *sosen-ni keii-o arawasu* (祖先に敬意を表す), or *sosen-ni keii-o harau* (祖先に敬意をはらう), "to pay (human) respect to the ancestors," (Toyozaki and Vernam-Atkin 2008, 188; Tateishi 2005, 249) are used.

In this context I want to comment on the commonly used term "ancestor worship." The Japanese word for "to worship," *ogamu* (拝む), is never used with regard to the ancestors. Quite differently, its synonym *reihai suru* (礼拝する) is frequently used in the compound *senzoreihai* (先祖礼拝), "ancestor worship." I suggest refrain from using this term, because I think it is not an innate Japanese term but rather the unreflected literal translation of the English term "ancestor worship,"³¹⁷ which, in turn, I consider factually inaccurate and pejorative.

Terms and concepts in the area of biblical archeology

In the area of biblical archeology scientific literature used various terms for "ancestor veneration":

- *Totenverehrung*, "veneration of the dead" (H. Schmid)
- *Ahnenkult*, "ancestor cult" (J. Lippert)
- *Seelenkult*, "soul cult" (J. Frey)
- *Ahnenverehrung*, "ancestor veneration" (M. Grundwald) (Lee 2001, 98–99).

---

314. Both mean "to venerate." *Agameru* (崇める) can also mean "to worship."

315. However, the boundaries are fluid as can be seen from the phrase *oya-to sosen-o uyamau-koto* (親と祖先を敬うこと), the "(divine) veneration of parents and ancestors" (Sasaki and Fujiwara 2000, 137). In the Japanese used in Christian churches, *uyamau* (敬う) is used for ancestors, and *agameru* (崇める) for God (Hara 2006, 192).

316. From what I understand, this verb is not used for ancestors. Aihara (相原鐵也) understands *sosen-o suuhai suru* (祖先を崇拝する), "to venerate the ancestors," as opposite to *kamisama-ya hotoke-sama-o toutobu suru* (神様や仏様を尊ぶ), "to cherish the gods or Buddha" (Aihara 2003, 137). If *toutobu* (尊ぶ), "cherish," is used in connection with the ancestors, it is not the ancestors themselves, but rather their teachings which are the object of cherishment (Rowe 2007, 17).

317. Turnbull also rejects the term "ancestor worship" and prefers "ancestor veneration" (Turnbull 1998, 197).

Lee suggests a categorical conceptual distinction between *Ahnenkult*, "ancestor cult," and *Totenkult*, "cult for/of the dead" or "cult of death." "Ancestor cult" presupposes the existence of a family, that is, relatives by blood.[318] "The ancestor is the object of cultic acts performed in the community of the house. Ancestor cult understood in that way has been called service for the ancestors, 'ancestor service,' or 'ancestor veneration'" (Lee 2001, 100). *Totenkult*, "cult for/of the dead" or "cult of death" concentrates on death itself (Hwang 1977, 343–344).

Towards a differentiated approach

I want to return to Figure 2.6 that I used earlier. But here I want to replace the field of "worldview" with the field of "theology." Ancestor veneration is a highly differentiated subject and is usually discussed under one aspect only. And this one aspect usually is theology. This leads to a one-sided evaluation and the common condemnation of ancestor veneration.

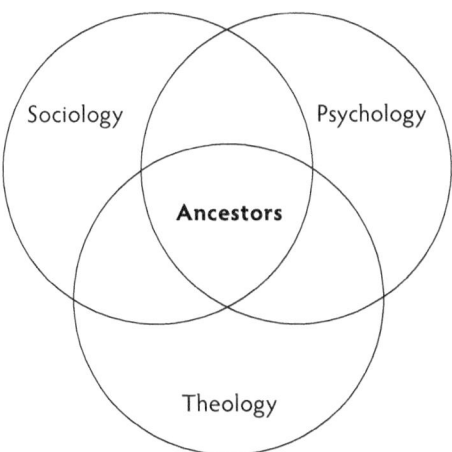

Figure 2.7 **Aspects of Ancestor Veneration (theology replacing worldview)**

The psychological dimension

In this section I want to focus on three aspects: Communal feelings, guilt feelings, and thankfulness.

---

318. This is different in China, where earliest sources testify to veneration of ancestors with extraordinary qualities rather than to veneration of relatives by blood (Hwang 1977, 346).

(1) Communal feelings

> A Japanese psychologist told us that she often prayed with her family to the ancestors. We asked what prayer means. She said that she had visited several American churches, and it seemed to her that prayer for the Japanese is not like prayer for American Christians. The Christians, she said, are asking for something. Prayer, for the Japanese, she said, is just being there, being with, and feeling together. The prayer is not petition. The common Western concept of prayer is grounded in the distance between God and humans. But in Japan the people are never really separated from other people or from the *kami* (神). Because, the psychologist explained, we are never really separated from other people, we are with the ancestors much as we would be with them when they were alive. It is not what we say to them as much as just being with them. (Goss and Klass 2005, 47)

This feeling is a form of the animistic "sentiment of holism." The communal feelings are based on the basic need of protection and recognition. The communal feeling is extended toward the deceased. This is a result of grief work[319] as well as an expression of the human desire for eternity beyond one's own lifespan. The Bible recognizes this desire but also objects to it. Man is not eternal but mortal. With his desire for eternity humans grasp for a divine attribute and cross the border which the above Japanese psychologist acknowledged.

> We have to emphasize that we do not understand the religious sphere as a projection of the immanent sphere; on the contrary, the primary imagination of man envisioning him as Divine-human after death (*kami* [神] or Buddha) is the constituent for the emotional integration of man into the shared world of his group. It is the very imagination of perfection, set against the experience of imperfection, which can serve as the standard for earthly relationships and mold them in a certain way. (Hildebrandt 1996, 165)

Hildbrand refers to Takeo Doi's *amae* (甘え)-concept. Doi wonders,

> whether "becoming a god or a Buddha" could possibly mean for Japanese, that the human personality of the respective individual, often ignored during his lifetime, – buried under formal

---

319. According to Nesbitt, talking to the dead in this sense cannot be considered as necromancy (58).

relationships or everyday worries – would get new attention and respect. (Hildebrandt 1996, 165)

The Japanese god-concept includes the notion, that "god is somebody beyond the tortures of unsatisfied *amae* (甘え), and this is the very essence of the Japanese god-concept" (165).

(2) **Guilt feelings**

Hildebrand's last quote points to the next psychological dimension of ancestor veneration, that is, that of guilt feelings toward the deceased. The Japanese "let" their deceased be gods so that at last they can have what they were not able to give them in their lifetime.[320] Hewer et al. (40) found that the reason for holding on to grief over an extended period of time could be "guilt feelings connected with ambivalent attitudes toward the deceased." "The grieving family members become victims of the struggle the deceased had with unresolved experiences of suffering in their lifetime. They pass these problems on to their bereaved" (Link-Wieczorek 1991, 263). Similar problems can be observed in the treatment of psychotraumas in the area of "survivor guilt" (Friedmann 2004, 177).

Japan (and other societies as well) has to deal with the particular "survivor guilt" toward aborted children:

> Some say that we in Japan enjoy peace at the expense of the A-bomb victims from Hiroshima and Nagasaki. Further do we enjoy our present prosperity at the expense of the sacrificed nameless embryos, disappearing into the dark. This is the new death cult in high-tech Japan, something nobody wants to open the mouth to talk about. Since World War II abortion has become very important as means of birth-control. (Ejima 1996, 99)

The fact that the blame for the increasing abortion rate after World War II is put on the Allies[321] does not change the guilt feelings toward these children.

---

320. According to Freud, these guilt-feelings toward the dead resulted in "deferred obedience" and were the reason for the evolution of paternal deities and the transformation of the "fatherless fraternity" into parentally organized societies (Baumann 1995, 178). I do not share this opinion.

321. The respective law, passed in 1948, legalized abortion and declared the aborted children as a new class of war victims as those who lost the struggle for survival and would have made life for the survivors difficult (Harrison 1996, 254). Abortion was considered an "inevitable evil." Between 1955 and 1964 there were more abortions than live births. Since 1948 more than 35 million children were aborted (registered abortions). In the 1980s 28% of all pregnancies ended in abortion, in 2000 the rate was down to about 22%. Tens of millions of women have an abortion history and the rate of aborting teenagers has risen alarmingly (Dominey 2005, 253–255).

Paradoxically did the guilt feelings[322] toward the dead children in Japan lead to a ritual praxis that treats them as "fully adequate humans" (Formanek 2008, 62). For the dead children similar rituals as those for the (adult) dead were created.[323] The aborted children are remembered through the ritual of *mizuko kuyou* (子供養), which is an adapted form of ancestor rituals. They are remembered as long as any survivor bears them in mind as distinct personalities (Harrison 1996, 253). "In the light of *mizuko kuyou* (水子供養) the Japanese attitude toward children as ancestors is in revision . . . Until now, they could not become ancestors because they were not full members of society" (265). Similar to the ancestor veneration rituals for deceased adults, the wish for postmortem safety (Dominey 2005, 257) as well as fear of curses from unappeased death spirits (263) play a role in the rituals for deceased children as well. However, the souls of deceased children are not honored through memorial services as often the souls of deceased adults are (Ooms 1976, 69).

---

322. Buddhism considers abortion as murder (Dominey 2005, 253, 260). According to Hardacre, *mizuko kuyou* (水子供養), the death rites for embryos, is rather economically driven than an answer to emotional needs (LaFleur 1999, 494).

323. In order to reevaluate aborted children not only this rite is used, but also postmortem marriages, *shiryou kekkon* (死霊結婚) or *meikon* (冥婚) (Formanek 2008, 86–88).

"Ancestor Rituals" for Deceased Children

Mizuko (水子), literally "water-child," means the unborn fetus inside the embryonic membranes (Dominey 2005, 256), but is used as a euphemism for an aborted child. "Regardless of the time since when the respective rituals were actually performed, the phenomenon of *mizuko kuyou* (水子供養) gained media attention and thus public attention in 1975, when the Japanese television broadcasted a cinematic documentation of such a ritual" (Formanek 2008, 52). A simultaneously occurring "spiritual boom" intensified the phenomenon (67). Even though *mizuko kuyou* (水子供養)-rituals have no verifiable roots in Buddhism, they are usually attributed to Buddhism, because they are usually executed in the context of other Buddhist rituals. Respective rituals in Shintoism emerged in the late 1990s (LaFleur 1999, 493–494).

In connection with the *mizuko kuyou houyou* (水子供養法要), the "death ritual for the souls of the [aborted] children," many temples use the *Sai-no kawara Jizou wasan* (賽の河原地蔵和讃), the "Hymnal to the Ksitigarbha (a bodhisattva) of the Sai-riverbed." Tradition attributes it to Kuuya Shounin (空也上人) (903–972), a prominent monk of the *Joudoshuu* (浄土宗), the Pure Land School, but it probably goes back only to the late medieval period of Japan. According to this hymnal, children who have died before they were able to repay their debt of obligation toward their parents or society, have to pile up stones and build pagodas in the riverbed of the *Sai-no kawara* (賽の河原). This is considered a meritorious deed, leading to Buddhahood or earning entrance into Buddha's *Pure Land*. However, demons riot the riverbed regularly and destroy the pagodas. It is only because of the savior-figure *Jizou Bosatsu* (地蔵菩薩), Ksitigarbha, who protects and aids the children, that they eventually can escape this hell. The ceremony appeals to Ksitigarbha and asks for his help (Formanek 2008, 53).

The name *Sai-no kawara* (賽の河原) means "riverbed of the *Sai* (賽). The Japanese reading of the Chinese character 賽 is *mukuimatsuru* (報い祀る), which means "to repay for the blessings received from the gods" (Gotou 1993, 148).

The content of the *Sai-no kawara Jizou wasan* (賽の河原地蔵和讃), the "Hymnal to the Ksitigarbha of the Sai-riverbed" includes depictions of deceased children piling up stones, of the blood flowing from their wounded fingers, of the demons *semeru*(ing), "blaming" and "torturing" them, and the Ksitigarbha protecting them (Hot Spring Culture Research Society Japan 2007, 199).

As an illustration for the suffering of these children, here is a text from the sermon-hymnal *Sahi-no Kawara-no Sekkyoubushi* (佐比河原の説教節):

> But there, how dreadful, demons appear, with eyes like fiery balls, evily staring at them: 'What kind of stupas have you built? Painful to see how poorly they are built! Stop crying all the time. You cannot gain Buddhahood when crying so much! Hurry up, build them again and pray that you may reach Buddhahood!' Thus they scold the children as they crack their iron whips and destroy their stupas completely. O, how painful this is. The little ones throw themselves on the ground, weeping, moaning, as the demons keep scolding them. We are all sinful, but the particular sin of the children is that they inflicted countless tortures on their mothers during their ten months in their womb, that they were born in pain, but that then they died at the age of three, five, or seven before father and mother imposing great pain to them. That is their first severe sin. They held on to the breasts of their mothers, and now as these breasts cannot give milk anymore, the mothers beat them in pain. The mothers have to endure the pain, and as they beat their breast, their now useless breasts, thunder roars at the bottom of the underworld, and it sounds like the drums of the Shura. The tears of the fathers turn into rains of fire, pouring down on the children. The tears of the mothers turn into sleet, and the grief causing bareness insults and tortures the children in the darkness. Because they loaded such sin upon themselves they have to wander the riverbed

> in the West, enduring tortures for a long time. In the riverbed a tiny rivulet flows, which reflects the torturing thoughts of their fathers and mothers, mourning their children on earth. And the children see their fathers and mothers, longing for them all the more, hoping they may still their hunger, creeping toward the nurturing breasts, but all of a sudden, they disappear and the water turns into blazing flames, burning their bodies... The smart ones among the children want to pluck flowers and offer them to Jizou Bosatsu in order to escape from the pain even for a short period of time. So they try to climb the blooming trees, but how pitiful they are, they are so small and slip off the trees, are pricked by the thorns here and there, so that they are covered in blood, until, eventually, they can pluck the flowers and offer them to Buddha. (Formanek 2008, 75–76).

(3) Thankfulness

Thankfulness is a decisive psychological element in Japanese ancestor veneration. In Japan thankfulness and feelings of guilt can hardly be distinguished. Nakajou (中条節子) describes this thankfulness owed to the ancestors as *oya-koukou* (親孝行), the "filial piety" owed to parents (119). The following conversation between a grandfather and his four-year-old grandchild is taken from the postscript of Asada's (浅田塘一) *Kouun-o yobu basou-no kagaku* (幸運を呼ぶ墓相の科学), literally "A Grave-Science Inviting Happiness." It is titled *Hakamairi-no kokoro* (墓参のこころ), "the heart of grave-visiting," and shows the connection between thankfulness and obligation – and feelings of guilt:

> "Grandpa, are we gonna pour the water here?"
>
> "You are right. We pour it from above over the gravestone. Be careful not to strike the stone with your water scoop. Otherwise the ancestor say 'Auch, auch!' Yes, you do a fine job." ...
>
> "Grandpa, who is in this grave?"
>
> "Your great-great-great-grandfathers and your great-great-great-grandmothers, very, very many of them. Because our ancestors

lived you could also be born into this world. Therefore, that you can live today is something you owe to them.[324] Therefore, you have to say thank you to your great-great-great-grandparents, right? When you pour the water like this, 'Thank you, thank you!' That surely makes them happy. And one more thing: The ancestors always watch over us from yonder world, and they wonder: 'Is this little boy going to be a good child?'" (Asada 2002, 243)

The Christian answer to the connection between obligation and feelings of guilt is not their heightening to "deferred obedience" and thankfulness, but forgiveness and release. In *In My Father's Image* (1993) Carlson and Schweitz point out the particular relationship to deceased fathers and warn about the following dangers: (1) tabooing and (2) suppression of faults and weaknesses of the deceased, (3) assuming responsibility for the guilt and sins of the deceased, and (4) misuse of the deceased by third persons who want to manipulate the bereaved.

Guilt needs to be accepted rather than suppressed. And even more, forgiveness can lead to acceptance of self through experienced acceptance by God. This liberates damaging self-destruction. According to Carlson and Schweitz (99–100), an excessive self-esteem is often the cause of self-reproach. "Humility is the escape hatch that can free you." Rather than endless obligation toward the deceased, humbly submitting everything to God's "strong hand" (1 Pet 5:6) is the Christian way.

The sociological dimension: Ancestor veneration in the Japanese history of law

The first Civil Code, enacted in 1898, related family and ancestor veneration as follows:

- Every *kazoku* (家族), "family," has to belong to a specific *ie* (家), "house";
- the *ie* (家), "house," is the smallest structural unit of the society;
- the *ie* (家), "house," itself is the prime legal corporation of ancestor veneration and the prime locus for the ancestral ceremonies, and therefore
- the *ie* (家), "house" (and with it the ancestral rituals) must "exist in perpetuity and must never be allowed to lapse."

"Because freedom of belief had been guaranteed by the 1889 constitution (now called the old or *Meiji*-Constitution, in effect until 1947), the old civil

---

324. *Ima kou yatte ikite irareru-no-wa gosenzosama-no okage nan da-yo* (いまこうやって生きていられるのはご先祖さまのおかげなんだよ).

code declared that ancestor worship was not a religion but a matter of national ethics." Even though "the current Civil Code, enacted after World War II, totally abolished the *ie* (家) system as a legal entity and thus nullified legal controls over ancestor worship," "the institution of *ie* (家) as a basis for ancestor worship survives widely in social behavior, and the fact that it survives has had to be acknowledged in legal practice" (Takeda 1976b, 129).

The stability of society

So far two extremely important corporative functions of ancestor veneration can be derived: One is the stability of the contextual framework of the national identity. Ancestor veneration is the key base of the *ie* (家) (Yonemura 1976, 177). The other is the continuity and authority of ethical values. If a nation wants to remain in existence, it cannot do without either of them.

In order to live together in lasting peace, people need a stable referential framework for their communal life. The ethical decay of many Western societies is sad proof of the futile attempt to find common and unifying values and characteristics solely in the present. Many nations – Japan is certainly among them – seek the unifying referential framework in history, or more specifically, with their common ancestors. The deeper the roots go into the past, the firmer the support, provided a nation is able to keep in vital touch with them. The livelier the memory of the ancestors – ancestors as close relatives commemorated in the *kuyou* (供養), the commemoration services, during *obon* (御盆), the festival for the dead in summer, or ancestors as distant "culture heroes" and their commemoration in folk tales – the stronger the national identity. In Japan ancestor veneration is not limited to a certain religion or religious sect, but it is integrated into the overarching religious system. The purpose of ancestor veneration is the continuation of social ties beyond death (Turnbull 1998, 196). According to Schwarz (159), ancestor veneration and the common grave have always been the foundation of social order. The ties of groups are founded on the ties with the ancestors:

> When individual identity is based on membership in a family or clan, we often find that the family or clan includes both the living and the dead ... To be sure, some ancestors might be distant cultural heroes, but most ancestors are deceased parents, grandparents, children, or friends. When the living are in contact with their deceased family members, they have a strong sense of social membership. (Goss and Klass 2005, 19)

The second social function of ancestor veneration is giving continuity and authority to ethical values that preserve the nation. Situational ethics on a day-to-day basis do not preserve values. Without lasting values, however, a nation descends into anarchy. Wiher (2003, 293) associates the preservation of the harmonious balance in the "animistic micro- and macrocosm" with the ancestors as the guardians of tradition. That does not mean that change is impossible by definition. But it does mean that especially in times of change forced upon a nation by external dramatic necessities, the attachment to the past and to tradition is of crucial importance.

> The family system plays a key role in the problem of social change. It brings the past into the present. The events of the present impinge upon it and try to alter it. Out of this past with its alterations we get the pattern generator for the culture of the future. (Zimmermann in Rushdoony 1973, 418)

In the light of these two crucial functions of ancestor veneration it is irresponsible to infringe upon the foundations of Japanese ethics without providing an adequate surrogate. As a matter of fact, one of the reasons of the severe persecution of Christians in the past has always been the fear of the destruction of Japanese ethics and the "loss of cultural identity" (Schrimpf 2001, 173) caused by the influence of Christianity. Shouzan Sakuma's (佐久間象山) (1811–1864) famous parole was: *touyou-no doutoku, seiyou-no gijutsu* (東洋の道徳、西洋の技術), "Eastern morals, Western technology" (Lüddeckens 2002, 87). He clearly feared the West as a threat to Japanese ethics. This fear led to the failure of the Treaty Revision (1889),[325] intensified and gave birth to a nationwide nationalistic surge which eventually demanded that "the moral obligation toward Emperor and nation" became the duty of every Japanese national. The AEPM also accepted "the veneration of Emperor and ancestors as indispensable loyalty of subjects" (Wippich 2001, 57).

Learning from Christian Keyßer's work in Papua New Guinea seems to be helpful. Drawing on Farnbacher's *Gemeinde verantworten: Anfänge,*

---

325. The text of the German *Staatsarchiv* reads: "In the year of 1889 Germany, after several other states preceded her in doing so, resolved to meet Japan's desire and conclude a new commercial contract with her, which was signed in Berlin, in the said year on the 11th of June. As soon hereafter heavy opposition against the treatise arose in Japan, the Japanese government chose to withdraw from the ratification of this treatise as well as of respective treatises colluded with third powers. The treatise of June 11th, 1889 therefore never came into effect, and was also never presented to the Federal Council and the Imperial Council" (Eoloff 1896, 288). For further information on the Treaty Revision and its rejection in Japan see the chapter "Civil Morality" in Gluck (1985), and pages 47–49 in Khan (1997).

Entwicklungen und Perspektiven von Gemeinde und Ämtern der Evangelisch-lutherischen Kirche von Papua-Neuguinea (1999), I try to find some answers for the situation in Japan. In the area of Madang, "the moral actions and the behavior expected by the group," so-called *lo*-determinatives were "constituted by the forefathers" and "confirmed by the ancestral spirits" (27). "The origin of *lo* is found in the ancestral cosmos. The deceased expect compliance with it. Thus they have the capacity to maintain the order of *lo*." Offences against the *lo* are repaid by the ancestors through withdrawal of blessings. "Interpreted thus, *lo* becomes the quality criterion and basic value of collective responsibility for functioning community life. Socio-religious reciprocity regulates and activates the obligation toward the ancestors." Farnbacher concludes that *lo* organizes life "by integrating individual behavior into a cosmic relational framework" (27). It is in the "interest of clan-identity that people ascertain the relational framework of the ancestral cosmos" (28). The "cosmic community includes the living and the dead, all things visible and invisible, beings, deities and various powers of the cosmos" (Fugmann in Farnbacher 1999, 42). This inclusive worldview explains "the natural living conditions as well as the entire framework of the cosmic relational structure." In this "cosmic community of obligation" the relationship with the ancestors documents the obligation toward tradition (42). This brief outline shows how similar this ancestor-concept is to its Japanese counterpart.

Keyßer did not perceive the sociological reality as a "bulwark against Christianity,"[326] and became the first to qualify the "clan-category" anew as *Volk Gottes*, as People of God, that lead to "the breakthrough in Christianization, to clan conversions as opposed to individual conversions, to the founding of churches, to a wide consideration of the pre-existing social structures, and to the fostering of cultural assets in worship service and proclamation" (Farnbacher 1999, 170–171). On the basis of this success Keyßer explained the obvious lack of success in mission work as a result of a "system error," that is, the "hereditary defect of church and mission" (Keyßer in Farnbacher 1999, 171).

> Understanding people means perceiving as its members a part of the collective to which tied. If mission only addresses individuals, without perceiving and honoring them as integral parts of their system, it must miss its objective. (172)

---

326. This is how the Friedrich Liederwald (pen name Nitzschkowsky) evaluated ancestor veneration in China: "The firmest, almost unconquerable bulwark mission has ever encountered is beyond any doubt the ancestral cult, a system by virtue of which this wonderful state colossus endured through millenniums" (Sun 2002, 157).

Keyßer's basic understanding was that "humans can only be addressed . . . collectively" (175).

In Keyßer's approach, the ancestors, too, were given a new function. "The ones we once considered dangerous spirits and the souls of our ancestors now have become our fathers and older brothers" (176).[327] After Christianity had gained strength "having more and more become the legitimator of a new social order" the religiosity based on the ancestors later decayed more and more (242).

The question is whether Keyßer's approach could be helpful in Japan. I see the following problems: (1) structurally Japan is very similar to smaller ethnic groups, but its size is hard to understand. Due to its size, Japan could not be transformed into a *Volkschristentum*, a "folk-Christianity" with the necessary speed. (2) The church history in Papua New Guinea shows that the initial success of this pragmatic approach later gave way to theologically rather questionable developments. The following enculturation example is theologically not tolerable anymore:

> A board of elders stated its conviction that through the ancestral chain, prayer could be directed back to a primordial deity as a symbol of the unity of all principalities. In addition, parallel ways of prayer to ancestors and the Christian deity offered a legitimate complementary methodology, said the board. (Farnbacher 1999, 386)

The theological dimension: Incompatibility of faith in God and ancestor veneration

Berentsen asks whether ancestor veneration is acceptable in the light of the Christian faith in God the Creator, who – as scholars on both sides think – is not compatible with the faith in Japanese deities (Berentsen 1985a, 148). Some totally reject attributing divinity to the ancestors[328] while others talk about a "blurred line" between the divine and the ancestors (Goss and Klass 2005, 9). The conflict between the Christian understanding of God and the Japanese *kami* (神)-concept has a strong bearing on the Christian attitude toward ancestor veneration. "The basic Christian confession of God as man's Creator,

---

327. In this context Keyßer's status as founder of a "new ancestral *lo*" is also problematic (Farnbacher 1999, 199–200). The hegemony of white people was later criticized by cargoism, and voices were rising that demanded that indigenous people should have a bigger part in the ancestral *mana* (331).

328. As Lederer states, "Ancestors are not gods, nor are they merely symbolic. In the Orient they are the past, which flows into the present, the tissue of inextinguishable life . . . Quite literally and concretely the anecstors are part of the present, despite the fact that they are dead" (Lederer in Gulick 1964, 83).

namely, a radical contradiction of the idea that the human and the divine are ultimately to coalesce within a comprehensive cosmic totality." According to the Christian faith, there is no cosmic interdependence between the human and the divine. It has always been "emphatically stated that man has to do with a God who is fundamentally beyond man's own limited dependent existence. God does not belong to cosmos" (Berentsen 1985a, 149).

Non-Christian scholars share in this judgment. Oono (大野健) equates gods and ancestors (91–92). According to him, *senzosuuhai* (先祖崇拝), the veneration of ancestors in old Shintoism of Japanese tribal groups, is a synonym for *kunitsugami suuhai* (国津神崇拝), the "veneration of the gods of the earthly rule" (93).[329] *Kamidana* (神棚), the "god-shelf," and *senzodana* (先祖棚), the "ancestor-shelf" (Smith 1976, 33) both mean the place of familial ancestor veneration and are mutually exchangeable synonyms. Fritsch-Oppermann (9) mentions ancestors and gods in one breath, von Siebold (88) talks about "deified ancestors." "The deification of men and women is a very widespread and very old custom in Japanese religion" (Smith 1974, 11), involving not only deceased emperors, but also "local heroes, famous personalities, and local warriors." They can be identified with the locally venerated *dousojin* (道祖神), the "ancestral patron deities for travelers." They also can be understood as *goryou* (御霊) or *goryoushin* (御霊神), "honorable spirits of the dead," and as *arahitogami* (荒人神), as "coarse man-gods" (York 2005, 29). According to Mabuchi (馬淵東一) (109), ancestors are deified on the occasion of their 33rd orbit. York judges, "It is perhaps the this-worldly orientation of Shinto, however, that more than anything else links it with pagan veneration." In the context of "paganism" – a term which York uses without any pejorative sentiment – he talks about "a belief in the oneness of god and humans, divinity and humanity" (29).[330]

Does this mean that faith in the God of the Bible excludes any kind of ancestor veneration? In order to answer this question, it is important to turn to the Old Testament and the encounter between ancestor veneration and the faith in Jahwe.

---

329. Takeda (竹田聴洲) calls the ancestors "holy beings," but he distinguishes more specifically. He explicitly does not equate them with the "gods of the Japanese mythology," but talks about "patron-deities" and "agricultural deities" (Takeda 1976a, 122).

330. On the basis of his observations on apparitions in Africa, Bammann judges similarly (Bammann 2004, 106).

Encounter in the Old Testament

Oswald Loretz's contribution

According to Oswald Loretz, "veneration of the dead and the ancestors are tangible only in a negative way . . . in the Old Testament; that is, in the prohibition of necromancy (Deut 18:11–12) and the command concerning honoring parents (Exod:20:12; Lev 19:3; Deut 5:19)" (Loretz in Wahl 1997, 135). That does not mean, however, that this is all. According to Loretz, the early Israelites partook in the "Canaanite death cult," which can be reconstructed from Ugarit texts. The "Canaanite death cult" was only subdued by the Jahwe-monotheism during the Exile and the post-exile period. Then it was substituted by the veneration of the biblical patriarchs. Death cult and ancestor veneration as "essential part of familial piety were thus corrected by Jahwism and integrated into the official religion" (Albertz 1992, 65). According to Loretz, ancestor veneration traditio-historically generated from "death cult."[331] "As ancestor veneration cannot be proved from the [biblical] texts and as it cannot be substantiated archeologically, indication for a possible praxis in Israel can only be found by means of comparative religious studies." Loretz thinks that texts from Ugarit provide the "necessary material for the reconstruction of the Canaanite ancestor cult." According to Loretz, Israel originally practiced ancestor veneration in the same way as its neighbors. "In the course of time the death cult caused a deification of the ancestors." Simultaneously with the prohibition of ancestor veneration (and together with it of necromancy; 1 Sam 28:3–25), the veneration of the patriarchs, considered to be the founders of the nation, generated. This coincidence "provides a temporal indicator." "From the viewpoint of history of religion, the prohibition of ancestor veneration was associated with the advent of the claim of exclusiveness of Jahwe,[332] who did not tolerate the veneration of divine ancestors" (Wahl 1997, 136).

---

331. He held "that the patriarchal narratives showed a paramount appreciation of the ancestral graves" what he considered "indisputable evidence for the existence of ancient ancestor veneration" (Lee 2001, 121).

332. This claim of exclusiveness would have prevailed against the ancestor veneration of the family religion. Karel van der Toorn's *Family Religion in Babylonia, Syria and Israel* sets out from Albertz and Vorländer: "Van der Toorn chose the term 'family religion' because the religious involvement of an individual has always to be seen in the context of the group to which the individual belongs." He talked about "the principle one being the family." "The essential common element of the religions of Babylon, Syria, and Israel was the connection between ancestor cult and the veneration of a family deity. It was only the Deuteronomist which declared these forms of family religion as illegitimate" (Fechter 1998, 29).

The suppression of the death cult led to a special formulation of the command concerning the honoring of parents and the formation of the patriarchal narratives. The ancestor veneration is historicized and becomes the starting point for the formation of the Jewish self-awareness, which from this point on understands Abraham as its starting point. (Loretz in Lee 2001, 111)

If Ugaritic texts are used for the understanding of "early Israelite" ancestor veneration, there are many parallels to Japanese ancestor veneration:

- The dead "partaking in the ancestral feasts" are called the "passers-by" (Loretz 1984, 84). This strongly reminds one of the Japanese *yuuke* or *yuuura* (夕占), the "evening oracle," in which passers-by served as mediums.
- "The evoked spirits are described as 'chirping' or 'gabbling' . . . The illustration of the dead as birds is duly documented in the texts of the Near East, which is proof of their ability to fly away from the underworld" (Schmidt 1994, 153). That the soul of a deceased person can flee in the form of a bird is a concept known to only a few in Japan,[333] but they are associated with divination.[334]
- Documents of the Akkadian Nuzi give evidence of the veneration of *ilani* (family deities) as well as *etemmu* (spirits of the dead). "It seems that the *ilani* represent the deified ancestors of a family" (Albertz 1992, 65).
- Albertz thinks that the תְּרָפִים (Gen 31:19, 34–35 and more) "can be seen as figurative representations of ancestors or spirits of the dead," to which he attributed "divination (Judg 18:14; Ezek 21:26; Zech 10:2) and miraculous healing powers (1 Sam 19:13, 16)." "They belonged to the familial house-cult (Judg 17:5), but are not identical with the family deities (Gen 31:53)" (Albertz et al. 2003, 363).
- In Ugarit, Baal held the title "Lord of the great deities," which is "Lord of the deified ancestors" (Herrmann 1999, 181).
- Holy stones, *il-ib*, were erected for the divine ancestors (Schmidt 1994, 53). The Ugaritic *il* is the equivalent of the Hebrew אֵל, the general term for "gods." The Ugaritic *ib* is associated with the Hebrew אָב and was possibly used as an adjective (54). According to

---

333. Exceptions are Itou (2007, 55) and Umezawa (梅沢恵美子) (23).

334. *Toriuranai* (鳥占い) is divination (占い) using birds (鳥) (*Encyclopedia of the Supernatural* 2001, 287).

Lambert's interpretation, the Old-Akkadian deity *Ilaba*, later known as *il-ib* "served all people as a private family-deity" (55).

- In Ugarit the ancestors were addressed as the *'rp'm* (the healers) because they ensured the continuation of the families in their progeny, thus securing continued provision for the deceased. At special occasions the ancestors were evoked with special incantations to descend from the lower god-realm to the world of humans (Lee 2001, 107).
- According to Ugaritic texts, it was the duty of the sons to succeed their fathers in the veneration of the family's deceased, who were seen as god-like beings. This was the most important duty of sons (Lee 2001, 108).

Even though the representatives of the "JHWH-faith" waged an intensive struggle against the Canaanite cults, the biblical texts show rudiments of ancestor veneration. Under the headline "Honoring parents and patriarchal traditions as an Israel-specific contextualization of the Canaanite death cult,"[335] Loretz names among others the following "rudiments":

- According to Loretz, the Old Testament as well as Ugaritic texts called the deceased ancestors רְפָאִים (the healers) (Isa 14:9; 26:14; Ps 88:11), but the editorial work on the Old Testament texts effectuated terminological adjustments. By changing the last consonant of the radical רף from א to ה, the "healers" became the "lame," to those who "collapse." This small conceptual change turned the healers, ancestors actively involved in the lives of people, into distant schemes of the kingdom of death. Thus the ancestors were neutralized and rendered harmless for everyday life.
- In the necromancy narrative in 1 Samuel 28:7–20 the spirit of the deceased is called אֱלֹהִים. Similar passages of the Ugaritic texts have *il* or *ilyn*, "integrating the dead into the lower sphere of gods." According to Moor, the deceased were buried "together with the *ilm'rs*, the "gods of earth." Thus the Ugaritic ancestors were seen as ancestral deities.
- According to Loretz, Deuteronomy 26:14 can be seen as a reference to Israelite provision for the dead. He is convinced that providing food for the deceased was common in Israel. Wächter also thinks

---

335. *Das Elterngebot und die Erzvätertraditionen als israelspezifische Kontextualisierung des kanaanäischen Totenkults.*

that this kind of provision was "at least likely." He understands the food described in Jeremiah 16:7 not as comfort for the bereaved but as grave goods. עַל־מֵת can also be translated with "for a dead person" (Lee 2001, 107–109).

Corporate Personality

In the context of this discussion Burks "re-introduced the term *corporate personality*, coined by H. Wheeler Robinson at the beginning of the last century."[336] The term *corporate personality* indicates a "spiritual communion" or a "spiritual unity" (Wiher 2003, 294).[337]

> The individual lives as part of a community which encompasses him spatially and temporally. A stream of life runs through him which neither started with him nor stops with him. In death the individual consciousness collapses, but that in which it participates lives on. (Schwienhorst-Schönberger 2003, 218)

This thought has already been discussed in the context of ancestor veneration as the Japanese way of fighting transience. I am going to introduce it into this discussion because it is here where its theological relevance becomes apparent.

> According to Gese, joining the family grave, that is, return to the ancestors, is not only a comfort for the dying, but it virtually constitutes the fulfillment of the life in the collective, as the individual totally immerses into the ancestors as the foundation of the collective. (Lee 2001, 121)

The "integration of the individual into the collective" explains the importance of ancestral graves in Israel. The individual is rooted in the community. This community is important for the living and the dead alike. Death does not lead to the termination of the relationship between the individual and the collective. "Death is merely the beginning of a new phase in the life in community" (Lee 2001, 121). Gese talks about the extended family as an organism, constituted by "the fact that children are born by parents," expressed in the veneration of parental ancestors. Awe and reverence are "collected and concentrated, and they focus on the deceased ancestors – even to the patriarchs . . . one descended from" (Gese in Lee 2001, 121). It is the

---

336. His main works are: *The Hebrew Conception of Corporate Personality* (1935) and *The Group and the Individual in Israel* (1937).

337. Wiher uses *seelische Gemeinschaft* and *seelische Einheit*.

concentration of the veneration of many generations which turn ancestors into ancestral deities.

Loretz's and Robinson's evolutionistic approach may be favored or rejected,[338] – I myself reject it – but the incompatibility of ancestor veneration and the "Jahwe-cult" is acknowledged by both sides. "The Old Testament considered the veneration of the dead as something in competition with the faith in God as exclusive power over the future of man" (Pannenberg 1993, 607).

Christian ancestor veneration: Possible or impossible
The example of Christian Keyßer shows both: (1) the Christian faith and ancestor veneration can coexist, and (2) if they do this leads to difficult problems. It is my opinion that the fear of syncretism must not keep Christians from struggling to find some practical way of Christian ancestor veneration. It may be a stony path, and he who walks it may stumble and even fall. But not walking it is not an option. In a panel discussion on African ancestor veneration leaning on Augustine's motion for using the term "gods" for demons and angels in his *Civitas Dei*,[339] Spaemann warned against "abandoning terrain" by not integrating non-Christian elements into Christianity. "There is a major Christian tradition of integrating non-Christian elements, but Protestantism has very much suppressed it" (Spaemann in a panel discussion documented by Koslowski 1985, 245).

According to Lee, this kind of integration was successful in Israel: "If there ever had been an ancestor cult in Israel, it was integrated into the JHWH-cult." Lee quotes H. C. Brichto according to whom "only such ancestor veneration remained besides the JHWH-cult which had no cultic elements." Brichto coined the following formula: "Veneration is not worship" (Lee 2001, 106). Similarly Chiu: "The Israelites of the Old Testament did not practice ancestor worship. But they had ancestral traditions which ensured that they paid respect and honor to the ancestors, without worshipping them" (Chiu in Lee 2001, 101).

---

338. Wahl opposes Loretz, who held that the Machpelah was a place of ancestor veneration. Wahl (137) said that this association was secondary. Albertz (65), too, doubted the correctness of Loretz's "hypothesis," because it exhibited conspicuous gaps. Robinson founded his studies on Lévy-Bruehl and Durkheim (Marttila 2006, 11; Low 2000, 286) whose approach I render inappropriate for a historical exegesis of biblical texts.

339. "If the Platonists prefer to call these angels gods rather than demons, and to reckon them with those whom Plato, their founder and mater, maintains were created by the supreme God, they are welcome to do so, for I will not spend strength in fighting about words. For if they say that these beings are immortal, and yet created by the supreme God, blessed but by cleaving to their Creator and not by their own power, they say what we say, whatever name they call these beings by" (Augustine 1888, 378).

Ancestor veneration without ancestor worship in Japan? There have always been voices theoretically demanding this way. Similar to the South Korean Catholic Church's interpretation of ancestral rituals as "cultural traditions" rather than "religious rituals" (Wippermann 2000, 190), Nobushige Hozumi (穂積陳重) (1855–1926)[340] argued:

> I look with sincere regret upon frequent conflicts between the missionaries or newly-converted Christians and our people who are ancestor-worshippers; for I am one of those who firmly believe that the practice of Ancestor worship is not incompatible with Christianity. It is not contrary to the First Commandment, because the ancestral spirit is nothing more than the outcome of the belief in the immortality of soul, and cannot be considered as 'gods,' which the 'jealous God' forbids to worship. If ancestor worship is . . . the extension of love and respect to distant forefathers, the manifestation of the love and respect in a certain harmless way may be regarded as realization of the Fifth Commandment to honor the parents; and nothing against Christianity, which is essentially a religion of love. (Hozumi 2008, xiii)[341]

Doi's interpretation of the "communion of saints" in the Apostles' Creed is similar. He holds that the "saints" originally meant "deceased saints" (1997, 128).

Ancestor veneration without ancestor worship? What does this look like in the praxis of Japanese Christianity? Churches as the Glorious Gospel Christian Church, the Original Gospel Tabernacle, or the Spirit of Jesus Church, all very much adapted to Japanese tradition, allow the prayer for deceased who have died without receiving salvation through Jesus Christ. They also allow the vicarious baptism (Hoffmann 2007, 116). However, Hwang warns against indifferently allowing ancestor veneration in the church (Hwang 1977, 351).

---

340. From 1882, Hozumi was the first Japanese professor for legal science and one of the fathers of the new Japanese constitution (Aoki 2001, 130). On the history of introduction of Western law see Sanders (2005).

341. The flaw in Hozumi's otherwise brilliant thought is the severance of love for God and love for parents. However, "the love of God should be placed over and above any other love. And loving the parents should be contained in the love of God. It is inappropriate to put the love of a father above that of God or to break one of God's commandments just to be nice to a father nor is it appropriate to be an accomplice in his wrong doing" (Shenouda 1997, 57).

In the article "Evangelical Church Forms & Ceremonies" Gotou, Martin, and Joseph presented helpful hints for Christian funerals:[342]

- If a picture of the deceased is exhibited this may encourage *reihai* (礼拝), "worship." Gotou et al. use the Christian word for the Sunday worship (234).
- Flowers can be used for the decoration of the church. However, the impression that these flowers are offered to the deceased must be avoided. The Japanese text uses *sonaeru* (供える), a term usually used for offerings to deities (234).
- Crematories usually provide Buddhist accessories. Therefore, the staff should be notified in advance that they are not desirable for Christian cremations (236).
- Gotou et al. strictly speak against bowing before the deceased (236). Even though bowing before the living is considered an expression of respect, bowing before the deceased is generally understood as an act of worship. Chua showed that חוה takes different meanings depending on the object: in the case of humans it means "to fall prostrate," in the case of God or gods "to worship." It is not the act itself that determines the meaning but its object (Nesbitt 2007, 63). In Japan the general understanding is that the deceased become gods. Therefore, Christians should not bow before the deceased no matter whether they consider them as gods or not.
- Gotou et al. suggest to refrain from reading telegram greetings during a funeral service, because the texts sometimes addressed the deceased directly. Gotou et al. (237) reject this as *ikyouteki* (異教的), literally as "belonging to another religion." For the same reason they suggest that all speakers deliver their speeches while looking at the bereaved.

Ongoing discussion is urgent and requires neutral terminology. I suggest refrain from *sosensuuhai* (祖先崇拝), "ancestor veneration," and *senzoreihai* (先祖礼拝), "ancestor worship" and rather use *sosen girei* (祖先儀礼), "ancestor etiquette," as Fujii suggested (Reid 1991, 130), or *sosen saishi* (祖先祭祀), "ancestral rituals" (Nesbitt 2007, 64).

---

342. I think that these hints are helpful, but I am also aware that they are followed only in the minority of churches. Nesbitt gives a good overview of various ancestral rites in big Christian movements in Japan (Nesbitt 2007, 71ff) as well as in the leading Christian denominations (Nesbitt 2007, 78ff).

Further, I think that distinguishing rituals following Arnold van Gennep and Victor Turner who distinguish the *rites de passage* as follows:

Table 2.6 Rituals (according to van Gennep 2005, 21; Goguel d'Allondans 2002, 41; Bleeker 1970, 44)

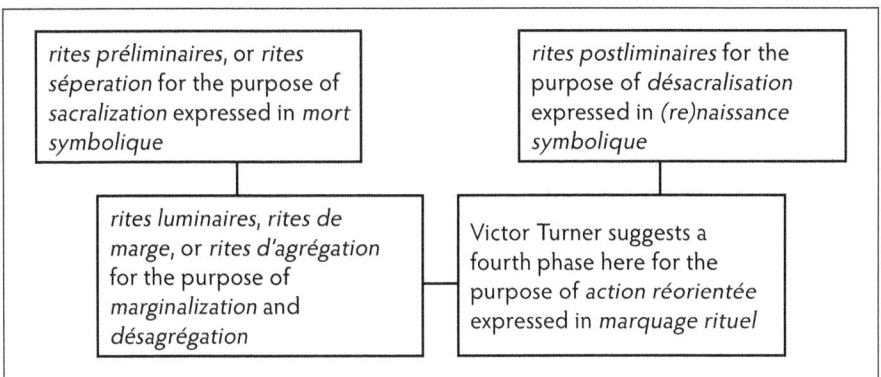

The *rites de marge* and *rites d'agrégation*, determined more than the others by the religious elements of a worldview, become less and less important with growing secularization. At the same time the *rites de séperation*, rather concerned with sociological issues such as obligation and thankfulness, gain more and more importance. I think that Christian ancestor rituals in the area of the *rites de séperation* need not to be rejected. One example are the memorial services of the *Lutheran Church of Japan* (Nesbitt 2007, 8ff).

The formula "ancestor veneration without ancestor worship" is good. That is, in theory good without any restrictions – yet in praxis, good with great caution and a multitude of justified concerns. There will always be Japanese Christians who, fearful of being unfaithful to God, reject any form of ancestor veneration.[343] Yet those not knowing any of these fears will always be there, too. Both extremes are wrong and the golden middle solution always desirable. It will always be crucial to watch the demarcation between ancestor veneration and ancestor worship. As salvation in Christ overcomes death the horizon of Christian salvation lies beyond death. This opens the way of martyrdom for the sake of a clear rejection of ancestor worship, an option that must not be

---

343. According to Mullins (135), the earliest pioneer missionaries and the evangelical missionaries in post-war Japan belong to this group.

forgotten in the struggle for a Christian answer to ancestor veneration as to any cultural encounter.

> In order to escape doom and to gain life we must be ready to make any sacrifice. The word of Jesus summons every single one individually before God. It makes salvation everyone's personal matter where the opinion of others cannot lead him. For the way every single one relates to God's grace and to God's justice brings forth for him either life or fall. (Schlatter 1977, 114–115)

Two case-studies:

(1) **Ancestor veneration of the Japanese "Crypto-Christians"**

In the religion of the Crypto-Christians the ancestors play an important role (Turnbull 1998, 206). In 1587, Toyotomi Hideyoshi (豊臣秀吉) (1537–1598) expelled the Jesuits from the country,[344] and "in 1614, the first Tokugawa-*Shogun* Ieyasu ((徳川家康) (1543–1616) prohibited practice of the Christian religion." He issued several orders aiming at the "repression" of Christians in Japan which were successful (Coulmas 2005, 140).[345] The Japanese *kakure kirishitan* (隠れキリシタン), "Crypto-Christians" went underground and preserved their faith for almost 250 years.[346] For the sake of camouflage and due to their syncretistic tendency they were mostly members of a Buddhist temple and a Shintoist shrine (Medd 2003, 71). They also integrated Buddhist and Shintoist elements into their faith. When the seclusion ended almost 250 years later, the Catholic Church refused their comeback into "the bosom of the Church," because their faith had drifted too far away from the Roman Catholic dogma (Coulmas 2005, 141).[347] However, the Crypto-Christians, too, rejected Roman Catholic orthodoxy for the sake of their own syncretistic mixture of

---

344. It is quite ironic that he expelled the Jesuits, among other reasons, because he saw Christianity as danger to his (postmortem) deification (Fox Young 2005, 161).

345. This triggered a cruel persecution of Christians with high death toll. However, it cannot be denied that the Catholic Christians provoked this with militant actions, and that Japan answered only after long forbearance (Hall 1968, 185). On this rather sad part of church history see Matsubara (1983), who writes from a Shintoist viewpoint.

346. Under the political control of the Tokugawa-Shogunate, which "used religion . . . for support of its feudal regime" not only the *kakure-kirishitan* (隠れキリシタン), the "Crypto-Christians," but also the *kakure-nembutsu* (隠れ念仏), "hidden followers of the Buddhist *Amida*-cult" went underground (Nakamaki 2003, 35).

347. This judgment is certainly an overgeneralization. Until 1873 some 14,000 of a total of 20,000 Crypto-Christians had returned to the Roman-Catholic Church (Bays and Grayson 2006, 509). Okano (岡野治子) talks about 20,000 to 50,000 Crypto-Christians that returned (2002, 139). Others talk about some 30,000 in 80 house churches (Yancey 2002, 313).

Catholic, Buddhist and Shintoist elements (Lim and Spaulding 2003, 206). They rejected Roman Catholic Christianity, reintroduced to Japan by French missionaries, as alien and have ever since been faithful to their "Iberian roots," inherited from the Portuguese missionaries of the sixteenth century (Whelan 2000, 369).[348] Today the relationship between the Catholic Church and the Crypto-Christians is much more relaxed, because of the Catholic Church's concessions with regard to ancestor veneration. Morioka quotes from the 1980 (Catholic) Catechism *Christiaens*:

> Question 14: I am son and heir of my *ie* (家), my "house," but because my ancestors and parents were Buddhists I have to have a Buddhist priest do the funeral with regard to my brothers, sisters, and other relatives. Is this allowed?
>
> Answer: Of course it is allowed. It contradicts the virtue of mercy to despise the religion of other people just because one is a Catholic Christian. This must never be forgotten. (Knecht 1986, 125)

The pantheon of the Japanese Crypto-Christians is merely part of the vaster pantheon of the Japanese religion. The great Christian *kamisama* (神様),[349] "gods," that is *Deusu-sama* (デウス様), *Iezu Kirisuto-sama* (イエズ・キリスト様), and *Santa Mariya-sama* (サンタマリヤ様) have a place among the other gods. "The Japanese *kami* (神), 'gods,' which the Jesuits renounced as devils, are far 'from being ousted from their thrones.' According to the understanding of the *kakure* (隠れ), the 'Cryptos,' they are only pushed aside in order to make space for other *kamisama* (神様), 'gods,' from Europe (Turnbull 1998, 206). In addition to "Christian gods" Shintoist gods were also "incorporated" into the "Christian pantheon." They were worshipped in a similar way as the Shintoist *kami* (神), "gods," whom they resembled not only in being the object of supplications but also in being the source of curses and calamities (Coulmas 2005, 141). Their worldview had not changed at all.[350] Sugiyama-Lebra calls this attitude "heterodoxy": "In the *Kakure* version of Christianity, we find a clear demonstration of the inseparability and intimacy of divine and human, noumenal and phenomenal, the transcendental and

---

348. The Crypto-Christians were "discovered" in 1865 by the French missionary Bernard-Thadée Petitjean (Knecht 1986, 124).

349. In this context Coulmas names a "category of higher beings" (2005, 141).

350. Another evidence for this is magical understanding of the Crypto-Christian *orashio* (オラシオ), which is derived from the Latin *oratio*. This prayer always ended with "Amen" and the Crypto-Christians believed that it invalidated and nullified the Buddhist prayers (Medd 2003, 71).

this-worldly (Sugiyama-Lebra 2004, 246). The judgment of non-Christians like Inoue (井上光晴) is interesting. In his novel, *The House of Hands*, Inoue has one of the main actors recite a widely accepted opinion:

> The people are Crypto-Christians, but a lot of them are Buddhist, too, and they've turned against the Christian church. Maybe, they've gotten their religion all mixed up after pretending to be Buddhist for such a long time. (Inoue 1994, 159)

The Christian saints were also turned into *kamisama* (神様), "gods" (Coulmas 2005, 141), namely the Japanese martyrs, called *Antou-sama* (殉道様)[351] in their terminology. And they were celebrated with ancestral rituals (Turnbull 1998, 204). Examples for the Crypto-Christian martyrs, venerated as ancestors, are *Paburou-sama* (パブロウ様),[352] the missionary and catechist *San Juan-sama* (サンフアン様), and *Bastian-sama* (バスティアン様), the Japanese co-worker of *San Juan-sama* (Turnbull 1998, 117). With regard to Turnbull's work Higashibaba (東馬場郁生) pointed out that the magical use of relics from martyrs venerated as saints was imported from Europe. As this popular Catholicism grew "it interacted with Japanese religion." "The polytheistic tendencies of popular Catholicism, in particular, resonated well with the Japanese beliefs in *kami* (神)" (Higashibaba 2001, 42).

There are other elements of Buddhist and Shintoist ancestor veneration Christianized by the Japanese Crypto-Christians which are interesting in the context of animism and its god-concept:

- The Buddhist *obon* (御盆), a festival of the dead in summer, as well as its "Christianized" version *otoborai*, *otogaborai*, or *ootomurai* (大弔い), similar to All Soul's Day are still observed by Crypto-Christians. They pray to "Santa Maria and Jesus" for the dead (Turnbull 1998, 204), and use lanterns to symbolically show them the way (197).
- The deceased were offered water, rice, and incense on the Buddha-altar. On Sundays, so-called *rokkan*-prayers were offered at the graves

---

351. *Antou* (殉道) is the Japanese pronunciation of the Chinese *xùndào* (殉道), which means "to take upon oneself self-sacrifice," "to give one's life for somebody else," or "to become a martyr" (*Chinesisch-Deutsches Online-Wörterbuch* der LEO GmbH).

352. *Paburou-sama* (パブロウ様), derived from "Pablo," whose Japanese name was Koushirou (幸四郎), was an officer of the Hirado-Clan, who was commissioned to persecute active Christians. He became blind and Christians administered to his needs. When he learned that it had been Christians that administered to his needs he himself became a Christian. He became later a martyr. Source: http://hagakurefuryu.web.fc2.com/sights/martyrs/ikitsuki/ikitsuki.htm (accessed 15 Oct 2012).

and rice wine was drunk together with the spirits of the deceased (Turnbull 1998, 204).[353] In Japanese the *rokkan*-prayers are called *rokkanon* (六観音). They are prayers of Mahayana-Buddhist origin and originally offered to the Indian Goddess of Mercy *Kuan-yin* (観音). The Crypto-Christians also worshipped dual idols, with *Kuan-yin* (観音) on one side and Mary on the other side, with crosses engraved on the back (Whelan 2000, 371).

- The *ihai* (位牌), wooden tablets on the Buddha-altar representing the dead, were used by Crypto-Christians as well. In addition to the *kaimyou* (戒名), the common postmortem Buddhist name on the back, they showed the baptismal name on the front (Turnbull 1998, 197).
- All Crypto-Christian rituals ended with a feast as was common in Shintoism. This custom served also as obfuscation for the purpose of protection during persecution (Turnbull 2006, 129).

(2) Ancestor veneration in MBB (Muslim Background Believers) churches

Sauma compared Islamic and Chinese ancestral cults and some of his findings are valid for Japanese ancestor veneration as well: "Muslim ancestor practices bear comparison with Chinese tradition. In both regions food is offered in memory of the dead, the rituals are communal, and visits to cemeteries and shrines are involved." Ancestor veneration invokes *baraka*, "blessings," that is "spiritual power." What is distinctively different in the Muslim context is that worship expressed in falling prostrate before the ancestors is considered inappropriate (Sauma 2002, 326). Sauma (325) points to the vexing fact that the Turkish religious language can distinguish between worship and veneration, but that the lines between the respective terms are blurred if they are used in a secular context. This is also true for the Japanese context.

"It is not mosque worship but the domestic ancestor cult that becomes problematic for MBBs. Their Muslim families and neighbors expect them to fulfill their filial responsibilities, including preparing, serving and eating memorial meals in honor of the dead" (Sauma 2002, 327). MBBs – just as many Japanese Christians – feel the tension between 1 Corinthians 8:10 and Exodus 20:12. Their solution could be helpful for Japanese Christians as well:

---

353. Eating before the *butsudan* (仏壇) or the *kamidana* (神棚) is interpreted as "participatory unity" (Nishioka 1997, 283).

- reference to Elisha's "permission"[354] of Naaman's prayer in the temple of Rimmon (Sauma 2002, 330, 334–336);
- distinction between "memorial for the deceased" as commanded in the Ten Commandments and "worship of their spirits" (331–332);
- assertion that the spirits of the dead are not to be solicited – only the Holy Spirit (332);
- supersession of memorial feasts by the Lord's Supper (334);
- committing the ancestors "into the hands of God, who is just and merciful" (334);
- assurance of God's protection from the wrath of vengeful ancestral spirits (334);
- permission of participation in family-feasts "in memory of the forebears" for the sake of being a Christian testimony (335–336);
- prohibition of participation in ancestral meals in public places of worship according to 1 Corinthians 10:21 (338).

2.5.3.3 *Amae* (甘え) ("dependence") and the Bible

In this passage I want to discuss the first two parts of Takeo Doi's *Seisho-to "Amae"* (聖書と「甘え」; The Bible and "Amae") (1997).

In his short reflection on the Bible from the viewpoint of *amae* (甘え), "dependence," Doi has two parts: First he asks where characters of the Bible are determined by *amae* (甘え), "dependence," in their interpersonal relationships. Then he asks what dogmatic stance the Bible takes concerning *amae* (甘え), "dependence."

(1)   *Amae* (甘え), "dependence" in the life of biblical characters

For the Old Testament, Doi lines up the following examples:

---

354. I think that rather than asking "permission," Naaman asked for "forgiveness in advance" (Spina 2005, 86). Elisha's "Go in peace!" is "hardly a stamp of approval on what Naaman was about to do. In fact, it seems hard to draw a firm conclusion from the facts about Elisha and Naaman" (Morton 2012, 26). The question Naaman asks rather is that for forgiveness: "for doing something which they both knew was wrong" (Tennent in Morton 2012, 27). Morton concludes: "The story of Naaman does not help the insider movements' argument. There is too much that is different." As Naaman sought forgiveness for his anticipated bow it is clear that he knew it was not pleasing to God for "people do not seek pardons for that which is lawful and pleasing to God . . . . . People seek forgiveness for disobedience, especially after they understand their disobedience. Naaman knows that bowing, even in the course of his professional duties, requires forgiveness. He knows it is wrong. Finally, Elisha replies, 'Go in peace.' While it seems that the prophet permits this inconsistency, it is more reasonable to suggest that Elisha simply dismisses Naaman without addressing the problem" (Roman 2000, 179).

- The remark that "Isaac loved Rebecca and received comfort from her instead of from his deceased mother" (Gen 24:67)[355] shows that there is an "emotional consistency" between the wife-husband-relationship and the mother-son-relationship (Doi 1997, 23).
- The fact that Joseph thought it the most natural thing that he would have the highest place in his family, is a sign of "extreme *amae* (甘え)" (24).
- Amnon's real desire was of an erotic nature; what he really demanded from Tamar was *amae* (甘え). According to Doi, this explains the fact that Amnon hated Tamar after raping her. He had not got what he wanted (25).
- According to Doi, Tamar also showed *amae* (甘え); she didn't want to be driven away, because "she expected to receive some kind of friendliness from Amnon" (26).

For the New Testament Doi lines up the following examples:

- Paul compares his relationship to the Christians in Thessalonica with the relationship of a mother with her children (1 Thess 2:7–8:27). The emotions addressed are those of *amae* (甘え) (28).
- On Philippians 2:25–28 Doi wrote, "The loving thoughtfulness[356] described in an extremely detailed manner shows that the decisive familiarity between Paul and Epaphroditus and Epaphroditus's relationship with the Philippians form an emotional unity" (30).
- In his letter to Philemon, Paul calls Onesimus "a child born by him," who is "his heart," and with whom he is "related in the Lord." According to Doi, this close relationship also shows signs of *amae* (甘え) (30–31).

(2) Amae (甘え), "dependence" and biblical teaching

At the beginning of this part, Doi makes the following statement: "In order to avoid any confusion, I want to clearly state it right at the beginning: faith in both, faith in God as the Almighty All-Creator, and faith in this God having a relationship with man, does not mean that this has anything to do with

---

355. *Isaku-wa Ribeka-o ai-shite, nakunatta haha-ni kawaru nagusame-o eta* (イサクはリベカを愛して、なくなった母に代わる慰めを得た).

356. The Japanese *omoiyari* (思いやり) can hardly be translated. "Thoughtfulness" comes closest.

amae (甘え)." However, Doi then admits, that humans can understand the relationship with God only in human interpersonal terminology (1997, 33).

Doi starts with the election of Israel and says that "in the electing love of God, the germ of *amae* (甘え) can be possibly included" (34). Then he asks the question of fundamental importance: Is God in favor of *amae* (甘え)? According to Doi, the example of Job shows that God in the end also sanctioned the *amae* (甘え), which Job demonstrated when he wanted to *amaeru* (甘える)[357] before his compassionate friends (34–37). From here Doi moves on to Psalm 131 and points out that verse 2 explicitly talks about a "weaned child." That means that a child before being weaned is one[358] with his mother, and that it is only during the process of weaning that the feeling[359] of the independence of the child becomes apparent; the mother is recognized as mother, and the child by his own accord desires the mother. And this is the very essence of *amae* (甘え) (38).

Faith and *amae* (甘え) are not the same, yet, says Doi, there is an interdependence between them (38). Doi interprets Psalm 22:10 as follows:

> This psalm expressed that man is in God's providence from the very onset of his existence,[360] and this is why the child's heart attitude toward his mother is the nucleus of the heart a man has toward God. That a child not only "*amaru*(es)" (甘える) with his mother, but also trusts her and experiences peace of mind,[361] is a metaphor of a man's trust in God. (39)

In a similar way Doi interprets Psalm 27 where David calls God his "refuge" (v. 1), and where he says – as Doi translates verse 4: "One thing I ask of the Lord, which I long for dearly, that I may live in the house of the Lord for all my life, and that I may, tasting the Lord's sweetness, know and behold his temple." *Koimotomeru* (恋い求める), "to long dearly," "to entreat," "to demand," as well as *shu-no umashisa-o ajiwaishiru* (主のうましさを味わい知る), "tasting the Lord's sweetness," are both phrases that are closely related with *amae* (甘え). For Doi it is significant that in the same psalm verse 10 is found as well, which, as Doi points out, states that faith in God surpasses the deepest human relationship, that between parents and children (40). "It is of

---

357. *Amaetaku naru* (甘えたくなる), "[he] gets into a state, in which he wants to *amaeru* (甘える)." "It was only through this empathetic gesture, through their compassion, that Job became able to express his grievance" (Dieterich 1989, 232).

358. *Ittai* (一体), literally "one body."

359. *Kokoro-no hataraki* (心の働き), literally "heart-labor."

360. *Kami-no setsuri-no naka-ni aru* (神の摂理の中にある).

361. *Kokoro-no yasuragi* (心の安らぎ).

greatest significance that, as far as the Old Testament is concerned, it can be deducted from the so-called human narratives that thoughts about God contain a *amae* (甘え)-like psychology" (41).

The starting point for Doi's survey in the New Testament is Matthew 11:25–30. "The peace[362] Jesus promised sufficiently gives testimony to the presence of *amae* (甘え)-like psychology" (43). In a similar way he interprets Matthew 7:11 and Romans 8:15 (44–45). *Amae* (甘え) is present in both Old and New Testament, but the significant difference between the two Testaments is that in the New Testament *amae* (甘え) permeates interpersonal relationships to a greater degree. Doi reduces this to the fact that through Christ humans can be sure of God's fatherly love (47–48).

2.5.3.4 Overcoming the *amae* (甘え)-mentality

I have previously dealt with this subject in the context of motherly god-concepts. This discussion needs to be resumed here.

Stressing the "fatherly attributes" of a strict, punishing God is as equally wrong as stressing the "motherly attributes" of a forgiving God. God's forgiving, "motherly" unconditional love, and his "fatherly" love demanding holiness without compromise, belong together. Endou's Christ has a motherly character. He can even demand that Christians deny him. He wraps everything in his forgiving love, even if "this causes him pain" (Kohler 1976, 55). In the foreword of the English translation of *Iesu-no shougai* (イエスの生涯; A Life of Jesus) Endou wrote:

> Jesus as I depict him is a person who lived for love and still more love and yet he was put to death for he chose to live without violent resistance. My way of depicting Jesus is rooted in my being a Japanese novelist. I wrote this book for the benefit of Japanese readers who have no Christian tradition of their own and who know almost nothing about Jesus. What is more, I was determined to highlight the particular aspect of love in his personality precisely in order to make Jesus understandable in terms of the religious psychology of my non-Christian countrymen and then to demonstrate that Jesus is not alien to their religious sensibilities.[363]
> The religious mentality of the Japanese is – just as it was at the time when people accepted Buddhism – responsive to one who "suffers

---

362. *Yasuragi* (安らぎ).

363. "Endou's novels deal with the question of how the non-theistic Japanese can embrace theistic Christianity" (Tang 2004, 93).

with us" and who "allows for our weakness," but their mentality has little tolerance for any kind of transcendent being who judges humans harshly, then punishes them. In brief, the Japanese tend to seek in their gods and Buddhas a warm-hearted mother rather than a stern father. With this fact always in mind I tried not so much to depict God in the father image that tends to characterize Christianity, but rather to depict the kind-hearted maternal aspect of God revealed to us in the personality of Jesus. (1978, 1)

The Japanese way of forgiving is different from the biblical way of forgiving. In the Bible sin is held against the sinner until it is exposed and confessed (e.g. Ps 32:3–5; 1 John 1:5–10). Here forgiveness means cancellation. But in Japan sin is not exposed in love but – on the contrary – "wrapped with love." This is not a problem because "sin does not seem to play an important role, rather seems to be a synonym of weakness." "It is clear that Christ here is described as the one who deeply understands the weakness" (Yewangoe 1987, 202). Thus salvation itself is redefined: "In *Shikai-no hotori* (死海のほとり, The Powerless Savior, 1979), Endou describes Jesus as the Sufferer. Endou sees Jesus Christ not as a Savior who abolished suffering from the world, but rather as one of the sufferers participating in the sufferings of this world. Endou views Jesus as the Co-Sufferer" (Yewangoe 1987, 202). Sin is not something to be repented from, something to be overcome. Consequently, salvation is not power that overcomes sin. Rather is sin weakness to be suffered under.

According to Yoshizawa, "the syncretistic peculiarity of the Japanese culture is founded in its traditional communal solidarity." "The traditional Japanese religion can be characterized as motherly religion,[364] which in a way

---

364. This phrase is quite old. It was coined by the European journalist Pfenninger, who talked about "a great mother" in 1974: "All (Japanese) are part of this body. All parts are happy, want to be glad with it, and suffer with it. Being cast out from this body is the worst that can happen to an individual" (Okano 2002, 145).

Masaaki Tezuka names "dependence on maternalistic personalities" as the first characteristic of the *nihonkyou* ((日本教), the "science of Japan" (Lundell 1995, 407). It is not by chance that the Japanese "High God" is the High-Goddess *Amaterasu-Oomikami* (天照大御神), "The Great and Honorable Deity Illuminating the Sky." Shintoism is one of the few religions that understand the sun as female (Cherry 1991, 16). In the 13th century the priestly family of the Watarai (渡会) created the *jinguu hiki* (神宮秘記), the so-called "secret books" where the *Toyouke* (豊受), revered by the Watarai (渡会), was made equal with *Amaterasu-Oomikami* (天照大御神) as co-creator under the name of *Ame-no Minakanushi* (天の御中主) or *Kuni-no Tokotachi* (国常立) (Teeuwen 1993, 225). This deity was the very first and originated by itself as is written in the *Kojiki* (古事記): "The names of the deities that originated in the beginning of heaven and earth in the Plain of the High Heavens were *Ame-no Minakanushi-no Mikami* (天之御中主神), the 'Lord of the Honorable Middle of Heaven,' as well as *Takami-musubi* (高皇産霊),

embraces man warm-heartedly" (185). Daisetsu Teitarou Suzuki, probably the most prominent representative of Zen Buddhism, thinks that here is one of the basic differences between the West and the East: "At the basis of the ways of thinking and feeling of the Westerner there is the father." But in the Orient it is the mother. The mother "enfolds everything in an unconditional love without difficulties or questioning. Love in the West always contains a residue of power. Love in the East is all embracing. It is open to all sides" (Daisetsu Teitarou Suzuki in Goss and Klass 2005, 30). According to Miyata, the climate of the "motherly religion" is a main motif in Shuusaku Endou's (遠藤周作) *Silence* (*chinmoku*, ちんもく) (1966). Endou has Ferraira say: "This country is a more terrible swamp than you can imagine. Whenever you plant a sapling in this swamp the roots begin to rot. The leaves grow yellow and wither. And we have planted the sapling of Christianity in this swamp" (1970, 237).

This "terrible swamp" kindles the opposition of Japanese theologians and psychologists against the all-pervading Japanese syncretism. Miyata rightfully doubts whether such a "Japanized Christianity" of motherly love is "Protestant Christianity."[365] The Roman Catholic Marian devotion "as a motherly religion" has the tendency "to dissolve into the Japanese climate," from which the "Protestant faith" with its "pungent awareness of sin," its "radical dogma of grace," and the resulting "deep awareness of the distance between God and man" sharply distinguishes itself.

> We can only then talk about the "gospel having taken root" when this transcendent faith truly takes root in the spiritual climate of Japan, when it radically changes the worldview and its concept on humanity, and thus creates a new power. (Miyata 1984, 180–181)

---

the 'High and Honorable Originator.'" Numazawa concludes that since time immemorial the Japanese scholars agreed that these three deities are the creators of the world and they reside in the Plain of Heaven (Numazawa 1970, 198–199).

The idea of a male creator-deity later re-occurs in the work of *Atsutane Hirata* (平田篤胤) (1776–1843) who was influenced by Christianity. He claimed that the *Taigen Kousoshin* (大元高祖神), the "first ancestral deity" by the name of *Ame-no Minakanushi-no Mikami* (天之御中主神) had "neither beginning nor ending," that he was "in heaven and had enough virtue to give birth to all creation." "Even though he permeates everything he rules creating in quietness." Here both principles are combined, the female principle of giving birth and the male principle, and the female deity *Amaterasu Oomikami* (天照大御神) is replaced. According to Hirata, the nature deities *Takami-musubi-no-kami* (高皇産霊神) and *Kami-musubi-no-kami* (神皇産霊神) emanated from *Ame-no Minakanushi-no Mikami* (天之御中主神), formed *Izanami* (伊弉冉 or 伊邪那美 or 伊耶那美 or 伊弉弥) and *Izanagi* (伊弉諾神 or 伊邪那岐命 or 伊耶那岐命), who in turn only then gave birth to *Amaterasu Oomikami* (天照大御神) (Devine 1981, 42).

365. *Evangelisches Christentum*.

Miyata explicitly speaks in favor of "draining the Japanese swamp" (Miyata 1984, 186), mainly because the motherly principle is by far not as tolerant and merciful as it seems to be. "'The path of mercy leads (only) over the abolition of one's own self.' This, however, is the demand of absolute power . . . Here the ugliness of this 'swamp' veritably shows" (183). Takeo Doi demanded the overcoming of *amae* (甘え) (185) as the motherly climate of the all-embracing Japanese syncretism. Because in the world of *amae* (甘え) there "is no freedom and independence in the strictest sense of the word," Doi demanded the "transcending" of *amae* (甘え) by means of the "discovery of subject and object" (185).

The psychiatrist Yuuichi Hattori (服部雄一) goes beyond Doi. In the discussion following a lecture on dual personality hosted by the *Missiology Forum* (*JEMA*), he said that Japanese collectivism could not be overcome by adoption of Western individualism, but only by a personal encounter of the individual with a "higher being," with God (Hattori 2010). In his clinical counseling, Hattori is mainly occupied with people and families suffering from *hikikomori* (引き篭り), a "typically Japanese" phenomenon, even though "studies suggest that this phenomenon is growing in other countries, too." "*Hikikomori* (引き篭り) is a complex form of withdrawal behavior, observed in Japan, that resembles the symptoms of schizoid personality disorder. Under the pressure of collectivism, mainly young males suppress their "true self"[366] and lose contact with their own emotions to an extent that they become unable to participate in communal life and therefore *hikikomoru* (引き篭る), "withdraw" to their own room, in some cases for years.[367] They

> shut themselves in the homes of their parents, seldom go out, and have very limited face-to-face contact with other people. They spend their days browsing the Web or chatting online and only occasionally see their parents, who continue to support their adult children financially. Economic and social conditions of contemporary Japan may contribute to this form of self-isolation. (Shiraev and Levy 2015, 238)

---

366. Hattori translates the Japanese *honne* (本音) with *true self*, *tatemae* (建前) with *false self* (Hattori 2010). *Honne* (本音) literally means the "true sound" that is, the true sound of the heart. *Tatemae* (建前) literally means that which is "set up in front." Kerr explains *tatemae* (建前) as follows: "People will strive to uphold the *tatemae* (建前) in the face of blatant facts to the contrary, believing it is important to keep the *honne* (本音), hidden in order to maintain public harmony" (105). In this context Kerr quotes Kawai (河合隼雄): "In Japan, as long as you are convinced you are lying for the good of the group, it's not a lie" (Kawai in Kerr 2001, 110).

367. When Hattori's book on *hikikomori* (引き篭り) was published in 2005, he estimated one million cases (10).

Part II

Peace as a Central Concept of Soteriology

"Theological anthropology inherently is peace anthropology" (Jüngel 2003, 30). Therefore *shalom* is rightfully also central in today's mission theology. According to Wrogemann, the major change in mission theology since 1960 has been, besides its geographical and organizational universalization, its "soteriological universalization" with *shalom* as its key concept (1995, 140–141).

> It is apparent that the whole width of human life has become the field where mission acts and proves itself valid. The goal of *missio Dei* therefore is the enforcement of worldwide *shalom*. As a result, the traditional order God-church-world has been reversed to God-world-church. Thus the primary goal of missions is not the planting of churches but the transformation and betterment of human, social and ecological status quos. (1995, 141–142)

This trend has continued since. The study document of the 2004 *Forum for World Evangelization* reads:

> *Shalom* as God's peace contains the vision of wholeness, of the good life and the flourishing for all humans as well as for the rest of creation, individually and collectively, in the mutual fellowship with God and among humans. *Shalom* as God's peace

encompasses all dimensions of human life, including the spiritual, physical, cognitive, social, and economical dimensions. *Shalom* seeks mercy, truth, justice, and peaceableness through personal surrender to Christ as well as through social transformation. (Schäfer 2005, 11–12).

In this part I am going to outline the Japanese concept of peace (和) as well as the biblical *shalom*-concept.

3

The Japanese Peace-Concept *Wa* (和)

Summary: The Japanese concept of peace *wa* (和) is a key concept of Japanese culture. It can be divided into the word-fields "sum," "harmony," "peace," and "Japan." Due to its strong focus on aesthetics the Japanese concept of peace has no strong sense of justice.

3.1 Word-Field Study of *Wa* (和)

First an old Japanese proverb:

> *Ten-no toki-wa chi-no ri-ni shikazu. Chi-no ri-wa hito-no wa-ni shikazu.*
>
> 天の時は地の利にしかず。地の利は人の和にしかず。
>
> Literal translation: Heaven's time, earth's benefit it equals not. Earth's benefit, man's *wa* it equals not.
>
> Meaning: Earthly benefits are better than heavenly gifts. Peace among humans is better than earthly benefits.

Conclusion: The most important is *wa* (和)! The maxim that "harmony between humans, between humans and their ancestors and other spirits, the Supreme Being, animals and plants, and 'inanimate' nature has to be maintained" (Wiher 2003, 293) applies to animistic societies in general.

> The more animistic an order of life is, the more cautiously and even the more anxiously – eventually the more harmony-attentively – the individual moves. He does so in order to make at least his

very own contribution towards harmony and thus possibly force the natural and numinous world to show benevolence. (Weggel 1997, 42)

As early as in the moral principles called *juushichikenpou* (十七憲法), the *Seventeen-Article Constitution*, published in 604 (Pye 2001, 6) by Prince Shoutoku (聖徳太子) (574–622) it says: "Consider *wa* (和) as the most valuable. This statement 'serves as an important marker for Japanese national identity'" (Triplett 2006b, 180). As שלם is a key concept of the Hebrew culture, *wa* (和) is a key concept for the understanding of the Japanese culture (Wetzel 2004, 105; Coll et al. 1998, 137).[1] To establish this, Wierzbicka quotes from the *Kokutai-no Hongi* (国体の本義):[2]

> When we trace . . . the progress of our history, what we always find there is the spirit[3] of harmony. Harmony is a product of the great achievements of the founding of the nation, and is the power behind our historical growth; while it is also a humanitarian Way[4] inseparable from our daily lives . . . Our country makes harmony its fundamental Way.[5] Herein indeed lies the reason why the

---

1. Wierzbicka (1997, 198) adds the also "untranslatable" key-concepts *amae* (甘え), dependence, *giri* (義理), duty, *on* (恩), obligation *enryo* (遠慮), restraint, *seishin* (精神), psyche or spirit, and *omoiyari* (思いやり) thoughtfulness. Hellen Deresky names the following key-concepts: *wa* (和), peace and harmony and *amae* (甘え), dependence, as the two principles that can explain the Japanese culture (Ootsu et al. 2002, 29). "No other term is used as much as *wa* (和) or 'harmony' to describe the nature of Japanese society" (Triplett 2006b, 179).

2. The *Kokutai-no Hongi* (国体の本義), the "*Cardinal Principles of the National Polity* "was published by the Bureau of Thought Control of the Ministry of Education in 1937 (Huffmann 1998, 25). The two million copies were to be used as school textbooks. One of the authors was the Shintoist philosopher Watsuji (Daston and Vidal 2004, 314), the "author of *sakkoku* (鎖国)," the "Seclusion," as Matsuoka called him (373). The *Kokutai-no Hongi* (国体の本義) is an appeal for Shintoist ideals and frequently refers to the *Kyougi-ni Kansuru Chokugo* (教育ニ関スル勅語), the *Imperial Rescript on Education* of the Meiji-Reform (Picken 2004, 105). It propagates the ideals of "familism, Emperor-loyalty, and patriotic devotion" (Fridell 1970, 823). Wierzbicka probably quotes from the translation of John O. Gauntlett published in 1949 (Seats 2006, 74). An extensive introduction into Watsuji's life and work, particularly into his Nazi propaganda can be found in Bellah's *Japan's Cultural Identity: Some Reflections on the Work of Watsuji Tetsuro* (1965).

3. *Seishin* (精神).

4. This translation is rather misleading. The Japanese *jinrin-no michi* (人倫の道) is better translated with "Way of human relations."

5. *Konpon-no michi* (根本の道).

ideologies of our nation are different[6] from those of the nations of the West. (Wierzbicka 1997, 248)

The part left out by Wierzbicka is very interesting:

Wa-no seishin-wa, banbutsuyuugou-no ue-ni ikiritatsu. Hitobito-ga akumade jiko-o shu-to shi, watakushi-o shutyou suru baai-ni-wa, mujuntairitsu nomiatsute wa-wa shoujinai. Kojinshugi-nioite-wa, kono mujuntairitsu-o chouseikanwa-suru-tame-no kyoudou, takyou, gisei-nado-wa ariete-mo, kekkyoku makoto-no wa-wa shoujinai. Sunawachi kojinshugi-no shakai-wa bannin-no bannin-ni taisuru tousou-de-ari, rekishi-wa subete kaikyuutousou-no rekishi-to-mo narau.

和の精神は、万物融合の上に峨り立つ。人々が飽くまで自己を主とし、私を主張する場合には、矛盾対立のみあつて和は生じない。個人主義に於ては、この矛盾対立を調整緩和するための協同・妥協・犠牲等はあり得ても、結局真の和は存しない。即ち個人主義の社会は万人の万人に対する闘争であり、歴史はすべて階級闘争の歴史ともならう。

The spirit of *wa* lives upon the unity of all things. If the people make Self the principal and insist on the private, it will lead only to contradictory confrontation and *wa* will not come about. As for individualism, even if things such as cooperation, compromise, and sacrifice were likely to exist to reconcile and alleviate its contradictory confrontation, true *wa* would never come about. That is, an individualistic society would be the war of all against all, and all history would eventually emulate the history of class struggle.

Miyata comments:

In short, in Japan all freedom of opinion will surely be unitized by that particular great harmony, which summarizes all different standpoints into one common origin. At the end of the process there is not conflict but harmony. Everything ends, not in destruction but in fulfillment. Here is the "Great Spirit" of Japan. (1984, 58)

---

6. The Japanese original is much stronger. It talks about a *konponteki-ni kotonaru moen* (根本的に異なる所以). A "fundamentally different way of doing [things]."

Wa (和) has four basic meanings:[7] (1) sum,[8] (2) harmony (order, peace of mind),[9] (3) peace (non-war),[10] and (4) Japan.[11]

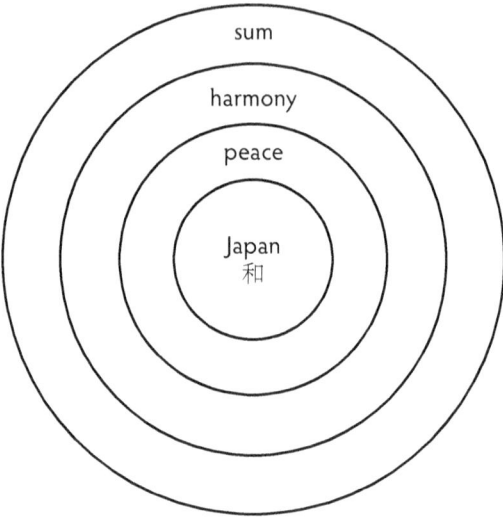

Figure 3.1 The Four Basic Meanings of *Wa* (和)

3.1.1 *Wa* (和) as Sum

Even though this meaning of *wa* (和) is rarely used in Japan today, I want to start here. *Wa* (和) almost always equates with "harmony," but the basic meaning of "sum" shows the basic texture and structure of *wa* (和): *wa* (和) is a state in which nothing lacks, and no area is secluded; in other words: *wa* (和) is a holistic term. In this sense Weggel (38) understands the pan-Asian peace concept. He talks about "harmony in entirety."

---

7. The *Kokugojiten* (国語辞典) divides into (1) be soft; (2) to be friends with others; (3) to be adapted; (4) to adapt a rhyme to a poem of somebody else; (5) sum.

8. The synonym Chinese character for 和 in this particular meaning is 合. The synonym Chinese character for 和 are discussed below.

9. The synonym Chinese characters for 和 in this particular meaning are 睦, 静, 穏, and 壅.

10. The synonym Chinese characters for 和 in this particular meaning are 平 and 緩.

11. The synonym Chinese characters for 和 in this particular meaning is 倭.

Souwa (総和), the compound of *sou* (総), "general," and *wa* (和), harmony, can be used as a synonym of *goukei* (合計). Both mean "sum." In the following mathematical phrases *wa* (和) also means "sum":

- *yon-to go-no wa-wa kyuu de aru* (四と五の和は九である), "the *wa* (和) of four and five is nine."
- *wa-o motomeru* (和を求める), "to determine the sum."

3.1.2 Wa (和) as Harmony

As indicated above, this meaning has to be divided into two parts: outward order in society and inward "peace of mind."

3.1.2.1 Wa (和) as interpersonal harmony

"The concept of *heiwa* (平和), peace, in Japan has been influenced by China and India." It is closer to the Chinese concept. *P'ing ho* (和平) as well as *heiwa* (平和) are concerned with political order. But *heiwa* (平和) can also mean the peaceful state of "peace of mind." "Furthermore, it places an emphasis on emotion, which distinguishes Japanese Confucianism from classical Chinese Confucianism." Another aspect of the Japanese concept of peace is aesthetics, which can probably be traced back to Shintoism (Ishida 1989, 125). Ootsu (大津誠) et al. (2002, 29) share this opinion as they hold that *wa* (和) is a genuinely Shintoist concept "which focuses on spiritual and physical harmony."

Here a comparison with verb *kasu* (和す), also written with 和 and expressing its basic meaning is interesting. The two basic meanings of *kasu* (和す) depict the collective cohesiveness of Japanese society: *wa* (和) as "being soft" and *wa* (和) as "being mingled."

The next two sections explore these two basic meanings, and the following section considers the connection between *wa* (和) and Japanese Confucianism.

Wa (和) as "being soft"

The general Japanese word for "soft" is *yawarakai* (和らかい, also written柔らかい and 軟らかい). In a literal sense it can mean things like a soft pillow, tender meat, overcooked rice, soft hands or soft wood. Charcoal produced from the particularly mild pine wood is called *nikosumi* (和柔炭), "soft charcoal," the downy feathers of birds' *nikoge* (和柔毛, 和毛, or毳), "soft or tender fur."

In a figurative sense *wa* (和) in the sense of "soft" or "soften" is used for eased pain, released stress, calmed anger, or a pacified mind. The intransitive *kokoro-ga yawaragu* (心が和らぐ), "the heart softens" is used as a synonym of *tagai-no kimochi-ga nagomu* (互いの気持が和む), the emotions of the other person are softened." The transitive *kokoro-o yawarageru* (心を和らげる), "to soften the heart" is used as a synonym of *tagai-no kimochi-o nagomaseru* (互いの気持を和ませる), "to soften the emotions of the other person."

The way to soften a heart or the way to get a soft heart is the way of *amanau* (和う). The alternative writing of *amanau* as 甘なう (using the Chinese character of *amae* [甘え], "dependence") shows just how close Wierzbicka's "key-concepts" *wa* (和) and *amae* (甘え) belong together. The word *nikibu* (和ぶ)[12] expresses the same. It means "to become mild." The *Kokugojiten* (国語辞典) adds *kutsurogi amanjiru*, written 寛ぎ安んじる and (!) 寛ぎ甘んじる as synonyms. It means "to relax." A human can experience *karaku* (和楽), "harmony and pleasure" which means that she *uchitokeru*(es) (打ち解ける)," that she, literally, "defrosts," that she unbends, "opens up," and enjoys. According to these words, "harmony" is that particular interpersonal "sweetness" in which everybody feels at home, where he can relax and expect and demand of the other whatever he wants. In this interpersonal relationship one part *aru koto-ni amanzuru* (あることに甘んずる) or *mansoku suru* (満足する), he is satisfied as his need (足) was fulfilled (満). The other part *kanju suru* (甘受する), "he accepts (受) the *amae* (甘え)-behavior of the other person." Then *wa* (和) and *wa* (和) are unified, which is expressed by the term *wagou* (和合). *Awaseru* (合わせる) means "to unify" and "to join." It is used in *fuufu-no wagou* (夫婦の和合), the "marital *wagou* (和合)," or in *ikka wagou* (一家和合), the "familial *wagou* (和合)," in which the husband (夫) and wife (婦) are together and the family (家) one (一).[13] Everybody cooperates – this is what is expressed with the word *wakyou* (和協), the "cooperating (協) *wa* (和)." The words used in this harmonious atmosphere are only *yawarakai* (和らかい), only "soft," also called *kangen* (甘言), *amae*(甘え)-words. Finally it is interesting that *amanau*

---

12. Sometimes also as *nikimu* (和む).

13. The closeness of *wa* (和) and *amaeru* (甘える) is an ambivalent issue. As much as adults, particularly men, yearn for this sweetness as long as they live, they are ashamed of this desire which makes them dependent on their wives. This shame is compensated in a number of depreciating words and phrases: *Yawaraka* (和らか, also written 柔らか and 軟らか), also written with *wa* (和), means "tepidity lacking toughness" is equated with the pejorative term *memeshii* (女々しい), "womanish" or "unmanly." *Nikitama* (和魂) (not to be confused with *nigimitama,* 和御魂, and not to be confused with *wakon,* 和魂), also a devaluating term, which literally means a *wa-tamashii,* a *wa*-soul is used for *onwa* (温和), the "mildness and weakness of women." They are considered *tawayame* (手弱女), literally "women (女) with weak (弱) hands (手)." The "mild" and "weak" hand of women is also called *nikote*, which means *wa*-hand (和手) or "soft hand" (柔手).

(和う or 甘なう), "soften the heart," *wakai suru* (和解する),[14] "reconcile," and *doui suru* (同意する), "to be of one opinion or will" are synonyms.

It seems that *wa* (和) is to be maintained at any cost. But this is not the case. The following proverb proves the opposite: *kunshi-wa wa shite dou zezu, shoujin-wa doujite wa sezu* (君子は和して同ぜず、小人は同じて和せず). It can be transliterated as follows: "A nobleman creates *Einheit*[15] without *Vereinerleiung*,[16] a commoner ends in *Vereinerleiung* without creating *Einheit*." In Japanese the difference between *Einheit* and *Vereinerleiung* is expressed with the opposites of *wa* (和) and *dou* (同). The *Koji Kotowaza-no Jiten* (故事ことわざの辞典) explains *dou* (同) as *muteiken-ni douchou suru* (無定見に同調する), "taking sides without principles."

Finally, "soft" can also mean "cultivated or "refined." *Nikoshi* (和し or 柔し) describes a "cultivated" state as opposed to *araarashii* (荒荒しい), "coarse" or "rude." *Nikishine* (和稲), soft (和) or cultivated rice (稲) as opposed to the wild (荒) rice (稲), *arashine* (荒稲).

Wa (和) as "being mingled"

If two different things are mingled or mixed, the process is called *aemaze* (和交 or 韲交), the result *aemono* (和物). Synonyms are:

- the intransitive *majiriau* (混じり合う), "being mingled"
- the intransitive *issho-ni tokeau* (一緒に溶け合う), "being melted into each other"
- the intransitive *choushi-ga au* (調子が合う), "to produce a convergent tone"
- the transitive *mazeawaseru* (混ぜ合わせる), to "mingle"
- the transitive *issho-ni suru* (一緒にする), "to bring together"
- the transitive *choushi-o awaseru* (調子を合わせる), "to tune"

The second basic meaning is almost identical with the meaning (but not with the usage!) of *wasuru* (和する): it is used for the union of two humans, particularly husband and wife in *fuufu aiwasu* (夫婦相和す),[17] the combination of two different things, particularly Ying and Yang in *inyou aiwasu* (陰陽相和す); also the sounding together of two tones is expressed with this term

---

14. Besides the meaning of "restoration of a relationship" *wakai* (和解) has the emotional notion that the heart becomes *nagoyaka* (和やか), "harmonious" and "likeable."

15. Unity.

16. Indifference.

17. In Japanese theater, passages talking about love are therefore called *wagoto* (和事), literally *wa*-things, and the actors playing these parts are called the *wagotoshi* (和事師).

as in *piano-ni washite utau* (ピアノに和してう歌う), "to sing to (together with) piano accompaniment"; the Japanese word for chord is *waon* (和音) the "*wa* (和) of sounds (音)," the word for harmonics is *waseigaku* (和声学), the "science (学) of joined (和) voices (声)," the word of the laws of harmonics *waseihou* (和声法), the "law (法) of joined (和) voices (声)." Two classic examples:

- When one received a poem in old Japan, one returned a poem in the same rhyme. The returned poem was therefore called *wain* (和韻), the "adapted (和) rhyme (韻)."
- The proverb *gun-wa ka-ni atte shuu-ni arazu* (軍は和にあって衆にあらず) means that in combat not the multitude (衆) of soldiers (軍), but the unity (和) is crucial.

"Mingling" can also have a negative meaning. *Aesagasu* (和えさがす) means that that which was said by somebody else is diffused and thus confused, which leads to *baka-ni sareru* (ばかにされる) or *gurou sareru* (愚弄される), the "fooling" of the speaker.[18] The Japanese word for "fornication" or "adultery" is *wakan* (和姦) which literally means people become affiliated in an inappropriate way. These phrases use *wa* (和) in a negative sense.

Wa (和) as harmony and Confucianism

Kisala (17) claims that before the *Meiji*-Era *wa* (和) meant "social order." The old proverb *wa-wa tenka-no tatsudou nari* (和は天下の達道なり), "*wa* (和) is the common moral under heaven" says that there are no relationships "under heaven" which are not governed by *wa* (和). This proverb reflects the ideal of Confucianism which Okakura (岡倉覚三) enthusiastically calls the "glory of Asia," that "glory" which lies "in that oscillation of peace which pounds in every heart; that harmony which brings together the Emperor and the peasant; that all-encompassing intuition which demands all sympathy and all politeness as its fruits" (142). Confucius aimed at peace and harmony which, according to him, would arrive if the leaders of the nation lived ethically. "If all members of a nation, those in the ruling class and the commoners, live ethically, social harmony will be the result" (Ootsu et al. 2002, 30). In Confucianism this harmony is connected with the reverence paid to those ranking higher in the hierarchy. "It is no voluntary or optional cooperation of people, but . . . is founded on the second value [of the Seventeen Articles], that is, on hierarchical

---

18. The otherwise neutral *aeru* (合える or 和える or 韲える or 齏える), "mix," "unify" can also be understood in this sense.

obedience" (Pye 2001, 6). Thus the phrase *wakeiseijaku* (和敬清寂) of the Zen-Buddhist tea ceremony joins *wa* (和) with *kei* (敬), "reverence."[19] This kind of sociological harmony influences even nature. The *Koji Kotowaza-no Jiten* (故事ことわざの辞典) explains the proverb *wa-o motte wa-o itasu* (和を以て和を致す), "*wa* (和) brings *wa* (和)," thus, that the humble heart of the nation leads to overflowing blessing for nature.[20]

It is here where the difference between traditional Chinese Confucianism and Japanese Confucianism is most significant. In his *Discours sur la théologie naturelle des Chinois*, published in 1705 and considered to be the culmination of his studies on China, Leibniz (26) names five Confucian virtues: (1) *Ren* (or more exactly *ren dao*, 人道), "humanity and love"; (2) *yi* (義), "uprightness and justice"; (3) *li* (理), "morality and standards of conduct"; (4) *zhi* (知), "knowledge and wisdom," and (5) *xin* (信), "credibility and trustworthiness." Van Ess (113) particularly emphasized "humanity, just behavior, wisdom, and lawful conduct, accompanied by prudence." Metzger (62) names *jun* (均), "balance"; *an* (安), "peace"; and *he* (平), "harmony" as the most important values of Confucianism and concludes, "Because of the personalization of values and morals the individual behavior is also the foundation of justice and social reason."

Quite contrary, the Japanese Confucianism is weak in the area of humanity and justice due to its emotional and esthetic components (Ishida 1989, 125). The Confucian proverb *rei-wa kore wa-o motte toutoshi-to nasu* (礼は之和を用って貴しと為す) means that social order, *rei* (礼), only leads to precious (貴し) results when exercised with gentleness or harmony, *wa* (和).[21] It warns against social order maintained with brutish harshness – and against this particular weakness. And it warns against neglecting justice for the sake of harmony.

Warning against neglecting humanity: According to De Mente, the Japanese concept of harmony contains not only the key-element of *on* (恩), "obligation," which determines the place of individuals in society, but also *sahou* (作法), etiquette, that is, rules of conduct to be followed meticulously. Morals were a matter of manners (De Mente 1994, 35). As a third key-element of the

---

19. This phrase describes reverence between host and guest as the adequate disposition of heart during the tea ceremony. The two Chinese characters at the end of the phrase describe this disposition of a heart of the tea house and the utensils as pure (清) and simple (寂).

20. *Kokumin-no yawaraida kokoro-ni yotte, shizen-ni housaku nado-no koufuku-o maneku* (国民のやわらいだ心によって、自然に豊作などの幸福を招く).

21. Another form of this proverb is *wa-o motte toutoshi-to nasu* (和を以て貴しと為す), which means the same.

Japanese harmony-concept de Mente (38) names the extreme homogeneity forced upon people by means of harsh collective punishment, something psychologically still present in Japan today. Breaking of etiquette – even for just reasons – was considered worse than the vilest crime and punished brutally. De Mente (36) reports the case of a certain farmer, Sogo, who went directly to the hamlet chieftain and bewailed the harsh taxes. He was made to watch the beheading of his three sons before he and his wife were crucified, because he had not followed correct etiquette. In Japanese morals, mercy is secondary to harmony, which can be seen in the proverb *wa-wa jin-no moto* (和は仁の基), "*wa* (和) is the foundation of mercy." Grotesquely, it is the Japanese love for beauty which – in the name of harmony – can use unspeakable cruelty.[22]

Today this cruelty is hardly tangible in public life. However, the strict Confucian rule of the world of work is still very much alive and demands its victims through *karoujisatsu* (過労自殺), "suicide caused by depression due to overwork" (Iwanami 2006, 106), and through *karoushi* (過労死), "death caused by overwork."[23]

---

22. This tragic tendency is further discussed under *Wa* (和) as non-war.

23. In 2004, 32,325 people in Japan committed suicide, in 2005, 32,522 people, and in 2006, 32,155. The death toll of suicide is four times higher than that of traffic accidents, amounting to an average of almost 90 people per day. About 70% of the victims are males, 34% over 60 years old. 47.9% are unemployed, 25.4% workers. Reasons are: health problems (about 39%), financial and other problems (about 33%), family-related problems (10%), and work-related problems (about 7%) (Tokyo Hokei Gakuin College Press 2007, 226; Sugitani et al. 2007, 208).

In 2016, "Japan is witnessing a record number of compensation claims related to death from overwork . . . Work-related suicides are up 45 percent in the past four years among those 29 and younger, and up 39 percent among women, labor ministry data show." White describes the present-day, economic context: "Labor demand, with 1.28 jobs per applicant, is the highest since 1991, which should help Prime Minister Shinzo Abe draw more people into the workforce to counter the effect of a shrinking population, but lax enforcement of labor laws means some businesses are simply squeezing more out of employees, sometimes with tragic consequences. Claims for compensation for *karoushi* (過労死) rose to a record high of 1,456 [with unrecorded cases being ten times higher], says Hiroshi Kawahito, secretary general of the National Defense Counsel for Victims of *Karoushi* (過労死)] in the year to end-March 2015, according to labor ministry data, with cases concentrated in healthcare, social services, shipping and construction, which are all facing chronic worker shortages . . . The problem has become more acute as Japan's workforce has divided into two distinct categories – regular employees, and those on temporary or non-standard contracts, frequently women and younger people" (White 2016).

According to the *Karoushi Bengodan Zenkoku Renrakukai* (過労死弁護団全国連絡会), the National Association of *Karoushi*-Lawyers, *karoushi* (過労死) is defined as "medical conditions of the brain, the heart, the respiratory system, the soul, and the like because of work-related stress, which worsen and lead to death" (Suwa and Irobe 2008, 12). However, it is extremely difficult to become eligible for a claim of *karoushi* (過労死). "A cardiovascular death is likely to be considered *karoushi* (過労死) if an employee worked 100 hours of overtime in the month beforehand, or 80 hours of overtime in two or more consecutive months in the previous

Warning against neglecting justice: Towards the end of the "bubble economy," more and more scandals surfaced, baffling Japanese and non-Japanese alike with its obvious apparent absence of any feelings of guilt. When *Daiwa Securities* paid protection money to corporate racketeers in order to prevent disturbances at shareholders' meetings, this was, legally speaking, a crime. However, the presiding judge said:

> It is true that there was a *fuuchou* (風潮) [a tendency] that the smooth operation of the shareholders' meeting is a priority of the management. Such a belief may have given the management a feeling of legitimacy to silence corporate racketeers who might disturb the meetings. (*Yomiuri Shinbun* 1998/10/15 in Chikudate 2015, 124–125)

The term *fuuchou* (風潮), literally "climate" or in a figurative sense "trend," "current of the times," belongs to the same semantic group as *kuuki* (空気), literally "air," figuratively "mood," and *ishiki* (意識), "consciousness," "that operate in the perceptions that are generated from an intersubjective lifeworld" (Chikudate 2015, 125). To my understanding, Chikudate explains here operational terms of *wa* (和) as harmony. Harmony is maintained if all "go with the flow," feel the "group-climate," and have a "consciousness" of what is going on. This is the principle with the highest priority. One of the *Daiwa Securities* executives said:

> Since we are just salary-men or employed white-collar workers, we all behave according to the *kotonakare-shugi* (事なかれ主義) (the principle of maintaining peaceful, stable, and continuous mundane workplace by ignoring troubles and problems even though people experience them).[24] In other words, it is the practice of *kusai mono-ni futa-o suru* (臭い物に蓋をする) (putting a lid over something smelly or dirty). (NHK in Chikudate 2015, 125)

Even Japanese Confucianism is distorted by the above shortcomings. It nevertheless played an important role in the formation of Japanese business

---

six. A suicide could qualify if it follows an individual's working 160 hours or more of overtime in one month or more than 100 hours of overtime for three consecutive months" (White 2016).

Kumagai (熊谷文枝) and Keyser directly associate *karoushi* (過労死) with the traditions that establish work conditions. Victims of *karoushi* (過労死) are men that "still adhere to the traditional ideology of dedication to work at the expense of one's personal life (Kumagai and Keyser 1996, 40).

24. In short "ostrich policy."

ethics. Ootsu et al. (39–40) compiled five Confucian principles singling out superior employees:

- Harmony: He functions as a group member. He does not breach the group order. He makes his interests second to those of the group.
- Hierarchy: He believes that organizational hierarchy is natural and necessary. He willingly accepts the authority of the management. He never disagrees with superiors. He does not envision subordinates as rivals.
- Grace, benevolence: He treats his subordinates graciously and sympathetically. He is fatherly rather than authoritarian. He readily and gladly helps and teaches his subordinates.
- Loyalty: He is loyal towards his superiors and to his company as a whole. He does his work with dedication. He is thankful for the benevolence with which his superiors treat him. He has strong emotional bonds with them. He identifies himself with his company.
- Lifelong learning: He loves to learn concerning his work ... He willingly undergoes further training outside his field of expertise.

3.1.2.2 *Wa* (和) as "peace of mind"

A large number of words and phrases using 和 describe what in English can best be expressed with words such as tranquility, placidity, quietude, and serenity.

The synonym for *heion* (平穏), "peaceful," *nodo* (閑和) is a compound of *nodoka* (閑) and *wa* (和). *Nodoka* explicitly means peace of mind as in the phrase *kokoronodoka-ni hi-o kurasu* (心のどかに日を暮らす), "to spend the days [of one's life] in peace of mind." *Das Ruigojiten* (類語辞典) explains: "*Nodoka* (閑) exists, when a human gets a quiet *kibun* (気分), a 'quiet feeling,' through his environment (seasons, temperature, landscape)." The corresponding verbs are *nodomaru* (和まる), *nodomeku* (長閑めく or 和めく), *nodomu* (和む), all meaning "to calm down," as well as *yurumeru* (緩める), "to ease."[25] The synonyms *nagomu* (和む) and *nikomu* (和む) mean "to become quiet." The nominal *nagushi* (和し) describes "peace of mind" as "cheerful state of mind." If something difficult, a *muzukashii mono* (難しいもの), is made *he-i* (平易), "plain and simple," this is called *yawarage* (和).

Terms from the realm of nature also describe this state:

---

25. The compound built from *yurumeru* (緩める) and *wa* (和) *kanwa* (緩和) means "relaxation" and is used for international détente policy as well as the care in hospices, *kanwa kea byoutou* (緩和ケア病棟).

- *Nagi* (和凪) is the quietness after the wind has ceased; *asanagi* (朝和凪) and *yunagi* (夕和凪) are the quietness at the seaside, at mornings and at evenings. The appearance of the sky can also be described with this term, as in the old phrase *kumo-mo naku nagitaru asa* (雲もなくなぎたる朝), "the morning is to be without clouds and quiet." The term *waki* (和気) describes quiet weather or the quiet ocean. The derived verb *nagu* (和ぐ or 凪ぐ) means "to quiet the heart and to contain oneself." In the same way *waki* (和気) can mean appeased emotions.
- *Wasuru* (和する) is the process that quiets the weather.
- The term *waki aiai* (和気靄靄 or 和気藹藹) describes quiet emotions or a friendly atmosphere and is also loaned from the realm of nature. The writing with 靄靄 uses the image of veils of mist, that with 藹藹 the image of a thicket to describe the inner life.

3.1.3 Wa (和) as "Non-War"

The key word used for "non-war" usually is *heiwa* (平和), "peace." Compounds are *heiwa kaigi* (平和会議), "peace conference," *heiwa koushou* (平和交渉), "peace talks" or "peace negotiations," and *heiwa kousaku* (平和工作), "peace initiative."

Even though *heiwa* (平和) is the common word for "non-war," some phrases and compounds use *wa* (和) by itself in the same way:

- *wa-o musubu* (和を結ぶ): to "tie" *wa* (和), that is, "to make peace";
- *ryoukokukan-no wa* (両国間の和): *wa* (和) between (間) two (literally both) countries (両国);
- *wakai* (和解): reconciliation;
- *waboku* (和睦): synonym of *wakai* (和解), it means as much as "peace agreements"; akin is the compound *waboku koushou* (和睦交渉), also meaning "peace talks" or "peace negotiations";
- *wagi* (和議): talks that lead to peace, particularly peace negotiations;
- *wasen* (和戦): "Peace and War"; akin is the compound *wasen jouyaku* (和戦条約), "peace treaty";
- *washin* (和親): friendship between nations; 親 means to be close and intimate; akin is the compound *washin jouyaku* (和親条約), "peace treaty" or "friendship treaty";
- *wakai* (和諧): "arbitration" (divorce law);
- *hito-no wa* (人の和): literally "person-*wa*" (和), is the *wa* (和) between people (人).

Japan has brought war to Asia like no other nation. And she did this particularly during the age of the Axis (1937–1945) under the banner of *Yamato* (大和), the banner of "Great Harmony" (大和). Is this a contradiction? According to Ishida (石田雄), the Japanese alliance of peace and harmony can even be an obstacle on the road to pacifism. Even though Japanese are interested in maintaining peace, they at the same time prefer the harmony in the existing order and therefore it is difficult for them to fight for peace. In the 1930s, it was the most important thing for the Japanese to hold on to national conformity in order not to disturb the social harmony. This is the reason why they were not able to resist war. The fusion of peace and harmony resulted in a marked lack of criticism concerning the established order. That in turn led to a mentality of harmony-at-all-cost, which tolerated injustice and even war (Ishida 1989, 144–145). This tragic irony can be seen in the term *yawasu* (和す), which means as much as *heiwa-ni suru* (平和にする), "to appease," but which also means *kijun saseru* (帰順させる), "to subject." *Kijun saseru* (帰順させる) is formed by "order," literally "sequence" (順), "to return" (帰), and the "to force (させる) (causative marker).[26] But the "non-existence of war cannot yet be called peace" (Kodama et al. 2004, 6). Therefore Kodama (児玉克哉) et al. include subjects such as North-South division (94), just language (109), multicultural societies (127), refugee problems (147), and environmental questions (167) into their *Peace-science for Beginners*.[27] However, theirs seems to be a lone voice.

3.1.4 Wa (和) as Japan

The old word for Japan is *Yamato* (大和).[28] It is written with the Chinese characters for "great" or "big" (大) and *wa* (和). However, the term is older than

---

26. What Nakane said about hierarchy is particularly interesting in this context!

27. For Kodama et al. (6, 10), *heiwagaku* (平和学), the "peace-science" is the "science born of remorse over the detestable wars," a *kibou-o tsukuridasu gakumon* (希望を創り出す学問), a "discipline to create hope."

28. For the sake of completeness, it needs to be mentioned that *wa* (和) is not the only Chinese character which means *Yamato*, the old or traditional Japan. The Chinese character 倭 is also read *Yamato* and found in various compounds: the indigenous Japanese are called *wajin* (倭人) or *wado* (倭奴), the original Japanese language *yamatokotoba* (倭語) or *wago* (倭語). The Japanese settlements in Korea in the 17th century were called *kyoriyan wakan* (草梁倭館) (Tai, n.d., 136). The oldest names for "Japan" are *Ooshima-no Kuni* (大八洲の国 or 大八島の国), "Land of Many Islands," *Shikishima-no Kuni* (敷島の国 or 磯城島の国), "Land of Scattered Islands," *Toyo Ashihara-no Nakatsu-Kuni* (豊葦原中つ国), "Land Amidst the Plentiful (Fruitful) Reed Plains," and *Chiihoaki Mizuho-no Kuni* (千五百秋瑞穂の国), "Land of Ears of Rice of 150

the usage of the Chinese writing system in Japan which used *dai-wa* (大和), "Great harmony," or *dai-Nippon* (大日本), "Great-Japan" for *Yamato*. Before that, *Yamato* probably meant "footprints in the mountains." In Chinese this would have been written 山跡 or 山迹. Interpreting *Yamato* as "footprints in the mountains" probably refers to an age "when heaven and earth were not completely separated, when the soil was muddy and not solidified and when people moving back and forth left footprints on the mountains." Another interpretation holds that the *to* in *Yamato* means 都, "habitat" or "capital." *Yamato* would then mean "mountain habitat" or "mountain capital." This could indicate that in ancient times people in Japan lived in the mountains (Picken 2004, 171). "We shall take the term 'Yamato' as the synonym of the prehistoric but discernible beginnings of national life. It represents the seat of the tribe whose valor and genius ultimately produced the Mikado system" (Griffis 1895, 65). The term is documented as early as the tenth century in the *Genji-Monogatari* (源氏物語), the *Tales of Genji* (Morris 1994, 10) and in *Meiji*-Era it becomes the crystallization point of national thinking (Lutum 2005, 247). In 1897 the *Kokumin Seishin Bunka Kenkyuujo* (国民精神文化研究所), the "Research Center of National Spiritual Culture" created the government-sponsored program *Kokumin Seishin Soudouin* (国民精神総動員), the "National Spiritual Mobilization," in which the term *yamato-damashii* (大和魂), "Spirit of *Yamato*" and its synonym *Nihon seishin* (日本精神), "Spirit of Japan" played an important role (Maraldo 1995, 337). In this process Shintoism played an important role but Zen-Buddhists – among them also Suzuki – expressed similar sentiments as well (Kirita 1995, 60). According to Zen master Shaku Souen (釈宗演), the term *yamato-damashii* (大和魂) stems from "a unique spiritual teaching, which emerged from a unique spiritual combination of Confucianism, Shintoism, and Buddhism." The "Buddhist contribution" was the idea of "self-sacrifice" (Victoria 1999, 95).[29]

Today the Chinese character *wa* (和) is used in various terms without its historical bias:

(Endless) Autumns" (Phillipps 2004, 10). The compound of the last *to* names to *Toyo Ashihara-no Chiaki Nagaioaki-no Mizuyoguni* (豊葦原之千秋長五百秋之水穂国) is also documented.

Similar to the Korean, the Manchurian and the Basque the Old-Japanese cannot be traced back to its origins (Suzuki 1999, 9).

29. The connections between Buddhism and National Socialism were studied rather reluctantly because during the post-war years it was much too personal for many scholars. It was also avoided by German Japanologists because it would have painfully raised questions concerning the *German Christians* churches and German National Socialism (Worm 1994, 156). For the sake of fairness, it must be said that there were some individuals within Zen-Buddhism that resisted war. For details see Victoria (1999, 113ff).

- *wayaku* (和訳) or *wage* (和解) is a translation into Japanese
- *wabun* (和文) is a text written in Japanese
- *wakan* (和漢) is the Japanese-Chinese international relationship[30]
- *wadoku* (和独) is the Japanese-German international relationship
- *wafutsu* (和仏) is the Japanese-French international relationship
- *wabei* (和米) is the Japanese-American international relationship
- *waro* (和露) is the Japanese-Russian international relationship
- *waei* (和英) is the Japanese-English international relationship
- *wasei* (和製) or *wasan* (和産 or 倭産) means "Made in Japan."

There are, however, a number of terms, in which *wa* (和) pointedly means the traditional Japan or things traditionally Japanese as opposed to modern things. In some phrases this can be clearly and easily seen:

- *yamato-goe* (和音 or 倭音),[31] is the Japanese reading of Chinese characters as opposed to the Chinese reading *go-on* (呉音);
- *yamato-e* (大和絵) is the medieval Japanese-style picture;
- *yamato-nadeshiko* (大和撫子) means a "daughter of Japan," literally a "carnation";
- *wagaku* (和学) is the study of that particular Old-Japanese culture.

In other phrases the connection to the old, traditional Japan is not so apparent:

- *wagin* (和琴) is the traditional *koto* (琴), a genuine Japanese stringed instrument;
- *wagaku* or *waraku* (和楽) is the traditional Japanese music;
- *waka* (和歌) or *wateki uta* (和的歌) is the traditional Japanese poem-like song in 31 syllables;
- *washi* (和詩 or 倭詩) is the Chinese poem in its Japanese form;
- *wasan* (和讃) is the Buddhist worship-song (Steffánsson 2002, 85);
- *waso* (和装) is traditional Japanese clothing;
- *wai* (和裁) or *wasai* (和裁) is the traditional method of clothing production;

---

30. However, this term is used only for historical international relations between Japan and China. For modern international relations between Japan and China, *nicchuu* (日中) is used. *Wakan* (和漢) and *nicchuu* (日中) must be distinguished. In a similar way the modern term *nichibei* (日米) is alternatively used for *wabei* (和米), *nichidoku* (日独) for *wadoku* (和独), *nichifutsu* (日仏) for *wafutsu* (和仏), and *nichiro* (日露) for *waro* (和露). Except for the term for the international relations between Japan and China all of them can be used interchangeably.

31. These Chinese characters can also be read *wa-on* or *ka-on*. Another term for *yamato-goe* (和音 or 倭音) is *wakun* (和訓 or 倭訓).

- *wagura* (和鞍) is the Old-Japanese saddle used until the *Meiji*-Era;
- *wagashi* (和菓子) is the traditional biscuit;
- *wasan* (和算) is the traditional way of calculating using a *soroban* (算盤);
- *washi* (和紙) is Japan-paper;
- *washitsu* (和室) is a room in the Old-Japanese style;
- *washuu* (和習) are traditional customs;
- *wago* (和語) is the native Japanese word;
- *washiki* (和式) is a general word for all things in a particular "Japanese-style" such as:
  - *washiki benjo* (和式便所), the Japanese-style toilet,
  - *washiki eihou* (和式泳法), the traditional Japanese swimming style;
- *wafuu* (和風) is in a similar way a marker for traditionally Japanese things such as:
  - *wafuu-no tatemono* (和風の建物), Japanese-style buildings,
  - *wafuu kenchiku* (和風建築), Japanese-style carpentry;
- *wafuu ryokan* (和風旅館), the Japanese-style inn;
- *wayou* (和様), literally *wa*(和)-like, is yet another marker for traditionally Japanese things;
- *wayou kenchiku* (和様建築), Japanese-style carpentry;
- all "things Japanese" are summarized under the term *wamono* (和物), "things Japanese" (De Bary and Kurata-Dykstra 2001, 390).

4

The Biblical Peace-Concept

Summary: According to Talmon (1997), the Hebrew concept of peace, *shalom*, can be divided into welfare, peace in interpersonal relationships, and peace among groups. The Hebrew concept of peace has a distinct eschatological dimension.

The concept of peace of the New Testament takes up the Hebrew concept of peace and confesses Jesus Christ as the author of the messianic peace. Furthermore, it introduces Greek elements into the biblical concept of peace.

4.1 The Hebrew *Shalom*-Concept

This word-field study is based mainly on Talmon's essay, *The Signification of* שלום *and Its Semantic Field in the Hebrew Bible,* published in 1977.

Talmon traces the Hebrew concept of peace back to the stem שלם and defines its basic meaning after comparing it to other Semitic languages as "wholeness," physically, spiritually (Talmon 1997, 81; similarly Jüngel 2003, 27),[1] as well as socially. He does so because in the Hebrew thinking *shalom* is a collective term and "indicates harmonious interpersonal and inter-group relations" (Talmon 1997, 81). According to Falcke, *shalom* is a "rational reality." "It is in the *shalom*-concept that the relationality of the Old Testament understanding of reality is bundled" (Falcke 1988, 38). As for personal

---

1. Others talk about "wholeness" and "Heilsein" of a personal relationship (Würthwein 1938, 98), "Unversehrtheit," intactness and integrity (Fohrer 1997, 285), "wholeness, well-being, salvation, and life in a holistic sense, encompassing its eternal as well as its temporal aspects, the relationship with God as well as the relationships with humans, the soul as well as the body, the individual as well as the community and the nations" (Mettner in Mette 2007, 345).

relationships "peace is concerned with the fellowship between humans and with the fellowship with God" (Kruhöffer 1999, 148). It means a "*Heilsein*" of the community in "all aspects" (150).[2] Eyselein (73) also talks about the "*Heilsein*" of "all basic human relationships."

In his analysis Talmon does limit himself to biblical references with the word שלום, but also includes its synonyms. Because, as he argues,

> a satisfactory understanding of the intrinsic connotation of שלום cannot be achieved by an etymological analysis alone. The identification of the root of a word does not yet disclose its inherent meaning in a given corpus of literature. As said, the signification and the scope of meaning of שלום can be more reliably ascertained by reviewing the use of the term intertextually and synoptically in the entire gamut of the biblical writings. In this process, the whole range of vocables and explanatory expressions must be brought under consideration which fall in the semantic field of שלום by collating synonyms and conterminuous idioms from a variety of passages. (89)

Talmon divides the שלום-concept into three groups of meaning:

- שלום pertaining to personal well-being, comfort, and safety (Pss 4:9; 37:11; 119:65; Prov 3:2; Job 5:23–24):
    - safety (Ps 4:9);
    - abundant prosperity (Pss 37:11; 119:165; Prov 3:2);
    - being in accord with nature (Job 5:23; Hos 2:20);
    - absence of danger and harm (Judg 6:22–23; Dan 10:12, 19; 1 Sam 20:21; 2 Sam 19:31) (82–84);[3]
    - The absence of שלום in the sense of "wholeness" is expressed with absence of "healing" (רפא) and "length (of life)" (ארך). Therefore, the terms of the semantic field of "health" also belong

---

2. As with many other German authors, Kruhöffer plays on the etymological relation between the German *Heil*, salvation, and *heilen*, to heal. *Heilsein* is a nominal form of *heilen* and means a state of being healed, being made well. I am well aware that this interpretation of the Hebrew peace-concept cannot be justified etymologically. However, the semantic connection is given.

3. In this sense Gen 28:21 as the probably oldest reference for שלום uses this word (Dinkler 1992, 265).

to the synonyms of שלום (Isa 57:18–19; Jer 14:19; 33:6; Hos 6:1; Mal 3:20) (91).[4]

- שלום pertaining to "interpersonal relations":
  - peaceful intentions (1 Sam 16:4–5; 1 Kgs 2:13; 2 Kgs 5:21–22);
  - as a greeting in "a situation in which the people involved do not harbor any suspicion" (Judg 19:20; 1 Sam 16:4–5) (84–87);[5]
  - in the psalms, שלום is used as synonym for "salvation" (ישעו), "justice" (צדק),[6] "covenant faithfulness" (חסד), "welfare" (הטוב), "glory" (כבוד), "trustworthiness" (אמת), "the fruit of the land" (יבול הארץ), and the verb "to dwell" (90) (שכן).[7]
- שלום pertaining to "intra-group and inter-group relations":
  - the cessation of internal discord or war with an external enemy, for whatever length of time, is often termed שלום (Judg 4:17; 21:13; Josh 9:6);[8]
  - also the "intermittent spells of suspended warfare in the period of settlement, whenever a 'judge' achieved a decisive victory over

---

4. In this sense the phrase "dying in peace" becomes the epitome of peace. Abram (Gen 15:15) (the promise that Abraham would die in peace was made in the face of the "life-threatening" childlessness (Ha 1989, 77–78).), Hilkiah (2 Kgs 22:20; 2 Chr 23:28), and Zedekiah (Jer 34:5) were to "die in peace," not so Joab (1 Kgs 2:6, 33). "Dying in peace" means that a person completes a full and satisfying life (Youngblood 1995, 732). Ziemer also stresses the importance of a burial. "Emphasis is placed . . . on the *quality* of the end of life, which essentially requires a burial . . . This quality . . . is expressed by 'in *peace*' and 'in *good age*'" (Ziemer 2005, 210). On the other side, Sailhammer interprets dying "in peace" in the context of Heb 13:20 as entering into eternal peace (Sailhamer 2010, Exegetical (Auslegung) Approaches). In Judaism the word שלום was generally used in commemorative prayers, blessings, and obituaries (Jacobson 1996, 641).

5. The intention of the "greeting of peace" that it "conveys peace itself . . . The greeting of peace . . . makes use of peace itself . . . Peace is . . . a realm into which the greeted is accepted and in which he is safe." But what actually happens in the greeting of peace? "Definitely something like an elementary pacification of existence . . . It is no accident that the greeting of peace is connected with . . . the assurance 'Fear not!'" (Jüngel 2003, 26). Judging from an animistic perspective, Ndabiseruye (184–185) arrives at a similar conclusion: In the background of formulas of greeting and parting we find an "almost magical understanding of reality." "One tried to ban the danger which one sensed whenever one met a stranger. The greeting assured host and guest that nothing would harm him. Upon parting the safe escort of the deity was evoked."

6. Falcke called peace and justice "twins" (46). As peace "justice is a communal concept" (Kruhhöffer 1999, 149). The connection between peace and justice is also known in other cultures. For Kirundi (a Bantu-dialect), Ndabiseruye (104) writes: "There is a correlation between peace and justice. Without justice there is no peace, and vice versa, without peace there is no justice.

7. Talmon shows this using Ps 85:9–14 as an example.

8. Including "imposed peace" or "negative peace" in the context of vassal treaties (Talmon 1997, 100–101).

- the one or the other enemy in a single campaign" can be called שלום (Judg 3:11; 5:31; 8:28) (87–89);
- in Isaiah 32:15–18 the synonyms "safety" (בטח), "quietness" (שקט), and "unbiased" (שאנן) are added; they are concerned with personal safety as well as with political peace in the sense of absence of war as "national ideal" (90–91).

In connection with this analysis the eschatological dimension of "positive peace"[9] seems to be of importance. Talmon talks about a "future era of unlimited positive peace."

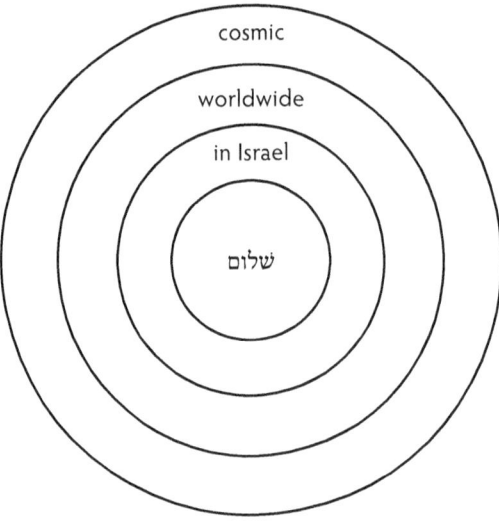

Figure 4.1 The Eschatological Dimensions of "Positive Peace"

This "national ideal" finds expression in a model of three concentric circles in which the term שלום and its semantic field are pivotal: Israel at peace internally; externally among all nations in a "world at peace"; and at peace in a "pacified universe." I am fully aware of the supreme creedal content of these visions. Nevertheless, I intend to highlight the "restorative" underpinning of their "utopian" make-up, that is to say, the basic historical realism which

---

9. "Positive peace" as opposed to "imposed" peace.

shows in them and the persuasive "factuality" of their formation. (Talmon 1997, 102)

In Figure 4.1, the inner circle of the three concentric circles is concerned with domestic peace in Israel as it was realized first and predominantly during the reign of Solomon (*pax Salomonica*) (Mic 4:4–5).[10] The ideal of domestic peace is the reunited kingdom of the future as envisioned by the "missionary" prophets Isaiah and Micah (Isa 9:5–6; 11:1–5, 10; Mic 5:1–4) (Talmon 1991, 107–110). However, the vision of these prophets surpasses the *pax salomonica* only for Israel (1 Kgs 5:5). The peace envisioned by the "missionary" prophets is peace for "all peoples" (113). This is the second circle of the three concentric circles. The third circle stands for the "cosmic peace." "The biblical concept of שלום also entails hope for cosmic peace. The apex of biblical Israel's hope for peace is reached in prophetic visions which transcend the horizon of human experience" (Isa 65) (114).

4.2 The Christian Peace-Concept

The Christian concept of peace is significantly determined by the Old Testament שלום-concept (Bakke 2001, 77; Dinkler 1992, 264). "The Old Testament concept of a messianic king bringing messianic peace together with his kingdom is transferred to Jesus of Nazareth" (Dinkler 1992, 264). According to Jüngel, God's demand to make peace with him (Isa 27:5) is continued in the New Testament. Because Isaiah 27:5 expresses that "the relationship between man and man cannot be well"[11] as long as the relationship with God is damaged. The "immediate presence of whole and undivided existence" can be accessed by humans only in the presence of God himself" (Jüngel 2003, 29). Jesus Christ is here, in the focal point of this demand: This is the very "grand mystery of the person of Jesus Christ that in him and through him God himself is actually present" (30). The "specific Christian concept of peace" was "established as an [interpretation] of the crucifixion of Christ by using the word εἰρήνη." Through the influence of Clemens Romanus the εἰρήνη-concept of profane Greek, affiliated with the antique concept of ὁμόνοια, was then introduced to the Christian thinking in the first century. This leads to the amalgamation of the concept "peace as salvation" and the concept of "peace as intra-worldly

---

10. Besides Mic 4:4–5, Talmon (107–108) also quotes references such as Mal 3:23–24; Mic 5:2; Zech 6:13; 8:16, and Hag 2:9 to describe the domestic peace.

11. Jüngel uses *heil*.

harmony and political non-war" (Dinkler 1992, 264). According to Kittel, the difference between the Hebrew and the Greek concept of peace is that שׁלוֹם means the quality of a relationship, whereas εἰρήνη means the condition of an existence (Ishida 1989, 121). This is how the "concept of peace of early Christianity was changed into a chapter of moral teaching." This concept was eventually combined with the "concept of order" and the "reference to Christ was no longer tangible" (Dinkler 1992, 300).

In the New Testament concept of peace, many different meanings are combined as can be shown exemplarily with Paul's usage of the term. It can be used:

- as virtue and as such as "fruit of the Spirit,"
- as false sureness jeopardizing the "apocalyptic vigilance,"
- as opposite to "disorder" or as "salfic good of the coming kingdom of God" (Dinkler 1992, 279–280).[12]

In his exposition, Dinkler starts from Ephesians 2:14, which he, together with Dibelius, interprets as an excursus that "establishes and explains the relationship between Isaiah 57:18f and Christ" (Dinkler 1992, 282). Through Christ, who "is our peace," all enmity is overcome by "destroying" the law. "This can only mean that the law as means of sin and as locus of sin signifies enmity as a disregard of God." The cross event is negatively developed as "mortification of the enmity," positively as "reconciliation with God." "The difficulty lies in the understanding of this twofold orientation of enmity and peace. They are attributed to the relationship between humans and God, and to the relationship between those close by and those far away, that is, Jews and Gentiles." Thus Christ becomes "the bringer of peace and the inaugurator of the access to God." He also inaugurates "the unity of those who formerly lived in the world as separated people, of those who objectively lived as enemies" (284–285). According to Dinkler, this thought is then further developed in Colossians 1:19f where, differently from Ephesians 2:14, the focus is not on peace among men but on peace with cosmic dimensions (287).

In a similar way Jüngel does not want to distinguish the "developing dimensions":

> Neither excludes the religious dimension of *shalom* . . . the worldly dimension of existential wholeness. As *shalom* is never a merely

---

12. Bakke (77) judged that Paul "internalized" and psychologized the Old Testament peace-concept. Dinkler shows that this was due to the Greek influence. Bakke's judgment is only partly true.

> "outward state of peace (as opposed to war)" it can never be a merely "inward peace without an intact[13] relationship with the environment." It rather is said that "righteousness and peace have kissed" (Ps 85:10). (Jüngel 2003, 28)

The promised age of the Messianic kingdom of peace is yet to come and stands "in harsh opposition to those experiences of Israel which identify the lack of peace as the judgment of God." The mere fact that Jeremiah brings his nation the promise of peace only during exile, that is the place of "total discomfort and restlessness,"[14] gives *shalom* a "new dimension": This new *shalom* is "connecting the peace for those that used to be Israel's enemies."

> Those in exile are to seek the *shalom* of the very land God has deported them to (Jer 29:7). As JAHWEH wills it, peace is possible even under circumstances that absolutely contradict peace. That fact that God has "thoughts of peace"[15] for the remnant of the nation can clearly be seen in the person of the Servant of God who suffered the punishment "to bring peace unto us" (Isa 53:5). Thus the peace of Israel is now dependent on God's acts of reconciliation and therefore "detached from yielding political power." It is now explicitly identified by God as "my peace" (Isa 54:10). It is JAHWEH himself who works peace.[16] (Jüngel 2003, 29)

---

13. *Heil.*
14. *Ungeborgenheit.*
15. Compare Isa 52:7; 54:10–13.
16. Compare Isa 45:7; Ezek 34:25; 37:26; Isa 57:19; 60:17; 66:12; Hag 2:9; Zech 8:12.

Part III

Four Aspects of Salvation in the Context of Japanese Animism

5

The Theological Aspect of Salvation

Summary: Distinctively different from the salvation concept of Japanese animism, the relationship with God is of basic importance for the biblical understanding of salvation. Judging from this theocentric viewpoint the calamity of humans is first and foremost rebellion against God. The central key concept of the Christian understanding of human calamity is "sin." Central key-concepts of Christian soteriology are forgiveness of sins and reconciliation with God.

"Theological" here means "concerning God" as opposed to "anthropological" or "sociological." The theological formulation of soteriology is of fundamental importance, because "since Christianity is a religion of redemption, it is greatly influenced by the views concerning the nature of sin" (Wiley 1940, II, 51). When it comes to defining *Unheil*,[1] the Bible is rather vague. *Unheil* is as wide as the pitiful state of humans and nature. However, if because of this wide view of *Unheil* conceptual clarification is abandoned and everything and anything is subsumed in a nebulous *Unheil*-wishy-washy, the flood gates to improper salvation concepts are opened. I speak against the assumption of Pieris and other Asian theologians[2] who make soteriology as

---

1. I am deliberately introducing a German technical term for convenience sake. *Unheil* means disaster, mischief, calamity, harm, or doom. In German, however, it serves – as the antonym of *Heil*, "salvation" – as a theological technical term defining the absence of salvation, so to speak "un-salvation."

2. C. S. Song suggests that the proper framework for doing theology is not redemption or salvation history, but rather creation (Niles 1982, 285).

common ground for Christianity and other religions the basis of all theology. Pieris's "theology of religions"

> is based on the assumption that soteriology is the basis of theology; and that Christianity can only relate to Asian religions of redemption only via soteriology. According to Pieris, the church must be baptized in the Jordan of Asian religiosity and at the cross of Asian poverty. (Rohls 1997, 726)

If Christianity is not baptized like this it will, according to Pieris, play no "authentic role" in the development of Asia (Levison and Pope-Levison 1994, 4).

This argument, however, obscures the fundamental question: Where does the *Unheil* come from? This question is so important because the answer defines, to a certain degree, the answer to the second question: Where does the *Heil*, the salvation, come from? There is no question that social structures of *Unheil* exist. But if the cause of *Unheil* is sought only in social structures, *Heil* is consequently sought in changing these structures.[3] There is no question that evil spiritual beings can be a *Unheil*-influence. But if the cause of *Unheil* is sought only there, sorcery will be its only cure.

The Bible defines *Unheil* in such a wide way that all that want to do theology in the spiritual ghetto must be alarmed. However, the cause of *Unheil* is defined in such a narrow and precise way that all soteriological approaches not aiming at the change, even the re-creation of the human heart must be nullified. "The Bible stresses that the existence and the experience of a state of *Heil* depends upon human acceptance of JAHWEH as the 'fountain of life' (Ps 36:9) and following his decrees" (Frohnhofen 1997, 3). *Unheil* began with human willful rebellion against God, with sin.[4] Sin is first and foremost a matter of the relation between God and man, what Nietzsche very well acknowledged when he rejected the doctrine of sin as "Jewish sentiment and Jewish invention."

---

3. This concept can be traced back to Pelagius who understood man as born without any tendency towards evil; evil is only what is done to man. It originates from the misuse of freedom (Wiley 1940, II, 72).

4. I deliberately chose this offensive and (to some) obsolete term, because it is precise and clear. Schlatter spoke against equating sin with calamity (*Unglück*) or error: "The term calamity (*Unglück*) defines that which inhibits the act of life." By doing so we distinguish ourselves from suffering. "Talking about sin, however, finds fault in us and judges us altogether." Judging ourselves as erring is also aimed at ourselves and partly painful. "However, the concepts of sin and error must be distinguished because the reproach of error does not concern our entire self . . . our will" (Schlatter 1911, 240).

According to Nietzsche, the doctrine of sin is determined and defined by the "God-concept of Judaism" (Pöhlmann 1980, 174).⁵

5.1 Preliminaries

The starkest and most glaring difference between the Japanese and the biblical concepts of gods/God (Allen and Springstedt 2007, XVI) is the biblical testimony of God Creator as absolute vis-à-vis to his creation. The "categorically different" God (Härle 1995, 411–413) does not exist in the Japanese worldview. As a consequence, Japanese soteriology makes no reference to God. In other words, it has no theological dimension.

The theological orientation of biblical soteriology has its equivalent in the cosmological orientation of soteriology in Japan. There are two forms of this cosmological orientation:

- The naturalistic form understands *Heil* as unity and harmony nature. Humans can assimilate the "nature-*kami*"(神) through prayer, and upright and faultless living (Rochedieu 1973, 79). They then are permeated by the divine (Rochedieu 1973, 227–228). Humans can also strive to reach *satori* (悟り) "enlightenment," through the absolute and perfect expressed in "pantheistic thought patterns," not discursively, but "spiritually and intuitively" (Schründer-Lenzen 1996, 11).
- The theogonistic form understands deities and humans as an original and unbroken unity as parts of "one world," one holistic reality. According to a Japanese proverb, children until the age of seven are "children" of God because they are pure, innocent, and holy (Itou 1996, 32). As such they are receptive for divine communication (Kamata 2000, 60): A child is *nanatsu mae-wa kami-no ko* (七つ前は神の子) "before [the age of] seven a child of the gods."⁶

---

5. On the other side, *Heil* cannot be confined to the place where *Unheil* began. *Heil* must start in the human heart and permeate the world as far as *Unheil* reaches. He who experienced *Heil* through the gift of a renewed and willing heart is under obligation to the world wherever it suffers under *Unheil*. If sin is only understood as rebellion against God, only as hubris, only as wrong attitude, the danger of the "sin of sloth" (Barth) is imminent, which "in traditional Protestantism was not stressed enough" (Pöhlmann 1980, 176–177). The omission of the good deed of standing up for justice and against *Unheil* is sin as well!

6. Another version of this proverb is: *nanasai made-wa kami-no uchi* (七歳までは神のうち), "until [the age of] seven in the gods/part of the family of the gods" (Kamata 2000, 60).

Neither of these forms is an equivalent for the relationship between God and humans as put forward in the Bible.

5.2 The Experience of *Unheil* under the Theological Aspect

In this section I shall outline the subject "sin as rebellion against God," not because this is all there is to human *Unheil*, but because I am convinced that this is the very root of human *Unheil*. "Sin as rebellion against God" does not have an equivalent in the Japanese worldview. In a discussion, Hirosachiya (ひろさちや) and Hayashi (林亮勝) agreed that since "in Japan there is one and only absolute God as in Judaism or Islam, it would be only fair that within his own sphere man decided what he had to do" (Hirosachiya et al. 1993, 189). Endou also, arguing that the Japanese were not able to imagine a transcendent God, defined sin exclusively sociologically (Mase-Hasegawa 2008, 68). In the Japanese context the Christian question of whether an action is a violation of a "command of God" is substituted by the question, whether an action *shuudan-no "wa"-o midasu* (集団の「和」を乱す), whether it "disturbs the harmony of the group."

> Japanese people value human relationships more than truth and principle . . . Because they are afraid of disturbing human relationships of their families and neighborhood . . . Japanese [people] make much of human relationships more than the truth . . . Those who harm the harmony are bad, whether they are right or not has been beside the question. (Okuyama in Kim 2014, 9)

Yobai (夜這い) for example, the "sleeping with your neighbor's wife" is not considered a sin, as the neighbor does not know about it (Hirosachiya et al. 1993, 39–40). "Because of the preferred principle of relationality the Japanese judgment of good and evil can be relativized according to any given situation. This constitutes the tendency to objectivize and universalize rules determining good and evil" (Court 2009, 435). In the West concepts of "good" and "evil" are understood as derived from given principles, often connected with a sense of guilt or sin. The ethical situation differs from that in that there is no sense for principles or sin. "Good" is what supports the harmony of the group and sustains the loyalty towards superiors. Respectively, evil is what disturbs the harmony of the group (Bucknall 2005, 40).

"In Germany the connection between guilt and atonement is grounded in individualism with its individual responsibility, in the modern conception of man with its rationality, and in Christianity" (Yasuda 2004, 28–29). There is a causal correlation between responsibility before God, Individualism, and individual responsibility independent from the collective. Of course, the Japanese language has lexical equivalents for the English word "sin," but they are explicitly not correlated with God.

5.2.1 The Theological Locus of Hamartiology

Even though Luther allowed for "the experience of the law and sin even for a non-Christian on the basis of a natural knowledge of God," he also maintained that "only through the preaching of Christ's suffering and dying" could sin be exposed in its very depth. This was, of course, radicalized by Barth on the basis of his categorical rejection of general revelation. Consequently, there is no hamartiology outside of and without Christology for Barth (Pöhlmann 1980, 175–176).[7] "We can never have the negative knowledge [of sin] except in [light of] this positive faith (Barth in Anderson 1999, 39). According to Barth, pondering over sin only leads into the knowledge of our limited human nature, possibly into despair and hopelessness. "But this is not what the Bible means by sin. The fathomless depth of sin can only be glimpsed under the tutelage of the Redeemer" (Anderson 1999, 39).

---

7. Althaus names two basic arguments for that in Barth's thought: (1) The teaching of general revelation violates the fact that "man has apostatized from God and is a lost sinner." Barth criticized the Reformers to stay Catholic in the question of how to find knowledge about God. "As a consequence of the teaching of justification we have to maintain that the knowledge of the true God is given to us only by grace and faith." Althaus in turn, criticizes Barth for unwaveringly equating and confusing "*Uroffenbarung* (primordial revelation) and a rational natural theology." More precisely, what is to be criticized is assertive claim of reason against revelation (Althaus 1947, 69). Man is not affiliated with God but tied into a relationship with God, which cannot be unmade by his being a lost sinner. He is lost yet not forsaken. "The '*gottlos*' (godless) man is just not *Gott los* (free from God), but his godlessness has its place in his ineradicable relationship with God, which he is well aware of. Without this [ineradicable relation with God] the term sin is rendered . . . utterly meaningless. This inevitably leads to meaninglessness of the term grace. Grace is for the sinner; but a man is and becomes a sinner in the primordial relationship with God revealed to him. This primordial relationship is the essence of being human and cannot be lost. Barth does not distinguish between the Divine presence, which constitutes man's guilt, and God's merciful presence, which constitutes the fellowship with the guilty." (2) Barth thinks that the concept of God is fragmented if we speak about a knowledge of God besides Jesus Christ. "Barth uses the formula of God's unity to flatly renounce a gradual revelation in the course of history" (Althaus 1947, 70).

5.2.2 "Original Sin"

In orthodoxy, sin was, based on Luther, divided into "original sin" (*Erbsünde*)[8] and misdeeds (*Tatsünden*) (Pöhlmann 1980, 172–173). Following these categories, I am first going to outline the "theological interpretament" (Weber) "original sin" (*Erbsünde*). According to Weber, it is derived from four biblical lines of thought:

(1) The term "original sin" (*Erbsünde*) is first derived from the generality of sin:[9] Paul connects Psalm 14:2–3 and 53:2–3 with Romans 3:9ff. "In humanity there is no sector … that is not being influenced by sin (Gen 6:5; 8:21; Pss 143:2; 130:3; 1 Kgs 8:46; Rom 11:32; Gal 3:22; 1 John 1:8–10) (Weber 1955, 658–659).

(2) Then it is derived from the characterization of humans as "flesh": "In the Bible the sinfulness of humans is affiliated with the general judgment that they are *flesh*. This does not mean that they 'have got' a fleshly or carnal 'aspect.' The background of the opposition against human hubris in Gen 6:3 is that they were made from earth and bound to die (Isa 40:6; Jer 17:5; Ps 63:1). In the New Testament 'the flesh' is literally 'hypostatized' (Gal 5:17; Rom 8:12), yet never equated with sin. The relationship between flesh and sin is expressed in the formula 'the flesh of sin' (Rom 8:3). The flesh is the 'carrier of ἐπιθυμία' (Gal 5:16; Eph 2:3; 1 John 2:16; 2 Pet 2:10)." "The σάρξ owns its own φρόνημα, which is death (Rom 8:6), the enmity against God (Rom 8:7). As the flesh characterizes humans per se (most clearly in John 3:6), by this *terminus* humans per se are understood as striving against God and as enslaved to vanity" (Weber 1955, 659–660). Similarly Schlatter states:

> When we use the word "flesh" our sinfulness is perceived as derived from our natural organization. We are sinners because our body is as it is, and because our inward life is as it is. This constitutes the dependency of our will and our thinking on organic impulses, and it judges the kind of this dependency as the origin of the moral dysfunctions. (Schlatter 1911, 272)

---

8. Kleffmann (1994, 26) understands the term *Erbsünde* (literally hereditary sin) as exclusively German neologism, which historically cannot be derived from the Latin *peccatum hereditarium*. According to Kleffmann, the German term *Ursünde* (primordial sin or original sin) developed only in the 19th century and was then at the latest used by Schleiermacher as an antonym for the German *Erbsünde* (1994, 29).

9. In a similar way Gestrich (258) wants to understand *Erbsünde* (hereditary sin) as *Allgemeinsünde* (general sin).

This judgment has its roots in the anthropology of the Old Testament:

> Before the holy God . . . man as בָּשָׂר is not only the *Hinfällige* (the frail), but also the *Anfällige* for sin (the one prone to sin), who therefore cannot stand before God's voice (Deut 5:6): "Who among all בָּשָׂר, that we heard the voice of the Living God from amidst the fire, could have saved his life?" Under the scorching wind of God's judgment all בָּשָׂר withers away like grass (Isa 40:6). According to the priestly sources, the judgment of the Flood comes over כָּל־בָּשָׂר, because "all flesh" per se has "corrupted its ways on earth" (Gen 6:12). (Wolff 1977, 55–56)

Even in the Old Testament, בָּשָׂר means not only physical weakness but also human "weakness of faithfulness and obedience towards the will of God. The creaturely weakness is joined by ethical weakness . . . This kind of 'flesh' is the absolute opposite of 'spirit' (Isa 31:3), which in turn is also its hope (Joel 3:1)" (Wolff 1977, 55–56).

Niebuhr pointed out that the church's teaching about original sin is almost identical with the Jewish teaching of evil inclination (יֵצֶר הָרַע). "Jesus used the terminology of the Rabbinic teaching of the evil inclination" (Niebuhr 1958, 350). According to Philo,[10] "the sinful" is "interwoven" with the human nature "through birth" (Carus 1809, 354). On the Christian side, Ambrose expressed that children are "licked by the evil [of original sin] even before birth." "This is the central thought of his teaching concerning original sin: Not only the suffering, but also the sin and guilt are transferred from parents to children in the act of procreation" (Lössl 1997, 335). Melanchthon, in the second article of the Augsburg Confession stated: "Further we teach that after the Fall of Adam (Gen 3) all humans born in a natural way are conceived and born in sin, that is, that all are full of inclination and lust for evil from the womb" (Melanchthon 1988, 24).

(3) There are "a few references . . . that correlate sin with the origin of humans." Weber translates Romans 5:12 as follows: "As a consequence of the sin of all, death pervaded to all." He explains: "Translating thus would mean that the coming of death into this world was the result of one man's sin, the pervading of death to all, however, caused by the fact that all sinned, once sin had entered 'into the world.'" Therefore, sin is not only deed, but "above all power, and as such antecedent to [sinful] deeds (Weber 1955, 660–661).

---

10. The teaching of the evil inclination is older than Philo. It goes back to the Rabbinate or Early Judaism (van der Horst 2003, 13).

According to Luther, original sin and "actual sins" are not two realities but two sides of one and the same reality. Fate and guilt paradoxically belong together inseparably (Pöhlmann 1980, 171).

The notion that the term *Erbsünde* (hereditary sin) is connected with the origin of sin is also present in the Japanese terminology. In Japanese original sin is called *genzai* (原罪). *Gen* (原) means origin, *zai* (罪) means sin or, in its secular usage, crime.

> God is the Creator and because he created humans with the intention that they would be obedient to him, obedient they must be. But they acted against this command and ate from the "tree of the knowledge of good and evil." Thus sin came into being. In Christianity this sin is called *genzai* (原罪), original sin. Humans commit countless sins, yet the origin of all those sins is the "original sin." (Soga 2001, 89)

(4) Finally, Weber (661) also derives the universality of sin from the universality of grace. "That sin really is the sin of all, can only be said, if also and even before that the fact is acknowledged that God is the Creator and Lord of all, which in turn is [only] revealed by his mercy through Jesus Christ."

5.2.3 "Original Sin" and the Sin of "Pre-existence of Souls"

It is necessary to deal with the sin of pre-existing souls as a particular form of the teaching of original sin, because in the Japanese context there exists a similar form.

According to Origen, souls exist in a "higher world" before their birth. For Origen, original sin has nothing to do with the sin of Adam, but humans have "original sin" because of the "fall of the spirits in the higher world, which led to the maculation of the souls during their state of preexistence" (Bauer 1967, 124–125). Based on that, Didymus distinguished "between the original sin, which is inherent to all humans because of their corporeality," and the "prenatal sin which the souls brought upon them by falling away from God" (TRE 1981, VIII, 744). In a similar way, Thomas Aquinas talked about ensoulment of the body and a sinful state before birth (Lohse 1994, 201). Equally influenced by Judaist Gnosis and Egyptian philosophy the idea of archons (third century) comprehensively explains how the souls are "maculated":

> Between heaven and earth were the seven planets, ruled by evil planetary divinities, the rulers of this world. Those are the archons,

demons of fate, as demons gnostically represented by the animal faces of the lion, the bull, the snake, the eagle, the bear, the dog, and the ass; they oppress man and place a blockade between him and heaven . . . Not only life itself, but even more its preexistence and postexistence, the state of the soul before birth and after death became the awesomely forbidding locality of the archon system. Because, as the souls descended from heaven to earth (the moon was considered to be the gate for the descent), it passed though the seven spheres and each of those spheres attached a spell to it determining its earthly fate. Then, after death, the soul upon its ascension must go by the same archons (the sun was considered to be the gate for the ascension), and at each station the old archon blocks its way as "God of destruction and the Second Death." (Bloch 1982, 1315)

As Colpe (110) showed, ideas of a heavenly journey of souls is "common all over the world in a confusing variety of forms," particularly in cultures with religions that show "shamanic structures." On the other side, the pre-existence of souls is not documented in Paul's (Schnackenburg 1982, 50; Schwindt 2002, 479) or John's thought (Heise 1967, 124). Augustine "rightly rejected this Origen notion" (Baur 1863, 174).[11]

In *Shintou*-Theology, there is no place for the dogma of "original sin" (Nitobe 2001, 30). With his subtle understanding of the "Japanese psyche," the Japanese theologian Kaiseki Matsumura (松村介石)[12] "rejected the Christian doctrine of original sin in favor of the Confucian understanding of human nature as essentially good," a doctrine called *seizensetsu* (性善説), the "doctrine of the good in man's character" (Mullins 1998, 76).[13] However, there are several teachings in Japan that know of an evil that befalls all humans.

In Japan, a basically negative attitude toward man is not the result of Christianity, but mainly a result of Buddhism:

---

11. Instead, Augustine teaches that God creates both, body and soul, of the new child in the womb (Hagenbach 1867, 234).

12. Matsumura (1859–1939) was a "leading intellectual figure" in the world of Japanese Christianity during the late-*Meji*-Era, the *Taishou*-Era, and the *Shouwa*-Era (Mullins 1998, 69). His movement started as a church movement, but eventually (1907) resulted in the foundation of a new religion (Mullins 1998, 70), the *Doukai* (道会), the "Society of the Way."

13. He understood religious life rather as "a process of self-cultivation that proceeds by stages, not as the once-and-for-all dramatic conversion so often emphasized in the Christian churches" (Mullins 1998, 76).

> *Shintou* has rescued Japan from being victimized by ecclesiastical doctrines of original sin and Hell. Buddhism has made Hells for punishment of the fallen, but *Shintou* has prevented them from having widespread terrorizing effect . . . Separation from the Unified All replaces original sin in Buddhism as the cause of evil. But, the *Shintou* insistence on the reality of the individual as a desirable and not detrimental spiritual fact of life has much mitigated in Japan the effect of this teaching. (Mason 2002, 141)

The Buddhist *Kagayaku Ake-no Myoujou-to Eien-no Seimei-o Manabu-Kai* (輝く明けの明星と永遠の生命を学ぶ会), the "Society which Teaches the Morning Star and Eternal Life," founded by Kazuyoshi Kajiwara (梶原和義), borrows much of its terminology from Jewish and Christian thought. For instance, it says on the official website of Kajiwara[14] that in Christ an era has come in which humans must not die anymore. The substance of death, the *shi-no jittai* (死の実体), as Kawajima sees it, is that humans have an "absolute self-awareness" called *jibun-to iu zettai ishiki* (自分という絶対意識), based on the assumption that the phenomenon, *genshou* (現象), perceived by the eyes, is absolutely existent. God created the earth and humans to that end, that death would destroy itself, *shi-o jimetsu saseru tame-ni, chikyuu-to ningen-ga souzou sareta-no desu* (死を自滅させるために、地球と人間が創造されたのです). In this context it is very interesting what Kajiwara writes about original sin, *genzai* (原罪):

> Christianity does not have the faintest idea about original sin. It uses the word original sin, but cannot explain its meaning. Original sin means sin from the origin.[15] From the origin means from before birth. In the previous world[16] they all have a misconception about God.[17] They have a misconception about their soul.[18] In the previous world they started have the awareness of being self. (Kajiwara 2002, 250)

With this idea Kajiwara does not stand alone. For Nishitani and the founders of the *Kyoto School of Philosophy*, Nishida and Hajime Tanabe (田

---

14. URL: http://www15.ocn.ne.jp/~kajiwara/toppage.html (accessed 19 Oct 2015).
15. *Genzai-to iu-no-wa, moto-kara-no tsumi-to iu imi-nanodesu* (原罪というのは、元からの罪という意味なのです).
16. *Zense* (前世).
17. *Torichigaeru* (取り違える).
18. *Tamashii* (魂).

辺元), too, self is radically evil, precisely because it exists. The problem is not self as an "intelligible *act*," but existence even as *self*. Self is radically evil as self" (Petersen 2005, 49). Therefore, it is "the loss of ego" is "the core of meditation" (Johnston 1970, 89).

In another place, Kajiwara (2001, 179) connects awareness with memory. "Memory[19] is the sin. The sensation of corporeality,[20] the sensation that the earth exists, that is the original sin of man."

5.2.4 Causes of Sin

Where does sin come from? Erickson names three causes:

- Ignorance[21] (ἄγνοιἄ, שגג and שגה, to err): "This word is often used in settings where it means innocent ignorance" (Rom 1:13; 2 Cor 6:9; Gal 1:22), in other cases the usage is not neutral yet God overlooked the error (Acts 3:17; 17:30; 1 Pet 1:14). Hebrews 9:7 talks about "sins committed in ignorance" where people are still "liable to punishment" (Erickson 2000, 583).
- Error (שגג and שגה): "The verb generally refers to an error in moral conduct." Contexts suggest that the person is liable for his actions. More common than either is תעה. Its basic meaning is "to err or wander about" with the notion of being "intoxicated." "The term refers to deliberate rather than accidental erring." The New Testament equivalent is πλανάω. The parabolic element of sheep is used to explain this kind of erring (Luke 15:3–7). Erring as πλανάω has a strong notion of "being deceived." The sources of this "leading astray" may be evil spirits (1 Tim 4:1; 1 John 4:6), other humans (Eph 4:14; 2 Tim 3:13), or oneself (1 John 1:8) (Erickson 2000, 584–585).
- Inattention (παρακοή), which means "to hear amiss or incorrectly." In several New Testament passages it refers to "disobedience as a result of inattention" (Rom 5:19; 2 Cor 10:6). The clearest case is Hebrews 2:2–3. The corresponding verb is παρακούω ("to refuse to listen") (Matt 18:17; Mark 5:36) (Erickson 2000, 585–586).

---

19. *Monogokoro* (物心).
20. *Buttai-ga aru-to iu kimochi* (物体があるという気持ち).
21. Sin is not ignorance because the conscious choice between evil and good is one of its prerogatives (Wiley 1940, II, 68). Erickson does not equate sin and ignorance. He names ignorance as one of the causes of sin.

5.2.5 The Nature of Sin

Erickson uses the following concepts to explain sin:

- "Missing the mark" (חטא and ἁμαρτάνω) is "probably the most common of those concepts."[22] In the Bible the word חטא "suggests not merely failure, but a decision to fail, a voluntary and culpable mistake." This sin is always "sin against God, since it is failure to hit the mark he has set, his standard" (586–587).[23]
- "Irreligion" (ἀσεβέω) is another character of sin. This is the negative of σέβω (to worship, to reverence). "Impiety . . . may be the best English rendering." The forensic term ἀδικία and its derivatives as well as ἀνόμως are used in this sense. "The word ἀνομία never refers to a breaking of the law in the narrow sense of the Mosaic regulations, but always a breaking of the law of God in the broader sense." For the violations against the Jewish law, Paul uses παρανομέω (Acts 23:3) (588–589).
- "Transgression" (עבר): This term occurs almost 600 times, usually in its literal sense "to cross over" or "to pass by." There are a number of references that connote the transgression of a command or "going beyond an established limit." The closest Greek equivalent is παραβαίνω with a "direct reference to the Jewish law" (Erickson 2000, 589–590).[24]
- "Iniquity" or "lack of integrity" (עול): The basic concept seems to be "deviation from a right course" (2000, 590).[25]

---

22. A literal usage is found in Judg 20:16 and Prov 19:2.

23. According to Erickson (587), the mark or standard is "perfect love of God and perfect obedience to him." The opposite is what Luther called *incurvatus in se ipsum*, "curved inward on oneself," not love of God but love always and only for oneself. The "self-seeking" man is always fixated on himself. He "cannot want that God is GOD" (Kettling 1993, 9). "The sinner *hates* God instead of loving him, despises God instead of fearing him, soars up haughtily, cramps up desperately, instead of trusting God (15).

24. According to Bruce, ἁμαρτία is objective and general, whereas παράβασις is subjective and personal (Wiley 1940, II, 83).

25. The sins listed so far (1–4) are concerned with the actions of man. Orthodoxy devides sins into (1) intentional sins and unintentional sins, (2) sins of commission and sins of omission, (3) sins of turning away from God and sins of turning to creature, (4) internal and external sins, (5) sins of the mouth, the heart, and deed, (6) sins against God and sins against man, (6) sins of the flesh and sins of the spirit, (7) secret sins and public sins, (8) venial sins and mortal sins (according to Gerhard in Pöhlmann 1980, 173). Barth divides sins according to Christology into sins of pride, sins of lethargy, and sins of deceit (Pöhlmann 1980, 176). Here ontological sin and sins of commission are not always distinguished as clearly as in Erickson's case. The sins he lists from here on (5–8) are concerned with the attitude of man.

- "Rebellion" (פֶּשַׁע: Isa 1:2; מרה: Isa 1:20; מרד: Ezek 2:3; סרר: Deut 21:18; Ps 78:8).[26] The most common terms in the New Testament are ἀπείθεια and derivatives (disobedience to parents; Rom 1:30; 2 Tim 3:2; Eph 2:2; 5:6), ἀφίστημι (1 Tim 4:1; Heb 3:12), and ἀποστασία (2 Thess 2:3) (590–591).
- "Treachery": מעל is used for treachery against humans (Num 5:12, 27, a woman's unfaithfulness against her husband; Josh 7:1; 22:20, Achan's unfaithfulness; Lev 26:40), בגד is mainly used for treachery against God (Ps 78:57; Jer 3:10; Mal 2:11). The New Testament equivalents παραπίπτω and παράπτωμα mean "to fall away" (Heb 6:6). "In both Testaments, there is a focus on the bond or covenant between God and his people" (592).
- "Perversion": (עוה, which means "to bend" or "to twist") (592).
- "Abomination" (שִׁקּוּץ and תּוֹעֵבָה): "These terms generally describe an act particularly reprehensible to God," such as idolatry (Deut 7:25–26), homosexuality (Lev 18:22; 20:13), wearing clothing of the opposite sex (Deut 22:5), sacrificing sons and daughters (Deut 12:31), sacrifice of blemished animals (Deut 17:1), and witchcraft (Deut 18:9–12). "These practices virtually nauseate God" (593).

5.3 The Experience of *Heil* under the Theological Aspect

The forgiving of sins and reconciliation with God are soteriological events. Yet they cannot be experienced by man. They are adjudged to him. As a result of that, man experiences various things. On one hand, the experience of *Heil* leads to "internal peace." Depending on the formation of his conscience, man may experience "internal peace" more as liberation from the fear of God's punishment (forgiving of sins), or more as rehabilitation (reconciliation with God).

However, the experience of "internal peace" must not be considered as all there is to salvation. On the other hand, experience of salvation must lead to "external peace." He whose sins are forgiven is liberated and obliged to forgive. Jesus inseparably joined being forgiven and forgiving (Matt 6:12–15; 18:23–35). Forgiving of sins is more than cancellation of punishment, but first and foremost annulment of the power of sin. He who is reconciled with God

---

26. In a similar way Pöhlmann (169) says that man "usurps" the throne of God. According to Soga (89), *hangyaku* (反逆), rebellion, is the "original sin."

is liberated and obliged to reconcile. The heart of reconciliation is love. Jesus inseparably joined the love for God and the love for others (Matt 22:37–40). Bloch's criticism of a merely "internalized salvation" (1982, 583) aims only at those who stop where salvation starts, but it does not hold good for those who understand "internal peace," being forgiving by and being reconciled with God as the foundation and starting point of a life engaged in "external peace."

6

The Cosmological Aspect of Salvation

Summary: In animism the cosmological aspect of human calamity is mainly experienced as fear of evil powers and forces under whose super-human power man is subjugated. In order to protect oneself from pending calamities, Japanese seek to foresee them by means of divination, mainly sought from female shamans. They seek protection against these powers and forces through amulets, talismans, and dedications. Another way of salvation, promoted by the Morita therapy, is the willful harmonious integration of man into the large context of nature.

In dialogue with Christian approaches, the fear of the Holy, a Christian encounter with satanic powers, a Christian answer to divination, and a comparison of shamanic and Christian leadership styles need to be addressed.

6.1 The Cosmological Aspect of Salvation in Japanese Animism

6.1.1 The Experience of Unheil *under the Cosmological Aspect*

Though persistently denied by those anthropologists that advocate cultural romanticism and the happiness of the heathen, fear is a constituting element of animism.¹ "Animistic peoples live with an all-pervasive fear of ancestors, spirits, magic, and witchcraft" (Van Rheenen 1996, 30; also Brown 2005, 86; Halverson 2004, 2–3; Zukeran 2008, 45, 48).² People with animistic worldviews understand themselves not only connected with, but also threatened by, the invisible world. "The animist is simply overwhelmed by the many powers allied against him" (Ndonga in Lwamba 2013, "Animism and the Spirit World in Africa: The Akamb Experience"). "In the degree that anything is unknown, it remains a source of dread, and therefore, of evil, since 'from fear of the invisible' spring the feelings of inferiority, helplessness and dependence" (Clodd 2012, "Man in the Making"). Animists live in "fear of souls, spirits and malicious people," and they are "enslaved by dread and fear of the unknown." In order to cope, they must "endlessly bargain, manipulate, or ward off invisible, sinister powers" (Lwamba 2013, "Animism and the Spirit World in Africa: The Akamb Experience").

> Acknowledgment of forces beyond individual understanding and desire to overcome confusion or fear in facing difficult and inexplicable aspects of life and death go hand in hand. (Nadin 1997, 413)

However, the object of animism is not – as usually assumed – only to be sought in the invisible world. Pieris understands the fear of visible things as the original fear. Cosmic religion³

> represents the psychological posture that the homo religious (residing in each of us) adopts subconsciously toward the mysteries of life – a sane attitude that an unwise use of technology can disturb. These mysteries relate to cosmic forces – heat, fire, wind and cyclones, earth and its quakes, oceans, rains, and floods – which we need and yet fear. (Pieris 1988, 71)

---

1. Hobbes' judgment that "the fear of things invisible is the natural Seed of Religion" still "holds the field" (Clodd 2012, "Man in the Making").

2. According to my understanding, fear is an instituting element of animism. At the same time, I am aware of the fact that fear is not the only feeling involved in the formation of worldviews and religions. Fear and ignorance were not enough for the creation of original religiosity. The feeling of dependency was also an important element (Bharathi 2000, 17). Samson names thankfulness as the dominating religious emotion of the Japanese (Samson 1978, 46). Hyslop acknowledges thankful reverence but he says that the original emotions were only those of fear (Hyslop 2003, 13).

3. Pieris prefers this term to "animism" which he rejects as pejorative (Pieris 1988, 71).

The Cosmological Aspect of Salvation

What is true for animism in general is also true for the Japanese animism. "Japanese are people that from the earliest prehistoric times until today fear the invisible power in the dark" (Seki 2004, 8). Naumann et al. write about the *Heian*-Era (794–1192) when people felt helplessly at the mercy of fate and the gods (Naumann et al. 1988, 242).

> In an age, in which humans feared that the natural phenomena of changes of heaven and earth were the work of god, the fear of god was probably the most natural thing. Before the power of the god who shook heaven and earth, powerless man could but plead and wait for god's heart to be appeased. And man could understand diseases and physical changes only as divine curses (*tatari*, 祟り).[4] (Onoyama 2004, 137)

In Japan, the negative influence of powers stronger than man is called *tsumi* (罪). The lexical translation of *tsumi* (罪) is "sin." The original meaning of *tsumi* (罪) can also mean natural calamities, physical deformations, and diseases (Matsumoto 1972, 15). "Snakebite, lightning and other mishaps polluted and were classified as *tsumi* (罪). *Tsumi* (罪) means both, guilt and calamity" (Gundert 1874, 21).[5] As for the origin of calamities, particularly, the New Religions answer:

> If man forgets that he is "kept alive" through the benefit of the Original Life, the relation between them will be destroyed. He will be severed from the life-force which sustains him, and consequently, he will be unable to realize the full potential of his life. (Tsushima et al. 1979, 146)

6.1.1.1 Fear of spirits

In addition to the inexplicable objectless fear of the *totaliter aliter* (Monnet 2007, 200), the fear of the Japanese has also had tangible objects:[6] the *ikiryou* or *seirei* (生霊), the spirits of "souls" of living people, the *shirei* (死霊), the spirits

---

4. "Commonly disasters, mishaps, and diseases are considered divine punishments (*tatari*, 祟り, literally "curses"). They can even be understood as a form of revenge" (Kalland 1991, 3). Dominey names nightmares, *kanashibari* (金縛), the "feeling of being suffocated in one's sleep," enuresis, and even insufficient performance at school (Dominey 2005, 263).

5. For the conceptual proximity of "sin" and "calamity" see under 8.1.1.2. The fuzziness of the Japanese "sin"-concept.

6. Most of my informants readily acknowledge the existence of evil spirits, share openly about (their own) possession, and admit that they feel (at times considerable) fear. At the same time, I have the impression that this subject is rather suppressed or rationalized in literature.

of the dead, and, since the beginning of the 1990s becoming more popular again (Gebhardt 2001, 13), the *goryou* (御霊), the "honorable spirits" are the most important. Even though "Japanese spirits . . . are basically neither good nor evil, but depending on how they are treated they can manifest in benevolent or malevolent ways" (Blacker 1999, 41).

The "fear" of spirits is very much alive in modern Japan. In the last fifty years, books on spirits have multiplied about one hundred times (Kreiner 2004, 431). In his book *Eternal Life: A Science of Bliss for the 21st Century* (2003), Ikuo Kinoshita (木下育生) writes:

> If one does not multiply the good spirits[7] in order not to be led astray toward evil by evil spirits[8] living in spiritual bodies,[9] if one does not eliminate the evil spirits [by multiplying good spirits], one will be occupied[10] by evil spirits at the next opportunity. The fight with the human self is the fight with the egocentric heart[11] and the fight with the evil spirits. As for the various kinds of evil spirits, we can say that in addition to the spirits of humans[12] there are also spirits living spiritually[13] based[14] in the world of ghosts[15] and the world of the evil.[16] These spirits are malicious spirits taking joy in leading humans astray and destroying them . . . If the evil spirits multiply as ruling spirits,[17] humans will get a defiled, evil heart as a result. The phenomenon commonly called "driven by the devil"[18] is the work of those evil spirits. In former times, evil deeds

---

7. *Zenryou* (善霊).
8. *Akuryoutachi* (悪霊たち).
9. *Reitai* (霊体).
10. I. Kinoshita uses *senryo* (占拠), a term from the world of military.
11. *Jigashin* (自我心).
12. *Jinrei* (人霊).
13. *Reiteki seibutsurei* (霊的生物霊). The *seibutsu* (生物) in *seibutsurei* (生物霊) means biological life.
14. Again, Kinoshita uses a term from the world of military, *honkyochi* (本拠地), "headquarter." His borrowing words from the world of military reminds of the worldview of "spiritual warfare."
15. *Yuukai* (幽界). This term is used as a synonym to *meido* (冥土 or 冥途), the "next world," the "other world" or the "world of the dead." The Shintoist term for death, *kiyuu* (帰幽), literally the "returning" (帰) into the "world of the spirits" (幽) belongs here.
16. *Makai* (魔界) is a Buddhist term identifying the realm of the *akuma* (悪魔), the "devil."
17. *Shihairei* (支配霊). *Shihai* (支配) means dominion or control.
18. *Ma-ga sashita* (魔が差した), literally "stung by [the] evil."

committed over and over again served as proof [of the influence of evil spirits]. These spirits first control the body of man[19] and cause spiritual damage,[20] but then they increase the spiritual energy[21] and live, if a certain level is reached, in the spiritual body[22] of man. There are many famous people who cause great anxiety in this world through such control of spirits. As long as they think they are normal, there is no remedy. (I. Kinoshita 2003, 40)

Fear of spirits of living persons

Ikiryou or *seirei*[23] (生霊), also called *ikisudama* (生魑魅 or 生霊), "living ghosts" are the *onryou* (怨霊), the vengeful spirits of living persons that can curse people (Nakae 1998, 225). Phenomena caused by these kinds of spirits have been described in the Genji-Monogatari (源氏物語). In modern Japan, they are explained in the context of telepathy and psycho-kinesis (*Encyclopedia of the Supernatural* 超常現象大事典 [*Choujougenshou Daijiten*] 2001, 63).

Fear of the spirits of the dead

Fear is the main reason/cause of veneration of the dead (Lwamba 2013, "Animism and the Spirit World in Africa: The Akamb Experience"). *Shirei* (死霊), "spirits of the dead" are thought to be living on earth and to be available for interaction (Goss and Klass 2005, 34). People can pray to them in "bad times" (Freed 2000, 17). But that does not mean that they are only benevolent. They are always needed and still need to be appeased if heirs and descendants want to live in peace (Byas 2005, 268). As long as they have not become Buddhas (*hotoke*, 仏) for sure they still can harm people (Goss and Klass 2005, 43). Malevolent spirits of the dead are called *goryou* (御霊), "honorable spirits."

Goryou (御霊), "honorable spirits,"[24] also called *mono-no ke* (物の怪) are *boukon* (亡魂), "lost souls" or "deceased souls." "Souls of those deceased holding a grudge against this world[25] are thought to have the capability of

---

19. *Nikutai* (肉体) means the biological body as opposed to spiritual body, *reitai* (霊体).
20. *Reishou* (霊障).
21. *Reiryoku-o appu suru* (霊力がアップする).
22. *Reitai* (霊体).
23. The second reading (*seirei*) of this word is identical with the Christian word for the Holy Spirit (聖霊). Therefore, Christians should be very cautious when using this word for the Holy Spirit when talking to non-Christians.
24. According to my experience these are the spirits which are most feared in present-day Japan.
25. *Kono yo-ni urami-o nokoshite shinda mono* (この世に怨みをのこして死んだもの).

cursing[26] the living." Therefore they are also called *tatarirei* (祟霊), "curse spirits."[27] Since the *Heian*-Era, malevolent spirits of the dead were feared and had to be appeased most attentively by "*teatsui chinkon-no girei* (手厚い鎮魂の儀礼)," laborious requiem masses (Kubota 1997, 61). Kubota (久保田展弘) explains the emergence of these rites:[28]

> On May 20th, 863 (early *Heian*-Era), in Kyoto's (then *heiankyou*, 平安京) Shinsenen (神泉苑) the *Goryoue* (御霊会)[29] was founded. Originally, deceased spirits of the Imperial Family were considered to be *goryou* (御霊) in the sense of *mitama* (ミタマ), but as time went by the meaning gradually changed to "souls of those who passed away by an unnatural death,"[30] and then even to "deceased."[31] The *Goryoue* (御霊会) became a rite for the appeasement of [all], which also were revengeful spirits.[32] (Kubota 1997, 65)

Spirits of the deceased cannot only be appeased through the rites of societies such as the *Goryoue* (御霊会), individuals can also make their peace with the deceased during the first forty-nine days after their passing. Psychics make contact with the deceased. The deceased appear mostly in dreams and let their bereaved know that they have forgiven them. Sometimes the sentiment of being forgiven can also be obtained without the help of psychics. They are able to let go of the ambivalent relationship with the deceased and the deceased are free to move on and become *hotoke* (仏), "Buddha" (Goss and Klass 2005, 43).

---

26. *Tatari-o nasu* (祟りをなす).

27. According to Tetsuma Hashimoto (橋本徹馬), they can curse humans in such a way that they suffer from heart problems, epilepsy, nightmares, suicidal tendency, neurosis, and cancer. Conflicts between parents and children can also be the result of curses (Formanek 2008, 66–67).

28. This quote shows where the name *goryou* (御霊) came from, why the spirits of the dead are called "honorable spirits." Originally only the spirits of the deceased members of the Imperial Family were venerated.

29. The *Goryou*-Society.

30. *Higyou-no shi-o togeta hito-no reikon* (非業の死を遂げた人の霊魂).

31. *Shisha* (死者).

32. *Onryou* (怨霊).

6.1.2 The Experience of Heil under the Cosmological Aspect

6.1.2.1 *Heil* as knowledge about the future, protection, and harmony

Japanese divination

Practices

Divination must not be confused with religion or religious practices. It considers itself as science.[33] Neither must it be confused with prophecy as prophecy is based on revelation by a super-human power. This is true even though the Japanese terms for divination, *shinsen* (神占) and *ekikyou* (易経), the "way of divination," which is the Chinese equivalent of the Japanese *shintou* (神道), the "way of the gods" (Mitsuhashi 1995, 10) connect divination with *shin* (神),[34] "god." In holistic and animistic worldviews, the line between science and religion is blurred, if it exists at all. Ono et al. define divination as (1) assurance of whether planned actions are "reconcilable with the will of god, or [assurance of] where the heart of god is"; and (2) the desire [of getting] a "certain sign" enquired by a defined method. Signs can be "phenomena in the environment" (Ono et al. 1985, 15). This definition shows two sides, (1) a religious side that inquires for "the will of god," and (2) a secular side that is concerned with the technique of divination.[35]

Dröge's observations concerning oracles are true for divination in general:

> The technique of oracles is recognizing the big in the small, capturing the hidden, causal relationships between things and forms of existence which cannot be recognized by means of reasoning . . . Oracle techniques are always closely connected with cosmology: When the cosmos is understood as a self-contained structure, the divinatory potency of the oracle is ultimately the result of knowledge of the hidden correspondence between the

---

33. In their article, *Eastern Determinism Reconsidered from a Scientific Point of View* (2002), Abe and Kobayashi discuss the originally Chinese *Yi-King* (*Chou*-divination) based on the theories of Yin and Yang and the Five Natural elements.

34. Mitsuhashi later juxtaposed the Chinese equivalent of Shintoism with *senjutsu* (仙術), "supernatural skill," *houjutsu* (方術), "divination" and in the widest sense with *reimyou-naru michi* (霊妙なる道), the "supernatural way" (Mitsuhashi 2007, 19).

35. On the other hand, there exist special divination deities: *uranaiwa-no kami* (卜庭神), the "deities of the divination-garden" and *Futonorito-no mikoto* (太祝詞の命) (Fairchild 1962, 59). The line between science and religion is blurred indeed.

micro-cosmos and the macro-cosmos, the result of prescientific[36] world observation. (Dröge 1992, 490)

Divination in Japan is attested for since ancient times. The old tale *How They Administered to the Mute Prince Homujiwake* (誉年治別) *and How He Eventually Was Able to Speak Again* tells the story of how Prince Aketatsu (明立) invoked a sign concerning the favorable outcome of a certain plan (Naumann and Naumann 1990, 7.390). Naumann et al. explain the *yuuke* (夕占), the "evening oracle" practiced in the *Heian*-Era thus:

> In the dusk, one would go to a crossroad in order to obtain an answer to one's questions by listening to the snatches of conversation of the passers-by. The evening oracle has very old rules, concepts almost lost even back then: the crossroad as a cosmic center where communication with the world of the dead is possible; the dark powers as those knowing about the future. (Naumann et al. 1988, 242)

In ancient times, divination was reserved for political affairs. Only officials were allowed to use it. Today it is widely used in the private sector (Ono et al. 1985, 15). In Japan, divination is as modern as it is old. Abe and Kobayashi judge: "In today's uncertain times, fortune telling has become increasingly popular in modern Japan" (Abe and Kobayashi 2002, 485). According to Lewis's research,[37] mainly young people use divination (Lewis 1993, 176). Special occasions are accidents with a suspected supernatural influence. Experts for divination are shamans (in Japan mainly female), and specialized priests and priestesses (Lewis 1993, 62). Other, more common, occasions are mate choice, medical problems, and inquiring with the dead (Lewis 1993, 165). However, only 2 percent of Lewis's informants have ever met with a psychic. Among Christians, counseling pastors can take the role of shamans (Lewis 1993, 177).[38]

---

36. I think that Dröge's "prescientific" is yet another example of Western ethnocentrism.

37. Lewis explained the methodology of his research in the foreword of *The Unseen Face of Japan* (Lewis 1993, xv–xvii). In a thorough selection process, he chose 667 usable surveys. To my understanding, Lewis interpreted and discussed his findings very cautiously. Instead of generalizing percentages he examined the sociological and biographical background of individual informants.

38. About 20% of Japanese believe in divination. Women between 25 and 29 are the biggest group (49%) (Kreiner 2004, 428–430).

Kokkurisan (狐狗狸さん)

Among the divination practices in Japan, *Kokkurisan* (狐狗狸さん) is very popular, particularly among primary school children.[39] For the practice of *Kokkurisan* (狐狗狸さん), a frame of three bamboo sticks – pencils and coins can also be used (Saruta 2002, 13) – is built within a circle of *hiragana*-syllable-characters (平仮名). The frame holds a bowl which all children touch with their hands. The bamboo sticks then move and point to different characters. At the beginning one person or all evoke *Kokkurisan* (狐狗狸さん) with an incantation called jumon (呪文). Two examples from literature:

> *Kokkurisan, Kokkurisan, koko-wa maru-ken, maru-shi-no- maru-machi, maru-choume, maru-maru desu. Yoroshikereba okoshi-kudasai* (こっくりさん、こっこりさん、ここは○県○市の○町○丁目○○です。よろしければお越しください); *Kokkurisan, Kokkurisan*, here is that and that prefecture, that and that ward of that and that city, that and that area and that and that house number. If thou art pleased would thou come hither? (Saruta 2002, 13)

> *Kokkurisan, Kokkurisan, irasshaimashitara okotaekudasai* (こっくりさん、こっくりさん、いらっしゃいましたらお答えください); *Kokkurisan, Kokkurisan*, if thou art here, make answer. (Yoshida 2002, 125)

The extraordinarily polite language shows the respect if not fear the children feel toward *Kokkurisan* (狐狗狸さん). Some of my informants reported that for that reason they used the less intimidating *Enjerusan* (エンジェルさん), the "Angel-san" instead of the dreaded *Kokkurisan* (狐狗狸さん). This fear also explains why the children sometimes want to make sure what spirit actually appeared (Yoshida 2002, 126). After the incantation, the children ask questions, usually on the level of "who loves whom?" If the circle of characters does not lead to satisfactory answers, the children also move on to yes-no-questions (Yoshida 2002, 126). In rare cases, *Kokkurisan* (狐狗狸さん) is asked to kill somebody (Yoshida 2002, 127).

---

39. Among young adults (20–24 years old) the rate of those who practice *Kokkurisan* (狐狗狸さん) drops to 20% (Lewis 1993, 167). As popular as the method is, it is not originally Japanese. It was introduced to Japan only around the end of the 19th and the beginning of the 20th century by American sailors (Lewis 1993, 167). The widely used *Bagua* (eight symbols) (Huang et al. 2012, 256) is also not originally Japanese but of Chinese origin (Chamberlain 1990, 670).

At the end of a session, *Kokkurisan* (狐狗狸さん) is asked to leave:

Kokkurisan, Kokkurisan, arigatou gozaimashita. Mou okaeri-kudasai. Wakarimashitara „Hai"-to okotae-kudasai (こっくりさん、こっくりさん、ありがとうございました。もうお帰りください。わかりましたら「はい」とお答えください); *Kokkurisan, Kokkurisan,* thank you very much. Please leave now. If you understood this, please answer with "yes." (Yoshida 2002, 127)

New Year lucky tickets *mikuji* (御籤 or 神籤)

The drawing of New Year lucky tickets (*mikuji*, 御籤 or 神籤)[40] has been popular since the *Kamakura*-Era (Tsuchiya 2008, 152). Happenstance is a crucial element. Nowadays, oracles are often obtained from vending machines and are generally rather shallow. Correspondingly, the attitude most Japanese have toward lucky tickets is also shallow.

The main headers of the lucky tickets are distributed as follows:

16%	*daikichi* (大吉)	Great Fortune
35%	*kichi* (吉)	Fortune
20%	*hankichi* (半吉)	Half Fortune
1%	*sue-shoukichi* (末小吉)	Almost Small Fortune
6%	*sue-kichi* (末吉)	Almost Fortune
30%	*kyou* (凶)	Misfortune. (Kitajima 2007, 91)

Under the main headers, also called *zentaiun* (全体運), "general fate," there are categories that further elaborate the oracle. Among others the categories are:

sagashimono (探し物)	things searched for
machibito (待ち人)	people waited for
kenkou (健康)	health
kin-un (金運)	monetary fate
shoubu-un (勝負運)	fate of winning and losing
seikatsu (生活)	(everyday) life. (Tsuchiya 2008, 152)

Lewis named three attitudes people have when drawing lucky tickets:

- It is better not to obtain a *mikuji* (御籤 or 神籤), because one does not want to know what misfortune may come;

---

40. The *kuji* (籤) used in a religious context is related to the secular *kuji* (くじ), the lottery ticket (Komatsu 1995, 150). Only the writing is different.

- The *mikuji* (御籤 or 神籤) is only regarded if it promises fortune;
- If the *mikuji* (御籤 or 神籤) promises misfortune, most people are scared, because they understand *un* (運), "fate," as something irrevocable. However, there is a chance of changing it through "prayers" (Lewis 1993, 173–174). Therefore people used to bind the lucky tickets that promised *kyou* (凶), "disfortune," to the trees in the temple- or shrine-precinct in order to receive *yousha* or, as Kitajimas reads it, *yurushi* (容赦) and *kago* (加護), "help," from the gods (Kitajima 2007, 91). Today, people also bind lucky tickets that promise *kichi* (吉) on the trees (Pye et al. 2007, 11). In doing so the connection to the deities is guaranteed (Tsuchiya 2008, 155) and the fortune thus bound cannot fly away. (Kitajima 2007, 91)

Palmistry

About 30 percent of Japanese use *kanshoujutsu* (観掌術), "palmistry." Palmistry is most popular on the *seijin-no-hi* (成人の日), the "Coming of Age Day." Young women consult the palmist for questions related to marriage, young men for questions related to career (Lewis 1993, 111). The attitude of the mainly young people is mostly that of seeking fun (Lewis 1993, 167–169).

Blood-type divination

In this context Lewis also discusses blood-type divination (Lewis 1993, 171), which has been very popular since about 1930 (Matsuda 1994, 194). It is based on the blood-type personality theory popularized by post-war writers Masahiko Nomi (能見正比古) and Yoshimasa Suzuki (鈴木芳正) (Yoshino 1997, 208). Lewis considers the blood-type personality theory "divination," because he cannot attribute any scientific basis to it. However, later scholars in the field of biological personality research acknowledge a significant correlation between blood-type and personality (Carducci 2009, 324). Matsuda (松田薫) also called attention to the relationship between astrology and the blood-type personality theory (Matsuda 1994, 1). However, he strictly distinguished between scientific typology research and "divination."

Astrology

Western astrology is perceived in a similarly shallow manner (Lewis 1993, 170), whereas with Chinese and the derived Japanese (Mori and Milenkovic 1995, 5.9), astrology is taken more seriously. Those interested can obtain the necessary *koyomi* (暦), "almanacs," from shrines, temples, and specialized book stores (Lewis 1993, 170–171).

Japanese astrology, called *kigaku* (気学), is based on the idea that a man is accompanied by the *ki* (気), *mana*, he received at his birth, and that this *mana* works synergistically with the *mana* of other people, increasingly or decreasingly (Mori and Milenkovic 1995, 15). As the *gaku* (学), "science" in *kigaku* (気学) shows, Japanese astrology explicitly understands itself as science.[41] Coulmas rightly commented that it was not about consulting an oracle, but rather about solving a mathematical problem (Coulmas 2000, 108).[42]

In this context Yamaguchi quotes Fan Li:

> Fortune and misfortune are dependent on the cyclic movements of the sun, the moon, the stars, and the planets, as well as on the recurring change of destruction and procreation (the four seasons) . . . But all the transformations are nothing else than (the deviation) in the fundamental, cyclic regularity (of the Yin and Yang in the Great Tao). (Yamaguchi 1997, 47)

Unlucky days and lucky days (1): The *Rokuyou* (六曜)-system

The Chinese *rokuyou* (六曜)-system was introduced during the *Ashikaga*-Era (Pike 1992, 8). The idea of lucky days and unlucky days as well as unlucky years – in Japan even more important – are influenced by Taoism (Aoki 1994, 203).[43] Lucky days and unlucky days are so important that they are printed in almost all Japanese calendars.

Japanese unlucky days are the *tomobiki* (友引),[44] the day of "pulling along friends." One must never conduct a funeral on such a day because friends may be pulled along into death (Coulmas 2000, 308). Lewis reports about a case where an impending funeral was postponed and the corpse was preserved with dry ice (Lewis 1993, 134–135). The *butsumetsu* (仏滅),[45] Buddha's death anniversary, is the "worst unlucky day, a kind of Good Friday for Buddhists (Coulmas 2000, 308). On this day, it is not advisable to start anything new. Change of residence or openings are taboo. Weddings are unthinkable. Pike

---

41. Long calls astrology "art, science, and pseudo-science" (Long 1981, 71; similarly Haack 1982, 13). Generally speaking, Käser calls animism explicitly "natural science" (Käser 2004, 27).

42. See the chapter "Zeit der Feste" in Coulmas's *Japanische Zeiten: Eine Ethnografie der Vergänglichkeit* (Coulmas 2000, 95ff).

43. 46% of the Japanese believe in lucky days and unlucky days (Kreiner 2004, 428).

44. On the other hand, Pye et al. understand the *tomobiki* (友引) as a lucky day on principle which bring misfortune only around noon (Pye et al. 2007, 248).

45. The 4th, 10th, 16th, 22nd, and 28th of the first and seventh lunar month is *butsumetsu* (仏滅), as well as every sixth day after the specific 28th (Pye et al. 2007, 235–236).

reports a case where a wedding hotel in Tokyo offered free weddings on *butsumetsu* (仏滅).[46] There were interested couples but they all cancelled their reservations under the pressure of family and friends (Pike 1992, 8).

Japanese lucky days are the *taian* or *daian* (大安), the "Day of Great Relief."[47] This day guarantees fortune for all activities. It was not by chance that the attack on Pearl Harbor was scheduled on a *taian* (大安) (Pike 1992, 8). On the *taian* (大安) dates wedding hotels are booked up months in advance (Coulmas 2000, 311).

Additionally, there are two days that can bring fortune **and** misfortune: the *sengachi*, *senkachi*, or *senshou* (先勝), brings fortune during the forenoon and misfortune during the afternoon. The *senbu* or *senmake* (先負) brings misfortune in the morning and is neutral during the afternoon. The *shakkou* (赤口) brings misfortune during the afternoon (Lewis 1993, 134–135). *Shakkou* (赤口), literally "red mouth" means the "wide open (and therefore red) mouth." This probably refers to a traditional Chinese proverb that talks about a mouth wide open and a tongue full of venom, which means a cursing mouth (Pye et al. 2007, 246). "This day is full of uncertainties, a day at which the slightest carelessness can evoke the curse of the gods" (Coulmas 2000, 309). Another interpretation of *shakkou* (赤口) is that the red (赤) refers to wounds afflicted by knives and the like. Particularly carpenters dislike this day (Pike 1992, 8).[48]

Unlucky days and lucky days (2): The *Juunichoku*(十二直)-system

In magazines and newspapers, usually printed under the horoscopes of the *rokuyou*(六曜)-system, there is also a column of the *juunichoku*(十二直)-system, also called *chuudanjuunichoku* (中段十二直). This system was created in consideration of the *Hokutoshichisei* (北斗七星), the "constellation of the Great Bear," and the *juunishi*(十二支)-system, a system of twelve "earthly branches" similar to the zodiac (Ooguri 2000, 125). In ancient China people believed that the power of the "Great Bear" revolving around the fixed polar star ruled all things (Uda 2007, 18).

---

46. In Japan, weddings can cost up to several hundreds of thousands of Euro. Kruth claims that the average spent for weddings in 2005 was YEN 3,820,000 (about €340,000 Euro) (Kruth 2007, 143).

47. The *taian* (大安) is on the 5th, 11th, 17th, and 29th of the first lunar month (Pye et al. 2007, 247).

48. Similarly, Coulmas (2000, 309).

The twelve categories of the *Juunishi*(十二支)-system, the system of the "earthly branches":

- *Tatsu* (建): The meaning of this Chinese character is "to build" or "to erect." This day is the luckiest among all lucky days, predestined for Shintoist and Buddhist festivities, weddings, store openings, changes of residence, starts of construction, travels, generally speaking for all kinds of new beginnings. However, for opening a warehouse this day is an unlucky day.
- *Nozoku* (除): The meaning of this Chinese character is "to leave out." Misfortunes are "left out" which makes this day a good day for seeing a doctor, sowing, or digging a well. However, for weddings this day is an unlucky day.
- *Mitsu* (満): The meaning of this Chinese character is "to be full" or "to fulfill." This day is an auspicious day for all kinds of plans.
- *Tahira* (平): The meaning of this Chinese character is "level" or "flat." Whatever is started on such days, becomes *byoudouheiwa* (平等平和), "even," "level," and therefore "peaceful." This is a lucky day for starting construction, travelling, sowing, civil weddings and other festivities. However, for digging ponds, ditches or holes this day is an unlucky day.
- *Sadan* (定): The meaning of this Chinese character is "to determine." This day gives stability and firmness to all plans: construction work, changes of residence, store openings, civil weddings, sowing, generally speaking for all kinds of new beginnings. However, for legal matters and travels this day is an unlucky day.
- *Toru* (執): The meaning of this Chinese character is "to do office work." This is a lucky day for Shintoist and Buddhist festivities, for producing things and for sowing. However, for spending and earning money as well as for asset management, this day is not a lucky day.
- *Yaburu* (破): The meaning of this Chinese character is "to tear." This day is an unlucky day for most everything, but particularly for legal matters.
- *Ayabu* (危): The meaning of this Chinese character is "danger." A moderate approach to all undertakings is advisable. This day brings misfortune particularly for travelling and mountain climbing. However, for making rice wine this day is a lucky day.

- *Naru* (成): The meaning of this Chinese character is "to become." Everything "becomes" as planned, everything leads to success. However, for legal matters and counseling this day is an unlucky day.
- *Osan* (収): The meaning of this Chinese character is "to gather," "to collect," or "to yield." This is a good day for harvesting grain and buying commercial goods. However, for weddings and marriage origination, this day is an unlucky day.
- *Hiraku* (開): The meaning of this Chinese character is "to open." This is a lucky day for building plans, store openings and civil weddings. However, for funerals and other defiling things, this day is an unlucky day.
- *Tozu* (閉): The meaning of this Chinese character is "to close." This is a lucky day for earning money, building graves or toilets. However, for starting construction, weddings, and store openings this day is an unlucky day (Sakade 2003, 4–5).

Unlucky ages

The observation of *yakudoshi* (厄年) "unlucky ages" is even more complicated. About half of the Japanese attach importance to unlucky ages (Lewis 1993, 148).[49] The ideas of *yakudoshi* (厄年) are based upon astrology, but were also influenced by Buddhism (Katsumoto 1992, 109). The *honyaku* (本厄), the "principal unlucky age" (Lewis 1993, 150), for women is 33, for men 42. The year before any unlucky age, called *maeyaku* (前厄) (Lewis 1993, 148) as well as the year following the principal unlucky age, called *atoyaku* (後厄), are also considered unlucky ages. For men the ages of 25 and 61, and for women the ages of 19 and 37 are also unlucky ages (Lewis 1993, 145). However, the entire *yakudoshi* (厄年) system is much more complicated:

Table 6.1 Unlucky Ages (according to Lewis 1993, 146)

	men	women
principal *yakudoshi* (厄年)	42	33
cardinal *yakudoshi* (厄年)	25, 61	19, 37

---

49. According to a survey conducted by Asahi-Shinbun (newspaper) in the 1980s, 55.5% of the women and 44.1% of the men showed consideration towards their *yakudoshi* (厄年) (Coulmas 2000, 316). According a newer survey, 54% believe in *yakudoshi* (厄年), whereby the rate of women in their thirties is particularly high (72%). Kreiner claims that the reason for this high rate is that the principal *yakudoshi* (厄年) for women is the age of 33 (Kreiner 2004, 428).

intermediate *yakudoshi* (厄年)	24, 26 41, 43 60, 62	18, 20 32, 34 36, 38
minor *yakudoshi* (厄年)	18, 19, 20 32, 33, 34 36, 37, 38	24, 25, 26 41, 42, 43 60, 61, 62
minor *yakudoshi* (厄年) without gender differences	1, 4, 7, 10, 13, 16, 22, 28, 40, 46, 49, 52, 55, 58	

When one recalls that not only the *yakudoshi* (厄年) is an unlucky age but also the previous and the following age, the question is whether from a certain age on there are any lucky ages.[50]

Shamanism

Introduction

"The term 'shaman' is originally a Tungusic word meaning 'a person influenced by spirits'" (Deppe and Deppe 2002, 187). Shamans are people with special skills. They serve others by obtaining information from realms of this world that cannot be accessed anymore by natural means. According to shamanic myths all people used to be able to access other realms,[51] but ever since the bridge between "heaven and earth"[52] was destroyed, only shamans know how to "travel" there (Storm 2000, 214). By means of possession[53] they are therefore considered to be able to live "in the middle zone between humans and the supernatural" (McKinney 2000, 869). "Possession bridges the gulf between humans and gods, spirits and ancestors, giving humans a deep sense of their presence and involvement in human lives" (Hiebert et al. 1999, 179; similarly

---

50. Divination with the Japanese zodiac, called *doubutsu uranai* (動物占い), literally "animal divination" (Pye et al. 2007, 236) and divination with crystal ball (Atoda 1990b, 18-21) are also known. From ancient times the *hatsuyume* (初夢), the "first dream" in the New Year, was ascribed divinatory importance (Hammitzsch 1969: 27). For divination with wounds see under 8.1.1.3 *Kegare* (穢れ) in connection with the body.

51. In Japan, there is a tale about a man who had to walk with a stoop because in his homeland the heaven was so low. The separation of heaven and earth took a long time (Fairchild 1962, 27).

52. In Japanese, this bridge is called *ama-no ukihashi* (天の浮橋), "the hovering bridge of heaven." *Izanami* (伊弉冉 or 伊邪那美 or 伊耶那美 or 伊弉弥) and *Izanagi* (伊伊弉諾神 or 伊邪那岐命 or 伊耶那岐命) were standing on it when they formed Japan (Fairchild 1962, 27).

53. Gro-Helen Tørum, for example, wrote about Lilli Bendriss, another neo-shaman: "She breathes herself into trance and surrenders herself completely to the primitive forces" (Tørum in Kalvig 2014, 339).

Blacker 1993, 152). There are two ways to obtain secret knowledge: Shamans are either possessed by a spirit,[54] or "their souls leave their bodies and ascend to the realm of the spirits" (McKinney 2000, 869; Oguro 1982, 27). The notion of "loss of soul" (Glottes and Lewis-Williams 1997, 23) is technically not correct.

In *Zur Struktur des Schamanismus* (1955), Schröder named seven characteristics for shamanism:

- "Shamanism is an institutionalized, fixed-ritual bound ecstatic contact with transcendental beings in order to perform a social function. It is not a religion, but is a religious phenomenon which fits in different religions."
- A shaman is neither a priest nor a prophet, mystic or magician. He is dependent on his patron spirit. Therefore, his office is not magical but religious.
- "Ecstasy is absolutely necessary for shamanism. It is a special kind of ecstasy – a transformation into another personality. By ecstasy the shaman contacts transcendental beings." There are two basic types of shamanism: migrating (contact outside the body) and possessed (transcendental beings enter the body).
- The patron spirit calls the shaman. During ecstasy the patron spirit determines the personality of the shaman.
- The training can be formal or informal.
- The investiture of a shaman is carried out through an initiation rite.
- The shaman is bound to a fixed form (costume, paraphernalia, rites, mode of performance) (Schröder in Fairchild 1962, 1–2).[55]

Japanese shamanism

History

Shintoism has always known incantation rituals (Köpping 1990, 20). According to Naumann, the migrating soul of the shamans is a basic element of their function, documented even in mythology (Naumann 1996, 52). According to Sansom, the earliest Japanese religion has much in common with the shamanic practices of Northeast Asia[56] (Sansom 1987, 8; similarly also Oyama 1995, 34;

---

54. The calling of the foundress of the "dancing religion" *Tenshoukoutaijinguukyou* (天照皇大神宮教), Sayo Kitamura (北村サヨ) is a typical example (Wendt 1970, 178).

55. To my knowledge Fairchild's *Shamanism in Japan* (1962) is the most comprehensive work on Japanese shamanism.

56. According to Campbell, Northeast Asia is still a stronghold of shamanism (Campbell 1991, I, 283).

Tsunoda et al. 1964, I, 21; Iida 1988). The worldview of shamanism is animistic (Sasaki 1980, 64–66): a "highest god," a "one and only" monotheistic deity, fundamental divorce of good and evil, let alone a dualistic distinction between God and Satan, are not acceptable (Oyama 1995, 111). "In Shamanism the divine-human continuum is manifested" (Inagaki 1990, 9).

In Japan, "women have had a leading role in cults . . . since ancient times" (Immoos 1991, 13).[57] This is also true for Shamanism (Immoos 1991, 20). The shaman office has been handed down along the matriarchal line (22) and in present-day Japan it is almost exclusively women who are shamans.[58] In the past there were also male shamans called *Jemmabo*, as Engelbert Kämpfer (1651–1712) reports in the journal of his Japan trip (1690–1692):

---

57. According to Hori, this is evident from the fact that there are no Japanese words for male shamans (Hori 1974, 181).

58. In pre-Buddhist Japan, women were highly esteemed. With Buddhism contempt for women entered Japan. According to Buddhism, women are "temptresses" and "full of sin," having the appearance of an "angel," yet "harboring in their hearts a devil." Therefore, they are to be feared more than anything else. Even today this Buddhist evaluation is seen in the proverbs such as *onna-no kokoro-to aki-no sora* (女の心と秋の空), "women's heart and autumn's sky [are equally changeable]" (Joseph 1982, 68) or *dansonjohi* (男尊女卑), "honoring men and despising women" (Gulick 1964, 82). Until 1925 women were equated with imbeciles (Neuss 1984, 41–42). The crucial reference for Buddhist discrimination against women is found in the Lotus-Sutra: "The female body is polluted; it is not a fit vessel for the Dharma" (Okano 2002, 175).

Two things need to be said for the rescue of the reputation of Buddhism:
(1) SGI-researcher Toshie Kurihara (栗原淑江) showed that for Buddhist monk practitioners, women were a "source of temptation . . . the greatest single impediment to their practice." Buddha himself "is recorded as having been very harsh in his condemnations of the deleterious effects of contact with women and of carnal desire." The world of enlightenment was open for monks only if they avoided "the lures of women" (Kurihara 2015, 37–38). When women were allowed for ordination they were under heavy rules and many more regulations than monks (39). Kurihara explains that "even the more vigorous rejection of femininity is best understood as warnings to men to avoid such distractions in their own pursuit of enlightenment" (42). After the death of Buddha there were changes in attitudes toward Buddhist nuns. "It is possible that male monks who did not welcome the presence of nuns presented their own views as the Buddhist words . . . Over time, the Buddha's original spirit was diluted and the ideas of these male monks were recorded as sutras, generating a philosophy of discriminatory and degrading views of women runs counter to its original spirit" (42). (2) Buruma holds that the negative evaluation of women dates back into pre-Buddhist Japan. It is a result of the fear men feel toward women. "As in other cultures, Japan also has many legends about this horrible aspect of female power" (Buruma 1985, 24). One reason for the popularity of shamanism among women could be that in the world of shamanism suppressed women find acknowledgment and power. Iida (1988) claims that this is true for Korean shamanism in Japan. In a similar way Schnabel points out to the fact that in societies where women are suppressed more women report about possession (Cook 1996, 178–179).

They pretend – through the power of certain ceremonies and power-words – to use domestic and foreign gods (*sintos* and *budsdo*), to evoke and ward off evil spirits. They notify of thieves and stolen goods, foretell the future, interpret dreams, heal diseases, uncover criminals, and determine guilt or innocence of those accused. In case of a disease, the patient has to give a full report on the evil that has befallen him to the *Jemmabo*. He in turn writes special characters on a piece of paper. These characters have a certain relation with the condition and constitution of such person. He then places this piece of paper in front of the idols, whose power then enters the paper through special ceremonies. The paper is the made into pills (*goof*) ... The *Jammaboes* use similar papers to find culprits, and [even] ... to extinguish fires. (Kämpfer 1777, 288–289)

Introduction

Together with Nakayama, Hori divides the Japanese female shamans into two groups and then adds a third:[59]

Graph 1

(1) The first group of female shamans are the so-called *kannagi* (巫 or 覡), which include the *miko* (巫). Today they exercise cultic functions, mainly in shrines. Their original functions and techniques have been lost. As they practice in *jinja* (神社), in "shrines," they are also called *jinja miko* (神社巫) (Hori 1974, 182).

Their functions are best explained with the Chinese characters in graph 1. The Chinese character for female shaman, *wu* (graph 1, left character), is formed by the radicals for the cosmic axis connecting heaven and earth (graph 1, center character) and two persons (graph 1, right character) dancing around the cosmic axis. Typical and representative is the preaching activity of Sayo Kitamura, foundress of "dancing religion" *Tenshoukoutaijinguukyou* (天照皇大神宮教). She preached "singing and dancing" (Wendt 1970, 178).[60]

---

59. Others classify shamans in other ways. Sasaki classifies according to the function of shamans into (1) possession shamanism, (2) prophetic shamanism, and (3) psychic shamanism (Sasaki 1980, 193).

60. This kind of "semantically based deciphering" of Chinese characters is actually not permissible, partly because of a very long history of changes and partly because of simplification reforms in the way the writing obscures the original form of the characters (Häffner 2009, 214). In addition, in this particular case, the original meaning of *miko* is not 巫, but 神子, "god" or "child of god" (Fairchild 1962, 57). However, what I am doing in the case at hand is not explaining the Chinese character *rei* (霊, 靈) (graph 3), but explaining what shamans do.

Campbell reports about a conversation between a Christian theologian and a Buddhist priest. The Christian theologian mentioned that regretfully he did not understand Japan's religion or ideology. The priest answered, "We have no religion. We have no ideology. We dance" (Campbell 1991, II, 564–565). The round dance of the shamans "keeps the cosmic processes going in their right order," says Immoos and quotes a song of a shaman acting in a *Nou*(能)-act: "I dance the dance that moves the palaces of the moon."[61] Generally speaking, female shamans have the function to balance the cosmic powers, to "serve as instruments of divine influence in this world" (Immoos 1991, 20).[62]

Graph 2

Another function of the shamans of this group seems to have been *amagoi* (雨乞 or 雨請), "rain magic." The old Chinese character for spirit, *rei* (靈) (graph 2, left character) is formed from three mouths (graph 2, center character) invoking rain (graph 2, right character).[63] *Rei* (靈) "expresses the spirit, the soul, where the power of the shamans is concentrated" (Immoos 1991, 19–20).

(2) The second group of female shamans are the *kuchiyose* (口寄せ), "literally "approaching mouth." The sedentary and migratory shamans, *ichiko* (市子), literally "city-shamans" and *sato miko* (里巫女), literally "country shamans" or "domiciled shamans" belong to this group. They master "telepathy, mediumship, necromancy, and divination." Their most demanded services are the communication with patron deities or patron spirits, ghosts, and the dead (Hori 1974, 182). The "psychic shamans" *kuchiyose miko* (口寄せ巫女) or *kuchiyose* (口寄せ) can be divided into three groups: (a) *kami kuchi* (神口), "those who are the mouth of the gods," (b) *iki kuchi* (生き口), "those who are the mouth of the living," and (c) *shini kuchi* (死に口), "those who are the mouth of the dead (Berentsen 1985a, 85; Nesbitt 2007, 58). While talking in their religious capacity, *kami kuchi* (神口) understand themselves as identical with the deity, or as the "pipe" of the god: *Watashi-wa kami-sama. Paipu dake* (私は神様。パイプだけ。), "I am god. Only a pipe" (Iwagou 2010). A shaman is called "to penetrate the curtain that veils the other world (mostly in ecstasy),[64]

---

61. Hiebert and Meneses report that in band societies, ecstatic dances are used for establishing contact with ancestors and gods (Hiebert and Meneses 1995, 61–62).

62. The element of dance in Shamanism is not limited to Japanese Shamanism. The Norwegian, female urban neo-shaman Gro-Helen Tørum calls herself a "dancer between the dimensions" (Kalvig 2014, 331).

63. The modern simplified form is 霊.

64. In Japanese, this kind of ecstasy is called *kamigakari* (神懸り or 神憑り), literally "to be under the guidance of a god," or *shinki*, alternatively *kamige* (神気), literally "the *ki* (気) of god."

to call good spirits and bring them messages, and to appease or ward off evil spirits" (Immoos 1991, 20).

Graph 3

(3) Hori adds a third group, the shamans of the New Religions. He calls these shamans *jussha* (術者), "magicians," and *gyousha* (行者), "practitioners" (Hori 1974, 183). A segment of their work is depicted in the Chinese character *shi* (graph 3, left character). It consists of the radical bamboo (graph 3, right character) and the lower part *miko* (巫),[65] "shaman" (graph 1, left character). The radical 竹, "bamboo" serves as radical in many Chinese characters that denote names of plants.

Presence

Even today and in the so-called "modern" (mostly meaning westernized) Japan, shamans are active (Oyama 1995, 171). However, they are not called shamans. In the last fifty years the interest in shamanism has rapidly increased. According to Kreiner, there are about ten times as many books on shamanism published now than in the 1950s (2004, 431). Today, there are five different categories of shamans:

(1) Among the Ainu, Japans oldest ethnic group, shamanism is still alive (Hori 1974, 185). The male shamans of the Ainu are called *tsusemkul*. According to Yewangoe, the Ainu-shamanism is the source of the Japanese *Shintou*-shamanism. One of the functions of the *tsumemkul* is to play the role of the game, that is, the bear, at the *Iomante*-festival.[66] The Ainu consider the bear as *kamui*, as "god." According to Taika there are two main aspects of the Ainu-religion, healing and divination, which are considered to be the heart of the "Ainu-soteriology." The *tsumemkul* master the *kamui-oroshi*,[67] literally the "calling down of a deity," as well as the *kuchiyose* (口寄せ), the evocation of a spirit of the dead (Yewangoe 1987, 157).

---

65. Köpping used the word *itako* (巫子) (Köpping 1990, 20–21) which was only used for the shamans in Northeast Japan (Yewangoe 1987, 157), where they are also called *kamisan* (上さん) (Sasaki 1980, 184) or *okamin* (おかみん) (Fairchild 1962: 70), which means "mistresses" or "ladies." *Itako* (巫子) are blind women. They still practice (Fairchild 1962, 62). In addition to the *itako* (巫子) in Northeast, there are also the mainly female *juta* of Okinawa (Schuster 2003, 248), the *waka* (若), derived from *waka-no miya* (若の宮), "young prince," or from *waka miko* (若巫女), "young *miko*" in Fukujima-prefecture, the *moriko* (もりこ), probably meaning "patrons," the *nono* (のの), a baby talk word for anything divine, and the *zatokata* (ざとかた), wives of priests (Fairchild 1962, 71–73). Some scholars called *miko* (巫女) the earliest prostitutes of Japan (Cherry 1991, 120).

66. *Iomante* literally means "Unleash the bear!"

67. *Kamui* is Ainu and means "god," but *oroshi* (卸し or 下ろし or 降ろし) is Japanese and means "lower" or "bring down."

(2) There are female shamans that withdrew into the "underground of folk religion where they ... survived all changes of society." Today they are active as healers, necromancers (Immoos 1991, 29), and psychics (Cecchini 1976, 275). Particularly in Northern Japan, shamanism is locally common. Wendt writes:

> Starting from the beginning of the 20th century, domiciled female shamans living in villages have taken the place of migrating female shamans ... An older female shaman choses a young girl as novice and with strict discipline trains her ... in trance techniques. The training lasts for three to five years and ends with an initiation-phase which consists of exams and a symbolic death and resurrection.[68] Traditionally the main functions of female shamans are divination under trance, prayers for the recovery of sick people, purification rites for building projects such as new houses and excavation of wells, and mainly communication with deities and with the souls of the dead. Bereaved families ask a shaman for her appearance, because the first communication with the deceased is considered an important rite of the funeral ceremony. It is called the "opening of the mouth of the dead." (Wendt 1970, 189)

(3) Then there are institutionalized forms of shamanism.

> In the ceremonies of the priests and priestesses at *Mt Ikoma* in Kansai and *Mt Osore* in Touhoku, ... one comes across the spirituality of Shintoism. Through a special disposition and hard training the priests and priestesses are able to make themselves accessible to the spirit of a god. (Oguro 1982, 96)

Oguro reports about a priestess who was possessed by a "divine spirit" which enabled her to see into the past and the future. She is very popular as a fortune teller. Ogura says that this is an "unequivocal sign of a shamanic religion" (Oguro 1982, 96).

Shamans can be found in Shintoist and Buddhist contexts. This particular feature is the result of the separation of shamanic theory and shamanic praxis, which is typical for Japan as Oyama (尾山令仁) pointed out. While in other countries such as Korea the shamanic theory controlled the shamanic praxis,

---

68. There are also texts that talk about an "animistic potion" through which a woman becomes a shaman (Usui 2009, 60).

shamanism in Japan welcomed practices from different religious sources and contexts (Oyama 1995, 167–168).

(4) The Japanese *shinshinshuukyou* (新新宗教), the "New New Religions"[69] have much to do with magic, healings and miracles. Their basic philosophies show shamanic features (Lewis 1993, 144) which can even be considered "central" (Hardacre 1996, 198). Most shamans practice in the context of the New New Religions (Oyama 1995, 171; 1990, 9). They are mostly founded by women whose "career shows criterions of Northeast Asia's shamanism to an astonishing degree." In their youth, most of these women showed traits of "arctic hysteria" (*piblokto*), which is considered a sign of shamanic calling. The symptoms are sickness, neurosis, and hysteria. Eventually, a god or spirit called them into service through a dream or ecstasy (Immoos 1991, 30). Examples are Miki Nakayama (中山みき), foundress of the *Tenrikyou* (天理教), Nao Deguchi (出口なお), foundress of the *Oomoto*-religion (大元教), and Sayo Kitamura, foundress of the "dancing religion" *Tenshoukoutaijinguukyou* (天照皇大神宮教).[70]

(5) Iida (飯田剛史) (1988) reports about the Korean shamanism in a group of "Korean temples" in the suburbs of Osaka, where the most Korean expats live in Japan. Iida calls this shamanism "a religious phenomenon" which syncretisticly mixes "Korean shamanism, Korean Buddhism, and Japanese mountain religion." The Korean folk religion in Osaka was revived mainly by women (Link-Wieczorek 1991, 262).[71] Men usually consider the rituals as "superstition." The Korean shamanism in the Osaka area is mainly concerned with healings, prayers for people suffering from diseases and infertility, and prayers for ancestors. The prayers are addressed to evoked deities.

Apotropaic magic in Japan

In this paragraph I mainly deal with practices that secure the protection of deities: amulets,[72] talismans, and dedication rites.

---

69. About 20% of the Japanese belong to the "New New Religions" (Hummel 1992, 451). The term was created by journalists and is religion-scientifically regarded not without controversy (Hardacre 1996, 198–199).

70. Comprehensively Thomsen: *Tenrikyou* (天理教) (Thomsen 1963, 33ff); *Oomotekyou* (大元教) (127ff); "dancing religion" *Tenshoukoutaijinguukyou* (天照皇大神宮教) (Thomsen 1963, 199ff; Wendt 1970, 178ff). Also Gerlitz (1977).

71. "In Korea shamanism is mainly a religion of women in two respects: there are many more female shamans . . . than male shamans, and the clients are also mostly women" (Wippermann 2000, 50).

72. Of course amulets are not limited to apotropaic magic. An entire group of amulets does not ward off evil, but invites good. Their function is *taiun* (待運), "waiting [for] good." These amulets are called *engimono* (縁起物), literally "things that raise up luck." It is believed that an inherent deity attracts luck (Reader and Tanabe 1998, 46). Some *omamori* (お守り) are

Amulets and talismans

Amulets are things with magic power to ward off calamities. In Japanese these things are simply called *omamori* (お守り), "protectors" or "patrons," or *mayoke* (魔除け), "off-warders." According to Kamata, *omamori* (お守り) work through the spiritual power thought to be present in them. In the *Manyou*(万葉)-Age[73] soldiers in combat carried along pubic and scalp hair of their wives or lovers. They thought that the inherent *reiryoku* (霊力), the female "spiritual power" would save them (Kamata 2000, 16). This folk belief is still alive. Kamata reports that in the 1970s, people believed that pubic hair of virgins helped in exams (18). Kamata calls this phenomenon *jubutsusuuhai* (呪物崇拝), "fetishism," literally "veneration of things with magic power" (16).

Omamori (お守り) also work through the inherent deities.[74] Therefore, as a Japanese joke says, it is not advisable to have more than one because the deities might start quarreling, which would lead to misfortune (Lewis 1993, 34). There are two basic understandings on how *omamori* (お守り) work:

(1) *Omamori* (お守り) are understood as *bunshin* (分神),[75] "offshoots" or "branches" of a certain deity, literally "parts of gods," or as their manifestation (Reader and Tanabe 1998, 46). A special kind of these *omamori* (お守り) are the *migawari omamori* (身代わりお守り). *Migawari* (身代わり) means "changing or substituting one's body." It refers to "the notion that a particular buddha, bodhisattva, deity, or other figure of spiritual power can offer itself in place of the person it protects and thus absorb any negative forces that might otherwise afflict the person" (46). The respective deities are mostly patron deities of the *ujigami*(氏神)-system of "family deities," in which the deceased are venerated as patron deities (Hori 1987, 202).[76] Deities evoked to protect through magic are not deities outside our world, but explicitly deities in this world. "Magic is the control of this-worldly supernatural forces, such as *mana*, by the use of proper chants, amulets and automatically effective rituals." It "does

---

made of the wood of the *nanten*(ナンテン)-bush and therefore bring luck. For the *nanten*(ナンテン)-bush see 8.1.2.6 Apotropaic rites: *mayoke* (魔除け).

73. Late 7th, early 8th century. In this age the *Manyoushuu* (万葉集) was written, a collection (集) of things to be passed on to endless (万) worlds (葉).

74. The border between these two groups of *omamori* (お守り) is not clearly defined. In Japan, nature force is often personified and worshipped as *kami* (神). *Kami* (神) are addressed in petition, but don't own personhood.

75. Others talk about *bunrei* (分霊), a part (分) of a spirit (霊).

76. Lewis reports about a case where people attributed so much power to the ancestors that they kept their valuables in the Buddhist house altar where the ancestors are thought to be present (Lewis 1993, 180).

not involve supplicating supernatural beings in the hope that they will respond" (Hiebert et al. 1999, 69). Quack said that in magic the contact to supernatural beings was "secondary" (1992, 382). As a result, the faith in the efficacy of the respective deities is rather shallow. For many people *omamori* (お守り) are nothing more than fashion accessories (Kamata 2000, 15). Even though 65 percent (Lewis 1993, 33) of his informants had a *omamori* (お守り), Lewis said that hardly any of them believed that the *omamori* (お守り) was the direct source of protection. *Omamori* (お守り) are not used because of a supposed inherent power, but because they give *kiyasume* (気休め) (Lewis 1993, 152), "peace," literally "rest of *ki* (気)," and *anshin* (安心), "relief," or *anshinkan* (安心感), the "feeling of relief" (Lewis 1993, 34, 101).

> Belief as a willingness to accept that rituals can indeed bring about the desired effects . . . is a . . . complicated matter, and the personal testimonies fall on both sides . . . Honda Souichirou narrates how a group of space engineers visited Tsukuba Shrine to pray for the successful launching of a Japanese telecommunications satellite: he notes that scientists are the most rational people in terms of their profession and must have the highest faith in their own abilities. Indeed, the leader of the group expressed no sense that the mission might not succeed. Yet, as Honda notes, they also recognized the limits of their (or science's) capacity to explain everything. The scientists certainly did not believe that the magical powers of a god were needed to launch the spacecraft they had so carefully constructed. But like anyone else who was prepared for an event, whether a school examination or a hospital operation, they were faced with the gap between knowledge and certainty, the space between desire and fulfillment, a territory where nothing is certain and the gods may be invoked to answer the emotional needs of the moment. (Reader and Tanabe 1998, 127)

Omamori (お守り) are usually long items,[77] such as *obi* (帯), "silk sashes," called *hadamamori* (肌守り), literally "skin-protector," when carried on the skin (Pye et al. 2007, 12.238), or, most commonly small, lengthy, cloth bags, with embroidery stating the name of the shrine and the kind of protection. The

---

77. Of course there are amulets with different forms as well. The *chi-no wa* (茅の輪), "rings made of *Miscanthus sinensis*" used as *gofu* (護符), "talisman" against *ekibyou* (疫病), "epidemic diseases," that were worn around the neck (Ichijou 2008, 107).

length guarantees "long" life (Lewis 1993, 152).[78] Among the *omamori* (お守り), *koutsuuanzenomamori* (交通安全お守り), "traffic safety amulets" as car-stickers or fastened to satchels, or the very powerful *happouyokeshugo* (八方除け守護),[79] are very popular. *Happouyokeshugo* (八方除け守護) "ward off" (除け) calamities coming from all "eight compass directions" (八方). There are *omamori* (お守り) for cars, factories, offices (Lewis 1993, 42), for the kitchen as a place with open fire, for the nursing period and for parenting (Lewis 1993, 100–101). A special group of *omamori* (お守り) are for protection at unlucky ages (Lewis 1993, 150, 152) and during pregnancy, the corset-like *hara-obi* (腹帯), literally "belly sash." *Haraobi* (腹帯) are put on for the first time in the fifth month of pregnancy[80] on the Day of the Dog, because they allegedly whelp easily (Lewis 1993, 99–100). There are, of course, scientific explanations for the effectiveness of *haraobi* (腹帯) and therefore some Christians put it on as well.

Dedication rituals

Another way to secure the protection of deities is to dedicate oneself to them. Respective rituals are used especially in times of transition. Rites of passage are found in all religions (Wach 1962, 255), because in times of transition the *reikon* (霊魂) or the *hakurei* (魄霊), the human "spirit," is particularly weak and vulnerable (Katsumoto 1992, 104). The respective Japanese rituals are:

- The *hatsu-miyamairi* (初宮参り), the first visit to the Buddhist temple after birth: After prayers and a purification rite, a Chinese character is written on the forehead of the children: *dai* (大), "big" for boys and *shou* (小), "small" for girls. These "signs" are signs of dedication and they secure that the deities see and protect the children (Lewis 1993, 103; Shimada 1993, 22).
- The *shichi-go-san* (七五三), literally the "seven-five-three," an initiation rite (Gerlitz 1977, 20). The ages seven, five and three are very meaningful: at the age of three, children usually start their kindergarten life, and the first grade at school at the age of six is protected by two rites at ages five and seven.

---

78. Coulmas interprets in a different way: "Long items or items with scale-patterns" are suitable, because "the deity *Ebisu* (恵比寿) sometimes takes the form of a serpent" (2000, 317). Ebisu (恵比寿) is the "god of affluence."

79. The *yokeru* (除ける) corresponds with the Greek ἀποτροπιάζομαι, which is used in "apotropaic" (Käser 2004, 80).

80. This is scheduled for the fifth month, because from then on the pregnancy is acknowledged. Then the spirit of the child has settled in the womb (Shimada 1993, 22).

- The *seijin-no-hi* (成人の日), the "Coming of Age Day" at the age of twenty: That is the age when women (used to) marry and men moved into a company dormitory (Lewis 1993, 112).[81]

Morita therapy: *Morita ryouhou* (森田療法)

In this context it makes sense to introduce the *Morita ryouhou* (森田療法), the "Morita therapy," named after its founder Shouma Morita (森田正馬). The *Morita ryouhou* (森田療法) is a therapy that understands healing as reintegration into nature. Its goal is the "reduction of an 'enlarged ego' and re-incorporation of the ego into a subject-decentralized relationship with the world"[82] (Lang 2003, 9). "Obedience to nature" is an important element (Iwai and Abe in Gielen et al. 2004, 285; Morita 1998, 18–19).[83]

The Japanese psychiatrist Shouma Morita (1874–1938) developed his therapy at the beginning of the twentieth century. "As one of the leading Japanese therapy methods it is deeply rooted in Japanese culture" (Hansch 2003, 169). Morita was convinced that Western therapy models of psycho-therapy and psycho-analysis could not be used in Japan, because Japan had different cultural traditions governing social life (he mainly referred to that of Zen Buddhism) (Schott and Tölle 2006, 470). Morita based his critique on the assumption that the symptoms a patient concentrates on are enforced just because the patient concentrates on them. He called this *seishin kougo sayou* (精神交互作用), the "psychological interaction effect" (Kawamura 2000, 51). This results in *shinkeishitsu* (神経質), "nervosity," the central term of Morita's neurosis-theory. Morita replaced the increasingly amplifying occupation with one's own emotions with the acceptance of negative emotions. He stressed the possibility to act controlled and responsibly in spite of negative emotions. As emotions cannot be influenced directly, too much self-attentiveness and reflection on one's condition are hardly fruitful, if not harmful. Positive actions, on the other side, yield positive emotions (Hansch 2003, 169). "It is essential

---

81. Katsumoto has a different explanation: As infant mortality used to be very high, the *shichi-go-san* (七五三) was celebrated as a triple festival of thanksgiving, when the children survived war. From the *Taishou*-Era on infant mortality declined significantly and the element of thankfulness fell into oblivion (Katsumoto 1992, 101).

82. *Subjektdezentriertes Weltverhältnis*.

83. The Morita-therapy is often discussed in connection with the *Naikan*-method (*naikanhou*, 内観法) (Hesselgrave 1983). Both are from Japan, but starting point and objective are completely different. The Morita-therapy sees man as a cosmological being, as part of nature. *Heil* (salvation) and *Heilung* (healing) are respectively understood as reintegration into nature. The *Naikan*-method sees humans as sociological beings. Its objective is the healing acceptance of dependence on others.

that the therapist comprehend the importance of dismantling the clients' contradictions by ideas when treating those with *shinkeishitsu* (神経質)" (Morita 1998, 18). How can he do this?

> The solution lies in assisting a client to discard artificial tactics and manipulations and to observe and obey nature. Trying to control the self by manipulation and willpower is like trying to choose numbers willfully on a thrown dice or to push the water of the Kamo River in Kyouto upstream. (Morita 1998, 18–19)

Morita suggests to submit to nature, to "obey" it. Schott and Tölle talk about "dispassionate acceptance of the world 'as is,' what also includes acceptance of the disease" (2006, 470). The goals of the Morita therapy are the following:

- recognition of facts
- obedience to nature
- focus on the present
- increase of spontaneous activities
- decrease of self-focused preoccupation
- elimination of indulgence in moods and emotions (*kibun hon-i*, 気分本位)
- withholding of value judgments
- reduction of intellectualizing
- cessation of escape into a sick role
- cultivation of a *sunao* (素直), a "humble" mind (Iwai and Abe in Gielen et al. 2004, 285).

The Morita therapy has four stages:

- one week of absolute isolation and bedrest[84]
- one week light labor
- one to two weeks hard labor
- two to three weeks practicing everyday life.

During this time the patient is to document his thoughts and discuss them with his therapist. However, he must refrain from complaining as much as possible (Schott and Tölle 2006, 470).

---

84. Kakar therefore juxtaposes the Morita-therapy with Ayurvedic sleep therapy (1984, 298).

6.2 Discussion with Biblical Concepts

Summary: A secularism which more and more denies and even replaces the fear of the Holy cannot be called Christian. On the other side, an involvement with affairs of the spiritual world needs to be criticized if it turns into fascination of the evil.

When speaking against divination Christians need to discern that God's goal for man is not his safety, but his transformation through fellowship with him.

In animistic cultures shamans have an important leadership role. This however is so powerful that it cannot be accepted in the Christian church without critically evaluating it.

6.2.1 At the Mercy of God

I showed that feeling at the mercy of powerful beings is a basic element of animism. I think that in this respect secularized people need to learn from animists. If there is one thing that is alien to secularized people it is awe for the holy. The "heathen" notion of the holy is much closer to the Bible. In the Bible, "holy" means "ghastly" to begin with. Is God "ghastly"? As C. S. Lewis showed, there are common concepts between paganism and Christianity which have been suppressed since the Enlightenment. He lets the children (raised in the Christian faith) ask fearfully:

"Is Aslan[85] quite safe?"

The Beaver answers: "Who said anything about safe? 'Course he isn't safe. But he's good. He's the King, I tell you" (Lewis 1986b, 75).

And when the proud stallion Bree meets Aslan for the first time, his whole body trembling, Aslan commands that he *should* touch him. "Do not dare not to dare!" he commands (Lewis 1986c, 157).

This kind of "horror" is not at all alien to the Bible. When Jacob woke from his dream, horror seizes him. Genesis 28:17 and Psalm119:120 clearly

---

85. In C. S. Lewis's fantasy world Narnia, the lion Aslan, the Son of the Great Emperor beyond the Sea, is a metaphor for Jesus Christ.

speak of the same horror: "My flesh trembles in fear of you; I stand in awe of your judgments."[86]

Where does this horror come from? The key word is "alien." God is the *totaliter aliter* and meeting with him is an "Encounter of the Third Kind." He is "alien" to mankind, utterly unfamiliar, different from all he knows. Humans can speak – and thus understand – about God only by means of metaphors. Metaphors are good if they nurture unequivocal and unwavering confidence. But they are not good if they invite undiscerning and blunt confidentiality. However, the secularized man is so blunt and indifferent, so "earthly-minded" that he cannot feel anything any more. Horror and science fiction films revive this basic fear of the "alien"; unspecified "aliens," invisible, yet seeing everything, nowhere, yet all the sudden appearing out of nowhere, formless, yet taking on any form, then horror strikes. "*It* is here!" All this is true for God. Bruce wrote about Hebrews 4:13: "Bare of all covering disguise and bare of all protection we are . . . utterly at his mercy" (Bruce 1990, 114). Ellens speaks about an "eerie feeling" people have toward "unconditional grace," because it leaves them bereft of any "leverage and control," totally "at the mercy of God's grace" (Ellens 2007, 37).

The secular man denies the existence of God, yet the fear of the numinous is cravingly evoked and even addictively consumed in a growing flood of horror and Sci-fi films. I think that one of the reasons is that the secularized man is still religious. He, too, needs the feeling of absolute powerlessness; the awe toward the "other" he can never control; who can see into the deepest places of his heart, yet is not visible to him; before whom he is naked and bare of any protection and defense; and whom he therefore – particularly therefore – can trust. "In the fear of the Lord (is) a strong fortress" (Prov 14:26).

Human beings' first, unconditional, and unreflected reaction toward the presence of God is horror. However, it is not the only feeling. The feeling of inadequacy follows unconditionally and unreflectedly. They recognize that they are not as they are supposed to be. They know – must know – that they are sinful. Depending on their character, different people react differently. However, they have one thing in common: they experience this situation as life-threatening.[87] The horrified nation sent Moses to meet with God: "Speak to

---

86. I oppose those who want to "dispel being afraid of God" no matter how well they mean. Schwarzwäller claims the "fear of God" does not mean "being afraid of a numinous deity" (Schwarzwäller 2000, 54). But yes, this is the original meaning of "fear of God"!

87. These primal emotions are only followed by the derived emotion of shame and by the rational fear of God's punishment. However, the latter must not be confused with the former.

us yourself and we will listen. But do not have God speak to us or we will die" (Exod 20:19). Manoah said to his wife: "We are doomed to die! We have seen God!" (Judg 13:22). The widow said to Elijah: "What do you have against me, man of God? Did you come to remind me of my sin and kill my son?" (1 Kgs 17:18). As a man of words, Isaiah recognized his sinfulness as impurity of "his lips" (Isa 6:1–6). Daniel reported: "I am overcome with anguish because of the vision, my lord, and I am helpless" (Dan 10:16). Leadership personality Peter asked Jesus – probably also as spokesman for the other disciples: "Go away from me, Lord; I am a sinful man!" The reason: "He and all his companions were awed at the catch of fish they had taken" (Luke 5:8–9). When the disciples recognized the transfigured Christ as God they were so horrified that they fell to the ground (Matt 17:6–7)!

The multitude of motion pictures that simulate this primal fear show yet something else: Only in very few of them the "alien" is good. In most of them the "alien" is understood as a threat that needs to be combated. Man knows that the relationship with the One he seeks is broken. But as fire is not "evil" just because children burn themselves with it, the *totaliter aliter* is not evil. God is love! Yet he is free, uncontrollable, not manipulatable by any power of magic, all-powerful, supernatural, omnipresent, the same from before the dawn of time, he does what he wants – man is well advised to fear him for he is the only one to be feared. He is not safe. But he is good.

In his unparalleled explanation to the Ten Commandments, Luther maintained the tension between love an fear: "We should fear and love God!" And this fear is not the fear of God's wrath upon those who do not keep his commandments, but "the fear of the unfathomable, hidden God" (Reinhuber 2000, 231). The co-existence of "awed and worshipping fear" and "fearful fear with the impulse of fleeing from God," in Luther's case, even "naked fear" leads into temptation (Reinhuber 2000, 232). In a similar way, Mayr and Uhrig explain Jerermiah 7:1–11 drawing on Luther's "fearing and loving God": "God is not a malevolent one who wants to destroy, but a benevolent one who forgives. Therefore, we must love him, and at the same time be fearful of not losing his love. He who does not want to better his life cannot be protected by God" (Mayr and Uhrig 2002, 300).

6.2.2 Kingdom-Theology *and* Power Encounter

In his speeches presented in 2003 in Ulaanbaatar at the symposium *Distinctively Christian, Distinctly Mongolian*, Gaiylin van Rheenen reached the conclusion that in conversion theology the "focus is too narrowly focused on human decision making rather than more broadly centered on God's sovereignty over his world." He stressed that the biblical message "had cosmic dimensions far beyond the conversion of individuals." An important aspect of God's dominion is the tension between the "already" and the "not yet." "The concept that the kingdom is already in the world but has not yet been consummated is termed *inaugurated eschatology*." Even though "the kingdom of God has come, the kingdom of Satan continues to exist . . . The arrival of the kingdom of God did not eradicate of the kingdom of Satan."

> This concept of inaugurated eschatology compels the animist who is overwhelmed by evil forces to wait for God to act. He knows that evil forces coexist in this world with forces of God. He must not "consult the mediums and wizards" (Isa 8:19) but "wait for the Lord" (Isa 8:17) and turn to "the law and to the testimony" (Isa 8:20). He must not "consult the dead on behalf of the living" (Isa 8:19). A Christian of an animist heritage knows that the kingdom of God and the kingdom of Satan coexist in this present world and is able to differentiate the two. (Van Rheenen 2003b, "Inaugurated Eschatology")

Van Rheenen concludes that "the church, like Jesus, actively confronts Satan's powers in all their manifestations in order to bring people under the sovereignty of God. Christians have the assurance that they will overcome because they have a greater power than that which is in the world (1 John 4:4)." This fight encompasses the physical world (healings, protection) as the spiritual world (exorcisms): it is holistic. Van Rheenen demands that all of culture be brought under God's sovereign rule. "Customs, mores, and laws which have been contorted by the influence of Satan must . . . be Christianized" (2003b, "Kingdom Proclamation in Animistic and Secular Contexts"). Peterson phrased it in a similar way. He talked about a spiritual war that does not leave any neutral place (Peterson 1997, 122–123).

I distance myself from certain so-called "spiritual warfare."[88] Van Rheenen warned against "a few Christian leaders" who emphasized "power so much that they implicitly incorporate animistic elements into Christian thinking and practice." Their encounter with animism was "paradoxically more animistic than Christian" (2003a). Where are the borders? "There are two equal and

---

88. Wright (1996) gives a good introduction into its history back to the Welsh revival in 1904.

opposite errors into which our race can fall about devils. One is to disbelieve in their existence. The other is to believe, and to feel an excessive and unhealthy interest in them" (Lewis 1986a, 8). Both extremes have to be avoided: the naturalistic extreme which reduces any and all supernatural phenomena to materialistically explainable ones; and the supernatural extreme which finds one and only one cause for everything that happens – demons (Wright 1996, 157).

I have a clear and unequivocal Yes for "spiritual warfare." The Bible testifies the existence of the unseen world (Rohrbach 1985, 36; Ferdinando 1996, 104; Deppe and Deppe 2002, 188–189). But that is not everything. Even though Christians in the West do not deny the existence of the unseen world, they locate the arena of the spiritual war into the "yonder world" which is mainly due to the Cartesian-dualistic thinking (Hiebert 2000). Animists on the other hand know that "territorial spirits" exist. Loewen's report from Nigeria is one example (Loewen 1991, 166ff). Wagner holds that their existence is detectable in the Old Testament (1992, 89–94). For Cullman, the existence of spiritual powers is an "important aspect in the teaching of the whole New Testament," mainly where "Christ's perfect dominion is discussed" (Green 1991, 180).[89] The encounter with animism can serve as a help and an eye-opener for Western Christians.

But then I have a clear No against "spiritual warfare"! Wolfram Kopfermann used to be one of the leading German protagonists of "spiritual warfare," but then turned away and distanced himself from its ideas in a fair and clear way. I think that the following points from Kopfermann's *Macht ohne Auftrag* (1994) are helpful for the encounter with animism:

- Experience and maximizing effectivity must never become the departing point or leading principle for exegesis. Wagner names an "increase of effectiveness for evangelism" as a motivation for spiritual warfare (Kopfermann 1994, 14). What serves the end of evangelism seems to be right. Kopfermann judges that scriptural proof is thus subordinated (38–39) and the authority of Scripture undermined (124).
- The "theocentric focus of the Christian faith" must not be compromised (Kopfermann 1994, 133; Ferdinando 1996, 130): The occupation with spiritual powers must not lead to Christian expertise in spiritism and the occult. Wagner's much-detailed

---

89. Noll (1996) gives a good summary on the history of Christian angelology.

specifications of territorial spirits (Wagner 1991, 43ff) and his concept of *spiritual mapping* (Kopfermann 1994, 37–40) is rather a testimony of unchristian dualism. In the Bible demons are not paid as much attention (Ferdinando 1996, 122; similarly Wright 1996, 158). According to Cullmann, the "original Christian faith" affirms the existence of spiritual powers, but it "attributes no independent existence to them." Thus it "avoids any kind of dualism" (Cullmann 1991, 198).[90] He who thinks dualistically places demons on the same level as God and relativizes the omnipotence of God (Ferdinando 1996, 122). However, according to the Bible, the realm of the demons is under God's sovereignty (1996, 123–124).

- "The practice of spiritual warfare distorts the (biblical) concept of prayer" (Kopfermann 1994, 128). The "prayer" as practiced in the spiritual warfare is a new way of prayer which is not addressed only to God, but also to "those powers" (Wright 1996, 160). Where theocentricity is abandoned, "demanding spirits in the name of Jesus" becomes prayer.[91] The "spiritual encounter" of Johann Christoph Blumhardt seems to be much more biblical: "He confined himself to mere supplication and fasting. He never confronted nor commanded the dark powers" (Kopfermann 1994, 103).[92] It is not against the Bible to address evil powers directly (1994, 103). However, Blumhardt's theocentric focus serves as a very good example. Blumhardt forwent the direct assault on dark powers because he wanted to avoid any kind of magic trusting only the "pure weapons of prayer and the word of God" (Rudert 1985, 35–36).

- The danger of "spiritual conceit" must never be let out of sight. Kopfermann furnishes some horrifying examples of how "spiritual warfare" created a "deceitful feeling of power" (Kopfermann 1994, 129ff). The driving concern of animism is power. Power, however,

---

90. There are some protagonists of "spiritual warfare" that are aware and maintain that God must be at the center of all spiritual encounters. Anne Gimenez (1991, 79) is an outstanding example.

91. A missionary to India said: "The biggest [obstacles] I've recently seen has been working to overcome the impression left by some well-intentioned American short-term missionaries. When they came to my village, they gathered and marched around the temple in the village, asking God to tear it down in the name of Jesus. Later one of the priests at the temple told me: 'You Christians are no different than we Hindus. We practice Hindu magic, and Christians practice Christian magic. I know because I saw those American Christians walking around our temple seven times praying. That's no different from what we do'" (Moreau 2012, 123).

92. Blumhardt commanded evil spirits, but he did not attack them (Rudert 1985, 32).

has the potential to make proud! The greatest danger of pride – also of "spiritual pride" – is the fact that "God opposes the proud" (1 Pet 5:5; Jas 4:5). Particularly Christians with an "animistic heritage must not view God's power as something to be manipulated and coerced." At the heart of Christian existence must not be power but a "loving, covenant relationship with Creator God" (Van Rheenen 2003a).

6.2.3 Divination and the Bible

Safety is a basic human need and so is the desire to know the future (Reichart 1964, 10). "In order to be able to do the little he can, man tries to know ahead of critical situations (and sometimes ahead of trifles) what is to come" (Naumann et al. 1988, 242). This basic need may in rare occasions be mingled with curiosity,[93] however, it is grounded in the deep desire for safety (Deppe and Deppe 2002, 192). The primal *Angst*[94] and the desire for safety prevalent in animistic cultures are value free. The moral evaluation aims not at the basic need but at how people react to it.

The moral evaluation of the Christian faith must aim at the question of pride and humility. In this case it must ask: Does a man humbly and willingly take the place assigned to him? Knowing the future is not in the "range of his power." Because "of his wise providence and love for his creatures God does not want them to know future and supernatural things, but he wants them to trust" (Reichart 1964, 10–11). Very much in line with this humility, the Hebrew time concept understands the future as that period of time which is *behind* man, invisible for him. Respectively the past is that which is displayed *before* him (Boman 1983, 128–129). However, humility must never be mistaken with irresponsibility, carelessness, or resignation. On the contrary, faith is obliged to act responsibly, even though the future is unknown (Bonhoeffer 1961, 22). Faith acts in obedience. God gave us "the present and his chief concern is that we are obedient 'now'" (Carlson 1981, 85).

Humility also stays clear of forcefully looking into the future when God choses to conceal it. This gives reason for the Christian to say no to oracles. He

---

[93]. The book titled *Bestrafte Neugier: Okkultismus* (Haack 1989), (*Curiosity Punished: Occultism*) may address a decisive motivation within the European context, but it misjudges the importance divination has for animists.

[94]. This kind of fear is only one among others. Riemann distinguishes four complementary basic fears and defines the one discussed above as "fear of change, experienced as transience and insecurity" (1995, 15). Transience is a constituting element of the Japanese culture.

who desires to glance into the future by means of oracles, blames God for "not adequately revealing his will so we cannot discern his leading" (Schlatter 1961a, 86), and for not being able to communicate his plan with us (Packer 1973, 259).

The Old Testament references ("Urim" and "Thummim," Gideon and Jonathan) cannot be used for the justification of a Christian oracle practice. Friesen and Maxson showed that the respective Old Testament characters acted not out of individual desire or even curiosity, but showed responsibility in the collective context of "Holy War." For the "age of the Church" this approach was "not appropriate" as the election of Matthias as apostle shows (Friesen and Maxson 1980, 226–227). In a similar way Waltke says that the missing of oracle practices in the New Testament shows its disapproval (Waltke 1995, 54).

In Christian ethics, empowering knowledge about the future must be substituted with obedience dependent on God (Carlson 1981, 87). What Käser wrote about magic in general is true for oracle practices in particular: "Magic can be . . . understood as the opposite what could be called 'true religion,' that is human surrender to and submission under the powers thought to be above himself. The magician does not submit himself [to the powers] but rather subjugates[95] them" (Käser 2004, 79).[96]

This dependence on God is central to Christian ethics. "We resolutely reject all conduct that cannot be aligned with the remembrance of God" (Schlatter 1961a, 59). Dependence on God is expressed by the term "leading of God." It is not that man obtains knowledge about the future and then plans his life accordingly, but God leads him as he trusts and obeys.

The pedagogical aspect of God's leading and his concealing the future is also very important. While humans strive primarily for safety, God rather aims at what kind of people they are and become (Carlson 1981, 82). He is mainly concerned that they "participate in his holiness" (Schmidt 1998, 57). It may therefore well be that God conceals the future, leaves Christians in (even painful) uncertainty, in order to "transform" us. In that case the use of oracle practice would run counter to God's will and plan.

> Divination sounds pious, but it may actually be ungodly because it shortcuts the Spirit's work in developing our character. It assumes you can know God's mind without having his heart and his Spirit.

---

95. Man "bemächtigt sich ihrer."

96. "Magic . . . is the hidden malignancy in all pagan religions, on account of which genuine reverence for the holy is nullified; since it was the means for bringing the sovereign will of God under human control and of using it for egotistical purposes" (Eichrodt in Rooker 2010, 64). "Magic is engaging in ritualized activity to gain power or influence" (Sprinkle 2001, 56–57).

But discerning the mind of God cannot be done apart from character development. You cannot divine God's heart, but you have available to you a way to develop a heart like his. He can work in your life through the Holy Spirit and his Word to foster virtue, and then you will have the mind of Christ. (Waltke 1995, 62)

6.2.4 Shamanism and Church Leadership

As I showed above, shamanism is quite alive, even in modern Japan. There are various reasons, one of them being the fact that the Japanese society is structured vertically. Japanese groups are structured vertically and hierarchically and need strong, charismatic leadership personalities – such as shamans. What Gerlitz wrote about the "New Japanese Religions" is also true for Japanese churches:

> The New Japanese Religions are all organized according to the parent-child relationship. The leader of a religion or its minister[97] takes the place of a father or a mother, while the church members or those seeking advice take the "subordinate role" of the child. Thus all members are "automatically tied into a vertical network of quasi-familial relations." (Gerlitz 1977, 32)

The vertical structure of Japanese churches is evaluated in different ways. Kraemer rightly recognized that the role of the Japanese pastor as fashioned according to the role of Confucian teacher evoked distrust on the part of the laity (Drumond 1961). Nevertheless, Engel maintains that the contextualization of church leadership forms calls for a "prominent role of the pastor," as "tradition demands respect for those with a higher social status" (Engel 1988, 126).

In the context of the "universal priesthood" its shamanic interpretation is discussed controversially,[98] but the shamanic understanding of pastoral

---

97. *Seelsorger*.

98. Schuster rightfully rejected the shamanic interpretation of the "universal priesthood" as suggested by Shaw. According to Shaw, Christians can utilize their relationship with God and for their relatives can obtain through prayer what non-Christians obtain through interaction with the spirits (Schuster 2003, 251). In South-Korea, there is the danger that Christian prayer is marred by self-effective magic as prevalent in shamanism (Underwood 1994, 73). Schuster rejects this notion because Christian prayer and shamanic practices cannot at all be compared (Schuster 2003, 251–252). In detail see Hunt and McMahon and their rejection of Morton Kelsey's "good witchcraft" (Hunt and McMahon 1986, 123–136). Ritchie's *Spirit of the Rainforest: A Yanomamö Shaman's Story* (1996) also shows impressively that Shaw also misjudges the social function of shamans. Shamans are a small, exclusive leadership guild. Their special skills and spiritual knowledge are kept secret.

authority has not yet been evaluated adequately. The Yawata-scandal[99] may serve as an introductory example:

> On April 6th, 2005 Pastor Paul Nagata (Tamotsu Kin), a Japan-born South Korean national, was arrested for sexually abusing four girls on eleven occasions between March 2001 and August 2004 in his office at the church in Yawata. The pastor claimed to have divine authority as God's representative. On this basis, he demanded total and unlimited obedience from his church members. For him, disobedience against the pastor was the same as rebellion against God. In the case of the four raped girls, he wanted to test their religious devotion and he warned them they would languish in hell if they acted against his will. [Pastor] Kin struck those who disobeyed him with his fists and belt. The victims were unable to defend themselves. The church had about 3,000 members before, but after the scandal became known, many members left the church. (Wood 2006, 18; *The Japan Times* 2005)

According to Wood the fundamental reason of this scandal is the distorted authoritarianism prevalent in many Japanese churches (Wood 2006, 19). Tateishi talks about manipulation by religious authority figures (Tateishi 2009, 23). The position of a pastor as often perceived by pastors and church members is that of a powerful shaman.[100] Some illustrations:

- The prayer of a pastor is more "powerful" than that of laymen.
- Only pastors can say the benediction at the end of a worship service.
- Only pastors can administer the sacraments.
- Pastors can prohibit church attendance in a different church.
- Pastors can arrange marriages.[101]
- In many churches, pastors hold the highest authority. The handbook of a Japanese denomination[102] explains the baptismal promises: "One promises that as a member of the church one gets used to the church life living to the glory of God *under the leadership of the pastor*" (italics mine) (Educational Department of DOMEI 2000, 31).

---

99. Sadly enough, this scandal is not the only one of this kind (Tateishi 2009).
100. I would not condemn the office of a shaman. Ritchie (1996) showed that converted shamans can become competent and socially accepted spiritual leaders.
101. Schiller (2007) reported similar things from Africa.
102. This denomination is not the one the Yawata church belonged to.

Wood concluded that the fundamental reason for the tragedy was the church tradition that simply trains Christians to obey their pastors without any spiritual discernment. He called for radical changes of church structures and for a return to biblical leadership principles (Wood 2006, 19). But what are "biblical leadership principles"?

6.2.4.1 Biblical leadership principles

Directive leadership styles

According to Hesselgrave, Paul formed his newly founded churches according to the presbyter principle of the synagogue, according to which at least ten men chose a leader who then delegated ministries to helpers and trained laymen (Hesselgrave 1980, 253–254). The shepherd of the Middle East walking ahead of the flock and thus leading it served as example. Such leadership, however, was never meant to be reckless self-assertion but rather serving by providing initiative (Sanders 1967, 187–188). In Japan, authoritarian leadership styles are prevalent. Therefore, I would caution against the introduction of biblical directive leadership styles for at least one to two generations.

Partnering leadership styles

According to Schlatter, the group around Paul was superficially fashioned according to discipleship groups of Pharisees, but Paul's co-workers never were dependent on him. Paul respected their freedom as independent persons with their own, individual calling. He talked to them as a free person to free persons. He never commanded, but rather argued (Schlatter 1961b, 39). Schlatter interpreted Matthew 23:8–10 to mean that the disciples were not to call each other "leader," because that term expressed what Jesus was for them (Schlatter 1961c, 342). The Greek καθηγητής occurs only in Matthew 23:10. The Hebrew equivalent מורה means "provider," "head," or "leader" (Strack and Billerbeck 1982, 919). According to Gesenius, the etymology of the root ידה is first "hand," then "point with the finger and show the way." Leaders are servants, not masters. Greatness is applied to service (Schlatter 1961c, 342). The service of leaders is to make decisions in a spirit of stewardship and compassion, without any arbitrariness (Armerding 1992, 109). I think this leadership principle is biblically ideal, but for Japan not feasible, as it runs counter to Japanese culture. Nevertheless, pastors and missionaries should not fail to work toward it.

Indirective leadership styles

According to Allen, Christian leaders never tell other Christians what they have to do. Paul rejected any leadership for himself because he wanted to walk the road of Christ and his Apostles (Newbigin in Allen 1962, i–ii; Newbigin's preface). Schlatter explained that Matthew 23:8 means that the church rejects "all religious authority," that it has no rabbi, but Jesus as its one and only teacher. According to Matthew 18:20, Christ is present in each individual Christian and therefore leads him or her individually. This guarantees both the unity and the freedom of the church (Schlatter 1982, 670). This is particularly exemplified in the way Paul treated Timothy – Paul acknowledged the faith of Timothy and therefore never relieved him from making his own decisions by giving him commands (Schlatter 1983, 216–217). I think this leadership style is desirable but judging from many years of pastoral work in Japan is presently not feasible for Japan.

6.2.5 Apotropaic Magic and Allegiance to God

The question of how Christians should deal with amulets is the frequent object of pastoral counseling. I am going to outline my personal approach and leave it for further discussion:

- I make it very clear that I consider the use of amulets as "superstition." In Japanese, superstition is called *meishin* (迷信), literally "confused faith" or "faith astray." The desire for protection is not "confusion" but a basic need to be acknowledged.
- I do not deny the existence of gods nor their power to protect.
- I explain protection with the Old Testament metaphor of "being under the canopy" of a deity. Then I explain that "being under the canopy" means as much as "being under dominion." He who gives himself to a deity can be sure of its protection.
- Finally, I explain that becoming a Christian means a change of dominion. Under God's dominion amulets are not only unnecessary, but also inappropriate.

7

The Sociological Aspect of Salvation

Summary: Under the sociological aspect, the *Unheil* of humans is mainly sensed as shame and dishonor, and experienced as loss of face and anthropophobia. This is due to the formation of the Japanese conscience, which is not only shame-oriented, as Benedict suggested. The Japanese conscience is basically guilt-oriented. Its shame orientation is superimposed. Therefore, it is rather doubtful whether it is helpful to distinguish between shame and guilt.

In Japan, *Heil* is experienced as rehabilitation through unconditioned, motherly forgiveness. Here the Japanese concept of salvation is in great need of extension by the concept of social justice.

7.1 The Sociological Aspect of Salvation in the Context of Japanese Animism

7.1.1 The Experience of Unheil under the Sociological Aspect

Wiher wrote about "animistic societies" in general: "In a society, where the community defines standards, sin is defined sociologically . . . Harmony and honor are core values of . . . an animistic society. It is therefore a sin to violate harmony and honor" (Wiher 2003, 296). Japan has been classified as "true shame-culture" with a tint of guilt (Cairns 1993, 28).

7.1.1.1 Japanese moral terminology

According to Kitano (北野菜穂), the post-*Edo* Japanese term for "ethics" is *rinri* (倫理). The *rin* (倫) in *rinri* (倫理) stands for a mass of people living together orderly and not in chaos. The *ri* (理) stands for a rational method, a rational way of acting. Therefore, *rinri* (倫理) literally stands for a "way by which order can be achieved and harmonious relationships can be maintained." Watsuji therefore holds that studying *rinri* (倫理) basically means the study of *ningen* (人間). *Ningen* (人間) means "man," "human," or "humanity." It is composed of *nin* or *hito* (人), "person," and *gen* or *ma* (間) "interspace," literally being the exact equivalent of the English "interpersonal."

> An example of *rinri* (倫理) can be observed in the concept of social responsibility. In Japan, responsibility in the sense of moral accountability for one's action already existed in the classical period, but the individual was inseparable from status (or social role) in the community. Each individual had a responsibility toward the community, and the universe that comprehends communities. Thus in Japan, social virtue lay in carrying out this responsibility relates to one's social role. (Kitano 2007, 3)

Kitano calls it a peculiarity of Japanese ethics that "social harmonization" is considered superior to "individual subjectivity." As a "practical example" he refers to the abduction and beheading of Shousei Koda (香田証生) in Iraq.[1] Koda and his family were condemned by the Japanese society. When Koda was forced to ask the Japanese government to withdraw their troops as a condition for his release from his abductors, he also apologized to the Japanese government and the Japanese society for the difficulties he had created. When Koda was found dead, "his parents first apologized publicly for disturbing the social peace. Rather than showing anger at the murder, or at the Japanese government for failing in setting their son free, his parents showed concerned about the social responsibility caused by their son breaking the social harmony" (Kitano 2007, 3).

---

1. 24-year-old Koda traveled in Iraq as an "adventurer," even though the Japanese government had commanded the evacuation of all Japanese from Iraq. On 10 October 2005, he was abducted by the al-Zarqawi-group because they thought he was connected to the Japanese troops. The group threatened to behead Koda if the Japanese government did not withdraw their troops. The prime minister rejected negotiations with the terrorists, but advocated diplomatic solutions (Tyner 2006, 127). Koda was beheaded in front of a running camera and his corpse was later discovered in Baghdad, wrapped in an America flag (Jones 2005, 6).

7.1.1.2 *Unheil* as shame

The central Japanese term for shame is "losing face." In Japanese psychology, the face is very important:

- *kao-o dasu* (顔を出す), literally "to bring your face outside," that is "how your face" "meets one's social commitments";
- people that are *kao-ga hiroi* (顔が広い), literally "having a broad face" have many useful connections;
- *kao-o kashite kudasai* (顔を貸してください), literally "please, lend me your face," is the Japanese equivalent of the American "May I use your name?";
- symbolically "face" means as much as a person's reputation.

"Losing face" is expressed by a different term:

- *menboku-o ushinau* (面目を失う), "losing face";
- *menboku maru tsubure* (面目まるつぶれ), literally, the "totally smashed *menboku* (面目)";
- after losing one's face, one *menboku-mo nai* (面目もない), "has no face at all";
- also one *awaseru kao-ga nai* (合わせる顔がない), "has no face anymore one could show," literally "make meet with other" (Matsumoto 1996, 20–21);
- he who wipes his *tsura* (面 or 頬), his "face," *haji-o koraeru* (恥をこらえる), "suppresses his shame," or *haji-o shinobu* (恥をしのぶ), "bears his shame."

Taijin kyoufu (対人恐怖) or *taijin kyoufushou* (対人恐怖症) (TKS), named thus since 1920 following Morita, is a Japanese culture-specific syndrome, which used to be very common (Okada 2005, 239). The closest translation of TKS is "eye contact-confrontation-phobia." Kasahara (笠原嘉) associates TKS with *sekimenkyoufushou* (赤面恐怖症),[2] "erythrophobia"; others associate it with anthropophobia. Today, the term *shakaikyoufu* (社会恐怖), "social phobia" or social anxiety disorder (SAD)" is used instead (Okada 2005, 239). People suffering from *taijin kyoufu* (対人恐怖) feel uncomfortable when they are looked at by *significant others*[3] besides their closest family and friends. The exaggerated impression of being looked at, triggers their staring at people, which in turn creates embarrassment in others (Kasahara 1986, 380–381).

---

2. If a person blushes with shame, he *tereru*(es) (照れる), he "radiates."
3. For the term *significant others* see Spiro and Spiro (1975, 408).

Kasahara blames this hypersensitivity on Japanese parenting (Kasahara 1986, 385). "The main reason is to be sought in those admonishments that make [children] focus on the eyes of other people (e.g. 'If you do that all will laugh at you!' or 'The others look at you funny!')" (Hoshino 2006, 191). Others also think it may be an inherited trait (Iwanami 2006, 48).

7.1.1.3 Formation of the Japanese conscience

Speaking against the shame-guilt-dualism

If, following Piers and Singer, conscience mechanisms are classified into shame-oriented and guilt-oriented,[4] shame orientation is prevalent in Japan.[5] Since Ruth Benedict's writing,[6] Japan has been classified as a "shame-oriented culture." The distinct need for harmony typical for societies with dominantly animistic worldviews[7] speaks in favor of this classification, which otherwise is only "fairly correct" at best, and may even be "confusing and not fruitful" (Yasuda 2004, 31), but in any case, it is too superficial. Takeo Doi lamented the fact that mainly "foreign scientists" stubbornly follow Benedict despite the criticism of "many Japanese scholars" (Doi 1982, 58ff).[8] Doi himself was totally opposed to Benedict's approach, mainly because her internalization of values in the guilt-oriented conscience as opposed to the external control in the

---

4. Today, this dualism is controversially discussed (Young 2005, 182). Even in 1965, P. M. Yap blamed the distinction between shame and guilt for being intellectualistic, arbitrary and without any empiric justification (Yap in Hesselgrave 1983, 464). "Anxiety, shame, and guilt are the natural, normal, and universal sequence of controls in human personality in every culture. There are no 'shame cultures' or 'guilt cultures' per se, but a culture may stress one of the three control patterns more than the others. All three processes occur in each person, group, and culture but to varying degrees and with different configurations" (Augsburger 1995, 113).

5. As Noble showed in *Naked and Not Ashamed*, Japanlogists' opinions on this matter vary greatly. While Ruth Benedict advocates the opinion that Japanese do not have enough sense of guilt, George de Vos talks about considerable feelings of guilt accompanied by shame (Noble 1975, 47).

6. For her biography, see Hesselgrave (1983). The explicit purpose of writing *The Chrysanthemum and the Sword* (1946) was "to understand the strangest enemy America ever fought against." Benedict had never been to Japan nor did she speak Japanese (Ikegami 1995, 373). Similarly Haring (1946, 13–16).

7. See Wierzbicka's quote from the *Kokutai-no Hongi* (国体の本義) under 3.1 Word-field study of *wa* (和).

8. Ruth Benedict developed the distinction between guilt-cultures and shame-cultures in *Patterns of Culture* (1934) and *The Chrysanthemum and the Sword: Pattern of Japanese Culture*: 菊と刀 (*kiku to katana*) (1946) (Augsburger 1995, 119).

shame-oriented conscience seems to carries unmistakable superior overtones (Doi 1993, 30).[9]

What seems to be shame-oriented parenting is in fact only superficially shame-oriented and works only with internalized guilt feelings.[10] "In contrast to Benedict, others studying Japan, such as De Vos (1973) and Lebra (1983), have pointed to the strong presence of guilt in Japanese culture. Lebra also describes the strong presence of shame, arguing that guilt and shame are not mutually exclusive, contrasting constructs but, in the case of Japan, mutually coexisting" (Schoenhals 1993, 191).[11] In the discussion after the presentation of the lecture *Soziale Kontrolle und Selbstkontrolle*, Sakuta (作田啓一) maintained that "the inner voice of the individual must be considered," and that internal control was crucial for the order between members of society (Sakuta 1986, 42), a fact that was not totally unknown to Benedict. "Although there was an emphasis in Japanese culture on the social sanction of shame, Benedict observed that in Japan, shame was not merely an external sanction but was often a very deep emotion" (Young 2005, 183).

Even though Japan is not exclusively shame-oriented, shame is a strong element in Japanese ethics. Benedict is right when she calls shame the root of virtue (Benedict 1986, 224). The phrase *haji-o shiranai otoko da* (恥を知らない男だ) can be translated either as "he doesn't know shame (恥)," or (!) "he doesn't know honor (恥)." A man like that is "worthless," as the following proverb says: *haji-o haji-to omowanu mono-wa yaku-ni tatanu* (恥を恥と思わぬ者は役に立たぬ), "He who doesn't consider shameful what is shameful is good for nothing."[12]

---

9. Schneider gives a good overview of the negative development in the evaluation of shame in Western philosophy (Augsburger 1995, 114). Even though anxiety, shame, and guilt are developed sequentially, "there is no basis for an evolutionary hierarchy suggesting superior or inferior cultural development for one predominant control vis-à-vis another... The negative valuation given to shame by Western theorists, therapists, and theologians betrays a bias (whether evolutionary, hierarchical, or philosophical) which both blinds one for the wisdom of other cultures and blocks one's own potential of growth" (Augsburger 1995, 113).

10. The Japanese conscience not only knows the internalized feelings of guilt, but also the underlying values, even if only the internalized judgment, about what is beneficial. Behind the much-praised Japanese group-loyalty, there is a strong "individuation" just like in other countries. "One is loyal to one's group because it pays" (Befu in Morisaki and Gudykunst 1994, 67).

11. According to Kitayama et al. this is true for all cultures (Pattison 2000, 55).

12. This seems to be universally valid for shame-oriented cultures. In a certain way, shame and honor are synonyms. A person with a sense of shame is a person with dignity and integrity. The shameless have lost all sense of honor (Noble 1975, 2).

According to Benedict, absence of shame has the same meaning in Japanese ethics as "being right with God" has in Western ethics (1986, 224). Japanese feel their "bad conscience" mostly as "shamed conscience," because they attach great importance to the evaluation of their *significant others*:

> Yet another characteristic of animism is the emphasis on community . . . The animist understands himself not as individual, but he believes that his real life consists in community with others . . . If there is one thing that is considered sin in the religious life of an animist, it is broken relationships . . . within a group. (Steyne 1993, 64–65)

The significant others in Japan

The mother as a significant other

Durant called the family the "true source of social order" (1985, 215). Within the family, the mother is the most important *significant other*. According to the American anthropologist and social psychologist De Vos, the mother is the "conscience-forming substance" (Linhart 1984b, 97–98).

> A nursling who watches the facial expression of his mother knows his own condition through the slightest change in his mother's face. The mother in turn, reads the demands of the nursling through his body language and non-verbal expressions and reacts respectively. We Japanese, who have exceptionally developed this non-verbal mutual understanding characteristic for the mother-child relationship, first put ourselves in the place of the other in all our considerations, and are used to adjusting our acting and speaking to the emotions of the other. (Okonogi 1990, 58)

The study of Caudill[13] and Weinstein is also interesting: Japanese mothers lull their babies more, hold them more, and cradle them more than American mothers. It seems they communicate physically more than verbally (Bock 1979, 25).

> The general findings indicate that the mothers in the two cultures engage in different styles of caretaking: the American mother seems to encourage her baby to be active and vocally responsive,

---

13. American anthropologist who conducted a long-term study on American and Japanese parenting methods in the early 1960s. He observed 40 Japanese and 30 American three- to four-month-old nurslings and their mothers.

while the Japanese mother acts in ways which she believes will soothe and quiet her baby. (Caudill and Schooler 1988, 15)

This behavior is mutual.

One controls oneself through the expectations of others[14] ... As to his effect ... the "other" is polarized into two aspects. One type is hierarchically higher, the other is in an inferior position ... Children choose their parents as their "individuals of reference,"[15] and parents in turn choose their children as "individuals of reference." However, the latter comes with a restriction: only nurslings and ... toddlers are chosen. (Sakuta 1986, 20)

Thus one's own interrelated "I" is from the beginning "really recognized as 'you' for the 'you.' That means that the self-image is changed from 'I' to 'you of you'" (Hamaguchi 1990, 146). The result is that "one's behavior is determined, contingent on and to a large extent organized by what the actor perceives to be the thoughts, feelings, and actions of others in the relationship." In order to construct one's own self, the Japanese need others (Markus and Kitayama in Chaudhuri and Fadil 2001, 265).

"The mother tries to lead her child in way so that he believes he does everything out of free will" (Linhart 1984b, 97–98). This obviously leads to an extremely ambivalent mother-child relationship. Christopher points to the Japanese word *mamagon* (ママゴン) (Christopher 1983, 73). *Mamagon* (ママゴン) is an artificial word combining *mama* (ママ), "mummy," and the last part of *doragon* (ドラゴン), "dragon." This word depicts the mother as an omnipresent, omnipotent, and all-dominating being. The Japanese proverb "Being loved is being pressed" (Treichlinger 1954, 8) expresses this sentiment. "Japanese children, while gradually experiencing[16] what is considered 'bad' from the standpoint of the maternal principle,[17] must grapple with that 'bad' within their own selves in forming a composite personality (Kawai 1986, 301).

---

14. "Learning social roles one is expected to play, is part of the process of enculturation" (Bock 1979, 144).

15. *Referenzindividuen*.

16. These experiences are induced by the suffering of the mother and by withdrawal of affection. Spiro and Spiro observed this process in parenting in an Israelite kibbutzim. They talked about an early period with much care followed by a period of relative withdrawal of care (Spiro and Spiro 1975, 400–401).

17. The close relationship with the mother which does not allow for any experience of frustration on the part of the child creates a deep dependency on the mother. The insecurity felt at the absence of the mother is dreaded so much that withdrawal of affection can be used as effective means of parenting (Sugiyama-Lebra and Lebra 1986, 144). Withdrawal of affection

The ancestors as significant others

It is the duty of the ancestors to watch over the moral of the family (Steyne 1993, 86). There are two mechanisms used:

- Parents refer to the ancestors: A textbook from the early 1960s assumed that it was a common experience for children "to be dragged before the house altar and then be asked 'Do you think you can find any excuse from the ancestors for what you did?'" In Japan, misbehaving children are not sent to their room but made to sit in front of the house altar where they can do some soul-searching "in the presence of their ancestors" (Goss and Klass 2005, 50–51).
- Ancestors actively interfere: The will of the ancestors has highest authority (Berentsen 1985, 265), enforced by either benevolent protection or punishing admonishments (267). This is the way how the ancestral souls watch over "weal and woe of the family" (Naumann 1984b, 1631).[18] All actions of the individuals are correlated to the family honor of prior and coming generations (Yamamori 1974, 16–17).

    The prosperity, unity, harmony, and honor of the house is considered the summum bonum. The ultimate ethical criterion, therefore, is neither to be found in universal standards transcending the social group, nor in individual happiness and edification. Whether the interests of the family – including living and dead – are served or not is ultimately the standard applied to a proper distinction between moral and immoral conduct. (Berentsen 1985b, 265)

Significant others outside the family

He who disturbs harmony among people brings shame and disgrace (Ejima 1996, 94). Therefore, breaches of law are only of importance if they also jeopardize one's own group (Triandis 1995, 32). "Stop it! Otherwise people laugh about our family!" and "When you grow up you must bring honor to the family!" are frequently used phrases in parenting (Haring 1946, 19). Neither "religion" nor "philosophy" but "a very human morality" plays an important role for the Japanese. "And this morality always governs people with the contemporary trends as a yardstick" (Nakane 1970, 150). "An ethical

---

can be threat of repudiation, exclusion from the home, and refusal of help (Sugiyama-Lebra and Lebra 1986, 150–152).

18. This function of the ancestors is very common (Huber 1992, 585–596).

obligation defined by the gods . . . that would have triggered feelings of guilt . . . were not known" (Naumann et al. 1988, 243).[19]

7.1.1.4 Interaction of shame and guilt

According to Doi, one and the same person can experience feelings of guilt and shame at the same time. "It seems that both have a very close relationship." Doi even said that it was "foolish" to believe Japanese had no sense of guilt (Doi 1993, 30–31). In Japan, both types of conscience formation exist. Spiro and Spiro gives the framework to understand their relationship:

> It is our hypothesis that societies in which the child is trained by only a few agents of socialization, who themselves administer punishment, produce individuals who not only internalize the values of the socializing agent but who "interject" the agent as well[20] . . . We also hypothesize that societies in which the child is trained by a number of socializing agents, or in which the trainers discipline the child by claiming that other agents will punish him, do not produce individuals with "guilt-oriented" superegos. . . . Because this punishment . . . is experienced as shame . . . we may refer to this type of super-ego as "shame-oriented." (Spiro and Spiro 1975, 408–409)

In Japan, the primary type of conscience is the guilt-oriented conscience, because children are brought up almost exclusively by their mother at least until the age of three. This time is the most important for the formation of the conscience. In 1983, 94.5 percent of one-year olds, 67 percent of the three- to four-year olds, and 33.8 percent of four- to five-year olds were brought up in the family (Lenz 1990, 83). But then the mother uses the obligation the children feel toward her to force them into obligation toward society.[21] Only then shame orientation generates. Shame orientation is merely superimposed. The apparently shame-oriented education in nurseries, kindergartens and schools does not work without a previously internalized sense of guilt:

---

19. Naumann writes about the *Heian-* and *Nara-*Era, but according to my experience this is true for modern Japan as well. (On the *Heian-* and *Nara-*Era see Dettmer 1987, 18–49.)

20. Western parenting values the development of autonomy and the internalization in the stirring superego, so that the child becomes autonomous as soon as possible (Augsburger 1995, 89).

21. The high level of lenience towards children correlates with the low level in Hofstede's dimension "indulgence versus restraint" which means that "Japan is a relatively restrained culture and that children are rather strongly socialized to fit into Japanese society" (Bebenroth 2015, 208).

> The processes in resolving early identification as well as assuming later adult social roles are never possible without some internalized guilt ... When shame and guilt have undergone a process of internalization in a person during the course of his development, both become operative regardless of the relative absence of either external threats of punishment or overt concern with the opinions of others concerning his behavior. Behavior is automatically self-evaluated without the presence of others. (De Vos 1986, 83)

Augsburger describes this double orientation full of "inner tension" with two continua: (1) external control–internal control; (2) external responsibility–internal responsibility. He understands the Japanese society as a society with external control (dependency on the mother and later dependency on the company) and internal responsibility (Augsburger 1995, 97–98):

> Internal responsibility is grounded in the deeply buried sense of guilt, reinforced by the high value placed on honor. It is exemplified by an executive who accepts full responsibility for a scandal in the company and commits suicide out of loyalty to the institution and responsibility turned against the self in self-destruction. (Augsburger 1995, 98)

How do guilt feelings generate through Japanese parenting? In short, "The Japanese mother has perfected the technique of inducing guilt in her children by quiet suffering" (De Vos 1986, 84).

> Toward the wishes of the child she appears extremely yielding. When the child behaves badly, she adopts a tolerant, even suffering attitude, so that the child by and by develops feelings of guilt and adopts his behavior to the expectations of the mother. (Linhart 1984b, 97–98)

> In his first years the child ... savors all imaginable liberties. Toddlers are totally pampered, they are allowed to do whatever pleases them ... Usually, mothers don't scold their small ones when they don't comply with standards, neither at home nor in public. (Lutherjohann 1998, 140–141)[22]

---

22. According to Haring, this is particularly true for boys (Haring 1946, 16).

This suffering of the mother ends only when the child enters a company. Then the child is transferred from the familial structures of the home to the familial structures of the company.

> The *kyouiku-mama* (教育ママ), the education-obsessed mother, waits in front of the school gate together with other mothers, full of hope that her son or her daughter may pass the exam[23] . . . It doesn't seem strange to the Japanese . . . that mothers accompany their "children" until they enter a company. Only with their entrance into a company their educational duty ends. (Lutherjohann 1998, 144)

Obligation "receives a strong effective push from the Japanese mother's devotion to her children's successful social development, which includes the standards of success set for the community" (De Vos 1986, 84). Children feel *giri* (義理),[24] "obligation" toward their mothers which forces children to adapt to members of society as new *significant others*. "Guilt takes the sharpest form for Japanese when it is generated from the awareness that one might possibly betray the social group one belongs to" (Doi in Sugiyama-Lebra 1976, 13).[25]

The shame orientation in Japan is therefore only formal or secondary. A child complies with its group's expectations because his mother expects it (Lanham 1986, 293). This "most natural and everyday state of mind" (Okonogi 1990, 38–39) for the Japanese, this double orentientation of their conscience, is also called Ajase-complex.[26] Kosawa explains:

> When children make a mistake this first induces a sense of guilt because of fear of punishment. But humans also have another sense of guilt on a higher level. When culprits are forgiven, a sense of guilt generates that is accompanied by deep remorse. (Kosawa in Okonogi 1990, 38–39)

---

23. Children taking exams expect their mothers to come to them when they call them to bring them snacks or sharpen their pencils (Fallows 1990, 74). What Fallows reports seems to be the exception.

24. *Giri* (義理) can be defined (1) as "return of favors of friends," (2) as "response to trust," and (3) as effort to protect one's reputation. "Group members that do not react to trust and don't return favors of friends are humiliated by their exclusive group and even ostracized. Out of this situation *giri* (義理) generates, either as an effort to protect one's reputation or as 'sense of honor'" (Minamoto 1986, 64).

25. Of course, this is not the only mechanism used to make individuals behave co-conformingly. "Threat of ridicule" is used most effectively (Linhart 1984b, 98). According to my own observations this is the most powerful mechanism.

26. For details see under *2.3.3.3 Repentance and forgiveness – or forgiveness and repentance?*

The Japanese technical term for the "attitude of the child toward parents, mainly toward the mother" is *amae* (甘え).[27] "The Japanese principle of dominion consists in inducing a spontaneous sense of guilt in the other, and then, by appealing to this sense of guilt, without fail dominating him and making him do things" (Okonogi 1990, 64–65).

This is reflected in the word *sumimasen* (すみません): The word *sumanai* (済まない)[28] is commonly used to express feelings of guilt. It is the negative form of *sumu* (済む) which means "to bring to an end." Even though *sumanai* (済まない) is commonly used to express a sense of guilt, it is rather an expression of an awareness that one did not meet the expectation of others, thus causing trouble and pain (Doi 1986, 122).[29] This phrase "is an ace in Japanese society. By using it one can live trouble-free."[30] He who blames himself, sheds tears, and is caught in an awkward situation is forgiven "without further ado" (Okonogi 1990, 46).

7.1.2 The Experience of Heil under the Sociological Aspect

7.1.2.1 *Heil* as rehabilitation

Because of the predominant orientation of their conscience (shame orientation) and the predominant structure of society (collectivism), Japanese experience *Heil* under the sociological aspect mainly as rehabilitation. In the West, *Unheil* is mainly understood as punishment (hell) and experienced as fear of punishment. Consequently, *Heil* is understood as cancellation of punishment. In Japan, *Unheil* is experienced as shaming and ostracism, *Heil* consequently as rehabilitation. In a study of twenty imprisoned female criminals,[31] Marran found that "conversion" can be perceived as the opposite of rehabilitation (Marran 2007, 84).

> Betty Latham (1967), an American anthropologist, has shown that Japanese folktales stress repentance and reform whereas Western folktales stress punishment and often death. Western societies seem to give up more quickly on people than Eastern ones. In a

---

27. For details see under *2.5.1.2 Takeo Doi (土居健郎): Amae* (甘え) *(dependence) as psychological key-term*.
28. *Sumimasen* (すみません) and *sumanai* (済まない) are identical in meaning.
29. De Mente explains *sumimasen* (すみません) as: "The guilt I sense is endless" (De Mente 1994, 48).
30. *Reibungslos*, literally "without friction."
31. In Japanese these women are called *dokufu* (毒婦), "women of poison."

Japanese translation of "Little Red Riding Hood," for example, the wicked wolf falls on his knees and tearfully promises to [change his way of life]. In the Western versions, the wolf is simply killed. (Braithwaite 1999, 64)

Braithwaite ascribes this to the Japanese view of man. Because man is ultimately good, he can correct himself. Therefore, he is treated with *amayakashi* (甘やかし),[32] with "indulgence" and "leniency" as soon as he shows signs of shame (Braithwaite 1999, 65). In Japan, an apology indicates that one wants to turn away from the evil inside. The evil inside is often depicted as *mushi* (虫), as "worm." Offenders are the victims of this "worm," but when extracted or extruded from man, he can rehabilitate as someone who is without guilt (Braithwaite 1999, 64).

Rehabilitation without betterment? Here is a fundamental difference between East and West. Whereas in the West, offenders are rehabilitated after showing signs of betterment in a "probation-period," in Japan he is rehabilitated because people believe in his ability to change for good, yes, collectivistically thinking, because people cannot believe that he cannot change. This is clearly exemplified in the *Naikan*-method (*naikanhou*, 内観法), which stresses shame (Hesselgrave 1983, 470).

Naikan-method: *naikanhou* (内観法)

Naikanhou (内観法), literally the "method of introspection," has been derived from the Buddhist concept of *mishirabe* (身調べ), "self-observation," an "ascetic method of introspection." Ishin[33] Yoshimoto (吉本伊信) (1916–1988) used this method first privately and avocationally (Reynolds 1993, 173ff), then, from 1954 on, with convicts in reformatories, and later for the treatment of mentally ill people (Sugiyama-Lebra 1976, 202).

The "*Naikan*-treatment involves a specific period of intense, guided self-reflection in isolation from all external stimuli" (Sugiyama-Lebra 1976, 203). Except for the hourly interviews with the therapist, there is no contact with the outside world. The patient has to wake and reflect all day, from 5:30 a.m. to 9:00 p.m. The goal of this introspection is that the patient reaches a point where he can "discover" or "grasp" the *jibun* (自分), the true "self" (Sugiyama-Lebra 1976, 204). The therapist abstains from any evaluation and trusts the confrontation with the past (Yahata 2007, 218). The questions guide the patient

---

32. For details see the the word-field *amae* (甘え) under *2.5.1.2 Takeo Doi* (土居健郎): *Amae* (甘え) *(dependence) as psychological key-term*.

33. Sugiyama-Lebra erroneously writes Yoshimoto's first name "Inobu."

to recognize what *sewa* (世話), what "assistance" or "help" he has received from his primary reference, mainly from his mother,[34] what *meiwaku* (迷惑), "troubles" and *shinpai* (心配), "worries," he caused, and what *okaeshi,* (お返し) what "return favor" he returned.

Eventually these questions help the patient to recognize himself as totally dependent self (Sugiyama-Lebra 1976, 207). The patient becomes aware of his absolute helplessness and how much he needs the indulgence of others. He then confesses to the therapist that he benefited to an overly great extent from the *sewa* (世話) of others. The next step is that the patient recognizes that he has not fulfilled his *on* (恩), his "universal obligation" (De Mente 1994, 39) toward others. Thus human failure complies with the view of man as held by the *Joudo Shinshuu* (浄土真宗), a Buddhist sect. This view of man portrays humans as "weak and sinful beings" that "cannot live if others don't help (Yahata 2007, 218). According to Hesselgrave, the patient must at this point not rationalize or become aggressive against others. He must feel guilt and (!) shame, according to Yoshimoto, two inseparable reactions to irresponsible behavior (Hesselgrave 1983, 473). This last point – reflection on the injury inflicted on others – constitutes the most important part of *Naikan*. As in other parts, the client is supposed to recall concrete incidents and experiences that definitely and irreversibly establish guilt, however trivial they may sound." And then the patient is "encouraged to resolve or reform himself (e.g. to abstain from alcohol, gambling, stealing, lying)" (Sugiyama-Lebra 1976, 209–210).

7.2 Discussion with Christian approaches

7.2.1 The Experience of Unheil under the Sociological Aspect

I first want to speak against the misconception that the Bible is mainly concerned with guilt. This judgment is not so much based on biblical scholarship, but on a theology that is overly influenced by the individualism of the Enlightenment. Guilt and shame exist side by side, deepening on the reference with varying emphasis. The guilt-shame-dualism is not helpful for a meaningful discussion of biblical concepts. Güs suggests talking about a "dialectical unity" on which "shame is always embedded with (!) guilt" (Güs 2006, 272). Klopfenstein[35] also

---

34. Reference persons can also be the father, the spouse, siplings (Yahata 2007, 218), superiors, and children (Kokubu 1998, 203).

35. In his thorough study of shame in the Hebrew Bible, *Scham und Schande nach dem Alten Testament* (1972), he examined among others the Hebrew roots בוש and כלם (Stiebert 2002, 44).

speaks in favor of a close connection between shame and guilt in the Hebrew Bible. For him, subjective shame and objective shaming are "symptoms of guilt" (Stiebert 2002, 45–47). It seems more adequate to contrast subjective sentiments and objective facts.

7.2.1.1 Subjective sentiments of shame and guilt

The Old Testament speaks much about shame. Shame and related terms occur over one hundred fifty times in the Old Testament; references with guilt and its related terms, on the other hand, are rather rare (Augsburger 1995, 139). The basic reference is the narration of the Fall. Härle states that "It is evident how much weight the *Urgeschichte* places on the phenomenon of 'being ashamed' (particularly Gen 2:25–3:21)." He draws the following conclusion: "It is remarkable that for the Bible, sentiments of shame are the first consequence of sin, not sentiments of guilt. This affirms . . . the observation that sin is primarily not understood as guilt, but as failure and disruption" (Härle 1995, 486).[36] In a similar way, more recent Protestant ethics distinguishes between remorse and shame. "Shame and remorse must not be confused. Remorse is felt when a man misses shame – then he misses something [does not have it]. Shame is older than remorse" (Bonhoeffer, *Ethik*).[37] "Remorse always is a moral judgment. Shame isn't. . . . Shaming always is accompanied by a notion of being ostracized from the social web (Trillhaas)" (Schröer 1977, 106). Where Härle and others attempt to distinguish, Luther connects unrighteousness and shame. In a sermon on Romans 6:19–23 he said:

> Beloved, remember our own life, how you – living free from righteousness – did nothing but what sin made you do and to what sin tempted you. Did you enjoy it or what did you benefit from it? Nothing but that which you have to be ashamed for to

---

36. As for shame, Islam has a similar view, also rooted in the narrative of the Fall. In her extended study on shame and guilt, mainly in the Turkish-Muslim context, Spychinger suggests understanding Kierkegaard's "object-undefined existential anxiety (*Angst*)" as "existential shame without external reason." If one suddenly becomes aware that one has been watched, one is ashamed even without having done anything bad. Spychinger understands Kierkegaard's "object-defined fear" as "social shame." One is ashamed when one transgressed a social norm. The first form of shame is the *Angst* and shame Adam and Eve felt in Paradise (Spychinger 2007, 86).

37. Klopfenstein opposes Bonhoeffer's understanding of the relationship between remorse and shame, "because the Hebrew Bible does not teach such a differentiation" (Stiebert 2002, 47). Takeo Doi, on the other hand, leans particularly on Bonhoeffer. "Leaning on D. Bonhoeffer's *Die Ethik*, Doi finds a similar structure in sin and the phenomenon of shame. . . . The basis of shame is not only *Angst* or fear of scornful reaction of society, but also of primal isolation from the Absolute. This can be definitely compared to the Christian concept of sin" (Court 2009, 435).

the present day . . . This is punished with two painful rods;[38] the one is that man must be ashamed before God and the world, just as Adam and Eve [were] in Paradise, ashamed in their hearts as they stood before God's eyes. The other is the eternal death and the fire of hell, which they must have on top of their shame. (Luther 1828, 13–14)

Daube's commentary on Deuteronomy examines the differentiation of shame- and guilt-cultures in the context of Old Testament studies. According to him, the existence of "the inner voice of authority" cannot be ruled out in Deuteronomy, but it foremost appeals to how people are judged by others. He justifies his judgment by the close relationship of Deuteronomy and wisdom literature where shame is stressed. He emphasizes "the centrality of public, visible shaming in Deuteronomy" and claims that in Deuteronomy the only reference is found where in Israelite law "punishment consists exclusively in shame (Deut 25:5–10)" (Stiebert 2002, 38–40).

Besides "God and world" as vis-à-vis of shame, Luther also names angels. In a sermon on Revelation 12:7–12, held at the occasion of Saint Michael's Day, he demanded that "we must learn to fear and be ashamed before the pure sons of heaven[39] who are so close around us" (Stier 1837, 789). Can shame be demanded? Or as Schlatter put the question: "Do we have to give pain to those who err, must we shame them?" Schlatter says that a Christianity that is not willing to shame those who err because that would hurt their feelings is an "effete" Christianity. Such a Christianity "reconciles itself with the world," while in reality it is under obligation to "perceive the sin of the other as a true evil, therefore treat it as such and subject it to infamy." According to Schlatter, fulfilling this obligation is a prerequisite for the health of Christianity" (Schlatter 1961a, 333–334).

7.2.1.2 Objective sin and guilt

The Old Testament is much closer to the Japanese "shame orientation" than Western cultures are. According to Westermann, the emphasis of the *shalom*-concept is on "wholeness and *Heilsein*[40] of a human society" (1978, 98). The Japanese concept of rehabilitation is included in this concept. But since neither *Unheil* nor *Heil* can be restricted to the psychological "inner life," feelings of

---

38. *Harte Ruthen.*
39. *Himmelskinder.*
40. Being *heil.*

shame and guilt must be complemented by objective facts. This is compliant with the biblical *shalom*-concept which also has a dimension of justice and injustice. The biblical concept of justice is equivalent with the biblical *shalom*-concept (Ndabiseruye 2002, 200). Justice is an "elementary prerequistite for peace." Peace and justice form an inseparable unity (Zimmer 2006, 16). According to Augsburger, this is particularly true for the New Testament which has almost no allusions to shame. In the New Testament the focus is not on sentiments, "but on the celebration of objective events of God's acting in incarnation, presence, acceptance, forgiveness, and liberation of humankind" (Augsburger 1995, 139).

A discourse on objective facts would not be complete without that which Luther called the "second rod," "eternal death, and the fire of hell, which they must have on top of their shame" (Luther 1855, 982). *Unheil* is certainly manifested in the conscience of humans being tormented by pangs of shame and guilt feelings (subjective-psychological manifestation). It is certainly manifested in various kinds of injustice in the world (objective manifestation). But on top of that, the Bible is unequivocally clear about an *Unheil* as the possible outcome of every individual human being, the "second death" (Rev 20:6, 14; 21:8). Referring to Isaiah 66:24, Jesus said that this *Unheil* would never end, that "their worm did not die, and the fire was not quenched" (Mark 9:48). Eternal *Heil* is not the only *Heil*, but it is by far more important than temporal and physical *Heil* (Matt 18:8–9; Mark 9:43–48).

7.2.2 The Experience of Heil *under the Sociological Aspect*

7.2.2.1 *Heil* as rehabilitation and justice

As I showed in the context of the Japanese god-concept,[41] the concepts of unconditional forgiving and God's motherly tenderness must be taken into account. In a discussion of shame-cultures as opposed to guilt-cultures, Kraus showed that in "guilt-oriented cultures" conflicts are solved by reconciliation through compensation or punishment, and that justifications bans guilt. In shame-oriented cultures, on the other hand, conflicts are solved by identification and communication with the shamed. Love bans shame (Green and Baker 2000, 156).

---

41. See *2.3.3.3 The mercy of God and motherly tenderness* and *Repentance and forgiveness – or forgiveness and repentance?*

Shame is experienced through exposure. All humans strive to hide their true self or things of which they are ashamed (Noble 1995, 3). In cultures mainly oriented on shame, a confession of sins, therefore, does not lead to emotional relief but, on the contrary, to emotional stress. Therefore, "shame-cultures have no acts of confession, not even before the gods" (Benedict 1986, 223). *Tsumi* (罪), in the Japanese context not only a culpable action, but much more an external defilement, can be washed off, warded off, or compensated. But never is there mention as to the nature of *tsumi* (罪). For Western thinking this is difficult to understand. What happens to justice when all that happens to punishment is that it is not mentioned anymore? What is the meaning of the cross where "the punishment that brought us peace was upon him" (Isa 53:5). The message of the cross as believed in the West hardly makes sense in Japan (Green and Baker 2000, 161).

According to biblical thinking, there can be two reasons for a conscience in "resting position." It is either in "resting position" because a person is not aware of anything wrong, rightly or wrongly; or it is in "resting position" because a person has lost his conscience altogether. In Japan, a shameless person is considered to be beyond hope, far from repentance;[42] but where there is hope, the Holy Spirit can use this hope to lead a person to repentance.[43] It is one of the main functions of the Word of God to reveal sin (Noble 1975, 35).[44] Therefore, if humans strive to cover and conceal sins, they work against God. God opposes this kind of pride, a fact David had to learn the hard way (Ps 32:4). In the voice of conscience "God's wrath has its say" (Delitzsch 1859, 256). The pangs of conscience want to lead a man into the opposite direction, toward confession. The shame-oriented conscience leads into the opposite direction. In confession "false and hypocritical honor is renounced and the shame adhering to guilt willingly endured" (Schlatter 1911, 289–290). The biblical message demands a confession, not in order to bring pangs of conscience, but to bring relief from sin through forgiving.[45]

> Forgiving is not being excused. As long . . . as there is excusing . . . there is no forgiving. Forgiving starts where excusing is not

---

42. Jer 6:15; 8:12; 3:3.
43. Ps 83:16.
44. Heb 4:12–13.
45. Ps 32 shows clearly that God reveals sin, but people strive to conceal it.

possible anymore, where guilt is acknowledged.⁴⁶ Then, the separation power of guilt is cancelled and community restored . . . Our share in God's salvation is of the renunciation of any kind of apology which may justify us. (Schlatter 1911, 261)

7.2.2.2 The death of Jesus on the cross in the context of the Japanese shame-culture

Kraus recognized that shame was connected with a concept of sin as defilement and impurity. He also maintained that the biblical concept of the cross is not distorted by a correlation with the Japanese concept of shame – that the cultural expression of shame is much more obvious in the Bible than Western readers are aware of (Green and Baker 2000, 157).

Kraus names four socio-psychological features of shame on which he builds his interpretation of the cross of Jesus in the context of the Japanese shame-culture:

- Shame is experienced by exposure before oneself and others. Some even say that shame is experienced most deeply when a person does not meet his own expectations;
- Shame is feared because a person cannot meet expectations and not, as in the guilt-fear-complex, because a person fears punishment;
- Shame can destroy relationships more profoundly than guilt can. Condemnation and punishment are communication processes, whereas shame is an isolating and alienating experience;
- Shame cannot be removed by punishment. It can only be removed by loving identification (Green and Baker 2000, 157–158).

In the Roman Empire, the emphasis was on the shame of the crucifixion, not on its pain.⁴⁷ The cross "was designed to be an instrument of contempt

---

46. Similarly, C. S. Lewis: "There is all the difference in the world between forgiving and excusing. . . . If one was not really to blame, then there is nothing to forgive. In that sense forgiveness and excusing are almost opposites. . . . The trouble is that what we call 'asking God's forgiveness' very often really consists in asking God to accept our excuses" (C. S. Lewis 1986d, 40).

47. The respective text is Marcus Tullius Cicero's speech Pro Rabirio (5:16): "The ignominy of a public trial is a miserable thing, – the deprivation of a man's property by way of penalty is a miserable thing, – exile is a miserable thing; but still, in all these disasters some trace of liberty remains to one. Even if death be threatened, we may die free men; but the executioner, and the veiling of the head, and the mere name of the gibbet, should be far removed, not only from the persons of Roman citizens – from their thoughts, and eyes, and ears. For not only the actual fact and endurance of all these things, but the bare possibility of being exposed to them, – the expectation, the mere mention of them even, – is unworthy of a Roman citizen and of a free man. Does not the kindness of their masters at one touch deliver our slaves from the fear

and public ridicule. The victim died naked, in bloody sweat, helpless to control bodily excretions." Leaning on Kitamori, Kraus suggests to understand the cross not so much as the act of an angry God, but as the act of a suffering God. Kraus argues that the cross is not reconciliation of the wrath of God, but a revelation of his love. His concept of the cross bases its soteriological significance on the shaming character of the crucifixion. In his love God willingly endured the shame (Green and Baker 2000, 163).

Because Jesus identified himself with the poor on the cross, Kraus can assure the Japanese and others exhausted by shame that Jesus comprehensively knows the fear of shaming ostracism (Green and Baker 2000, 164). Jesus's solidarity with the shamed and ostracized of his age led to the ultimate experience of shame – to the crucifixion. In the eyes of his prosecutors, Jesus was contaminated by his communion with tax collectors and sinners. But Jesus did not shun others in order to protect his own moral purity and his reputation (165).

According to Kraus, Japanese can change and realize a new identity as children of God on the basis of Jesus's identification with the shamed. The vicarious nature of Jesus's death on the cross consists in Jesus's experience of the ultimate shaming ostracism as a substitute for the shamed. They are therefore liberated from the burden of shaming ostracism, both already experienced and feared (Green and Baker 2000, 166).

This does not mean that Kraus alters the categories of sin from transgression and guilt to defilement and shame. He does not deny the category of transgression and guilt. Rather he gives shame an authentic moral content and an internalized standard, that is, exposure before the eyes of the God who sees everything, who is righteous and just, and who loves. The judgment of God is explicitly a public exposure of shameful things we rendered hidden (Luke 12:1–3). The reinterpretation of an external social standard as an internalized theological standard is important for Christian ethics, particularly in societies where public shaming remains the primary sanction against undesirable behavior. Without this reinterpretation, the conscience remains attached to relative authorities such as tradition and local social recognition (Kraus in Green and Baker 2000, 166–167).

---

of all these punishments; and shall neither our exploits, nor the purity of our past life, nor the honours which you have conferred on us, save us from the scourge, from the hangman's hook, and even from the dread of the gibbet?" (Yonge 1856). Berger and Colpe explain: "This text is striking proof (compare *Pro Rabirio* 4:12) not only for the horror of crucifixion, but also its concomitant circumstances and its infamy which grades the culprits lower than slaves" (Berger and Colpe 1987, 87).

In a similar way, the Lutheran theologian Tokuzen (徳善義和) applied Luther's thought to the Japanese context of shame orientation. Man can either remain *coram hominibus* (before man), or he can be lead to the place where he suddenly recognizes himself fully *coram Deo* (before God) (Tokuzen 1981, 569). Tokuzen correlates Ebeling's "*coram*-relation" with the Japanese *sekensama* (世間様) versus *kamisama* (神様),[48] with the ethical orientation towards others or towards gods or God. Tokuzen's choice is masterly appropriate. Western theology is much concerned with conceptualized abstraction and describes relation with nouns. Relational ontology uses relative pronouns to describe relations. "The preposition *coram* is etymologically rooted in the phenomenon of countenance, similar to the Hebrew equivalents לִפְנֵי and עַל־פְּנֵי." The countenance is the place of actively seeing and passively being seen. Ebeling places more emphasis on the passive aspect (Redeker 2011, 59).[49] As I showed before,[50] the face is the central organ of the Japanese understanding of shame and therefore also for Japanese ethics.

7.2.2.3 Social justice in Japan

Koperski called attention to the fact that justice is, according to Philippians 3:9, an integral part of Christian soteriology (Koperski 1996, 191). As I showed above,[51] the Japanese peace concept has a dangerous tendency toward internalization. In Japan, the social dimension of salvation is in danger of being restricted to rehabilitation only, leaving out justice. Even if justice is discussed in the Christian context, it is exclusively discussed as "righteousness before God." However, just as the love for God must not be separated from the love of the neighbor, the "righteousness before God" must not be separated from social justice. Here internalized soteriologies as well as the internalized Japanese concept of peace are in need of a strong, biblical correction.

Besides the ethnic minority of the Ainu, the indigenous Japanese ethnicity pushed far into the North of Hokkaido (Leroi-Gourhan and Leroi-Gourhan

---

48. See under *2.5.3.1 Japan as example for extreme collectivism.*

49. The *coram*-relation defines the human existence ontologically in three aspects: Being is being together, being linguistic, and being responsible. These three aspects of existence are then asserted in a threefold relation: as being before God (*coram Deo*), being before the world (*coram mundo* [almost identical with *coram hominibus*]), and being before "myself" (*coram meipso*). All three *coram*-relations are interrelated. According to Ebeling, relational ontology provides precisely by that "an interpretation framework, in which the entirety of the Christian faith can be articulated and structured, not in an abstract, theoretical way, but in a way that signifies the relation to real life" (Rehfeld 2012, 25).

50. See under *7.1.1.2 Unheil as shame.*

51. See under *3.1.2.1 Wa (和) as harmony and Confucianism.*

1995) and the *burakumin* (部落民),[52] the outlaws of Japan, descendants of the *eta* (穢多) (Zöllner 2009, 62–63)[53] and guilds of various "unclean professions" as they were called in the *Edo*-Era, there are to my knowledge no bigger ethnic or social groups that are discriminated or suppressed. *Ainu* and *burakumin* (部落民) are guaranteed equal opportunity before the law, but these rights are frequently refused in practice.[54] Mayer and Clammer also name other discriminated minorities: third-generation Koreans living in Japan,[55] the inhabitants of Okinawa (also Kaneko 1993, 14), the victims of the atomic bombing of Hiroshima and Nagasaki and their descendants, the boat people and illegal foreign laborers (mainly in the sex-industry) (Mayer 1994, 119–124; Clammer 2001, 117), Davis Jr. adds the *nikkeijin* (日系人), children of Japanese emigrants having returned to Japan (Davis Jr. 2000, 110).

The fact that there are only a few ethnical minorities must not lead to the illusion that the remaining over 90 percent of the Japanese are not socially suppressed. The majority of suppressed people are not found in a few homogenous ethnic groups. Those suffering violence are found in all strata of society, among the poor and among the rich. Social injustice cannot be defined by economic standards only. There is social injustice among rich people. First of all, there are those suffering under the pressure of a society that is extremely oriented towards achievement and profit. They are exhausted because of external stress (school, work place) and internal stress (denial of negative emotions).

The performance pressure caused by worshipping economic growth demands its toll, not only when people become victims of *karoushi* (過労死),[56] of "death due to overwork," but long before in childhood. In order to be hired by a good company, one needs to graduate from a good university; in order to enter that one needs to be enrolled in a good *high school*, for that in

---

52. According to Mayer, they account for up to 6% of the Japanese population (Mayer 1994, 119–224).

53. In his novel *Hakai* (破戒) (English title: *The Broken Commandment*) (1906), Touzon Shimazaki (島崎藤村) shows mainly the psychological aspects of the discrimination of the late 19th century *eta* (穢多) in an impressive way.

54. As for their constitutional rights, the *burakumin* (部落民) today are better off than ever (Davis Jr. 2000, 113–114). However, as a thesis of the *Buraku*-Liberation League (*Buraku Kaihou Doumei*, 部落開放同盟) from 1961 states, they are not granted equal rights in the field of career choice (Kaneko 1993, 13). In his study on Japanese emigrants in America Spickard showed that *eta* (穢多) are discriminated and ostracized even today. They are called "unclean," and marriage with them is avoided. They live in constant fear of being found out (Spickard 1991, 94–95).

55. For their history see Kaneko (1993, 14ff).

56. *Karoushi* (過労死) has become known worldwide as a loan-word from the Japanese.

a good *junior high school* – the pressure can sometimes be traced back even into kindergarten age. There are kindergartens with entry exams! In Japan, the children are the victims. Among the economically rich countries, Japan has the highest rate of infant and juvenile suicide.[57]

Fathers who neglect their families because of work-related stress harm their children poignantly (Hemfelt et al. 1995, 63–69). Neglected wives are in danger of harming their children by emotional incest (68). In cases of overly strong attachment, emotional incest leads to sexual abuse. Sexual abuse of boys by their mothers is comparatively high in Japan. Children abused in such a way need a lot of energy to deny or process the resulting problems as adults, which again leads to fatigue.

There is also a strong countermovement against the Japanese performance society, triggered mainly by the collapse of the bubble economy:[58]

- Even in Japan, the second richest country in the world, poverty becomes a more and more undeniable social reality. In the 1990s the social divide between rich and poor did not seem to be wide. The general *souchuuryuu ishiki* (総中流意識), the "consciousness of the middle class" was still strong into the mid-1990s (Schad-Seifert 2007, 105). However, today, Japan is considered a country with a *kiboukakusashakai* (希望格差社会), literally a "society with hope-disparity," a society with unequal opportunity (Schad-Seifert 2007, 116).
- Indicators of the decay of the middle class are the growth of the *parasite singles* (*parasaito shinguru*, パラサイトシングル),[59] and growth of the *furiitaa* (フリーター) and *NEET*.[60]

---

57. In detail see Teichler (1994, 402–403).

58. "By 1993, the great boom of the 1970s and 1980s for Japanese business was at an end. Japan's Prime Minister Kiichi Miyazawa (宮澤喜一), acknowledged on 29 January 1993, that the collapse of Japan's bubble economy had occurred . . . Growth for the rest of the economy would remain flat. Miyazawa admitted that changes in the economy were needed. As late as 2014, Japan was still trying to find the right combination of government and private sector reforms to make needed change happen" (McNabb 2016, "What Went Wrong?").

59. For details see Koide (2000), Matsumoto (2001), Japan Echo Inc. (2000), and Curtin (2001).

60. *Furiitaa* (フリーター), a term used for male, part-time workers aged between 15 and 34 (Nishiyama 2006, 182), is composed of the English loan-word derived from "<u>free</u>" and the suffix of the German word for "worker," *Arb<u>eiter</u>*. In 2001, there were 4,170,000 "*freeters*" (21.2% of the total work force). "Recent data has revealed that, in 2010, 1.83 million freeters were working in Japan" (Ogawa 2015, 150). *Freeters* are either without permanent employment or in training, seeking a part-time job (*NEET* for <u>N</u>ot in <u>E</u>ducation, <u>E</u>mployment, or <u>T</u>raining), or they are working part time. More the 70% of the "*freeters*" are in this group involuntarily.

- More and more men become homeless because they cannot bear the shame of unemployment. The unemployment rate – particularly among middle aged men (Oshige 2003, 9–10) – is constantly growing.[61]
- More and more young families with a desire to have children think they cannot have children because of low income. This accelerates the aging of society (Thränhardt 1994, 431).[62]

Churches must work toward social justice, cooperating with professional therapists. They must emphasize the primacy of personal relationships over work achievement. They must help individuals to spend time for themselves and others in spite of the demands of economy. They must prophetically criticize the existing primacy of economy. On the other side, they must speak in favor of the political responsibility of individuals for maintaining the population and work force. In the field of pastoral theology, they must change the way of "keeping the Sabbath." Presently, Christian families are under a lot of pressure due to the expectations of church activities on Sundays. Christian families are separated even on Sundays.[63]

According to the *Ministry of Health, Labour and Welfare* (*MHLW*) more than 60% of these young people have either never applied for a job or stopped applying. One of the main reasons was fear of social contacts on the job (Nishiyama 2006, 182). Characteristics of the *furiitaa* (フリーター) are not so much their low wages but "a poor accumulation of knowledge, a high social insecurity, and a bad social prestige as prospective marriage partners" (Schad-Seifert 2007, 116–118).

61. For details see Hosaka (穂坂光彦) and Shimokawa (1999), and the *Japan NGO Report Preparatory Committee* (1999).

62. "The Japanese population has the lowest birth rate, the longest life expectancy, and hence a growing population of aged people" (Sano 2003, 135). The aging process in Japan is faster than that in other countries (Nishiyama 2006, 182).

63. Christian's comments on the "hallowing of the seventh day" can be helpful: "The hallowing of the seventh day is predicated upon God's resting on the seventh day of creation. Thus Sabbath remembering is a recognition that life and the world come to us as a gift from the working, but also from the resting, God. Rest reflects the character of God as truly as does activity and labor. Therefore, it is an integral part of the cosmic order. But the Sabbath is not merely memorial; it is also commanded for the benefit of the human race in its creaturely limitation. Pausing for restoration is recognition that we are men and women and not God. We do not have unlimited strength and resources" (Christian 2004, 118).

8

The Anthropological Aspect of Salvation

Summary: In Japanese thinking, defilement of any kind plays about the same role as "sin" in Western Christianity. Calamities, self-inflicted or not self-inflicted, as well as salvation sought in liberation from them, are mainly expressed in terms of defilement and purity.

In order to create a tool for clearer understanding of Japanese concepts, and in order to prepare the ground for an encounter with biblical concepts, I introduce into the discussion the aspect of guilt, which is alien to Japanese thinking.

8.1 The Anthropological Aspect of Salvation in the Context of Japanese Animism

Summary: The uncritical equation of Western and Christian concepts and Japanese animistic concepts is misleading. Therefore, they need to be explained and understood from within their original context.

Humans experience the absence of salvation as defilement: (a) as self-inflicted and not self-inflicted *kegare* (穢れ), as "defilement" and/or as *tsumi* (罪), "sin"; (b) as self-inflicted *tsumi* (罪), "crime"; (c) as *yogore* (汚れ), "dirtiness."

Respectively salvation is experienced (a) through *harae* (祓え), "atonement rituals and/or purification rituals; (b) through *misogi* (禊ぎ) and *kiyome* (清め),

"purification rituals"; and (c) through *mayoke* (魔除け), "apotropaic magic"; and (d) through hygienic cleanliness.

In this context, I use "anthropological" not in the sense of "anthropology" in the widest sense, but in the narrow sense of "concerning humans per se." Under the anthropological aspect, *Unheil* is mainly experienced as defilement and impurity. *Heil* is experienced respectively as purification in the widest sense. The most common terms are the following:

Table 8.1 Sin and Defilement and Its Remedies

tsumi (罪) "sin"	*kegare* (穢れ) "defilement"	*yogore* (汚れ) "dirtiness"
harae (祓え)¹ "atonement"	*misogi* (禊ぎ), *kiyome* (清め) "purification"	*arai* (洗い) "washing"
	mayoke (魔除け) "apotropaic magic"	

8.1.1 The Experience of Unheil as Impurity

8.1.1.1 The myth of the "happy heathen"

The Japanese correlation of the Western concept of sin as being evil or an evil action is the concept of impurity, *tsumi* (罪), what is commonly used as translation of the English "sin" (Matsumoto 1972, 15). The lexical equation of terms used in different religious traditions has been causing much confusion in comparative religious science, as can be seen from the following text:

> Let us compare *Izanagi* (伊弉諾神 or 伊邪那岐命 or 伊耶那岐命) and *Izanami* (伊邪那美命 or 伊弉冉尊) with Adam and Eve. The latter were expelled from the Garden of Eden, because Eve had eaten from the apple of knowledge. They had acquired the ability to distinguish between good and evil, and were thus able to sin. Japan does not know such a myth. *Izanagi* (伊弉諾神 or 伊邪那岐命 or 伊耶那岐命) and *Izanami* (伊弉冉 or 伊邪那美 or 伊耶那美 or 伊弉弥) were not punished for any particular action,

---

1. Besides *harae* (祓え), *harai* (祓い) is also used. I prefer the term *harae* (祓え). As for the usage of Chinese characters for *harae*, the usage of 払え is more common nowadays than 祓え. For details see below under *8.1.2.1 Differentiation between the rites of* harae (祓え) *and* misogi (禊ぎ).

they were not even expelled from a Garden of Eden. Their crisis occurred as *Izanagi* (伊弉諾神 or 伊邪那岐命 or 伊耶那岐命) was seen by his spouse in her impurity. The *Unheil* stemmed from their shaming, not from anything they would have committed deliberately. The gods could enjoy sex unpunished, yet they were terribly afraid of impurity, particularly of the impurity of death. After *Izanagi* (伊弉諾神 or 伊邪那岐命 or 伊耶那岐命) has seen the decayed corpse of his sister, he hardly escapes death. One can even say that impurity is the Japanese version of hereditary sin. (Buruma 1985, 19)

The ostensible antithesis of sin and impurity has ignited the polemic controversy between "anthropologists" and "missionaries," going back to Herman Melville's *Typee and Omoo* (1846), Somerset Maugham's *Miss Thompson* (before 1922), and Peter Matthiessen's *At Play in the Fields of the Lord* (1965) (Priest 1993, 88–90), and the cultural romanticism and the myth of the "happy heathen" evoked therein. Benedict's, Durant's, and Campbell's interpretations of the Japanese culture are but examples of this cultural romanticism – according to Japanese philosophy, the "flesh" was not evil; to enjoy what is enjoyable was "no sin" (Benedict 1986, 189–190); "carnal desire" was as natural as hunger or thirst (Durant 1985, 217);[2] or Campbell: "It is the basic ethical idea that natural processes cannot be bad. The conclusion is that the pure heart follows the natural processes. Man – a natural being – is not bad per se, but is, in his pure heart, in his natural state, divine" (Campbell 1991, II, 548).

As it will become clear from the following, such an interpretation of the Japanese ethos is neither correct nor helpful. It is rather wishful thinking (of some anthropologists) which defines the outcome of the survey beforehand.

> To Western sensibilities, a "sin" directly affects the individual's soul like a filthy cloak which only a priest of the church or the direct forgiveness of God intuited by prayer can remove via absolution. . . . However, . . . *tsumi* (罪) do not affect the "real" person but are thought as temporary separations from the harmonious interaction of body, soul, and world. Western preoccupations with virtue do not apply to Shinto conceptions of impurity and purity, mainly because *tsumi* (罪) are not antithetical

---

2. "Under the *Tokugawa*-regime (mid-15th century) monks drank a lot, publicly kept mistresses, and committed pederasty" (Durant 1985, 220).

to virtue or harmony. They are simply a fact of existence afflicting all of us, *kami* (神) included, *but they can be completely obliterated*, with no lingering guilt complexes. (Nelson 1996, 104)

In Japan, *tsumi* (罪) is not related with God or the gods. This is the most important difference between the Christian concept of sin and the Japanese animistic concept of impurity. In Shintoism, the relationship with the gods is not disturbed. There is no "hereditary sin" (Matsumoto 1972, 16). Instead of "hereditary sin" Shintoism rather advocates "hereditary grace":

> We directly receive from the *kami* (神)³ via our ancestors a specific gift of inclinations and abilities; if we let these hereditary dispositions express themselves naturally, we spontaneously put parental love, honesty, and love for our neighbors into practice. (Rochedieu 1973, 114)

The moral indifference concerning "good and evil" also stems from the fact that, according to Ueda, *kami* (神) like animals are beyond "good and evil." Moriyama summarizes Ueda's position as follows:

> Logical standards are a human phenomenon that cannot be applied to other animals. . . . Humans lead a life based on societal relationships, but fox and badger spirits [Ueda equates these spirits with *kami* (神)] live in a world that lacks such norms. Theirs is a primal existence. (Moriyama in Fessler 1996, 4)

In his moral concept, Ueda went as far as to say that religious practices are a hindrance on the way to becoming a *kami* (神): "The *kami* (神) are divine entities; humans cannot follow religious [Buddhist] practices and someday become a *kami* (神)" (Fessler 1996, 4).

8.1.1.2 The fuzziness of the Japanese "sin"-concept

There are three reasons for the (alleged) fuzziness of the Japanese term *tsumi* (罪):

1. Equating sin with *tsumi* (罪) and impurity with *kegare* (穢れ) in a slavish lexical meticulousness is obtrusive and deceptive. The fact that *tsumi* (罪) and *kegare* (穢れ) share common features does not mean that Japanese are unable to distinguish between sin and impurity. Nomura's (野村玄良) etymological observations are useful. He interprets *kegare* (穢れ) as a compound formed by

---

3. In Rochedieu's quote, *kami* (神) does not denote the God of the Bible, but Japanese gods which are immanent beings.

ke (ケ or 気 or 息 or 生気)⁴ and *kare* (枯れ), "dried up" (Nomura 2001, 171). Thus, *kegare* (穢れ) describes cause and effect of the drying up of the *mana*-force. Kitagawa and Ludwig talk about "life-hindering pollution" (Kitagawa and Ludwig 1984, 1638). Nomura deduces the *tsu* in *tsumi* (罪) from *tsume* (爪), "finger nail," here meaning the "tip of the finger" as a metaphor for attack; he deduces the *mi* in *tsumi* (罪) from *mi* (霊 or 精霊), "spirit" or "spirit of life." *Mi* (霊 or 精霊) and *ki* (気) belong close together. Thus, *tsumi* (罪) describes the attack on the Holy (Nomura 2001, 190), that is, the *mana*-force. Aoki defines *tsumi* (罪) as "hindrance of the *life-force*" (Aoki 1994, 265). Court defines *kegare* (穢れ) as "acting against the common good of the community" (Court 2009, 435). Thus, in the context of the Japanese language, the terms *tsumi* (罪) and *kegare* (穢れ) belong together.

2. However, not only the inflexible equation with Western terms and concepts suggest conceptual fuzziness. The ideological encounter with Buddhism also introduced a confusing element into the discussion: the element of differentiation of "physical" and "spiritual" things.

In the early Shintoist purification rituals *misogi* (禊), as reported in the *Kojiki* (古事記), the focus was only on the purification of the physical body. Under the influence of Buddhism, its "nature-religious" notion was gradually changed into an "rational" notion in which the purification right was thought not only to purify the body but also the *seishin* (精神), the "mind" or the *kokoro* (心), the "heart" (Triplett 2004, 153–154). Thus, two aspects, originally unified in Japanese animism, were separated.

3. The third reason for the conceptual fuzziness is that there are many approaches towards *tsumi* (罪). In her comprehensive study *Tsumi: Offence and Retribution in Early Japan* (2003), William showed six different approaches to the understanding of:

   a. Norinaga's approach;⁵
   b. the approach of western Japanologists who want to equate *tsumi* (罪) with sin [and then come to the conclusion that Japanese don't have a sense of sin];

---

4. For the Japanese *mana*-concept see *2.2 The Japanese* Mana*-concept* ki (気).

5. For Norinaga *tsumi* (罪) "meant whatever people hate and abominate as evil, including not simply evil deeds, but also diseases, various disasters, filthy things, ugly things, and so forth ... *Tsumi* (罪) broadly referred to 'filthiness or impurity, physical and spiritual,' only a part of which was concerned with morality. '*Tsumi* (罪) was pollution of the senses.' This being the case, there was no clear distinction between moral guilt on the one hand and physical disaster and pollution on the other" (Higashibaba 2001, 113–114).

c. the juridical approach which understands *tsumi* (罪) as "crime";

d. the anthropological approach which focuses on the study of purification rituals and mythological sources;

e. a philosophical approach which studies *tsumi* (罪) in the context of Japanese intellectual history;

f. the approach of comparative historical research (Williams 2003, 2–3).

Mitsuhashi points to a similar conceptual fuzziness created by the usage of the term in different religious traditions:

a. The Shintoist concept of sin is complicated and diverse. In the juridical sense, there are transgressions of laws. They are called *hanzai* (犯罪), "crimes."

b. In ethics, an offense against the *hito toshite mamorubeki michi* (人として守るべき道), against the "way one has to keep as human," is called *zaiaku* (罪悪), "evil of sin."

c. In Buddhism, *tsumi* (罪) is turning one's back on Buddha's rules. This is called *zaigou* (罪業), "deed of sin," *zaishou* (罪障), "hindrance of sin," and *zaika* (罪科), "ogling with sin" (Mitsuhashi 2007, 169).

8.1.1.3 Sin *tsumi* (罪) – dirtiness *yogore / kegare* (汚れ) – defilement *kegare* (穢れ)

In Japan, impurity is expressed with three different terms:

Figure 8.1 Japanese Terms for "Impurity"

The central term is *kegare* (穢れ). It is central because it encompasses both *tsumi* (罪), here meaning impurity with guilt, and – though to a much smaller degree – *yogore/kegare* (汚れ), impurity without guilt. Figure 8.1 shows that *kegare* (穢れ) and *tsumi* (罪) are almost congruent, while *yogore/kegare* (汚れ) and *kegare* (穢れ) have hardly any common features.

I am well aware of the fact that Japanese scholars and theologians do not use guilt/innocence as a discriminating criterion. They distinguish classically into *kunitsutsumi* (国津罪), "sins committed on earth," and *amatsutsumi* (天津罪), "sins committed in heaven" (Williams 2003, 42). In the present they distinguish anthropologically like Suzuki:

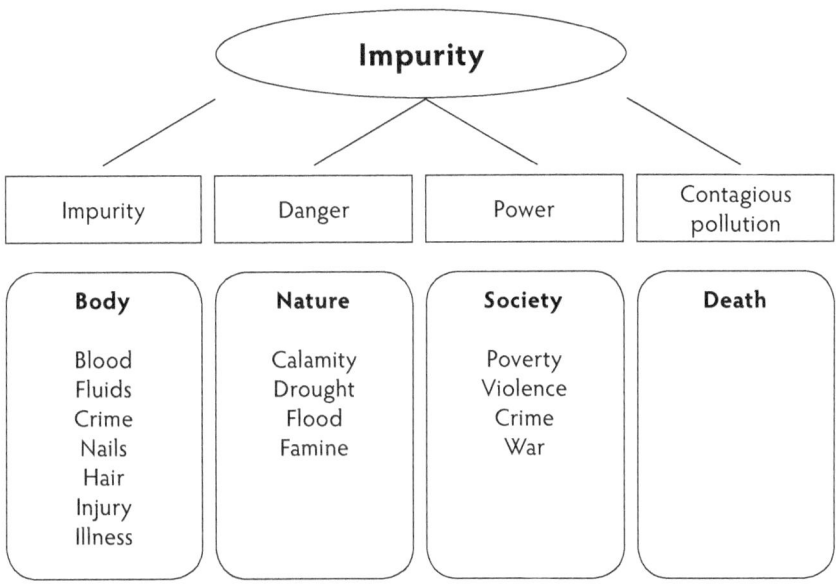

Figure 8.2 Impurity (according to Suzuki in Nesbitt 2007, 26)

Suzuki's model shows where "impurity" in the broadest sense occurs. The moral evaluation is not a distinguishing feature for Suzuki. Figure 8.2 attempts to bridge the gap between indiscriminately mixing impurity, blameworthy or not on the Japanese side, and a rigid terminological orthodoxy on the Western side. However, within the structure of my graph above, I divide according to Suzuki.

Defilement as *kegare* (穢れ)

The field of *kegare* (穢れ) with guilt

This field is congruent with that which Suzuki categorized as "power" and "society." In this field *kegare* (穢れ) and *tsumi* (罪) are congruent. It is mainly concerned with various sexual "sins." Mitsuhashi, as well as Ono and Kaneko name among others: *ono-ga ko okasu tsumi* (おのが子犯す罪), "incest with a natural child"; *haha-to ko-to okasu tsumi* (母と子と犯す罪), "fornication with a woman and her child"; *kemono okaseru tsumi* (畜犯せる罪), "sodomy" (Mitsuhashi 2007, 171; Ono and Kaneko 2004, 40). Further "sins" in this sense are murder (von Siebold 2001, 97) and desecration of corpses (Sansom 1978, 52).

The field of *kegare* (穢れ) without guilt

In this field, *kegare* (穢れ) and *tsumi* (罪) are almost congruent.

Kegare (穢れ) in connection with the body

In this field, there are first diseases (Antoni 1998, 29) in general, and wounds in particular. Kubota points to the phonetical proximity of *kegare* (穢れ) and *kega* (怪我), "wounds," and concludes: *kega* (怪我), "wounds," are a result of *kegare* (穢れ), "defilement" inside the body (Kubota 1997, 177; similarly Sansom 1978, 51). However, wounds afflicted from the outside, particularly snake bites, also defile (Blacker 1999, 42). According to Rumi Iwagou, the connection mentioned by Kubota is the basis of a comprehensive divination system, according to which wounded body parts refer to interpersonal problems. Some examples:

- wounds of the hands signify problems in the future, because hands point forward;
- wounds of the feet or legs signify problems in the past, because those point backward;
- wounds of thumbs and big toes signify problems with parents, because they are called *oyayubi* (親指), literally "parent-finger."

Closely connected with diseases and wounds are the *aka fujou* (赤不浄), the "red defilement," also called *chifujou* (血不浄), the "blood defilement," and the *kuro fujou* (黒不浄), the "black defilement" by anything affiliated with death. Both occur in professions that deal with animal cadavers, in ancient Japan pursued by the ostracized *eta* (穢多), the "unclean." *Eta* (穢多) literally means "much (多) defilement (穢)" (MacFarlane 1997, 277), in this case 穢 being a synonym of 汚 (unclean). *Aka fujou* (赤不浄), "red defilement," is caused mainly by the blood of women (Okano 2002, 23), mainly menstrual blood (MacFarlane 1997, 277).[6] Besides death the blood of women falls under the Japanese taboo-concept *imi* (忌 or 斎).[7] In the case of blood the special word *chiimi* (血忌), "blood-taboo," is used.

Kegare (穢れ) in connection with nature

Among the calamities which also fall under *kegare* (穢れ), Mitsuhashi lists among others: *hau mushi-no wazawai* (昆虫の災), "calamities due to creeping insects," *takatsukami-no wazawai* (高つ神の災), literally "calamities due to high gods," that is, calamities through fire and lightning, and *takatsutori-no wazawai* (高つ鳥の災), literally "calamities due to high birds," that is, damage on the roof by birds of prey (Mitsuhashi 2007, 171).

Kegare (穢れ) in connection with death

According to traditional Shintoism, everything connected with death is unclean.[8] The main *kuro fujou* (黒不浄), "black defilement," is (besides dirt) death. This defilement is called "black," because this color is generally considered to be unclean (Nawrocki 1998, 360). Humans are defiled by "deaths of biological relatives" or when coming in contact with a corpse (von Siebold 2001, 97). Therefore, people try to avoid everything related with death. The fact that in ancient Japan the realm of the dead was thought to begin right outside the village boundaries reveals an extreme fear of death, the fear to be pulled along or to be contaminated. Corpses used to be abandoned in the mountains and people would flee them immediately (Naumann 1984b, 1591). In Shintoism, there is also an esthetic rationale. Drawing from the myth of *Izanami* (伊弉冉 or 伊邪那美 or 伊耶那美 or 伊弉弥) and *Izanagi* (伊弉諾

---

6. In pre-Buddhist Japan, menstrual blood was considered powerful rather than defiling (Edwards 2001, 234).

7. *Imi* (忌み or 忌) or *monoimi* (物忌み or 物忌) is a term from the *onmyoudou* (陰陽道). In Shintoism, the term *saikai* (斎戒) is used instead. The general term for taboo is *kinki* (禁忌) (Toya 2006, 199), literally "prohibited taboo." *Monoimi* (物忌み) is avoiding *kegare* (穢れ) through "historically determined days of bad luck, contact with unclean things, or the violation of geomantic rules (*"Genjimonogatari Daijiten" Henshuu Iinkai* [『源氏物語大辞典』編集委員会], the board of editor of the *Genji-Monogatari*-Encyclopaedia 2008, 194). *Onmyoudou* (陰陽道) is the Chinese teaching of the Five Elements (Wu Xing) (Schedler 2004, 53). Others call it the "cult of the Yin-Yang-doctrine" (Taira 1990, 190). It is assumed that *onmyoudou* (陰陽道) is a system of ancient Japanese practices of determining fate through observing natural phenomena and divination in the area of interpersonal relationships. They were influenced by ideas from Taoism, Buddhism, and Shintoism and took their present shape in the late 7th century (Naturalists 2008, 394).

8. However, in the moral teaching of the samurai, death "represents highest freedom and the height of purity" (Ejima 1996, 95).

神 or 伊邪那岐命 or 伊耶那岐命), Ejima points out that "death is somehow connected with shame" (1996, 94), because the deceased *Izanami* (伊弉冉 or 伊邪那美 or 伊耶那美 or 伊弉弥) didn't want *Izanagi* (伊弉諾神 or 伊邪那岐命 or 伊耶那岐命) to see her repulsive and therefore "shameful" decay.

Even today, death is widely taboo. This can be seen from various rules of etiquette, such as the taboo of sticking chopsticks into rice vertically (as it reminds people of the incense offered to the dead), or passing on food directly from chopstick to chopstick (as it reminds people of the habit of passing on bones from one relative to another after cremation, again with special chopsticks). However, since the early 1990s, the growing popularity of *shizensou* (自然葬), "natural burial" with its shattering of ashes at places that were meaningful for the deceased shows that the concept of defilement due to death is weakening (Nesbitt 2007, 42).

The notion that birth defiles a woman should also be mentioned here (Sansom 1978, 51). However, birth does not bring *aka fujou* (赤不浄), "red defilement," but *kuro fujou* (黒不浄), "black defilement." Because of a high rate of infant mortality in ancient Japan, birth has always been affiliated with death (Coulmas 2005, 35). Another reason is that children and old people were always considered to be particularly close to the realm of death. Through birth, women were in touch with the "other world." They were considered unclean for seven days after birth, or, according to the *Sasekishuu* (砂石集), a medieval Buddhist source, for fifty days after the death of a relative. There are two reasons: (1) Birth is considered the beginning of death (Steineck 2007, 55);[9] and (2) women giving birth are in contact with babies, people in "a marginal state" that are often treated as "both vulnerable and dangerous" (Douglas 2002, 118).

Kegare (穢れ) in other contexts

Other reasons for defilement are possession after certain Shintoist festivals (Plutschow and O'Neill 1996, 86), sorcery (Sansom 1978, 52), and sexual intercourse (Sansom 1978, 51).

---

9. This was established by the ritual rules of the *Engishiki* (延喜式), implementation rules of the *Engi*-Era, compiled in 905–927. Others talk about 57 days (Bownas and Brown 2004, 69). In ancient Japan, the *ubuya* (産屋) were common, the "birthing-huts," where women lived after giving birth and partly also during their menstrual period, separated from society (Coulmas 2005, 35).

Defilement only as *yogore/kegare* (汚れ)

According to Oonuki-Tierney, the thinking of ritual impurity has changed, but ancient notions still determine concepts of hygiene (Oonuki-Tierney 1984, 37–38). 汚れ can also be read *yogore* which means "dirt" without any ritual or moral notion, *and* it can be read *kegare* which includes moral defilement. This double reading of 汚れ mirrors the historical development of the thinking about defilement.

Dirt particularly means *hitogomi* (人ごみ), the "dirt from the body of others," experienced as "germs" and warded off by wearing masks and white gloves (Oonuki-Tierney 1984, 31). "Dirt from the body of others" is mainly hair and dandruff, as well as the dirt under fingernails. This is the reason for the historical fact that the Dutch were considered "the *least* unclean" foreigners – they trimmed their beards and cut their fingernails (MacFarlane 1997, 277).

Defilement only as *tsumi* (罪)

The graph under 8.1.1.3 shows that this area is very small. Violations against laws belong here, offenses that are not necessarily considered morally condemnable. These are in the widest sense offenses that are prosecuted. The typical example is offenses against the traffic law. Those offenses are not called *tsumi* (罪) with a moral notion, but *hanzai* (犯罪) with a juridical notion.

8.1.2 The Experience of Heil *under the Anthropological Aspect*

Purification rituals are a common part of nature religions (Soete 1992, 594–596). The belief that water can purify from *tsumi* (罪) and *kegare* (穢れ) is belief in the power of nature (Abe 2004, 133). The "central concern of Shintoism is purity" (Schwalbe 1970, 52). Therefore, according to "naturalist Shintoism" and the "folk religions" of Japan, *Heil* is a state of purity (Triplett 2004, 153). Purification and purity have something to do with the communion with the divine. All existence is revived upon its return to its original place (Steffánsson 1993, 16). Purification is the "integration of human life into the life-giving power of the deity" (Kitagawa and Ludwig 1984, 1638).[10] Further, purity forms the foundations of Japanese ethics, because it is equated with "good" (Matsumoto 1972, 15).

---

10. Compare with Nomura's explanations on the etymology of *kegare* (穢れ, 汚れ) and *tsumi* (罪) under *8.1.1.2 The fuzziness of the Japanese "sin"-concept.*

Japanese Understanding of Salvation

Kunio Yanagita combines the terms "life-force" (ケ or 気), "defilement" (ケガレ or 穢れ), and "ritual" (ハレ)[11] into a comprehensive cosmology correlated with terms of Greek cosmology. In attributing central importance to the concepts of purity and impurity, the mundane and the holy, and the ordinary and the extraordinary, Yanagita represents an entire generation of *kokugaku*(国学)-scientists, the Japanese term for "Japanologists":

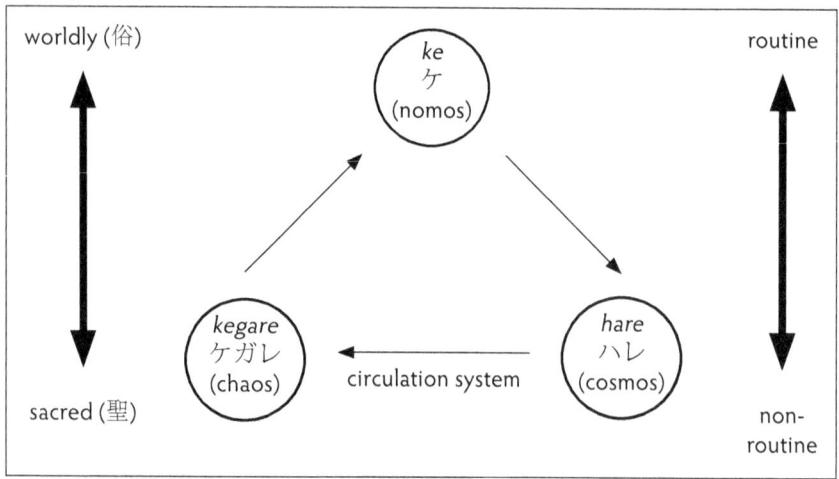

Figure 8.3 Japanese Cosmological Terms Correlated to Greek Cosmological Terms (according to Bak 2008, 4)

In the section on the experience of *Unheil*, I showed that the respective terms overlap. This is a common phenomenon. Huber writes that sin, "according to the faith of many peoples, implies an inner maculation, which brings about *Unheil*, if not rectified through divinatorily revealed rituals of purification, atonement, or reconciliation, or partly through confession and compensation" (Huber 1992, 585–586).

Huber mentions "rituals of purification, atonement, or reconciliation" in the same breath, because quite often they cannot be distinguished conventionally. In the area of impurity/sin the distinction was fairly complicated, but in the following area of rituals with *Heil* they are very confusing. The word-fields can be correlated in a similar way as those of impurity/sin:

---

11. *Hare* (ハレ) refers to "space, time, objects and phenomena outside the normal" (Oonuki-Tierney 1989, 140).

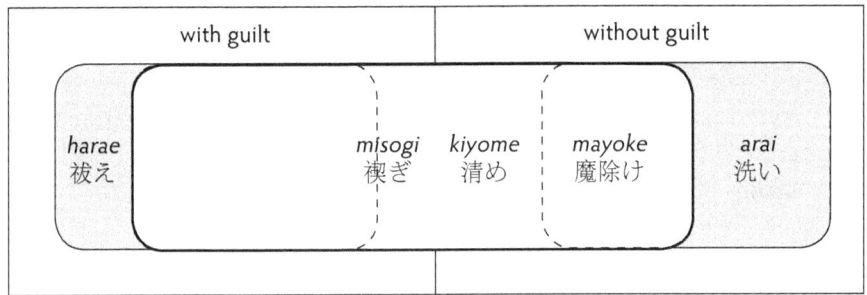

Figure 8.4 Japanese Terms for "Purification"

8.1.2.1 Differentiation between the rituals of *harae* (祓え) and *misogi* (禊ぎ)

The graph above shows that the terms *harae* (祓え) and *misogi* (禊ぎ) have much in common. In fact, in present-day Japanese, they are hardly distinguishable. The reason is that *tsumi* (罪) and *kegare* (穢れ) are almost equated due to the absence of the differencing criteria of guilt/non-guilt (Mitsuhashi 2007, 201).

Harae (祓え) is derived from the mythologeme in which *Susanoo* (素戔嗚尊 or 須佐之男命)[12] "is levied . . . with an atonement payment" in form of a material compensation for damage caused by his indecent pranks, here called *tsumi* (罪) (Naumann et al. 1988, 69–73). In this case "*tsumi* (罪) means a 'debt' to be settled. The *harae* (祓え) consisted in settling this debt by means of compensation . . . It brings about the **total** annihilation of the *tsumi* (罪)." Thus, *harae* (祓え) became a rite for which each household had to give an atonement offering called *mi-agamono* (身購物), literally a "thing as atonement for self" (Naumann et al. 1988, 168–171).

Misogi (禊ぎ), on the other side, "is derived from the myth of *Izanagi*'s (伊弉諾神 or 伊邪那岐命 or 伊耶那岐命) return from the land of the dead[13] when he washed off the *kegare* (穢れ), the defilement caused by contact with death" (Naumann et al. 1988, 69–73; Yamakage et al. 2006, 90).

After the eighth century, the discriminating difference between *harae* (祓え) and *misogi* (禊ぎ) fell into oblivion. Until then, the strict rule was applied, that punishment followed "sin" and that *harae* (祓え) or a *aganai* (購い), a "ransom payment" was necessary. Respectively, the unity of the terms

---

12. *Susanoo* (素戔嗚尊 or 須佐之男命) is a destructive deity of the Japanese mythology. For details see Naumann et al. 1988, 69–82.

13. For details see Naumann et al. 1988, 62.

tsumi (罪) and *batsu* (罰), that is, the punishment following *tsumi* (罪), also were gradually forgotten. Both Chinese characters, 罪 and 罰, used to be read *tsumi* (Mitsuhashi 2007, 168–169). In present-day Japan, the connection is remembered only in the fact that fines and prison sentences are sometimes considered to be *harae* (祓え). We have here, as Naumann et al. call it, "a subtle change of the guilt-concept (Naumann et al 1988, 168–171). That which could only be paid off by an atonement offering or a compensation, is today simply washed off by a purification rite. In modern Shintoist theology, *harae* (祓え) and *misogi* (禊ぎ) are connected to *misogi-harae* (禊祓え). One of the important incantations used during the rite of *misogi* (禊ぎ) is the *misogi-no ooharai* (禊ぎの大祓い) (Evans 2002, 3), also called *kiyoharae* (清祓). Particularly in the *misogi-no ooharai* (禊ぎの大祓い) it says:

Moromoro-no	*magagoto*	*tsumi kegare-o*	**harai-tamae**	**kiyome-tamae**	*to mousu koto-no yoshi-o*
もろもろの	凶言	罪穢れを	祓い給え	清め給え	と申しことの由を
All kinds of	calamity,	"sins," [and] defilement	atoned	[and] purified	may be

(according to Evans 2002, 3; similarly Itou 2001, 159)[14]

The difference between the two aspects of this rite is that *misogi* (禊ぎ), also called *kessai* (潔斎), which consists of a symbolic rinsing of the mouth and hands, is considered "introductory," the following *harae* (祓え), however, is considered as a "ban and purification" (Kitagawa and Ludwig 1984, 1638).

8.1.2.2 Atonement rituals/purification rituals: *harae* (祓え)

Ooharae (大祓), the "Great Purification"
Nelson called *harae* (祓え) "one of the central themes running through the core of Shinto practice" (Nelson 1996, 101). The so-called "Great Purification," *ooharae* (大祓), are conducted in shrines, one on 1 January, and the *natsugoshi-no harae* (夏越の祓) on 30 June.[15] They are understood as *shinji* (神事), rituals

---

14. For the difference between *misogi* (禊ぎ) and *kiyome* (清め) see below under *8.1.2.3 Differentiation of* misogi (禊ぎ) *and* kiyome (清め).

15. Besides the *natsugoshi-no harae* (夏越の祓), the "summer solstice-*harae* (祓え)," the *toshikoshi-no harae* (年越の祓), the "turn of the year-*harae* (祓え)" on 31 December was also offered in former times (Kouunsha Publisher 2008, 71).

at which *shirazu-ni shirazu-ni karada-ni tsumotta tsumi-ya kegare-o harai, sorekara, hantoshi-no aida-no wazawai-o nozoku* (知らずに知らずに体に積もった罪やけがれをはらい、それから、半年の間の災いを除く), "the 'sins'[16] unknowingly, yes, unknowingly accumulated in (or on) the body are washed off,[17] and thus calamities[18] warded off for half a year" (Ichijou 2008, 107). The *harae* (祓え) that washes off all "sins," including those committed unknowingly, is called the *issaijouju-no harae* (一切成就祓) (Mitsuhashi 2007, 193), the "purification fulfilling all."

In these rituals, there is (1) an aspect of purification in the sense of washing off or wiping off of *kegare* (穢れ) or *tsumi* (罪), as well as (2) an aspect of banning and expelling: In the first ritual, a *haraigushi* (祓い串) or *harainusa* (祓い幣), a "wand with white paper streamers" is "waved over the objects of area or people being purified" (Nelson 1996, 105; Yamakage et al. 2006, 101). In the second, *hitogata* (人型), literally "human form," "paper dolls . . . cut into the shape of a kimono" are shattered over the believers like confetti. Those that land on the head of the believers are "magnets" that magically pull those *tsumi* (罪), "sins" out of the body that can be removed more easily.[19] In the next step, the paper dolls are

> removed from the envelope to begin a circuitous route over the body . . . Before putting the doll back into the envelope, everyone exhales mightily upon it, allowing it to further absorb the impurities deep with the body's nether regions. Now filthy with contaminations of all sorts, the envelopes are collected quickly. (Nelson 1996, 106)

---

16. *Tsumi* (罪).
17. *Harai* (祓い).
18. *Wazawai* (災い).

19. "There is another means of purifying the body in the Shinto tradition, which involves purifying materials. We are told that in the ancient style of *misogi harai* (禊き祓い) (purification and cleansing), participants rolled up their sleeves with a cotton sash and held some plants called *torimono* (執物 or 取物) (meaning 'things to hold') to perform *misogi* (禊き). These plants were sedge plants, a hemp leaf, a miscanthus plant, or summer greens. It is probable that the body was stroked with *torimono* (執物 or 取物) to let the plant absorb all kinds of sin, faults, uncleanness, or *mono-no ke* (ものの気), meaning vengeful ghosts, specters, and low-energy vibrations. The plants were then thrown into the river." (Yamakage et al. 2006, 99)

During the incantation of a *norito* (祝詞) they are thrown into the water of the pond of the shrine. They are washed over a waterfall into a river where the "*kami* (神) of purification" . . . will claim them (Nelson 1996, 107–111).[20]

The *kami* (神) of purification or the "deity of the depth" is further specified in the recited *norito* (祝詞).[21] Here it is important to explain what a *norito* (祝詞) is: It is a figure of speech coming from the innermost and working *seiryoku* 精霊), *mana*-power, here referred to as *kotodama* (言霊), literally the "spirit of the word" (Nomura 2001, 285). It is believed that "language owes a kind of mystical spiritual power which controls good luck and bad luck, blessing and calamity."[22] According to this belief, a *magagoto* (凶言), literally a "bad luck word," that is, a curse, works bad luck through a *akuryou* (悪霊), an "evil spirit," whereas a *yogoto* (吉言), literally a "good luck word," that is, a "blessing," works good luck through a *zenrei* (善霊), a "good spirit" (Tsugita 2008, 15).

The *hadaka matsuri* (裸祭) at *Kounomiya* Shrine (国府宮神社)

Hadaka matsuri (裸祭) are held at various locations and with various traditions in January and February. The largest and oldest is the one held at the *Kounomiya* Shrine (国府宮神社) in Inazawa (Aichi), on 13 January 13, "where some 10,000 men in loin-cloths and wooden sandals, strive to touch the *shin otoko* (紳男), literally a "god-male," a naked man chosen to act as scapegoat, and divest the community of all evil and back luck" (Melton 2011, 359). This particular *hadaka matsuri* (裸祭) is another example of a purification ritual. Shared elements are the medium to be loaded with the undesired evil, the way of transferring it (e.g. through physical contact), and the sending away of the medium. The origin goes back to the year 767, when Emperor Shotoku (574–622) ordered all . . . temples across Japan to offer invocations to dispel plagues" (Melton 2011, 359). In its early history, the villagers used to seize any traveler passing by, without telling him anything about their plans, and unloaded all their evil into him and then chased him out of the community. After 1744, they discontinued this custom and instead selected a villager to play this role (Plutschow 1996, 18–19; Kankou Shiryou Hogo Zaidan 1976, 474–475).

The circumstances of the origin of this festival indicates what kind of evil was to be done away with. Emperor Shotoku ordered this ritual after an

---

20. Nelson gives a detailed report on the *natsugoshi-no harae* (夏越の祓え) on 30 June celebrated at the Suwa-Shrine (諏訪神社) (Nelson 1996, 101ff).

21. See the full text of the respective *norito* (祝詞) in Appendix 3.

22. *Kikkyoukafuku-o sayuu suru* (吉凶禍福を左右する). Therefore the words a Shinto priests utters as blessing (or curse) are also called *kamu-goto* or *kan-goto* (神言) (Holtom 1941, 378).

epidemic (Plutschow 1996, 18) as *akueki taisan-no tou* (悪疫退散の祈), "prayer for expelling epidemics" (Kankou Shiryou Hogo Zaidan 1976, 474–475). As epidemics are thought to be caused by either *ekiki* (疫鬼), "epidemic demons," or *yakubyougami* (疫病神),[23] "epidemic gods," the expelling takes on the form of an exorcism. One word for exorcism or dispossession is *na* (儺).[24] Its synonym is *tsuina* (追儺), "the driving away of the *na* (儺)."[25] For this reason, the *shin otoko* (紳男) is also called *naoinin* (儺負人), the "person carrying the *na* (儺)" (Nihon Minzoku Gakkai 1999, 71), and the respective ritual *natsuishinji* (難追神事), the "ritual of driving away *na* (難)" (Yamaguchi and Bates 2014, 460). Today, the object of the disposition has widened. "In an Edo-period (1600–1868) print, . . . the person is depicted with three candles tied to his hair. This conjures up a traditional image of someone who tries to curse someone or an entire community. Thus the villagers tried to get rid of all possible influences that might affect the village in the year to come" (Plutschow 1996, 18–19). Therefore, the ritual is today affiliated with the idea of *yaku* (厄), the "evil" of the *yakudoshi* (厄年), the "unlucky ages."[26] The *shin otoko* (紳男) has to be a *yakudoshi-no hito* (厄年の人), a "man of a critical climacteric age" (Yamaguchi and Bates 2014, 460). The men that strive to transfer their *yaku* (厄) are mostly 23- and 42-years-old which are also considered to be unlucky years for men (Fodor's 2014, Hadaka [Naked Festival]).

As in the "Great Purification," the evil is transferred by physical contact. The basic idea of the *hadaka matsuri* (裸祭) at the *Kounomiya* Shrine (国府宮神社) is "that the *shin otoko* (紳男) around whom the ritual is built has the power to receive and carry away the evil of all the men who make contact with him." The men try to touch him "in order to pass to him their sins and bad luck" (Melton 2011, 359). They *furete yaku-o otosou-to momiau* (触れて厄

---

23. Because these "evils" are caused by demons and gods and not by humans they are also called *amatsutsumi* (天津罪), "sins committed in heaven," which Takikawa considers a synonym of *na* (儺) (Takikawa 1984, 312).

24. The character *na* (儺) is used in the following ways: The *daina* (大儺), the "Great *na* (儺)," also called *dainakou* or *daina-no kimi* (大儺公), the "*daina* (大儺) divine ruler," is the *housoushi* (方相氏), an exorcist with a yellow, four-eyed mask, who plays the main role in the ritual of *tsuina* (追儺), "the driving away of the *na* (儺)." The children bustling about him are called the *shouna* (小儺), the "small *na* (儺)," also called *shounakou* or *shouna-no kimi* (小儺公), the "*shouna* (小儺) divine ruler." The soy beans thrown at the demons in order to drive them away at the event of *setsubun* (節分) (see under *8.1.2.6 Apotropaic rituals*: mayoke, 魔除け) are called *namame* (儺豆), "*na* (儺)-soy beans" (Shinmura 1995). Apotropaic rituals and purification rituals are closely related and can, at times, hardly be distinguished.

25. It is a common feature of animistic thinking that the evil to be driven away and the ritual of driving it away are not always clearly distinguished.

26. See under *6.1.2.1 Heil as knowledge about the future, protection, and harmony*.

を落とそうともみあう), "jostle to touch him and transfer their *yaku* (厄)" (Yamaguchi and Bates 2014, 460).

The *shin otoko* (紳男) "has to run, tumble, and crawl to the other side of the sea of men . . . They in turn are all out to chase him, jump on him, and pummel him in their frantic attempts to touch him, so as to transfer onto him the evils of their community and draw from him some luck for the coming year" (Roy 2005, 302). Thus the *naoinin* (儺負人) becomes a *nuhi* or *dohi* (奴婢), a "servant" or "slave" who carries on his shoulders the *haraeyareru na* (祓えやられる儺), the "*na* (儺) to be taken away through purification" (Hagihara 2004, 31).

This brings up the question as to how the evil is ultimately done away with. There are two prominent, converging ideas: One is the idea affiliated with purity, the other with the concept of the scapegoat:

- The concept of purity is taken up in the preparatory "lengthy purification process that includes shaving all of his body hair" (Melton 2011, 359).[27] After being touched, the *naoinin* (儺負人) "must carry a big load of mud in the form of a *kagamimochi* (鏡餅)-rice cake on his back, indicating the weight of the evil and misfortune he has accumulated" (Plutschow 1996, 18; Kankou Shiryou Hogo Zaidan 1976, 474–475). The fact that it is made of mud could indicate the impurity, which is later driven out of him by Shinto priests (Yamaguchi and Bates 2014, 460).

- The second concept is that of the scapegoat. Hori talks about a *hyuuman sukeepugooto* (ヒューマン・スケープゴート) (Takikawa 1984, 312), a "human scapegoat." In ancient times, the villagers would chase the *shin otoko* (紳男) out of the community (Plutschow 1996, 18). Today this is reduced to symbolism (Roy 2005, 302).

---

27. The *Nihon Minzoku Gakkai* (日本民族学会, The Folklore Society of Japan) explains: That evil and bad luck is transferred to the *naoinin* (儺負人) is only the interpretation of the Shrine. But the power of the naked man that actually partakes in the ritual goes way beyond the official interpretation. Because of that the *naoinin* (儺負人) has to shave and get naked for his own protection, also has to be protected from four sides by *kamimamori* (神守り), literally "god-protectors," so he can safely go through the midst of the naked males with their *sakki* (殺気), their "drive to kill." The violence is controlled and dramatized (Nihon Minzoku Gakkai 1999; 71), however, the festivals often lead to stampedes and "regularly result in serious injury to participants" (Fodor's 2014: Hadaka (Naked Festival)).

Joya-no kane (除夜の鐘), the "Bell on New Year's Eve"
The Buddhist custom of *joya-no kane* (除夜の鐘) shows again that apotropaic rites and purification rites are very similar. In the late evening of *Oomisoka* (大晦日), New Year's Eve, 108 chimes of the Buddhist temple bell are to drive away 108 *bonnou* (煩悩), "literally nuisances and distresses," the Buddhist technical term for "worldly desires." The declared objective is that *hito-no kokoro-ni aru bonnou-o harau* (人の心にある煩悩を祓う), that "the worldly desires in the heart of man are driven away" (便利・わかりやすい冠婚葬祭マナー＆ビジネス知識 (*benri, wakariyasui kankonsousai manaa & bijinesu chishiki*), n.d.). "Driving away" is here expressed with *harau* (祓う), "purify." That *harau* (祓う) is understood as driving away can also be seen from other words and phrases used in this context: *nozokisaru* (除き去る), literally "removing and driving away" of worldly desires, so that man gets a *sappari shita kimochi* (さっぱりした気持ち), a "cheerful feeling," and *jibun-no hontou-no kokoro-o torimodosu* (自分の本当の心を取り戻す), "regains his true heart" (Matsunaga 2008, 229–230).

Death as purification
It seems that after death, there is also something like *harae* (祓え). The dead that cannot become Buddhas gather at the River *Sanzu* (三途河) which marks the border between this and the yonder world. Then they cross it on *jigoku-kara mukae-no fune* (地獄から迎えの船), the "courtesy ship from hell." On the other side they are undressed by *Datsueba* (奪衣婆 or 脱衣婆), a female demon. *Ken-e-ou* (懸衣翁), another female demon, then hangs their clothes on the tree *Eryouju* (衣領樹).[28] Tobe calls these demons *onibaba* (鬼婆), "evil old witch hags." This process can be understood in a positive way as *mouja-no tsumi-ya kegare-o haraiotoshi* (亡者の罪や穢れを祓い落とし), as "atoning removal of 'sin' and 'defilement' of the dead" (Tobe 2007, 179–180).

8.1.2.3 Differentiation of *misogi* (禊ぎ) and *kiyome* (清め)
In the same way in which *harae* (祓え) and *misogi* (禊ぎ) cannot be clearly distinguished, so the purification rituals *misogi* (禊ぎ) and *kiyome* (清め) overlap. One difference between the two can be seen when the category "guilt" is applied, which is alien to Japanese thought. When applying this category, *kiyome* (清め) covers the area of purification from *kegare* (穢れ) without guilt.

---

28. The weight of the sins can be read from the way the clothes hang down from the tree (Ichijou 2009, 243).

8.1.2.4 Purification rituals: *misogi* (禊ぎ)

Misogi (禊ぎ) is also a central rite of Shintoism (Yamakage et al. 2006, 89). *Misogi* (禊ぎ) originally means *misogi* (身削ぎ), "to scrape (削ぐ) the body (身)" and thus remove the impurity. Later, *misusugi* (身滌ぎ or 身濯ぎ), "rinsing of the body" was used (Mitsuhashi 2007, 203). The objective is not only purity of the body but also of the heart ("*Genjimonogatari Daijiten*" *Henshuu Iinkai* (『源氏物語大辞典』編集委員会), the board of editor of the *Genji-Monogatari*-Encyclopaedia 2008, 194) and of community: "*Misogi* (禊ぎ) aims to restore the *wa* (和) of the community"[29] (Hirosachiya et al. 1993, 47). The best phrase to describe the objective of *misogi* (禊ぎ) is *semei seichoku* (清明正直), "clean, bright, right, and straight." "The words seem simple, but together they form the most important first principles for human life, out of which all else that is of value emerges." *Seimei* (清明) means "a clean and happy attitude of inner mind, that is, without impurity together with a bright, happy or clear mind." *Seichoku* (正直) means "right action or behavior as well as the social aspect of being right (that is, not committing any sin, crime, or offense), and behaving with honesty, openness, and frankness toward others" (Yamakage et al. 2006, 88). Body and heart belong together and are both important:

> *Misogi* (禊ぎ) is not simply a matter of washing and cleansing the body. When the physical body is made clean by water, our heart and mind are purified at the same time. The act of washing our hands before worshipping at a shrine is about more than the magical cleansing power of water. We also make a distinction within ourselves between the secular and the sacred by that act, and thus we change our attitude and our mindset. In so doing, we wash away uncleanliness. We purify our heart and mind so that we may connect with the spirt of *kami* (神) with a heart and mind that is clean, bright, right, and straight. This is the most important goal of *misogi* (禊ぎ). (Yamakage et al. 2006, 94–95)

It is interesting that the water basins for purification sometimes bear the inscription *shinsen* (心洗), "washing of the heart." Steffánsson shows the connection between purification and the desire for personal integrity:

> At all Shinto shrines there are places of purification, and the ritual purification gives purity to body and soul which leads to

---

29. For "community," Hirosachiya uses *kyoudoutai* (共同体), literally "common (共同) body (体)."

honesty. A key concept in Japanese ethics is *shoujiki* (正直)[30] . . . Through purification the connection to the divine is restored, and all existence is revived by being taken back to its original plane and source. (Steffánsson 1993, 16)

8.1.2.5 Purification rituals: *kiyome* (清め)

The notion that calamities can be warded off by purification is alive down to the present. This can be seen from the multitude of car owners who bring their car to a shrine on New Year's Day to have it purified from the evil accumulated during one year in order to avoid accidents (Oonuki-Tierney 1984, 72). "Companies have their technically highly developed factories purified by Shinto priests in order to avoid accidents" (Takenaka 1972, 83). Oonuki-Tierney interprets these rituals as "microcosms of rural Japan," as rural magic wrapped in commerce (Oonuki-Tierney 1984, 144).

Fire, water (von Siebold 2001, 96), wind (Oonuki-Tierney 1984, 37), and salt[31] are considered to have purifying power, a belief connected with the belief in nature's power (Abe 2004, 133). Talismans, other cultic objects, and sometimes even familiar tools (Kitano 2007, 2) are not simply thrown away (defilement), but ritually burnt (purification) at a shrine. This belief is even present in secular sayings such as *mizu-ni nagasu* (水に流す), "wash away into water," "meaning to forget or forgive one's [own] as well as other's misfortunes and misconduct" (Higashibaba 2001, 108). This phrase is an expression for "forgiving" and shows the power of water.

Some examples for the purifying power of salt:

- The *sumou*(相撲)-ring is purified before the athletes enter it. It must be pure so that the contest can be used as oracle (Schwalbe 1970, 43).[32]
- Besides being offered the *chouzu-no gi* (手水の義), the "ritual of [pouring] water over hands" upon their arrival at the house of mourning after the ceremony at the crematory, the mourners are sprinkled with salt for purification (Petroschkat 2008, 14; Hoffmann

---

30. 正直 can be read *seichoku* and *shoujiki*.

31. "Seawater was considered to be especially efficacious, and if it was not available, salt could serve as substitute" (Köck 2015, 242).

32. *Sumou*(相撲)-fighting was originally used as oracle ritual. Stimac, however, holds that is was used for appeasing the gods and for bringing fertility to the fields (2004, 181).

1998, 33). The hosts sprinkle a pinch of salt over each chest, shoulder, and shoes (Kondou 2008, 107).

- *Morishio* (盛り塩), small heaps of salt at the entrance of private houses, restaurants and particularly bars and "massage-saloons" (houses "where pleasure can be bought") also ward off defilement.

8.1.2.6 Apotropaic rituals: *mayoke* (魔除け)

The usage of salt for purification particularly in connection with funerals shows how closely purification rituals are connected with apotropaic rituals. When Yamakage et al. call *misogi* (禊ぎ) a way of "breaking of contact with unclean spirits" (2006, 89), they blur the lines between purification rites and apotropaic rites. It is only for the sake of classification that I hold on to the differentiation of *misogi* (禊ぎ) and *mayoke* (魔除け).

There are many rituals and customs that are to ward off the influence of evil spiritual beings. So-called "wild-gods" need to be "detained" in a *kamidana* (神棚),[33] the Shintoist house altar, to keep them from causing calamities (Stucki 1978, 105). Stucki reports about Japanese builders that out of fear of a vengeful territorial deity would not start with the construction unless it would be appeased (Stucki 1978, 93). Demons can also endanger the building process and houses. In order to ward them off it is important to build and furnish houses according to the geomantic rules derived from the Chinese *feng shui* (classical: 風水; simplified: 风水) (Hiebert et al. 1999, 139). Experts, mostly Shinto priests or *onmyoushi* (陰陽師), practitioners of the *onmyoudou* (陰陽道), provide information concerning the *omote kimon* (表鬼門), "front entrance" for (evil) powers, and the *ura kimon* (裏鬼門), the "back entrance" for demons. The "gate for demons" faces northeast. This explains why Buddhist temples are often found in the northeastern areas of cities; they are to ward off evil (Chamberlain 1990, 28). The north is generally considered to be the direction from which calamities come. Therefore, it is not advisable to sleep with one's head facing north. In order to protect oneself from evil spirits the *kimon* (鬼門), the "demon-gates" must be kept clean. The interior is also set up according to geomantic criteria. Yellow things on walls facing west promise prosperity, because yellow stands for gold and therefore prosperity. Walls facing north are best decorated with white things, because white stands for purity

---

33. According to Gantemby, the word *kamidana* (神棚) is not an original Japanese word, but the direct translation of the English *god-shelf* used by cultural outsiders for describing the board suspended from the ceiling of the living room where people keep objects of veneration (Miller 1993, 266).

which wards off the evil coming from the north. Spells and the *nanten*(ナンテン)-bush can also ward off calamities.³⁴

Many customs are concerned with caution against demons. Others explicitly drive them away. The most important of the exorcism festivals is *setsubun* (節分), literally "spring festival" on 3 or 4 February. With loud shouts: *fuku-wa uchi, oni-wa soto* (福は内、鬼は外) (Joseph 1982, 61), "Blessing inside – demons outside!" and with wild *mamemaki* (豆撒き), "throwing of beans" people dressed up as demons are driven away. The people dressed up as demons stand for the *ekiki* (疫鬼), "sickness demons" or s*akubyougami* (作病神), literally "gods making diseases," and generally for all calamities. Calamities, diseases, and evil are thought to be inside the beans. By throwing the beans out, the calamities must go, too (Katsumoto 1992, 92–93). The New Year custom of *hagoita* (羽子板), a kind of badminton played with wooden rackets was originally also an exorcism of "winter demons" that were driven away with powerful blows (Wendt 1970, 187).

Besides apotropaic rituals there are many "superstitious" actions and behaviors that are believed to ward off evil:

- When seeing a hearse one must quickly hide one's *oyayubi* (親指), literally "parent-fingers," "thumbs" within the fists, lest one's parents be claimed by an untimely death.
- For the same reason, it is not advisable to sleep with one's socks on.
- If one sees a crow three times one must spit on the ground in order to ward off calamities. If one hears it cry, someone has to die.
- When children lose their milk teeth, those from the upper jaw must be thrown away in a straight downward movement, those from the lower jaw in a straight upward movement. Thus malocclusion, a misalignment or incorrect relation between the teeth can be avoided.
- In order to make money stay longer in one's purse it is advisable to put the bills into the purse with the faces on the bills facing inward.

The importance of the *nanten*(ナンテン)-bush shows how magically powerful words are. Many apotropaic rituals and customs are explained by word games based on homophones. The word of the bush *nanten* (ナンテン) has various homophones: two of them are *nanten* (難点) "difficult issue," and *nanten* (難転), "turning of difficulties" (Lewis 1993, 84–85).

---

34. Other plants and fruits useful for warding off demons are the peach (Holtom 1941, 364), calamus, and mugwort. If demons touch them their bodies decay. They are set up at the entrance of houses (Munakata 1976, 30).

Other customs are:

- It is not advisable to have fruit trees in one's garden, because *mi-ga narisagaru* can mean "bearing fruit" (実が生り下がる) or "being unlucky" (身が成り下がる) (Lewis 1993, 84–85).
- It is advisable to dedicate girls on their 33rd day, because 33 can be read *sanzan* (三三), which also means "abundance in birth" (産山) (Lewis 1993, 107).
- On the Coming of Age Day young women donate five Yen, which is pronounced *goen* (五円). *Goen* (御縁) or *goensama* (御縁様) means lover. These young women want to secure a lover by donating five yen (Lewis 1993, 111).
- Several five-yen coins bring even more luck, because *juujuu goen* (重々御縁) means much luck. *Juujuu* (重々) means "piled up."
- Because 四, "four," and 死, "death" are both pronounced *shi*, many buildings have no fourth flour, the house number 4, parking lot number 4, or ticket window 4 in airports are omitted (Hielscher 1995, 10).
- The 42nd year of life is considered to be an unlucky year for men, because the digits 4 and 2 can also be read *shi ni* (四二), which also means *shi-ni* (死に), "toward death."
- Women that were born in the 42nd year of the Chinese Sexagenarian cycle are considered to be dangerous as prospective marriage partners, because they have a reputation of killing their husbands (Coulmas 2000, 319).
- For women, the 33rd year of life is considered an unlucky year, because *sanzan* (三三) cannot only stand for *sanzan* (産山), "abundance in birth," but also for *sanzan* (散々), "terrible" (Kamata 2000, 23).
- Giving a sick friend a potted flower is a sign of bad taste and rudeness, because *nezuku* (根付く), "striking roots" and *netsuku* (寝付く) "lying [on the sickbed]" are pronounced almost the same.
- Some people worship the frog, because *kaeru* means "frog" (蛙 or 帰る) and "return" *kaeru* (帰る). They hope that the money they spent returns (Horikoshi 1993, 45).
- For the same reason, some people put a little frog figure into their purse.

- Sea breams are frequent wedding presents, because the Japanese word for sea bream, *tai* (鯛), sounds like the last syllable of *medetai* (めでたい), "auspicious" (Hielscher 1995, 10).[35]
- The *kaimyou* (戒名), the Buddhist postmortem name, also belong into this category. The more money is spent – at times tremendous amounts of money – the more powerful the *kaimyou* (戒名), and, the safer the journey to the Pure Land.[36]
- Words are powerful and must be used cautiously. The Buddhist proverb *kuchi-wa wazawai-no kado* (口は災いの門), "the mouth is the gate of calamities," warns against careless speaking, because things said carelessly can "invite calamities (災い)" (Matsubara 1994, 115).

Because words are so powerful, the choice of names is a very serious matter.[37] *Seimeihandan* (姓名判断), literally "name-judgment," the determination of one's fate by one's name is practiced by more than half of the Japanese.[38] The stroke count of the first Chinese character of the family name and the stroke count of the Chinese character(s) of the given name determine the *jinseiun* (人生運), the "life-fate," the stroke count of the second Chinese character of the family name and the stroke count of the Chinese character(s) of the given name the *shakaiun* (社会運), the "social fate." The *seichouun* (成長運), the "growth-fate," and the *souun* (総運), the "general fate" can be evoked in a similar way (Lewis 1993, 161–162).

8.1.2.7 Hygiene and ritual purity

"Bathing is cult," Buruna says cryptically (1985, 25). He is right. "The rinsing of hands and gurgling before the shrine visits, even the daily hot bath, are originally cultic and are based on Shintoist purification rituals" (Schwalbe 1970, 43). Reader pointed to the close connection between everyday cleaning processes and religious purity (Reader 1995, 228). However, today Japanese are

---

35. According to McVeigh, the power of words is a divine power called *kotodama* (言霊), literally the "spirit of words," which is put in effect by vocalizing them (McVeigh 1992, 62).

36. According to Joseph, this Buddhist custom was fashioned according to the Christian custom of giving baptismal names. He claims that Buddhist priests interpreted baptismal names as magical names and used them in the form of postmortem names in order to raise income (Joseph n.d., 210–211). Goss and Klass explain that this custom was derived from the giving of new names on the occasion of the ordination of Buddhist priests (2005, 46).

37. As the Japanese fairy tale *Der lange Name* shows, the life expectancy rises with the length of the name (Hammitzsch 1969, 236–237).

38. 57% in investigation of Lewis (Lewis 1993, 163).

not always aware of the connection "between hygiene behavior and religious ritualization" (Bergler 2009, 25).

Thus, other ways of categorization must be found. One could be Oonuki-Tierney's "spatial categories," according to which Japanese hygiene practices are derived from the basic Japanese symbolic structure of spatial categories:

Table 8.2 Spatial Categories (according to Oonuki-Tierney 1984, 31)

inside	outside
above	below
purity	impurity

Not all Japanese concepts in the context of hygiene, however, can be captured with Oonuki-Tierney's spatial categories. Douglas's definition seems to be wider and can be adapted more appropriately. "Dirt . . . is never a unique, isolated event. Where there is dirt there is system. Dirt is the by-product of systematic ordering and classification of matter, in so far as ordering involves rejecting inappropriate elements" (Douglas 2002, 44). "In Japan, the 'normal' is equated with 'purity'" (Henshall in Vollmer 2011, 341).

8.2 Discussion with Christian Concepts

Summary: The close relationship between sin and impurity can be observed in the whole Bible. But the Bible differentiates between ritual, not self-inflicted impurity and moral, self-inflicted sin which defiles man. Therefore, the concepts of self-inflicted guilt, the concept of fundamental human depravity and the concept of the new creation of the heart as opposed to merely its purification need to be introduced into Japanese thinking.

8.2.1 The Experience of Unheil *under the Anthropological Aspect*

8.2.1.1 Biblical concepts of impurity and sin

Even though secularized people in the West have almost no awareness of the concept of purity, it still is a central theme in the Bible, particularly in the holiness code and laws of purity in Leviticus. Jesus did not abolish the laws, but rather radicalized them, by his critique of their superficial observation. The Old Testament concepts of ritual purity and impurity, the concepts of sickness and death, as well as the Exile as a form of punishment, point to a shame orientation, rather than a guilt orientation (Kraus in Green and Baker 2000, 157). Similar to the Japanese notions of purity, sin and impurity are closely linked, particularly in the New Testament (1 John 1:9).

The question is, how are they linked? Keil wrote about the Levitical laws of purity:

> The Mosaic Law calls certain physical states and circumstances as defiling for the citizens of the kingdom of God, in order to create an awareness of sin and its consequences. It also provides regulations for the removal and extinction of those impurities. (Keil 1858, 268)[39]

These regulations are not sanitary, but they are "religious regulations for the promotion of sanctification and the moral life in God," which signifies an interesting parallel to Japanese concepts. Keil explained:

> Sin opposes sanctification, and the life in God is abrogated through death, the consequence of sin. However, sin permeates the whole person, defiling not only the soul where it has its roots. Sin not only separates the soul from God, but also defiles the body as it permeates it and turns it into death dust. (Keil 1858, 277)

As for their phenomenology, Japanese and biblical concepts of purity and impurity hardly differ. However, as for the relationship of impurity with sin, Japanese and biblical concepts differ categorically. In the context of Japanese animism, impurity *is* sin. In the Bible, impurity is *a consequence* of sin. Klawans, who understands ritual and moral impurity as two "different impurity systems," acknowledges the connection between sin and impurity and explains that certain "grave sins" own a particularly strong "defiling force" (Klawans 2004, 21). Even though contact with certain things defiles a person according to the laws of purity, the contact itself is not sin. Klawans justifies this with the fact that the contact with defiling things is nowhere prohibited (2004, 24). However, in an alleviated form, there is a certain causal relationship:

> Even though ritual impurity is not sinful, a few biblical narratives view at least one form of ritual defilement as a punishment for moral shortcomings. Moses' sister Miriam was afflicted with "leprosy" when she spoke against her brother's Cushite wife

---

39. Keil categorizes them into impurity of death, impurity of leprosy, and impurity of various discharges (Keil 1858, 268–276).

(Num 12), and the Judean King Uzziah was similarly afflicted when he asserted priestly prerogatives (2 Chr 26:21). (Klawans 2004, 25)

In the case of "moral impurity" the relation between sin and defilement is clear. Certain deeds are so abominable that the biblical sources name them explicitly as defiling. Among others these are sexual sins, idolatry, and bloodshed. Moral impurity is the direct consequence of such sins (Klawans 2004, 26).[40]

8.2.1.2 Unclean spirits

This section would not be complete without reference to the "unclean spirits" frequently mentioned in the Gospels. In his detailed study, *Jesus and the Impurity of Spirits in the Synoptic Gospels* (2004), Wahlen gives various explanations as to why they are considered "unclean": (1) they are "unclean" because a person can be obsessed by them by committing unclean deeds; (2) possession by unclean spirits leads to "estrangement from God"; (3) the unclean spirits are considered unclean because they are a source of impurity; (4) impurity is demonized (Wahlen 2004, 3–7).

In this case, impurity is – at least partly – something that confronts humans from the outside, without their sinful involvement. Can this be juxtaposed with the Japanese animistic concept of sin/impurity? Drawing on Cyprian, Wahlen rejects this. Cyprian held that even though unclean spirits seduced humans to sin, it was the humans who sinned. "When the Holy Spirit begins dwelling in a person, wicked spirits depart. However, if the person's faith begins to fail and they begin to sin, the impure spirit returns" (Wahlen 2004, 66).

8.2.2 The Experience of Heil *under the Anthropological Aspect*

As I showed above, concepts of impurity, defilement, and purification are not alien to the Bible. Many references use sin and defilement, as well as forgiving and purification in parallel (Lev 12:6, 8; 14:19, 31; Job 33:9; Ps 51; Prov 20:9; Matt 15:18–20; Heb 1:3; 1 John 1:9). But it would certainly be wrong to ignore one essential difference between the animistic and the biblical understanding of

---

40. According to Oppenheimer and Levine, this is addressed particularly in the prophetic message of the Old Testament (1977, 52).

purity.⁴¹ The biblical concept of impurity is complemented by the more radical concept of "sin" as "rebellion against God." This is important for missiology in general and for the missiological encounter with Japanese animism in particular. Again, it is Shuusaku Endou's unparalleled keen eye that recognized the importance of the subject of "sin" for missiology. He discussed it in at least three of his works:

- The embittered suspended French missionary and apostate Durand in Shuusaku Endou's novel *Volcano* (*Kazan*, 火山) charges the Japanese pastor Satou, faithful to the Roman Catholic doctrine, that Christianity would never strike root in Japan because "the Japanese had no feeling for sin at all" (Endou 1959, 41). Later, he tries to lead a young believer away from the faith: "You don't really . . . believe in God, do you? . . . He who feels no guilt, cannot believe in God. And you Japanese, you don't feel any guilt, do you?" (Endou 1959, 127).
- On a similar note, the writer Kanou in Shuusaku Endou's *Scandal* says (*Sukyandaru*, スキャンダル), "Sadly enough, I have no idea what sin is, because I am irreligious" (Endou 2000, 13).
- In *Meer und Gift* (1984) (*The Sea and Poison, Umi-to Dokuyaku*, 海と毒薬), Shuusaku Endou also developed this thought, using criminal profiles of medical doctors who conducted vivisections on American prisoners of war during World War II. On one side, there is the main character of the novel, Jiro Suguro, who hopes that God exists, so that he can be delivered from the fate of his lack of conscience (1984, 70). On the other side is the conscienceless medical doctor Tsuyoshi Toda (1984, 92ff), who cannot feel any remorse over his abominable deeds and is shocked that everything leaves him cold. "Whether there is a God or not has long been all the same to me" (1984, 70) is his attitude toward God. By murdering American prisoners of war, he desperately seeks "anguish of mind and pangs of conscience" – and is disappointed because he does not find them (1984, 130; similar 141). "An awareness of guilt and pangs of conscience I absolutely do not feel" (1984, 139).

According to Shintoism and Buddhism, sin and defilement come from the outside and defile man. They are *mi-ni tomaru akuji* (身に泊まる悪事) (Hearn

---

41. The *Original Gospel Tabernacle* uncritically uses Japanese purification rituals like the *oomisogi* (大禊), *hiwatari* (火渡り), the walking on embers, and *takiabi* (滝浴び), "waterfall-bathing" for spiritual purification and for inurement (Mullins 1998, 124–125).

2015, Japanese Buddhist Proverbs), "evil things that adhere to the body." Man itself is considered good and evil is – even if considered to be inside – only a "worm" (Braithwaite 1999, 64). However, according to Christian doctrine, man *is* a sinner. Particularly in the encounter with Jewish purification rituals, Jesus said that man was not defiled from the outside, but by what comes from his heart (Matt 15:2ff).

This categorically different sin-concept calls for a categorically different salvation, as introduced in Psalm 51. The climax of Psalm 51 is verse 10: "Create in me a pure heart, O God, and renew a steadfast spirit within me." The old, sinful heart cannot be purified. A new heart of integrity must be "created." David deliberately uses בָּרָא, a root used (almost) exclusively for God's creative work.[42]

---

42. Exceptions are Josh 17:15, 17; 1 Sam 2:29; Ezek 21:24; 23:47, which possibly use a completely different root (Harris et al. 1981).

Part IV

The Dimensions of Salvation

9

The Animistic Focus on Salvation in this World

Summary: The central concept of Japanese religious sentiment is *gense riyaku* (現世利益), "this-worldly benefits." This concept is discussed controversially between Buddhism and Shintoism. The most popular representatives of this kind of religious sentiment are the "Seven Auspicious Deities," *Shichifukujin* (七福神). They provide people with prosperity and safety, fertility, interpersonal and psychological happiness, as well as cultural values.

Gense riyaku (現世利益) is an animistic concept:
- "The animistic concept of *Heil* is holistic and includes elements such as well-being, harmony, honor, longevity, prosperity, and power" (Wiher 2003, 295). These things are the central concern of *gense riyaku* (現世利益), "this-worldly benefits."
- The connection between *gense riyaku* (現世利益) and a magic worldview makes it an animistic concept. Ishii (石井進) and Iyanaga (彌永貞三) understand *gense riyaku* (現世利益) in the context of the religious-magical Japanese *shizen shuukyou* (自然宗教), "nature religion" (Ishii and Iyanaga 2002, 1831). Ono et al. call Shintoism explicitly a *gensechuushinshugi-no shuukyou* (現世中心主義の宗教), a "religion centering on this world" (Ono et al. 1985, 191). *Chuushin* (中心) means "central." This means that this material world is the center of Japanese religiosity. "According to Japanese sociologists, an important feature of Japanese folk religion is the

dominance of 'magical' rituals oriented to 'this-worldly benefits' (*gense riyaku,* 現世利益)" (Poewe 1994, 97).[1]
- Finally, the pragmatism of *gense riyaku* (現世利益) qualifies it as an animistic concept. Hajime Nakamura (中村元) "made it clear that what he calls Japanese 'this-worldliness' and a lack of interest in religious belief actually reflects a kind of critical empiricism and pragmatism" (Paul 2001, 131).

According to Hori, *gense riyaku* (現世利益) is the selection criterion by which the Japanese select those elements of foreign religions they want to assimilate. "The religious identity of the Japanese is this-worldly and emphasizes participation in traditional rituals over a transcendental faith" (Hoffmann 2007, 189). Shintoism "postulates . . . an almost absolute this-worldliness, because it doesn't know any otherworldly salvation and is, in this respect, not far away from the materialistic thinking of the West" (Schlieper 1997, 108). Kornicki and McMullen called *gense riyaku* (現世利益) one of the most significant themes of Japanese religiosity (1996, 273). However, it was the study *Practically Religious: Worldly Benefits and the Common Religion of Japan* by Reader and Tanabe that brought *gense riyaku* (現世利益) to international awareness as the central theme of Japanese religiosity.

9.1 An Outline of *Gense Riyaku* (現世利益), "This-Worldly Benefits"

9.1.1 Definition

> Our basic argument is that *gense riyaku* (現世利益) is a normative and central theme in the structure and framework of religion in Japan – sought through numerous ritual practices, symbolized by various religious objects such as talismans and amulets, and affirmed in doctrinal terms in various religious organizations as well as through textual traditions. (Reader and Tanabe 1998, 14)

Gense riyaku (現世利益) literally means "benefits (利益) in this (現) world (世)." The opposite of "this world" is *gose* (後世), the "world thereafter," or *raise* (来世), the "coming world."[2] The "coming world" does not mean the Christian

---

[1]. On the other side, faith in *gense riyaku* (現世利益) requires more than a magical worldview. Faith in the personal compassion and the power of personal deities is also important (Hall 1988, 542). In the *Soukagakkai* (創価学会), *gense riyaku* (現世利益) is connected with *kudoku* (功徳), a (divine) act of compassion (White 1970, 31).

[2]. *Gense* (現世) can also mean the material world.

"new heaven and a new earth" (Rev 21:1), but the world into which the dead proceed even today, the world that "comes" after death. *Gense riyaku* (現世利益) can be translated in many different ways. Reader and Tanabe suggest "this-worldly benefits," "practical benefits in this lifetime," or simply "practical benefits" (1998, 2). In *The Illustrated Encyclopedia of Zen Buddhism* (2002), Baroni defines: "'Worldly benefits' that may be gained in this life through the practice of Buddhism.[3] These benefits include long life, physical health, monetary wealth, safety in childbirth, and protection from various calamities" (Baroni 2002, 108). Other benefits are "delightful marriage" (Shillony 2004, 35), and, according to a survey of NHK, "spiritual balance ... necessary for the moral education and the stabilization of everyday life" (Katsumoto 1992, 39). Generally speaking, the benefits guarantee a "fruitful human life" (Reader and Tanabe 1998, 13–14). However, *gense riyaku* (現世利益) must not be confused with "materialistic benefits," because things as *anshin* (安心), "peace of mind," *shinkou* (信仰), "faith," and *kyuusai* (救済), "salvation" are also sought (Reader and Tanabe 1998, 16–17). Material and spiritual aspects cannot be separated. *Anshin* (安心) "cannot properly exist in normal terms without material substance" (1998, 19).

9.1.2 History

The subject of *gense riyaku* (現世利益) has a long and controversial history of mutual influence and accusation between Buddhism, Shintoism and Christianity. Probably due to Reader and Tanabe's contribution, it is today accepted as justified religious orientation. Hirata even attributes to their work that today *gense riyaku* (現世利益) is considered to be the "moral glue" which holds society together (Hirota 2000, 218).

But this has not always been the case. Particularly Buddhism used to criticize *gense riyaku* (現世利益) heavily. For example, Buddhist scholars held that "the Japanese folk religion" debased the Buddhist focus on spiritual benefits in a way "that material pleasures were included." Thus they condemned the so-called New Religions because of their focus on this-worldly benefits as *jakyou* (邪教), "wrong religion," *ruiji shuukyou* (類似宗教), "quasi-religion,"

---

3. Of course, the "practice of Buddhism" is not the only means. Most everything can be done to secure *gense riyaku* (現世利益): the observation of astrological laws (Shively and McCullough 1999, 541–542) or the "remembering" the dead, and "by carrying out practices that ensure that they will settle into buddhahood and become beneficial ancestors." If properly memorialized, the dead become "sources of blessings in this world," *gense riyaku* (現世利益) and offer protection (Ivy 1995, 150).

or *shinkou shuukyou* (新興宗教), "new fad religion" (Reader and Tanabe 1998, 3).[4] This reproach was, however, factually inaccurate. It was long before its encounter with Japanese religiosity that Buddhism was "immanentized" (Eisenstadt 1996, 235). Even before Buddhism reached Japan, its "preoccupation with the meaning of human existence in the phenomenal world" in China

> contributed to the shift in outlook from other-worldliness to this-worldly, in objective from individual salvation to universal salvation, in philosophy from extreme doctrines to synthesis, in methods of freedom from religious discipline and philosophical understanding to pietism and practical insight, and in authority from the clergy to the layman himself. (Wing-tsit Chan in Kitagawa 1987, 206)

This has something to do with the difference between Indian and Chinese thinking. Contrary to Indian thinking which is focused on the "other world," Chinese thinking is focused on "this world" (Fung 1983, 238). The same is true for Korea where Buddhist blessings were almost invariably understood as material blessings (Underwood 1994, 72).

In Japan, Buddhism influencing Shintoism took turns with Shintoism influencing Buddhism. When Buddhism entered Japan, it influenced Shintoism toward a stronger focus on the coming world. In the *Shasekishuu* (砂石集 or 沙石集), a *setsuwa* (説話)-collection, a collection of Buddhist narratives of the *Kamakura*-Era, the transformation of the *kami* (神), the Japanese "gods" under the influence of Buddhism can be observed. The *Shasekishuu* (砂石集 or 沙石集) portrays the *kami* (神) as deities "with a profound desire . . . to turn humans away from this lowly world, to take them away from seeking *gense riyaku* (現世利益), and this concern is accompanied by a marked insistence on the future life *gose* (後世) as the only thing of value" (Rotermund 1993, 276). Later, Confucianism awakened and strengthened the focus in Shintoism on this world which in turn influenced Buddhism. Judging by the books published,

---

4. The New New Religions are all syncretistic and draw from Christian influence. Some of them are even registered as Christian sects. "What they borrowed from Christianity . . . stems right from the center of the Christian *kerygma*" says Gensichen and means particularly kingdom theology and the universal priesthood (Gensichen 1985a, 15). Watanabe's (渡辺楳雄) article *Modern Japanese Religions: Their Success Explained* (1957) is a very good introduction into the *shinkou shuukyou* (新興宗教), the "new fad religions." In this article he names additional features such as (1) the fascination of a "mysterious" element, mostly a revelation; (2) the miracles; (3) the gullibility of uneducated masses; (4) greatly simplified doctrines; (5) a minimum of ceremonies; (6) a small financial burden; (7) a coordinated member recruitment; (8) the founder's personal attention in the life of the members; (9) the leaders' strong example (Watanabe 1957, 157–162).

the turning point from the focus on the coming world to the focus on this world was in the *Kanbun*-Era. Before that three-quarters of the books were of Buddhist content; thereafter, more books dealt with Confucianism and this world. Japanese Confucianists and scholars of the Japanese Classic attacked Buddhism for its other-worldliness. Some Buddhists open to reformation changed their traditional attitude (Nakamura 1998, 527), going back to the previous this-worldly orientation.

With the impoverishment of the people in the late *Tokugawa*-Era, this tendency grew stronger. Hur writes about *Edo* (江戸) (today Tokyo) of the late *Tokugawa*-Era, that is it was a "forlorn city" overwhelmed by epidemics (smallpox, measles, influenza, syphilis), fire, floods, storms, a high infant mortality (70%–75%), malnutrition (eye diseases, beriberi), food poisoning, limited access to the production of food, clothing, and shelter. "In their helplessness, the Edoites took refuge in prayer and threw themselves on the mercy of the deities. No doubt the world of the *kami* (神) and Buddhas was the most familiar source of hope and comfort. However, the prayer culture of Edoites in the late Tokugawa period was … quite distinct from the prayer culture of earlier periods." According to Hur there are two aspects that were different:

- (a) "There was a great concern for 'this-worldly benefits' (*gense riyaku*, 現世利益), which included even this-worldly solutions to other-worldly wishes." Because of their struggle with daily predicaments here and now, "compensation in the other world was less meaningful than it had been."

- (b) "Edoites of the late *Tokugawa* period were suspicious of the religious efficacy of traditional deities." This led to a remarkable increase in new deities (*Benzaiten,* 弁財天; *Kannon,* 観音; *Yakushi,* 薬師; *Fudou,* 不動; *Amida,* 阿弥陀; *Jizou,* 地蔵; *Inari,* 稲荷) in the hope of finding answers to newly felt needs, e.g. cure of diseases. "These new deities were not immune to the fate of many older deities, however … Edoites were quick to take up the worship of new deities and just as quick as to discard them." As long as they served their purpose (alleviation of misfortune and suffering and the acquisition of good luck, health, and prosperity) they were worshipped.

Bakufu leaders and Confucian intellectuals were highly critical of this tendency, and they accused Buddhism of creating values premised on "vanity" and desires premised on "fantasy." Armed with Confucian ethics, government officials castigated the *gense riyaku* (現世利益) form of Edo Buddhism as a stumbling block to rationalistic efforts to improve conditions in this world. Despite their scorn, *gense riyaku* (現世利益) remained unabated. (Hur 2000, 202–204)

"In present-day Japan, all the big Buddhist schools promise health, success in business, and happy married life" (Shillony 2004, 35). The objection that prayer for this-worldly benefits and success in business was not true religion[5] is thus refuted by Jitsudou Matsumoto (松本実道):[6]

> Religion absolutely has to be something for the living human beings. Religion itself, along with showing us the existence of the gods and buddhas, provides the spiritual foundations for human life, releases us from its sufferings and pains, gives rise to a joyful life, and teaches us an awareness of the way toward respecting the true nature of human beings. In the end, seeking the Pure Land and praying for its realization are nothing if not a this-worldly activity: after all, if there are no this-worldly benefits there can be no salvation. Is not, after all, seeking entry into the Pure Land a request for an extension of this-worldly benefits? Since present and future are inseparable, to disregard the present is in effect to disregard the future. (Matsumoto in Reader and Tanabe 1998, 23)

In present-day Japanese Buddhism there are the "New Religions," *Shinshuukyou* (新宗教), founded in the late nineteenth and early twentieth century, and the so-called "New New Religions," *Shinshuukyou* (新新宗教), founded after World War II. They differ in the horizon of their propagated salvation. Shimazono write about the *Shinshuukyou* (新宗教):

> An extremely large number of Japanese new religions do not preach reliance on the power of God, the power of Buddha, the power in this or that holy person, but preach that happiness cannot be attained unless one changes one's own mental attitude and manner or daily life. . . . This-worldly orientation . . . is linked with

---

5. *Tadashii shuukyou de-wa nai* (正しい宗教ではない).

6. In 1974, Jitsudou Matsumoto was the 69th Head priest of the Buddhist *Houzanji*-Temple (宝山寺) near Osaka. He specialized in this-worldly benefits. The following quote is from his book *Kankiten shinkou-e-no michi* (歓喜天信仰への道), "The Road to Faith in Kankiten." *Kankiten* (歓喜天) is also known as *Kangiten* (歓喜天), *Kangiten-sama* (歓喜天様), *Shouten* (聖天), or *Daishou-Kangiten* (大聖歓喜天), and in English as *Deva of Bliss*. *Kanki* (歓喜) means "bliss," *Shou* (聖) "holy" in the sense of "pure."

an immanentist view of the divine that recognizes the divinity of the human being and recognizes divinity in existence in the present world in general. These characteristics were lacking in traditional religions with their strong tendency to be affirmative with regard to the other world and negative toward this world. It is easy to understand why such this-worldly orientation and an immanentist view of the divine are attractive to people living in competitive society where industrialization and urbanization have advanced and changes are extreme. (Shimazono in Hoffmann 2007, 42)[7]

Main protagonists of the "New New Religions," *Shinshinshuukyou* (新新宗教), are *Aum-Shinrikyou* (オウム真理教), infamous after the 1995 Tokyo subway sarin attack, and the *Koufuku-no Kagaku* (幸福の科学), the *Research Institute for Human Happiness* (Schrimpf 2008, 2).[8] They, on the contrary, emphasize salvation on the other world, similar to medieval Buddhism (Hoffmann 2007, 42).[9] It seems that the overwhelming problems in this world can trigger two antithetical reactions: acceptance of these problems (Edoites of the late *Tokugawa*-Era) and prayer for this-worldly salvation; or denial and suppression of these problems and escape into a salvation that is sought in the other-world.

9.2 The "Seven Auspicious Deities" *Shichifukujin* (七福神)

Under the headline *fuku-no kami-no shinkou* (福の神の信仰), "faith of the gods of blessing,"[10] Miyata (宮田登) asks what "blessing" is. He understands "blessing" basically as *gense riyaku* (現世利益), divided in *gense riyaku* (現世利益) that averts evil, and *gense riyaku* (現世利益) that secures good (Miyata 1998, 60). The most popular symbols of *gense riyaku* (現世利益) are probably

---

7. Here must have been a change in the orientation of the *Shinshuukyou* (新宗教). In the beginning of the 20th century, that is shortly after their formation, Mori (森作太郎) judged that particularly the faith in the existence of the afterlife was their foundation: *shigo-no seizon-o kiso-to suru shinshuukyou* (死後の生存を基礎とする新宗教), "the New Religions that make the afterlife their foundation (Mori n.d., 143ff).

8. On the life of its founder Ryouhou Ookawa (大川隆法), see Schrimpf (2008).

9. At the beginning of the 20th century, Kagawa (賀川豊彦) attributed the admiration of the medieval Japanese for Christianity to its other-worldly orientation. Because of the persistent threat of natural calamities, the tragic side of life was blindingly illuminated (Kagawa 2007, 9–10).

10. *Shichifukujin* (七福神) is usually translated by "Seven Auspicious Deities," the "Auspicious" obscuring the connection to "blessing" in the literal translation "*Seven Deities of Blessing*."

the "Seven Auspicious Deities," the *Shichifukujin* (七福神). Miyata calls them the "most central"[11] deities (62). *Gense riyaku* (現世利益) and *fuku* (福), "blessing," can be equated. *Shichi* (七) means "seven." *Jin* (神) means the deities that bring *fuku* (福), "happiness" in the widest sense. Their names are *Ebisu* (恵比寿), *Daikokuten* (大黒天), *Benzaiten* (弁財天), *Bishamonten* (毘沙門天), *Juroujin* (寿老人), *Fukurokuju* (福禄寿), and *Hotei Oshou* (布袋和尚) (62). As to their level of familiarity and popularity, Ashkenazi associates the "Seven Auspicious Deities" with the Santa Claus in Western countries, particularly as they are portrayed in many department stores (Ashkenazi 1993, 166).

The "Seven Auspicious Deities" on board their *takarabune* (宝船), the "treasure-ship," enter port on New Year's Eve. On the night of 2 January, it is advisable to put a picture of them under one's pillow. Anyone who has pleasant dreams during that night will have luck in the New Year (Matson 2004, 165). Those who have nightmares must throw the picture in to a river so that the evil of the past year may not harm them (Shintani 2006, 28). According to another narration, the "Merry Seven" meet once a year to chat about the "old days" and dine together. Then they turn to "business," that is the arrangement of marriages in the coming year. They have many bundles of white and red silk which represent the fate of those to get married. White stands for males, red for females. The "Seven Auspicious Deities" seek the threads of silk and tie them together so they fit perfectly. As long as they do their "job" seriously and diligently, the marriages are going to be happy. However, after a while they become lazy and frolic about. That is the reason why so many marriages are without luck (Griffis 2008, 86–87).

Following Gerhart, the *Shichifukujin* (七福神) can be grouped according to their religious-historical background:

Table 9.1 The "Seven Auspicious Deities" Grouped by Religious-Historical Background (according to Gerhart 1999, 175)

Buddhism	Hinduism	Taoism	Shintoism
Hotei Oshou (布袋和尚)[12]	Benzaiten (弁財天)	Juroujin (寿老人)	Daikokuten (大黒天)
Bishamonten (毘沙門天)		Fukurokuju (福禄寿)	Ebisu (恵比寿)

---

11. *Ichiban chuushinteki* (一番中心的).

12. Miyata says that *Hotei Oshou* (布袋和尚) also shows strong Taoist influence (Miyata 1998, 33).

Or they can be grouped according to their countries of origin, which seems better:

Table 9.2 The "Seven Auspicious Deities" Grouped by Countries of Origin (according to Matson 2004, 165)

India	China	Japan
Daikokuten (大黒天)	*Hotei Oshou* (布袋和尚)	*Ebisu* (恵比寿)
Bishamonten (毘沙門天)	*Juroujin* (寿老人)	
Benzaiten (弁財天)	*Fukurokuju* (福禄寿)	

Miyata writes about the meaning of the number "7" that besides the numbers "1," "3," and "5," is one of the most important. It is considered to be particularly *sei-naru* (聖なる), "holy." The number "7" is used in the following traditions:

- the *oshichiya* (お七夜),[13] the seventh night after birth;
- the *shonanoka* (初七日),[14] the seventh day after death;
- the *shichidaiji* (七大寺), the seven "great temples" in Nara (since the *Heian* Era), an institution important for prosperity;[15]
- the *shichikousan* (七高山), the seven "high mountains";[16]
- the *shichikanon* (七観音), the seven *Kannon* Statues;[17]

---

13. A festivity of naming and prayer for health. According to a Japanese proverb *shichiya-no uchi-no kaze-wa isshou tsuku* (七夜の内の風邪は一生つく), a cold caught before the *oshichiya* (お七夜) stays for life.

14. A Buddhist celebration on the seventh day after death.

15. These are the *Toudaiji* (東大寺), the *Koufukuji* (興福寺), the *Saidaiji* (西大寺), the *Gagouji* (元興寺), the *Daianji* (大安寺), the *Yakushiji* (薬師寺), and the *Houryouji* (法隆寺).

16. These are *Mt Hieizan* (比叡山) and *Mt Hirasan* (比良山) in Shiga-Prefecture, *Mt Ibukiyama* (伊吹山) in Gifu-Prefecture, *Mt Adagosan* (愛宕山) in the Kyoto-District, *Mt Shinbousan* (神峰山) in the Osaka-District, *Mt Kinbusan* (金峰山) and *Mt Katsuragisan* (葛城山) in Nara-Prefecture. *Mt Katsuragisan* (葛城山) in Nara-Prefecture is sometimes substituted by *Mt Kouyasan* (高野山) in Wakayama-Prefecture.

17. These are the *Kannon* at the *Gyouganji* (行願寺) in Kyoto's *Koudou* (革堂)-District, the *Kannon* at the *Seiwain* (河崎清和院) in Kawasaki, *Kannouji* (感応寺), the *Kannon* at the *Kichidenji* (吉田寺), the *Kannon* at the *Kiyomizudera* (清水寺), the *Kannon* at the *Rokuharamizuji* (六波羅蜜寺), the *Kannon* at the *Rokkakudou* (六角堂), and the *Kannon* at the *Rengeouin* (蓮花王院).

- the Buddhist *shichinansokumetsu* (七難即滅), the "seven calamities,"[18] which some consider a direct cause for the "7" in the "Seven Auspicious Deities" (Miyata 1998, 63).

The date of the origin of the *Shichifukujin* (七福神) is uncertain. They probably emerged in the late *Muromachi*-Era or the early *Edo*-Era (Miyata 1998, 61; Chaudhuri 2003, 27). They are fashioned along Chinese lines and symbolize the seven virtues of Confucius: "longevity, luck, popularity, candor, kindness, dignity, and magnanimity" (Chozanshi et al. 2006, 206). The main reason for their emergence was human strife for material goods. In the era in which they emerged there was a sutra that said that a person would without fail get great riches and become lucky, if on the first three days of every month they cleansed their bodies, wore clean clothes, and acclaimed the name of *Vaisravanas*[19] in a North-Western direction (Chaudhuri 2003, 27).

The origin, the characteristics, and the blessing of the *Shichifukujin* (七福神) clearly depict how Japanese understand *gense riyaku* (現世利益). Therefore, I would like to introduce them.

9.2.1 Ebisu *(*恵比寿*)*

Ebisu (恵比寿),[20] also called *Ebisuten* (恵比寿天) is probably the most popular of the "Seven Auspicious Deities" (Seiyaku.com 2006). He probably entered Japan as a tribal god of immigrating fishers from the South Pacific (Volker 1975, 158). Even though his name is not completely explored (Guichard-Anguis 1995, 70), it indicates this origin. According to Jacob Raz, it means "*Ainu*,[21] stranger, foreigner, savage, somebody from a far-off country." "Therefore, *Ebisu* is a god that comes from a far-off country and brings good luck and happiness" (Baptandier 2001, 143).

---

18. The seven calamities are *taika* (大火), "conflagration," *taisui* 大水), "floods," *taifuu* (大風), "typhoon," *tentai-no ihen* (天体の異変), "change in the planets," *heika* (兵火), "conflagration due to war," *touzoku* (盗賊), "robbery and theft," and *ekibyou* (疫病), "epidemics" (Miyata 1998, 63).

19. *Vaisravanas* is venerated in Japan as *Bishamonten* (毘沙門天), one of the "Seven Auspicious Deities."

20. These Chinese characters can also be read *Emishi* (Guichard-Anguis 1995, 70).

21. Griffis also holds that *Ebisu* (恵比寿) is an ancient word meaning "Ainu" (Griffis 2006, 15).

Japanese mythology explains his origin in a different way. Here he is identified with *Sukunabikona-no kami* (少名毘古那神),[22] *Kotoshironushi-no-kami*[23] and *Hiruko* (蛭子) (Iwao and Iyanaga 2002, 489; Ashkenazi 2003, 142; Whelan 1996, 85). *Hiruko* (蛭子) was born as the first child of *Izanami* (伊弉冉 or 伊邪那美 or 伊耶那美 or 伊弉弥) and *Izanagi* (伊弉諾神 or 伊邪那岐命 or 伊耶那岐命).[24] He was born in the form of jellyfish. Being the firstborn made him the older brother of the sun goddess *Amaterasu-Oomikami* (天照大御神), the ruler-of-the-moon *Tsukiyomi-no-Mikoto* (月読尊), and the storm-god *Susanoo-no-Mikoto* (素戔嗚尊 or 須佐之男命). His name means "leech-child." When he was born, his parents did not approve of his form (Turner and Coulter 2001, 220). As a leech without limbs (Ooiwa et al. 2001, 37) he was not able to stand by himself, even at the age of three (Guichard-Anguis 1995, 70), so his parents abandoned him on a raft.[25] His raft stranded on the beach of Ebisu (恵比寿). That is why he was called *Ebisu* (恵比寿) (Turner and Coulter 2001, 220).

In the Japanese pantheon, *Ebisu* (恵比寿) holds the office of a *rusugami* (留守神), a "house-sitting deity." In October, when the gods meet for the *kami-ai-sai* (神会い際), their annual meeting at *Ookuninushi-no-Mikoto*'s (大国主命) palace in *Izumo* (出雲),[26] *Ebisu* (恵比寿) stays home because he is deaf – or just pretends to be deaf (Ashkenazi 2003, 142).

---

22. *Sukunabikona-no kami* (少名毘古那神) was a dwarf-deity, one of the 1,000 sons of *Kamimusubi-no-kami* (神皇産霊神 or 神産巣日神) (according to the *Kojiki*, 古事記), or of *Takamimusubi-no-kami* (高御産巣日神 or 高皇産霊神) (according to the *Nihonshoki*, 日本書紀). In cooperation with *Ookuninushi* (大国主) *Sukunabikona-no kami* (少名毘古那神) finished the work of creating Japan, left uncompleted by *Izanami* (伊弉冉 or 伊邪那美 or 伊耶那美 or 伊弉弥) and *Izanagi* (伊弉諾神 or 伊邪那岐命 or 伊耶那岐命) (Ashkenazi 2003, 82–83).

23. Ashkenazi probably means *Yaekotoshironushi-no-kami* (八重言代主神). In a similar way, Picken sees a connection to *Kotoshironushi-no-mikoto* (事代主命), venerated at Osaka's *Imamiya-Ebisu-Jinja* (今宮戎神社) (Picken 1994, 119).

24. However, within the group of the "Seven Auspicious Deities" *Ebisu* (恵比寿) is considered to be the son of *Daikokuten* (大黒天) (Ashkenazi 2003, 142; Seiyaku.com 2006).

25. *Ebisu* (恵比寿) is frequently portrayed as having other "handicaps" or "disfigurements"; as deaf, monocular, lefthander, hermaphrodite, or humpback (Whelan 1996, 85). According to an old folk belief in Japan, children born with handicaps or disfigurements bring good luck to their families. Hanada makes an interesting observation that most of the *Shichifukujin* (七福神) are "abnormally" portrayed. They seem to have such "disabilities" as cerebral palsy, obesity, or hydrocephalus. However, "this association of disability with affluence and happiness does not exist in modern Japan (Kramer 2003, 126–127).

26. As all the gods gather in *Izumo* (出雲) in October and are not present in their usual territory, October is also called *kaminazuki* or *kannazuki* (神無月), the month (月) without (無) gods (神), in most of Japan. Only in *Izumo*, where the gods meet at the *Izumo Taisha* (出雲大社), October is called *kamiarizuki* (神在月), gods-here-month (Seitousha Henshuubu 2016, 149).

Ebisu (恵比寿) became the patron deity of fishers (Guichard-Anguis 1995, 70) only from the late *Heian* Era. He is a *marebito*,[27] a "deity visiting humans, better to be treated with respect." He reveals himself either as a sojourner or as a whale (Knight 2004, 77), or he visits the fishers by allowing them to catch him in his nets. Then he changes his form into a "strangely formed stone." If this stone is properly worshiped by sacrifices and the *Ebisu-mai* (恵比須舞 or 戎舞), "*Ebisu*-dances" (Plutschow and O'Neill 1996, 221), *Ebisu* (恵比寿) grants good catches (Ashkenazi 2003, 142). *Ebisu* (恵比寿) is also the patron deity of all seafarers (Seiyaku.com 2006).

Starting from the twelfth century, *Ebisu* (恵比寿) was more and more affiliated with trade (Picken 1994, 119). On land, he is worshiped as the patron deity of farming, particularly the rice paddies. He also is very popular with traders because he brings prosperity.

Ebisu's (恵比寿) distinctive mark is a fish,[28] either carried under his left arm or dangling from a fishing rod in his right hand. His headware is the *kazeori eboshi* (風折烏帽子), a kind of pointed huntsman's hat, and behind his neatly trimmed beard one can see a merry smile (Seiyaku.com 2006). Special days dedicated to him are 9–11 January. January 10th is *Hatsu-Ebisu* (初恵比寿), the "first *Ebisu* (恵比寿)". It is also called *Tooka-Ebisu* (十日恵比寿), because it is on the tenth, *tooka* (十日). The eve of *Hatsu-Ebisu* (初恵比寿) is called *Yoi-Ebisu* (宵恵比寿), "*Ebisu*'s Eve," and 11 January is called *nokori-fuku* (残り福), which means "leftover of blessings" (Sasaki et al. 2002, 14).

9.2.2 Daikokuten *(*大黒天*)*

Daikokuten (大黒天) has a long history. Originally, he is considered a form of the Indian deity *Shiva*, Hinduism's high-god, lord of destruction and creation (Naka 2006, 192). He is also considered a form of an angry patron-deity, protecting the right faith (Keown et al. 2003, 163). Later he became a Buddhist patron-deity protecting Buddhist monasteries as *Mahakala*, the "Great Black" (Pye et al. 2007, 236). He was also worshipped a bringer of great prosperity, particularly food (Chaudhuri 2003, 67–68). *Mahakala*'s Japanese name is

---

27. The term used by Ashkenazi is – in this form – rather elusive. *Marehito, marebito, maroudo* or *marouto* (客 or 賓) means "guest." The reading *marehito* or *marebito* alludes to 稀人, "a person rarely seen." Here, *mare* (稀) means "hardly existing." In *maremono* (稀者), *mare* (稀) means "rare," and therefore "prominent." The element of the strange and special is a typical animistic feature (Käser 2004, 91–94).

28. Usually this is the *tai* (鯛), the "red sea bream," the *koi* [鯉], the "carp," the *tara* (鱈), the "cod," or the *suzuki* (鱸), the "sea bass" (Seiyaku.com 2006).

Daikokuten (大黒天); *dai* (大) means "big," *koku* (黒) "black," and *ten* (天) "heaven" or "god." In Japan, *Daikokuten* (大黒天) is equated with the Shintoist deity *Ookuninushi-no-Mikoto* (大国主命). The reason is that the *kuni* (国) in *Ookuninushi-no Mikoto* (大国主命), meaning "land" is read *koku* (国) in its Chinese pronunciation. *Koku* (黒), meaning "black" in *Daikokuten* (大黒天) is pronounced the same way (Miyata 1998, 65; Chaudhuri 2003, 67; Iwao and Iyanaga 2002, 389; Pye et al. 2007, 236).[29] *Ookuninushi-no Mikoto* (大国主命) means "Great king of the land" (Masaki and Nakao 2007, 75). He is the main representative of the *kunitsukami* (国津神), the "gods that rule the land." He can be called the hero of Japanese mythology. As such, he has got many names:

- *Ashiharashikoo-no-kami* (葦原色許男神): Japan's strongest male deity;
- *Yachioko-no-kami* (八千矛神): deity bearing many (literally 8,000) weapons;
- *Oomononushi-no-kami* (大物主神): deity of great spiritual power (Masaki and Nakao 2007, 74);
- *Ooanamuchi-no-mikoto* (大己貴命): great honorable lord;
- *Makyaraten* (摩訶迦羅天) or *Onmakyara* (御摩訶迦羅): one of his Tibetan names; however, he has nothing in common with the respective Tibetan deity (Nientiedt 2007, 85–86).

According to the *Kojiki* (古事記), he and *Sukunahikona-no-kami* (少名毘古那神) came over the ocean, multiplied the knowledge of agriculture, medicine, and trade, and thus developed the country (Masaki and Nakao 2007, 74). It is probably for this reason that in Southern Japan he is frequently equated with the *ta-no kami* (田の神), the "god of the rice paddies" (Iwao and Iyanaga 2002, 389; Hockley and Isoda 2003, 155).

In present-day Japan, *Daikokuten* (大黒天) has two main characteristics due to his long history: He is a frightening warrior and at the same time the god of the kitchen (Miyata 1998, 65; Chaudhuri 2003, 67). As god of the kitchen he is mainly worshiped by farmers, traders, and cooks. He is mostly portrayed wearing archaic courtly hunting clothes and sitting on a rice sack. His corpulence is a sign of the prosperity he promises to bring. Slung over his left shoulder is a sack with mysterious treasure inside. In his right hand he

---

29. *Naka* (中瓜生) explains that in the beginning there was some confusion concerning the first two Chinese characters of the two deities. The *ookuni* (大国) in *Ookuninushi-no Mikoto* (大国主命) is read *daikoku* (大国), if separated from the rest of the name, exactly the same as the *daikoku* (大黒) in *Daikokuten* (大黒天). Naka therefore talks derogatorily of *kondou* (混同), "confusion" (Naka 2006, 192).

holds *uchide-no-kozuchi* (打ち出の小槌), a magic hammer often decorated with the *tomoe* (巴 or 鞆絵)-motif which is said to bring good luck (Seiyaku.com 2006).[30] In Japan, *Daikokuten* (大黒天) is almost always worshiped in his less scary form. However, there are Japanese mandalas (曼荼羅 or 曼陀羅) that portray him with three faces and six arms as a warrior with tangled hair and scary features, driving away evil (Naka 2006, 192).

9.2.3 Benzaiten *(弁財天)*

Benzaiten (弁財天), also called *Benten* (弁天), is the only female deity among the *Shichifukujin* (七福神). Originally, she was *Sarasvati*, one of the three main Indian deities. *Sarasvati* is the goddess of fine arts: music, painting, sculpture, dance, and literature. She is therefore portrayed holding a *biwa* (琵琶), the Japanese lute (Seiyaku.com 2008).

The *sara* in *Sarasvati* means "excellent," the *sa* "rhetorical," and the *vati* "talent." *Sarasvati* can be translated with "excellent music" (Chaudhuri 2003, 50). The name *Benzaiten* (弁財天) is the Chinese translation of *Sarasvati*. However, in China the name *Benzaiten* is written 弁才天 and not 弁財天 as in Japan. *Sai* (才) means "talent." During the *Muromachi*-Era the original *sai* (才), "talent," was changed to *sai* (財) which means "financial riches" (Chaudhuri 2003, 49). Thus the original deity of music became the deity of financial power in Japan (Miyata 1998, 66).

In Japan, *Benzaiten* (弁財天) is worshiped as the deity of good luck, happiness, love, eloquence, education, and the fine arts particularly by students, artists, geishas (芸者), and entertainers. Her virtues are gladness, prosperity, and longevity. She protects from natural calamities and graces people with wisdom for victory in battle. As a sign for the help in battle she is often portrayed with eight arms beating weapons (Watsky 2004, 233).

However, she has one negative character trait. She is jealous. Her jealousy is depicted by a sea serpent or the serpent[31] on which she rides. Because of her jealousy, couples avoid coming before her together (Seiyaku.com 2008). The

---

30. The *tomoe* (巴 or 鞆絵)-motif consists of three commas of tears following each other in a circle (Seiyaku.com 2006).

31. Others portray her as riding on a dragon (Ashkenazi 2003, 126). Yet other traditions claim that *Benzaiten* (弁財天) is the daughter of the dragon king *Ryuu-ou* (竜王) and rose from the sea (Turner and Coulter 2001, 97) which is why she is also worshiped as sea goddess or rover goddess (Suzuki 2007, 172; Griffis 2008, 85). Because of her affiliation with water she is mainly worshiped in the area of the Japan Inland Sea, *Seto Naikai* (瀬戸内海), where 6,000 sanctuaries are dedicated to her (Pelletier 1992, 137).

serpent often has the head of a woman and bears the name of a prominent fertility deity, *ugajin* (宇賀神) (Ashkenazi 2003, 126).³²

In a Japanese fairy tale about *Benzaiten* (弁財天) and a horse drover, she falls in love first with his beautiful song, then with himself. She appears to him in the form of a beautiful woman and they spend a night together. As a token of her gratitude she gives him a sack of gold which (upon keeping certain rules) will never run empty (Hammitzsch 1969, 267). This fairy tale combines three of the above features of *Benzaiten* (弁財天): music, love, and prosperity.

9.2.4 Bishamonten *(*毘沙門天*)*

The bearded *Bishamonten* (毘沙門天), also called *Bishamon* (毘沙門),³³ is married to *Kisshouten* (吉祥天), the original Indian goddess of beauty (Kimura 2003, 72). He is also called the "god of dignity" of "harbinger of good fate" (Hatsumi 2005, 187). Originally, he was the Hindu demigod *Vaisravana* (Chaudhuri 2003, 20) or *Kubera* (*Kuvera*) (Hopkins 1969, 142; Leeming 2001, 183).³⁴ *Brahma's* spiritual son *Pulastya* had himself also a spiritual son, *Vaisravana*, who left him and went to *Brahma* who rewarded him with immortality (Wilkins 2004, 321). In India *Vaisravana* was one of the four patron deities and the king over the *Yaksha*, the "spirits of nature" (Leeming 2001, 184), over the *Gandharva*,³⁵ the *Kinnara*³⁶ and others (Aiyangar

---

32. This cult was a secret fertility cult. Buddhist priests considered it "too barbarian" and did not tolerate it (Johnson 1994, 168). Therefore, the official (Buddhist) explanation of her name obscures the original affiliation with the fertility cult: It explains *uga* as derived from *uke* or *uka* (食) which means food, particularly *ina* (稲), "rice." She is the called *ugajin* or *ukajin* (宇賀神) and as such worshiped as a Buddhist supplier deity who (in Buddhist terminology) *subete-no shujou-ni fukutoku-o sazukeru* (すべての衆生に福徳を授ける), who "bestows grace to the host of living beings." She is also worshiped as a Buddhist deity who *bodai-ni michibiku* (菩提に導く) the dead, who "leads [the dead] to buddhahood."

33. Derived from *visana* (毘沙拏), the horn of the rhinoceros (Soothill and Hodous 1987, 306). Exegetes of the *Rhinoceros Sutra* are divided over whether *visana* means "rhinoceros" or the "rhinoceros horn." Both symbols stand for solitariness and seclusion, the rhinoceros because it is a loner, its horn because it is a single horn (Salomon and Glass 2000, 10; Wiltshire 1990, 51). In religious medicine *visana* also plays a role. However, exegetes are not sure whether it is a plant or a horn (Zysk 1992, 211).

34. Called *Jambhala* in Tibetan Buddhism (Waddell 1972, 368).

35. *Gandharvas* are "heavenly entertainers and musicians" (Chaudhuri 2003, 93), allegedly numbering 6,333 and populating the middle world in the mountains between heaven and earth (Sharma 2004, 149).

36. *Kinnaras* are human-like beings with horse heads (Wilkins 2001, 401). Others portray them as heavenly musicians, half man, half bird (Zimmer and Campbell 1972, 120).

1987, 412). Others call him the "Indian Pluto"[37] who originally was an evil spirit (Soothill and Hodous 1987, 306). *Yaksha*, *Gandharva*, and *Kinnara* are sometimes called "a host of demonic beings" who "pledged to protect . . . the teaching of Buddha" (Linrothe 1999, 20; Obeyesekere 1984, 37).

Buddhism adopted *Bishamonten* (毘沙門天) as one of the four heavenly kings (Ruppert 2000, 210), called *shiten-ou* (四天王) in Japanese.[38] As patron of the righteous and symbol of authority *Bishamonten* (毘沙門天) protects the northern territories and the chair of Buddha. He resides in earth's core, in the fourth stratum under *Mt Sumeru*.[39] In Japan, *Bishamonten* (毘沙門天) originally had no special status among the *shiten-ou* (四天王) (Chaudhuri 2003, 22). Because of a legendary miracle in China, where *Vaisravana* saved the Chinese army from the Tibetan army in 742, and because of a special theophany of *Vaisravana* in Japan in 766 in Japan, he became more and more popular (Chaudhuri 2003, 24).

As symbols of his help in war he bears defensive and offensive weapons (Seiyaku.com 2008). *Bishamonten* (毘沙門天) also carries a jewel that grants wishes (Ruppert 2000, 210), and the *tahoutou* (多宝塔) literally the "tower of many treasures," a pagoda as sign of the prosperity he grants.[40] It is not by accident that the patron of the North is worshiped as bringer of prosperity, because it is the North where the treasure chambers of the world are thought to be (Ashkenazi 2003, 128). *Bishamonten* (毘沙門天) distributes his treasures among poor people that are worthy of them and whom he then protects. However, as they are few, *Bishamonten* (毘沙門天) sometimes destroys his treasures (Seiyaku.com 2008).

In his comprehensive study on male homosexuality from the medieval period to the twentieth century, Pflugfelder calls the *Bishamonten* (毘沙門天) of the Kyoto *Kuruma*-Shrine (車神社) with its affiliation with male-male erotic, dating back to the medieval period "mediator of erotic texts" (Pflugfelder 1999, 50). Urushiya attributed an affiliation with male-male

---

37. Pluto is the lord over hell (Guerber 2003, 159). Turner and Coulter equate *Vaisravana* with the giant serpent *Vasuki* (Turner and Coulter 2001, 489).

38. The patron of the East is *Jikokuten* (持国天), that of the West *Koumokuten* (広目天), that of the South *Zoujouten* (増長天), and that of the North *Tamon* (多聞) or *Bishamonten* (毘沙門天). Others also equate *Tamonten* (多聞天), *Vaisravana* and *Bishamonten* (毘沙門天) (Petter 1997, 117; Saso 1991, 65).

39. *Mt Sumeru* is also called the "central mountain" (Lopez 2007, 13). In India he abides in the Himalayas (Aiyangar 1987, 412).

40. Others understand the pagoda as the symbol of his authority (Renard 2002, 23), or as the source of healing of all kinds of injuries (K. Furuya 1996, 204).

erotic to *Fudou* (不動) properly *Fudou-Myou-Ou* (不動明王), to *Yakushi* (薬師) properly *Yakushi-Nyorai* (薬師如来), and to *Bishamonten* (毘沙門天) who all kept their *douji* (童子 or 童児), their "boys" (Pflugfelder 1999, 67). Crompton called these deities "patron deities of male love" (Crompton 2006, 413). In Shintoism, homosexuality was neither condemned nor suppressed, and Japanese Buddhism therefore allowed homosexuality as "tolerable vent for the emotions of monks" (West and Green 1997, 69). Schmidt understands this tolerance in the context of Shintoism where women are considered as defiled, "but nevertheless necessary beings for conception" (Schmidt 1995, 136). "Homosexuality is a formative component of the homoerotic culture of both the warrior class and the monasteries, and remains an attractive variation of erotic art[41] in present-day pop culture" (Kersten 1997, 90). The affiliation between homosexuality and Shintoism is also apparent in present-day Japan as pictures of Shintoist *hadaka matsuri* (裸祭), "Naked Festivals" serve as stimulants in gay-discos (McLelland 2000, 133).

Why is it *Bishamonten* (毘沙門天) who is thus affiliated with sexuality? I suggest that his name as a derivative of "horn" affiliates it with Shintoist phallus cults. Shintoism is a nature religion and "phallus worship is a form of worshiping the life-force" (Paley 2000, 51). The phallic cult of Early Shintoism forms an integral part of its essential naturalism. As Shintoism understands fatherhood as the most prominent of divine mandates, it worships the instrument of fatherhood in naive simplicity (Revon in Underwood 2007, 41). "It is the naturalistic orientation of the *kami* (神) that is the cornerstone of Shinto. This includes ancestor worship and spreads into the areas of shamanism and phallicism" (York 2005, 29).

Shimada holds that Japan fosters an "openness towards the sexual act and genitals." In the context of Shintoism they are not "seen within the framework of individual intimacy, but rather symbolized in 'public' communal events of religious festivals." Sexuality is tied into communal life and symbolized as common life-force and fertility (Kersten 1997, 88–89).

> At many roads there are ... stone sculptures in the form of an erected penis (phallus) that are to protect travelers and to remind them of all the joys they had and will have. At the annual *Jibeta-Matsuri* (地べた祭り) in Kawasaki (April 15th), a big, colorfully decorated phallus, measuring several meters, is still carried around the city, as families buy souvenirs in the form of small phalli, and

---

41. *Geschlechtsdarstellungen*.

children eat lollipops in the respective form – without anybody being offended. (van Dijk 2007, 83)

In all these festivities, the phallus is explicitly not the symbol of sexual lust, but the symbol of fertility, and therefore of the sustaining of life. The close affiliation between phallus worship and Shintoist agricultural rites shows that the basic principle is that of fertility (Underwood 2007, 41). The phallus symbols of the deity *Chimata-no-kami* (巷神 or 岐神 or 衢神) are frequently found in spas where men with sex problems and women with a desire for children stroke the sculptures in hope of improvement (Ashkenazi 2003, 129). Even today farmers have sex in their fields in order to improve the yield. Until 1953 the city of Chiba hosted a festival where a wooden phallus had ritual sex with a vagina made of straw, before both were "anointed" with milky rice beer (Paley 2000, 51).

9.2.5 Juroujin (寿老人)

Because of their common country of origin and their shared religious-historical roots, *Juroujin* (寿老人) and *Fukurokuju* (福禄寿) are closely connected. They are at times even considered to share one body (Drew and Telesco 2003, 209). Others call *Juroujin* (寿老人) "a kind of repetition" of *Fukurokuju* (福禄寿) (Chamberlain 1990, 306). For these reasons they are frequently confused, but the one distinctive feature is *Fukurokuju*'s (福禄寿) smile. He is a bald-headed, merry dwarf. *Juroujin* (寿老人), on the other hand, does not laugh (Ashkenazi 2003, 185).

Juroujin (寿老人) comes from China (Chozanshi et al. 2006, 206), and is at times considered to be identical with *Roushi* (老子), Lao-Tze (Nakajima 2003, 87) or with the South Pole Star (Plutschow and O'Neill 1996, 253).[42]

Juroujin (寿老人) is portrayed as a "skinny, old man wearing the cloak of a sage" with a long, white beard (Seiyaku.com 2006). His prominent feature is his high head which, as can be seen in the pictures of Kyousai Kawanabe (河鍋暁斎) (1831–1889), sometime takes up two-thirds of his body height

---

42. Canopus, the brightest star in the southern constellation of Carina (keel) is called *Nangyokuroujin* (南極老人), *Roujinsei* (老人星), *Nangyoku-Juroujin* (南極寿老人), or *Jusei* (寿星) in Japanese and equated with *Juroujin* (寿老人) (Yato 2005, 159). *Nangyoku* (南極) means "south pole."

(Blomberg 2000, 27). He leans on a long staff and sometimes carries a jewel.[43] He is accompanied by a stag and a crane, sometimes also by a tortoise.

The *makimono* (巻物), the "scroll," fastened to his staff is a symbol of *Juroujin*'s (寿老人) wisdom. It contains "all wisdom of the world" (Jiménez 2005, 9), that is the yield of his life-long learning about the world and the mystery of longevity (Seiyaku.com 2006), yes, even the mystery of "eternal life" (Ashkenazi 2003, 185). As deity of longevity, the ability to banish diseases, cure illnesses, and prevent infections are attributed to him (Villiers 1996, 96). Others understand the mystery of his scroll less positively, claiming that the names of all living and their dates of death are listed in it (Rowthorn et al. 2003, 68). That is the reason why he is not always welcome, particularly if he has read in his scroll right before his visitation (Drew and Telesco 2003, 209).

The main feature of longevity is enforced by the symbolism of the accompanying animals, the crane, the messenger tortoise, and *Genroku* (玄鹿), the stag (Naka 2006, 365; Seiyaku.com 2006). Crane and stag are also the symbols of happiness and bliss (Ashkenazi 2003, 185).[44]

9.2.6 Fukurokuju (福禄寿)

Fukurokuju (福禄寿) also comes from China. In China, *gense riyaku* (現世利益) is divided in *fuku* (福), *roku* (禄), and *ju* (寿). *Roku* (禄) stands for material benefits, *ju* (寿) for longevity, and *fuku* (福), for blessing. These three terms were used to form the name of *Fukurokuju* (福禄寿) (Miyata 1998, 61). His place among the *Shichifukujin* (七福神) is not as strong as that of the others. In some images of the *Shichifukujin* (七福神) he is substituted by the female deity *Kichijouten* (吉祥天) who is of Indian origin like *Benzaiten* (弁財天) (Pye et al. 2007, 237; Komatsu 2005, 83).

Juroujin (寿老人) is also affiliated with Lao-Tze, and is sometimes considered to be his avatar (Ashkenazi 2005, 155). He also carries a staff with a scroll of wisdom fastened to it. He also is accompanied by a stag, a crane, and a tortoise.[45] Like *Juroujin* (寿老人) he has a high, bald head (Seiyaku.

---

43. The jewel stands for prosperity (Huish 2008, 63) which by no means is *Juroujin*'s (寿老人) main concern.

44. In olden days, the stag could also be an evil demon who once even attacked the emperor, oversized and with shining, red eyes, with a humungous mouth showing "teeth like daggers." Due to the continuous influence of Buddhism, the stag became an innocent being, sometimes even considered to be an incarnation of Buddha (Volker 1975, 42) or as symbol of the teaching of Buddha (Turner and Coulter 2001, 252).

45. He is also accompanied by a stork (Hackin and Couchoud 2005, 446).

com, 2006), so high that he himself cannot shave it (Schnell 1999, 75). He maintains a close relationship with mountain ascetics (van der Veere 2003, 78) and is regarded as philosopher and benefactor for humanity (Bradway and McCoard 1997, 75). *Fukurokuju* (福禄寿) is a deity of material riches (Pye et al. 2007, 237),[46] mainly, however, known as a deity of wisdom, virility, fertility, longevity (Chozanshi et al. 2006, 206), gaiety (Pye et al. 2007, 237), and, at times, of carnality (Ashkenazi 2005, 155). Sometimes he is also affiliated with the blessing of *jinbou* (人望), "fame" (Pye et al. 2007, 237).

The shape of his head resembles the phallus (Chozanshi et al. 2006, 206), and thus he is often portrayed in the form of the *harigata* (張形), the traditional dildo.[47] In China, longevity and Taoist wisdom are associated with sex, the male-female principles of Yan and Ying. Therefore, his and *Juroujin*'s (寿老人) pictures are frequently found in Japanese red-light districts (Ashkenazi 2005, 155).

9.2.7 Hotei Oshou (布袋和尚)

Hotei Oshou (布袋和尚), often called only *Hotei* (布袋), got his Japanese name from the *hotei* (布袋), the "cloth bag" hanging over his shoulder (Pye et al. 2007, 239). He is portrayed as being extremely obese,[48] his body having the shape of a rice cake. He has lopped ears hanging down to his shoulders and double chin. He is unshaven and rather a tramp with little social skills (Dobbins and Williams 2004, 327).

Behind *Hotei* (布袋) stands the historical person of the likable Zen-monk Pu-Tai (Seiyaku.com 2006) or Pu-Tai Ho-schang (Gómez 1987, 163)[49] of the *Ch'an*-tradition who lived in the tenth century and traveled the country with a sack over his shoulder (Pye et al. 2007, 239). He died in 916 (Brinker 1987, 28). Pu-Tai Ho-schang was a wandering mendicant with supernatural powers. He preferred wandering to the safety of temples (Leighton and Halifax 2003, 258). He passed the panhandled goods like cakes and fruit on to children (Aitken 1997, 8) and was considered their friend. In his bag, he also collected other

---

46. The phrase *Fukurokuju-no ichidachi* (福禄寿の市立ち), literally "*Fukurokuju* stepping on the market place," is used when a rich man comes to the market place. The opposite phrase is *zeninashi-no ichidachi* (銭無しの市立ち). A *zeninashi* (銭無し) is a person who does not even have small change.

47. The picture of *Benzaiten* (弁財天) is frequently used likewise (Hopkins 2007, 237).

48. His obesity is a sign of his importance (Thomas and Pavitt 1994, 49).

49. In Europe he is known under the name Pusa (Hackin and Couchoud 2005, 446), in Japan also under the name Budai (Brinker 1987, 28).

things that people would throw away. In his bag there was "trash, wonderful trash. Everything that children love. Things that everyone else has thrown away, and thought of as valueless, this Buddha collects and gives away to children" (Watts 1999, 37–38). He also used the trash to tinker toys for children (Dobbins and Williams 2004, 327). When his bag was empty he laughed and let the children play with it. Not only his gifts but also his kindness made him the friend of children. Sometimes children teased him while he was asleep. But when he woke, he smiled at them, hugged them, and told them stories (Eden 2005, 101). Leighton called him a "scruffy Buddhist Santa Claus" (Leighton 2001, 160), and Bing compared him to Friar Tuck, the good-natured companion of Robin Hood (Bing 2005, 351).

For Zen-Buddhists, Pu-Tai Ho-schang stands for the wandering monk who found peace through the studies of Zen (Turner and Coulter 2001, 224). Even though he was poor and destitute – or possibly for this very reason[50] – he became the patron of and father of bliss and happiness. Besides the said cloth bag he called nothing his own but a worn-out cape and a *ougi* (扇), a hand fan (Dobbins and Williams 2004, 327). "He slept under bridges, his knees drawn up" (Miyata 1998, 40). His bag served as bed and as raft (Eden 2005, 101). He was always merry and a "pure-hearted 'fool'" (Leighton 2001, 160). His sermon was laughter. When he entered a village, he used to roll on the ground, laugh, and jump around, until the whole village laughed. If enquired concerning Buddha, he laughed, concerning enlightenment, he burst with laughter, concerning the truth, he laughed. His message was laughter (Capitani 2006, 78).

No wonder that his eccentric appearances earned him the scorn of his colleagues. However, in the encounter with them, his superior wisdom prevailed, as the following story shows:

> "*Hotei* (布袋), we have heard that you are just playing a role, acting," his colleagues asked him.
>
> "We have heard that you are a Zen master, so why do you go on wasting your time just giving toys to children? And if you are really a Zen master then show us what Zen is."
>
> *Hotei* immediately dropped his sack.
>
> "What does it mean?" they asked.
>
> "That is all. If you drop the burden. That is all."

---

50. Eden therefore calls him the "Diogenes of Japan" (Eden 2005, 101).

"Well. And what is the next step?"

He picked up his sack and went on: "That is the next step. But now I do not carry. I know now that the burden is not me. The whole burden has become just toys for children, and they are going to enjoy them."

(according to Osho 1997 17)[51]

Therefore it is said of him: "He goes his way without following the steps of the ancient sages" (Watts 1999, 37–38).

This can be said about the "historical" *Hotei* (布袋). The question is why a man would join the ranks of the *Shichifukujin* (七福神). The answer: The form of the priest is only a "cover" (Hackin and Couchoud 2005, 446). Miyata calls *Hotei* (布袋) a "variation of the Chinese Maitreya-faith" (Miyata 1998, 100). He is considered to be a re-incarnation of Maitreya (Nakamaki 2003, 102; Seiyaku.com 2006). In present-day China, he is as such completely identical with Maitreya (Leighton 2001, 160). In the *Jikkinshou* or *Jikkunshou* (十訓抄), a collection of sermons from the *Kamakura* Era, *Hotei* (布袋) is called *miroku-no shosa* (弥勒の所作), the "[dance-] moves of the future" (Miyata 1998, 100). According to mythology, Maitreya, the future Buddha is to appear "undercover" in the form of a fool. In this case, the heavenly Bodhisattva is not only a savior and worker of miracles, but also a model for humane living. This mythology shows that the virtues of the Bodhisattva are not to be found among sages and holy men, but that the Bodhisattva is sent to live with the humble. The immanence of the Bodhisattva veils his holiness (Gómez 1987, 163). In this sense Miyata deeply asks: "Has *Hotei* (布袋) shown the way to *shifuku* (至福) (the highest bliss) by the way he lived?" (Miyata 1998, 42).

The Maitreya-identity of *Hotei* (布袋) explains the various miracles and the evidence of supernatural power (Leighton and Halifax 2003, 258):

- his body did not get wet even though he slept on snow (Miyata 1998, 40);
- his big ears were a sign of his omniscience (Turner and Coulter 2001, 224)
- his prophesies concerning the *kikkyou* (吉凶), the fate of people never missed (Miyata 1998, 72).

---

51. This story is often told without the explaining comments (Kopp 2004, 51; Reps and Senzaki 1998, 32; Leighton 2001, 160–161).

As *Benzaiten* (弁財天) has been modified to a deity of prosperity once she entered Japan, *Hotei* (布袋) was also modified in the same way.[52] According to Pye et al. he is mostly affiliated with granting *tairyou* (大量), "full measure" (Pye et al. 2007, 239). The Japanese monk, Ryoukan Ninshou (忍性良観), in the late thirteenth century already shows the *Hotei* (布袋) as a person who gives money to beggars (Locher and Zwingli 1981, 65). Similar to *Daikokuten* (大黒天), *Hotei* (布袋) is considered to be a "deity of abundance," whose stock of rice in his bag is never exhausted. This is the reason why he can be so generous. In Japan, the example of contentment became the deity of "joy and satisfaction in trade" whose statue is therefore often seen at the entrance of stores (Seiyaku.com 2006).

9.2.8 Summary

The "blessings" of the "Seven Auspicious Deities" *Shichifukujin* (七福神) can be summarized under six key words: prosperity, safety, fertility, interpersonal happiness, psychological happiness, culture.[53]

Prosperity and safety are the most important. The high desire for safety correlates with Japan's extremely high value on the area of "uncertainty avoidance" (Dainton and Zelley 2015, 101).[54] All of the "Seven Auspicious Deities" are affiliated with them. In the oracle *Koutaijin Takusen* (皇太神託宣), sent from the sun goddess *Amaterasu-Ookami* (天照大神) to Princess *Yamato-hime* (倭姫),[55] it is written: "To receive divine beneficence, you must give priority to prayer; to obtain protection, you must make uprightness the

---

52. Not only in Japan, but also in China, *Hotei* (布袋) is worshiped as "fat, laughing lord of prosperity," to whom petitions can be made in times of financial crisis, "when you must promptly pay off your debts" (Illes 2002, 32).

53. See Appendix 4.

54. "Uncertainty avoidance" is related to anxiety and need for security (Hofstede in Omran et al. 2007, 84). It is one of the six cultural dimensions Geert Hofstede developed in order to measure cultural differences. "Geert Hofstede is a Dutch management researcher who developed an inductive theory of culture. Specifically, he gathered statistical data from 100,000 employees of IBM around the world to determine the values on which cultures vary. In the process, he surveyed workers from 50 countries and three regions" (Dainton and Zelley 2015, 97). "Hofstede's ... cultural dimensions have become the most-quoted in cross-cultural studies and have been applied to a variety of research (Khosrow-Pour and Information Resources Management Association, USA 2015, 2755). Compared with 52 other countries (Hofstede 1993, 91), Japan rates extremely high (Dainton and Zelley 2015, 101): 92 of 100 (The Hofstede Center, http://geert-hofstede.com/japan.html).

55. Written in the *Houki Hongi* (宝基本紀), *Yamato-hime-no Mikoto Seiki* (倭姫命世記), and *Gochinza Denki* (御鎮座伝記), Shintoist texts of the 13th century (Itou 2003, 105).

basis" (Teeuwen 1993, 228).[56] In principle, Japanese folk religious *sukui* (救い), "salvation," is "two-dimensional". It is concerned with warding off of calamities and dangers, and sustaining *inochi* (命), "life" (Shimazono 1999, 90).

As the short outline of the blessings of the "Seven Auspicious Deities" showed, they are "means to an end."[57] They have to serve the happiness of humans and are "domesticated" and "belittled" to that end. Almost nothing is left of the awe-inspiring, even dreadful power of the Indian deities. *Sarasvati*, one of the three main deities of India, became beautiful and gentle *Benten* (弁天) as the indispensable element of banter and pastime (Blomberg 2000, 23). *Shiva*, Hinduism's highest deity, lord of destruction and creation (Naka 2006, 192), became a good-natured fellow who fights with *Ebisu* (恵比寿), because his rat gnaws on his sea bream (Blomberg 2000, 24). The great sage *Hotei* (布袋) became a drinker of wine (Dobbins and Williams 2004, 328). *Juroujin* (寿老人) as well as the Chinese imaginary character *shoujou* (猩猩), at times substituting him, also love rice wine (Turner and Coulter 2001, 252; Miyata 1998, 62) At their meetings, the "Seven Auspicious Deities" lazily frolic like big boys (Griffis 2008, 87). On a more positive note, it can be said that they are not anymore feared as gods but rather treated with emotional cordiality (Huish 2008, 62). At the same time, their worship has become rather shallow. They are

> popular among young people today, but their abiding concern seems to be collecting the stamps available from the railway stations on the pilgrim's route. This phenomenon, that sees shrines transformed into tourist sites, is not of course confined to shrines. It applies more generally to all sacred places. If veneration is never entirely absent, it is subordinated to the pleasure, entertainment dimension. (Inoue 2003, 196)

---

56. The original text reads: 神垂以祈祷為先冥加以正直為本 (Abe 2000). Interpretation of Hideto Kinoshita (木下秀人): *Kami-no shide, kitou-o motte saki-to nashi, myouga, shoujiki-o motte moto-to nasu* (神垂、祈祷をもって先となし、冥加、正直をもって本となす) (H. Kinoshita 2003). Based on this text, the following four compounds of two Chinese characters are very important in Shintoism: *kami-no shide* (神垂), "blessing," *kitou* (祈祷), "prayer," *miyauga* (冥加), "protection," and *shoujiki* (正直), "uprightness" (Saeki 1935, 350).

57. See Watanabe's quote under 2.5.1.1 *Chie Nakane* (中根千枝): "vertical society *tateshakai* (タテ社会) as sociological key-term; *Collectivism and individualism in the Japanese context*.

10

Discussion with Christian Concepts

Summary: As the discussion of the this-worldly orientation of Japanese salvation concepts clearly shows, salvation and suffering, in stark opposition to the Christian understanding of salvation, exclude each other. Furthermore, Christian salvation concepts exist always between extreme poles: (a) "this world" and "yonder world," (b) "this world" and "the coming world," (c) redemption and emancipation.

In this chapter I attempt to compare Japanese salvation concepts and Christian salvation concepts, to show congruities and contradictions. The next section is without a corresponding equivalent in Japanese animism, as there – as well as in many newer Christian theologies – suffering is understood as the complete opposite of "salvation."

The following two sections owe their structure to the key concept of the Japanese salvation concept, *gense riyaku* (現世利益). *Gense riyaku* (現世利益) is an ambivalent term, because the *gen* (現) in *gense* (現世) means both the "real" or "material" world as opposed to the dream world or the "spiritual" world,[1] and the present world and age[2] as opposed to the coming world. These

---

1. Opposites of *gense* (現世) as "real world" are *yume* (夢), "dream" and *maboroshi* (幻), "phantom." The Japanese term for secularism is *genseshugi* (現世主義), "*gense*-ism." *Gense* (現世) in this sense it's opposite of the now existing, spiritual world.

2. Opposites of *gense* (現世) as "present world" are *shourai* (将来), "future," *genzai* (現在), "presence" is a synonym. The following proverbs are testimonies of this usage: *gense-no hate-o mite, kakomirai-o shiru* (現世の果てを見て過去未来を知る), "Look at the ends of *gense* (現世) and know past and future"; *genzai-no inga-o mite, kakomirai-o shiru* (現在の因

two aspects cannot be separated completely, but I want to discuss the given subject according to these two meanings of *gen* (現) (*10.2 Between "this" world and "yonder" world*[3] and *10.3 Between "this" world and the "coming" world.*).

And as the boundary between the gods and man are fluid, the fourth set of extreme poles is also important (*10.4 Between redemption and emancipation*) (Westhelle 1998, 1210).

10.1 Salvation and Suffering

> **Summary:** Pain and suffering are indispensable elements of the Christian faith, especially of the Christian ethics, the Christian eschatology (Kitamori), and the theology of missions (Vicedom).

10.1.1 Kazou Kitamori (北森嘉蔵) (1916–1998)

In his *Theology of the Pain of God* (1965)[4] Kitamori placed the pain of God in the center of ethics and in the center of eschatology. Leaning on Romans 6:3–8; Galatians 2:19; 5:24; 2 Corinthians 1:5; Philippians 3:10; 1 Peter 2:21, 24; 4:13, Kitamori talks about the "mysticism of the pain of God" (Kitamori 1972, 69)[5] that establishes the new life of Christians and their ethics:

果を見て過去未来を知る), "Look at the (Buddhist) law of cause and effect in the *gense* (現世) and know past and future."

3. As collectivism is a prominent feature of Japanese society, sin and salvation need to be discussed as collectivistic principles in the context of Christian theologies. See *10.2.4 Collectivistic concepts*.

4. According to Levison and Pope-Levison, Kitamori developed his theology "in the wake" of bombardments of Hiroshima and Nagasaki (Levison and Pope-Levison 1994, 7). Asian theologians such as Chung, of course, strongly oppose this positivistic interpretation: "Actually, Kitamori's book was completed at the very height of the war. Written during the war, Kitamori idealizes and even fetishizes the tragic suffering of the Japanese people, through which one perceives and comprehends the pain of God, while completely ignoring the innocent victims who suffered under Japan in other Asian countries. Kitamori completely eradicates the real victims of WW II, those suffering and murdered during the period of Japanese colonization" (Chung 2015, 319).

5. Kitamori conceptually distinguishes between his "healthy" mysticism of pain from Bernard of Clairvaux's "unhealthy" mysticism of suffering. With regard to the content, he distinguishes mysticism of pain from mysticism of suffering by saying that the mysticism of suffering lacks reflection, and that, as self-contained system, it furthers meritoriousness. According to Kitamori, a healthy mysticism must not be a self-contained system, because then it is not in need of the grace of God (Kitamori 1972, 75–77).

> When I am dissolved in the pain of God, that is, when I am unified with God in pain, then this is for me *the joy* itself, there is no higher bliss for me. In the pain of God my pain is healed, my old self dies; then I am overcome and awakened to new life. This takes place, because the pain of God is substantiated love of God. (Kitamori 1972, 70)[6]

It is this very mysticism that establishes ethics:

> When we are dissolved in the pain of God and when we are unified with him in pain, the lusts and desires of the flesh lose their power. The most efficient means of mortifying sin is to continually put on the pain of God ... The mysticism of pain gives birth to the driving force of sanctification. (Kitamori 1972, 75)

The pain of God thus has the function to serve as a "conduit" for the unification with God. According to Boutroux, the transforming grace of God enters man through this "conduit." "It is our sole desire to be unified with God in pain" (Kitamori 1972, 77–79). As ethics is established through the mysticism of pain, it also consists in pain, because "true ethics is made possible through *truthfulness* of love." True neighborly love "rejoices with those who rejoice and mourns with those who mourn" (Rom 12:15). Therefore, an ethic appropriate to "our times of pain" is "*made possible only through truthfulness of pain*" (Rom 9:2) (Kitamori 1972, 84).[7] For this "ethics of love," Kitamori names the following core values:

- The mere fact that two humans are unified in pain does not make their pain an ethic of pain. For that to occur, the pain of both must be unified with the pain of God (Kitamori 1972, 85).
- The pain of man must, through the grace of God, be sanctified, cleansed and removed from all natural sources, liberated to the "equality of the truthfulness of pain." "If *every* neighbor feels the *truthfulness* of the pain that parents feel who attend a child through suffering to death, only then the ethic of pain becomes possible." If this happens this is a "blessed experience." The feeling of being blessed gives us "*joy* amidst pain" (Kitamori 1972, 86–87).

---

6. Kitamori justifies the connection between love and pain by the double meaning of המה, which means pain and love (Ogawa 1965, 39–40).

7. In a similar way, Bosch (*Witness to the World*, 1980) named *compassion* as one of the four roots of a biblical understanding of missions (Triebel 1988, 3).

- The neighbor is also the neighbor who does not believe. Equal love for believers and unbelievers demands that both are considered as such who stand in the "order of light," who cannot be lost. "An ethic, according to which the unbeliever must be loved in the same way as the believer, must develop into a *theology*, according to which the unbeliever stands in the same order of light as the believer." God's love welcomes and receives people who by the standards of God's justice he cannot welcome and receive. This establishes the pain of God, the 'love' of the cross" (Kitamori 1972, 88–89).
- It is the "basic principle of the gospel" and of the pain of God that God loves him who cannot be loved, and that therefore he lets his son die. According to Nygren, God's love is not dependent on man, on the sinner, but dependent alone on God. He who eagerly follows this love of God loves his enemies (Rom 5:10). "For us who carry our cross, who follow the cross of the Lord, who eagerly follow the pain of God through our own pain, for us ethics must be determined by love, that is, by the pain of God. We must not linger in the love that loves only those who deserve our love (Luke 6:32–34)" (Kitamori 1972, 90–93).

With reference to the speech of the Last Days, particularly Luke 17:25, Kitamori also connected eschatology with the pain of God. The "coming of the kingdom of God" takes place through the love of God in "the gospel of the pain of God." "Truly the rule of God only [comes] if the gospel prevails all over the world." For Kitamori this is the same as the pain of God prevailing all over the world (1972, 139–141). For Kitamori, eschatology means that man is caught in an unsolvable contradiction (Phil 3:12) which he can bear only in "hope." The contradiction consists between the "forgiveness of sin as the pain of God," which means "complete *redemption*," and sanctification on which the unfolding of the pain of God toward love aims. However, different from forgiveness, sanctification has *not yet been redeemed*. "The pain of God is the principle that envelops all. And because the pain of God is now connected with eschatology, eschatology also shows the all-enveloping character (Kitamori 1972, 143–144).[8]

---

8. "Enveloping" seems to be a typical term of Kitamori. His Japanese colleagues called his theology which envelopes everything in the hermeneutical principle of pain *furoshiki*(風呂敷)-theology. A *furoshiki* (風呂敷) is a piece of cloth used for packing up groceries and the like for transportation. In Japanese philosophy, this term is used to describe Hegel's dialectic synthesis (Michalson 1962, 61).

10.1.2 Georg Friedrich Vicedom (1903–1974)

In this context, Vicedom's *Das Geheimnis des Leidens der Kirche* (1963) and Triebel's discussion of the same about two and a half decades later, *Leiden als Thema der Missionstheologie* (1988), are of interest.

After an introduction into the history of persecution and suffering of the Christian church Vicedom demands:

> The church can only do her service, if she clearly knows that her service is tied to suffering. She must learn again that suffering for the sake of God[9] is a privilege. God wants to make the service of the church fruitful through suffering. Therefore, avoiding suffering can become betrayal. The church must live in Christian hope again, and particularly overcome the impulse of taking fright and avoiding suffering,[10] so she may be free to truly testify for the gospel. (Vicedom 1963, 12)

Kitamori talked about the "pain of God"; Vicedom about "suffering through God." Kitamori talked about the joy in the pain of God; Vicedom about a "divine privileged."[11] Both connected Christian ethics with pain or suffering. Both talked in this context about the Christian hope. Both saw the mystery of the pain of God as being revealed on the cross (Vicedom 1963, 12).[12]

On the other side, the difference between the two theologians is evident: Kitamori established the pain with reference to Luther's *"da streydet Gott mit Gott,"* with the conflict in God himself (Terazono 1987, 186). Vicedom

---

9. *Leiden durch Gott*, literally "suffering through God."

10. Vicedom uses the word *Leidensscheu*, a compound of Leiden, "suffering," and *Scheu*, which in this case is derived not from the adjective *scheu*, "shy," but from the verb *scheuen*, "to balk" or "to take fright."

11. *Gottes Bevorzugung*, literally "God's preference" [of those who suffer in his service].

12. The parallels are surprising. Vicedom obviously knew Kitamori's work. The English translation of Kitamori's *Theology of the Pain of God* was published in 1965. At the same time Keiji Ogawa's (小川圭治) comprehensive report about Kitamori's theology (*Die Aufgabe der neueren evangelischen Theologie in Japan*) was published. The German translation of Kitamori's *Theology of the Pain of God* was published only in 1972. Also in 1972, Kitamori published an article called *The Problem of Pain in Christology* in *Christ and the Younger Churches: Theological Contributions from Asia, Africa and Latin America* published by Vicedom. Only then his thoughts became known more widely. In his preface to Karl Barth to the Japanese translation to his *Einführung in die evangelische Theologie* (*fukuinshugi shingaku nyuumon*, 福音主義神学入門) in 1962, Karl Barth criticized Kitamori's attempt of a Japanese theology (Koizumi 2006, 53). Vicedom was co-publisher of *Theologischen Stimmen aus Asien, Afrika und Lateinamerika*, a magazine in which Kitamori introduced his work as early as 1968 (Wrogemann 2012, 2.1 *Interkulturelle Theologie* – Theologische Entwürfe aus der Dritten Welt?). The question is: Did Vicedom know Kitamori's work back in 1963?

established the suffering of Christ and his church with reference to the powers fighting each other in the drama of *Heilsgeschichte*, the power of God and the power of the enemy (Vicedom 1963, 13). Christians suffer for the sake of Jesus, they suffer because they live as upright people in a world of lies, they suffer because the world scorns them for their testimony, and they suffer because the world fights against the church (Vicedom 1963, 17–18).

Because the mission of Jesus was fulfilled in his suffering, the discipleship of Jesus is carried out particularly in suffering. Even though the suffering of Christians can never be *imitatio* of the suffering of Christ (Vicedom 1963, 15), it still is the means through which God (Kitamori talked about the "conduit" of God [1972, 77]) brings "redemption to humans." "God chose a paradoxical way. Through the suffering of the church he makes visible that he is the Lord" (Vicedom 1963, 20). Kitamori said that the kingdom of God prevails not in power but in love, which in his case means "through power" (1972, 139). While the powerful of this world rule firmly, Christ rules "in powerlessness, in the counterplay of power." Vicedom concluded: "Therefore, the church must allow herself to be included in the suffering of persecution, into downfall, into dying (1 Cor 15:30–31; 2 Cor 4:8–12; Phil 1:12–14)" (Vicedom 1963, 20), in order to have a testimony with missionary integrity. "Like the incarnation, the crucifixion must find its reduplication in the messengers of Christ" (Kantonen in Vicedom 1963, 22). Or in Chung's words:

> The missional church is grounded in God's reconciliation through Christ's suffering. It does not escape the suffering. In suffering, it receives the mandate to suffer vicariously for the world. The church participates in the rule of Christ and thus becomes an eschatological reality. The missional church is characterized as the one engaged in the ministry of reconciliation that assigns the ministry to prepare the church for times of suffering (Acts 14:22). (Chung 2013, 71–72)

Like Kitamori (even though in a different order), Vicedom connects ethics not only with suffering, but also the communion with Jesus that establishes ethics. "In suffering the Lord Jesus is one with his church" (Vicedom 1963, 26).

Vicedom explicitly objects to the "pagan concept of life," that particular "concept of salvation" so well portrayed in the soteriology of the *Shichifukujin* (七福神): "We have widely adopted the pagan concept of life which makes us think that faith in Christ must make us perfectly happy, particularly in the social sphere." This is justified by misusing John 10:10, even though Jesus said these words in the context of his suffering (John 10:15). However, the discipleship of Jesus must be discipleship of the cross (Matt 16:24; Mark 8:34) (Vicedom 1963, 14–15).

10.1.3 Reflection

While the conceptual similarities between Kitamori and Vicedom seem striking, their basic concepts root in different traditions, traditions which in turn are not at all compatible. As long as Kitamori is discussed vis-à-vis Vicedom or even in accord with Luther, and outside his Asian context, or to be more precise, outside his Korean-Japanese context, the irreconcilable differences may go unrecognized. However, Miyamoto sees a compatibility between Song,[13] Park, Koyama, Endou, and Kitamori. Crossreading Kitamori with them it becomes clear that "God is basically in suffering because of God's all-embracing love . . . Regarding the view of God, all of them . . . are aiming to depict the character of the All-embracing" (Miyamoto 2010, 62). In the Japanese context, Endou's "theology of the cross" is the closest to Kitamori's *Theology of the Pain of God* (Fritsch-Oppermann 2000, 230). Even though Kitamori is a Lutheran theologian, it is not Luther who defines the meaning behind Kitamori's choice of words, but Endo.

Kitamori explains this notion of love rooted in pain by using the three orders of love:

- "The first order of love is the immediate, smooth, and flowing love to a human being."[14]
- "This first love becomes pain because of human sin, disobedience against God."
- "However, God is determined to embrace fallen humans by reason of God's deepest essence of love. It is not immediate love, but love mediated by pain of God. The love rooted in the pain of God accompanies the forgiveness of sin. The cross is the locus to reveal the 'process of his agonies,' by which God embraces those who

---

13. Kitamori influenced Song (Pope-Levison and Levison 1992, 85).

14. That love of God that is not accepted by humans and that consequently rules over them in the form of the law. The true and living God delivers the rebel, the sinner to death (Terazono 1987, 186).

cannot be embraced, forgives those who cannot be forgiven, and loves those who cannot be loved" (Miyamoto 2010, 33–34).[15]

At this point it is Kitamori himself who distinguishes his theology from Luther. "In order to distinguish between the first order and the third order, Kitamori even criticizes Luther in that he recognizes the 'wrath of God' as the 'means of revealing God's love.' He considers the wrath of God as the real reaction to real sin" (Miyamoto 2010, 34).

> Luther's "hidden God" is important because the concept is fundamental to our faith; we cannot live a Christian life without it ... The theological basis for the concept of the "hidden God" is this: the wrath of God is the *means* of revealing his love. Consequently, faith is to have an insight into God's love veiled *under* his wrath ... However, we cannot overlook one great *problem* in connection with this idea. That is, is it sufficient to consider the wrath of God only as the "means" of revealing his love? Rather is it not true that the wrath of God implies something other than the means of revealing his love? (Kitamori 2005, 108)

Kitamori then quotes Luther:

> For God's working must be hidden, and we cannot understand its way. For it is concealed so that it appears to be contrary to what our minds can grasp ... In this way he acted in his own proper work, in that which is the foremost of his works and the pattern of them, i.e. in Christ. When he wanted to glorify him and establish him in his Kingship, he made him die, he caused him to be confounded and to descend to hell. (109)

From there, I see three steps. First Kitamori concludes:

> Since Christ is the example (*exemplum*) as well as the gift (*donum*) to the believers, these words are not inapplicable but the significance of Christ's death must be found elsewhere. The wrath of God which Christ bore in himself was never a means for his love, but rather his actual response to man's rebellion. (109)

---

15. The term "pain of God" thus describes the tension between the love of God and the wrath of God. The pain of God consists in the fact that God cannot forgive those he loves. And it consists in the fact that he forgives even though he cannot forgive. By quoting Luther's "*da streydet Gott mit Gott*" (thus God striveth with God) Kitamori claims: "The God who must deliver the sinner to death, strives with the God who loves the sinner. The fact, that in both cases it is the very same God, this is the pain of God" (Terazono 1987, 186).

Then Kitamori relates the wrath of God and the pain of God: "When the love of God bears and overcomes his wrath, nothing but the pain of God takes place. The solution of the wrath of God must be sought in the pain of God before it can be sought in the 'hidden God.' In Luther's thought some idea corresponding to that of the pain of God can be found" (2005, 109). "In God's pain, God's wrath is overcome, because it took place in the suffering life of the Son" (Chung 2013, 72). The last step is that from this "mutual relationship" of "the hidden God" and the "pain of God" he makes the pain of God the ruling principle.

Because Christ has already overcome the reality of God's wrath, we are allowed to perceive it in faith as *means* of his love. Faith in the "hidden God" becomes a truth only after it finds its basis in the pain of God. Love rooted in the pain of God provides the place where faith in the "hidden God" can be realized. Because of God's love, the wrath of God can be used a means (Kitamori 2005, 109). In leaving "the problem unresolved" Luther was, according to Kitamori, "confused" and failed to root the concept of the "hidden God" in the pain of God (109).

It is exactly here where, as I understand it, in his attempt to "re-root the gospel of Christ for the Japanese mind" (Miyamoto 2010, 34), Kitamori departs from orthodoxy. The cross becomes the place of the pain that is generated by loving the unlovable. In other words, it generates from tolerating the intolerable. This kind of suffering love is Endou's all-embracing motherly love. In Luther's thought, the cross is the place where the wrath of God is put on his beloved Son and thus overcome. Sin is not tolerated in pain but put away with through suffering. In Endou's thought the unlovable will always be the unlovable, and thus pain must prevail as principle. In biblical thought, as I perceive it, the unlovable becomes the "beloved child of God," because the "beloved Son of God" became sin. Not embracing the sinner and tolerating his sin or weakness, but overcoming sin and the new creation of the just is the biblical principle, not helpless and weak vicarious (Chung 2015, 318) co-suffering,[16] but victorious suffering – the suffering Servant is also the heroic *Heiland* (Savior), the *victor quia victima*!

---

16. "Kitamori's notion of pain is deeply rooted in the Japanese experience and understanding of tragedy: *tsurasa* (辛さ). *Tsurasa* (辛さ) is neither bitterness nor sadness. It is realized when one suffers and dies, or makes someone else that one loves suffer and die" (Thornton 2003, 210). Kitamori equates the "pain of God" with helpless *tsurasa* (辛さ) found in Kabuki-theater. "A good example can be found in the play *Terakoya* (寺子屋). There the hero, Matsuomaru (松尾丸), learns that the enemy wants to kill the son of his feudal lord. Matsuomaru (松尾丸) and his wife deliberately send their own son into the same school (*Terakoya*, 寺子屋) where the

Kitamori's "re-rooting of the gospel of Christ" went as far as re-interpreting the gospel, and by putting it into a different interpretative frame-work, alienating it. And this new and clearly governing context is Buddhism. The concentration on suffering is "a clear symptom of the Buddhist context" in which Kitamori's theology is formulated (Brinkman 2014, 111).

> After his studies in the Lutheran seminary, he studied further at Kyoto University. He primarily attended the lectures of Tanabe Hajime (1885–1962), who was influenced by Jodo (Shin) Buddhism and who, after Zen Buddhist philosopher Nisida Kitaro (1870–1945), was the leading personality in the Kyoto school of philosophy. Thus Kitamori was very strongly influenced by Jodo (Shin) Buddhism. His statement that Jesus Christ heals our human wounds by his own wounds is echoed in the Buddhist proposal that illness (for humans, the result of foolish love) can be healed by illness (the mercy of the Amida-Buddha). (Terozono 2006, 224)

10.2 Between "This" World and "Yonder" World

> **Summary:** According to Takakura (高倉徳太郎) a Christianity without a transcendent reference and man in its center is not a Christianity "according to the gospel." Without this reference, the depth of human lostness and subsequently salvation are belittled. Takenaka (竹中正夫) as well maintains that God is the center of the Christian faith and the center of salvation, but he also promotes the idea that salvation manifests itself differently according to different contexts of human suffering.
>
> The opposite position is represented by Pieris who promotes a soteriological orientation solely on this-worldly, non-Christian religions. The concepts of *han* (Park) and the socio-oriented salvation (liberation theologies) also promote a prevalent (and sometimes exclusive) orientation on immanent salvation.

---

lord's son is, in order to let their son die in his place. When Matsuomaru (松尾丸) learns that his son has died as a substitute and that the son of his lord has escaped, he cries silently with his wife and says to her, 'Be glad, wife, that our son has done his duty'" (Terazono 2006, 224).

Proper Christian soteriology must keep the balance between both extremes. In Japanese Christian discussion, the conflict between salvation in "this" world and salvation in the world "yonder" is disputed between (conservative) Protestantism on one side and Liberalism and Pentecostal churches on the other. While Japanese Protestantism "has been isolated in an intellectual middle-class ghetto" rightly criticizing "mass religiosity,"

> . . . pentecostal forms of Christianity, on the other hand, share a great deal in common with the New Religions flourishing in contemporary Japan. Both emphasize religious experience and this-worldly benefits. One Japanese Pentecostal leader, for example, explained that Evangelicals[17] have long taught the message of salvation from "sin," but failed to teach the biblical message of healing and economic blessings from God. (Poewe 1994, 97)[18]

Hoffmann also concludes that Christian groups in Japan that are "more popular" and more "indigenized" such as the Non-Church Movement *Mukyoukai* (無教会) "emphasize this-worldly Bible study rather than other-worldly salvation" (Hoffmann 2007, 116). An even more typical example is the Pentecostal Spirit of Jesus Church (*Iesu-no Mitama Kyoukai*, イエス之御霊教会) introduced by Mullins:[19] "The version of Christianity advanced by the Spirit of Jesus Church tends to appeal to those Japanese already deeply rooted

---

17. Naming "the Evangelicals" as protagonists of salvation exclusively in the world "yonder" is a generalization that has its faults. The Mormon theologian Hoffmann sees a parallel between the frequent and strong emphasis on miraculous healings in Japan's New Religions and the tradition of faith healing in American Evangelicalism and Pentecostal churches (Hoffmann 2007, 41). "Moreover, it is not uncommon for Western Christians to see their faith and religious practices as tied to their health, romantic relationships, or even their wealth" (Hoffmann 2007, 74).

18. Sickness and healing were widely excluded from the realm of religion. But "now a change emerges, initially taking place outside official mainstream religion, for example in Pentecostal churches or in the esoteric scene. According to Fritz Stolz, *Heilung* and *Heil* may come closer in Post-Modernity" (Neuhold 2000, 80).

19. The Spirit of Jesus Church was founded in 1941 by Jun Murai (村井屯) under the influence of the Chinese True Jesus Church from which it adopted teachings such as the washing of feet and baptism for the dead (Shew 2005, 498; Berentsen 1985a, 195; Holder 2005, 170). Today, the Spirit of Jesus Church is probably the biggest Pentecostal church in Japan (McLeod 2006, 101).

in folk religious traditions. Considerable emphasis is placed on . . . *gense riyaku* (現世利益), or the worldly benefits of religion (Mullins 1998, 101).[20]

In the following section, I will turn first to an evangelical Japanese theologian (Takakura), an ecumenical Japanese theologian (Takenaka), and a Catholic Sri Lankan theologian (Pieris). Then I am going to discuss "sin" (Park) and "salvation" (Liberation Theologies) as collectivistic concepts.

10.2.1 Tokutarou Takakura (高倉德太郎) (1885–1934)

Takakura, a student of Masahisa Uemura (植村正久) who was strongly influenced by evangelical missionaries such as Brown, Hepburn, and Ballagh, was professor at the Tokyo Theological Seminary from 1918. During his studies under H. R. Mackintosh and W. Paterson in Scotland (from 1921), he was deeply influenced by Troeltsch, particular by his *Grundprobleme der Ethik* where he describes the relationship between Christianity and culture (Jennings 2005, 168). The theologian he felt most connected with was Peter Taylor Forsyth (Inagaki and Jennings 2000, 24). After Uemura's death, Takakura became his successor as president of the Tokyo Theological Seminary (Satou 1997, 48–49). Takakura identified himself as an "Evangelical" theologian. He understood "Evangelicalism" as a Christianity that was founded on the Bible, beginning with the prophets, and that was revived through the reformers.[21] He used "Evangelical" as a sharp contrast to "Catholic" and "liberal" (Kim 2008, 121).

In his paper *Salvation in the Japanese Context*,[22] Takenaka characterizes the salvation concept of the first period of Evangelical missions (from 1859) by which he himself was influenced as "ethical liberation from the old way of life." Evangelical missions owed this emphasis to the many samurai who converted

---

20. South Korean churches show similar traits. Ma writes about David (Paul) Yonggi Cho's message of hope and blessing. This message shows great potential to create dangerous syncretism with shamanism as well as an egocentric gospel of prosperity. Presently, many Asian church leaders emphasize this kind of fascinating message which poses a profound question as to what the true meaning of blessing is. Ma objects to their interpretation of blessing which advances the idea that materially blessed Christians are more spiritual. Faith and material blessing are blended together (Ma 2007, 28). Cho's interpretation of blessing is holistic and aims at spiritual well-being, material affluence and health. Cho justifies this with 3 John 2. Of course, Cho's teachings were criticized for advancing humanism and shamanism (Ma 2007, 29).

21. Takakura was frequently referred to as Calvinist, yet always objected. All he wanted to do was to know Christianity as the religion of the Bible (Dohi 1991, 82).

22. Japanese title: 現代における救い (*gendai-ni okeru sukui*) which means "salvation in the present."

to Christianity (Takenaka 1972, 80) and showed a great zeal for evangelism and devotional pietism. They understood salvation as "liberation from personal sin" (Takenaka 1972, 81). The late Takakura was oriented towards Barth (McGrath and Forrester 1995, 282).

In his principal work *Fukuinteki Kirisutokyou* (福音的基督教), "Christianity according to the Gospel" (1955), Takakura offers four reasons why it came to its "present, weak condition":[23]

- "'Those who advocate a so-called liberal Christianity have fallen into religious subjectivism. Having received the influence of rationalism, naturalism, [and] humanism, the transcendental, objective side of the Christian faith has been neglected, and God's immanent side has been emphasized.' This subjective Christianity has taught people to find God in the 'depths of the soul,' to penetrate the soul's life, and thus to seek a 'fusion' or 'identity of the soul and God.' This thinking neglects objective grace, however, and it blurs the fundamental, biblical line between Creator and creature. It has thus resulted in a loss of 'true prayer' as well as of any 'certainty of salvation.'"
- "Subjective Christianity views humanity optimistically. The biblical understanding is that of a sinful creature having a fundamental, tragic inner dualism who stands in need of Divine '*grace*.' The contemporary, optimistic interpretation on the other hand sees humanity as weak, yet ever progressing towards its ideal through education and enlightenment."[24]
- Christianity has thus become "a human-centered, experience-oriented religion which sees God as a means to fulfilling humanity's religious desires. This so-called cultural and philosophical Christianity turns out to be simply utilitarian, e.g. only providing service for the state, and is exemplified by the imported American *Social Gospel*. It offers no manifestation of the biblical religion of conscience, of calling, of living for God's glory" (Jennings 2005, 229–230).

This does not, however, mean that Takakura did not show any interest in social or political matters. On the contrary, he was interested in these matters,

---

23. I refer to only three of the four reasons and show the fourth under *10.3.3 Between world and heaven*.

24. With his objection to this humanistic optimism Takakura encountered the fundamental philosophy of Japanese religiosity. He demanded that Christians had to cleanse the Japanese culture and rebuild it on the foundation of the cross (Van Lin 2002, 150).

but he did not want to make them the starting point, heart and purpose of theology. This can be clearly seen from his lecture series on Romans 13:1–7[25] in which he adopted a clear political position in a most sensitive age. "I seek to love and suffer for the homeland, believing with my whole heart in our God that a 'righteous and holy state' (*seigi kokka*, 正義国家) will be built in our homeland." He strongly emphasized that in order to do so it was first necessary to "lay the homeland before the Gospel of the Lord." Particularly the "Spirit of Fraternity" (*douhou-no seishin*, 同胞の精神) must be "*judged* according to the cross." "*Put on trial* the narrow-minded patriotism that is controlling our fellow countrymen!" (Miyata and Vanderbilt 2009, 69).

*10.2.2 Masao Takenaka (*竹中正夫*) (1925–2006)*

Over five decades Masao Takenaka was a leading ecumenical thinker in Asia. For forty-one years he taught ethics and religious philosophy at *Doshisha University* (同志社大学) in Japan (Kobia 2006). He lamented the row between the Japanese churches over their different concepts of salvation and suggested the following position as common ground:

> We need to grasp the comprehensive meaning of salvation. Salvation is not a static concept, but it is a dynamic event that has happened and is happening, and will be happening continuously throughout history. It has an equal impact on history by bringing the whole of creation into a right relationship with God. This saving power of God has manifested itself in the person and ministry of Jesus Christ who is the fulfillment of God's promise: Immanuel, God is with us. We need constantly to search for the deeper and more comprehensive grasp of salvation without absolutizing our relative understanding and response. (Takenaka 1972, 84)

By introducing the Immanuel-concept into soteriology, Takenaka ran the risk of blurring the line between God as the subject of salvation and man as its object, a risk he was aware of.

Because Christians are the "first fruits of the new humanity," Takenaka called for the presence of Christians in unjust societies. Wherever there is suffering, injustice and exploitation of life Christians have to partake in the fight for the restoration of humanity in any given concrete social context. Takenaka was well aware that this was very complicated, particularly in the

---

25. Held from the mid-1920s to the early 1930s, published in 1964.

Japanese context. As the humanity in Christ, Christians must be open, not closed. Reconciliation must never be understood as a merely spiritual concept (Yewangoe 1987, 212). "In search for the meaning of salvation we [rather] need to think concretely, within the particular context of today" (Takenaka 1972, 85). For Takenaka "thinking concretely" meant to be oriented on the deepest suffering:

> Certainly God cares for all people and for all things he created. But his love is not like hair-spray, distributed thinly in general. It is not like the harmonious rainbow of the ideal world. The cross is the center of God's love. It signifies concretely his solidarity with those who are weak, poor, despised, helpless, and sinful. It is hard to read the Bible with the interest of the rich and the right since it reveals God's love in the uplifting of the meek and those of low degree. (Takenaka 1972, 85)

Even though Takenaka saw the "immense value" for the "the process of humanization" (85), he never put humans in the center of theology, but clearly advocated God-centeredness (Yewangoe 1987, 212). For Takenaka, "humanization" did not mean an unbalanced concentration on human this-worldly needs, but a counter movement against mechanization (Takenaka 1972, 86). The "world" or the *Unheil* in the "world" must never write the agenda for Christian action. Takenaka warned that "the church's present interest in interreligious dialogue could not always be deduced from the inner structure of the message of Jesus, but was rather a product of the religious pluralism of this age." He even held that the early church's mode of encounter with other religions was confrontation and not dialogue. Takenaka was sure that the present-day attempts at dialogue would fade if they were not rooted in the inner core of the message of Jesus (Odagaki 1997, 127).

Takenaka also spoke against humans being the subject of their own salvation. Humans can only be the conduit through which God's will manifests itself in concrete situations in Asia (Takenaka in Yewangoe 1987, 212).

10.2.3 Aloysius Pieris (1934–)

The liberation theologian, Aloysius Pieris, is a Jesuit priest and the director of the Tulana Research Center (Dialogue Center) in Sri Lanka. According to Hodgson, Pieris has a similar function in Asia as Gutiérrez has in Latin America (Hodgson 1994, 70).

Pieris starts out with the religious-sociological observation that a "meta-cosmic religion" cannot be deeply rooted (and that means "enculturated") into tribal societies in the context of their "cosmic religions," even though "a cosmic religion is an open spirituality that expects transcendental orientation from a meta-cosmic religion." The encounter can never be a competing either-or, but rather a supplementation that leads to a "two-dimensional soteriology" with a healthy tension between the cosmic *Now* and the meta-cosmic *Yonder*. According to Pieris, in most Asian countries (he does not list Japan among the exceptions) it was not Christianity that achieved the supplementation through a meta-cosmic religion. Therefore, the European model of Christianization through supplementation would not work any more in Asia (Pieris 1988, 54).[26] He therefore calls for the genesis of "an indigenous church identity emerging from soteriological perspectives of Asian religions." On this path, he sees three signposts:

- An already existing two-dimensional soteriology of a non-Christian religion where a cosmic participation is aligned with a meta-cosmic orientation on the future, continuously relativizing the here and now, serves as a ready referential framework for Christian spirituality, liturgy, the testimony of the church, social engagement, and theological formulating.
- Asian theology is not the result of excogitation but rather a process of explication, or, more specifically, a Christian apocalypse in the struggle for liberation.
- Because we not only explicate theology implicated in pre-existing, non-Christian soteriologies, the method of choice is "instrumentalization" of non-Christian schemes, but one of assimilation through participation in the non-Christian ethos, a baptism in the Jordan of our ancestors' religiosity[27] . . . which allows "Christ's little flock" to freely graze on the Asian pastures which it trampled for centuries (Pieris 1988, 55).

---

26. In Japan as well as in many other Asian countries, Buddhism played this role.

27. As a "positive" example, Pieris mentions a certain Benedictine monk who was baptized in the waters of Hinduism (Pieris 1988, 55). Pieris objects to a missiology that wants to bring Christ into a region where he was not known previously. According to him, Christ is already there before the missionaries arrive. The Asian church must learn to recognize the "christhood" of the poor (Barnes 2002, 250).

10.2.4 Collectivistic Concepts

10.2.4.1 Sin as collectivistic concept (Andrew Sung Park)

In *The Wounded Heart of God* (1993), a study on an Asian sin-concept, Park introduces the sin-concepts of some Western theologians and concludes that Western theologies emphasize "the private self in relation to God through Christ."[28] However, Park (and others) want to understand sin not only as a private or family matter, but rather as a matter in a "political and social context." Here Park introduces the Asian concept *han*[29] which also describes the suffering of the victims (Carmichael 2003, 61–62).

Even though *han* has individual layers (Bacote 2002, 105), its main focus is on collectivistic and structural layers (Park 2009, 41). According to Park, *han* is the suffering of the innocent, of those "caught in evil situations of helplessness" (Park 2001, 47). He compares *han* with "black holes": "In a similar way, when a victim's pain expands beyond his or her capacity for perseverance, the soul collapses into a deep, dark abyss" (Park 2000, 82). T. Kim talks about a deep emotion born from the unjust, massified and condensed experience of suppression (Bacote 2002, 105). Park sees biblical prototypes of the *han*-concept in the story of Cain and Abel ("the crying blood is the voice of *han*") (Park 2001, 48) or in the story of Job who suffered the agony of *han* (Park 2001, 51); in Job's case the absence of God in his suffering is his *han* (Park 2001, 52). Jesus also particularly administered to the needs of the suppressed.[30] "Thus, it is necessary for Christians to read the Bible chiefly from the viewpoint of the downtrodden." However, traditional theology was mainly occupied with suppressors, because the ruling powers have long controlled Christianity and its Bible (Park 2001, 45–46). Park concludes:

> In pulpits we have preached the one-sided theology of the sin-repentance mode for everyone, including the sinned-against and

---

28. In a similar way the 2nd Latin American Episcopal Council in Medellín (1968) corrected this one-sided sin-concept. They spoke about "the sinful character of institutional violence" (Gensichen 1985b, 137).

29. The term *han* has also (or even mainly) been promoted by the plenary presentation of Hyun Kyung Chung in Canberra (1991). "In her presentation, Chung explained the Holy Spirit as the one identifying with those spirits [that feel *han*], who cries with them and actively struggles for their liberation in a greedy and torn world of death." As such Chung identified the Holy Spirit with *Kwan In*, the goddess of mercy and wisdom (Kim 2004, 350). Chung is concerned to seek a "spirituality that promotes the immanence of God, the sanctity of this world, and the wholeness of body, sensuality, and sexuality" (352).

30. Park thoroughly elaborates this under the headline "*Han*" in the New Testament (Park 2001, 52ff).

the wounded: "Repent of your sin and be saved." Toward victims, we have done wrong. The God of Job is angry at this simplistic sin-repentance formula the church has applied to the victims of sin and tragedy. Our present one-dimensional theology is under God's wrath. Theologians owe burnt offerings to God and our apology to the victims. (Park 2001, 51)

In the days of Jesus, the "most poor and powerless people were called 'sinners' by the religious leaders because poverty prevented them from observing the Sabbath law of purification" (Park 2001, 53). Park demands that the problem of sin and *han* be seen "from the Christian point of view" and that they "must be discussed and treated together," because they are "indivisible in their relationship to one another." The church has "paid a great deal of attention to the spiritual well-being of sinners, while generally neglecting the healing of the sinned-against" (Park 2000, 83).

Of course, Park's *han*-concept is not new. He articulates for the Korean (and thus Asian)[31] context what has been said by mainly Latin American liberation theologies that interpret "situations of suppression . . . as structural sin" (Greinacher 1988, 68). According to this thought, sin expands horizontally through society and vertically from generation to generation (Wright 2006, 431). Therefore, the kingdom of God must also "be established in the relations between human beings" (Boff and Boff 1986, 13). Park seems to be aware of this connection because he quotes Moltmann even though he objects to his notion that God's suffering generates from the love for the son: "The cross represents God's full participation in their *han*, and in turn, every victim's *han* is emblematic of God's crucifixion" (Park 2000, 89). Park understands the cross as Jesus's solidarity with the victims (Park 2009, 42).

Under the leadership of Joseph Ratzinger the Congregation for the Doctrine of the Faith (mainly in its Instruction on certain aspects of the "Theology of Liberation," 1984) corrected the Latin American tendency towards sin as structural evil. Ratzinger did not reject liberation theology, but he criticized its one-sidedness (Min 1989, 81), because it was guilty "of the denial of the integrity of salvation in its three dimensions; transcendence, individuality,

---

31. The collectivist aspect of sin in Japan has already been discussed in *5.2 The experience of* Unheil *under the theological aspect*. Asia tends to be more collectivistic than the West and therefore a collectivistic sin-concept can be apprehended more easily. The Japanese religious scientist Iwanami (岩波明) compared the prototypes of evil, Jude in Christianity and Devadatta in Buddhism and observed that "following the Judaist legalism Christians rather fear punishment . . . This makes sin in Christianity a personal matter" (von Brück and Lai 2000, 355).

and wholeness" (70). The instruction further reads: "For some it even seems that the necessary struggle for human justice in the economic and political sense constituted the essence of salvation. For them, the gospel is reduced to a purely earthly gospel" (80). Ratzinger further criticized that liberation theology tends to "localize evil principally or uniquely" in "social sin" or "structural sin." Thus they ignore "the full ambit of sin" or "the totality of effects of sin of which social sin is only one dimension. It fails to recognize that sin, which is always primarily personal, not evil structures, is the cause of evil." This leads to the "destruction of the 'wholeness' of salvation" (81).

There is also opposition from Korean theologians. Kim writes about the concept that the term "sin" belongs to the vocabulary of the ruling class, and the term "*han*" to the vocabulary of the *Minjung*:

> This leads to a literally "superficial" hamartiology[32] that localizes sin not anymore in the relation between God and man, but transforms it into a purely worldly category which then is just a synonym for social injustice. This concept is opposed to the biblical understanding of sin according to which all are guilty before God and sinners. (Kim 2002, 155)

In Japan, the respective critique is expressed by the political scientist and theologian Mitsuo Miyata: "Of course, the gospel is not a message of political salvation. The Christian confession transcends politics." On the other hand, Miyata warns against a political voicelessness of the gospel. Precisely because the gospel "transcends" politics, it can be of indispensable service for both Christians and non-Christians by making political [common] sense truly rational and objective. By doing so Christians in Japan can contribute to the strengthening of "democracy and social justice" and to the advancement of a future of peace (Miyata 1984, 67).

10.2.4.2 Salvation as collectivistic concept (liberation theologies)

The Latin American liberation theologies have to do something with the Japanese salvation concept insofar that they understand salvation (at least partially) as a collectivistic and this-worldly concept. According to Rahner, all theology is soteriology that must never be limited to a singular doctrine of forgiveness of sins (Manzanera 1974, 46). In a fictitious discussion between a liberation theologian, a parish priest, and a liberation theology activist Clodovis

---

32. This critique is certainly too general. In a lecture on the subject of forgiveness, Park clearly opposed a singularly psychological and inter-personal concept of forgiveness (Park 2003).

Boff makes the activist make an accusation that needs to be heeded: Those who spiritualize terms do so, because this is easier, and because they cannot face reality (Boff 1985, 74).

In this regard, Waldenfels pointed to the fact that redemption and salvation were originally worldly concepts. Redemption used to be the freeing of slaves, salvation a military term: "Open room is to be created for somebody with armed force, and he shall be delivered from the power of his enemies" (Waldenfels 1974, 114). In the Hebrew Bible the terms for salvation are derived from יָשַׁע, which in Arabic means "making wide space" or "making sufficient." The opposite is צָרַר, "narrow," "being limited," "being cramped," "being constricted," or "bring into trouble" (Harris et al. 1981). "If the soul can develop without limited forces around, it is wide." Therefore "salvation" is the "development of the human soul," "unlimited prosperity, happiness, and safety under the protection of a powerful God, and elimination of all dangers." The salvation concept of the Hebrew Bible is this-worldly (Goldsmith 1994, 83).

Influenced by the Enlightenment[33] and as a countermovement to the *Great Reverse*, the Evangelicals went through a period of individualistic narrowness after Wheaton 1966 (Walldorf 1996, 231). After Lausanne 1974 they started asking the anxious question whether their understanding of salvation was too narrow (Hindmarsh 2002, 43). "The salvation we claim should be transforming us in the totality of our personal and social responsibilities" (*Lausanne Covenant* 1974). John Stott who was the leading thinker certainly started a process of rapprochement between Evangelicals and liberation theologies. While liberation theologies warn against materializing metaphors and thus depriving them of their transcendence (Boff 1985, 79),[34] Evangelicals point out that the "emphasis on salvation of the soul for eternal life is not the only feature of Evangelicalism" (Bacote 2002, 97). The Evangelical Wheaton professor Vincent Bacote named four categories of a soteriology focusing on this life:

---

33. In the Christian tradition from which the modern mission movement emerged, salvation was localized in the inner experience of the individual. The individual stood before God alone (Bosch 1983, 500). Early Pietism was unequivocally concerned with the salvation of individuals. According to Zinzendorf the Christian mission was limited to "save more souls" (Müller 1985, 71). On the other side, Hindmarsh showed that Wesley advanced the primacy of the poor and ostracized and showed great interest in the physical healing of the sick (Hindmarsh 2002, 48–53). Also, early Evangelicals were very much interested in transformation of society (Hindmarsh 2002, 56–57).

34. Society is one – and only one – of the *topoi* of the realization of salvation (Boff 1985, 83). This warning is not new. Freytag warned against a "pan-missionism in a sense that the church's responsibility for this world per se was 'mission.'" Müller called the equation of Christian responsibility and mission an "erosion of the gospel" (Müller 1985, 74).

- Public character of salvation: Salvation must go beyond the experience in one's own heart. According to Andrew Sung Park, the cross of Luke 9:23 is a symbol of protest against suppression (Bacote 2002, 107). The Christian faith must criticize those forms of community that can bring death to their members. The question posed to Evangelical soteriology is: Are we willing to advance the proclamation of salvation as costly identification with a Messiah who brings salvation in this life by means of the suffering of a cross-bearing community?[35] The public character of the gospel leads to an incitement to justice (108–109).
- Political character of salvation: A sin-concept that also addresses (like Millard Erickson) collectivistic sin is prerogative. Biblical examples are Achan (Erickson 2000, 592; Bacote 2002, 109), in Daniel 9, and Micah 3. In order to be a "nation of the book," Christians need to permeate political systems that practice open and hidden forms of suppression and not just read Paul's "sin-individualism"[36] (Bacote 2002, 110).
- Pneumatological character of salvation: According to Van Ruler, the Spirit instructs us to have an enthusiastic dedication for the world.[37] Van Ruler also claims that the Spirit of God not only dwells in Christians, but also in nations and cultures, as they are established in the covenant [with God]. Bacote wants to learn from this that

---

35. In a similar way, Bosch demanded that a "missionary theology" must be a theology of *costly discipleship* that embraces elements of suffering and servanthood (Bosch 1983, 493). "The church must truly participate in the suffering of others and must make their suffering its own. In order to do so it must theologically recognize the presence of Christ in the brokenness of human existence" (Boesak 1985, 55–56). Tutu talked about the "costly matter" of "identification with the poor." It is costly because it leads into "defamation and ostracization" (Tutu 1987, 33). Triebel explained, "He who follows Jesus cannot ignore the injustice in this world. Showing *compassion* [a term introduced into missiology by Bosch] he will take sides with the suppressed, with those who suffer under injustice, and he will endeavor to step up for them, not for the sake of political activism and political interests, but for the sake of his faith" (Triebel 1988, 11–12).

36. This accusation does not apply to Paul, but to the Liberal Protestant interpretation of his thought. "In principal, *Heil* as well as *Unheil* have a communal character. Nothing is further from Paul's intention than religious individualism; the fact that around [the year] 1900 Liberal-Protestantism (then hailed as the religion of the future) (Adolf von Harnack) attributed a distinctive religious individualism particularly to Paul. This has blocked its understanding of the phenomenon Church until today." In contrast, "for the Jew Paul the net of cooperative relationships . . . is primal also for religion" (Berger 2002, 11).

37. The Brazilian liberation theologian Gorgulho: "The life according to the Spirit is realized in the praxis of love" (Gorgulho 1984, 95).

the Spirit opens our eyes not only for eternity but also for the here and now (111).[38]
- Geographical character of salvation: Salvation requires a place in the geographical sense (112).

10.2.5 My Own (Preliminary) Opinion

> We must never hide behind our prayers, because that would never be an authentic Christian spirituality. But neither must we be satisfied with worldly things and the fulfillment of our material duties. (Tutu 1987, 31)

> The danger lurking today, is that traditional soteriology is almost meaningless for secularized people, and that at the same time, it loses its Christian validity because of theological efforts that attempt to do justice to the problems of humanity and to strive for adaption. (Jhi 2006, 15)

These two quotes accurately depict the dilemma. The efforts to answer to the needs of people with a this-worldly soteriological outlook must not lead to the sellout of Christian truths. Theology must

> answer to the soteriological question of present-day people while remaining faithful to the Christian tradition, to the origin of the salvific event and concept. It must do justice to the changing questions of modern people, but must never abandon its roots for the sake of adaption. (Jhi 2006, 28)

The often condescendingly spoken of salvation concept of the Old Testament (Jhi 2006, 22) may well serve as a model for a vital tension between salvation in this and the yonder world. According to Lash, Max Weber's analysis of Judaism shows its "co-existence of an extraordinary this-worldliness and an extreme other-worldliness" (Lash 1999, 374). This model is of interest for this book as well, because "even though the world of Judaism and the world of Shintoism are . . . totally separated" they show "surprising commonalities":

---

38. This thought is certainly problematic for Bacote. On the website of Wheaton College he introduces himself with a quote from Abraham Kuyper: "There is not a square inch in the whole domain of our human existence over which Christ, who is sovereign over all, does not cry: Mine!" He concludes: "This quote gets to the heart of the way I view theology and the Christian faith. It is important to recognize that our faith is not reserved for some kind of Christian ghetto. It ought to impact every facet of our lives and society" (Bacote 2008).

> The psychology of both religions is basically different, but both are interested in the present rather than in the coming world. This is different from Christianity and Buddhism that – historically speaking – put the world after death first. A pious Jew does not fulfill his religious duties in order to obtain eternal salvation, but because God commanded him to do so. The rewards and punishments given by the Mosaic Law are clearly not concerned with the coming world but with this world. (Shillony 2004, 34)

In search for the "roots" evoked by Jhi, I want to start out with Martin Luther's soteriological leading question, "*Wie kriege ich einen gnädigen Gott?*," "How do I get a gracious God?" Luther wrote on Galatians 3:15ff:

> Nay, God can reward our good works, for example with fair weather, earthly peace,[39] riches, health, through protection from all calamities, and (and that is true for the justified) in heaven with special advantages and freedom.[40] But the principal part,[41] the forgiveness of sins and the gain of a gracious God, that is too rich and noble[42] to be earned with works. (Luther 1987, 372)

And on Luke 16:1–9 Luther preached on the second Sunday about the Trinity:

> He who truly considers such blessing, even though he be lacking earthly[43] blessings, even though he be poor, despised, wretched,[44] and laden with sundry adversities, all this is a lowly thing to him; because he sees that always he retains more than he loses. If money and goods be not there, yet he knows that he has a gracious God; if the body be weak and sick, yet he knows that he has been called to eternal life. (Luther 1862, 386)

Luther knows both salvation as "fair weather," "peace," and "riches," yet also and more important than the others "the principal part, the forgiveness of sins and that we may get a gracious God." It is this most important of all questions that is not undisputed anymore. "Today it cannot be a matter of whether we

---

39. *Zeitlichem Frieden.*
40. *Im Himmel mit sonderlichem Vorteil und Freiheit.*
41. *Das Hauptstück.*
42. *Hoch und hehr.*
43. *Zeitlich.*
44. *Unglückhaft.*

undisputedly accept Luther's question, [how he may get a gracious God], as crucial" (Adam 1999, 282).[45] Jüngel explains the fact that today nobody is concerned with the "gracious God" anymore:

> The question for God has become irrelevant, because people don't ask for grace anymore when they inquire of "God" . . . As soon as I think I can ask for *God* while *bypassing* the question of grace the inquiry for God ceases to exist. Because then the discourse abstracted from revelation of the gracious God goes past the crucial issue. But if the crucial thing about God is not said, any discourse about God becomes meaningless, because with losing the crucial in regard with God also denies the crucial in regard with man: faith. Any inquiry for God that bypasses the grace of God ignores the fact that God and faith belong together, as Luther put it. (Jüngel 2000, 74–75)

"We must never be so easily taken in tow by this kind of modern question, nor must we short-circuitedly say, we as modern people have replaced Luther's question by questioning God's existence per se" (Thielicke 1979, 72). The criteria for probing our questions can never be whether they are "old-fashioned" or "modern." We must rather consider "whether we modern people have forgotten and buried the realities that drove the old to ask such hard and annoying questions. We want to assume that the religious reality has changed. However, what if only we have changed? What if we have but become shallow?" (Thielicke 1979, 82). Instead of pushing aside or even dropping altogether the inquiry for the gracious God and consequently making humans and their needs the center of soteriology,[46] this inquiry must again be made central and reformulated for modern people.

> The transcendent relationship of man with God by which premodern man[47] was directly affected and which was by no means exceptional for him must be . . . retained in modern man's inquiry for salvation; otherwise soteriology forfeits its constituting cause from the very beginning and expires in sciences such as social

---

45. This was the subject of discussion at the Assembly of the Lutheran World Federation in 1963 (Adam 1999, 282).

46. As, for example, postulated by Schütz: "Modern man defined by Enlightenment . . . cannot directly ask for God anymore, because he does not anymore accept God – perhaps even as a God of wrath – as a matter of course" (Schütz 1973, 32).

47. *Frühere Menschen.*

ethics ... In order to retain and preserve the Christian origin and tradition it is important to correctly classify man as a sinner before God, and the experience of *Unheil* as outside and without God. This classification ... is indispensable, even for present-day's soteriology. Because without this prerogative the constitutive element of Christian soteriology, that is the Christ event, and mainly the cross, can hardly be established. (Jhi 2006, 28–29)

As important and fundamental as the inquiry for a gracious God is, it cannot become the only concern of Christian soteriology. Neither must the concern for "peace with God" replace the concern for "peace on earth," nor must "the biblical understanding of salvation be dissolved into the social-ethic dimension" (Berneburg 1997, 233). Modern salvation concepts repeat the historical mistake of Stoicism and Gnosticism, that is, to consider man as good in principle and as the ultimate good. Modern man seeks the fault mostly outside and not inside. Therefore, salvation is sought in liberation from weakening, external influences (Watts 2002, 39). Berneburg warns against the danger of a soteriological "horizontalism" (Boff 1985, 68) explicitly because "in human life the vertical and the horizontal dimensions cannot always be distinguished." And this is the very reason why "theological discernment is all the more necessary" (Berneburg 1997, 232).[48]

Beyerhaus offers a kind of "theological discernment" in a comment on 2 Corinthians 5:18:

> [This passage] is first concerned with the reconciliation between God and us; however, this opens the opportunity of reconciliation between us and our neighbors. The most important task of missionaries is to go to not yet reconciled people and to beseech them to be reconciled with God ... This reconciliation is offered through proclamation, and is consummated through the integration into the body of Christ through faith and baptism. But to make the reconciling love of God visible, the word is accompanied by deeds of mercy. (Beyerhaus 1975, 9–10)

As to the relationship between the horizontal mandate of the church in social, caricatural and economic help he writes:

---

48. Boff claims that even though salvation and liberation belong together in praxis, they don't "in the head" (Boff 1985, 82). "All suppression is sin, but not all sin is suppression. Therefore, all liberation is grace, yet not all grace liberation, at least not in the political sense" (78).

> All help offered in these areas can be considered as an expression of genuine Christian mission, if the salvation event in the gospel it's concerned with is its origin and purpose: the reconciliation of man with God through forgiveness of sins, which also liberates us from the captivity under demons and endows us with true life. (Beyerhaus 1975, 10)

While theologians like Beyerhaus strive for discernment and conceptual clarification, others tend to (or deliberately) aim at conceptual ambiguity that blurs the line between the horizontal and the vertical. One example is Jhi: "All humans strive for happiness and fulfillment of life. In religious-soteriological terminology this could be expressed thus: all seek salvation" (Jhi 2006, 11). Another, even more marked example is Nürnberger:

> The discrimination between *Heil* and welfare[49] cannot be sustained. *Heil* is *heil* life. *Heil* life is comprehensive welfare in peace with God and the whence and whither of experienced reality. If wellness[50] is to be whole and comprehensive it has to be thought of in concentric and expanding contexts: the psyche needs to be regarded in the context of corporeality, the individual in the context of community, the community in the context of nature, nature in the context of cosmic processes. Wellness is not divisible. (Nürnberger 2003, 115)

This quote shows the ultimate consequence of a soteriology that puts the vertical side by side with the horizontal, a soteriology that roots itself in anything else and aims at anything else than God alone: it leads to outright naturalism. The ultimate – and thus ultimately determining – value of salvation in Nürnberger's quote is the cosmos. His outlook is that of the Japanese *gense riyaku* (現世利益) and thoroughly pagan.

On top of that, I cannot help but feel that this kind of reasoning that speaks of putting the vertical and the horizontal side by side conceals its true intention of replacing the vertical by the horizontal. Social justice, health, and happiness are all *Heil*, salvation, *shalom*. But they do not save from the wrath of God. However, "spiritual salvation is forgiveness of sins and fellowship with God the father" (Boff 1985, 77). Jesus explicitly warned against losing vertical

---

49. *Wohl.*
50. *Wohlergehen.*

salvation for the sake of horizontal salvation: "What good will it be for a man if he gains the whole world, yet forfeits his soul?" (Mark 8:36; cf. Matt 16:26).

The Argentinian theologian Eduardo Pironio advocates a well-balanced view:

> The Spirit liberates us in Christ . . . The day shall come in which we are completely free. The Spirit who raised Christ from the dead, will also bring our mortal body to life (Rom 8:11), and then at last we shall be "lords" of creation forever. Until that day comes, the Holy Spirit who leads us impresses into us the image of Christ, the new Man, ever more deeply and in our innermost being gives rise to love, joy, and peace (Gal 5:33) as our default attitude. (Pironio 1984, 35)

The tasks of this new person are:

- first return oneself, inwardness, contemplation; as a man of contemplation the new man is a man enabled for dialogue. Praying means to be aware of one's destitution before God and to enter into the community of his will (Pironio 1984, 35–36).
- "The new man – a man of Easter – lives the disappropriation of self in Christ" which carries the characteristic of steadfastness because one has to "die frequently" (36–37).
- The new man is a man of joy, a trait long lost in a secularized "fun"-world. Joy is the sister of hope. Joy is the assurance of the coming of Jesus, of his being near even today (Phil 4:5). The joy of Christians is not rejection of the cross. On the contrary, if deep and true, it has its origin in the cross. Neither is it an escape from a shocking and harmful reality. It is rather founded in the steadfast conviction that salvation has come to us (37–38).

10.3 Between "This" World and the "Coming" World

Summary: An overly strong orientation to this world can result in ethical shallowness (*Shichifukujin*, 七福神), an overly strong orientation to "the coming world" to a dangerous ethical relativism. The example of *Aum-Shinrikyou* (オウム真理教) shows that an exclusive orientation to salvation in "the coming world" can be totally oblivious of salvation "here and now" and thus create unspeakable suffering.

When understanding eschatology as a principle, salvation is mainly sought in "this world." When understanding eschatology as history, salvation is mainly sought in "the other world." However, the hope of "the coming world" must neither be lifted up to a principle and thus deprived of its historical truth, nor must this hope itself lack historical reality.

Only if the glory of God and not human happiness (this-worldly or not this-worldly) is in the center of soteriology, can the balance between salvation in "this world" and salvation in "the coming world" be kept.

According to Pieris, the function of a meta-cosmic religion is to provide a cosmic religion with a meaningful interpretative "referential framework" that "constantly relativizes the here and now" (Pieris 1988, 54–55). The question that was painfully posed by the Japanese sect *Aum-Shinrikyou* (オウム真理教) is just how much the "here and now" can and may be relativized. That there is "too much" of relativizing became clear when Asahara used the "referential framework" of Tibetan Tantra-Buddhism to legitimize mass murder. And it is particularly its "transcendental" values that are used as justification for the until then unthinkable violence. Religiously motivated terrorism "assumes a transcendent purpose and therefore becomes a sacramental or divine duty" (Hoffman in Parachini and Furukawa 2007, 532). Therefore, in the first paragraph I am going to review the worldview of *Aum-Shinrikyou* (オウム真理教) in the light of the tension between "this" world" and the "coming" world.

However, there can also be "too little" provision of meaning. This happens when in the name of Post-Modernity the scepter of meaninglessness is raised and all "meta-stories" – including that of Tibetan Tantra-Buddhism – are refuted. "The Post-Modern society of the present confines basic metaphysical problems such as the inquiry for salvation to the realm of questions that cannot be answered scientifically. Classic references to philosophy and religion are refuted" (Hille 2004, 362) and thus devalued. According to Ernest Becker (1962) "Post-Modernity [thus] . . . disintegrates the teleological yield of the history of humanity and raises the scepter of meaninglessness, the conceivableness that human existence might possibly be without any inherent value" (Lose 2003, 19). What remains after the destruction of all (metaphysical) meta-stories are "language games" and "paralogies,"[51] eventually meaningless even in the smallest societal entities.

The outline on the *Shichifukujin* (七福神) showed meaninglessness and thus moral shallowness of a consequently this-worldly orientation. The fact that Japan as one of the richest countries in the world, as a country that provides more this-worldly and horizontal "salvation" than most other countries, suffers from one of the highest suicide rates in the world is sad and alarming. Japan is an example of a country that is rich enough to give its citizens all that is physically necessary. However, Japan is poor in spiritual things and in the kingdom of God (Toujou 1992, 180).

After the paragraph on *Aum-Shinrikyou* (オウム真理教) I am going to discuss various different theological concepts under the viewpoint of two fields of tension: *10.3.2 Between eschatology as principle and eschatology as history* and *10.3.3 Between world and heaven.*

10.3.1 Aum-Shinrikyou *(*オウム真理教*)*

On 18 March 1995, members of the Japanese *Aum*-Sect committed a nerve-gas[52] attack in the Tokyo subway system killing ten[53] and injuring over 5,000 people (Deutsche Gesellschaft für auswärtige Politik e.V. 2004, 35). The goal was to kill 30,000 people (Schmidt and von Weizsäcker 2007, 213).

Asahara Shoukou (麻原彰晃), the leader of the *Aum*-Sect, was sentenced to death for multiple murders on 27 February 2004 (Gardner 2009). The verdict has been under appeal until recently. The appeal for reopening of the lawsuit, submitted by Asahara's daughter in 2008 was timely rejected by the Tokyo District Court on the fourteenth anniversary of the attack (Itou 2009). Until recently Japan has been struggling with the questions raised by the attack. It was not only an act of terror but it touched on basic questions of Japanese culture.

---

51. "Language games" (Wittgenstein) are freely invented and temporary figures of speech, the sum of which forms a language. A "meta story" is a story that claims a broad universality and represents an ultimate and absolute truth. A paralogy is a stimulating interlocutory form that creates ideas, but does not necessarily lead to compliance (Shawver 2008, 462).

52. Sarin was "selected after a long research history with biological weapons (Langbein et al. 2002, 160) and then used in the attack in Tokyo. It was originally developed by German scientists in the 1930s under Hitler's preparations for World War II. In the 1980s it was used against the Kurds and by Iraq against Iran. It is 26 times as poisonous as cyanide. A drop the size of a pinhead can kill a person" (Gräfe in Murakami 2002, 11).

53. Others talk about 12 casualties (Kaplan and Marshall 1996, 388; Langbein et al. 2002, 158).

In the 1970s, the time of origin of *Aum-Shinrikyou* (オウム真理教), Japan experienced a "spiritual boom." Hundreds of new religious groups endeavored to fill the spiritual void in the hearts of the nation (Kaplan and Marshall 1996, 23). The trend of those days was the occupation with the extraordinary and the fantastical. "Particularly the young generation enthusiastically delved into the world of the unreal" (42). This withdrawal into an unrealistic world was understandable. Where else could those young people have withdrawn in a disillusioned post-bubble world that had before systematically destroyed any individualism?

> Talented, young people were broken in this educational machinery. What counts in this world are only adaption, obedience, and mere memorizing. Japanese students must not analyze, not question, but only accumulate facts and then reel them off . . . in endless exams. (Kaplan and Marshall 1996, 43)

Chizuo Matsumoto (松本智津夫), born in 1955, came into contact with yoga through the New Religion *Agon-Shuu* (阿含宗). In the early 1980s he founded the group *Aum Shinsen-no-kai* (オウム神仙の会), the "*Aum* Circle of Divine Hermits" (Parachini and Furukawa 2007, 534). In 1987 he changed his name to Asahara Shoukou (麻原彰晃), and the name of his group to *Aum-Shinrikyou* (オウム真理教), "Aum-Teaching of the Absolute Truth." Asahara saw himself as being called to missionary work in Japan by a comment of the Dalai Lama (Repp 1997, 15–17).[54] Asahara's "empire" consisted of twenty organizations all over Japan, thirty companies of various branches (also foreign), a trading company in Taiwan, a sheep breeding farm in Australia, a tea plantation in Sri Lanka, radio and TV programs in Russia, a computer chain, restaurants, fitness-centers and a clinic. In its heyday *Aum-Shinrikyou* (オウム真理教) had 40,000 members (Langbein et al. 2002, 159), 10,000 in Japan and 30,000 in Russia (Parachini and Furukawa 2007, 534). After the attack, Asahara was officially deposed. *Aum-Shinrikyou* (オウム真理教) lived on under the name *Aleph* (アーレフ) and speedily recovered. As early as 1997, it had rebuilt fifteen local centers and recruited about 5,000 members (Langbein et al. 2002,

---

54. "The Dalai Lama had met Asahara (as he had many other Japanese religious leaders), been photographed with him and exchanged compliments through formal letters. These items (the letters and photographs) have since be utilized by *Aum* to construct the image of a close and approving relationship (since refuted by the Dalai Lama, who has pointed out that such violent activities as *Aum* has been accused of are contrary to Buddhism teaching). This pattern, of using foreign religious leaders so as to enhance one's own image and religious status is very common in Japan, with the Pope and the Dalai Lama being the two most targeted religious leaders" (Reader 1996, 17).

161). However, in 2009 they counted about 1,500 members (Ellington 2009, 168). In 2012 there were 1,200 to 1,300 members with a growth rate of about two hundred new members every year (*Japan Today* 2012).

The unspeakably cynical violence baffled many as it marked "a new era of terrorism." *Aum-Shinrikyou* (オウム真理教) did

> what most government and private experts believed terrorists would eschew: the use of a military-grade chemical agent, although with degraded quality, indiscriminately on ordinary citizens with the intent to cause mass murder. Until this attack, most observers assumed terrorists wanted as much public attention with as little death and destruction as they could get away with. (Parachini and Furukawa 2007, 531)

Concerning the Tokyo sarin attack Juergensmeyer wrote: "The religious tradition in which one least expects to find violence is Buddhism, and the location for which a violent act of religious terrorism is least anticipated is modern urban Japan" (Juergensmeyer 2003, 103).[55] How did this kind of violence come about? What are its religious sources? How can it be that in a country of which harmony is the highest value such readiness to use violence could emerge under the cloak of such harmony (Repp 1997, 67)? The sad example of *Aum-Shinrikyou* (オウム真理教) shows that a religion's one-sided focus on the "coming world" or a "coming age" can lead to extreme cynicism. Both religious sources of *Aum-Shinrikyou* (オウム真理教) seek salvation as something yet to come; the one in a future life within the cycle of rebirth, the other in a coming kingdom after an apocalyptic catastrophe.

10.3.1.1 Tibetan Tantra-Buddhism

The term "*Aum*" is originally a Sanskrit word meaning the powers of destruction and re-creation of the universe (Reader 1996, 15). Asahara identified himself with *Shiva*, the "central object of [*Aum*'s] worship" (Repp 1997, 18). Shiva represents the "chaotic-dynamic element in the Hinduist pantheon that leads to destruction and re-creation" (Repp 1997, 26; Schopenhauer 1859, 324–325).

Aum as religion goes back to Gilbert Bourdins' (1923–1998) Aumism. In his late twenties, Bourdins dedicated himself to the search for the "divine," he

---

55. Those more acquainted with Japan and its culture do not share his bafflement. Martin Repp wrote: "Many Japanese are baffled by the violence of *Aum* . . . But what about the aggressive driving style that is a threat to pedestrians and cyclists? And what about the savage destruction of the traditional Japanese culture? (Repp 1997, 67–68).

became a member of the Theosophical Society and the French *Grande Loge Nationale*, became actively involved in various societies affiliated with Rose-Cross, Martinism, the Kabbalah, and Alchemism, and showed interest in the Holy Grail. In the early 1960s he travelled to Rishikesh (in the Himalayas) and became acquainted with the influential guru Swami Sivananda, the founder of the *Divine Life Society* (Zoccatelli 2005, 215–216), from whom, at the occasion of his initiation as *sannyasin*, he received his new name, Hamsananda Sarasvati. He founded Aumism sometime in the 1970s or 1980s (Zoccatelli 2005, 217).

In Tibetan Buddhism, salvation is sought in a coming life within the cycle of rebirth. That leads to the dangerous cynicism that devalues the life in the here and now to something merely preliminary. According to Asahara, suffering is merely the result of bad karma that needs to be overcome by religious liberation. "Freedom is freedom from karma" (Asahara in Repp 1997, 28).

> The suffering you now experience is the suffering of the wretched realms [of existence, that is the realm of hell, the world of the Hungry Ghosts and the world of the animals] that you would have had to suffer in your next life. Therefore, you should suffer much and practice much in order to overcome suffering and reach true freedom, joy, and happiness. (Asahara in Repp 1997, 28)

In addition to this suffering *Aum-Shinrikyou* (オウム真理教) also knows the suffering of the "Affirmation of Suffering Vow" that pledges vicarious suffering for others (Repp 1997, 28–29). It was probably composed by Asahara and reads as follows: *Jiko-no kurushimi-oyorokobi-to shi, ta-no kurushimo-o kurusimi-to suru* (自己の苦しみを喜びとし、他の苦しみを苦しみとする) (Irokawa and Miyata 1997, 77), "I make my suffering my joy; I make others' suffering my own suffering" (Asahara in Repp 2014, 204). It is here that the specific influence of the Tibetan Tantra-Buddhism leads to the devastating sanction of evil means to a (supposedly) good end:

> Parents accumulate bad deeds because of their children. They work hard; they even lie for their children. . . . However, when the children attain enlightenment and start to save other beings, the bad deeds instantly change into good deeds. This is a Tantric way of thinking. The parents go to the higher world because their children could not live if they had not committed bad deeds. (Asahara in Repp 2014, 205)

In the esoteric Buddhism of Tibet, the killing of an evil person is called *poa*. *Poa* is a euphemism for murder. It means that according to the karma the lifetime of a certain person has ended and that the one who kills him actually does him a favor by helping him to go on to the next existence. What (according to this thinking) only looks like murder is in truth a great help, because the evil person does not have to go to hell – or any other wretched form of existence – but by means of *poa* has better starting conditions in his next existence (Repp 1997, 33). "Aum's leaders justified the organization's violence in religious terms, suggesting that . . . the victims benefited from death because it purified them of the earthly evils that afflicted them" (Parachini and Furukawa 2007, 531). Kaplan and Marshall talk about a "transfer of the soul into a higher level," about "wiping off of bad karma." The murderer himself can thus "draw closer . . . to the nirvana, because it is 'a good deed to eliminate people who persistently do evil and are condemned to go to hell'" (Kaplan and Marshall 1996, 71). In this sense Asahara said about the victims of the Tokyo Sarin attack: "It is good that the victims lost their souls to the holy leader – and to the god Shiva (Asahara in Kaplan and Marshall 1996, 335).

Asahara's attitude stands in stark opposition to a religiosity that "seems to exist solely for the advancement of individual happiness" (Asahara in Repp 1997, 81).

> Asahara aimed at the value called *gense riyaku* (現世利益). . . . Most New Religions founded in post-war Japan started out with the promise of giving this-worldly benefits to their believers, such as healing from diseases, solving of problems, happiness, and riches. Buddhism is also involved in such kinds of religiosity, although its true purpose of its teaching and praxis is a fundamental solution to human misery. (Repp 1997, 81)

No matter what the "true" purpose of Buddhism is, even *Aum-Shinrikyou* (オウム真理教) needs at least a pinch of *gense riyaku* (現世利益), "this-worldly benefits." In *Aum-Shinrikyou* (オウム真理教) those are mainly riches and fame (Asahara in Repp 1997, 29). The name of the sect's periodical, *Enjoy Happiness* (Kaplan and Marshall 1996, 129) also alluded to this-worldly benefits.

10.3.1.2 Apocalyptic thought from the West
In addition to Buddhist sources, Asahara was also influenced by Christian thought. In 1988, he began reading the Revelation of John from which he

also borrowed terms like "Armageddon"[56] or the "Four Horsemen" frequently occurring in his books.

> Besides being the savior foretold by Nostradamus, he also identified himself as the Christ (most notably in his two-volume series *Kirisuto Sengen* (キリスト宣言), translated as *Declaring Myself the Christ*), who had come to save the world or, as he also at times prophesied, to be sacrificed in order that the world might be saved. (Reader 1996, 18)[57]

In the 1970s, advanced by the writings of Nostradamus, apocalyptic thought became popular in Japan (Repp 1997, 34).[58] Goshima's Japanese translation (1973) of the *Prophecies of Nostradamus* attracted broad attention and was much "used" in the New Religions. Yoshihiro Inoue, who joined the sect at the age of 17 (Reader 1996, 117) and became its "Minister of Intelligence" (Parachini and Furukawa 2007, 562), devoured books on the supernatural as well as Nostradamus's books while still being in high school (Kaplan and Marshall 1996, 280). At least the Japanese translation suggests that a "spiritual savior" would arise from the East. "Not surprisingly, many of the religious leaders who follow a millenialist line in Japan (including Asahara) have identified themselves with this savior, and have read into Nostradamus's work a prediction of their own coming" (Reader 1996, 14). *Aum-Shinrikyou* (オウム真理教) focused particularly on the prophecy ch 10, no.72:

> In the year 1999 and seven months,
> From the skies shall come an alarmingly powerful king.
> To raise again the great King of the Jacquerie,
> Before and after, Mars shall reign at will.
> (Nostradamus in Shimazono 2011, 63)

---

56. In Buddhism, there is a term that is similar to the biblical term "Armageddon": *mappo*, "the age of chaos, when the world forgets the teachings of Buddha and sinks into anarchy." However, Asahara preferred the biblical concept and soon he and his disciples talked about the coming of Armageddon (Kaplan and Marshall 1996, 31).

57. Because of the missionary activities in America, Americans also became members of the sect. One of them was David who studied theology at Columbia University. In an interview given in 1995, he said that what impressed him most in Asahara was "his desire to end the suffering of all human beings in the universe, and to sacrifice his own happiness and peace of mind in order to give peace to others" (Kaplan and Marshall 1996, 135).

58. Nostradamus was not the only one who occupied himself with Japan. Edgar Cayce (and others with psychic gifts) also prophesied "cataclysmic events" for Japan, such as volcano eruptions that would lead to the breaking apart of the islands and sinking into the ocean (Mann 1995, 10, 13, 145).

This prophecy has always been understood as prediction of a major catastrophe. Asahara's interpretation: Not the destruction of humanity, but a catastrophe almost as bad, out of which a "new humanity" would be born. Such a cataclysm would create an "*Übermenschheit*," a superhuman race. According to Nostradamus, the advent of the "alarmingly powerful king" would be followed by an age of peace (Mann 1995, 128).

Aum-Shinrikyou (オウム真理教) endeavored to enter politics, but the sect's *Shinritou* (真理党), "*Truth Party*" (Parachini and Furukawa 2007, 538), suffered an abysmal failure in 1989/90 (Repp 1997, 19). From then on, Asahara's sermons revolved more and more around the pending and imminent catastrophe (Kaplan and Marshall 1996, 69). "It takes political action to do what a religion cannot do" (Asahara in Repp 1997, 19). According to Asahara, the Third World War would be not of political or military, but of religious nature, a war between East and West, between Buddhism and Christianity.

> Religious wars break out all over the world. Christianity controls the world and there is no doubt that it persecutes other religions ... Everything happens according to the law of karma. Those who persecute must be persecuted, and those who suppress must be suppressed. I am certain that the last religious war on earth will be a confrontation between Buddhism and Christianity. (Asahara in Repp 2004, 169)

Asahara saw the end of the Christian era. After that all countries would become Buddhist and *Aum-Shinrikyou* (オウム真理教) would be the center of the world (Repp 2004, 169). In other apocalyptic religions, Armageddon is understood as a supernatural event. Asahara, however, planned to bring about Armageddon by himself (Repp 1997, 103). In August 1993, Asahara ordered Masami Tsuchiya, the sect's chief chemist, to "start construction of a sarin producing facility to produce seventy tons of sarin to disperse over major cities in Japan" (Parachini and Furukawa 2007, 541). It was his plan to then blame the United States and thus trigger the Third World War, his "Armageddon."

10.3.2 Between Eschatology as Principle and Eschatology as History

10.3.2.1 Eschatology as principle

In the first paragraph I am going to briefly outline the approaches of Albert Schweitzer, Ernst Bloch, and Jürgen Moltmann. I am going to use Schweitzer's approach, because his work marks a new beginning in eschatology after the epoch of liberal theology (Bosch 1991, 501), and because he heavily influenced

Bloch as well as Moltmann. I am going to use Bloch's approach, because he referred to the Bible more than any other "atheist thinker," even though he did so only to "bequeath" it (Böhm 1979, 93), and because he influenced Moltmann not only in his thought but also in his terminology (Allen 2000, 115). I am going to use Moltmann's approach, because it is a bridge to liberation theology and thus serves as a non-Japanese dialogue partner in the discussion on a theological justification of *gense riyaku* (現世利益).[59]

Albert Schweitzer (1875–1965)

Albert Schweitzer's approach of consequent eschatology (Schwambach 2006, 293) or consistent eschatology (Blocher 2004, 114) was born from the simple discovery he made during his Strasbourg lectures (1903). He found that it would be the "most natural" starting point for a lecture on Jesus to start with his eschatological proclamation (Schweitzer 1998, 417–418).[60] Schweitzer perceived Jesus as wholly embedded in the context of the Judaist-eschatological worldview (Schwambach 2006, 293). Jesus's outlook on the kingdom of God would thus be part of the eschatology of Late Judaism (Schweitzer 1995, 386) which centers around ethics. The connection between the Day of the Lord and ethics is as old as the Old Testament apocalyptic Amos (Schweitzer 1998, 371).

> Not only did he bring to life the notion of the Day of Yahweh throughout history, he also *loaded it with ethics*. Judgment is about to come over the nations, because they sinned ethically, and not because – this would be the antique notion – because they are the enemies of Israel. The Day of Yahweh is thus not a day of winning for Israel but a day of winnowing. (Schweitzer 1998, 371–372)[61]

With John the Baptist "the prophetic and the ethical return to eschatology" (Schweitzer 1998, 414). Jesus then carries on this thought which was already present in Henoch: "Ethical behavior is synonymous with *suffering and persecution for the sake of hope*. Suffering and persecution are the trademark of those predestined for the kingdom of God" (Schweitzer 1998, 420). Jesus did not "spiritualize" the ethics of Late Judaism. On the contrary, he made it "a vessel of his powerful and profound ethic of love" (Schweitzer 1995, 386).

---

59. I am aware that others associate these three with a historical eschatology (Sobrino 1985, 62–63). However, I am going to show that they started out with a historical eschatology, and then transformed it into a principle.

60. In doing so, Schweitzer followed Johannes Weiss (Palu 2012, 14–15).

61. With "winning" and "winnowing" I want to transcribe Schweitzer's agnomination of "*Siegestag*," "day of victory," and "*Sichtungstag*," "day of sifting" or "day of winnowing."

According to Schweitzer, Jesus anticipated the eschaton during his lifetime, or at his death the latest (Schwambach 2006, 293). He justified this with Matthew 10:23, which he interpreted so that Jesus thought the Son of Man would come before the disciples had finished preaching to the cities of Israel (Künzi 1970, 118; Palu 2012, 197). "The disappointment of Early Christianity's imminent expectation not only necessitated a mere rethinking of eschatology," but it rather "mortally wounded the very essence of Early Christianity" (Ebeling 1993, 29). The death of Jesus "differed from that of other martyrs and prophets, for they died with the intention that their death should serve as their last act in defense of their cause." Their death was "in *continuity* with their life" and was thus meaningful to them. "By contrast Jesus dies in total *discontinuity* with his life and his cause. The death he experienced was not only the death of his person, but also the death of his cause" (Sobrino 1985, 218). "It is hard for us to accept that Jesus who possessed the spirit of God in a unique way, and who is for us the highest revealer of religious and spiritual truth, did not precede time as the significance he has for all ages would have called for" (Schweitzer 1995, 386). In his paper "A Comparison of Buddhism and Christianity to a History of Problems," Schweitzer's disciple Fritz Buri wrote on the "theological embarrassment" of the delay of Parousia ("stopgap solution"):

> Jesus and his community saw themselves placed in question by the actual course of the world – Jesus on the cross and perhaps earlier, and his community after his death. The solution to the problem of meaning had been sought in the imminent end of the world which did not take place. He proclaimed the nearness of the kingdom and thought to bring about a new aeon by his atoning death. In doing so he not only set aside an illusion, . . . but he also proclaimed a state of the world and required conduct corresponding to this situation which would make one capable of participation in the kingdom. By his own actions he tried to reach a goal which, like his message, proved to be illusionary in its eschatological expectation. It was possible, contrary to the factual course of history, to see a manifestation of the coming world in the resurrection of the crucified Jesus, in his appearances and in the reception of the spirit and its effects, and so to postpone the coming of the end, to continue to expect it in the future. But, on the one hand, these occurrences were only partial appearances of the promised and expected end, and, on the other, through the necessary postponement of the end one fell into contradiction

with the message of its original imminence. In this way the faithful found themselves forced to make some sort of compromise with the existing world, to find some sort of place in it. This could only happen in a way which contradicted the requirements which Jesus had made for the attainment of fulfillment of meaning in the kingdom of God. (Buri 1986, 18–19)[62]

The consequence was the "de-eschatologizing of religion" (Künzi 1970, 117). According to Martin Werner,[63] the "emergence of dogmatic was a decay product of the self-dissolution of consistent eschatology" (Ebeling 1993, 29). "The awareness that the Parousia was going to be delayed and that the original expectation of its nearness could not be maintained played an essential role in the development of early Christian theology" (Strecker 2000, 211). "According to Werner, the vacuum created by the delay of the Parousia is now filled by the history of the Christian dogma" (Hoekema 1994, 111). What remains after this disappointment is only the ethical teaching of Jesus (Schwambach 2006, 293).

Ernst Bloch (1885–1977)

Bloch begins his magnum opus *Das Prinzip Hoffnung* (*The Principle of Hope*)[64] with the programmatic words: "Primarily, man lives in the future, because he strives, past things only come later, and as yet the genuine present is almost never there at all" (Bloch 1982, 2). "Hopelessness is itself, in a temporal and factual sense, the most insupportable thing, downright intolerable to human needs" (3).

---

62. Kümmel (1987, 30–31) and Ciampa (2007, 290) opposed the notion of the "stop-gap solution" and justified this with the fact that the so-called "eschatological tension" was evident as early as the Post-Exile. Cullmann wrote on Matt 11:5: "Even then it is confirmed how closely the faith of Jesus . . . and mainly the connection between his faith and the 'already,' together with the hope of the consummation of the 'not yet' was linked with his self-conception (*Selbstbewußtsein*); the kingdom of God *is* present, because he who *will* bring it is already present. Wherever he is at work, we are dealing not only with portents, but he himself is already the consummation" (Cullmann 1975, 46). "For Jesus, the juxtaposition of present and future statements cannot pose a problem, because he sees the kingdom realized in his person. Thus, *a problem of delayed Parousia cannot possibly exist for himself*" (Cullmann 1965, 175).

63. Besides Fritz Buri, Martin Werner is Schweitzer's most prominent disciple. Buri attempted – against Schweitzer himself – to associate Schweitzer with existentialism. Therefore, Schweitzer recognized his disciple Martin Werner as the one who had the "courage" to represent and complete his theology. He wrote of him: "You will lead theology into the problem of worldview. It will buck like the cow that must enter a new stable, but that will do nothing to help" (Schweitzer in Grässer 1979, 232).

64. Bloch's work can by no means be outlined in this book. I want to highlight only on what he wrote on biblical eschatology.

Under the headline "Biblische Auferstehung und Apokalypse" [Biblical Resurrection and Apocalypse], Bloch wrote that the Jews were "as this-worldly as the Greeks," yet "at the same time lived with an incomparably stronger focus on the coming and on goals." Bloch justifies this with references to death cult and the Medium of Endor (Bloch 1982, 1323). However, the "breakthrough to immortality" occurred only "through the work of the prophet Daniel (around 160 BC), and the driving force behind this cannot be sought in the old desire for a long life and this-worldly benefits, now extrapolated into transcendence." Bloch views Daniel in the context of Job and the prophets and argues – like Schweitzer – ethically. According to Bloch, the driving force was the "thirst for justice, and so the wish became a postulate, the postmortem scene by all means a tribunal. The faith in [eternal] survival thus became a means to soothe the doubt about God's justice on earth; most importantly, the resurrection became a juridical-moral resurrection" (Bloch 1982, 1324). The "essential novelty, that which should disturb the rich and powerful in their placidity, was added much later in Israel. Because now the leitmotif[65] of the thus demanded resurrection now becomes a threat, it now means the *making up of the missing earthly judgment* . . . (Dan 12:2f)." However, this resurrection has nothing in common with the general resurrection of the dead. Only a few shall be resurrected, "that is the faithful Jewish martyrs, and among the unjust only the worst blood hounds. And even those not to be sent to hell, but to receive shame and disgrace, and that they may see the triumph of the just" (Bloch 1982, 1325).[66]

---

65. *Grundmotiv*, "basic motive."

66. Shame "means the loss of every honor – the opposite of the glory of the redeemed." Except here, the word "shame" occurs only in Isa 66:24 and "denotes something one repels as unacceptable, that is, as an object of loathing, that is, it denotes an objective abomination. Those are the ones that cannot find a place in the kingdom of God because of their impurity" (Maier 1982, 412). "However, verse 2 [of Dan 12] contains a substantial problem. Who are the 'many'? One group of expositors believes that 'many' means 'all.' But this interpretation fails due to the explicit wording . . . Are they . . . only certain groups of Israelites, for example the 'particularly pious' and the 'archivillains' ('*Erzbösewichter*') [as Baumgartner, Botterweck, Bright, Fenz, and Rowley claim]?" (Maier 1982, 413–414). In the Apocrypha and the pseudepigraphic works these "archvillains" are called the godless (Libertines). Enoch 102:6ff: "When you (the just) die, the sinners say about you: 'As we die, so the just die. What did they benefit from their (good) works? From now on we are all equal. What will they receive and behold in eternity? For behold, they are dead, too, and from now on they do not behold (anymore) the light in all eternity'" (Strack and Billerbeck 1982, 885–886). Maier also considers other interpretations: "Could it possibly be that we have to define more narrowly, that we have to – as Culver does – consider a limited resurrection, limited to Israel, immediately after the Great Tribulation yet before the general resurrection of the dead? If one observes more closely, one recognizes that verse 2 does, contrary to verse 1, not speak about Israel anymore. And even more: In chapters 9:27 and 11:44 the 'many' concern the heathen . . . The context of the entire Bible, however, suggest the following solution: Dan 12:2 relates to the first resurrection which takes place immediately

As Schweitzer, Bloch saw Jesus as completely embedded in the context of this "Jewish-apocalyptic wordview." Like Schweitzer, Bloch argued on the basis of Matthew 11: "The great logion in Matt 11:25–30 is [about] this world, not yonder world;[67] it is [a] government degree of the Messiah-King who brings to end suffering of any kind, [of the messiah-King] as the one who has been given all things so he may turn around everything." Bloch translates Luke 17:21 this way: "The kingdom of God is among you" and notes that with this sentence Jesus addressed "the Pharisees . . . and not the disciples." This sentence means: "The kingdom is already alive among you, the Pharisees, as an elected community, in these disciples." Bloch concludes: "Therefore, the sense is a social and not an inward, invisible sense." In John 18:36 Jesus "did not offer to Pilate an alibi by means of cowardly otherworldly pathos." The meaning is rather chronological, according to the "astral-religious speculations of the Old Orient, that is, the teaching of the eons." "This world" means the "present aeon." The "other world" is not someplace else but chronologically the "future aeon." Bloch concludes: Jesus therefore means "not a geographical distinction between this world and yonder world, but *a world chronologically-succeeding on the very same stage located here.* 'That world' is the utopian earth under a utopian sky."[68] Jesus expected "an upheaval that would not leave one stone unturned, and he expected it in the next moment, from nature, from the super-weapon of a cosmic catastrophe." Therefore, he could "render unto Caesar what was Caesar's." Jesus thus expressed the "contempt for the state" with regard to "its imminent doom" (Bloch 1982, 575–582). "Jesus demanded the leap, not the leap . . . from this world into the inner world or the yonder world, but a new and as a fresh start into this world" (583). In this sense, Bloch called Jesus "eschatology from scratch" (1491). "Jesus precisely is the opposing sign against the authority, and it is precisely this sign the world opposed and answered with the gallows: the cross is the world's answer to the Christian love" (1489).[69]

---

before the Millennium (Matt 24:31; 1 Cor 15:23ff; 1 Thess 4:14ff; Rev 19:20). This is actually a resurrection to eternal life for 'many.' However, at the same time the Antichrist and the False Prophet – possibly a group of people – are already thrown in the 'Lake of Fire' (Rev 19:29). This 'Lake of Fire' is nothing else than the place of eternal condemnation, so that this could be a called a resurrection 'unto eternal shame and disgrace' (John 5:29; Rev 20:10, 14f). However, this solution is merely a suggestion and not absolutely compelling" (Maier 1982, 413–414).

    67. *Diesseits, nicht Jenseits.*

    68. *Himmel.*

    69. Later I want to address the cross-interpretation of liberation theologies. They were influenced by Schweitzer via Bloch and Moltmann.

As Schweitzer, Bloch understood the cross of Jesus not as continuation of his work, but as discontinuity and disruption (Sobrino 1985, 218). "So unshakingly did Jesus believe in himself being the bringer of the imminent Zion that this faith left him only on the cross (Bloch 1969, 175). As Schweitzer and liberation theologies with their selective referral to the "historical Jesus," Paul and his theology mean nothing to Bloch.[70] According to Bloch, Paul started building the foundation of his thought at zero, at the failure of Jesus of Nazareth. "Instead of accepting the historical reality of the death of Jesus, Paul starts forming a new god. With his own interpretation of the cross, Paul virtually stabs Jesus in the back" (Böhm 1979, 115).[71] According to Bloch, Jesus is the Messiah not in spite of the cross but because of the cross (Böhm 1979, 116). "The life goal of the actual Jesus of Nazareth, as Bloch could only perceive him according to his presuppositions, has been thoroughly destroyed by his apostles: that is, to domicile man in this world alone . . . Paul reinstated the ruling Above . . . Man remains dependent" (Böhm 1979, 117).

The salvation-historic interpretation of the cross, as Paul advanced it, according to which the cross is "a burden God cast upon his son vicariously for mankind," is to Bloch an "unparalleled twist" (Böhm 1979, 115–116). "In order to justify itself, the same world [that brought Jesus to the cross], later used heathen myths and made his death on the cross a voluntary sacrifice" (Bloch 1982, 1489).

Jürgen Moltmann (1926-)

Only hope can be called "realistic," because only hope takes seriously the possibilities that the presence is pregnant with (Moltmann 2002, 10). Moltmann was strongly influenced by Schweitzer and Bloch (Bühler 1981, 293). As he works with theological metaphors this is not always obvious. Therefore, it is important to first look at some of his basic theological assumptions:

Moltmann's concept of God

According to Cobb, Moltmann is opposed to a theistic God. He rather wants to see God in the suffering of Jesus. Although Moltmann speaks a great deal about God, he rarely addresses directly the question, "Who is God?" On one occasion, he writes as follows:

---

70. Bloch probably got his respect for Jesus and his aversion for Paul from Nietzsche (Watts 2002, 39).

71. The German has an impressive word game here: *Er fällt gewissermaßen dem wirklichen Jesus mit seiner eigenen Kreuzesauslegung in den Rücken.*

> The image of the authority in heaven ... is past. The judging God is found in the man who argues with God ... We abandon the centuries-old, weak Christianization of the God concept and are on the way towards a fuller understanding of God in the crucified Christ. Who is "God" in the Christ event? He is the power of transformation of the world in vicarious suffering. Who is "God" in the corresponding event of belief in unbelief? He is the word of the justification of the godless. Who is "God" in the event of love and alienation? He is the power of freedom in self-surrender. Who is "God" in the event of hope and in the face of death? He is the power of a qualitatively near future. Finally, who is "God" in the new creation? He is the eternal presence of the victory of the crucified Christ. (Moltmann in Cobb 1982, 68)

Moltmann's concept of resurrection

In the final analysis, the resurrection is, according to Moltmann, nothing that could be historically validated. The resurrection of Jesus "from the dead, through [the power of] God has never been perceived as a validation miracle true only for Jesus. It was rather understood as the beginning of the general resurrection of the dead." It must therefore be seen "in the context of a universal hope of the eschatological faith that was kindled by it" (Moltmann 1987, 149). It must be without "historical proof of its truth," because the resurrection of Jesus *from the dead* will only be validated through the general resurrection of *the dead*. It takes faith, specifically the faith in the anticipated matter, to recognize the "eschatologically anticipated" in the sequence of interdependent and each other confirming historical anticipations. Moltmann concludes that the resurrection withdraws itself from that which in Modernity is called "historically factual evidence. The resurrection of Jesus through [the power of] God does not yet speak the language of 'facts,' but so far only the language of faith and hope, that is, the 'language of promise'" (Moltmann 1987, 159–160). "The hermeneutic word for the understanding of the Christian resurrection faith must therefore be sought in the open, unanswerable, yet irrenouncable question concerning justice in the history of suffering into his world." The dispute concerning the resurrection of Jesus is all about justice in history (Moltmann 1987, 165–166).

Moltmann's concept of eschatology

"If Christianity be not altogether thorough-going eschatology, there remains in it no relationship whatever with Christ" (Barth 1999, 298). With reference to this famous quote from Karl Barth's second edition of his *Commentary on Romans*, Moltmann gives eschatology a central place in his theology:

> Christianity is completely and utterly – not only in its appendix – eschatology; it is hope, anticipation, and forward focus, and therefore also departure and transformation of the presence. The eschatological is not something *within* Christianity, it virtually is the medium of Christian faith, the note its everything is tuned to, the color of dawn of a new day everything in this world is bathed in. For the Christian faith lives on the resurrection of the crucified Christ and reaches out towards the promise of the universal future of Christ. Eschatology is the *Leiden* and the *Leidenschaft*[72] kindled by the Messiah. Therefore, eschatology can never be [only] a part of Christian teaching. Rather is the character of all Christian proclamation, any Christian existence, and the whole church focused eschatologically. (Moltmann 1966, 12)

Maier's judgment of Barth's "eschatologism"[73] is also valid for Moltmann. According to Maier, Barth's notion of eschatology totally "crosses out" all chronological meaning. According to Barth, Romans 13:11 "can never be grasped in chronological categories. The apostle rather leads us before the 'overhanging wall of God,' before the 'suspension of all time'" (Maier 1981, 548). "Contradictions to the anchoring (compare to Exod 14:31) of faith in God's historical acts, faith is established beyond history. The 'last things' thus stand opposite all things of the concrete world, yes, they are 'radically superior,' they are the 'origin of time.'"[74] If the eschatology that is based on the resurrection of Jesus is thus understood "platonically," the historicity of the resurrection itself is out of the question. In this sense Barth said: "The tomb [of Jesus] may ultimately be proved to be empty or sealed, it does not really matter." For Barth, the general resurrection of the dead is nothing more but "a transliteration of

---

72. I left the two words *Leiden* and *Leidenschaft* in the translation. They both mean passion. *Leiden* is *passion* in the sense of suffering, *Leidenschaft* is *passion* in the sense of fervor.

73. This term was coined by Philipp Bachmann (1921), one year before the publication of the second edition of Barth's *Commentary on Romans* (Maier 1981, 553).

74. According to Newbigin, the cyclic sense of time complies with the cyclic processes found in nature. Therefore, it is mainly agrarian cultures that have a cyclic sense of time and correspondingly a deist concept of god. In addition, they cannot perceive the "qualitative difference" between God and humans (Koyama 1968, 54–58). However, according to Cullman, the basis for the thinking of early Christianity was not the spatial antithesis "this world–yonder world," defined by Greek cyclic sense of time, but rather the chronological distinction between "before-now-then" (Schlaudraff 1988, 54–55).

the word of God." Paul does not present "future things but things superior." He understands eschatology as a dogma of being and meaning. Eschatology expresses a quality, the quality of the eternal, yes, God himself. Maier judges: "In a magnificent way, eschatology is declared to be the entire content of the New Testament, and at the very same moment, it is totally 'rescinded' as biblical eschatology" (Maier 1981, 551–552).[75]

So much for the theological prerogatives of Moltmann. Founded on these prerogatives nothing remains standing but an ethic of love (compare Schweitzer 1995, 386; Schwambach 2006, 293). For Moltmann faith is crossing those borders in hope and expectation that the resurrection of the crucified broke down (Moltmann 2002, 6). In this sense, "the future has already . . . begun. Through the resurrection of Jesus the otherwise impossible became possible, reconciliation amidst conflict, the justice of grace amidst judgment, and love amidst legalism" (Moltmann 1987, 158). Wholly in accordance with Bloch's "leap . . . as a fresh start into this new world," Moltmann's ethic remains within the horizon of this world: "On earth," the "unbroken-other kingdom of God" "settled down" and,

> The discipleship of the Crucified creates . . . the power for the incarnation of love in those opportunities one has got and finds. This love embraces this life as if it was everything, and yet it knows that that which is not everything. It empties itself so passionately as if death would put an end to everything, yet it sets its hope on the resurrection of the dead. It finds God in the concrete, yet it knows that all concrete is transcended by God. (Moltmann 1971, 69–70)

10.3.2.2 Eschatology as history

The term *Heilsgeschichte* (henceforth: salvation history) was coined by the Erlangen theologian J. Chr. K. von Hofmann (1810–1877) (Schlaudraff 1988, 50–51). "Salvation history can be understood as a view of history that can be derived from the books of the Old and New Testament" (Afflerbach 2006, 174). Oscar Cullmann adopted this term but did not share von Hofmann's "biblicistic

---

75. "Later, Barth adopted futurist eschatology more strongly. He even showed understanding for the Millennium. As early as 1923 he said: 'Without Chiliasm, even the smallest quantum of it, no ethic'" (Maier 1981, 552).

concern" (Schlaudraff 1988, 51).⁷⁶ He was aware that many theologians had an aversion to the term "salvation history." They are "virtually afraid to run with bad theological [meaning Pietistic] company if they affirmed salvation history" (Cullmann 1965, 56). Even though Pannenberg was influenced by Oscar Cullmann (Sobrino 1985, 65) and was himself respected by him (Cullmann 1965, 39), Pannenberg called the historical view of salvation history "a notion incompatible with an enlightened understanding of the world (Afflerbach 2006, 178). Schweitzer and Bultmann called salvation history "a stopgap solution" or "aberration" that originated because of the problems of the non-appearance of the kingdom of God, even though they did not deny its existence in the New Testament (Cullmann 1965, 11).

In Japanese theology, Zenta Watanabe (渡辺善太) (1985–1978) was the protagonist of a salvation-historical-eschatological view. Departing from Karl Löwith's⁷⁷ *Weltgeschichte und Heilsgeschehen: Die theologischen Voraussetzungen der Geschichtsphilosophie* (1964), Watanabe translated the German *Heilsgeschichte* literally with *kyuusaishi* (救済史), "salvation history," and *Heilsgeschehen* with *kyuusai-no dekigoto* (救済の出来事), "salvation event" (Sunohara 2009). He understood salvation history as an approach to harmonize the "discrepancies and contradictions in the Bible" (Yagi 1967, 33–34).

Worldview framework

"The history of redemption approach to Scripture seeks to uncover the biblical authors' own understanding of the events and their significance within the unfolding narrative context in which they are found" (Ciampa 2007, 254–255). But what exactly is this "narrative context"?

- It is a historical context that "assumes a coherent, special divine event encompassing the past, the presence, and the future" (Cullmann 1965, 3). For Luther, eschatology was "in essence extension of soteriology and Christology into the future" (Maier 1981, 284). This approach attempts to systematize the biblical history that coherently links the biblically attested salvation events. Salvation-historical

---

76. According to Schlaudraff, Cullmann was not affiliated with the salvation history theologians of the revivalist movement. His approach to salvation history was rather founded in historical-critical thinking (Schlaudraff 1988, 253).

77. Löwith taught at the Imperial University (today Touhoku University) in Sendai, Japan, from 1936 to 1941.

thinking "constructs unbroken causal connection of history" (Afflerbach 2006, 179).[78]
- For the salvation history theologians, however, "above or behind the visible and time-defined world history" stands the "invisible eternal world of ideals, the only truly real world" (Afflerbach 2006, 185). In this sense, Sauer leaning on Bettex spoke about the "eternal ideas" of God (Sauer 1983, 212).
- The "narrative context" of salvation history develops in the Bible. This has a bearing on the understanding of Scripture. Most salvation history theologians adhere like Sauer to the infallibility of the Bible in matters of natural science and history (Afflerbach 2006, 183).[79] Historical and salvation-historical statements are mixed and the history the Bible bears witness to is generally understood as historically reconstructible history (179).
- Salvation history approaches seek for biblical criteria that aid them in a meaningful partitioning of the biblical narrative. Under the influence of Covenant Theology, Sauer partitions salvation history according to the biblical covenants (Afflerbach 2006, 173). Cullmann, on the other hand, said that salvation history could not always be described as historical continuum, but that the development was of biblical-theological nature (Schlaudraff 1988, 226). Yet another example is Ciampa's SER-structure[80] of Israel as a nation, in turn

---

78. According to Afflerbach this is exactly the reason why school theology criticizes salvation history, because in doing so "an extraneous pattern of modern understanding of history is artificially superimposed on the Bible" (Afflerbach 2006, 179). Boman's research showed that the Hebrews are psychologically speaking "timeless." Humans keep all their memories, yet always remains the same. "The awareness encompasses a whole life and cannot be divided like space. An event is also a coherent whole. It is objectively inadmissible to divide or define this wholeness by a sequence of sections or rapidly consecutive points of time" (Boman 1983, 118). For the Hebrews content of time is as important as the content of space for the Greek (Boman 1983, 120–121). Then, however, Boman strictly distinguishes between physical time (without content, simple continuation like the arms of a clock) and psychological time (with content, "that is, a successive sequence of experienced events"). Chronology is a historically later scientific achievement, necessary for ordering historical data (Boman 1983, 122). Even though the Bible knows a timewise sequence of events, it does not know any chronology (123). On the other hand, von Rad claimed that Israel gradually developed a linear understanding of history as the number of experienced salvation events of God increased (Schlaudraff 1988, 236). "Over against the Greek cyclic view of time, Cullmann asserts that the biblical understanding of time bears a rectilinear shape sloping upwards towards Christ as its midpoint" (Palu 2012, 20).

79. "Salvation history can only be maintained, if one accepts any kind of inspiration of the Scripture" (Afflerbach 2006, 179).

80. **Sin-Exile-Restoration.**

being embedded in the greater CSER-structure[81] of world history (Ciampa 2007, 256–257). He claims that Rabbis agree (261). The great CSER-structure of world history serves as a framework for Israel's SER-structure (264).

- According to Sauer, everything in this world comes to God and returns to God making the whole of world history a cyclic movement (Afflerbach 2006, 184). God sovereignly controls everything as the "absolute Lord of history" (Isa 13:19; Jer 49:13; Deut 32:8; Acts 17:26; Dan 7:11–12; Luke 1:52) (Salomon 1980, 102–103). As "eschatology recapitulates protology," salvation "cannot be understood properly" apart from creation (Watts 2002, 18). "For Sauer, world history is ultimately salvation history," because "the history of humanity is the history of God . . . World history is the scaffolding of salvation history." Sauer concludes: "As we recognize God as the ruler of the nations' history who *never* confines his work to but *one* nation, the whole of humanity's history bears a divine stamp" (Sauer in Afflerbach 2006, 188). In a similar way, Hodgsons understands universal history as preservation history (Müller-Fahrenholz 1974, 129). "Not only does revelation have a history, history itself is revelation. It is not only 'work,' but also the inspiring 'word' of God. It is a realm of power, grace, and judgment of the nation-controlling potentate over the world" (Sauer in Afflerbach 2006, 185). The reservation must be made, however, that even though salvation history is universal and as such existent also outside the biblical history, it is only within and dependent on the biblical tradition that it is recognized as such (Müller-Fahrenholz 1974, 109).

"Eschatological tension" and the "interim period"

Cullmann talked about a "salvation-historical intermission" between the "eschatologically already decisive date of Christ's resurrection" and the "date of Christ's second coming" (Künzi 1970, 135). "He offers a helpful scheme of time based on the chronological distinction between D-Day and V-day in World War II" (Palu 2012, 21).

> If Christ's resurrection is the starting point of Christian theology, this means that, according to the New Testament, we are in an interim period, between Jesus's resurrection which has taken place

---

81. Creation-**S**in-**E**xile-**R**estoration.

already, and our resurrection which will take place only at the end. However, it also means that the power of life,[82] the Holy Spirit,[83] is working among us already. (Cullmann 1962, 49)

In his small yet adversely disputed book, *Unsterblichkeit der Seele oder Auferstehung der Toten?: Antwort des Neuen Testaments* [Immortality of the Soul or Resurrection of the Dead?: The Answer of the New Testament] (1962), Cullmann portrays the Christian hope of resurrection as flat out opposite to the Greek immortality of the soul.[84] Exactly because the New Testament does not recognize this Greek doctrine, the message of Easter was so powerful: "Christ has risen! That means: We have already entered *into the new aeon* where death has been conquered through the Holy Spirit, where the corruptible is no more" (Cullmann 1962, 45). For Cullmann the resurrection thus becomes the decisive event for the understanding of the New Testament. "Christ has risen, death has already been conquered, the new creation does already exist. The period of resurrection *has been initiated*! Of course, only initiated, yet initiated *in a decisive way*: for death is still at work, and Christians still die" (46). For Cullmann, this constitutes a disposition for *salvation* history. "For it is *characteristic for all New Testament salvation history that between Christ's Resurrection and his Second Coming there is an interim period, its nature being determined by this very tension*" (1965, 181).[85]

> Thus we stand in a section of time in which we are already redeemed through Christ, in which we already have the Holy Spirit, who is characteristic of the new section of time, but in

---

82. *Lebensmacht*.

83. Hoekema stresses the pneumatic element, too (Hoekema 1994, 68).

84. His judgment is founded in the attitude the Old Testament takes toward death. According to Green, there are three affirmations: "First, human existence is marked by finitude; second, death is absolute; and third, death is regarded as the sphere within which fellowship with YAHWEH is lost. Death is the common destiny of all living creatures; it allows no survivors – neither any persons nor any parts of persons . . . Death is the cessation of life in all of its aspects, and especially the severance of all relationships – relationships with God and with every person and with everything in the cosmos . . . Death is never a question merely of biological cessation, and attempts at segregating death into its 'aspects' (physiological versus spiritual, for example) . . . tame the concept and experience of death, from an Old Testament perspective" (Green 1991, 190).

85. For Cullmann, one distinctive feature of this interim period is mission. Referring to 2 Thessalonians 2:6–7 and the Jewish tradition according to which there must come for Israel a time of conversion before the Messianic age, he argued that it was the proclamation of the Gospel to the heathen that is holding back the end (Cullmann 1966).

which also the sin characteristic of the entire period before the Parousia is not done away. (Cullmann in Palu 2012, 22)

In the interim period of this earthly life the new existence in Christ must [still] be related to the old existence in sin. In this interim period new life begins, expressed in good works. On the foundation of justification through faith, the Christian lives in sanctification and dies to his old nature. Here the eschatological tension between being and becoming become apparent. In this present age, the new being of the Christian remains veiled from himself and the world. Therefore the Christian lives between this and world and that, this aeon and that. (Schwambach 2006, 300)[86]

While Cullmann establishes the eschatological tension with regard to Christology, Hoekema finds other reasons in the New Testament:

- The New Testament doctrine of the two aeons: The New Testament talks about "that aeon" (Luke 20:35), the "coming aeon" (Luke 18:30), and the "aeon to come" (Matt 12:32). Other references are Hebrews 6:5; Ephesians 2:7 (Hoekema 1994, 18).
- Also the Bible verifies two historical development lines: that of the kingdom of God and that of the kingdom of evil, explicitly portrayed in the parable of the tares and the wheat (Matt 13:24–30, 36–43). "Here again we see the ambiguity of history. History does not reveal a simple triumph of good over evil, nor a total victory of evil over good. Evil and good continue to exist side by side. Conflict of the two continues during the present age, but since Christ has won the victory, the ultimate outcome of the conflict is never in doubt" (Hoekema 1994, 35). Because God ultimately controls even evil, the Christian "understanding of history is basically optimistic" (38). The

---

86. Interpreting Cullmann's notion of the "intermission" as "interim period" and then talking about "works of love" places Cullmann's in conceptual proximity to Schweitzer's "profound ethic of love" that was also valid for a short interim period. Kümmel radically opposes this argument, "because Jesus could not motivate the demand of doing God's will with the imminent coming of the kingdom of God. He rather referred to God's way of acting . . . Matt 5:44f and called for an imitation of God . . . Luke 6:36" (Kümmel 1987, 43–44). Kümmel called the ethic of Jesus the "ethic of the salvation age" or the "ethic of the new covenant" (Kümmel 1987, 44). "The tension, therefore, is not only a later 'stopgap solution' . . . Jesus proclaimed the kingdom of God for the *future*, but on the other hand he proclaimed that it had *already descended*" (Cullmann 1962, 47).

parallel existence of evil and good, however, must not be equated with the parallel existence of "the world" and the church (37).
- It is only in the light of this tension that the kingdom of God can be perceived as present and future reality: The parables Matthew 13:44–46; Luke 14:28–33 and the present-tense Beatitudes (Matt 5:3–10) show that the kingdom of God is already present (Hoekema 1994, 48–49). But Jesus also taught the kingdom of God as something in the future: Matthew 7:21–23; 8:11–12; 22:1–14; 13:24–30, 36–43; 13:47–50; 25:1–13; 25:14–30 (Hoekema 1994, 49–50). This dualism is also found in Paul's thought: The kingdom of God is present (e.g. Rom 14:17) and future (2 Tim 4:18; 1 Cor 6:9) (Hoekema 1994, 50). "Of course, Paul presupposes in some references . . . that the entrance into the kingdom of God as an event concurs with the final judgment (Gal 5:21; 1 Cor 6:9; 15:50; 2 Thess 1:5)."[87] But there are also references that portray the kingdom of God as "present existence of Christians" (Rom 14:17; 1 Cor 4:20; Col 4:11). These references show "that for Paul – as for Jesus – the kingdom of God was not *only* a matter of hope" (Kümmel 1987, 126–127).

Continuity passing through discontinuity

The phrase in this heading, *Kontinuität durch Diskontinuität hindurch*, was coined by Schwambach who holds that this distinction is "vitally crucial[88] . . . and ultimately critical for the distinction between true and false theology." According to Schwambach, the definition of the "*transitions between the created world to the fallen world, from the fallen world to the redeemed world, from the already redeemed yet under trial to the redeemed world free from trial*" are crucial and "any dogmatic has to answer for its position theologically" (Schwambach 2006, 304).

Sauer's salvation-historical approach advocates discontinuity. The "destination" of history is not the "result" of history (Afflerbach 2006, 191): The world as a whole and the hearts in particular are going to be renewed radically, yet not by means of an evolution of human resources unto the full deployment of highest ideal humanity, but by means of God's providence[89]

---

87. According to Ciampa, the New Testament term "heritage" implies a "not-yet" (Ciampa 2007, 303).
88. *Lebenswichtig*.
89. *Hinführung*.

leading to divine goals. To that end God uses powerful miracles intervening in power and love (Sauer in Afflerbach 2006, 190).

> [The kingdom of God] does not come from bottom to top, but from top to bottom . . . It does not come as a result of progress, but through upheaval . . . Not Christianization of the world eventually achieving a Christian culture,[90] but growing hostility of the world until culture eventually rejects Christianity – that is the process prophesied in the Bible (2 Thess 2:3–12; Rev 13). (Sauer in Afflerbach 2006, 191)[91]

On the same note, Cullmann, even though he understood salvation history as a "process proceeding organically," strongly opposed any notion of progression. "The 'age of the church' does not progress us towards the good . . . On the contrary, it is also part of the early Christianity's eschatological expectation that 'evil increases in the last days'" (Schlaudraff 1988, 250–251).

According to Sauer, there will be "collapses and worldwide catastrophes" in the course of this progress (Afflerbach 2006, 191), already bearing features of the judgment of the nations. For them, "the presence is a season of ripening unto . . . judgment" (Salomon 1980, 107). Jesus's logion of the "entering into the kingdom of God" (Kümmel 1987, 30) also talks about separation. The promise of entering into the kingdom of God is given only "to the 'little flock' the Father has decreed to give the kingdom (Luke 12:32) . . . As much as Jesus promises the participation in God's salvation, it does not apply to simply everybody, but it is tied to certain conditions" (Kümmel 1987, 32).

In missiology, the approach of discontinuity was advocated mainly by Karl Hartenstein and Walter Freytag. According to Beyerhaus, Hartenstein used a fourfold hermeneutical key concerning the religions:

---

90. *Bis zur erfolgten Verchristlichung der Kultur.*

91. The notion of eschatological discontinuity is the absolute opposite of the hope of the Industrialization Age (Moltmann 1971, 48). Saint-Simon expressed this hope thus: "All nations move toward the same goal. The goal towards which they move is away from a feudalist-militarist power-system, toward an industrial, peaceful administration-system. There is no power that could withstand this movement (Saint-Simon in Moltmann 1971, 48). On a similar note, Comte thought "that one could move from the religious state to the political state, and from there to the industrial state." He also believed "that thus the three stages of history would be completed and that the industrial society of humanity would be the 'end of history'" (Moltmann 1971, 48–49). "Thus the modern industrial society is welcomed as the fulfillment of any form of Christian hope" (Moltmann 1971, 50). This industrial aspiration was at times the driving force behind liberation theologies (Câmara 1969, 16–20). I shall deal with this subject below.

- the key of revelation theology: In the light of the religion of the Bible, religions must be considered as fruitless, human attempts to get in touch with God.
- the key of soteriology: Salvation is sought by man, however, it is brought only by God, completed in the salvific work of Christ. This also includes the rejection of both the humanization of God and the deification of man.
- the key of ecclesiology: The church is unified by its confession of faith in salvation through Christ alone. In its exclusiveness, it stands in opposition against all other religions.
- the key of the interim period: Hartenstein has a double focus: (a) The salvation of the church in the interim period points towards the salvation of the nations in the consummation; (b) in the interim period there will be a growing polarization between the church and non-Christians (Schuster 2002, 64–65).

However, the aspect of discontinuity must be put into perspective:

> According to Jesus, the kingdom of God does not come through a continuous development, but suddenly directly from God. However, this event will end a process that is not meaningless. It is rather [even before God's sudden intervention] a divinely planned process, even though it is also marked by human sinfulness and *Unheil*. (Cullmann 1965, 211)

On a similar note, Sauer holds that "the new world . . . will not be without any cohesive correlation with the old world. The coming earth is not 'another' earth, but a 'new' earth" (Sauer 1983, 213). Salvation-history theologians reject a developmental connection between the old and the new world. Sauer sees a material connection (Sauer 1983, 213). According to my opinion, the only valid connection between the old and the new world can be sought in the faithfulness of God, which, according to Schwambach, is the "bridge between the old and the new world":

> The line of continuity between the originally promised and the eschatological creation can therefore only be recognized as something going through discontinuity, because the world is fallen. Continuity through discontinuity is possible because the discontinuity is overcome in Christ and through the Spirit. Thus the continuity is not established through immanent resources of the cosmos or humanity . . . In faithfulness to his promise

God constantly establishes the connection between himself and fallen man. And therefore he does not let go of man – not even in death ... The very same is true for the whole cosmos that is now being under the powers of destruction (sin, death, devil), enslaved, yet in hope (Rom 8:19ff). (Schwambach 2006, 308–309)

10.3.3 Between World and Heaven

As one of the causes of the "weakness" of Christianity in Japan, Takakura named the fact that secularism and the "this-worldliness" disposition of the present Christianity "nullified" the "healthy other-worldly, eschatological spirit of the Christianity of the Bible" of biblical Christianity (Jennings 2005, 230). In the following two paragraphs I am going to outline these two orientations of Christianity:

10.3.3.1 Focus on "this world"

The focus on the "world" is mainly advocated by "the" liberation theology.[92] Liberation theologians stress "the oneness of history" and reject "the differentiation between God's salvation history and profane history" (Greinacher 1988, 68). God does not work only in the heart and conscience, but he is also the lord of history (Boff 1985, 90). "Eschatological reality and history stand in multivalent proximity to God's dominion in history." God's dominion "sets history in motion, breaks open its immanence, and provokes new beginnings of liberation, justice, and reconciliation in history. The anticipation of the eschatological peace in history thus changes history ... into an open process" (Falcke 1988, 32). Leaning on Augustine,[93] the "kingdom," yes, even "the whole Christ" is perceived as "being borne in the womb of the history of humanity." The Second Vatican Council phrased it thus: "Here the body of a new humanity is growing" (Boff 1985, 84). While these arguments are of historical-political nature, others argue on the basis of Christology and ethics. Sobrino points out that Jesus preached "in the context of a sinful world" (Sobrino 1985, 50). Moltmann argues that if the "last things" are postponed to the very "last day," they lose its "directive, encouraging, and critical meaning for all the days we are to live until the end of history" (Moltmann 2002, 1).

---

92. The origin of liberation theology either dates back to 1971, when Gutiérrez' *Teología de la Liberación* was first published, or back to the Latin American Episcopal Conference in 1968 in Medellín (Altman 1998, 1207).

93. "*Historia gravida Christi*," "history is pregnant with Christ."

The influence of Marxism

According to Cobb, Moltmann's thinking was heavily influenced by Bloch's Marxism.

> Bloch believed that "the ultimate, enduring insight of Marx is that truth does not exist for its own sake but implies emancipation, and an interpretation of the world which has the transformation of the world as its goal and meaning, providing a key in theory and leverage in practice." Drawing on this tradition, Moltmann writes that unless truth "contains initiative for the transformation of the world, it becomes a myth of the existing world." (Cobb 1982, 57)

The encounter between salvation on earth and salvation in heaven can be traced back to Ludwig Feuerbach. Because Man desires "eternity, deep eternity" yet cannot get it, he projects the goal of this desire into yonder world (Böhm 1979, 63). The Greeks were satisfied with a "postponed death," but the Christians sought yonder world (65). Feuerbach's postulate "Remaining faithful to the earth" (Böhm 1979, 76) shows Hegel's influence who wrote in a letter to Carl Ludwig von Knebel (1807): "On the basis of my experience I have been convinced of the truth of the biblical logion which I have made my guiding star: Seek ye first food and clothing; and the kingdom of God shall be added unto you" (Hegel in Hoffmeister 1969, 186). "Karl Marx is basically in agreement with the left-wing Hegelians according to whom religion and metaphysics are to be rejected, because they have been invented for but one specific reason: that is to make the misery of man bearable, at least in his mind" (Böhm 1979, 79).

In order to liberate man from the illusion of religion, from the "fantastical gold coating covering the real misery" of humanity, Marx demanded "abolition of religion as illusory happiness of the people" in order to lead them to "true happiness" (Böhm 1979, 86–87).[94] Bloch called this a novelty in regard to the utopian (Bloch 1982, 161). According to Marx, the alienation is abolished by dialectic materialism aiming at the establishment of "Primitive Communism" (Jansen 1979, 31–32). For Bloch, Marxism is the practicable way, found at last,

> which leads to the realization of all that has always been potentially present in man and nature, foreboding light beckoning from

---

94. According to Marx, the classification of humanity into the class that rules and the class of those who are ruled over was consolidated through religion. "Humanity was enslaved even more and then necessarily fed with false hopes" (Böhm 1997, 82). Even though Marx's critique is not valid for genuine Christianity, it touches sore points of a depraved Christianity (Böhm 1997, 82).

beyond all alienation, shining from day dreams, utopias, the natural law, philosophy, art, and religion, even from the hieroglyphs of nature, humanized nature, naturalized man. (Seidel 2001, 77)

Because Bloch discussed his Marxism vis-à-vis Christianity, he "materialized Christianity" (Zwerenz and Zwerenz 2003). Right after entering "historicity" – according to Bloch – with the Exodus-event (Bloch 1982, 575), the nation praying in its misery[95] is opposed by an energetic founder who "started out by killing a foreman" (Bloch 1982, 1453).[96] Bloch postulates that the unrealistic promises of Christianity that God would helpingly intervene have "until now sentenced humanity to inactivity." "Therefore, demanding the abolition of God is not an act of malice, but rather the overripe fruit of the necessary." According to Bloch, the basic prerequisite for the creation of a whole world is its "liberation from the ruling above, that is, the abolition of God" (Böhm 1979, 101). "Bloch accuses Christians of hoping for a whole world[97] on the basis of the impossible; that is, they expect the help to come vertically from above. Bloch's approach to hope, however, works with the notion of the possible" (Böhm 1979, 103).

The "materialization of Christianity" is also found in liberation theologies. According to Moltmann, liberation means,

1. economically: "fulfillment of the material needs of man with regard to health,[98] food, clothing, and habitation";

---

95. For Bloch, the greatest "misery" is hunger: "The stomach is the first lamp into which oil must be poured. Its longing is precise; its drive is so unavoidable that it cannot even be repressed for long" (Bloch in Moisio, n.d., 245). In this context Bloch criticizes psychoanalysis: Because it fails to satisfy hunger and the economic needs of man, psychoanalysis is "limited to certain classes" that – with their filled stomachs – can afford pondering about the soul (Bloch 1982, 71–73). Bloch's critique also applies to any kind of Christianity in which soteriology is limited to "counseling."

96. The Jesuit theologian E. J. Laje speaks against an overly political interpretation of the Exodus-event. He thinks that the theological theme of the covenant is prevalent (Frieling 1984, 74). "Laje reminds us that Jesus never engaged in political-revolutionary action in order to liberate the suppressed. Jesus wanted to change the very core of man. Humans thus changed from inside out then from the new nation of God in this world." Laje recognizes structural and collectivistic sin, but "liberation is possible only if those responsible are called to repentance, and if they see to a peaceful way toward justice" (Frieling 1984, 75). Laje seems to be a "lone voice" in the context of liberation theology.

97. *Heile Welt*.

98. With regard to health, Bloch seems to be rather cynical and nihilist. He finds fault in the "underlying final plan, the ultimate medical wishful thinking, which is the "abolition of death" (Bloch 1982, 539). "Diseases are not done away with, but their ultimate outcome – death – has bafflingly been pushed back. If only the exploited life to which so many are given back to was worth anything, if only one war made up for the omitted dying of years, the physician

2. politically: democracy. "We mean by this human dignity in assuming responsibility. This includes participation in and control over economic and political exercise of power";
3. culturally: "liberation from the vicious cycle of alienation" and "identity in the recognition of others." "We mean with this the 'human emancipation of man'" (Marx);
4. ecologically: "liberation from the vicious cycle of industry destroying nature" and "peace with nature" (Moltmann 1987, 309–310).

In spite of the close similarity to Marx, liberation theologians are well aware that Marx's atheist ideology cannot be adopted (Gutiérrez 1986, 50–54). Gutiérrez seeks the dialogue between theology and social science and not the dialogue between theology and social analysis (56). The one thing sociology cannot offer is the (evaluative) interpretation of its findings. "No sociology will ever recognize sin to be at the very heart of unjust social realities: breaching the relationship with God is therefore breaching the relationship with others" (58).

After the breakdown of the "modern Communist societies" (Jansen 1979, 72), the basic critique of Marxism is Marx's unrealistic historical-political approach. "The historical evolution aims at the paradisiac and classless society . . . Karl Marx does not ask how history really wants this . . . He construes according it to his preconceived opinion" (Jansen 1979, 33). Czech Marx-expert, Jan Milič Lochman, also criticized the high significance Marx placed on the historical work process:

> The history of production is an essential part of world history. However, it is not salvation history. Work is man's just claim, but it is no claim for his justification[99] . . . The abolition of God is not a necessary postulate for the liberation of man, but a decision of faith, in this case, the decision of unbelief: a worldview dogma . . . What does it mean to "abolish God"? According to my understanding this is not a mere intellectual operation of worldview cosmetics. It is rather "revaluation of all values," in Marx's case with a concrete meaning: shifting the absolute from the "world of God" to the "world of man." (Lochman 1975, 71)

---

could have been halfway content for a hundred years" (528). But "what is that life of most for which the physician makes them 'capable'? What is a health that merely makes people ready to be harmed again, wasted, and shot?" (545). "However, humans don't get a straight gait as long as life in society is still skewed" (546).

99. *Die Arbeit ist das Recht, nicht aber die Rechtfertigung des Menschen.*

My personal position is that I rather oppose Marx's model of social analysis and his "Historical Materialism" (Jansen 1979, 31) as an interpretative tool providing meaning for Christian theology, because of Marx's atheism and his unethical lifestyle[100] under apparent occult influence (Jansen 1979, 19).[101]

10.3.3.2 Focus on "heaven"

Along with the "Instruction on Certain Aspects of the 'Theology of Liberation'" of the *Congregation for the Doctrine of the Faith* (1984) liberation theologians have always criticized if not rejected Marxism as ideology: Marxism must not be adopted as "comprehensive and coherent ideology," because this renders impossible the "true liberation of the poor" (Boff 1986, 109). According to Frieling, liberation theology criticizes Marx's theory of alienation for not being radical enough, that is, for not rooting the problem in its origin, the alienation from God. "Full liberation is found only in the faith in Jesus Christ, because there is no other mediator for the reconciliation with God" (Frieling 1984, 80).

Bloch made hunger the first of human needs (Bloch 1982, 71–73). So did Jesus. Bloch placed psychological needs second. So did Jesus, because the need for clothing is first and foremost a psychological need. But in stark

---

100. The German Communist Moses Hess said about Marx who had just immigrated to Paris: "What a pity, what a shame, that the ego of the most brilliant man of our movement cannot content itself with the recognition paid to him, but that he seems to demand self-subjugation" (Hess in Jansen 1979, 21). This and many more contemporary witnesses should alert: he had an illegitimate child with his housekeeper, harbored a strong hatred against Jews in general and against Jewish Communists (Ferdinand Lassalle, Moses Hess) in particular, hatred against all that did not share his opinion; Carl Schurz said about Marx that he never met anybody whose behavior was so "provocative and unbearable"; together with Engels he destroyed the first Communist International; he brought fighting to all parties (Jansen 1979, 23–27).

101. Jansen wrote about the changes of the young Karl Marx during his student years: "We can draw some conclusions from a hardly known drama of Marx with the title 'Oulanem.' [A telling quote]: 'Until I go crazy and my heart is completely changed, behold this sword – the prince of darkness sold it to me. Because he beats the time and he gives the signs. Ever bolder I play the dance of death, and they, too, are Oulanem, Oulanem. This name sounds like death, keeps sounding until it dies away in a wretched creeping. While the chasm yawns for the both of us, into which you will descend, into which I will follow you laughing as I whisper into your ears: Descend! Come with me, my friend! I want to take revenge on the One who reigns there above. If there is anything that destroys, I will jump into it, even though I may bring the whole world to its ruins, the world between myself and the abyss, I shall scatter it to pieces with my unceasing curses. I shall wrap my arm around the world's coarse reality. In my embrace the world will vanish in silence and then sink down into utter nothingness, destroyed, without existence – that's the true meaning of life!' . . . 'Oulamen' is a distortion, an anagram of the word Emanuel . . . Such name distortions are used in the occult praxis of black magic. The sword mentioned in the quote belongs to the rituals of higher consecration in satanic cults. The candidates bought a sword that secured their success. He paid by signing with his own blood that after his death his soul would belong to the devil" (Jansen 1979, 18–19).

contrast to Bloch, Jesus made both basic human needs second to the kingdom of God (Matt 6:25–34). Everything Bloch wrote about "hope" Jesus simply forbade. His kingdom is not from this world.[102] It can neither be anticipated not acquired. Jesus calls such attempts running after things like the pagans do (Matt 6:32). Cortesi rightly criticized "a spirituality that aims only at satisfaction of needs," because "the Christian faith does not serve . . . the satisfaction of personal desires." Cortesi poses the crucial question: "Is the Christian faith able to proclaim salvation in its eschatological meaning, or does it reduce it to a human construct?" And then he judges: "An unreflected spirituality only supports the re-mystification of the world. This is clearly apparent in Neo-Paganism with its mythological features" (Cortesi 2004, 63).

10.3.4 My Own (Preliminary) Opinion

> It is for the sake of eternal life that everybody must be a Christian. In fact, it is solely for the sake of eternal life that we are Christians. We must be religious for the sake of the other life where there will be no evils at all. You became Christians not for the sake of the present life, but because of the future life. (Augustine in Böhm 1979, 65–66)

This classic word of Augustine is one pole of Christian soteriology. If this pole is abandoned, Christian soteriology slowly sinks below the horizon of this world. In this sense Schwambach wrote: "In biblical terminology, hope means confidence . . . in eternal life." The opposite of this hope is "human hope."[103] Human hope "does not hope against hope, but is oriented towards the possibilities each perspective presence holds. It is limited to that which is visible and already present, and from there it forefeels the future." Christian hope goes beyond the horizon of experience. "Its basis is not experience (compare Heb 11:1f), but it becomes the basis of experience" (Schwambach 2006, 314).

The word of Augustine is a pole. Yet it is *only* a pole. "The 'salvation' brought by Jesus is to be applied to the wholeness of the humanity of those who need salvation" (Kertelge 1974, 93). Then Kertelge enumerates exorcism, mainly exorcism of demons of sickness, liberation from legalistic narrowness, liberated createdness, and "not least" forgiveness of sins (94–97). According to

---

102. I do not share Bloch's view of chronological/successive interpretation (Bloch 1982, 580).

103. Bloch's "clearest consciousness" (Bloch 1982, 161–199) also falls under this judgment.

Cullmann it is a "wrong understanding of early Christianity's eschatology" if Christian hope paralyzes Christian action in this world: "Genuine Christian hope does not inhibit Christian action in this world. On the contrary, Christian action, particularly the action of missionary proclamation, belongs to the eschatological salvation plan of God as an integral part thereof" (Cullmann 1941, 98).

The pole focusing on eternal life and the pole focusing on the life in this world belong together, joined together by the highest purpose of salvation: the glory of God (Eph 1:4; 4:15) (Serman 2002, 138). Overcoming evil in this world as well as God's new creation serve God's glory. Judging from Hebrews 13:13–15 it can be argued that *gense riyaku* (現世利益) cannot be the *summum bonum* of Christian ethics. In the context of Hebrews 13:13–15, Evans talks about obligatory thankfulness. I think this concept is particularly helpful for the Japanese context because obligation (*on*, 恩), thankfulness (*kansha*, 感謝), and the duty to return favors (*okaeshi*, お返し) play an important role:

> This is the measure of gratitude for which the author of Hebrews calls the congregation to go out to him "outside the camp, bearing his reproach," . . . not thinking of how best to preserve their enjoyment of this world's goods as they chart their future course, but only thinking of what kind of loyalty, service, and witness Jesus merits for the immense generosity he has lavished upon them, giving up his own honor and life in this world on their behalf. (Evans 2005, 254)

According to Collins, the obligation is the key to all exhortations of Hebrews (Collins 1994, 46). It calls the believers to a "liminal" status.[104] With

---

104. The term "liminality" goes back to Arnold van Gennep and Turner. Victor Witter Turner (1929–1983), representative of symbolic anthropology (Manchester School of Anthropology), did research mainly in Southern Africa. He adopted the term of "liminality" from van Gennep's *rites de passage* of which the second phase is called the "marginal" or "liminal" phase. "During the intervening 'liminal' period, the characteristics of the ritual subject (the 'passenger') are ambiguous; he passes through a cultural realm that has few or none of the attributes of the past or coming state" (Turner 1995, 94). "The attributes of liminality or of the liminal *pasonae* ('threshold people') are necessarily ambiguous, since this condition and these persons elude or slip through the network of classifications that normally locate states and positions in cultural space. Liminal entities are neither here nor there; they are betwixt and between the positions assigned and arrayed by law, custom, convention, and ceremonial . . . Thus, liminality is frequently likened to death, to be seeing the womb, to invisibility, to darkness, to bisexuality, to the wilderness, and to an eclipse of the sun or moon. Liminal entities . . . may be represented as possessing nothing, . . . they have no status, properties, insignia . . . indicating rank or role – in short, nothing that may distinguish from their fellow . . . initiands" (Turner 1995, 95).

Jesus as their forerunner the believers are called to "run with perseverance" (Heb 12:1) the track that Jesus ran before. Following Jesus they have already left "the camp" (Heb 13:13). Back in the "normal" life, the Christians were Jews and heathen and thus separated. As they became Christians they had suffered the loss of their possessions and their reputation that tied them to their former status. Now they are called to follow Jesus outside the camp. They are called to enter the space of liminality sacrificing being "at home" and "belonging" as a token of their gratitude for Jesus who also had left the camp. In this space they are between the community they have left and the kingdom they are to receive (Heb 12:28; 13:11–14). In this space they experience both humiliation and ordeal on one hand, yet sacrality and power on the other. They "bear the reproach" of Christ (Heb 13:13), they are the target of the enmity and the humiliation techniques of society. Yet they also are in a space of holiness in which they are privileged to "come boldly unto the throne of grace" (Heb 4:16). They have an altar of which the Levitical priests have no right to eat (Heb 13:10) (DeSilva 2000, 310–311).

> Within the liminal state they have been brought together into a community marked by cooperation, sharing, and equality, within which they are rendered sacred for intimate access to God and being fitted for their new, glorious, normal state, which they shall enter at the eschatological shaking of the natural realm. The rest of the believer's life is therefore to be lived out in this liminal state, in the margins between status in this world and the next. The author urges the addressees to continue to persevere in the margins, for the margins of society are pregnant with promise as the threshold over which they, like Jesus, will pass into the unshakeable realm, the full presence of God. (DeSilva 2000, 311)

Those living in this liminal state between leaving home ("the camp") and coming home to the "Father's house with many mansions" (John 14:1–3) can bear the "eschatological tension" only

- if sustained, encouraged and comforted by the hope of being together with Jesus "under one roof" in "personal and local community with the Father" (Peres 2003, 155);
- if in a communicating relationship with God: "The eternal life is presence and future at the same time. It is present insofar that the judgment of the eschaton, deciding over life and death, is

executed through the Son's coming into our mortal life (flesh) and then through the word of his mission (and exaltation), given unto faith, and insofar that the believers are in the Son and He in them (John 14:20; 15:4–10), as He is in the Father and the Father in Him (John 14:10, 20)." This presence, this "being-in" the reality of a communication process (Kleffmann 2003, 51);
- if this communication process is in essence "partaking in the life of the Son who came and who came back, partaking in motion of the Logos, partaking in His loving *Condescendencia* toward that which He created" (Kleffmann 2003, 51–52).

10.4 Between Redemption and Emancipation

Summary: The tension between the teaching that understands human beings as the sole subjects of soteriological action, and the teaching that makes them solely the object of God's soteriological action, is hard to bear, but must never be resolved.

Wherever humans are the sole or co-operating subject of salvation, the understanding of humans and world is hamartiologically optimistic. Salvation is seen as developing horizontally, eventually overcoming all religious perimeters.

As for "vertical salvation," that is, the relationship of humans with God, humans clearly are the sole object of God's soteriological action. As for Christian action, humans are summoned to act "in the Lord."

The incidents concerning the *Aum*-Sect also pose the following question: Who is the subject of salvation? Repp observed that the *Aum*-Sect as well as other apocalyptic sects attempt to induce "Armageddon" by their own actions (Repp 1997, 103). For those who understand humans as the subject of salvation, this must be a critique worthy of consideration (Jhi 2006, 24). Those who make themselves the subject of salvation attempt to take the place of God just as Ashara did with his *Kirisuto Sengen* (キリスト宣言), translated as *Declaring Myself the Christ* (Kaplan and Marshall 1996, 135).

10.4.1 The Hubris of Feuerbach

"The feeling of dependency which people have is the ground of religion. The object of this feeling of dependency . . . is originally nothing but nature. Nature is the first and original object of religion, as the history of all religions and peoples fully shows" (Feuerbach 1908, 31; Feuerbach in Wartofsky 1982, 389). Therefore, faith in the supernatural is nothing more than faith in the freedom of subjectivity before the judgment bars of nature – and thus faith of man in himself (Feuerbach 1849, 3). The leading principle is the liberation of man from his dependency on God – the hubris of humans. Feuerbach criticizes Luther for exorbitantly degrading man by his doctrine of grace and thus doing humanity the poorest service (Böhm 1979, 70). "What Luther takes away from man he restores unto you in God a hundredfold. Luther is inhuman toward man only because he has a humane God and because the humanity of God discharges man from his humanity" (Feuerbach 1846, 268). Harvay judges: "Luther declared himself entirely and unqualifiedly for God and against man" (Harvay 1997, 152). In doing so, Feuerbach turned away from theology, because theology "does not satisfy me, because it does not give me what I demand, what I urgently need" (Feuerbach 1972, 154). He saw it as his duty to "radically liberate man from the thought of God in the name of man" (Böhm 1979, 62).[105] His motto was "*Homo homini deus est*," "the human being is a god to humanity" (Feuerbach 1837, 277). Feuerbach's approach must be considered as a possible worldview background of the missiological talk of human emancipation in salvation.

10.4.2 Anthropocentrism

10.4.2.1 Positive encounter

The Catholic understanding of grace, according to which the grace of God has always been "latently" present in man, and according to which – as L. Boff put it – man has always lived in the "milieu of grace," creates the framework within which Catholic liberation theologians combine divine and human action (Frieling 1984, 15). This combination goes so far that man "cooperates

---

105. In this sense Bloch said in a TV interview in 1975: "The fact that the dreamer man wrapped his dreams in religious wishes shows how deeply he is moved by hope. His longing has just been misguided. Even though cunning persons misused these desires by making them completely otherworldly, this doesn't mean that under many layers the true roots come to light. Man has only been made aware that his hope is not founded in the reality of God, but in his own reality" (Böhm 1997, 98).

in the all-inclusive process of redemption . . . through his work in creation" (Schwambach 2006, 296). On the Protestant side of liberation theology there is the confession to the uninterrupted relationship between God and man: "By man's . . . accession to power over the earth, and by his advancement of God's blessing in peace, he vicariously and representatively partakes in God's world dominion and the blessing of creation" (Moltmann 1976, 223).

On one side, such thinking naturally goes with an optimistic evaluation of man and his abilities: "God wants to return life and the world into the hand of the *mündig*[106] man," because freedom – for Cox an equivalent *Shalom*[107] – first means "freedom to maturity" (Schütz 1973, 38). This "new Christian Humanism" endows man with the right to "rule the earth and to continue creation" (Câmara 1969, 20).

On the other side, such thinking owes an overly positive interpretation of the history of humanity. "Feasibility is the horizon within which the post-theistic, enlightened and secularized man understands his presence and future" (Schütz 1973, 34). The churches are also "drawn into this vortex" (Schütz 1973, 35). That can be seen from the following quote:

> Far from being angry with man, the Father sends his divine Son to this world. The Son conceives the longing of man to become

---

106. "*Mündig*" means literally "coming of age," thus "having the right to open one's *Mund*, one's mouth," figuratively: "politically mature."
The notion of the "responsible man" goes back to Bonhoeffer who talked about the "world coming of age" ("*mündig gewordenen Welt*"), the "responsible world" ("*mündige Welt*") or the "irresponsible world" ("*unmündigen Welt* "), about the "responsibility of the world and of man" ("*Mündigkeit der Welt und des Menschen*"), and about our "coming of age maturing into a true knowledge of our situation before God" ("*Mündigwerden zu einer wahrhaftigen Erkenntnis unserer Lage vor Gott*") (Jhi 2006, 19). However, "Bonhoeffer . . . was not concerned about the responsible world's claim on Christ, but conversely about Christ's claim on a world that has come of age" (Daub and Radbruch 2006, 554). "The responsible world is a world without religion. 'We are headed towards a totally irreligious age,' Bonhoeffer wrote, an age in which God, as he understood him, was not the almighty God, but God who was weak and powerless in this world. He was a suffering God, the God on the cross. And it is the fate of humans to suffer together with God. It is not the religious deed that defines a Christian, but his participation in the suffering of God." Bonhoeffer's notion of free and responsible action was the acknowledgment of a responsible world and the compassion with God's suffering by accepting the drama of guilt and redemption. Bonhoeffer's decision for resistance and tyrannicide was therefore . . . justified by his *theologia crucis* (von Klemperer 1995, 415).

107. Moltmann demands: "Theology of modern times must necessarily be theology of freedom. The modern world is the product of liberation movements and is still involved in the movements. Many liberation movements allied with atheism because church and theology hung on to the traditional 'authoritarian principle' for too long." In this context, Moltmann talks about freedom of religion, freedom of faith, freedom of conscience, freedom of church, and freedom of theology (Moltmann 1988, 32–33).

God, and he knows that man – no matter how great he may be – will always be indefinitely far apart from the divine life; and as he knows this the Son of God becomes man, God-man, in order to realize man's dream to become God. Therefore, evolution[108] is for us a holy and infinite struggle. (Câmara 1969, 13)

Back in the 1960s, Câmara was still driven by the reverence for progress ... nuclear fission, man's landing on the moon, satellites, genetic engineering, petrochemistry, automation ... (Câmara 1969, 16–17).[109] "We envisioned a jealous and small-minded God ... insisting on creating everything directly and personally, not willing to share the creational gift with one of his creatures" (17). However, according to Pope John XXIII we are at the "dawn of the first day of creation." "The Christians of the Second Vatican Council have faith in God's work through man, his co-creator." Today, the "homogeneous and harmonious evolution of mankind" is not utopia anymore. Câmara justifies this with the technical progress that "overcomes famine" and "prevails against misery" (18). The "new Christian humanism" knows that "for the first time in history mankind has at its command the means to sweep away all misery from earth" (20).

10.4.2.2 Negative encounter

Such kinds of optimism did not go unchallenged. Watts called attention to the fact that modern salvation concepts repeat the historical mistake of Stoicism and Gnosticism. They believed that man was good in himself, that he even was the supreme good. "Modernity seeks fault on the outside, not inside. Thus salvation is sought in liberation from weakening, external influences" (Watts 2002, 39). Jaffin opposes:

> As much as I cherish peace, as desirable it may be, I am ... not an optimist ... We will never control evil and hatred. We may possibly be able to suppress these powers inside ourselves, but then they turn against ourselves, and one day envy, hatred, and

---

108. *Entwicklung*.

109. Is it mere coincidence that Bloch said the same almost word by word, in his *Das Prinzip der Hoffnung*, published some ten years earlier? "If only we would give technology as much freedom in the general field as we grant freedom in military technology!" Then he named inorganic chemistry, artificial oil, petrochemistry, polymer chemistry as the new miracles of technology. "Artificial fertilizers, artificial irradiation, are on the way – or could be on the way – to enliven the soil to yield a hundredfold, [competing] in a hubris, an 'anti-Demeter-movement' unparalleled" (Bloch 1982, 1054–1055).

all destructive powers break forth. The world cries out for peace, yet there is no peace, as the prophets have proclaimed it long ago. (Jaffin 1981, 12)

"We cannot make it [God's kingdom] come," Cullmann summarizes the "overall witness of the New "Testament" (Cullmann 1941, 99). According to Schütz, "God's salvation event[110] aims ... at the reconciliation between God and man." The call, "Be reconciled to God!" (2 Cor 5:20) is a "demonstration of the non-feasibility, the cannot-do[111] of salvation." "The New Testament assertion of the non-feasibility of salvation, of the uselessness of inner-worldly salvation, and of preliminary realization of inner-worldly salvation through God as the foundation of all humanitarianism is hard to take and a scandal for enlightened thinking" (Schütz 1973, 42).

10.4.3 Horizontalism

After the Second Vatican Council God's salvation work is considered to be "present among all mankind from the very beginning." It provokes "the longing for salvation[112] and the search for sanctification"[113] (Müller-Fahrenholz 1974, 183). Müller-Fahrenholz concludes that "the evolutionary-dynamic understanding of history ... allows for the acceptance of a universal process towards one grace and [one] truth in which all religions ... participate. The ultimate and concrete epitome of this process is the Catholic Church (Müller-Fahrenholz 1974, 184).

In Protestant theology, this universalism is established by "Israel's confession of the One God" which also claims that not only for Israel but also for the other nations there is no God besides the only one. "Thus the nations and the entire creation live because of the mercy of the one and only [God]! The all-including unity of all creation can be concluded from the exclusive uniqueness of Yahweh" (Maurer 1976, 51). On this basis, the history of the world and of humanity can be seen "in view of a non-dialectic, linear leavening with truly humane life. Any human effort of humanization of the world can fully be considered as God's work in and for our age" (Cox in Schütz 1973, 38).

---

110. *Heilsveranstaltung.*
111. *Nichtmachbarkeit.*
112. *Heil.*
113. *Heiligung.*

10.4.3.1 Paul F. Knitter

According to Odagaki (小田垣雅也), Knitter considers salvation – centered not on theory but on praxis – as the common denominator of the basis for the dialogue between religions (Odagaki 1992, 171). In this paragraph, I want to focus mainly on the Knitter's article "Mission and Dialogue", published in 2005. Knitter calls the "shift from church-centeredness to kingdom-centeredness[114] in the Christian understanding of missions" a "seismic shift."[115] "The kingdom of God ... is the biblical symbol for what we can call in more contemporary terms, a new world order – a new way for humans to live with each other, a new way of structuring society in which the foundational values for all laws and economic policies and international relationship will be a compassion that calls for and animates justice" (Knitter 2005, 201). Drawing on Sobrino, Knitter claims that the kingdom of God was the main concern of the historical Christ. When Christians see only the "divinity of Jesus" and not the man, when the "proclaimer" becomes the "proclaimed," when they don't recognize Jesus as a prophet, then they "no longer have the original, the authentic Jesus." In this context Sobrino talks about the "Jesuanic Principle" (Knitter 2005, 203). Being oriented on the kingdom of God means being oriented on the victims. "God makes our final salvation depend on what we do with the poor" (Sobrino in Knitter 2005, 204). In order to work for the poor, Christians must work together also with adherents of other religions.

Other theologians think similarly. Maurer asks: "What biblical forces motivate the present-day Christianity to unite with various extra-Christian efforts in order to get involved in a common construction of humane life in the entire world" (Maurer 1976, 53)? In a similar way, the World Council of Churches in 1967 asked "what the function of the church would be with regard to 'the unification plan of God for this world'" (Pannenberg 1976, 7). The church is not an end in itself. In the church

> the future community of the kingdom of God is manifested even today, the community that embraces the entire human race, namely the renewed human race which has passed through the judgment of God; for the community of the human race is only

---

114. The influence of Bloch and his interpretation of the "kingdom" (Bloch 1982, 575–582) is obvious.

115. When Knitter studied in Rome in the early 1960s, it was still taught that "the primary purpose of missionary activity was *plantatio ecclesia* – the planting of churches in new cultures and regions." Today, "the primary mission is to plant the kingdom" (Knitter 2005, 202).

realizable through the overcoming of the evil in its midst, through God's judgment of all evil. (Pannenberg 1976, 8)

Pannenberg writes about this "unified human race": "It is not in man's hand to bring it about, but working towards it results from the sacramental character of the church as an operative sign of this future destiny of the human race." "The community of the human race in peace in justice . . . is part of the hope for the kingdom of God. As an operative sign for the hope . . . the church serves peace and justice among mankind" (Pannenberg 1976, 8). Pannenberg demanded: "Because religion is essentially not a private matter, its contribution towards the unification of the human race must be considered" (Pannenberg 1976, 14–15).

In this process, the dialogue with adherents of other faith communities is an indispensable element. Drawing from Jensen, Knitter establishes this-kenotic Christology: "Jesus Christ is the One who embodies openness to others. He is the One who empties himself on behalf of us, enfleshing our right relations with each other and humanity's relation with God" (Jensen in Knitter 2005, 205). Together with Jensen, Knitter concludes: "As those who confess Jesus as the Christ, Christians are likewise called to open themselves to others, particularly those who profess different religious communities" (205–206). Jensen and Knitter go as far as to say that "in order to become more faithful disciples, Christians need the insights of persons who profess distinctly different religious commitment" (206). Knitter explicitly opposes the idea that mission includes dialogue. "Mission = dialogue in service of God's kingdom" (Knitter 2005, 207).[116] Knitter is aware that critics of his position fear that mission as dialogue makes impossible the proclamation of the gospel. In order to "attempt a dialogue with such fellow-Christians," Knitter suggests: Interreligious dialogue is not only *speaking with* others, it is also *speaking to* others, that is, proclaiming "what one has found to be life-giving truth." The prerequisite of "real conversation between two religious believers is "Both of them must be as fully committed to their own truth as they are open to that of others. They must want to persuade others of their truth and at the same time be ready to be persuaded by them" (Knitter 2005, 207).

The center of mission is the kingdom of God, explicitly not the kingdom of Christ. Together with John Hick, Raimondo Panikkar, and others, Knitter

---

116. Beyerhaus passionately opposes this: "Christian mission essentially is . . . one-way traffic." He is aware that in the past oftentimes culture rather than the gospel was conveyed under this motto. But these mistakes cannot be undone by new "vogue-theologies," so Beyerhaus (Beyerhaus 1999, 121–122).

demands a theocentrism as opposed as to Christocentrism.[117] Therefore, Knitter no longer defines conversion as conversion to the church, but to the "kingdom of compassion and justice" as equivalent for the kingdom of God (Knitter 2005, 208).

> A Christian missionary who has no baptisms to report but who has helped Muslims, Hindus, Buddhists, and Christians to live together and work together lovingly and justly is a successful disciple of Christ; a missioner who has filled his or her church with converts without seeking to change a society that condones, for instance, dowry deaths or bonded labor is a failure. (Knitter 2005, 208–209)

Conversions are something that "may occur." "The Christian missionary will accept them, and be happy." But the missionary is not to "seek them, or proselytize for them, as the primary goal of missions." On the contrary, the Christian missionary "will also be happy to accept, and be happy if members of the Christian community are so moved by the Spirit to become members of the Buddhist or Islamic community." Leaning on John 14:1–3, Knitter demands that "in this new understanding of church, Christians acknowledge that there is no one way, and there is no one religion, to bring about what Jesus envisioned as the kingdom of God" (Knitter 2005, 209).[118]

10.4.3.2 God's "preferential option for the poor"

"God makes our final salvation depend on what we do with the poor (Sobrino in Knitter 2005, 204).

Ethical justification

Sobrino establishes God's "preferential option for the poor" ethically. According to him, ethics are explicitly defined by Christology (Sobrino 1985, 1–2). He interprets Matthew 25:31–46 thus, that Jesus is "incarnated" in the poor,[119] and that going to the poor is coming to God (Sobrino 1985, 223). Sobrino's

---

117. According to Takizawa they are not compatible (Odagaki 1992, 157).

118. Cullmann interpreted John 14:1–3 differently. Even though Christ rules over both church and world, they are not one and the same but concentric circles and separated. It is only in the future that they come into one kingdom (Schlaudraff 1988, 83–86).

119. The Brazilian Franciscan Leonardo Boff even goes as far as to say that God "privileged the poor as sacrament of his self-disclosure" (Boff 1984, 59). "Christian faith knows that the sacramental presence of Christ reaches an exceptional density in the poor" (64). After having temporarily been imposed with penal silence, Boff left the Catholic Church in 1992 (Altmann 1998, 1208–1209).

interpretation in particular and the notion of God's "preferential option for the poor" follow the general tendency of Latin American liberation theologians and their focus on the "historical Jesus" as leader and giver of orientation (Sobrino 1985, 10).[120] Waldenfels expressed this as follows: "In the final analysis, the acceptance of the Christian message of redemption does not consist in the celebrating contemplation of past events, but in the consequence of personally following [Jesus]" (Waldenfels 1974, 118). According to Rahner, orthodoxy (among others orthodox Christology) and orthopraxis (that is, acting as a follower of Christ) are mutually dependent in a "primary, nameless unity" (Manzanera 1974, 44). The cross is the result of the historical way of Jesus; therefore, Christian spirituality cannot be reduced to a mysticism of the cross. Christian spirituality must consist in walking the way of Jesus. Christian ethics is not an ethic of suffering but ethic of following [Jesus] (Sobrino 1985, 215).

Eschatological justification

While Sobrino establishes God's "preferential option for the poor" retrospectively and ethically, other liberation theologians establish it prospectively and eschatologically. "It can be said that the political and historical events of liberation *are* the growth of the kingdom (of God), *are* events of salvation. However, neither are they the *coming* of the kingdom nor are they the *total* redemption . . . Without liberation initiatives in history the kingdom of God will not be able to grow" (Gutiérrez 1973, 171).

> The novelty of the Christian faith is that it doesn't await the Son of Man and his kingdom at the end of humanity's history of suffering, but that amidst this very history of suffering it perceives in the Christ who is victorious through suffering the genesis of this distant future. Therefore, the practical application of Christian hope is established by Jesus, the Son of Man, not by patient perseverance until the end, but in following the self-emptying Son of Man, and in world-changing love for the estranged man. (Moltmann 1976, 229)

---

120. Under the headline of *The Death of Jesus and Liberation in History*, Sobrino theologically establishes the notion of the cross as solidarity with the suffering (Sobrino 1985, 179ff).

10.4.4 My Own (Preliminary) Opinion

Surely the call for Christian action in responsibility for this world seeks to correct a one-sided emphasis on grace:

> It has been criticized that the emphasis on the transcendence of salvation, on God's unique salvific acting, and on the *sola gratia* has led to the traditional exclusive notion that reserves the completion of salvation to God's action and not only excludes the necessity of the activity of man towards his own salvation, . . . but furthermore polemically and derogatively considers any human action and effort as presumptuous attempt of self-redemption and impairment of God's gracious acting. (Jhi 2006, 22–23)

As oftentimes, it is necessary to resist the temptation of resolving the tension. Above all, however, it is imperative to clearly define the problem. Luther's notion of the all-sufficient *sola gratia* talks about a salvation perceived as vertical event! As for his relationship with God, as for his *Unheil* under the wrath of God, man can never be the subject of his own salvation. With this regard, Luther's *sola gratia* must remain. On the other hand, Luther's horizontal *sola gratia* must not be applied to God's horizontal salvation. As for God's horizontal salvation, God does not exclude the active participation of humans, but includes it. Singe concludes from the observance of Jesus's actions "that Jesus is not beyond healing-liberation praxis but in it (Singe 2006, 56). God calls, empowers and obliges those whom he freely – *sola gratia* – saves from his wrath and makes them his children. It is alone God's grace that works salvation. God's omnipotence does not need human help. It is because he is omnipotent that he is able to and wants to use man. Takenaka's notion of humans as conduits of God's will (Yewangoe 1987, 212) is a beautiful image.

Another tension is the one between an utterly un-Christian, pessimistic passivity on one side and a euphoric activism to create heaven on earth on the other.[121] Even though the "humanization of the world" brought about by "actions of God through secular processes" (Schütz 1973, 38) cannot be the focus of Christian hope, this must never result in passivism and irresponsibility. According to Hartenstein, the eschatological outlook of mission results in

---

121. For Seeberg, the kingdom of God is an inner-worldly evolution or process. He expects "the redemptive kingdom of God to prevail in humanity thus that humanity becomes the kingdom of God" (Maier 1981, 548). According to Harvey Cox's *Theologie für die säkulare Stadt* (Moltmann 1988, 26) the task of present-day Christians consists in "creating a world of humans worth living in" (Schütz 1973, 45).

a joyous assurance of the Christian hope that does not give in neither to passivism nor to activism aiming at a secular millennialism (Spohn in Schuster 2002, 73). Even though I reject the prerogatives of Moltmann's theology, I think what he wrote about (Christian) pessimism is great: sin is usually equated with human hubris that they want to be like God, but the "other side of such pride is hopelessness, resignation, inertia and melancholy" (Moltmann 2002, 8).

> God has exalted man and given him the prospect of a life that is wide and free, but man hangs back and lets himself down. God promises a new creation of all things in righteousness and peace, but man acts as if everything were as before and remained as before. God honors him with his promises, but man does not believe himself capable of what is required of him. That is the sin that most profoundly threatens the believer. It is not the evil he does, but the good he does not do, not his misdeeds but his omissions, that accuses him. They accuse him of lack of hope. For these so-called sins of omission all have their ground in hopelessness and weakness of faith. "It is not so much sin that plunges us into disaster, as rather despair," said Chrysostom. (Moltmann 1966, 18)

11

Epilogue

11.1 Summary

In this book I aimed at showing that the primary worldview of Japan is that of animism. In order to do so I looked at basic worldview concepts (*mana*-concept, god-concept, soul-concept) as well as sociological issues, mainly collectivism and groupism with its particularly animistic application of the inclusion of the *living dead*. I further critically discussed the findings with Christian and biblical positions. The overall result of this discussion is that while many animistic concepts may not be compatible with Western Christianity, they seem to be much closer to biblical concepts (part 1).

As a bridge to the discussion of soteriology in the context of Japanese animism, I took up the concept of harmony or "peace" as one more animistic key concept. I choose this concept because it is at the same time a core concept of biblical soteriology. The studies showed that while formal similarities exist, mainly the inclusive character of *wa* (和) and *shalom*, it became clear that the Japanese concept fails to integrate justice (part 2).

The next part was dedicated to outlining salvation in the context of Japanese animism under four aspects. The first aspect was that of theology. While the Bible consequently defines *Unheil* as well as *Heil* only in connection with God, God plays no role in Japanese soteriology because he does not exist in the context of Japanese animism. The second aspect was that of cosmology. In the context of (Japanese) animism *Heil* is sought and experienced as knowledge about the future, protection, and harmony, all of them being basic and legitimate human needs. The Bible does not deny these needs, but it discusses them strictly in the context of theology. The third aspect was that of sociology, the major issues being that of guilt orientation versus shame orientation, and respectively *Heil* as forgiveness of sins and sociological rehabilitation. The fourth aspect was that of anthropology. Human beings experience *Unheil* as life-endangering impurity; *Heil* is respectively sought in rituals that either purify humans or keep away impurity (part 3).

In the last part I discussed dimensions of soteriology. Besides "peace," the overarching principle of the Japanese salvation concept is *gense riyaku* (現世利益), "this-worldly benefits." They define Japanese soteriology as two-dimensional, while biblical soteriology clearly aims beyond the horizon of this world (part 4).

11.2 Critique

Almost six years have passed since I submitted the original version of this book as doctoral thesis. I have been continuing my studies and implemented into this publication whatever could be implemented without changing the basic structure and the basic scope. However, my studies have not only led to more insight along the same lines, they have also changed my outlook.

I have come to the point where I find fault in the way many missionaries and missiologists – including myself – conduct their cultural studies. They are traditionally so indebted to and entangled by comparative religious science and anthropology that they tend to focus on historical and traditional material. I criticize this approach and my own work along with that of many others for having this particular, narrowed approach with its limited awareness of contemporary developments and present-day status quo. This critique has surfaced at times in the justified and accurate critique that the German publication of my thesis lacks practical application. It does and it cannot help doing so, for prevalent occupation with tradition hardly ever yields findings with practical relevance.

On the other hand, any more "practical application" would have gone way beyond the scope of a doctoral thesis. The justified critique touches not so much upon the scope and design of this book, but rather upon a bias in missiological and cross-cultural research methodology. The call for more practical application is the call for another book. This book-to-be must correct the bias of this present book on theory, if it wants to venture into missiological, pastoral, and social praxis. I came to believe that comparative religious studies together with biblical studies suffice as long as only the question of truth (*Wahrheit*) is asked. But as soon as the question of reality (*Wirklichkeit*) becomes relevant, basic religious studies must be complemented with present-day data found much more in research dedicated to economy, health and education. Both questions, that for *Wahrheit* and that for *Wirklichkeit* are crucial, orthodoxy and orthopraxis are both indispensable for missiology and mission to remain faithful to their calling.

11.3 Horizon

"Behind the invisible curtain, over there, somebody is smiling" (Hoshino 1992, 99). In Japanese, the word for curtain, *maku* (幕), is a cypher for the Shogunate, the rule of the shoguns (将軍), the Japanese warlords, stretching 1186 to 1867 over several eras (Okakura 2006, 67). They ruled from behind the curtains, the doors of their tent headquarters in the army camps. Political decisions were not made openly at the Imperial Court anymore, but "behind the curtain." Thus the Japanese for Shugunate is *bakufu* (幕府), "government (府) from behind the curtain (幕)" (Turnbull 2008, 16).

In the poem quoted on page xvi at the beginning of this book, the Christian Hoshino uses this cypher to state that God, invisible for man, rules. Just as little as the bustle of the Imperial Court was able to control the course of history during the age of the *bakufu* (幕府) (Richie and Reischauer 1994, 63; Irokawa and Jansen 1988, 14), all human hubbub, neither its achievements nor its defeats, can make any final decisions on *Heil* or *Unheil*. As differently and controversially as people in different cultures and adherents of various faiths interpret the world and define *Heil* and *Unheil*, it will remain crucial for the Christian understanding of salvation that God is its beginning and end, its sole source and only purpose.

In Hoshino's poem, he introduces God as the one "behind the curtain," the one "over there." This message is crucial, particularly in the context of Japanese animism with it numberless immanent gods: God is not "one of them," not part of this world," not a product of human thought, and therefore neither limited by their comprehensive faculty nor answerable to their hopes and desires.

Nevertheless, Hoshino does not portray God as apathetic and blissfully elevated above all human suffering. The "one" behind the curtain "is smiling." This is surprising as Japanese theology knows about the "pain of God." It is even more surprising when one considers Hoshino's tragic life story. From the age of twenty-four, Hoshino was paralyzed from his neck down due to a sports accident in 1970, leaving him with the ability to move only his mouth (Hoshino 2001, 94). Can God smile in the face of this world's suffering? He could not if he wasn't able to eventually overcome all *Unheil*. God's love and power unquestionably can and eventually will overcome all *Unheil*. Eventually. This makes Christian soteriology intrinsically eschatological. Unquestionably. This makes Christian soteriology intrinsically joyful. Joy is the trademark of Christianity (Pironio 1984; Kitamori 1972; Schnabel 2002, 217). It cannot be and shall not that

> the demand of the loveless and the self-imprisoned that they should be allowed to blackmail the universe: that till they consent to be happy (on their own terms) no one else shall taste joy: that theirs should be the final power; that Hell should be able to veto Heaven. (Lewis 1946, 124)

God's smile is not the apathetic smile of a tranquilly blissful God enraptured from all suffering. It is the smile of the one who joyfully works *Heil*, already growing amidst and despite of the *Unheil* of this world. It is the smile of joyful anticipation of that day when all encapsulating horizons shall crack open – and we shall see his face, as Hoshino's poem below so intriguingly puts it.

ここは何かの中なのでは
ないでしょうか
木の実の中の一粒の種のように
ある日空がパッカリ割れて
そこにあなたの顔があるように
そんな気がして
ならないのです

星野富弘

Koko-wa nanika-no naka na-no de-wa
nai deshou-ka
Ki-no mi-no naka-no hitotsubu-no tane-no you-ni
Aru hi sora-ga pakkari warete
soko-ni anata-no kao-ga aru-you-na
Sonna ki-ga shite naranai-no desu

> Could this here be the inside of something?
> I wonder.
> Myself, a seed inside a pomegranate.
> One day, ha! Heaven burst open
> and there, I see your face
> –
> I cannot help but feel that way.

Tomihiro Hoshino

Appendices

Appendix 1:   Incantations for *reiki* initiation-rites
Appendix 2:   Japanese Bible translations and key-references of Wolff's *Anthropologie des Al-ten Testaments*
Appendix 3:   The incantation of the "Great Purification"
Appendix 4:   The "blessings" of the *Shichifukujin* (七福神)

Appendix 1

Incantations for *reiki* initiation-rites

While tracing the respective "symbols" during *reiki* initiation-rites the following incantations are chanted:

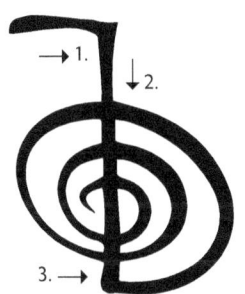

While tracing the first symbol *Choku-Rei* (直霊):[1]
(1) I go into infinity.
(2) I take a decision.
(3) I enfold and reach the core of divine nature with all energies.

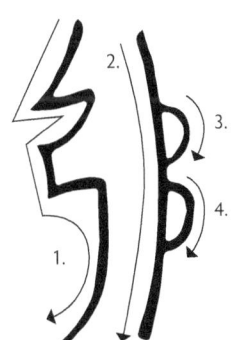

While tracing the second symbol *Sei-Heki* (青碧):[2]
(1) I go to the higher self, to the intermediate self, to the inner child.
(2) I build the protection.
(3) I hold the key and under the protection I unlock (Dalberg 1997, 217).

---

1. *Chokurei* (直霊) means "direct *rei* (霊)." According to Hauth, it is a protective mantra that means "all energy of the universe is here" or "God is here" (Hauth 2008, 86).
2. *Seiheiki* (青碧) means "azure blue." This symbol stands for spiritual balance. Hauth calls it a mental symbol of symbol of harmony (Hauth 2008, 87).

Japanese Understanding of Salvation

While tracing the third symbol *Hon Sha Ze Sho Nen*:[3]
  (1) I go into infinity.
  (2) I take a decision,
  (3) (4) to set up the divine conduit.
  (5) I remember infinity.
  (6) I need a foundation
  (7) to build a bridge
  (8) (9) (10) for the house
  (11) of the humane,
  (12) which foundation is the earth.
  (13) I go into the depth,
  (14) out of which I remember infinity.
  (15) I build the protection
  (16) (17) for the evolving divine conduit on earth
  (18) without beginning, without ending
  (19) I have access to the inner child,
  (20) the divine bowl,

---

  3. The characters Dahlberg and others refer to, do not comply with Japanese rules in their writing and as well as stroke order. The closest interpretation of the symbol *Hon Sha Ze Sho Nen* could be 本者正念. In this combination, 本者 could mean "the person himself," 正 "justice" or "right", and 念 "the sentiment." Thus: The person himself and the (up)right sentiment. The text of the incantation has absolutely nothing in common with the meaning of the Chinese character radicals. Hauth calls this symbol the space-time-symbol (Hauth 2008, 88).

(21) (22) in which I place my hands trusting (Dalberg 1997, 217–218).

There is also another version for the third symbol:
- (1) The spirit of God
- (2) lowers down,
- (3) (4) unto the roof of the world,
- (5) unto man,
- (6) unto the level of his consciousness.
- (7) The spirit of God lowers down further,
- (8) (9) (10) onto the roof of the house,
- (11) where man lives,
- (12) and into the level of his conscience.
- (13) The spirit of God lowers down further,
- (14) wide,
- (15) deep,
- (16) (17) into the roof,
- (18) into man,
- (19) into the Divine,
- (20) into the heart ventricle,
- (21) (22) in order to combine the heart valves (Dalberg 1997, 218).

Japanese Understanding of Salvation

While tracing the master-symbol *Dai Komio*:[4]

(1) I go into infinity.
(2) (3) I am aware of the divine conduit.
(4) On earth, in the world.
(5) (6) (7) Man, eyes opened aspiring towards light.
(8) (9) I go into the depth to experience the female and male forces.
(10) Shell –
(11) protection of the soul remembering
(12) giving
(13) and receiving.
(14) Shell –
(15) protection of the soul remembering
(16) impression
(17) and expression.
(18) And: This is the light shining in the deep
(Dalberg 1997, 225).

---

4. The symbol shown in the graph is the equivalent of 大光明, 大 meaning "big" or "great," 光 meaning "light," and 明 meaning "bright." Thus: "great, bright light." Again, the text of the incantation has absolutely nothing to do with the Chinese radicals of the characters.

Appendix 2

Japanese Bible Translations and Key-References of Wolff's *Anthropologie des Alten Testaments*

In the first column there are the key-references quoted by Wolff. In the second column (Wolff) are his explanantions. The page numbers there are those in his *Anthropologie des Alten Testaments* (1984). In the third column (Oogushi) there are Oogushi's translations in 旧約聖書の人間論 (*kyuuyaku seisho-no ningenron*; *Anthropologie des Alten Testaments*) (1983) with their respective page numbers. The following columns are the translations of the following Japanese tranlsations::

- *Kougoyaku Seisho* (語訳聖書); a classical Bible translation, which deliberately wanted to use "spoken Japanese" (口語);
- *Shinkyoudouyaku* (新共同訳); a newer revision of a classical Bible translation, widely used in high churches; used by *The Gideons International in Japan* (日本国際ギデオン協会);
- *Shinkaiyaku Seisho* (新改訳聖書), third, revised edition; a mostly easy to understand translation; widely used in evangelical churches;
- *Ribingu Baiburu* (リビングバイブル); an equivalent of the *Living Bible*.

נֶפֶשׁ (*nefesh*):

Ref.	Wolff	Oogushi	1. 口語	2. 新共	3. 新改	4. リビ
Gen 2:7	Atem; breath (25–26)	iki (息); breath (33)	ikita mono (生きた者); living being	ikiru mono (生きる者); living being	ikimono (生きもの); living being	ikita jinkaku-o motsu mono (生きた人格をもつ者); living being with personality
Isa 5:14	Schlund, Rachen, Kehle; gullet, pharynx, throat (26)	shokudou (食道); pharynx, intou (咽頭); larynx, nodo (のど); throat (34)	yokubou-o ookiku suru (欲望を大きくする); enlarge the desire	nodo-o hirogeru (喉を広げる); widen the throat	nodo-o hirogeru (のどを広げる); widen the desire	shita-name-zuri suru (舌なめずりする); lick the lips
Eccl 6:9	die nicht zu stillende Gier der Kehle; the voracity that cannot be stilled (27)	nodo-no kyouyoku (「のど」の強欲); the strong desire of the throat (35)	yokubou (欲望); desire	yokubou (欲望); desire	kokoro-ga akogareru koto (心があこがれること); that which the heart longs for	akogarete iru mono (あこがれているもの); the things longed for

Japanese Bible Translations and Key-References

Ref.	Wolff	Oogushi	1. 口語	2. 新共	3. 新改	4. リビ
Prov 10:3	*bedürftiger Mensch*; needy human (27)	*konkyuu shita ningen jishin* (困窮した人間自身); the needy human as is (36)	*hito-o uesasenai* (人を飢えさせない); not let a man hunger	*hito-o uesaserareru koto-wa nai* (人を飢えさせられることはない); not let a man hunger	*mono-o uesasenai* (者を飢えさせない); not let a man hunger	*hito-o uejini sasemasen* (人を飢え死にさせません); not let a man starve
Prov 27:7	*Sitz des Geschmackssinnes*; locality of taste (28)	*mikaku-no kikan* (味覚の器官); organ of taste (37)	*mono* (者); human (form expressing humility)	*hito* (人); man	*mono* (者); human (form expressing humility)	*ohara* (お腹); abdomen
Jer 2:24	*Organ der Atmung*; respiratory organ (29)	*kokyuuki* (呼吸器); respiratory organ (38)	*yokujou* (欲情); lust (sexual)	*yokujou* (欲情); lust (sexual)	*yokujou* (欲情); lust (sexual)	*yokujou* (欲情); lust (sexual)
Ps 105:18	*Nacken*; neck (31)	*kubi* (くび); neck (40)	*kubi* (首); neck	*kubi* (首); neck	*yosefu* (ヨセフ); Joseph	*kare* (彼); he
Jer 4:10	*Hals*; neck (32)	*nodobue* (のど笛); windpipe (41)	*inochi* (命); life	*nodo* (喉); throat	*nodo* (のど); throat	*juumin* (住民); population

Ref.	Wolff	Oogushi	1. 口語	2. 新共	3. 新改	4. リビ
Ps 35:25	Verlangen, Begehren, Sehnen, Trachten; yearning, desire, craving, striving (33)	yokkyuu (欲求); craving, setsubou (切望); yearning, netsubou (熱望); hot craving, akogare (あこがれ); longing (43)	negatta koto (願ったこと); that which one asked for	umaku itta (うまく行った); it went well	nozomi (望み); hope	mattaku omoidoori-ni koto-ga hakonda-na (全く思いどおりに事が運んだな); that went just as one thought it would go
Prov 23:2	Mensch, dessen Verhalten ganz und gar vom Trieb der Kehle ... bestimmt ist; a man totally governed by the drive of his throat (33)	ousei-na shokuyoku (旺盛な食欲); excessive appetite (43)	shoku-o tanoshimu mono (食をたのしむ者); a man who enjoys eating	shokuyoku ousei-na ningen (食欲旺盛な人間); a man with an excessive appetite	shokuyoku-no sakan-na hito (食欲の盛んな人); a man with a strong appetite	
Prov 16:26	Hunger; hunger (34)	ue (飢え); hunger (45)	shokuyoku (食欲); appetite	yokubou (欲望); craving	shokuyoku (食欲); appetite	taberu (食べる); to eat

Japanese Bible Translations and Key-References 499

Ref.	Wolff	Oogushi	1. 口語	2. 新共	3. 新改	4. リビ
Deut 23:25	Hunger; hunger (34)	mitasarete-inai setsubou (満たされていない切望); unfulfilled desire (45)	N/A	omou zonbun manzoku suru made (思う存分満足するまで); until one gets as much as he wishes for		soko-de taberu bun (そこで食べる分); that which one (can) eat there
Exod 23:9	Seele . . . Bedürfnisse und Wünsche; soul . . . needs and desires (35)	tamashii (魂); soul . . . setsubou (切望); desire, ganbou (願望); craving, desire (46)	kokoro (心); heart	kimochi (気持); emotion	kokoro (心); heart	kokoro (心); heart
Job 30:25	Organ des Mitgefühls mit dem Bedürftigen; organ of sympathy for the needy (36)	nayameru ningen-no chuushinteki kikan (悩める人間の中心的器官); main organ of a sympathetic human (46)	tamashii (魂); soul	kokoro (心); heart	tamashii (たましい); soul	kokoro (心); heart

Ref.	Wolff	Oogushi	1. 口語	2. 新共	3. 新改	4. リビ
Job 6:11	*Geduld*; patience, longsuffering (36)	*nintai* (忍耐); patience (48)	*taeshinobu* (耐え忍ぶ); persevere	*taeshinobu* (耐え忍ぶ); persevere	*taeshinobu* (耐え忍ぶ); persevere	*gaman suru* (我慢する); persevere
Prov 8:35–36	*Leben*; life (37)	*inochi* (命); life (49)	*inochi* (命); life	*tamashii* (魂); soul	*jibun jishin* (自分自身); self (strong form)	*jibun* (自分); self
Prov 7:23	*Leben*; life (37)	*inochi* (命); life (49)	*inochi* (命); life	*yokubou* (欲望); craving	*inochi* (いのち); life	*unmei* (運命); fate
Lev 17:11	*Leben*; life (38)	*inochi* (命); life (50)	*inochi* (命); life	*inochi* (命); life	*inochi* (いのち); life	*inochi* (いのち); life
Exod 21:23	*Leben*; life (39)	*inochi* (命); life (51)	*inochi* (命); life	*inochi* (命); life	*inochi* (いのち); life	*shikei* (死刑); capital punishment
Prov 3:22	*Person, Individuum, Wesen*; person, individuum, being (41)	*jinbutsu* (人物); person, *kojin* (個人); private person, *sonzai* (存在); existence (54)	*tamashii* (魂); soul	*tamashii* (魂); soul	*tamashii* (たましい); soul	*ikiru chikara* (生きる力); power for living

Japanese Bible Translations and Key-References 501

Ref.	Wolff	Oogushi	1. 口語	2. 新共	3. 新改	4. リビ
Num 6:6	tote Person; dead person (43)	shinda jinbutsu (死んだ人物); dead person (56)	shitai (死体); corpse	shitai (死体); corpse	shitai (死体); corpse	shitai (死体); corpse
Judg 16:30	"ich"; Personalpronomen, I, personal pronoun (45)	watakushi (私); equivalent for "I", daimeishi (代名詞); pronoun (59)	watashi (わたし); equivalent for "I"	watashi-no inochi (わたしの命); my life		
Job 16:4	"ich"; Personalpronomen, I, personal pronoun (46)	watakushi (私); equivalent for "I" (60–61)	anatagata (あなたがた); equivalent for "you" (2p, pl) watashi (わたし); equivalent for "I"	anatatachi (あなたたち); equivalent for "you" (2p, pl), watashi (わたし); equivalent for "I"	watakushi (私); equivalent for "I", anatagata (あなたがた); equivalent for "you" (2p, pl)	washi (わし); equivalent for "I"

רוּחַ (*ruach*):

Ref.	Wolff	Oogushi	1. 口語	2. 新共	3. 新改	4. リビ
Gen 1:2	*Wind*; wind (58)	*ugoiteiru kuuki* (動いている空気); moving air (79)	*rei* (霊); spirit	*rei* (霊); spirit	*rei* (霊); spirit	*rei* (霊); spirit
Exod 10:19	*kräftiger Seewind*; strong onshore wind (58)	*tsuyoi toufuu* (強い東風); strong east wind (80)	*seifuu* (西風); west wind	*seifuu* (西風); west wind	*seifuu* (西風); west wind	*seifuu* (西風); west wind
Ps 78:39	*schwacher Windhauch*; a gentle breeze (58)	*soyokaze* (微風); gentle breeze (80)	*kaze* (風); wind	*kaze* (風); wind	*kaze* (風); wind	*kaze* (風); wind
Isa 42:5	*Atem*; breath (58)	*iki* (息); breath (81)	*iki* (息); breath	*iki* (息); breath	*rei* (霊); spirit	*iki* (息); breath
Ezek 37:6	*Atem*; breath (59)	*iki* (息); breath (81)	*iki-o ataeru* (息を与える); give breath	*rei-o fukikomu* (霊を吹き込む); breathe in spirit	*iki-o ataeru* (息を与える); give breath	*iki-o fukiireru* (息を吹き入れる); breathe in breath
Ps 146:4	*Atem*; breath (59)	*iki* (息); breath (81)	*iki* (息); breath	*rei* (霊); spirit	*kokyuu* (呼吸); breathing	*rei* (霊); spirit

Japanese Bible Translations and Key-References

Ref.	Wolff	Oogushi	1. 口語	2. 新共	3. 新改	4. リビ
Job 34:14	*Lebenso-dem*; breath of life (59)	*seimei-no ibuki* (生命のいぶき); breath of (biological) life (82)	*rei* (霊); spirit	*rei* (霊); spirit	*Mitama*(御霊); Honorable Spirit, meaning the Holy Spirit	*rei* (霊); spirit
Jer 2:24	*Atemluft*; air for breathing (60)	*kuuki* (空気); air (83)	*kaze* (風); wind	*iki* (息); breath	*iki* (息); breath	*kunkun-to hana-o narasu* (くんくんと鼻を鳴らす); strongly snort with the nose
Job 19:17	*Atemgeruch*; odor of breath (60)	*nioi* (臭い); (bad) smell (83)	*iki* (息); breath	*iki* (息); breath	N/A	*iki* (息); breath
Ps 33:6	*schöpferische Lebenskraft*; creative life-force (60-61)	*seimeiryoku* (生命力); life-force of (biological) life (83); *inochi-o souzou suru chikara* (命を創造する力); power that creates life (84)	*iki* (息); breath	*ibuki* (息吹); breath	*hitokoto* (ひと言); one word	*ibuki* (いぶき); breath

Ref.	Wolff	Oogushi	1. 口語	2. 新共	3. 新改	4. リビ
Gen 41:38	that which gives aus-serordent-liche Begabung to a human, extraordinary talent (61)	tokubetsu-na sainou-ga hito-ni ataerareru (特別な才能が人に与えられる); an extraordinary talent is given to a person (85)	rei (霊); spirit	rei (霊); spirit	tokubetsu-no chikara (特別の力); extraordinary strength	rei (霊); spirit
Isa 11:2	Kraft, Vollmacht; strength, authority (62)	chikara (力); power, zenken (全権); (absolute) authority (85)	rei (霊); spirit	rei (霊); spirit	rei (霊); spirit	rei (霊); spirit
2 Kgs 19:7	"unsichtbares selbstän-diges We-sen," "das ganz seiner" [of God] Verfügung untersteht; invisible, independent being, under God's control and in his service (62–62)	me-ni mienai dokuritsushita sonzai toshite kare-no shihai no moto mattaku fukushitehairu (眼に見えない独立した存在として・・・かれの支配の下で全く服してはいる); direct translation (86)	rei (霊); spirit	rei (霊); spirit	warui shirase (悪い知らせ); bad news	rei (霊); spirit

Ref.	Wolff	Oogushi	1. 口語	2. 新共	3. 新改	4. リビ
1 Kgs 10:5	ihr stockte der Atem, Ohnmacht, fassungsloses Staunen; she was left breathless, perplexed amazement (64)	kokyuu-ga tomatta (呼吸がとまった); breathing stopped, kizetsu (気絶); faint, torimidashita kyoutenjoutai (取り乱した驚天状態); bewildered, shocked state (88)	mattaku ki-o uwabarete shimatta (全く気を奪われてしまった); ki was totally taken away	iki-mo tomaru you-na omoi de-atta (息も止まるような思いであった); that was a thought that even left one breathless	iki-mo tomaru bakari de-atta (息も止まるかりであった); it just left one breathless	iki-mo tomaru bakari deshita (息も止まるかりでした); it just left one breathless
Job 15:13	Erregung, Unmut; agitation, annoyance (64)	fungeki (憤激); indignation, anger, wrath, fukigen (不機嫌); bad mood (88)	ki-o iradateru (気をいらだてる); irritate the ki	muzukari-o kaesu (憤りを返す); return a bad mood	iradatsu (いらだつ); become irritated	
Prov 14:29	Ungeduldiger; impatient person (64)	sekkachi (せっかち); impatient, hasty (88)	ki-no mijikai mono (気の短い者); person with "short ki"; impatient person	tanki-na mono (短気な者); person with "short ki"; impatient, literally "short-tempered" person	ki-no mijikai mono (気の短い者); person with "short ki"; impatient, literally "short-tempered" person	

Ref.	Wolff	Oogushi	1. 口語	2. 新共	3. 新改	4. リビ
Eccl 7:8	*Langmütiger*; longsuffering person, *Hochmütiger*; haughty person (64)	*gaman-tsuyoi hito* (がまん強い人); persevering person, *agatta hito* (上がった人) a "raised" person (89)	*taeshinobu kokoro* (耐え忍ぶ心); a persevering heart, *takaburu kokoro* (高ぶる心); a haughty heart	*ki-ga nagai no* (気が長いの); something with long "*ki*", *kigurai-ga takai* (気位が高い); with great haughtiness (literal meaning: on a high ki-level)	*nintai* (忍耐); patience, *unubare* (うぬばれ); conceit	*nintai* (忍耐); patience; *kouman* (高慢); haughtiness
Prov 18:14	*seelische Disposition*; psychological disposition (65)	*kokoro-no joutai* (心の状態); condition of heart (89)	*kokoro* (心); heart	*rei* (霊); spirit	*kokoro* (心); heart	*yuuki* (勇気); courage
Ezra 1:5	*Träger energischer Aktionen des Willens*; organ of energetic actions of will (65–66)	*ishi-no eneru-gisshi-na katsudou* (意思のエネルギッシュな活動); energetic action of will (90)	*kokoro-o kandou sareta mono* (心を感動された者); a person with an emotionally agitated heart	*kokoro-o ugokasare-ta mono* (心を動かされた者); a person with an agitated heart	*rei-o furuita-tasareta mono* (霊を奮い立たされた者); a person with an agitated spirit	*kokoro-o karitaterarete* (心を駆り立てられて); with a perturbed heart
Isa 29:24	*Geist*; spirit (67)	*rei* (霊); spirit (92)	*kokoro* (心); heart	*rei* (霊); spirit	*kokoro* (心); heart	

לֵב/לֵבָב (leb/lebab):

Ref.	Wolff	Oogushi	1. 口語	2. 新共	3. 新改	4. リビ
1 Sam 25:37	Herz als Organ; heart as organ (cor) (69), gesucht im Leibesinneren; localized inside the body (70)	shinzou (心臓); heart as organ (96), karada-no naibu (体の内部); internals of the body (97)	kokoro (心); heart	ishiki-o nakushi (意識を無くし); faint, lose consciousness	ki-o ushinatte (気を失って); lose ki	ishikifumei (意識不明); unconsciousness (medical term)
Jer 4:19	Wände meines Herzens; walls of the heart, Herzan-Fall, heart attack (70–71)	shinzou-no kabe (心臓の壁); walls of heart, shinzou-hossa (心臓発作); heart attack (98)	shinzou (心臓); heart as organ (cor)	shinzou (心臓); heart as organ (cor)	shinzou (心臓); heart as organ (cor)	shinzou (心臓); heart as organ (cor)
1 Kgs 21:7	das Herz wird gebessert, der Mensch gestärkt; the heart improves, man is strengthened (71–72)	shinzou-o naoshinasai (心臓をなおしなさい); heal your heart! (99)	genki-o dasu (元気を出す); be of good courage!; literally: show the original ki	genki-o dasu (元気を出す); be of good courage!; literally: show the original ki	genki-o dasu (元気を出す); be of good courage!; literally: show the original ki	

Ref.	Wolff	Oogushi	1. 口語	2. 新共	3. 新改	4. リビ
Jonah 2:4	unergründliche Tiefe der hohen und unerforschten See; unsearchable depths of the unexplored high seas (72)	taiyou-no hakari-shiranai kaien (大洋の測り知らない海淵); the unfathomable abyss of the ocean (100)	umi-no mannaka (海のまん中); the innermost of the sea	kagefu-no soko (陰府の底); bottom of the shadows	umi-no mannaka-no fukami (海の真ん中の深み); the depths in the middle of the sea	ooumi-no fukami (大海の深み); depths of the ocean
Deut 4:11	dem Menschen unerreichbare Höhe des Himmels; the heights of the skies, unreachable for man (72)	ningen-ni-wa toutei tassuru koto-no dekinai takasa (人間にはとうてい達することのできない高さ); heights man cannot possibly reach (100)	chuuten (中天); high above in the skies/heaven	chuuten (中天); high above in the skies/heaven	chuuten (中天); high above in the skies/heaven	ten (天); sky/heaven
1 Sam 16:7	das Unerforschliche; the unexplorable (73)	mattaku hakari-shirenai, himitsu-na mono (全く測り知れない、秘密なもの); something no one can possibly know, a secret (101)	kokoro (心); heart	kokoro (心); heart	kokoro (心); heart	kokoro (心); heart

Japanese Bible Translations and Key-References   509

Ref.	Wolff	Oogushi	1. 口語	2. 新共	3. 新改	4. リビ
Ps 44:22	der Herzen Geheimnisse; the secrets of the hearts (73)	shinzou-no himitsu (心臓の秘密); secret(s) of the heart as organ (102)	kokoro-no himitsu (心の秘密); secret(s) of the heart	kokoro-ni kakushite iru koto (心に隠していること); things hidden in the heart	kokoro-no himitsu (心の秘密); secret(s) of the heart	kokoro-no oku-no oku (心の奥の奥); the innermost of the innermost of the heart
Ps 25:17	Sensibilität und Emotionalität; Weite die Verengung meines Herzens!; sensitivity and emotionality; Widen the confinement of my heart! (74)	kanjusei (感受性); receptivity, kansei (感性); sensitivity (102); watakushi-no shinzou-no semasa-o hirogete kudasai (私の心臓の狭さをひろげて下さい); Widen the confinement of my heart as organ! (103)	kokoro-no nayami (心の悩み); suffering of the heart	nayamu kokoro (悩む心); suffering heart	kokoro-no kurushimi (心の苦しみ); pain of the heart	

Ref.	Wolff	Oogushi	1. 口語	2. 新共	3. 新改	4. リビ
Prov 14:30	"Gemütsverfassung", "Stimmung" (74); mood	kibun (気分); mood, ningen-no funiki (人間の雰囲気); atmosphere of man (103)	kokoro (心); heart	kokoro (心); heart	kokoro (心); heart	kokoro (心); heart
Ps 21:3	Verlangen und Begehren; yearning and desire (76)	yokubou (欲望); desire, setsubou (切望); yearning (105)	kokoro (心); heart	kokoro (心); heart	kokoro (心); heart	negai (願い); (strong) request
Job 31:7	verborgenes Begehren; hidden desire (76)	kokoro-no naka-de omoiukabete iru yokujou (「心の中で」思い浮かべている欲情); lust ascending in the middle of the heart (106)	kokoro (心); heart	kokoro (心); heart	kokoro (心); heart	

Japanese Bible Translations and Key-References   511

Ref.	Wolff	Oogushi	1. 口語	2. 新共	3. 新改	4. リビ
1 Sam 17:32	the heart *fällt in Mutlosig-keit*; falls into discourage-ment (77)	*genki-no nai joutai-ni ochikomu* (元気のない状態に「落ち込む」); fall into a state in which one has no "original *ki*" anymore (106)	*ki-o otosu* (気を落とす); let the *ki* fall down	*ki-o otosu* (気を落とす); let the *ki* fall down	*ki-o otosu* (気を落とす); let the *ki* fall down	*goshinpai-ni-wa oyobimasen* (ご心配には及びません); this does not disturb one
Deut 29:3	*Verstehen*; understanding (78)	*rikai* (理解); understanding (108)	*kokoro-ni satorasenai* (心に悟らせない); one is not nade having enlightenment in the heart	*satoru kokoro* (悟る心); an enlightened heart	*satoru kokoro* (悟る心); an enlightened heart	*wakatte inakatta* (わかっていなかった); one did not know

Ref.	Wolff	Oogushi	1. 口語	2. 新共	3. 新改	4. リビ
Prov 15:14	*Einsicht*; insight (78)	*rikai* (理解); understanding (108)	*kokoro-wa chishiki-o tazuneru* (心は知識をたずねる); the heart inquires into knowledge	*kokoro-wa chishiki-o motomeru* (心は知識を求める); the heart demands knowledge	*kokoro-wa chishiki-o motomeru* (心は知識を求める); the heart demands knowledge	*nesshin-ni shinri-o motomeru* (熱心に真理を求める); eagerly demand knowledge
Prov 18:15	*vernehmende Vernunft*; receptive reason (79)	*kiite shiru risei* (「聞いて知る」理性); hearing and knowing reason (109)	*kokoro-no chishiki-o eru* (心は知識を得る); gain knowing of the heart	*kokoro-no chishiki-o kakutoku-suru* (心は知識を獲得する); acquire knowing of the heart	*kokoro-no chishiki-o eru* (心は知識を得る); gain knowing of the heart	
Gen 31:20	*jemanden um die Einsicht bringen, täuschen*; to take away insight, deceive (80)	*dousatsu-o ubaitoru* (洞察を奪いとる); rob insight, *damasu* (だます); deceive (110)				

Japanese Bible Translations and Key-References 513

Ref.	Wolff	Oogushi	1. 口語	2. 新共	3. 新改	4. リビ
Isa 65:17	*ins Bewußtsein kommen*; come into awareness (81)	*omoidasu* (思い出す); remember (111)	*oboerareru koto* (おぼえられること); being reminded	*omoiokosu mono* (思い起こす者); a person who makes one remember	*omoidasare-nai* (思い出されない); one does not remember	*omoidasa-nakunaru* (思い出さなくなる); one does not remember
Judg 16:18	*Wissen*; knowledge (81–82)	*chishiki* (知識); knowledge (112)	*kokoro* (心); heart	*kokoro-no naka* (心の中); in the heart	*kokoro* (心); heart	*hontou-no koto* (ほんとうのこと); the truth
Prov 28:26	*Organ der … Überlegun-gen*; organ of consideration (82–83)	*jukuryo-no kikan* (熟慮の器官); organ of cautious pondering (113)	*kokoro* (心); heart	*kokoro* (心); heart	*kokoro* (心); heart	*jibun* (自分); self
Job 12:3	*Verstand*; reason (83)	*rikairyoku* (理解力); power of understanding (114)	*satori* (悟り); enlightenment	*kokoro* (心); heart	*satori* (悟り); enlightenment	
Prov 16:9	*Wille, Erwägen*; will, pondering (84)	*ishi* (意志); will, *kouryo* (考慮); pondering (115–116)	*kokoro* (心); heart	*kokoro* (心); heart	*kokoro* (心); heart	

Ref.	Wolff	Oogushi	1. 口語	2. 新共	3. 新改	4. リビ
1 Sam 24:6	Gewissen; conscience (85)	ryoushin (良心); conscience (116)	kokoro-no seme-o kanjita (心の責めを感じた); one felt the reproach of the heart	koukai shita (後悔した); one regretted	kokoro-o itameta (心を痛めた); the heart hurt	kokoro-wa itamidashita-no desu (心は痛みだしたのです); the heart began hurting
2 Sam 7:3	Absicht; intention (86)	ito (意図); intention (118)	kokoro (心); heart	kokoro (心); heart	kokoro (心); heart	kangae-no mama-ni (考えのままに); as one thought it would be
Exod 35:21	Willensan-trieb; urge of will (87)	ishi-no douki (意思の動機); motivation of will (119)	kokoro (心); heart	kokoro (心); heart	kokoro (心); heart	kokoro (心); heart

Appendix 3

The Incantation of the "Great Purification"

The English text was translated by Philippi (1959). The notes on the Japanese original are taken mainly from Ogasawara (2001). The Japanese text was provided by *Kototama & 100 deities* (言霊百神).[1]

> Hear me, all of you assembled princes of the blood,
> princes, court nobles, and all officials.
>
> Thus I speak.
>
> The various sins are to be exorcised, are to be purified in the
> great exorcism of the last day of the sixth month –
>
> Hear me, all of you.
>
> The eight myriad deities were convoked in a divine
> convocation and spoke these words of entrusting:
>
> "Our Sovereign Grandchild is to rule the Land of the Plentiful Reed
> Plains, of the Fresh Ears of Grain, tranquility as a peaceful land."
>
> Having thus entrusted the land, they inquired with a divine inquiry of the
> unruly deities in the land, and expelled them with a divine expulsion;
>
> They silenced to the last leaf the rocks and the stumps
> of the trees, which had been able to speak,

---

1. Source: http://homepage2.nifty.com/studio-hearty/kototama_ver.1/lecture/ooharai_norito/ooharai_norito.pdf. Unfortunately, this source is not available anymore. A similar text can be accessed from WikiSource: https://ja.wikisource.org/wiki/六月晦大祓祝詞 (accessed on 2012/10/22). A video clip of a similar incantation can be found here: https://www.youtube.com/watch?v=xzeVeoz6K4Y (accessed on 2017/07/26).

And caused him to descend from the heavens, leaving the
heavenly rock-seat, and pushing with an awesome pushing
through the myriad layers of heavenly clouds –

Thus they entrusted the land to him.

The various sins perpetrated and committed by the heavenly
ever-increasing people to come into existence in this land
which he is to rule tranquilly as a peaceful land;

First, the heavenly sins:
breaking down the ridges,[2] covering up the ditches,[3]
releasing the irrigation sluices,[4]
double planting,[5] setting up stakes,[6]
skinning alive,[7] skinning backwards,[8]
defecation[9] –

Many sins such as these are distinguished and called the heavenly sins.

The earthly sins:

cutting living flesh,[10] cutting dead flesh,[11]
white leprosy,[12] skin excrescences,[13]
the sin of violating one's own mother,[14]
the sin of violating one's own child,[15]
the sin of violating a mother and her child, or a child and her mother,[16]

---

2. *Ahanachi* (畔放ち).
3. *Mizoume* (溝埋め).
4. *Hihanachi* (樋放ち).
5. *Shikimaki* (重播き or 頻蒔き). The additional sowing on the paddy of a neighbor, adversely affects the growth of rice.
6. *Kushizashi* (串刺).
7. *Ikihagi* (生き剥ぎ).
8. *Sakahagi* (逆剥ぎ).
9. *Kusodo* (糞戸 or 屎戸).
10. *Ikihadatachi* (生膚断). Flaying and subsequent bloodshed.
11. *Shinhadatachi* (死膚断). Postmortem section.
12. *Shirahito* (白人). Literally "white person". 白人 as racial specification is written the same way but pronounced *hakujin*.
13. *Kokumi* (胡久美), also called *semushi* (傴 or 僂).
14. *Ono-ga haha okaseru tsumi* (己が母犯せる罪).
15. *Ono-ga ko okaseru tsumi* (己が子犯せる罪).
16. *Haha-to ko-to okaseru tsumi, ko-to haha-to okaseru tsumi* (母と子と犯せる罪、子と母と犯せる罪).

the sin of transgression with animals,[17]
woes from creeping insects,[18]
woes from the deities on high,[19]
woes from the birds on high,[20]
killing animals, the sin of witchcraft[21] –

Many sins as such shall appear.

When they thus appear, by the heavenly shine usage,
let the Great Nakatomi[22] cut off the bottom and cut
off the top of heavenly pieces of wood,

and place them in abundance on a thousand tables;

Let him cut off the bottom and the top of heavenly
sedge reeds and cut them into myriad strips;

and let him pronounce the heavenly ritual, the solemn ritual words.[23]

When he thus pronounces them,

the heavenly deities will push open the heavenly rock door, and
pushing with an awesome pushing through the myriad layers
of heavenly clouds will hear and receive these words.

Then earthly deities will climb up to the summits of
the high mountains and the low mountains,

and pushing aside the mists of the high and low
mountains, will hear and receive these words.

---

17. *Kemono okaseru tsumi* (畜けもの犯せる罪).
18. *Hau mushi-no wazawai* (昆虫災).
19. *Takatsukami-no wazawai* (高津神の災). Calamities by lightning.
20. *Takatsutori-no wazawai* (高津鳥の災). In another prayer, this line reads *tobu tori-no wazawai* (飛ぶ鳥の災), "calamities by flying birds". This signifies damage birds of prey cause on roofs.
21. Killing of animals is here called *kemonotaoshi* (畜仆し). This text, however, is about killing of animals for the sake of *kodou* (蠱道)), here called *majimono* (蠱物), "malevolent sorcery", as the 畜 shows.
22. The *Nakatomi* (中臣) clan was an influential clan of priests in ancient Japan.
23. *Amatsu Miyagoto mochite, Oonakatomi, amatsu kanagi-o, honuchi kiri, sueuchi tachite, chikura-no okikura-ni okiashira hashite, takatsu sugaso-o, hon-uchi tachi, sueuchi kirite, hachi hari-ni torisakite, amatsu norito-no otonoritogoto-o nore* (天津宮事以ちて、大中臣、天津金木を、本打切り、末打断ちて、千座の置座に置足らはして、天津菅麻を、本刈断ち、末刈切りて、八針に取辟きて、天津祝詞の太祝詞事ふとのりとごとを宣のれ).

> Then, beginning with the court of the Sovereign Grandchild,
> in the lands of the four quarters under the heavens,
>
> each and every sin will be gone.
>
> As a result of the exorcism and the purification, there will be no sins left.
>
> They will be taken into the great ocean by the goddess called Seoritsu-hime,[24] who dwells in the rapids of the rapid-running rivers which fall surging perpendicular from the summits of high and low mountains.
>
> When she thus takes them, they will be swallowed with a gulp by the goddess called Hayaakitsu-hime,[25] who dwells in the wild brine, the myriad currents of the brine,
>
> when she thus swallows them with a gulp,
>
> the goddess called Hayasaura-hime,[26] who dwells in the land of Hades, the under-world,[27] will wander off with them and lose them.
>
> When she thus loses them,
>
> beginning with the many officials serving in the Emperor's court,
>
> in the four quarters and the heavens,
>
> beginning from today,
>
> each and every sin will be gone.
>
> O diviners of the four lands, carry them out to the great river and cast them away.
>
> Thus I speak.

(Philippi in Nelson 1996, 108–111)

---

24. 瀬織津姫.
25. 速開津姫.
26. 速佐須良姫.
27. *Ne-no kuni soko-no kuni* (根国底国). Literally: "the deepest land of the Land of Roots".

みなづきのつごもりのおおはらへ （しはすはこれにならへ）[1]
六月晦大祓　（十二月は之に准へ）

うごなはりはべるみこたち　おほきみたち　まへつぎみたち　もものつかさのひとども　もろもろききたまへよと　のたまふ
集はり侍る親王　諸王　諸臣　百官人等　諸聞食へよと宣ふ

すめらがみかどにつかへまつる　ひれかくるとものを　たすきかくるとものを　ゆぎおふとものを　たちはくとものを
天皇が朝廷に仕奉る　比礼挂くる伴男　手襁挂くる伴男　靱負ふ伴男　剣佩く伴男

とものをのやそとものををはじめて　つかさづかさにつかへまつるひとどもの　あやまちおかしけむくさぐさのつみを
伴男の八十伴男を始めて　官官に仕奉る人等の　過犯しけむ雑雑の罪を

ことしみなづきのつごもりのおおはらへに　はらいたまひきよめたまふことを　もろもろききたまへよと　のたまふ
今年六月の晦の大祓に　祓給ひ清給ふ事を　諸聞食へよと宣ふ

たかまのはらにかむづまります　すめむつかみろぎかむろみのみこともちて
高天原に神留り坐す　皇親神漏岐神漏美の命以ちて

やほよろづのかみたちを　かむつどへにつどへたまひ　かむはかりにかはりたまひて　あがすめみまのみことは
八百万の神等を　神集へに集へ賜ひ　神議に議賜て　我が皇孫之尊は

とよあしはらのみづほのくにを　やすくにとたひらけくしろしめせとことよさしまつりき
豊葦原の水穂の国を　安国と平けく所知食と事依し奉き

かくよさしまつりしくぬちに　あらぶるかみたちをば　かむとはしにとはしたまひ　かむはらひにはらひて
如此依し奉し国中に　荒振神達をば　神問しに問し賜ひ　神掃に掃賜ひて

こととひしいはね　こだち　くさのかきはをもことやめて
語問し磐根　樹立　草の垣葉をも語止て

あまのいはくらはなち　あまのやへぐもをいつのちわきにちわきて　あまくだしよさしまつりき
天磐座放ち　天の八重雲を伊頭の千別に千別て　天降依し奉き

かくよさしまつりしよものくになかと　おおやまとひたかみのくにをやすくにとさだめまつりて
如此依さし奉し四方の国中と　大倭日高見之国を安国と定奉て

したついはねにみやばしらふとしきたて　たかまのはらにちぎたかしりて
下津磐根に宮柱太敷立て　高天原に千木高知て

1　The text is taken from http://www.geocities.jp/sizen_junnosuke/minaduki-ooharae_norito.html.

すめみまのみことのみづのみあらかつかへまつりて　あまのみかげ　ひのみかげと
かくりまして
皇御孫之命の美頭の御舎仕奉て　天之御蔭　日之御蔭と隠坐て

やすくにとたひらけくしろしめさむくぬちに　なりいでむあまのますひとらが　あ
やまちおかしけむくさぐさのつみごとは
安国と平けく所知食む国中に　成出む天の益人等が　過犯けむ雑々の罪事は

あまつつみと　あぜはなち　みぞうめ　ひはなち　しきまき　くしざし　いきはぎ
　　さかはぎ　くそへここだくのつみを
天津罪と　畔放　溝埋　樋放　頻蒔　串刺　生剥　逆剥　屎戸　許々太久の罪を

あまつつみとのりわけて
天津罪と法別て

くにつつみと　いきはだたち　しにはだたち　しろひと　こくみ　おのがははおか
せるつみ　おのがこおかせるつみ
国津罪と　生膚断　死膚断　白人　胡久美　己が母犯罪　己が子犯罪

ははとこおかせるつみ　ことははとおかせるつみ　けものおかせるつみ
母と子と犯罪　子と母と犯罪　畜犯罪

はふむしのわざわひ　たかつかみのわざわひ　たかつとりのわざわひ
昆虫の災　高津神の災　高津鳥の災

けものたふしまじものせるつみ　ここだくのつみいでむ
畜仆し蟲物為罪　許々太久の罪出でむ

かくいでば　あまつみやごともちて　おおなかとみ　あまつかなぎをもとうちきり
すえうちたちて
如此出ば　天津宮事以て　大中臣　天津金木を本打切末打断て

ちぐらのおきくらにおきたらはして　あまつすがそをもとかりたちすえかりきりて
千座の置座に置足はして　天津菅曽を本苅断末苅切て

やはりにとりさきて　あまつのりとのふとのりごとをのれ
八針に取辟て　天津祝詞の太祝詞事を宣れ

かくのらば　あまつかみはあまのいはとをおしひらきて　あまのやへぐもをいつの
ちわきにちわきてきこしめさむ
如此乃良ば　天津神は天磐門を押披て　天之八重雲を伊頭の千別に千別て聞食む

くにつかみはたかやまのすえひきやまのすえにのぼりまして
国津神は高山乃末短山之末に登坐して

たかやまのいほりひきやまのいほりをかきわけてきこしめさむ
高山の伊穂理短山の伊穂理を撥別て所聞食む

かくきこしめしてば　すめみまのみことのみかどをはじめて　あまのしたよものく
ににには　つみといふつみはあらじと
如此所聞食てば　皇御孫之命の朝廷を始て　天下四方国には　罪と云ふ罪は不在と

The Incantation of the "Great Purification"

しなとのかぜのあまのやへぐもをふきはなつことのごとく
科戸之風の天之八重雲を吹放事之如く

あしたのみきりゆうべのみきりを　あさかぜゆうかぜのふきはらふことのごとく
朝之御霧夕之御霧を　朝風夕風の吹掃事之如く

おおつべにおるおおふねを　へときはなちともときはなちて　おおうなばらにおしはなつことのごとく
大津辺に居る大船を　舳解放艫解放て　大海原に押放事之如く

おちかたのしげきがもとをやきがまのとがまもちて　のこるつみはあらじと　はらひたまひきよめたまふことを
彼方之繁木が本を　焼鎌の敏鎌以て打掃事之如く　遺る罪は不在と　祓賜ひ清賜事を

たかやまのすえひきやまのすえより　さくなだりにおちたきつはやかわのせにますせおりつひめといふかみ
高山之末短山之末より　佐久那太理に落多支都速川の瀬に坐す瀬織津比咩と云神

おおうなばらにもちいでなむ　かくもちいでいなば
大海原に持出なむ　如此持出往ば

あらしほのしほのやほぢのしほのやほあひにますはやあきつひめといふかみ
荒塩之塩の八百道の八塩道之塩の八百会に坐す速開都比咩と云神

もちかかのみてむ　かくかかのみてば　いぶきどにますいぶきどぬしといふかみ　ねのくにそこのくににいぶきはなちてむ
持可可呑てむ　如此可可呑てば　気吹戸に坐す気吹主と云神　根国底之国に気吹放てむ

かくいぶきはなちてば　ねのくにそこのくににますはやさすらひめといふかみ　もちさすらひうしなひてむ
如此気吹放てば　根国底之国に坐す速佐須良比咩と云神　持佐須良比失てむ

かくうしなひてば　きょうよりはじめてつみというふつみはあらじと
如此失てば　今日より始て罪と云ふ罪は不在と

たかまのはらにみみふりたててきくものと　うまひきたて
高天原に耳振立聞物と　馬牽立て

ことしみなづきのつごもりのひの　ゆふひのくだちのおおはらへに
今年六月の晦日の　夕日之降の大祓に

はらひたまひきよめたまふことを　もろもろききたまへよとのたまふ
祓給ひ清給ふ事を　諸聞食へよと宣ふ

よくにのうらべども　おおかわぢにもちまかりいでて　はらへやれとのる
四国の卜部等　大川道に持退り出でて　祓へ却れと宣る

Appendix 4

The "Blessings" of the *Shichifukujin* (七福神)

	Ebisu (恵比寿)	Daikokuten (大黒天)	Benzaiten (弁財天)	Bishamon-ten (毘沙門天)	Juroujin (寿老人)	Fukuro-kuju (福禄寿)	Hotei Oshou (布袋和尚)
prosperity	fishery; trade; agriculture	agriculture; prosperity	money	wishing jewel; tower of riches	jewel as symbol for prosperity	material riches	contentment and affluence for others; in Japan material affluence
safety	seafaring	protection of monaste-ries; protection in the kitchen	longevity; protection from natural calamities	patron-deity granting protection for the teaching of Buddha	longevity	longevity	safe oracles
fertility			her serpent is a fertility-deity	phallus-symbolism		virility and fertility	
interper-sonal happiness			marital happiness; sexual pleasure	sexual pleasure		carnality, fame	friendship
psycholo-gical happiness			cheerfulness		bliss		"highest bliss" independence from prosperity; wisdom
culture		agriculture; medicine; trade	talents: music, painting, sculpture, dance, literature			wisdom	

Bibliography

便利・わかりやすい冠婚葬祭マナー&ビジネス知識 (*benri, wakariyasui kankonsousai manaa & bijinesu chishiki*) [Practical and easy-to-understand knowledge about social events and business]. No year; http://www.jp-guide.net/manner/sa/joya-no-kane.html (accessed 2012/10/12).

聖書が教えている教会生活: 教会生活入門てびき (*seisho-ga oshiete iru kyoukaiseikatsu: kyoukaiseikatsu nyuumon tebiki*) [What the Bible teaches about church life: An introductory handbook to church life]. 2000. Tokyo: Nihon Domei Kirisuto Kyoudan Kyouikubu (Education Departments of the DOMEI-Denomination) (日本同盟基督教団教育部).

美しい日本の習慣 (*utsukushii Nihon-no shuukan*) [Beautiful customs of Japan], edited by Kouunsha-Verlag (幸運社). 2008. Kyoto: PHP Kenkyuujo (PHP研究所).

Abe, Akio (阿部秋生). 2000. 日本思想体系３９近世神道論前期国学 (*Nihon shisou taikei 39 kinsei shintouron zenki kokugaku*) [Japanese Thought System: 39 Modern Shintou-Approaches: First Semester Studies in Japanology]. Tokyo: Iwanami Shotenkan (岩波書店刊); http://1gen.jp/1GEN/NAN/J6.HTM.

Abe, Masamichi (阿部正路). 2004. 神道がよくわかる本 (*shintou-ga yoku wakaru hon*) [A book for better understanding of Shintoism]. Kyoto: PHP Kenkyuujo (PHP研究所).

Abegg, Lily. 1970. *Ostasien denkt anders: Eine Analyse des westlich-östlichen Gegensatzes*. First revised edition. Munich: Verlag Kurt Desch.

Adam, Gottfried. 1999. "Rechtfertigung." In *Theologische Schlüsselbegriffe: Biblisch, systematisch, didaktisch*, edited by Rainer Lachmann, Gottfried Adam, Werner H. Ritter, 277–292. Göttingen: Vandenhoeck & Ruprecht.

Adami, Norbert R. 1991. "Ideal und Wirklichkeit." In *Ideal und Wirklichkeit: Essays zur japanischen Gegenwart*, edited by Norbert R. Adami and Ulrich Pauly, 13–88. Munich: Iudicium Verlag.

Afflerbach, Horst. 2006. *Die heilsgeschichtliche Theologie Erich Sauers* (original title of doctoral thesis (Pretoria): Die heilsgeschichtliche Theologie Erich Sauers im Kontext missionarischer Verantwortung). Wuppertal: R. Brockhaus Verlag; Gießen: Brunnen Verlag (Theologische Verlagsgemeinschaft, TVG).

Aihara, Tetsuya (相原鐵也). 2003. 鎌倉幕府のリスクマネジメント (*Kamakura Bakufu-no risukumanejimento*) [Risk-Management of the Kamakura-Government]. Tokyo: Bungeisha (文芸社).

Aitken, Robert. 1997. *Original Dwelling Place: Zen Buddhist Essays*. New York: Basic Books.

Aiyangar, Narayan. 1987. *Essays on Indo-Aryan Mythology*, volume 1. New Delhi: Asian Educational Services.

Akima, Toshio (秋間俊夫). 1982. "The Songs of the Dead: Poetry, Drama, and Ancient Death Rituals of Japan." *The Journal of Asian Studies* 41 (3): 485–509. Edited by the Association for Asian Studies.

Albertz, Rainer. 1992. *Religionsgeschichte Israels in alttestamentlicher Zeit*, volume 1 (Grundrisse zum Alten Testament; ATD Ergänzungsreihe Volume 8/1). Göttingen: Vandenhoeck & Ruprecht.

Albertz, Rainer, Gabi Kern, Ingo Kottsieper, and Jakob Wöhrle. 2003. *Geschichte und Theologie: Studien zur Exegese des Alten Testaments und zur Religionsgeschichte Israels*. Berlin and New York: Walter de Gruyter.

Allen, Diogenes, and Eric O. Springstedt. 2007. *Philosophy for Understanding Theology*. Second edition. Richmond, VA: Westminster John Knox Press.

Allen, John L. Jr. 2000. *Pope Benedict XVI: A Biography of Joseph Ratzinger* (Original title: Cardinal Ratzinger: The Vatican's Enforcer of the Faith). London and New York: Continuum.

Allen, Roland. 1962. *Missionary Methods: St. Paul's or Ours?* American Edition. Grand Rapids, MI: Eerdmans.

Althaus, Paul. 1947. *Die christliche Wahrheit*. 2 vols. Gütersloh: C. Bertelsmann Verlag.

Altmann, Walter. 1998. "Befreiungsbewegung, kirchengeschichtlich." In *Religion in Geschichte und Gegenwart: Handwörterbuch für Theologie und Religionswissenschaft (RGG)*, fourth completely revised edition, edited by Hans Dieter Betz, Don S. Browning, Bernd Janowsky and Eberhard Jüngel, 1207–1209. Tübingen: Mohr Siebeck.

Anderson, Gary A. 1999. "*Necassarium Adae Peccatum*: The Problem of Original Sin." In *Sin, Death, and the Devil*, edited by Carl E. Braaten and Robert W. Jenson, 22–44. Grand Rapids, MI: Eerdmans.

Anderson, Joseph L., and Donald Richie. 1982 (1959). *The Japanese Film: Art and Industry*. Enlarged edition. Princeton, NJ and Chichester, West Sussex: Princeton University Press.

Andou, Junko (安藤純子). 2001. "Rezeption der subjektiven Freiheitsrechte in der frühen Meiji-Zeit." In *11. Deutschsprachiger Japanologentag in Trier 1999: Sprache, Literatur, Kunst, Populärkultur, Medien, Informationstechnik*, edited by Hilaria Gössmann and Andreas Mrugalla, 45–50. Berlin, Hamburg and Münster: LIT Verlag.

Ankerberg, John, and John Weldon. 2001. *Fakten über ganzheitliche Medizin und alternative Heilmethoden: Können wir unseren Ärzten noch vertrauen?* Pfäffikon: Verlag Mitternachtsruf; http://bitflow.dyndns.org/german/JohnAnkerbergUndJohnWeldon/Fakten_Ueber_Ganzheitliche_Medizin_Und_Alternative_Heilmethoden_2001.pdf (accessed 13 May 2016).

Anrich, Gustav. 1990. *Das antike Mysterienwesen in seinem Einfluss auf das Christentum*. Hildesheim, Zürich, New York: Georg Olms Verlag.

Antoni, Klaus J. 1998. *Shintō und die Konzeption des japanischen Nationalwesens (kokutai)*. Leiden: Brill.
Aoki, Eiichi (青木栄一). 1994. *Japan: Profile of a Nation*. Tokyo: Koudansha International, New York: Koudansha America.
Aoki, Hitoshi (青木人志). 2001. "Nobushige Hozumi: A Skillful Transplanter of Western Legal Thought into Japanese Soil." In *Rethinking the Masters of Comparative Law*, edited by Annelise Riles, 129–151. Oxford: Hart Publishing.
Aoyagi-Usui, Midori (青柳みどり), Henk Vinken, and Atsuko Kuribayashi (栗林敦子). 2003. "Pro-environmental Attitudes and Behaviors: An International Comparison." *Human Ecology Review* 10 (1): 23–31 (accessed 12 Oct 2012).
Araki, Michio (荒木美智雄). 2003. "Popular Religions and Modernity in Japan." In *Beyond Primitivism: Indigenous Religious Traditions and Modernity*, edited by Jacob Olupona, 214–223. Oxford: Routledge, Taylor & Francis Group.
Armerding, Hudson T. 1992. *The Heart of Godly Leadership*. Wheaton, IL: Crossway.
Asada, Youichi (浅田塘一). 2002. 幸運を呼ぶ墓相の科学 (*kouun-o yobu basou-no kagaku*) [A grave-science inviting happiness]. Tokyo: Bungeisha (文芸社).
Ashkenazi, Michael. 1993. *Matsuri: Festivals of a Japanese Town*. Honolulu: University of Hawaii Press.
———. 2003. *Handbook of Japanese Mythology*. Santa Barbara, CA: ABC-CLIO.
Asoya, Masahiko (安蘇谷正彦). 1994. 神道とはなにか (*shintou-to-wa nani-ka*) [What Is Shintoism?]. Tokyo: Perikansha (ぺりかん社).
Augsburger, David W. 1995. *Pastoral Counseling across Cultures*. Richmond, VA: Westminster John Knox Press.
Augustine, Aurelius. 1888. *The City of God*. Edited by Marcus Dods. Edinburgh: T & T Clark.
Ayabe, Henry. n.d. [1992]. *Step Inside: Japan: Language–Culture–Mission*. Tokyo: Japan Evangelical Missionary Association.
Bacote, Vincent. 2002. "What Is This Life For?: Expanding Our View of Salvation." In *What Does It Mean to Be Saved?: Broadening Evangelical Horizons of Salvation*, edited by John G. Stackhouse, Jr., 95–113. Grand Rapids, MI: Baker Academic.
———. 2008. Self-introduction on the website of Wheaton College; http://www.wheaton.edu/Theology/Faculty/bacote/ (updated 2008/12/5; accessed 15 Apr 2009); now: http://www.wheaton.edu/Academics/Faculty/B/Vincent-Bacote (accessed 12 Oct 2012).
Badcock, Gary D. 1997. *Light of Truth and Fire of Love: A Theology of the Holy Spirit*. Grand Rapids, MI: Eerdmans.
Bairy, Maurice. 1969. "Motivational Forces in Japanese Life." In *The Japanese Employee*, edited by Robert J. Ballon, 41–60. Tokyo: Sophia University; Rutland, VT and Tokyo: Charles E. Tuttle Co.
Bak, Mikyung. 2008. *Animism Inside Japanese Animations: Focused on Animations by Hayao Miyazaki*, presented at the occasion of the 京都国際デザイン会議クム

ルス 2008 (*Kyouto Kokusai Dezain Kaigi Kumurusu* 2008; International Kyoto-Lecture Cumulus 2008); http://www.kyoto-seika.ac.jp/cumulus/e_programs/posterpdf/s2_4.pdf (accessed 12 Oct 2012).

Bakke, Odd Magne. 2001. "Concord and Peace: A Rhetorical Analysis of the First Letter of Clement with an Emphasis on the Language of Unity and Sedition." Revised version of a doctoral thesis presented at the University of Oslo. Tübingen: Mohr Siebeck.

Bammann, Heinrich. 2004. "Zur Diskussion gestellt: Geisterphänomene in Afrika." *Evangelikale Missiologie* 3 (4): 100–108.

Bancroft, Emery H. 1976. *Christian Theology: Systematic and Biblical*, 2nd revised edition. Grand Rapids, MI: Zondervan.

Baptandier, Brigitte. 2001. *De la malemort en quelques pays d'Asie*. Paris: KARTHALA Editions.

Barnes, Michael. 2002. *Theology and the Dialogue of Religions*. Cambridge: Cambridge University Press.

Baroni, Helen Josephine. 2002. *The Illustrated Encyclopedia of Zen Buddhism*. New York, NY: Rosen Publishing Group.

Barr, James. 1993. "Biblical Faith and Natural Theology: The Gifford Lectures for 1991." Delivered in the University of Edinburgh. Oxford: Oxford University Press.

Barrett, Charles Kingsley. 1991. "Paulus als Missionar und Theologe." In *Paulus und das antike Judentum*, Wissenschaftliche Untersuchungen zum Neuen Testament 58, edited by Adolf von Schlatter, Martin Hengel and Ulrich Heckel, 1–16. Tübingen: Mohr Siebeck.

Barrett, Gregory. 1989. *Archetypes in Japanese Film: The Sociopolitical and Religious Significance of the Principal Heroes and Heroines*. Cranbury, NJ: Associated University Presses.

Barth, Karl. 1970. *Die Kirchliche Dogmatik: Erster Volume, Zweiter Teil*. Zollikon-Zürich: Evangelischer Verlag.

———. 1982. *Die christliche Dogmatik im Entwurf*, volume 1. Zürich: Theologischer Verlag.

———. 1985. *Die Kirchliche Dogmatik*, volume 4: *Die Lehre von der Versöhnung*, Zweiter Teil, Fourth edition. Zürich: Theologischer Verlag.

———. 1999 (1922). *Der Römerbrief* (second version). 16th edition. Zürich: Theologischer Verlag.

Barth, Ulrich. 2005. *Gott als Projekt der Vernunft*. Tübingen: Mohr Siebeck.

Basu, Dipak, and Victoria Miroshnik. 2016. *Structural Revolution in International Business Architecture: Political Economy*, volume 2. New York: Palgrave MacMillan.

Baumann, Heinz. 1995. *Individualität und Tod: Psychologische und anthropologische Aspekte der Todeserfahrung*. Originally presented as doctoral thesis at the University of Zürich, winter semester 1993/94. Würzburg: Königshausen & Neumann.

Baur, Ferdinand Christian. 1863. *Geschichte der christlichen Kirche.* Tübingen: Verlag und Druck von L. FR. Fues.

———. 1867. *Lehrbuch der christlichen Dogmengeschichte.* No date: The book is at the University of Oxford.

Bays, Daniel H., and James H. Grayson. 2006. "Christianity in East Asia: China, Korea, and Japan." In *The Cambridge History of Christianity: World Christianities C. 1815–C. 1914*, edited by Sheridan Gilley and Brian Stanley, 493–512. Cambridge: Cambridge University Press.

Beardsley, Richard K. 1965. "Religion and Philosophy." In *Twelve Doors to Japan*, edited by John Whitney Hall, and Richard K. Beardsley, 310–347. New York, St. Louis, San Francisco, Toronto, London, Sydney: McGraw-Hill.

Bebenroth, Ralf. 2015. *International Business Mergers and Acquisitions in Japan.* Tokyo, Heidelberg, New York, Dordrecht and London: Springer.

Beck, J. T. 1862 (1843). *Umriß der biblischen Seelenlehre: Ein Versuch.* Second enlarged and revised edition. Tübingen: Verlag von Albert Moser.

Becker, Ernest. 1962. *The Birth and Death of Meaning: A Perspective in Psychiatry and Anthropology*, volume 450. Glencoe, IL: Free Press of Glencoe.

Bellah, Robert N. 1965. "Japan's Cultural Identity: Some Reflections on the Work of Watsuji Tetsuro." *The Journal of Asian Studies* 24, no. 4 (August 1970): 573–594. Edited by the Association for Asian Studies.

Ben-Dasan, Isaiah.[1] 1972 (Japanese original 1970). *The Japanese and the Jews* (ユダヤ人と日本人, *yudayajin to nihonjin*). Second English edition. New York and Tokyo: Weatherhill.

Benedict, Ruth. 1986 (first published in 1946). *The Chrysanthemum and the Sword: Patterns of Japanese Culture*: 菊と刀 (*kiku to katana*). 41st edition. Rutland, VT, and Tokyo: Charles E. Tuttle Co.

———. 2005 (1934). *Patterns of Culture.* New York, NY: Houghton Mifflin Harcourt.

———. 1993. "Shame Cultures and Guilt Cultures." In *Japanese Religions: Past and Present*, edited by Ian Reader, Esben Andreasen, and Finn Stefánnson, 28–30. Honolulu: University of Hawaii Press.

Berentsen, Jan-Martin. 1985a. *Grave and Gospel.* Presented as doctoral thesis in Oslo, 1982. Leiden: Brill Archive.

———. 1985b. "Ancestor Worship in Missiological Perspective." In *Christian Alternatives to Ancestor Worship:* 祖先崇拝問題 (*sosen suuhai mondai*) [Problems of ancestor veneration], edited by Bong Rin Ro. Taichung, 261–285. Taiwan: Asia Theological Association.

Berger, Klaus. 2002. *Paulus.* Volume 2197 in the Beck'schen Reihe: Wissen. Munich: Verlag C. H. Beck.

Bergler, Reinhold. 2009. *Psychologie der Hygiene.* Berlin: Springer.

---

1. Ben-Dasan is the pen-name of Shichihei Yamamotos (山本七平) (Lundell 1995, 407).

Berneburg, Erhard. 1997. "Das Verhältnis von Verkündigung und sozialer Aktion in der evangelikalen Missionstheorie: Unter besonderer Berücksichtigung der Lausanner Bewegung für Weltevangelisation (1974–1989)" (in Systematisch-theologische Monographien [STM]). Presented as thesis at the University of Tübingen, 1996. Wuppertal: R. Brockhaus Verlag; Gießen: Brunnen Verlag (Theologische Verlagsgemeinschaft, TVG).

Beyerhaus, Peter. 1975. *Mission in urchristlicher und endgeschichtlicher Zeit.* Gießen and Basel: Brunnen-Verlag.

———. 1999. "Das Einheimischwerden des Evangeliums und die Gefahr des Synkretismus." In *Kein anderer Name: Die Einzigartigkeit Jesu Christi und das Gespräch mit nichtchristlichen Religionen: Festschrift zum 70. Geburtstag von Peter Beyerhaus,* edited by Thomas Schirrmacher, 116–135. Nürnberg: Verlag für Theologie und Religionswissenschaft.

Beyreuther, Sabine. 2000. "Die absolute Hingabe an den Augenblick." In *Buddhismus verstehen: Sympathie-Magazin,* 31–33. Ammerland/Starnberger See: Studienkreis für Tourismus und Entwicklung.

Bharathi, K. S. 2000. *Mahatma Gandhi: Man of the Millennium.* Ram Nagar, New Delhi: S. Cand & Co.

Bienert, Wolfgang A. 1972. *"Allegoria" und "Anagoge" bei Didymos, dem Blinden von Alexandria.* Revised edition of doctoral thesis presented in Bonn, 1970. Berlin and New York: Walter de Gruyter.

Bing, Samuel. 2005. *Artistic Japan. Illustrations and Essays,* volume 5. Boston: Elibron Classics, Adamant Media Corporation.

Blacker, Carmen. 1993. "Shinto and Folk Religion." In *The Cambridge Encyclopedia of Japan,* edited by Richard Bowring and Peter Kornicki, 152–157. Cambridge: Cambridge University Press.

———. 1999. *The Catalpa Bow: A Study in Shamanistic Practices in Japan.* Third edition. London: Routledge.

Bleeker, Jouco C. 1970. "The Conception of Man in the Phenomenology of Religion." *Studia Missionalia: man, culture and religion: homme, culture et religion* 19: 13–38. Rome: Gregorian Biblical BookShop.

Bloch, Ernst. 1969. *Atheismus im Christentum: Zur Religion des Exodus und des Reichs* (vol. 14 der Gesamtausgabe). Frankfurt am Main: Suhrkamp.

———. 1982. *Das Prinzip Hoffnung.* Eighth edition of the edition revised in 1953 and 1959, in 3 volumes. Frankfurt am Main: Suhrkamp Verlag.

Blocher, Henri. 2004. *Evil and the Cross: An Analytical Look at the Problem of Pain.* Grand Rapids, MI: Kregel.

Blomberg, Catarina. 2000. *The West's Encounter with Japanese Civilization, 1800–1940.* London and Philadelphia: Routledge.

Bock, Philip K. 1979. *Modern Cultural Anthropology: An Introduction.* Third edition. New York: Alfred A. Knopf.

Bockmühl, Klaus. 1993. *Christliche Lebensführung: Eine Ethik der Zehn Gebote*. Gießen & Basel: Brunnen-Verlag.
Boesak, Allan A. 1987. *Gerechtigkeit erhöht ein Volk: Texte aus dem Widerstand*, translated and edited by Heinz-Herrmann Nordholt. Neukirchen-Vluyn: Neukirchener Verlag.
Boff, Clodovis. 1985. "Society and the Kingdom: A Dialogue between a Theologian, a Christian Activist, and a Parish Priest." In *Salvation and Liberation*, edited by Leonardo Boff and Clodovis Boff, 67–118. Maryknoll: Orbis; Melbourne: Dove.
———. 1986. "Die ambivalente Haltung der 'Instruktion zur Theologie der Befreiung gegenüber dem Marxismus.'" In *Theologie der Befreiung und Marxismus*, edited by Peter Rottländer, 109–116. Münster: edition liberación.
Boff, Leonardo. 1984. "Von der Spiritualität der Befreiung zur Praxis der Befreiung." In *Spiritualität und Befreiung in Lateinamerika*, edited by Eduardo Bonnín, übersetzt von Antonio Reiser, 58–72. Würzburg: Echter Verlag.
Boff, Leonardo, and Clodovis Boff. 1986. *Liberation Theology: From Dialogue to Confrontation*. San Francisco: Harper & Row.
Böhm, Heinz. 1979. *Die Generation der Hoffnungslosen: Ernest Hemingway, Jean-Paul Sartre, Albert Camus, Ludwig Feuerbach, Karl Marx, Ernst Bloch*. Neuhausen-Stuttgart: Hänssler Verlag.
Bolt, Peter G. 1996. "Jesus, the Daimons and the Dead." In *The Unseen World: Christian Reflections on Angels, Demons, and the Heavenly Realm*, edited by Anthony N. S. Lane, 75–102. Carlisle, Cumbria: Paternoster.
Boman, Thorleif. 1983. *Das hebräische Denken im Vergleich mit dem griechischen*, seventh edition. Göttingen: Vandenhoeck & Ruprecht.
Bonhoeffer, Dietrich. 1961. *Widerstand und Ergebung: Briefe und Aufzeichnungen aus der Haft*, edited by Eberhard Bethge. Munich and Hamburg: Siebenstern Taschenbuch Verlag.
———. 1985 (1939). *Gemeinsames Leben*, 20th edition. Munich: Christian Kaiser Verlag.
Borengässer, Norbert Maria. 1992. "Indianische Hochkulturen." In *Lexikon der Religionen: Phänomene, Geschichte, Ideen*, edited by Hans Waldenfels, 300–306. Second edition. Freiburg, Basel, Wien: Verlag Herder Freiburg im Breisgau.
Bosch, David J. 1983. "An Emerging Paradigm for Mission." *Missiology* 11 (4): 485–510.
———. 1991. *Transforming Mission: Paradigm Shifts in Theology of Mission*. Maryknoll: Orbis.
Bownas, Geoffrey, and Pauline Brown. 2004. *Japanese Rainmaking and Other Folk Practices*. Routledge Library Editions: Anthropology and Ethnography. London: Routledge.
Bowring, Richard. 1993. "Language." In *The Cambridge Encyclopedia of Japan*, edited by Richard Bowring and Peter Kornicki, 114–121. Cambridge: Cambridge University Press.

Bradshaw, Bruce. 1996. *Bridging the Gap: Evangelism, Development and Shalom: Innovations in Missions*. Second edition. Monrovia, CA: MARC, A Division of World Vision International.

Bradway, Kay, and Barbara McCoard. 1997. *Sandplay: Silent Workshop of the Psyche*. Oxford: Routledge.

Braithwaite, John. 1999. *Crime, Shame, and Reintegration*. Cambridge: Cambridge University Press.

Brinker, Helmut. 1987. *Zen in the Art of Painting* (original title: Zen in der Kunst des Malens). London: Taylor & Francis.

Brinkman, Martien E. 2014. *The Non-Western Jesus: Jesus as Bodhisattva, Avatara, Guru, Prophet, Ancestor or Healer? Cross-Cultural Theologies*. London and New York: Routledge (Taylor & Francis Group).

Brown, Arthur Judson. 2005. *The Mastery of the Far East: The Story of Korea's Transformation and Japan's Rise to Supremacy*. Whitefish, MT: Kessinger.

Buber, Martin. 2004. *I and Thou*. Second edition. London: Continuum.

Bucknall, Kevin B. 2005. *Japan: Doing Business in a Unique Culture*. Raleigh, MC: C&M Online Media.

Bühler, Pierre. 1981. *Kreuz und Eschatologie: eine Auseinandersetzung mit der politischen Theologie, im Anschluss an Luthers theologia crucis*. Vol. 17 of Hermeneutische Untersuchungen zur Theologie. Tübingen: Mohr Siebeck.

Bulatao, Jaime. 1966. *Split-Level Christianity*. Quezon City: Ateneo University Press.

Buri, Fritz. 1986. "A Comparison of Buddhism and Christianity to a History of Problems." In *Buddhist-Christian Dialogue: Mutual Renewal and Transformation*, edited by Paul O. Ingram, and Frederick J. Streng, 15–33. Honolulu: University of Hawaii Press.

———. 1997. *The Buddha-Christ as the Lord of the True Self: The Religious Philosophy of the Kyoto School and Christianity* (original title: Der Buddha-Christus als der Herr des wahren Selbst: Die Religionsphilosophie der Kyoto-Schule und das Christentum). Translated by Harold H. Oliver. Macon, GA: Mercer University Press.

Burnett, Gary W. 2001. *Paul and the Salvation of the Individual*. Leiden: Brill.

Buruma, Ian. 1985. *Japan hinter dem Lächeln: Götter, Gangster, Geishas*. Translated by Bernd Rullkötter. Frankfurt/Main, Berlin, Wien: Verlag Ullstein GmbH.

Byas, Hugh. 2005. *Government Assassination*. Whitefish, MT: Kessinger.

Cairns, Douglas L. 1993. *Aidōs: The Psychology and Ethics of Honour and Shame in Ancient Greek Literature*. Oxford: Oxford University Press.

Câmara, Dom Hélder. 1969. *Revolution für den Frieden*. Freiburg im Breisgau: Herder-Bücherei.

Campbell, Joseph. 1991. *Mythologie der Urvölker: Die Masken Gottes*. Vol. 1 and 2. Basel: Sphinx-Verlag.

Capitani, Paola. 2006. *Scuola domani*. Rome: FrancoAngeli.

Carducci, Bernardo J. 2009. *The Psychology of Personality: Viewpoints, Research, and Applications*. Second edition. Chichester: Wiley-Blackwell.

Cardullo, Bert. 2010. *Screen Writings: Genres, Classics, and Aesthetics*. London: Anthem.

Carlson, Dwight L. 1981. *So erkenne ich den Willen Gottes für mein Leben: Ein praktischer Ratgeber zur Entscheidung in allen Lebensfragen*. Bad Liebenzell: Verlag der Liebenzeller Mission.

Carlson, Randy, and Rita Schweitz. 1993. *In My Father's Image: A Workbook for Discovering Your Father's Impact on Your Life*. Chicago: Moody Press.

Carmichael, Kay. 2003. *Sin and Forgiveness: New Responses in a Changing World*. Hants: Ashgate.

Carr, Jay. 2002. *The A-List: The National Society of Film Critics' 100 Essential Films*. Cambridge: Da Capo Press.

Carter, Robert Edgar. 2008. *The Japanese Arts and Self-Cultivation*. Albany: State University of New York Press.

Carus, Friedrich August. 1809. *Psychologie der Hebräer*. Leipzig: Johann Abrosius Barth und Paul Gotthelf Kummer.

Cary, Otis. 1995. *A History of Christianity in Japan*. London: Routledge.

Caudill, William A., and Carmi Schooler. 1988. "The Family as an Ethical System." In *Inside the Japanese System: Readings on Contemporary Society and Political Economy*, edited by Daniel I. Okimoto and Thomas P. Rohlen, 15–17. Stanford, CA: Stanford University Press.

Cecchini, Sister Rose-Marie. 1976. "Woman and Suicide." In *Woman in Changing Japan*, edited by Joyce Lebra, Joy Paulson and Elizabeth Powers, 255–296. Stanford, CA: Stanford University Press.

Chamberlain, Basil Hall. 1891. *Things Japanese: Being Notes on Various Subjects Connected with Japan, for the Use of Travelers and Others*. London: K. Paul, Trench, Trübner & Co.

Chaudhuri, Kaushik, and Paul A. Fadil. 2011. "Linkages between Preceived Occupational and Organizational Commitments of General Employees in Japanese Organizations." In *Business Research Yearbook: Balancing Profitability and Sustainability: Shaping the Future of Business*, vol. 18 (1), edited by Margaret A. Goralski, H. Paul Leblanc III, and Marjorie G. Adams, 264–270. N.p.: International Academy of Business Disciplines (IABD); http://www.unf.edu/~s.gupta/pubs/G40115_BRY_2011_volume1.pdf#page=245 (accessed 2 Feb 2016).

Chaudhuri, Saroj Kumar. 2003. *Hindu Gods and Goddesses in Japan*. New Delhi: Vedams eBooks.

Chikudate, Nobuyuki (築達延征). 2015. *Collective Myopia in Japanese Organizations: A Transcultural Approach for Identifying Corporate Meltdowns*. New York, NY: Palgrave MacMillan (eBook).

Cherry, Kittredge. 1991 (1987). *Womansword: What Japanese Words Say about Women*. Tokyo, New York, London: Koudansha International.

Cho, EunSik. 1998. "The Great Revival of 1907 in Korea: Its Cause and Effect." *Missiology* 26 (3): 289–300.

Chozanshi, Issai, and Chozan Niwa. 2006. *The Demon's Sermon on the Martial Arts*. Translated by William Scott Wilson. New York, Tokyo, London: Koudansha International.

Christian, C. W. 2004. *Covenant and Commandment: A Study of the Ten Commandments in the Context of Grace*. Macon, GA: Smyth & Helwys.

Christopher, Robert C. 1983. *The Japanese Mind: The Goliath Explained*. Tokyo: Charles E. Tuttle Co.

Chung, Hyun Kyung. 1988. "Following Naked Dancing and Long Dreaming." In *Inheriting Our Mothers' Gardens: Feminist Theology in Third World Perspective*, edited by Letty M. Russell and Ada Maria Isasi-Diaz, 54–74. Richmond, VA: Westminster John Knox.

Chung, Paul S. 2008. *Martin Luther and Buddhism: Aesthetics of Suffering*. Second edition. Cambridge: James Clarke & Co.

———. 2010. *Public Theology in an Age of World Christianity: God's Mission as Word-Event*. Basingstoke: Palgrave Macmillan.

———. 2013. *Hermeneutical Theology and the Imperative of Public Ethics: Confessing Christ in Post-Colonial World Christianity*. Missional Church, Public Theology, World Christianity, 2. Eugene, OR: Pickwick (Wipf & Stock).

———. 2015. "Martin Luther and Reformation Theology: An East Asian Perspective." In *Die Reformation radikalisieren: Befreiung von Gewalt zum Leben in Frieden / Radicalizing Reformation: Liberation from Violence for Life in Peace* (vol. 4), edited by Ulrich Duchrow and Craig Nessan, 316–337. Münster and Berlin: LIT Verlag.

Ciampa, Roy E. 2007. "The History of Redemption." In *Central Themes in Biblical Theology: Maping Unity in Diversity*, edited by Scott J. Harmann and Pauls R. House, 254–308. Grand Rapids, MI: Baker.

Clammer, John. 2001. *Japan and Its Others: Globalization, Difference and the Critique of Modernity*. Melbourne: Trans Pacific Press.

Clodd, Edward. 2012. *Animism: The Seed of Religion*. The Sacred Books Collection, #419. Altenmünster: Jazzybee Verlag Jürgen Beck (eBook).

Clowney, Edmund P. 1994. "A Biblical Theology of Prayer." In *Teach Us to Pray: Prayer in the Bible and the World*, edited by D. A. Carson. Second edition. Grand Rapids, MI: Baker; Carlisle: Paternoster.

Cobb, John B. 1982. *Process Theology as Political Theology* (on the basis of the Ferguson lecture delivered at the University of Manchester, 1980). Manchester: Manchester University Press; Philadelphia, PA: Westminster.

Coll, Cynthia T. García, Janet L. Surrez, and Kathy Weingarten. 1998. *Mothering Against the Odds: Diverse Voices of Contemporary Mothers*. Hove, East Sussex: Guilford Press.

Collins, Raymond F. 1994 (1988). *Letters That Paul Did Not Write: The Epistle to the Hebrews and the Pseudepigrapha,* vol. 28 of Good News Studies. Collegeville, MN: Liturgical Press.

Colpe, Carsten. 2003. *Iranier–Aramäer–Hebräer–Hellenen: Iranische Religionen und ihre Westbeziehungen: Einzelstudien und Versuch einer Zusammenfassung.* Tübingen: Mohr Siebeck.

Connell, George. 2000. "Against Idolatry: Heidegger and Natural Theology." In *Postmodern Philosophy and Christian Thought.* Indiana Series in the Philosophy of Religion, edited by Merold Westphal, 144–168. Bloomington, IN: Indiana University Press.

Cook, Robert. 1996. "Devils & Manticores: Plundering Jung for a Plausible Demonology." In *The Unseen World: Christian Reflections on Angels, Demons, and the Heavenly Realm*, edited by Anthony N. S. Lane, 165–184. Carlisle, Cumbria: Paternoster.

Cornell, Laurel L. 1996. "Infanticide in Early Modern Japan? Demography, Culture, and Population Growth." *The Journal of Asian Studies* 55 (1): 22–50. Edited by the Association for Asian Studies.

Cortesi, Alessandro. 2004. "Pfade heutiger Suche nach dem Heil in Europa." In *Heil in Differenz: Dominikanische Beiträge zu einer kontextuellen Theologie in Europa* [Salvation in Diversity: Dominican contributions to a Contextual Theology in Europe], edited by Christian Bauer, Stephan van Erp, 56–69. Berlin, Hamburg and Münster: LIT Verlag.

Corwin, Charles. 1978. "Japanese Bonsai or/and California Redwood." *Missiology* 6 (3): 297–310.

Coulmas, Florian. 1999 (1996). *The Blackwell Encyclopedia of Writing Systems.* Illustrated reprint. Oxford: Wiley-Blackwell.

———. 2000. *Japanische Zeiten: Eine Ethnografie der Vergänglichkei*t. Reinbek bei Hamburg: Kindler Verlag GmbH.

———. 2005. *Die Kultur Japans: Tradition und Moderne.* Munich: Verlag C. H. Beck.

Court, Jürgen. 2009. *Wege und Welten der Religionen: Forschungen und Vermittlungen.* Frankfurt am Main: Verlag Otto Lembeck.

Cox, Ralph. 1998a. *God Is, God Spoke, God Came.* Lookout Mountain, TN: Milton.

———. 1998b. 日本人と神、聖書、キリスト (*Nihonjin-to kami, seisho, Kirisuto*) [The Japanese, God, the Bible, and Christ]; translation of *God Is, God Spoke, God Came*), edited by Sachiko Niimi. Tokyo: Inochinokotobasha (いのちのことば社).

Cox, Rupert A. 2003. *The Zen Arts: An Anthropological Study of Aesthetic Form in Japan.* London and Philadelphia: Routledge.

Crim, Keith. 1981. "Ainu Religion." In *Abingdon Dictionary of Living Religions*, edited by Keith Crim, 17. Nashville, TN: Abingdon.

Crome, Peter. 1985. "Konfuzius und Co." *GEO - Das Bild unserer Erde* 10: 74–94.

Crompton, Louis. 2006. *Homosexuality & Civilization*. Cambridge, MA, and London: Harvard University Press.

Cullmann, Oscar. 1941. "Eschatologie und Mission im Neuen Testament." *EMM* 85: 98–108.

———. 1962. *Unsterblichkeit der Seele oder Auferstehung der Toten?: Antwort des Neuen Testaments*. Stuttgart: Kreuz-Verlag.

———. 1965. *Heil als Geschichte: Heilsgeschichtliche Existenz im Neuen Testament*. Tübingen: Mohr Siebeck.

———. 1966 (1936). "Der eschatologische Charakter des Missionsauftrags und des apostolischen Bewußtseins bei Paulus: Untersuchung zum Begriff des κατέχον (κατέχων) in 2. Thess. 2, 6–7." In *Oscar Cullmann: Vorträge und Aufsätze 1925–1962*, edited by Karlfried Fröhlich, 305–336. Tübingen: Mohr Siebeck.

———. 1975. *Die Christologie des Neuen Testaments*. Fifth edition. Tübingen: Mohr Siebeck.

———. 1991. "The Subjection of the Invisible Powers," (excerpt of *Christ and Time*, 1950). In *Engaging the Enemy: How to Fight and Defeat Territorial Spirits*, edited by C. Peter Wagner, 193–202. Ventura, CA: Regal Books.

Curtin, J. Sean. 2001. *Parasite Singles: International Perspective and Analysis*; http://academic.csuohio.edu/makelaa/history/courses/his373/ParasiteSingles.htm (accessed 13 May 2016).

Dainton, Marianne, and Elaine D. Zelley. 2015. *Applying Communication Theory for Professional Life: A Practical Introduction*. Los Angeles, London, New Delhi, Singapore and Washington DC: SAGE.

Dalberg, Andreas. 1997. *Der Weg zum wahren Reiki-Meister: Mit den Symbolen, Mantren und Einweihungsritualen aller Reiki-Grade*. Munich: Droemersche Verlagsanstalt Th. Knaur Nachfolger.

Dale, Kenneth J. 1998. "Why the Slow Growth of the Japanese Church." *Missiology: An International Review* 26 (3): 277–288.

Dambmann, Gerhard. 1989. *25xJapan: Weltmacht als Einzelgänger*, Fifth edition. Munich & Zürich: R. Piper GmbH & Co. KG.

Daston, Lorraine, and Fernando Vidal. 2004. *The Moral Authority of Nature*. Chicago, IL: University of Chicago Press.

Daub, Hans Friedrich, and Gustav Radbruch. 2006. *Die Stellvertretung Jesu Christi: Ein Aspekt des Gott-Mensch-Verhältnisses bei Dietrich Bonhoeffer*. Berlin, Hamburg and Münster: LIT Verlag.

Davies, Roger J., and Osamu Ikeno. 2002. *The Japanese Mind: Understanding Contemporary Japanese Culture*. North Clarendon, VT, and Tokyo: Tuttle Publishing; Singapore: Berkeley Books Pte. Ltd.

Davis, John H. Jr. 2000. "Blurring the Boundaries of the Buraku(min)." In *Globalization and Social Change in Contemporary Japan*, edited by Jerry S. Eades, Tom Gill, and Harumi Befu, 110–122. Melbourne: Trans Pacific Press.

Deats, Paul. 1986. "Introduction to Boston Personalism." In *The Boston Personalist Tradition in Philosophy, Social Ethics, and Theology*, edited by Paul Deats and Carol Robb, 1–14. Macon, GA: Mercer University Press.

De Bary, William Theodore, and Yoshiko Kurata-Dykstra. 2001. *Sources of Japanese Tradition*. Second edition. New York: Columbia University Press.

De Castro, Erwin, D. J. Oropeza, and Ron Rhodes. No year (probably after 1993). *Enter the Dragon?: Wrestling with the Martial Arts Phenomenon; Part One: The Historical-Philosophical Backdrop*. Statement DM066. Santa Margarita, California: Christian Research Institute; http://home.earthlink.net/~ronrhodes/Martial1.html (Accessed 12 Oct 2012).

Delitzsch, Franz. 1859. *Commentar über den Psalter: Erster Teil, Übersetzung und Auslegung von Ps. I–LXXXIV*. Leipzig: Dörffling & Franke.

De Mente, Boye Lafayette. 1994. *Japanese Etiquette & Ethics in Business: A Penetrating Analysis of the Morals and Values That Shape the Japanese Business Personality*, sixth edition. New York: McGraw-Hill.

De Mooij, Marieke. 2014. *Global Marketing and Advertising: Understanding Cultural Paradoxes*, fourth edition. Thousand Oaks, London and New Delhi: SAGE.

Deppe, Werner, and Monika Deppe. 2002. *Auswege oder Wege ins Aus?: Weltreligionen, Esoterik, Sekten*. Bielefeld: Christliche Literaturverbreitung; http://bitflow.dyndns.org/german/WernerUndMonikaDeppe/Auswege_Oder_Wege_Ins_Aus_2002.pdf (accessed 13 May 2016).

DeSilva, David Arthur. 2000. *Honor, Patronage, Kinship & Purity: Unlocking New Testament Culture*. Downers Grove, IL: InterVarsity Press.

Desser, David. 1997. "Introduction: A Filmmaker for All Seasons." In *Ozu's Tokyo Story*, Cambridge Film Handbooks Series, edited by David Desser, 1–24. Cambridge: Cambridge University Press.

Dettmer, Hans Adalbert. 1987. *Einführung in das Studium der japanischen Geschichte* (Orientalische Einführungen in Gegenstand, Ergebnisse und Perspektiven der Einzelgebiete). Darmstadt: Wissenschaftliche Buchgesellschaft Darmstadt.

Deutsche Gesellschaft für auswärtige Politik e.V. 2004. *Jahrbuch Internationale Politik 2001–2002*. Munich: Oldenbourg Wissenschaftsverlag GmbH.

Devine, Richard. 1981. "Hirata Atsutane and Christian Sources." *Monumenta Nipponica* 36 (1): 37–54. Edited by Sophia University.

De Vos, George. 1986. "The Relation of Guilt toward Parents to Achievement and Arranged Marriage among the Japanese." In *Japanese Culture and Behavior: Selected Readings*, edited by Takie Sugiyama-Lebra and William P. Lebra, 80–101. Honolulu: University of Hawaii Press.

Dieterich, Michael. 1989. *Handbuch Psychologie und Seelsorge*. Wuppertal: R. Brockhaus Verlag.

Dietrich, Walter, and Ulrich Luz. 2002. *The Bible in a World Context: An Experiment in Contextual Hermeneutics*. Grand Rapids, MI: Eerdmans.

Dihle, Albert. 1990 (1933). "Judentum." In *Theologisches Handwörterbuch zum Neuen Testament*, volume 9, 630–633. Stuttgart, Berlin, Köln: Verlag W. Kohlhammer.

Dijkstra, Meindert. 2001. "Women and Religion in the Old Testament." In *Only One God?: Monotheism in Ancient Israel and the Veneration of the Goddess Asherah*, edited by Bob Becking, Meindert Dijkstra, and Karel J. H. Vriezen, 164–187. London: Continuum.

Dinkler, Erich. 1992. "EIRENE: Der urchristliche Friedensgedanke." In *Im Zeichen des Kreuzes: Aufsätze von Erich Dinkler*, edited by Otto Merk and Michael Wolter, 263–304. Berlin and New York: Walter de Gruyter.

Dobbins, Frank S. and S. Wells Williams. 2004 (1901). *Story of the World's Worship*. Whitefish, MT: Kessinger.

Dohi, Akio (土肥昭夫). 1991. "Die erste Generation: Christliche Führungspersönlichkeiten der ersten Periode." In *Theologiegeschichte der Dritten Welt: Japan*, edited by Theo Sundermaier and Norbert Klaes, translated by Martin Repp and Frank Biebinger, 33–73. Munich: Chr. Kaiser.

Doi, Masatoshi (土居真俊). 1979 (English original 1976). "Religion und Natur." In *Wie Christen in Asien denken*, edited by Douglas J. Elwood; translated by Radegundis Stolze, 79–88. Frankfurt am Main: Verlag Otto Lembeck.

Doi, Takeo (土居健郎). 1973. *The Anatomy of Dependence: The Key Analysis of Japanese Behavior*. Tokyo, New York, San Francisco: Kondansha International.

———. 1982. *Amae – Freiheit und Geborgenheit: Zur Struktur der japanischen Psyche* (American edition: The Anatomy of Dependence; title of the Japanese original, 1973: 甘えの構造 (*amae -no kouzou*) [The structure of amae]. Translation of the American version by Elmar Holenstein. Frankfurt am Main: Suhrkamp Verlag.

———. 1986. "Amae: A Key Concept for Understanding Japanese Personality Structure." In *Japanese Culture and Behavior: Selected Readings*, edited by Takie Sugiyama-Lebra and William P. Lebra, 121–129. Honolulu: University of Hawaii Press.

———. 1993. "Sin and Shame." In *Japanese Religions: Past and Present*, edited by Ian Reader, Esben Andreasen, and Finn Stefánnson, 30–32. Honolulu: University of Hawaii Press.

———. 1994. 信仰と「甘え (*Shinkou-to "Amae"*) [Faith and "amae"]. Second edition. Tokyo: Shunjuusha (春秋社).

———. 1997. 聖書と「甘え (*Seisho-to "Amae"*) [The Bible and "amae"]. Kyoto: PHP Kenkyuujo (PHP研究所).

———. 2001. 甘え」の構造 (*"Amae"-no kouzou*) [The Structure of "amae"], sequel (The content is different from the book published in 1971 under the same title). Tokyo: Koubundou (弘文堂).

Doi, Takeo (土居健郎), and Keigo Okonogi (小此木啓吾). 1990. "Anlehnung und Moratorium: Ein Gespräch zwischen Doi Takeo and Okonogi Keigo." In *Die kühle Seele: Selbstinterpretationen der japanischen Kultur*, edited by

Jens Heise, 80–87. Frankfurt am Main: Fischer Taschenbuch Verlag GmbH (Fischer Sozialwissenschaft).

Dominey, Mark. 2005. "Abortion and *Mizuko* Rites in Japan: How Buddhists Respond to Needy Women." In *Sharing Jesus Holistically with the Buddhist World*, edited by David Lim and Steve Spaulding, 253–280. Pasadena, CA: William Carey Library.

Dorrien, Gary J. 2001. *The Making of American Liberal Theology: Idealism, Realism & Modernity: 1900–1950*. Louisville, KY: Westminster John Knox Press.

Douglas, Mary. 2002 (1966). *Purity and Danger: An Analysis of Concept of Pollution and Taboo*. London and New York: Routledge Classics.

Douglas, Robert K. 1895. *Confucianism and Taouism* (Non-Christian Religious Systems), fourth corrected and revised edition. London: SPCK.

Drew, A. J., and Patricia Telesco. 2003. *God/Goddess: Exploring and Celebrating the Two Sides of Wiccan Deity*. Franklin Lakes, NJ: Career Press.

Dröge, Christoph. 1992. "Orakel." In *Lexikon der Religionen: Phänomene, Geschichte, Ideen*, edited by Hans Waldenfels, 490–491. Second edition. Freiburg, Basel, Wien: Verlag Herder Freiburg im Breisgau.

Drumond, Richard H. 1961. "Hendrik Kraemer in Japan." *The International Review of Missions*, Bd. L (200).

Dufty, Cynthia. 1995. "Human Relations and Leadership in the Japanese Protestant Congregation." Unpublished MA Dissertation presented at the Alliance Theological Seminary. Nyack, New York.

Dülfer, Eberhard, and Bernd Jöstingmeier. 2008. *Internationales Management in unterschiedlichen Kulturbereichen*, seventh edition. Munich: Oldenbourg Wissenschaftsverlag.

Dumoulin, Heinrich. 2005. *Zen Buddhism: A History. Vol. 2: Japan*. Translated by James W. Heisig und Paul Knitter. Bloomington, IN: World Wisdom.

Durant, Will. 1985. *Kulturgeschichte der Menschheit: Der Ferne Osten und der Aufstieg Griechenlands*, vol. 2. Köln: Naumann & Göbel Verlagsgesellschaft.

Dyrness, William A. 1990. *Learning about Theology from the Third World*. Grand Rapids, MI: Zondervan.

Ebeling, Gerhard. 1982. *Lutherstudien* (vol. 2): *Disputation de Homine* (2.Teil). Tübingen: Mohr Siebeck.

———. 1993. *Dogmatik des christlichen Glaubens: Volume 3: Der Glaube an Gott, den Vollender der Welt*, third revised edition. Tübingen: Mohr Siebeck.

Eberhard, Wolfram. 1983. *Lexikon chinesischer Synonyme: Geheime Sinnbilder in Kunst und Literatur, Leben und Denken der Chinesen*. Köln: Eugen Dietrichs Verlag.

Ebina, Chou. 1976. "Die dämonische Spinne." In *Japanische Märchen*, edited and translated by Toshio Ozawa, 36–37. Third edition. Frankfurt am Main: Fischer Taschenbuch Verlag GmbH.

Eden, Charles Henry. 2005 (1877). *Japan: Historical and Descriptive*. Boston: Elibron Classics, Adamant Media Corporation.

Edwards, Linda. 2001. *A Brief Guide to Beliefs: Ideas, Theologies, Mysteries, and Movements*. Richmond, VA: Westminster John Knox.

Ehmcke, Franziska, and Heins-Dieter Reese. 2000. *Von Helden, Mönchen und schönen Frauen: Die Welt des japanischen Heike-Epos* (Japanisches Kulturinstitut, Köln). Köln and Weimar: Böhlau Verlag.

Eichrodt, Walther. 1967. *Theology of the Old Testament*, volume 2. Louisville, KY: Westminster John Knox.

Eisenstadt, Shmuel Noah. 1996. *Japanese Civilization: A Comparative View*. Chicago: University of Chicago Press.

Ejima, Masako (江島正子). 1996. "Die Wiederherstellung der Harmonie: Todeskult versus Schande." In *Harmonie und Konformität: Tradition und Krise japanischer Sozialisationsmuster*, edited by Agi Schründer-Lenzen, 94–102. Munich: Iudicum Verlag.

Ellington, Lucien. 2009. *Japan* (Asia in Focus). Santa Barbara, CA: ABC-CLIO.

Encyclopedia of the Supernatural, 超常現象大事典 (*Choujougenshou Daijiten*), edited by Rei Hani (羽仁礼). 2001. Tokyo: Seikoushobo (成甲書房).

Endou, Shuusaku (遠藤周作). 1959. *Der Vulkan* (original title: 火山; *kazan*; Volcano). Freiburg, Basel, Wien: Herder.

———. 1970. *Silence* (original title: ちんもく; *chinmoku* [Silence]). Third edition. Rutland, Vermont and Tokyo: Charles E. Tuttle Publishers.

———. 1974 (1959). *Wonderful Fool* (original title: おバカさん; *obakasan* [Mr. Idiot]), translated by Peter Owen. Rutland, Vermont and Tokyo: Charles E. Tuttle Publishers.

———. 1978. *A Life of Jesus*. Translated by Richard A. Schuchert. Mahwah, NJ: Paulist Press.

———. 1984 (1958). *Meer und Gift* (original title: 海と毒薬; *umi-to dokuyaku* [Sea and poison]). Frankfurt am Main: Fischer Taschenbuch Verlag.

———. 1986 (1974). *Eine Klinik in Tokyo* (original title: 口笛を吹くとき; *Kuchibue-o fuku toki* [When I whistle]). Translated from the English edition by Rainer Rönsch. Second edition. Berlin: Verlag Volk und Welt.

———. 1997 (1980). *The Samurai* (original title: 侍; *samurai* [Samurai]), translated by Van C. Gessel. New York: New Directions.

———. 2000 (1986). *Scandal* (original title: スキャンダル; *sukyandaru* [Scandal]). Translated by Van C. Gessel. Third edition. Boston, Rutland, Vermont, Tokyo: Charles E. Tuttle Publishers.

"Energy Medicine: An Overview." 2005. In *Backgrounder*. N.p.: National Center for Complementary and Alternative Medicine. http://www.healthy.net/Health/Article/Energy_Medicine_An_Overview/2407 (accessed 2012/10/12).

Engel, James F. 1988. *Zeitgemäße christliche Kommunikation: Evangelische Missionslehre, Reden und Aufsätze*. Second revised edition. Bad Liebenzell: Verlag der Liebenzeller Mission.

Engelland, Hans. 1961. "Der Ansatz der Theologie Melanchthons." In *Philipp Melanchthon: Forschungsbeiträge zur vierhundersten Wiederkehr seines Todestages dargeboten in Wittenberg 1960*, no editor, 56–75. Göttingen: Vandenhoeck & Ruprecht.

Eoloff, Gustav, ed. 1896. *Das Staatsarchiv: Sammlung der officiellen Actenstücke zur Geschichte der Gegenwart*. Vol. 58. Leipzig: Verlag von Duncker & Humblot; https://archive.org/stream/staatsarchiv58inst/staatsarchiv58inst_djvu.txt (accessed 2 Oct 2015).

Erickson, Millard J. 2000. *Christian Theology*. Second edition. Grand Rapids, MI: Baker.

Erlinghagen, Helmut. No year (probably in the early 1980s). *Japan: Eine Landeskunde*. Munich: Verlag C. H. Beck.

Eswein, Mikiko. 1999. *Die Rolle der Berufsbildung beim sozialen Wandel in Japan*. Institut für Ostasien-Wissenschaften an der Universität Duisburg. http://www.uni-due.de/in-east/fileadmin/publications/gruen/paper11.pdf (accessed 12 Oct 2012).

Evangelical Lutheran Synod of Missouri, Ohio, and Other States. 1921. *Triglot Concordia: The Symbolical Books of the Evangelical Lutheran Church: German-Latin-English*. Published as a memorial of the quadricentenary jubilee of the Reformation anno Domini 1917. St. Louis: Concordia. http://bookofconcord.org/info.php (accessed 12 Feb 2014).

"Evangelisation ist mehr als Wortverkündigung." In *idea.de: das christliche nachrichtenportal*, 17. 4. 2008. Wetzlar: idea e.V. 2008. http://www.idea.de/index.php?id=891&txtt news%5Bttnews%5D=63777&tx_ttnews%5BbackPid%5D=18&cHash=758f76ec56.

Evans, Ann Llewellyn. 2002. *Shinto Norito: A Book of Prayers*. Bloomington, IN: Trafford.

Evans, Craig A. 2005. *John's Gospel, Hebrews-Revelation*. Vol. 3. The Bible Knowledge Background Commentary. Colorado Springs, CO: David C. Cook.

Evans, William. 2014 (1922). *The Great Doctrines of the Bible*. Glendale, CA: Bibliotech Press.

Eyselein, Christian. 1993. *Segnet Gott, was Menschen Schaffen?: Kirchliche Einweihungshandlungen im Bereich des öffentlichen Lebens*. Stuttgart: Calwer Verlag.

Fairchild, William P. 1962. "Shamanism in Japan." *Folklore Studies* 21, nos. 1–122. The Nanzan Institute for Religion and Culture.

Faix, Wilhelm. 2004. "Bindung als anthropologisches Merkmal: Die Bedeutung der Eltern-Kind-Beziehung als Prävention für eine gesunde Persönlichkeitsentwicklung aus biblischer und entwicklungspsychologischer Sicht und gemeindepädagogische Folgerungen." In *Ein Mensch–was ist das?: Zur theologischen Anthropologie; Bericht von der 13. Studienkonferenz des Arbeitskreises für evangelikale Theologie (afet), 14–17 Sept. 2003 in Bad Blankenburg; Helmut Burkhardt zum 65. Geburtstag gewidmet*, edited by Rolf Hille, Helmut Burkhardt and Herbert H. Klement, 260–291. Wuppertal: R. Brockhaus Verlag.

Falcke, Heino. 1988. "Theologie des Friedens in der einen geteilten Welt." In *Friedenstheologie, Befreiungstheologie: Analysen, Berichte, Meditationen*, edited by Jürgen Moltmann, 17–66. Munich: Chr. Kaiser (Kaiser Taschenbücher).

Fallows, Deborah. 1990. "Change Comes Slowly for Japanese Women." *National Geographic* 177 (4): 52–82.

Farnbacher, Traugott. 1999. "Gemeinde verantworten: Anfänge, Entwicklungen und Perspektiven von Gemeinde und Ämtern der Evangelisch-lutherischen Kirche von Papua-Neuguinea." (Presented as thesis at the Augustana-Hochschule in Neuendettelsau, 1998.) Berlin, Hamburg and Münster: LIT Verlag.

Fasching, Gerhard. 1999. *Das Kaleidoskop der Wirklichkeiten: Über die Relativität naturwissenschaftlicher Erkenntnis*. Wien and New York: Springer.

———. 2000. *Phänomene der Wirklichkeit: Okkulte und naturwissenschaftliche Weltbilder*. Wien and New York: Springer.

Fazzioli, Edoardo. 2003. *Gemalte Wörter: 214 chinesische Schriftzeichen – vom Bild zum Begriff: Ein Schlüssel zum Verständnis Chinas, seiner Menschen und seiner Kultur*. Translated by Anna Eckner. Fifth edition. Wiesbaden: Fourier Verlag.

Fechter, Friedrich. 1998. *Die Familie in der Nachexilszeit: Untersuchungen zur Bedeutung der Verwandtschaft in ausgewählten Texten des Alten Testaments*. Presented as habilitation treatise at the University of Erlangen-Nürnberg, 1997. Berlin and New York: Walter de Gruyter.

Ferdinando, Keith. 1996. "Screwtape Revisited: Demonology Western, African and Biblical." In *The Unseen World: Christian Reflections on Angels, Demons, and the Heavenly Realm*, edited by Anthony N. S. Lane, 103–132. Grand Rapids, MI: Tyndale House; Carlisle, Cumbria: Paternoster.

Fessler, Susanna. 1996. "The Nature of the Kami: Ueda Akinari and Tandai Shoshin Roku." *Monumenta Nipponica* 51 (1): 1–15. Edited by Sophia University.

Feuerbach Ludwig. 1837. *Darstellung, Entwicklung und Kritik der Leibniz'schen Philosophie*. Ansbach: Carl Brügel.

———. 1846. *Ludwig Feuerbachs sämtliche Werke*. Leipzig: Verlag von Otto Wiegand.

———. 1849. *Das Wesen der Religion*. Second edition. Leipzig: Verlag von Otto Wiegand.

———. 1908. *Ludwig Feuerbachs sämtliche Werke: bd. Vorlesungen über das Wesen der Religion, nebst Zusätzen und Anmerkungen*. Edited by Wilhem Bolin, Friedrich Jodl and Hans-Martin Sass. Jena: F. Frommann (E. Hauff).

———. 1972. *Kleinere Schriften*. Vol. 10. Berlin: Akademie-Verlag.

Figel, Astrid. 1994. *Der Beitrag der Sprache zum Verständnis der Kultur*. Unpublished presentation at the Freie Hochschule für Mission – AEM, Korntal.

Fodor's. 2014. *Fodor's Japan*. Vol. 21. Fodor's Travel Publications. London: Penguin Random.

Fohrer, Georg, and Hans Werner Hoffmann. 1997. *Hebräisches und aramäisches Wörterbuch zum Alten Testament*. Third revised edition. Berlin & New York: Walter de Gruyter.

Formanek, Susanne. 2008. "Mizuko kuyo: Moderne Ausprägungen und historische Hintergründe der buddhistischen Totenrituale für Ungeborene in Japan." In *Universität Hamburg, Zentrum für Buddhismuskunde*, vol. 11–K05: 51–97; http://www.buddhismuskunde.uni-hamburg.de/fileadmin/pdf/digitale_texte/Bd11-K05Formanek.pdf (accessed 12 Oct 2012).

Fox Young, Richard. 1990. "New 'New Religions' in the New Era: Magic and Morality in Modern Japanese Exorcistic Technologies: A Study of Mahikari." In *Heisei: A New Era or More of the Same?: Missiological Issues in the '90s; Hayama Seminar Annual Report*, edited by Robert Lee and Barry L. Ross, 31–49. Tokyo: Tokyo Mission Research Institute.

———. 2005. "Christian Spirituality in Africa, Asia, Latin America, and Oceania." In *The Blackwell Companion to Christian Spirituality*, edited by Arthur G. Holder, 156–174. Oxford: Blackwell.

Fraenkel, Peter. 1961. "Fünfzehn Jahre Melanchthonforschung: Versuch eines Literaturberichts." In *Philipp Melanchthon: Forschungsbeiträge zur vierhundersten Wiederkehr seines Todestages dargeboten in Wittenberg 1960*, no editor, 11–55. Göttingen: Vandenhoeck & Ruprecht.

Freed, Anne O. 2000. "Therapeutic Interventions with Elders of Japanese Ancestry." In *Therapeutic Interventions with Ethnic Elders: Health and Social Issues*, edited by Sara O. Aleman, Tanya Fitzpatrick, Thanh V. Tran, and Elizabeth W. Gonzalez, 5–26. Philadelphia, PA: Haworth Press.

Fridell, Wilbur M. 1970. "Government Ethics Textbooks in Late *Meiji* Japan." *The Journal of Asian Studies* 29 (4): 823–833. Edited by the Association for Asian Studies.

Friedmann, Alexander. 2004. *Psychotrauma*. Berlin: Springer.

Frieling, Reinhard. 1984. *Befreiungstheologien: Studien zur Theologie Lateinamerikas*. Second revised edition. Göttingen: Vandenhoeck & Ruprecht.

Friesen, Carry, and J. Robin Maxson. 1980. *Decisionmaking & the Will of God: A Biblical Alternative to the Traditional View*. Portland, OR: Multnomah.

Fritsch-Oppermann, Sybille. 2000. *Christliche Existenz im buddhistischen Kontext: Katsumi Takizawas und Seiichi Yagis Dialog mit dem Buddhismus in Japan*. Berlin, Hamburg and Münster: LIT Verlag.

Frohnhofen, Herbert. 1997. *Ganzheitliche Heilungsprozesse in Jesus Christus: Einige Aspekte einer zeit- und kontextbezogenen Erlösungslehre*. Lecture presented at the Jahreskonferenz der katholischen Religionslehrer/innen an beruflichen Schulen der Diözese Augsburg on 11 April 1997 in St. Ottilien;[2] http://www.theologie-beitraege.de/erloesung.pdf (accessed 12 Oct 2012).

Fukada, Robert M. 1965. "New Frontiers of Encounter and Witness: The Task of the Church in the Industrial Society of Japan." *International Review of Missions* 54 (214): 173–183.

Fung, Yu-lan. 1983. *History of Chinese Philosophy, volume 2: The Period of Classical Learning from the Second Century BC to the Twentieth Century AD*. Princeton, NJ: Princeton University Press.

Furui, Yoshikichi (古井由吉). 1990. "Das Tal." In *Zeit der Zikaden: Japanisches Lesebuch: Erzählungen der Gegenwart*, edited by Tadao Araki and Ekkehard May, 22–42. Munich and Zürich: Piper.

Furuya, Kensho. 1996. *Kodo Ancient Ways: Lessons in the Spiritual Life of the Warrior/Martial Artist*. Lancaster: Black Belt Communications.

Furuya, Yasuo (フルヤヤスオ). 1996. *A History of Japanese Theology*. Grand Rapids, MI: Eerdmans.

Gardner, Richard A. 2009. "The Sentencing of Asahara: Victims and Victimizers." In *The Asia-Pacific Journal: Japan Focus* (アジア大平洋誌：焦点日本 (*Ajia Taiheiyou Shi: Shouten Nihon*) [The Asia-Pacific journal]), 21/3/2009; http://japanfocus.org/-Richard_A_-Gardner/1953 (accessed 13 May 2016).

Gates, Alan Frederick. 1979. *Christianity and Animism in Taiwan*. San Francisco: Chinese Materials Center.

Gebhardt, Lisette. 2001. *Japans neue Spiriutualität*. Wiesbaden: Verlag Otto Harrassowitz.

Geering, Lloyd. 2015. *Tomorrow's God: How We Create Our Worlds*. Wellington, NZ: Bridget Williams Books (eBook).

Geldsetzer, L. *Japanische Philosophie: Vorlesung im WS*. 1996/1997 an der HHU Düsseldorf (URL no longer available).

"Genjimonogatari Daijiten" Henshuu Iinkai (『源氏物語大辞典』編集委員会; Editorial Committee of the unabridged Genji-Monogatari-Dictionary). 2008. 源氏物語入門 (*genjimonogatari nyuumon*) [Introduction into the Genji-Monogatari]. Tokyo: Kadokawagakukei Shuppan (角川学芸出版).

Gensichen, Hans-Werner. 1985a (1966). "Der Synkretismus als Frage an die Christenheit heute." In *Mission und Kultur: Gesammelte Aufsätze*, edited by Theo Sundermeier and Wolfgang Gern, 13–24. Munich: Chr. Kaiser Verlag.

———. 1985b (1977). "Europäische Überlegungen zur lateinamerikanischen Theologie der Befreiung." In *Mission und Kultur: Gesammelte Aufsätze*, edited by Theo Sundermeier and Wolfgang Gern, 130–140. Munich: Chr. Kaiser Verlag.

---

2. Similar edition: "Ganzheitliche Heilungsprozesse in Jesus Christus. Einige Aspekte einer zeit- und situationsgemäßen christlichen Erlösungslehre." In *Informationen für Religionslehrerinnen und Religionslehrer* (Bistum Limburg) 1 (1996): 3–12, abridged version in *RHS* 40 (1997): 12–22.

Gerhart, Karen M. 1999. *The Eyes of Power: Art and Early Tokugawa Authority*. Honolulu: University of Hawaii Press.

Gerlitz, Peter. 1977. *Gott erwacht in Japan: Neue fernöstliche Religionen und ihre Botschaft vom Glück*. Freiburg im Breisgau: Verlag Herder.

Gese, Hartmut. 1991 (1981/5/13). "Die Frage nach dem Lebenssinn: Hiob und die Folgen: Peter Stuhlmacher zum fünfzigsten Geburtstag." In *Alttestamentliche Studien*, edited by Hartmut Gese. Lecture within the Ringvorlesung der Evangelisch-theologischen Fakultät Tübingen on "Lebenssinn und Schulderfahrung." Tübingen: Mohr Siebeck.

Gesenius, Wilhelm. 1962 (1915). *Hebräisches und Aramäisches Handwörterbuch über das Alte Testament*. 17th edition. Revised by Franz Buhl. Berlin, Göttingen, Heidelberg: Springer Verlag.

Gestrich, Christof. 1995. *Die Wiederkehr des Glanzes in der Welt: Die christliche Lehre von der Sünde und ihrer Vergebung in gegenwärtiger Verantwortung*. Tübingen: Mohr Siebeck.

Gielen, Uwe Peter, Jefferson M. Fish, and Juris G. Draguns. 2004. *Handbook of Culture, Therapy, and Healing*. London and Philadelphia: Routledge.

Gigliardi, Alessandro. 2003. *Postmodernity in Recent Japanese Literature and Science*. http://psychology.rutgers.edu/~eklypse/Postmodernity.pdf (accessed 13 May 2016).

Gilmore, George William. 1919. *Animism: Or, Thought Currents of Primitive Peoples*.
I. The Animistic Stage of Culture –The Case Stated
http://www.sacred-texts.com/sha/anim/anim03.htm (accessed 12 Oct 2012)
II. The Discovery of the Soul
http://www.sacred-texts.com/sha/anim/anim04.htm (accessed 12 Oct 2012)
III. The Soul's Nature
http://www.sacred-texts.com/sha/anim/anim05.htm (accessed 12 Oct 2012)
IV. The External or Separable Soul
http://www.sacred-texts.com/sha/anim/anim06.htm (accessed 12 Oct 2012)
V. Parity of Being
http://www.sacred-texts.com/sha/anim/anim07.htm (accessed 12 Oct 2012)
VI. Belief in "Free Spirits"
http://www.sacred-texts.com/sha/anim/anim08.htm (accessed 12 Oct 2012)
VII. "Free Spirits" – Their Construction and Activities
http://www.sacred-texts.com/sha/anim/anim09.htm (accessed 12 Oct 2012)
VIII. Logical Consequences of Parity of Being
http://www.sacred-texts.com/sha/anim/anim10.htm (accessed 12 Oct 2012)
IX. Death Not Always Regarded as Inevitable
http://www.sacred-texts.com/sha/anim/anim11.htm (accessed 12 Oct 2012)
X. The Continued Existence of the Soul
http://www.sacred-texts.com/sha/anim/anim12.htm (accessed 12 Oct 2012)

XI. Modifications of the Idea of Continuance
http://www.sacred-texts.com/sha/anim/anim13.htm (accessed 12 Oct 2012)
XII. Condition of the Discarnate Soul
http://www.sacred-texts.com/sha/anim/anim14.htm (accessed 12 Oct 2012)
XIII. The Home of the Soul
http://www.sacred-texts.com/sha/anim/anim15.htm (accessed 12 Oct 2012)
XIV. Descensus Averni
http://www.sacred-texts.com/sha/anim/anim16.htm (accessed 12 Oct 2012)
XV. Worship
http://www.sacred-texts.com/sha/anim/anim17.htm (accessed 12 Oct 2012)
XVI. Residua of Animism
http://www.sacred-texts.com/sha/anim/anim18.htm (accessed 12 Oct 2012)

Gimenez, Anne. 1991. "Battle in the Heavenlies." In *Engaging the Enemy: How to Fight and Defeat Territorial Spirits*, edited by C. Peter Wagner, 77–82. Ventura, CA: Regal Books.

Ginsberg, Leonard. 2008. *Rhapsody on a Film by Kurosawa*. Bloomington, IN: Trafford.

Glottes, Jean, and David Lewis-Williams. 1997. *Schamanen: Trance und Magie in der Höhlenkunst der Steinzeit*. Sigmaringen: Jan Thorbecke Verlag.

Gluck, Carol. 1985. *Japan's Modern Myths: Ideology in the Late Meiji Period*. Studies of the East Asian Institute. Princeton, NJ: Princeton University Press.

Goguel d'Allondans, Thierry. 2002. *Rites de passage, rites d'initiation: lecture d'Arnold van Gennep*. Lectures Québec, Québec Lectures: Les Presses de l'Université Laval. Saint-Nicholas: Presses Université Laval.

Goldhill, Simón. 1986. *Reading Greek Tragedy*. Cambridge: Cambridge University.

Gómez, Lois O. 1987 (1984). "From the Extraordinary to the Ordinary: Images of the Bodhisattva in East Asia." In *The Christ and the Bodhisattva: Symposium Papers*, edited by Donald S. Lopez, and Steven C. Rockefeller, 141–192. Albany, NY: SUNY Press.

Goodenough, Ward Hunt. 1981. *Culture, Language, and Society*. Second edition. Menlo Park, CA: Benjamin/Cummings.

Gorgulho, Gilberto. 1984. "Die Erinnerung und der Geist der Armen." In *Spiritualität und Befreiung in Lateinamerika*, edited by Eduardo Bonnín, 81–97. Translated by Antonio Reiser. Würzburg: Echter Verlag.

Goss, Robert, and Dennis Klass. 2005. *Dead but Not Lost: Grief Narratives in Religious Traditions*. Lanham, MD: Rowman Altamira.

Gotou, Akio (後藤昭雄). 1993. 平安朝漢文文献の研究 (*heianchou kanbun bunken-no kenkyuu*) [Research on Kanbun-Literature in the Heian-Era]. Tokyo: Yoshikawa Koubunkan (吉川弘文館).

Gotou, Mitsuzo, David Martin, and Kenny Joseph. 1982. "Evangelical Church Forms & Ceremonies." In *The New Combined Language Handbook*: 聖書を英語で学ぶためのハンドブック (*seisho-o eigo-de manabu tame-no handobukku*) [Handbook

for Bible studies in English], edited by Kenny Joseph and Russell Stellwagon, 183–240. Uda, Nara and Wilmington, DE: Dawn Press (暁屋).
Grässer, Erich. 1979 (1976). *Albert Schweitzer als Theologe*. Tübingen: Mohr Siebeck.
Graves, William. 1972. "Living in a Japanese Village." *National Geographic* 141 (5): 668–693.
Grayson, James Huntley. 2001. "The Shintō Shrine Conflict and Protestant Martyrs in Korea, 1938-1945." *Missiology* 29 (3): 287–305.
Green, Joel B., and Mark David Baker. 2000. *Recovering the Scandal of the Cross: Atonement in New Testament & Contemporary Contexts*. Downers Grove, IL: InterVarsity Press.
Green, Michael. 1991. "Principalities and Powers." In *Engaging the Enemy: How to Fight and Defeat Territorial Spirits*, edited by C. Peter Wagner, 177–191. Ventura, CA: Regal Books, A Division of Gospel Light.
Greinacher, Norbert. 1988. "Der Konflikt um die Theologie der Befreiung." In *Friedenstheologie, Befreiungstheologie: Analysen, Berichte, Meditationen*, edited by Jürgen Moltmann, 67–90. Munich: Chr. Kaiser (Kaiser Taschenbücher).
Greschat, Hans-Jürgen. 1992. "Animismus." In *Lexikon der Religionen: Phänomene, Geschichte, Ideen*, edited by Hans Waldenfels, 23. Second edition. Freiburg, Basel, Wien: Verlag Herder Freiburg im Breisgau.
Griffis, William Elliot. 1895. *The Religions of Japan*. N.p.: Plain Label Books.[3]
———. 2006 (1876). *The Mikado's Empire: A History of Japan from the Age of the Gods to the Meiji Era* (*660 BC–AD 1972*). Tokyo: Yohan Classics, IBC Publishing.
———. 2008. *Japanese Fairy World: Stories from the Wonder-Lore of Japan*. Charleston, SC: Biblio Bazaar, Biblio Life.
Griffiths, Michael. 1972 (English original: *Take off Your Shoes*, 1971). *Christus im modernen Japan*, translated by Sibylle Lehmann. Gießen: Brunnen-Verlag GmbH; Zürich: Überseeische Missionsgesellschaft.
Großes Deutsch-Japanisches Wörterbuch: 独和大辞典 (*dokuwa daijiten*) [German-Japanese comprehensive dictionary]. 1990. Shougakukan (小学館).
Grundmann, Walter. 1981. *Das Evangelium nach Matthäus*, fünfte Auflage (Theologischer Handkommentar zum Neuen Testament, 1). Neuhausen, Stuttgart: Hänssler Verlag.
Grunlan, Stephen A., and Marvin K. Mayers. 1981. *Cultural Anthropology: A Christian Perspective*. Fifth edition. Grand Rapids, MI: Zondervan.
Gudykunst, William B., and Patricia San Antonio. 1993. "Approaches to the Study of Communication in Japan and the United States." In *Communication in Japan and the United States*, edited by William B. Gudykunst, 18–48. Albany: State University of New York Press.

---

3. The connection between Plain Label Books and Google seems to be obscure. See http://blog.stephenleary.com/2007/04/google-books-plain-label-books.html.

Guerber, H. A. 2003. *Myths of Greece and Rome*. Whitefish, MT: Kessinger Publishing.

Guichard-Anguis, Sylvie. 1995. "The Parish of a Famous Shrine: The Influence of Rites and Ceremonials on Urban Life. The Sanctuary of Ebisu in Nishinomiya." In *Ceremony and Ritual in Japan: Religious Practices in an Industrialized Society*, edited by Jan van Bremen and Dolores P. Martinez, 67–82. London: Nissan Institute/Routledge Japanese Studies.

Gulick, Sidney Lewis. 1964. *The East and the West: A Study of Their Psychic and Cultural Characteristics*. Second edition. Rutland, Vermont and Tokyo: Charles E. Tuttle Company.

Gundert, Hermann. 1874. *Evangelisches Missionsmagazin*. Basel: Verlag des Missions-Compoirs.

Gunkel, Hermann. 1985 (1933). *Einleitung in die Psalmen: Die Gattungen der religiösen Lyrik Israels*. Göttingen: Vandenhoeck & Ruprecht.

Güs, F. 2006. "Transkulturelle Psychoanalyse: Ein Psychotherapieansatz für Migranten." In *Transkulturelle Psychiatrie – Interkulturelle Psychotherapie: Interdisziplinäre Theorie und Praxis*, edited by Wohlfart Zaumseil, 239–275. Wien and New York: Springer.

Gutiérrez, Gustavo. 1973. *Theologie der Befreiung*. Volume 11 of Gesellschaft und Theologie. Seventh edition. Munich: Verlag Kaiser.

———. 1986. "Theologie und Sozialwissenschaften." In *Theologie der Befreiung und Marxismus*, edited by Peter Rottländer, 45–76. Münster: Edition Liberación.

Ha, John. 1989. *Genesis 15*. Revised edition of the thesis presented at the Pontifical Biblical Institute, 1986. Berlin and New York: Walter de Gruyter.

Haack, Friedrich-Wilhelm. 1982. *Astrologie*. Fourth revised edition. Munich: Evangelischer Pressevervolume für Bayern.

———. 1989. *Bestrafte Neugier: Okkultismus*. Munich: Junge Municher Reihe.

Hackin, J., and Paul Louis Couchoud. 2005. *Asiatic Mythology 1932: A Detailed Description and Explanation of the Mythologies of All the Great Nations of Asia*. Whitefish, MT: Kessinger Publishing.

Häffner, Sonja. 2009. "Kanji: Eine symboltheoretische Einordnung." In *Philosophie der Schrift*, edited by Elisabeth Birk and Jan Georg Schneider (Germanistische Linguistik), 205–220. Tübingen: Max Niemeyer Verlag.

Hagenbach, Karl Rudolf. 1867. *Lehrbuch der Dogmengeschichte*. Stuttgart: S. Hirzel Verlag.

Hagihara, Hidesaburou (萩原秀三郎). 2004. 鬼の復権 (*oni-no fukken*) [The Reinstatement of the Demons]. Tokyo: Yoshikawakoubunkan (吉川弘文館).

Hall, John Whitney. 1968. *Fischer Weltgeschichte: Das Japanische Kaiserreich*. Frankfurt am Main: Fischer Bücherei.

———. 1988. *The Cambridge History of Japan: Medieval Japan*. Cambridge: Cambridge University Press.

Halpern, Jack. 1991. *New Japanese-English Character Dictionary:* 新漢英辞典 (*shin kan-ei jiten*) [Neues chinesisch-englisches Schriftzeichen-Lexikon]. Fourth edition. Tokyo: Kenkyuusha (研究社).

Halverson, Dean. 2004. *Animism* (A Religion Profile from International Students). Colorado Springs, CO: International Students; http://www.thetravelingteam.org/sites/default/files/Animism%202004.pdf (accessed 12 Oct 2012).

Hamaguchi, Eshun (浜口恵俊). 1990. "Ein Modell zur Selbstinterpretation der Japaner – 'Intersubjekt' und 'Zwischensein.'" In *Die kühle Seele: Selbstinterpretationen der japanischen Kultur*, edited by Jens Heise, 138–147. Frankfurt am Main: Fischer Taschenbuch Verlag GmbH.

Hammitzsch, Horst, ed. 1969. *Japanische Volksmärchen* (Die Märchen der Weltliteratur). Transliterated from the Japanese by Ingrid Schuster and Fritz Rumpf. Düsseldorf-Köln: Eugen Diederichs Verlag.

———. 1984. "Religion: Die Hauptströmungen im religiösen Bereich Japans." In *Japan-Handbuch*, edited by Horst Hammitzsch, 1515/1516–1539/1540. Second edition. Stuttgart: Franz Steiner Verlag Wiesbaden GmbH.

Hanegraaff, Hank. 1991. "Should a Christian Practice the Martial Arts?" In *Christian Research Newsletter* 4 (1). Statement CP1300. Santa Margarita, CA: Christian Research Institute; http://www.equip.org/article/should-a-christian-practice-the-martial-arts/. But the author is B. J. Orepeza (accessed 12 Oct 2012).

Hansch, Dietmar. 2003. *Erste Hilfe für die Psyche*. Wien and New York: Springer Verlag.

Harbeck-Pingel, Bernd, and Michael Roth. 1977. "Vernunft III." In *Theologische Realenzyklopädie*, volume 35 (Vernunft III – Wiederbringung aller), edited by Horst Robert Balz, Gerhard Krause and Gerhard Müller, 1–15. Berlin and New York: Walter de Gruyter.

Hardacre, Helen. 1996. "*Shinmeiaishinkai* and the Study of Shamanism in Contemporary Japanese Religious Life." In *Religion in Japan*, edited by Peter Francis Kornicki, James McMullen, 198–219. Cambridge: Cambridge University Press.

Harder, Günther. 1979. "Seele." In *Theologisches Begriffslexikon zum Neuen Testament*, volume 2. Edited by Lothar Coenen, 1112–1119. Fifth edition. Wuppertal: Theologischer Verlag R. Brockhaus.

Haring, Douglas G. 1946. "Aspects of Personal Character in Japan." *The Far Eastern Quarterly* 6 (1): 12–22. Edited by the Association for Asian Studies.

Härle, Wilfried. 1995. *Dogmatik*. Berlin and New York: Walter de Gruyter.

Harris, R. Laird, Gleason L. Archer, and Bruce K. Waltke. 1981. *Theological Wordbook of the Old Testament*, volumes 1 and 2. Second edition. Chicago: Moody Press (electronic edition under BibleWorks for Windows, Version 7.0.012g [2006]).

Harrison, Elizabeth G. 1996. "*Mizuko kuyou*: The Re-Production of the Dead in Contemporary Japan." In *Religion in Japan: Arrows to Heaven and Earth*, edited by Peter Francis Kornicki, and James McMullen, 250–266. Cambridge: Cambridge University Press.

Harrison, Roland Kenneth. 1969. *Introduction to the Old Testament with a Comprehensive Review of Old Testament Studies and a Special Supplement on the Apocrypha*. Grand Rapids, MI: Eerdmans.

Hartung, Constance. 2005. *Der "Weg der Väter": Ostafrikanische Religionen im Spiegel früher Missionarsberichte*. Berlin, Hamburg and Münster: LIT Verlag.

Harvay, Van A. 1997. *Feuerbach and the Interpretation of Religion*. Cambridge Studies in Religion and Critical Thought. Cambridge: Cambridge University Press.

Harvey, Graham. 2005. *Animism: Respecting the Living World*. Kent Town, South Australia: Wakefield Press.

Hasenfratz, Hans-Peter. 1992. "Okkultismus." In *Lexikon der Religionen: Phänomene, Geschichte, Ideen*, edited by Hans Waldenfels, 479–480. Second edition. Freiburg, Basel, Wien: Verlag Herder Freiburg im Breisgau.

Hasenhüttl, Gotthold. 1991. *Schwarz bin ich und schön: Der theologische Aufbruch Schwarzafrikas*. Darmstadt: Wissenschaftliche Buchgesellschaft.

Hastings, John A. 2003. *Encyclopedia of Religion and Ethics*. Part 17. Whitefish, MT: Kessinger Publishing.

Hatsumi, Masaaki (初見良昭). 2005. *Advanced Stick Fighting*. Translated by Bruce Appleby and Doug Wilson. Tokyo: Koudansha International.

Hattori, Yuuichi. (服部雄一). 2005. ひきこもり：家族トラウマ (*hikikomori: kazoku torauma*) [*Hikikomori: Family Trauma*]. Tokyo: NHK出版 Publishing.

———. (服部雄一). 2010. "The Dual Personality System in Japanese Psychology: How This Affects our Mission." Lecture on the occasion Missiology Forum (JEMA) at the Ochanomizu Christian Center, Tokyo, 2010/2/8.

Hausmann, Jutta. 1995. *Studien zum Menschenbild der älteren Weisheit (Spr 10ff.)* (Forschungen zum Alten Testament, 7). Revised edition of the habilitation treatise presented at the Hochschule Neuendettelsau, 1992. Tübingen: Mohr Siebeck.

Hauth, Rüdiger. 2008. *Taschenbuch Esoterik: Von Bachblüten bis Yoga: Ein kritischer Leitfaden*. Witten: R. Brockhaus-Verlag im SCM-Verlag.

Hearn, Lafcadio. 1971. *Japan: An Attempt at Interpretation*. 11th edition. Rutland, Vermont and Tokyo: Charles E. Tuttle Company.

———. 2015 (1899). *In Ghostly Japan*. Worcestershire: Read Books (eBook).

Heine, Steven. 1994. "Tragedy and Salvation in the Floating World: Chikamatsu's Double Suicide Drama as Millenarian Discourse." *The Journal of Asian Studies* 53 (2): 367–393. Edited by the Association for Asian Studies.

Heine, Wilhelm. 2005 (1860). *Japan und seine Bewohner*. Boston, MA: Adamant Media; Elibron Classics.

Heise, Jens. 1990. *Die kühle Seele: Selbstinterpretationen der japanischen Kultur*. Frankfurt am Main: Fischer Taschenbuch Verlag GmbH (Fischer Sozialwissenschaft).

Heise, Jürgen. 1967. *Bleiben: Menein in den johannesischen Schriften* (Hermeneutische Untersuchungen zur Theologie 8). Edited by Gerhard Ebeling, Ernst Fuchs, and Manfred Mezger. Tübingen: Mohr Siebeck.

Hemfelt, Robert, Frank Minirth, and Paul Maier. 1995. *Mut zur Liebe*. Fourth edition. Asslar: Schulte & Gerth.
Hennecke, Susanne, and Ab Venemans, eds. 2015. *Karl Barth – Katsumi Takizawa: Briefwechsel 1934–1968* (einschließlich des Briefwechsels Charlotte von Kirschbaum - Katsumi Takizawa). Göttingen: Vandenhoeck & Ruprecht.
Hennig, Kurt. 1992 (1962). *Das Grundgesetz Gottes: Eine Auslegung der Zehn Gebote*. Stuttgart: Quell Verlag.
Hermann, Kai, and Alberto Venzago. 1992 (1990). *Yakuza: Ein Insider-Report über die japanische Mafia*. N.p.: Goldmann Verlag.
Herrmann, Wolfram. 1999. *Von Gott und den Göttern: Gesammelte Aufsätze zum Alten Testament*. Berlin and New York: Walter de Gruyter.
Hesselgrave, David J. 1978. *Communicating Christ Cross-Culturally: An Introduction to Missionary Communication*. Grand Rapids, MI: Zondervan.
———. 1980. "Missionary Elenctics and Guilt and Shame." *Missiology* 11, no. 4 (October 1983): 461–483.
———. 1983. *Planting Churches Cross-Culturally*. Grand Rapids, MI: Baker.
Hewer, Walter, Wulf Rössler, and Josef Aldenhoff. 2007. *Akute psychische Erkrankungen: Management und Therapie*. Munich: Elsevier GmbH Deutschland.
Hiebert, Paul G. 1982. "The Flaw of the Excluded Middle." *Missiology* 10 (1): 35–47.
———. 2000. "Spiritual Warfare and Worldviews." *Direction* 29 (2): 114–124; http://www.directionjournal.org/article/?1052 (accessed 12 Oct 2012).
———. 2002. Lecture at a workshop of the Annula Meeting of the Japanese Church Planting Institute (CPI) in Hakone, Japan.
Hiebert, Paul G., and Eloise Hiebert Meneses. 1995. *Incarnational Ministry: Planting Churches in Volume, Tribal, Peasant, and Urban Societies*. Grand Rapids, MI: Baker.
Hiebert, Paul G., R. Daniel Shaw, and Tite Tiénou. 1999. *Understanding Folk Religion: A Christian Response to Popular Beliefs and Practices*. Grand Rapids, MI: Baker.
Hielscher, Gebhard. 1995. *Japan*. Munich: Polyglott-Verlag.
Higashibaba, Ikuo (東馬場郁生). 2001. *Christianity in Early Modern Japan: Kirishitan Belief and Practice*. Leiden: Brill.
Hijiya-Kirschnereit, Irmela. 1988. *Das Ende der Exotik: Zur japanischen Kultur und Gesellschaft der Gegenwart*. Frankfurt am Main: Suhrkamp Verlag.
Hildebrandt, Mathias. 1996. "Politische Kultur und Zivilreligion." Presented as doctoral thesis at the Univeristy of Erlangen-Nürnberg, 1992. Würzburg: Verlag Königshausen & Neumann.
Hill, Harriet. 2007. "The Effects of Using Local and Non-Local Terms in Mother-Tongue Scripture." *Missiology* 35 (4): 383–396.
Hille, Rolf. 2004. "Die Auseinandersetzung der frühen Kirche mit dem Heilsuniversalismus in Theologie und Mission – heute wieder aktuell?" In *Wahrheit und Erfahrung: Themenbuch zur systematischen Theologie* (volume 3: Heiliger Geist, Kirche, Sakramente, Neuschöpfung), edited by Christian

Herrmann, 362–380. Wuppertal: R. Brockhaus Verlag; Gießen: Brunnen Verlag (Theologische Verlagsgemeinschaft, TVG).

Hindmarsh, D. Bruce. 2002. "Let Us See Thy Great Salvation: What Did It Mean to Be Saved for the Early Evangelicals?" In *What Does It Mean to Be Saved?: Broadening Evangelical Horizons of Salvation*, edited by John G. Stackhouse, Jr., 43–66. Grand Rapids, MI: Baker.

Hirosachiya (ひろさちや), Ryoushou Hayashi (林亮勝), and Takeshi Mitsuhashi (三橋健). 1993. みそぎ考日本史に見る罪と罰 (*misogikou Nipponshi-ni miru tsumi-to batsu*) [Concerning misogi: in and retribution in Japanese history]. Tokyo: Suzuki Shuppan (鈴木出版).

Hirota, Dennis. 2000. *Toward a Contemporary Understanding of Pure Land Buddhism: Creating a Shin Buddhist Theology in a Religiously Plural World*. Albany, NY: SUNY Press.

Hockley, Allen, and Koryuusai Isoda ((礒田湖龍斎). 2003. *The Prints of Isoda Koryūsai: Floating World Culture and Its Consumers in Eighteenth-century Japan*. Seattle, WA: University of Washington Press.

Hodgson, Peter Crafts. 1994. *Winds of the Spirit: A Constructive Christian Theology*. Richmond, VA: Westminster John Knox Press.

Hoekema, Anthony A. 1994 (1979). *The Bible and the Future*. Grand Rapids, MI: Eerdmans.

Hoffmann, John P. 2007. *Japanese Saints: Mormons in the Land of the Rising Sun*. Lanham, MD: Lexington.

Hoffmeister, Johannes. 1969 (1952). *Briefe von und an Hegel*, volume 1 (volume 235 of Philosophische Bibliothek). Third edition. Hamburg: Felix Meiner Verlag.

Hofstede, Geert. 1993. "Cultural Constraints in Management Theories." *Academy of Management Executive* 7 (1): 81–94.

———. 2013 (1991). *Interkulturelle Zusammenarbeit: Kulturen – Organisationen – Management*. Wiesbaden: Gabler.

Holder, Arthur G. 2005. *The Blackwell Companion to Christian Spirituality*. Oxford: Wiley-Blackwell.

Hölldobler, Bert. 2010. "Der ganze Staat ist das Hirn." *Der Spiegel* no. 5/1.2.10: 102–106.

Hölldobler, Bert, and Edward O. Wilson. 1990. *The Ants*, volume 514. Third edition. Cambridge, MA and London, England: Harvard University Press.

Holtom, D. C. 1940a. "The Meaning of *Kami*. Chapter 1. Japanese Derivations." *Monumenta Nipponica* 3 (1): 1–27. Edited by Sophia University.

———. 1940b. "The Meaning of *Kami*. Chapter 2. Interpretation by Japanese Writers." *Monumenta Nipponica* 3 (2): 392–413. Edited by Sophia University.

———. 1941. "The Meaning of *Kami*. Chapter 3. *Kami* Considered as *Mana*." *Monumenta Nipponica* 4 (2): 351–394. Edited by Sophia University.

Hooker, Richard. 1996. "*Mono No Aware*: Sensitivity to Things." *Japan Glossary*. http://richard-hooker.com/sites/worldcultures/GLOSSARY/MONO.HTM.

Hopkins, Edward Washburn. 1969. *Epic Mythology*. Cheshire, CT: Biblo & Tannen.

Hopkins, Jerry. 2007. *Asian Aphrodisiacs: From Bangkok to Beijing – the Search for the Ultimate Turn-on*. North Clarendon, VT and Tokyo: Tuttle Publishing.

Hori, Ichirou (堀一郎). 1974. *Folk Religion in Japan: Continuity and Change*. Edited by Joseph M. Kitagawa and Alan L. Miller. Chicago: University of Chicago Press.

Hori, Ichirou (堀一郎). 1987. "The Appearance of Individual Self-Consciousness in Japanese Religion and Its Historical Transformations." In *The Japanese Mind: Essentials of Japanese Philosophy and Culture*, edited by Charles A. Moore, 201–227. Eighth edition. Honolulu: University of Hawaii Press.

Horikoshi, Nobuji (堀越暢治). 1994. "God, Nature and Thankfulness." In *The Harvester's Handbook: Evangelism and Church Planting in Japan: A Compilation of Articles from the Japan Harvest, 1984–1994*, edited by Ron Sisco, 207–208. Tokyo: Japan Evangelical Missionary Association.

Hosaka, Mitsuhiko (穂坂光彦), and Peter M. Shimokawa. 1999. *The State of the Urban Poor in Japan*. http://www.achr.net/sup_japan.htm (accessed 2012/10/12).

Hosaka, Takahiro (保坂幸博). 2003. 日本の自然崇拝、西洋アニミズム：宗教と文化/非西洋的な宗教理学への誘い (*nihon-no shizensuuhai, seiyou animizumu: shuukyou-to bunka / hiseiyouteki-na shuukyou rigaku-e-no izanai*) [Japanese Nature Veneration, Western Animism: Religion and Culture: Towards a Science of Non-Western Religions]. Tokyo: Shinhyouron (新評論).

Hoshi, Shinichi (星新一). 1990. "Der Mann im Park." In *Zeit der Zikaden: Japanisches Lesebuch: Erzählungen der Gegenwart*, edited by Tadao Araki and Ekkehard May, 48–58. Munich and Zürich: Piper.

Hoshino, Tomihiro (星野富弘). 1992. 速さのちがう時計 (*hayasa-no chigau tokei*) [The Clock that ticks differently]. Tokyo: Kaiseisha (偕成社).[4]

———. 2001. 鈴の鳴る道：花の詩画集 (*suzu-no naru michi: hana-no shigashuu*) [Road of the Tinkling Bell: Paintings, Poems, and Essays]. Tokyo: Kaiseisha (偕成社).[5]

Hoshino, Yoshihiko. (星野仁彦). 2006. 気づいて！こどもの心のSOS：こどもの心の病全書乳幼児、小学生、中高生、青年期の若者対象 (*kizuite! kodomo-no SOS: kodomo-no kokoro-no yamai zensho nyuuyouji, shougakusei, chuukousei, seinenki-no wakamono taishou*) [Pay Attention! To the SOS of Childrens' Heart: Complete Volume Heart Aches of Children: For the Target Group of Young People of Baby Age, Elementary School Age, Junior High School Age, High School Age, and Youth]. Tokyo: Voice.

Hot Spring Culture Research Society Japan (日本温泉文化研究会, *Nihononsenbunkakenkyuukai*). 2007. 温泉の文化誌: 論集〈温泉学I〉(*Onsen-*

---

4. Hoshino's poem quoted at the beginning of the book is taken from page 99 of his book.
5. Hoshino's poem quoted at the end of the book is taken from page 79 of his book.

no bunkashi: ronshuu (onsengaku I)) [Magazine for Onsen Culture: A Collection of Treatises (volume 1 of Hot Spring Science)]. Tokyo: Iwata Shoin (岩田書院).

Hozumi, Nobushige (穂積陳重). 2008 (1901). *Ancestor-Worship and Japanese Law.* Charleston, SC: BiblioBazaar, LLC.

Huang, Ning, Roman Retzbach, and Knut Kühlmann. 2012. *China-Knigge: Chinakompetenz in Kultur und Business.* Munich: Oldenburg Verlag.

Huber, Hugo, SVD. 1992. "Schuld/Sünde: Religionsethnologische Sicht." In *Lexikon der Religionen: Phänomene, Geschichte, Ideen,* edited by Hans Waldenfels, 585–586. Second edition. Freiburg, Basel, Wien: Verlag Herder Freiburg im Breisgau.

Huffmann, James L. 1998. *Modern Japan: An Encyclopedia of History, Culture, and Nationalism.* London: Taylor & Francis.

Huish, Marcus B. 2008. *Japan and Its Art.* Alcester, Warwickshire: Read Books.

Hummel, Reinhart. 1992. "Neureligiöse Bewegungen: In Asien." In *Lexikon der Religionen: Phänomene, Geschichte, Ideen,* edited by Hans Waldenfels, 451–453. Second edition. Freiburg, Basel, Wien: Verlag Herder Freiburg im Breisgau.

Hunt, Dave, and T. A. McMahon. 1986. *The Seduction of Christianity: Spiritual Discernment in the Last Days.* Ninth edition. Eugene, OR: Harvest House.

Hur, Nam-Lin. 2000. *Prayer and Play in Late Tokugawa Japan: Asakusa Sensōji and Edo Society.* Cambridge: Harvard University Asia Center.

Hwang, Bernard. 1977. "Ancestor Cult Today." *Missiology* 5 (3): 339–365.

Hyslop, James H. 2003 (1919). *Contact with the Other World: Latest Evidence as to Communication with the Dead.* Whitefish, MT: Kessinger Publishing.

Ichijou, Shinya (一条真也). 2008. 開運!パワースポット「神社」へ行こう (*kaiun! pawaasupotto "jinja"-e ikou*) [Improvement of good luck!: Let's go to the powerspot "Shrine"] Verbesserung des Schicksals! Auf zum powerspot "Schrein"). Kyoto: PHP Kenkyuujo (PHP研究所).

———. 2009. 天国」と「地獄」がよくわかる本: 千年王国からヴァルハラ、八大地獄、タルタロスまで (*"tengoku"-to "chigoku"-ga yoku wakaru hon: sennenoukoku-kara waruhara, hachidaijigoku, tarutarosu-made*) [A Book for an improved understanding of "heaven" and "hell": From the millennium and eightfold hell to the tartaros]. Kyoto: PHP Kenkyuujo (PHP研究所).

Ibsen, Michael. 2000. "Takizawa, Katsumi." *Biographisch-Bibliographisches Kirchenlexikon* XVII: 1347–1358. N.p.: Verlag Traugott Baut.

Iga, Mamoru. 1986. *The Thorn in the Chrysanthemum: Suicide and Economic Success in Modern Japan.* Berkeley, Los Angeles, and London: University of California Press.

Iida, Takafumi (飯田剛史). 1988. "Folk Religion among the Koreans in Japan: The Shamanism of the 'n Temples.'" *Japanese Journal of Religious Studies* 15: 2–3.

Iimura, Akiko (飯村昭子). 1997. "Medical School Doctors Study 'Ki.'" *OCS-News* (552): 1–2. http://www.ryokukai.com/articles/images/OCS_23-Eng.pdf (accessed 12 Oct 2012).

Ikegami, Eiko (池上英子). 1995. *The Taming of the Samurai: Honorific Individualism and the Making of Modern Japan*. Fifth edition. Cambridge, MA, and London: Harvard University Press.

Iles, Timothy. 2007. "Familie, Father, Film: Changing Images from Japanese Cinema." In *Japanstudien: Jahrbuch des Deutschen Instituts für Japanstudien: Familienangelegenheiten*, volume 19, edited by Peter Backhaus, 189–206. Munich: Iudicum Verlag.

Illes, Judika. 2002. *Emergency Magic!: 150 Spells for Surviving the Worst-Case Scenario*. Beverly, MA: Fair Winds Press.

Illius, Bruno. 2002. "Schamanismus: die Vorstellung von 'ablösbaren Seelen.'" In *Der Begriff der Seele in der Religionswissenschaft*, edited by Johann Figl and Hans-Dieter Klein, 87–100. Würzburg: Verlag Königshausen & Neumann.

Immoos, Thomas. 1991. "Das Land der mächtigen Frauen: Archaisches im Gegenwärtigen: Frauen in schamanistisch-kultischen Funktionen." In *Japan – ein Land der Frauen?*, edited by Elisabeth Gössmann, 13–33. Munich: Iudicum Verlag.

Inagaki, Hisakazu (稲垣久和). 1990. "Post-Modern 'Japanism': Worldview and Contextual Horizon." *Japan Harvest* 40 (3): 8–14. (This article is an abridged version of the original article.)

Inagaki, Hisakazu (稲垣久和), and Nelson J. Jennings. 2000. *Philosophical Theology and East-West-Dialogue*. Amsterdam and Atlanta, GA: Editions Rodopi B. V.

Inoue, Mitsuharu (井上光晴). 1994. "The House of Hands." In *The Crazy Iris and Other Stories of the Atomic Aftermath*, edited by Kenzaburo Oe, 145–168. Translated by Ivan Morris, and Frederick Uleman. N.p.: Grove Press.

Inoue, Nobutaka (井上順孝). 2003. "The Modern Age: Shinto Confronts Modernity." In *Shinto: A Short History*, edited by Nobutaka Inoue, 159–197. London and New York: RoutledgeCurzon (Taylor & Francis Group).

Ion, A. Hamish. 1993. *The Cross and the Rising Sun, Volume 2: The British Protestant Missionary Movement in Japan, Korea, and Taiwan, 1865–1945*. Waterloo, ON: Wilfrid Laurier University Press.

Irie, Chiyoko. 1976. "Froschfrau." In *Japanische Märchen*, edited and translated by Toshio Ozawa, 50–51. Third edition. Frankfurt am Main: Fischer Taschenbuch Verlag GmbH.

Irokawa, Daikichi (色川大吉), and Marius B. Jansen. 1988. *The Culture of the Meiji Period* (Princeton Library of Asian Translations). Princeton, NJ: Princeton University Press.

Irokawa, Daikichi (色川大吉), and Noboru Miyata (宮田登). 1997. 転換期の世相 (*tenkanki-no sesou*) [The Turning Point (or The Transition Phase) of Social Conditions]. Tokyo: Shougakukan (小学館).

Ishida, Takeshi. 1989. *Japanese Political Culture: Change and Continuity*. Piscataway, NY: Transaction Publishers.

Ishii, Susumu (石井進), and Teizou Iyanaga (彌永貞三). 2002. *Dictionnaire historique du Japon (L-Z)*. Paris: Maisonneuve & Larose (Maison Franco-japonaise).
Ishizaka, Masanobu (石坂正信). 2009. *Christianity in Japan, 1859–1883*. N.p.: BiblioBazaar.
Itou, Ichirou (伊藤一郎). 2009. 松本死刑囚：再審請求を棄却…新証拠退ける東京地裁 (*Matsumoto shikeishuu: saiban seikyuu-o kikyaku . . . Shinshouko shirinozokeru; Toukyou Chisai*) ["Candidate for death Matsumoto: Appeal for reopening of the process denies . . . new evidence denied; Tokyo Court."] Mainichi Shinbun (毎日新聞), 19 March 2009; http://mainichi.jp/select/jiken/news/20090319k0000m040088000c.html.
Itou, Satoshi (伊藤哲). 2003. "The Medieval Period: The Kami Merge with Buddhism." In *Shinto: A Short History*, edited by Nobutaka Inoue, 63–107. London and New York: RoutledgeCurzon (Taylor & Francis Group).
Itou, Shigeru (伊藤茂). 2001. 戦場ケ原異聞 (*Senjougahara ibun*) [The Strange Stories of Senjougahara]. Tokyo: Bungeisha (文芸社).
Itou, Shinobu (伊東信夫). 2007. 成り立ちで知る漢字のおもしろ世界 (*naritachi-de shiru kanji-no omoshiro sekai*) [The interesting world of Chinese characters, as perceived from their origin]. Tokyo: 3anet (スリーエーネットワーク).
Itou, Toshiko (伊藤,敏子). 1996. "Das 'Gute Kind': Ein gezwungener Hoffnungsträger der Gesellschaft?" In *Harmonie und Konformität: Tradition und Krise japanischer Sozialisationsmuster*, edited by Agi Schründer-Lenzen, 32–51. Munich: Iudicum Verlag.
Ivy, Marilyn. 1995. *Discourses of the Vanishing: Modernity, Phantasm, Japan*. Chicago and London: University of Chicago Press.
Iwanami, Akira (岩波明). 2006. 臨床心理学がよくわかる本：現代人の「心の病」を治療する (*rinshou shinrigaku-ga yoku wakaru hon: gendaijin-no "kokoro-no yami"-o chiryou suru*) [Comprehensive Book on Clinical Psychology: Treating the 'Heart-Aches' of Young People Today]. Tokyo: Shuuwa System (秀和システム).
Iwao, Seiichi (岩生成一), and Teizou Iyanaga (彌永貞三). 2002. *Dictionnaire historique du Japon (A-K)*. Paris: Maisonneuve & Larose (Maison Franco-japonaise).
Jacob, Edmond. 1990. "Die Anthropologie des Alten Testaments." *Theologisches Handwörterbuch zum Neuen Testament* 9: 614–629. Stuttgart, Berlin, Köln: Verlag W. Kohlhammer.
Jacobson, Howard. 1996. *A Commentary on Pseudo-Philo's Liber Antiquitatum Biblicarum: With Latin Text and English Translation* (Arbeiten Zur Geschichte des Antiken Judentums und des Urchristentums, volume 31). Leiden: Brill Academic.
Jaffin, David. 1981. *Die Welt und der Weltüberwinder*. Bad Liebenzell: Verlag der Liebenzeller Mission.
Jaichandran, Rebecca, and B. D. Madhav. 2003. "Pentecostal Spirituality in a Postmodern World." *Asian Journal of Pentecostal Studies* 6 (1): 39–61. http://

www.apts.edu/aeimages/File/AJPS_PDF/03-1-RJaichandran.pdf (accessed 12 Oct 2012).

James, Grace. No year. "Matsuyama Mirror." In *Japanese Fairy Tales*, edited by Grace James. Los Angeles, CA: Bookpubber.

Jansen, Albert. 1979. *Marx oder Jesus: Antworten als Hilfe zur Lebensbewältigung*. Neuhausen-Stuttgart: Hänssler Verlag.

Japan Echo Inc. 2000. "'Parasite Singles' Multiply: And Parental 'Hosts' Don't Seem to Mind." http://web-japan.org/trends00/honbun/tj000508.html (accessed 13 May 2016).

Japan NGO Report Preparatory Committee. 1999. *Women 2000, Japan NGO Alternative Report: Women and Poverty in Japan*. http://www.jca.apc.org/fem/bpfa/NGOreport/A_en_Poverty.html (accessed 12 Oct 2012).

Jennings, Nelson J. 2005. *Theology in Japan: Takakura Tokutaro (1885–1934)*. Lanham, MD: University Press of America.

Jhi, Jun-Hyung. 2006. *Das Heil in Jesus Christus bei Karl Rahner und in der Theologie der Befreiung*. Göttingen: Vandenhoeck & Ruprecht.

Jiménez, Lina Maria Arias. 2005. *Los 7 Rituales Orientales de la Prosperidad Y la Abundancia*. Colombia: La Llama Trina.

Johnson, Buffie. 1994. *Lady of the Beasts: The Goddess and Her Sacred Animals*. Rochester, VT: Inner Traditions/Bear & Company.

Johnston, James L. 1999. *The First Japanese Freemason*. http://www2.gol.com/users/lodge1/history-e/papers/johnston04.html (accessed 12 Oct 2012).

Johnston, William. 1970. "The Notion of Man in Zen." *Studia Missionalia: Man, Culture and Religion: homme, culture et religion* 19: 87–100. Rome: Gregorian Biblical BookShop.

Jones, Ronald H. 2005. *Terrorist Beheadings: Cultural and Strategic Implications* (Carlisle Papers in Security Strategy). N.p.: Strategic Studies Institute.

Jorissen, Hans. 1992. "Transzendenz/Immanenz." In *Lexikon der Religionen: Phänomene, Geschichte, Ideen*, edited by Hans Waldenfels, 678–681. Second edition. Freiburg, Basel, Wien: Verlag Herder Freiburg im Breisgau.

Joseph, Kenny. 1982. "Japanese Proverbs and Colloquial Sayings." In *The New Combined Language Handbook:* 聖書を英語で学ぶためのハンドブック (*seisho-o eigo-de manabu tame-no handobukku*) [Handbook for Bible Studies in English], edited by Kenny Joseph and Russell Stellwagon, 57–72. Uda, Nara und Wilmington, DE: Dawn Press (暁屋).

———. *Jiso vs. Jesus in Japan: 1800 Years of Erased Christian History*; 日本の地蔵対ジィーザス (*Japan's Jisou contra Jesus*). Pre-edition for research purpose. No publisher.

Jost, Peter Samuel. 2004. "Die Bedeutung der Wirklichkeit Gottes für die Mission der Kirche hinsichtlich der Diesseitsorientierten Plausibilitätsstruktur nachchristlicher Gesellschaften." Dissertation presented at the University of South Africa. http://

etd.unisa.ac.za/ETD-db/theses/available/etd-11172005-115001/unrestricted/dissertation.pdf.

Juergensmeyer, Mark. 2003. *Terror in the Mind of God: The Global Rise of Religious Violence*. Berkeley and Los Angeles: University of California Press.

Jüngel, Eberhard. 2000 (1968). "Gottes umstrittene Gerechtigkeit: Eine reformatorische Besinnung zum paulinischen Begriff δικαιοσύνη θεου." In *Unterwegs Zur Sache (sechzehn Aufsätze und Vorlesungen zwischen 1963 und 1971)*, edited by Eberhard Jüngel. Second edition. Tübingen: Mohr Siebeck.

———. 2003 (1983). "Zum Wesen des Friedens: Frieden als Kategorie theologischer Anthropologie." In *Ganz werden: Theologische Erörterungen*, edited by Eberhard Jüngel, 1–39. Tübingen: Mohr Siebeck.

Juniper, Andrew. 2003. *Wabi Sabi: The Japanese Art of Impermanence*. Rutland, VT and Tokyo, Japan: Charles E. Tuttle Company.

Kagawa, Toyohiko (賀川豊彦). 2007 (1934). *Christ and Japan*. Translated by William Axling. Alcester, UK: Read Books.

Kahlert, Johanna. 2003. "Möglichkeiten interreligiösen Lernens am Beispiel deutscher Jugendlicher in Japan und japanischer Jugendlicher in Deutschland." Doctoral thesis accepted by the Carl von Ossietzky University Oldenburg, social science.

Kajiwara, Kazuyoshi (梶原和義). 2002. ユダヤ人に与えられた永遠の生命 (*yudayajin-ni ataerareta eien-no seimei*) [The Eternal Life Received from the Jews]. Tokyo: Bungeisha (文芸社).

———. (梶原和義). 2001. ユダヤ人が立ち直れば世界が見事に立ち直る (*yudayajin-ga tachinaoreba sekai-ga migoto-ni tachinaoru*) [If the Jews recover, the world shall recover wonderfully]. Tokyo: Bungeisha (文芸社).

Kakar, Sudhir. 1984 (1982). *Schamanen, Mystiker und Ärzte*. Authorized translation by Holger Fliessbach. Munich: Biederstein Verlag.

Kalland, Arne. 1991. "Facing the Spirits: Illness and Healing in a Japanese Community." Presented at Traditional Folk Belief Today in Tartu Estonia, 1990. Copenhagen: Nordic Institute of Asian Studies (NIAS).

Kalvig, Anne. 2014. "Popularity of – and Controversy in – Contemporary Shamanism." In *Controversial New Religions*, edited by James R. Lewis, and Jesper A. Petersen, 331–347. Second edition. Oxford and New York: Oxford University Press.

Kamata, Touji (鎌田東二). 2000. 神道とは何か：自然の霊性を感じて生きる (*shintou-to-wa nanika: shizen-no reisei-o kanjite ikiru*) [What is Shintoism?: Living with an awareness of the spirituality of nature]. Kyoto: PHP Kenkyuujo (PHP研究所).

Kaminsky, Joel S. 1995. *Corporate Responsibility in the Hebrew Bible*. New York, NY: Continuum.

Kämpfer, Engelbert. 1777. *Geschichte und Beschreibung von Japan*, volume 1. Lemgo: Verlag der Meyerschen Buchhandlung.

Kaneko, Martin. 1993. *Textilarbeiterinnen in Japan: Die Frauen aus Buraku und Okinawa*. Wien, Köln, Weimar: Böhlau Verlag.

Kang, C. H., and Ethel R. Nelson. 1998 (1979). *Erinnerungen an die Genesis: Die Chinesen und die biblische Urgeschichte*. Neuhausen-Stuttgart: Hänssler.

Kankou Shiryou Hogo Zaidan (The Foundation for the Preservation of Tourist Material, under the Japanese Agency for Cultural Affairs (観光資源保護財団, 文化庁). 1976. 日本民俗芸能事典 (*nihon minyou geinou jiten*) [Dictionary on Japanese Folk-Entertainment]. Tokyo: Daiichihoukishuppan (第一法規出版).

Kaplan, David, and Andrew Marshall. 1996. *Aum: Eine Sekte greift nach der Welt*. Translated by Eckhard Böhme. Düsseldorf and Munich: Metropolitan Verlag.

Kasahara, Yomishi (笠原嘉). 1986. "Fear of Eye-to-Eye Confrontation among Neurotic Patients in Japan." In *Japanese Culture and Behavior: Selected Readings*, edited by Takie Sugiyama-Lebra and William P. Lebra, 379–388. Honolulu: University of Hawaii Press.

Käser, Lothar. 1995. *Animismus: Einführung in seine begrifflichen Grundlagen*. Bad Liebenzell: Verlag der Liebenzeller Mission.

Katou, Tsuneaki (加藤常昭). 2005. *Japanischer Katechismus: Kirchenlehre der evangelischen "Yuki no Shita"-Gemeinde in Kamakura/Japan*. Translated by Stefan Jäger. Waltrop: Hartmut Spener.

———. 2004. "Lecture Anthropology." Akademie für Weltmission, Korntal.

Katsumoto, Masami (勝本正實). 1992. 日本の宗教行事にどう反応するか (*nihon-no shuukyougyouji-ni dou hannou suru-ka*) [How to respond to religious rites of Japan]. Third edition. Tokyo: Inochinokotobasha (いのちのことば社) (Word of Life Press).

Kaufmann, Rolf. 2006. *Alte und neue Religiosität: ABC einer Metamorphose*. Stuttgart: opus magnum.

Kawai, Hayao (河合隼雄). 1986. "Violence in the Home: Conflict between Two Principles – Maternal and Paternal." In *Japanese Culture and Behavior: Selected Readings*, edited by Takie Sugiyama-Lebra and William P. Lebra, 297–306. Revised edition. Honolulu: University of Hawaii Press.

Kawakami, Youichi. 2002. "つわり：独自の「座薬」漢方でにおい嫌悪を解消" (*tsuwari: dokuji-no "zayaku"-kanpou-de nioi keno-o kaishou*) [Morning sickness: Elimination of odour intolerance using original suppositories of Chinese traditional medicine]. In 漢方辞典：名医と治す (*kanpoujiten: meii-to naosu*) [Encyclopedia of Chinese tranditional medicine: Healing together with the physician], edited by weekly journal Shuukan Asahi (週刊朝日), 122–123. Tokyo: Asahi Shinbunsha (朝日新聞社).

Kawamura, Shouichi (河村正一). 2000. 神経症の逆療法: 森田療法の功罪を評す (*shinkeishou-no gyakuryouhou: Morita ryouhou-no kouzai-o hyousu*) [Therapy against nervosity: A commentary on advantages and disadvantages of the Morita-Therapy]. Tokyo: Bungeisha (文芸社).

Kawano, Satsuki. 2010. *Nature's Embrace: Japan's Aging Urbanites and New Death Rites*. Honolulu: University of Hawaii Press.

Kawasaki, Yufuji (川崎ゆふじ). 2002. 幽霊が見える: 幽霊なんて絶対信じないあなたに (*yuurei-ga mieru: yuurei nante zettai shinjinai anata-ni*) [Ghosts are visible: For you who would never ever believe in stuff like ghosts]. Tokyo: Bungeisha (文芸社).

Kawashima, Takeyoshi (川島武宜). 1988. "Die familiale Struktur der japanischen Gesellschaft." In *Japan ohne Mythos: Zehn kritische Essays aus japanischer Feder, 1946–1963*, published and translated by Karl Friedrich Zahl, 60–81. Published in the Chuuou Kouron, 1946, published as a book in 1948 日本社會の家族的構成 (*Nipponshakai-no kazokuteki kouzou*) [The familial structure of the Japanese society]. Munich: Iudicium Verlag GmbH.

———. 2000. 日本社会の家族的構成 (*Nipponshakai-no kazokuteki kouzou*) [The familial structure of the Japanese society]. First published 1946 in the Chuuou Kouron (中央公論), first published as a book in 1948. Tokyo: Iwanami Gendaibunko (岩波現代文庫).

Keil, Carl Friedrich. 1858. *Handbuch der biblischen Archäologie* (erste Hälfte: Die gottesdienstlichen Verhältnisse der Israeliten). Frankfurt am Main und Erlangen: Verlag von Heyder & Zimmer.

———. 1871. *The Twelve Minor Prophets*. In Biblical Commentary on the Old Testament by C. F. Keil and F. Delitzsch. Published in Theological Library, fourth series, volume 27. Edinburgh: T & T Clark.

Keown, Damien, Stephen Hodge, and Paola Tinti. 2003. *A Dictionary of Buddhism*. New York, NY: Oxford University Press US.

Kerr, Alex. 2001. *Dogs and Demons: Tales from the Dark Side of Japan*. New York: Hill & Wang (a division of Farrar, Straus & Giroux).

Kersten, Joachim. 1997. *Gut und (Ge)schlecht: Männlichkeit, Kultur und Kriminalität*. Berlin and New York: Walter de Gruyter.

Kertelge, Karl. 1974. "Jesus als Befreier." In *Theologie und Befreiung*, edited by Heribert Bettscheider, 85–103. N.p.: Steyler Verlag.

Kettling, Siegfried. 1993. *Typisch evangelisch: Grundbegriffe des Glaubens*. Second edition. Gießen and Basel: Brunnen Verlag.

Khan, Yoshimitsu. 1997. *Japanese Moral Education Past and Present*. Madison, NJ: Fairleigh Dickinson University Press.

Khosrow-Pour, Mehdi; Information Resources Management Association, USA. 2015. *Encyclopedia of Information Science and Technology*. Third edition. Hershey, PA: IGI Global (Information Science Reference).

Kikuchi-Brinkley, F. n.d. *A History of the Japanese People From the Earliest Times to the End of the Meiji Era*. Alexandria: Library of Alexandria.

Kim, Chun-Shik. 2001. *Ostasien zwischen Angst und Bewunderung: Das populäre deutsche Ostasienbild der 1930er und 40er Jahre in Reiseberichten aus dem japanischen Imperium*. Berlin, Hamburg and Münster: LIT Verlag.

Kim, Joseph. 2014. "Kankei, Wa, and Evangelism." *Japan Harvest* 65 (3): 8–10. Tokyo: JEMA.

Kim, Kirsteen. 2004. "Spirit and 'spirits' at the Canberra Assembly of the World Council of Churches, 1991." *Missiology* 32 (3): 349–365.

Kim, Sebastian C. H. 2008. *Christian Theology in Asia*. Cambridge: Cambridge University Press.

Kim, Yong Sung. 2002. "Theodizee als Problem der Philosophie und Theologie: zur Frage nach dem Leiden und dem Bösen im Blick auf den allmächtigen und guten Gott." Volume 3 of *Forum Religionsphilosophie*. Münster: LIT Verlag.

Kim-Sawa, Young. 1987. "My Journey in Mission: A Korean-Japanese Woman Pastor's Story." *Missiology* 15 (3): 347–356.

Kimura, Naoji (木村直司). 2003. *Der "Ferne Westen" Japan: Zehn Kapitel über Mythos und Geschichte Japans*. St. Ingbert: Röhrig Universitätsverlag.

———. 2009. "Ethische Begründung des Liebestodes in der japanischen Literatur aus komparatistischer Perspektive." In *Grenzen des Lebens - Grenzen der Verständigung*, edited by Heinz-Dieter Assmann, Karl-Josef Kuschen, and Karin Moser v. Filseck, 111–122. Würzburg: Königshausen & Neumann.

Kindler, Jürgen. 2003. "Was ist Reiki." http://www.reiki-land.de/artikel/grundlagen/was-ist-reiki-01-einfuehrung.html (accessed 12 Oct 2012).

Kinoshita, Hidehito (木下秀人). 2003. 和辻哲郎「尊王思想とその伝統」1943, 全集14巻 1962 (*Watsuji Tetsurou: "sonou shisou-to sono dentou" 1943, zenshuu 14-kan 1962*) [Watsuji Tetsurou: "The Idea of Emperor Venaration and its Tradition" 1943, Complete Edition Scrole 14, 1962]. http://www8.plala.or.jp/hkino/file3-6-3.htm (accessed 16 May 2016).

Kinoshita, Ikuo (木下育生). 2003. 永遠のいのち―二十一世紀の幸福論 (*eien-no inochi: nijuuisseiki-no koufukuron*) [Eternal life: A bliss-science for the 21st century]. Tokyo: Bungeisha (文芸社).

Kirita, Kiyohide (桐田清秀). 1995. "D. T. Suzuki on Society and the State." In *Rude Awakenings: Zen, the Kyoto School, & the Question of Nationalism*, edited by James W. Heisig, and John C. Maraldo, 52–74. Honolulu: University of Hawaii Press.

Kisala, Robert. 1999. *Prophets of Peace: Pacifism and Cultural Identity in Japan's New Religions*. Honolulu: University of Hawaii Press.

Kitagawa, Joseph Mitsuo. 1987. *On Understanding Japanese Religion*. Princeton, NJ: Princeton University Press.

Kitagawa, Joseph Mitsuo, and Theodore Ludwig. 1984. "Shinto." In *Japan-Handbuch*, edited by Horst Hammitzsch, 1632–1640. Second edition. Stuttgart: Franz Steiner Verlag Wiesbaden GmbH.

Kitajima, Hirotoshi (北嶋廣敏). 2007. 日本人の「縁起」と「ジンクス」：なぜ大晦日(おおみそか)に蕎麦(そば)を食べるのか (*Nihonjin-no "engi"-to "jinkusu": Naze oomisoka-ni soba-o taberu-ka*) ["Good omens" and "bad omens" of the Japanese: Why do we eat soba noodles on December 31st?]. Kyoto: PHP Kenkyuujo (PHP研究所).

Kitamori, Kazou (北森嘉蔵). 1968. "Das Problem des Leidens in der Christologie." In *Theologische Stimmen aus Asien, Afrika und Lateinamerika*, volume 3, edited by Georg F. Vicedom et al., 112–121. Munich: Chr. Kaiser Verlag.

———. 1972. *Theologie des Schmerzes Gottes* (Theologie der Ökumene, volume 11). Göttingen: Vandenhoeck & Ruprecht.

———. 2005. *Theology of the Pain of God*. Eugene, OR: Wipf & Stock.

Kitamura, Kazuyuki (喜多村和之). 1985. *Japan – im Reich der mächtigen Frauen*. Berlin & Wien: Ullstein.

Kitano, Naho (北野菜穂). 2007. "Animism, Rinri, Modernization: The Base of Japanese Robotics." Lecture presented as part of the Fullday Workshop on Roboethics on 14 April 2007, at the 2007 IEEE International Conference of Robotics and Automation, 10–14 April 2007, Rome, Italy. http://www.roboethics.org/icra2007/contributions/KITANO%20Animism%20Rinri%20Modernization%20the%20Base%20of%20Japanese%20Robo.pdf (accessed 12 Oct 2012).

Kitayama, Osamu (北山修). 2005. "Cross-Cultural Varieties in Experiencing Affect." In *The Language of Emotions: Development, Psychopathology and Technique*, edited by Salman Akhtar and Harold Blum, 33–48. Lanham, MD: Rowan & Littlefield.

Klaes, Norbert. 2000. "Shinto, Shintoismus." In *Lexikon für Theologie und Kirche*, volume 9, third completely revised edition, 544–550. Freiburg, Basel, Rom, Wien: Herder.

Klawans, Jonathan. 2004. *Impurity and Sin in Ancient Judaism*. New York, NY: Oxford University Press.

Kleffmann, Tom. 1994. "Die Erbsündenlehre in sprachtheologischem Horizont." Presented as doctoral dissertation at the University of Göttingen, 1992. Tübingen: Mohr Siebeck.

———. 2003. "Nietzsches Begriff des Lebens und die evangelische Theologie: Eine Interpretation Nietzsches und Untersuchungen zu seiner Rezeption bei Schweitzer, Tillich und Barth." Habilitation treatise at the University of Göttingen, 2001. Tübingen: Mohr Siebeck.

Klein, Hans-Dieter. 2002. "Der Begriff der Seele in Philosophie und Religion." In *Der Begriff der Seele in der Religionswissenschaft*, edited by Johann Figl and Hans-Dieter Klein, 27–44. Würzburg: Verlag Königshausen & Neumann.

Kleine, Christoph. 2002. "Religion im Dienste einer ethnisch-nationalen Identitätskonstruktion: Erörtert am Beispiel der 'Deutschen Christen' und des japanischen Shinto." *Marburg Journal of Religion* 7 (1). https://www.uni-marburg.de/fb03/ivk/mjr/pdfs/2002/articles/kleine2002.pdf (accessed 16 May 2016).[6]

Kliesow, Olaf. 2001. „Aktionärsrechte und Aktionärsklage in Japan: Gesetzliche Regelungen und soziale Wirklichkeit." Disertation at the Westfälischen Wilhelms-Universität Münster, 2000, Tübingen: Mohr Siebeck.

Klumbies, Paul-Gerhard. 1992. *Die Rede von Gott bei Paulus in ihrem zeitgeschichtlichen Kontext*. Göttingen: Vandenhoeck & Ruprecht.

Knecht, Peter. 1986. "Funeral Rites and the Concept of Ancestors in Japan: A Challenge to Christian Churches?" In *Building the Church in Pluricultural Asia* (Inculturation: Working Papers on Living Faith and Cultures), edited by Robert Hardawiryana, Arul M. Varaprasadam, Kees Bertens, J. B. Banawiratma, Maria Elena Chong-Javier, Peter Knecht, and Joseph Dinh Duc Dao (Pontifical Gregorian University), 121–144. Rome: Editrice Pontificia Università Gregoriana.

Knight, John. 2004. *Wildlife in Asia: Cultural Perspectives*. London: Routledge.

Knitter, Paul F. 2005. "Mission and Dialogue." *Missiology* 33 (2): 200–210.

Knörer, Ekkehard. 2001. *Sen to Chihiro no Kamikakushi / Spirited Away (Regie: Hayao Miyazaki, Japan 2001): Kritik*. Jump Cut-Magazine. http://www.jump-cut.de/filmkritik-spiritedaway.html (accessed 12 Oct 2012).

Kobayashi, Chieko (小林千枝子). 2004. 「天の恵」騒動記:高齢妊婦・出産・育児の記録 (*"ten-no megumi" soudouki: koureininpu, shussan, ikuji-no kiroku*) [Diary of "heaven's blessings": pregancy at an advanced age, birth, parenting records]. Tokyo: Bungeisha (文芸社).

Kobia, Samuel. 2006. "Tribute to Prof. Dr. Masao Takenaka." In *Ökumenischer Rat der Kirchen* (website). https://www.oikoumene.org/en/resources/documents/general-secretary/tributes/masao-takenaka (accessed 16 May 2016).

Koch, Kurt E. 1984. *Okkultes ABC*. Schwäbisch Gmünd: Bibel-und Schriftenmission.

Köck, Stefan. 2015. "Washing Away the Dirt of the World of Desire: On Origins and Developments of Notions of Ritual Purity in Japanese Mountain Religions." In *Discourses of Purity in Transcultural Perspective (330-1600)*, edited by Matthias Bley, Nikolas Jaspert, and Stefan Köck, 240–268. Leiden and Boston: Brill.

Kodama, Katsuya (児玉克哉), Yasunobu Satou (佐藤安信), and Hisae Nakanishi (中西久枝). 2004. はじめて出会う平和学: 未来はここからはじまる (*hajimete deau heiwagaku: mirai-wa koko-kara hajimaru*) [Peace-science [for those who] encounter [this subject] for the first time: The future begins here]. Peace Studies for Beginners. Tokyo: Yuuhikaku Aruma (有斐閣アルマ).

Kohler, Werner. 1976. "Japanische christologische Versuche." In *Das asiatische Gesicht Christi*, edited by Heribert Bettscheider. Nettetal: Steyler Verlag.

---

6. This is the written version of Christoph Kleine's test lecture before the habilitation committee of the department 03 at the Philipps-Universität, Marburg, presented 19 Dec 2001.

Koide, Natsuko. 2000. "Parasite Single: What's the Matter." http://law.ris.ac.jp/ilc00/contents/981l00174/.

Koizumi, Ken (小泉健). 2006. *Das Wort, das Gemeinde ruft: Japanische Übersetzung deutscher Homiletik.* Inaugural doctoral disertation presented at the Theological Faculty of the Ruprecht-Karls-Universität, Heidelberg; http://archiv.ub.uni-heidelberg.de/volltextserver/7164/ (accessed 16 May 2016).

Koji Kokugo Dai Jiten Dictionary (故事国語大辞典) [Historical Japanese comprehensive dictionary]. 1986. Tokyo: Shougakukan (小学館).

*Koji Kotowaza Proverb Dictionary (*故事ことわざの辞典 (*koji kotowaza-no jiten*)). 1988. Tokyo: Shougakukan (小学館).[7]

Kokubu, Yasutaka (國分康孝). 1998. カウンセリング心理学入門 (*kaunseringu shinrigaku nyuumon*) [Introduction into counseling psychology]. Kyoto: PHP Kenkyuujo (PHP研究所).

Komatsu, Kazuhiko (小松和彦). 1995. "おみくじ (*omikuji* [Oracle])." In 日本を知る101章 (*nihon-o shiru 101shou*) [101 Chapters of knowledge about Japan], edited by Hiroshi Shimonaka (下中弘), 148–150. Tokyo: Heibonsha (平凡社).

———. 1999. "ノロイ・タタリ・イノチ (*noroi, tatari, iwai*) [Incantation, curse, festivity]." In 民俗宗教を学ぶ人のために (*minzokushuukyou-o manabu hito-no tame-ni*) [For people who learn folk religion]), edited by Tetsuo Yamaori and Nimitsu Kawamura, 40–59. Kyoto: Sekaishisonsha (世界思想社).

Komatsu, Mihoko (小松美保子). 2005. 神さま仏さま探訪記: ご利益をたどれば日本人が見える (*Kamisama hotokesama tanbouki: Gorieki-o tadoreba Nihonjin-ga mieru*) [Documentation of a Study s(on) (Japanese) gods and buddhas: If welfare is traceable the Japanese is visible]. Tokyo: Bungeisha (文芸社).

Kondou, Tamami (近藤珠實), ed. 2008. 日本の作法ハンドブック (*Nihon-no sahou handobukku*) [Handbook of Japanese etiquette]. Kyoto: PHP Kenkyuujo (PHP研究所).

Kondou, Tomie. 1995 (近藤富枝). "あわれ (*aware* [pitiable])." In 日本を知る101章 (*nihon-o shiru 101-shou*) [101 chapters of knowledge about Japan], edited by Hiroshi Shimonaka (下中弘), 238–240. Tokyo: Heibonsha (平凡社).

Koperski, Veronica. 1996. „The Knowledge of Christ Jesus my Lord: The High Christology of Philippians 3:7–11." Doctoral thesis at the Catholic University of Leuven, Belgium, 1991. Leuven: Peeters Publishers.

Kopfermann, Wolfram. 1994. *Macht ohne Auftrag: Warum ich mich nicht an der "geistlichen Kriegführung" beteilige.* Emmelsbühl: C&P Verlags-GmbH; Rothrist, Schweiz: Koinonia-Verlag.

Kopp, Zensho W. 2004. *Der große Zen-Weg: Der Weg zur Erleuchtung mitten im Leben.* Darmstadt: Schirner Verlag.

---

7. A dictionary for old proverbs.

Köpping, Klaus-Peter. 1974. *Religiöse Bewegungen im modernen Japan als Problem des Kulturwandels.* Köln: Wieland Verlag.

———. 1990. *Die neuen Religionen Japans: Traditionelle Denkmuster hinter revolutionärer Rhetorik*, (OAG aktuell; Vorträge, Materialien; No. 44). Tokyo: Gesellschaft für Natur- und Völkerkunde Ostasiens (OAG).

Kornicki, Peter Francis, and James McMullen. 1996. *Religion in Japan: Arrows to Heaven and Earth.* Cambridge: Cambridge University Press.

Koschnick, Wolfgang J. 1998. *Management and Marketing: Encyclopedic Dictionary, English – German.* Berlin and New York: Walter de Gruyter.

Koslowski, Peter, ed. 1985. *Die religiöse Dimension der Gesellschaft: Religion und ihre Theorien.* Tübingen: Mohr Siebeck.[8]

Koyama, Kousuke (小山晃佑). 1968. "'Zorn Gottes' und thailändische *theologia gloriae*." In *Theologische Stimmen aus Asien, Afrika und Lateinamerika*, volume 3, edited by Georg F. Vicedom et al., 50–60. Munich: Chr. Kaiser Verlag.

Kramer, Eric Mark. 2003. *The Emerging Monoculture: Assimilation and the "Model Minority."* Westport, CT: Greenwood.

Kranewitter, Rudolf. 2005. *Dynamik der Religion: Schamanismus, Konfuzianismus, Buddhismus und Christentum in der Geschichte Koreas von der steinzeitlichen Besiedlung des Landes bis zum Ende des 20. Jahrhunderts.* Berlin, Hamburg and Münster: LIT Verlag.

Kraus, Manfred. 1987. *Name und Sache: Ein Problem im frühgriechischen Denken.* Amsterdam: John Benjamins Publishing.

Krause, Ingrid. 1985. "Kindererziehung in Japan als Geburtsstunde der Amae-Mentalität." Unpublished seminar paper in the field of anthropology, CBS and FHM Korntal.

Kreck, Walter. 1987. *Grundentscheidungen in Karl Barths Dogmatik: Zur Diskussion seines Verständnisses von Offenbarung und Erwählung.* Berlin: Evangelische Verlagsanstalt Berlin.

Kreiner, Josef. 1992. "Shinto, Shintoismus." In *Lexikon der Religionen: Phänomene, Geschichte, Ideen*, edited by Hans Waldenfels, 607–610. Second edition. Freiburg, Basel, Wien: Verlag Herder Freiburg im Breisgau.

———. 1995. "Religionen heute." In *Länderbericht Japan: Geographie, Geschichte, Politik, Wirtschaft, Gesellschaft, Kultur*, edited by Hans Jürgen Mayer and Manfred Pohl, 505–509. Darmstadt: Wissenschaftliche Buchgesellschaft.

———. 2004. "Religion." In *Modern Japanese Society*, edited by Ulrich Möhwald and Hans-Dieter Ölschleger, 417–434. Leiden: Brill.

Kruhöffer, Gerald. 1999. *Der Mensch – das Bild Gottes* (Biblisch-Theologische Schwerpunkte, volume 16). Göttingen: Vandenhoeck & Ruprecht.

---

8. This book contains contributions presented at a conference of the CIVITAS Gesellschaft zur Förderung von Wissenschaft und Kunst e.V., Munich, held from 4–7 November 1984.

Kruth, Jörg. 2007. "Gedanken über die Zukunft der Familie in Japan – Eine Studie vorehelicher Partnerschaften." In *Japanstudien: Jahrbuch des Deutschen Instituts für Japanstudien: Familienangelegenheiten*, volume 19, edited by Peter Backhaus, 129–150. Munich: Iudicum Verlag.

Kubota, Nobuhiro (久保田展弘). 1997. 日本多神教の風土 (*Nihon-no tashinkyou-no fuudo*) [The climate of Japanese polytheism]. Kyoto: PHP Kenkyuujo (PHP 研究所).

Kumagai, Fumie (熊谷文枝), and Donna J. Keyser. 1996. *Unmasking Japan Today: The Impact of Traditional Values on Modern Japanese Society*. Westport CT: Greenwood Publishing.

Kümmel, Werner Georg. 1987. *Die Theologie des Neuen Testaments nach seinen Hauptzeugen Jesus, Paulus, Johannes* (Grundrisse zum Neuen Testament, NTD, Ergänzungsreihe 3). Fifth edition. Göttingen: Vandenhoeck & Ruprecht.

Küng, Hans, and John Bowden. 2006. *Tracing the Way: Spiritual Dimensions of the World Religions*. London: Continuum.

Künneth, Walter. 1954. *Politik zwischen Dämon und Gott: Eine christliche Ethik des Politischen*. Berlin: Lutherisches Verlagshaus.

Künzi, Martin. 1970. "Das Naherwartungslogion Matthäus 10, 23: Geschichte seiner Auslegung." Revised version of the thesis presented in Basel, 1967. Tübingen: Mohr Siebeck.

Kurihara, Toshie (栗原淑江). 2015. "Gender Equality of Buddhist Thought in the Age of Buddha." *The Journal of Oriental Studies* 25: 37–44. (Special Series: The Challenge of Global Transformation). Tokyo: Institute of Oriental Philosophy.

Kurita, Isamu (栗田勇). 2005. "Setsugekka: Japanese Art and the Japanese View of Nature." Special Exhibition at the MOA Museum of Art: Snow, Moon, and Flowers ("The Japanese View of Nature"). http://groups.yahoo.com/group/worldkigolibrary/message/200 (accessed 2012/10/12).

Kuroda, Toshio (黒田俊雄). 1981. "Shinto in the History of Japanese Religion." *The Journal of Japanese Studies* 7 (1): 1–21. Translated by James C. Dobbins and Suzanne Gay. Edited by the Society for Japanese Studies.

Kuroi, Senji (黒井千次). 1990. "Die Finger." In *Zeit der Zikaden: Japanisches Lesebuch: Erzählungen der Gegenwart*, edited by Tadao Araki and Ekkehard May, 59–79. Munich and Zürich: Piper.

Kusuyama, Masao (楠山正雄). No year. 松山鏡 (*matsuyama kagami*) [The Matsuyama Mirror]. Google Play Books. http://books.google.de/books?id=PMucQ-P7CFoC&dq=%E6%9D%BE%E5%B1%B1%E9%8F%A1&source=gbs_navlinks_s (accessed 13 Oct 2014).

LaFleur, William R. 1999. "A Comment Concerning Abortion Rites in Japan." *Journal of Japanese Studies* 25 (2): 493–495. Edited by The Society for Japanese Studies.

Lande, Aasulv. 1993. "The Japanese Language." In *Japanese Religions: Past and Present*, edited by Ian Reader, Esben Andreasen, and Finn Stefánnson, 21–24. Honolulu: University of Hawaii Press.

Lang, Hermann. 2003. *Wirkfaktoren der Psychotherapie*. Würzburg: Verlag Königshausen & Neumann.

Langbein, Kurt, Christian Skalnik, and Inge Smolek. 2002. *Bioterror: Die gefährlichsten Waffen der Welt: Wer sie besitzt. Was sie bewirken. Wie man sich schützen kann*. Stuttgart and Munich: Deutsche Verlags-Anstalt.

Lanham, Betty B. 1986. "Ethics and Moral Precepts Taught in Schools of Japan and the United States." In *Japanese Culture and Behavior: Selected Readings*, edited by Takie Sugiyama-Lebra and William P. Lebra, 280–296. Honolulu: University of Hawaii Press.

Larbi, Emmanuel Kingsley. 2002. "The Nature of Continuity and Discontinuity Of Ghanaian Pentecostal Concepts of Salvation in African Cosmology." *Asian Journal of Pentecostal Studies* 5 (1): 87–106. http://connection.ebscohost.com/c/articles/6635574/nature-continuity-discontinuity-ghanaian-pentecostal-concept-salvation-african-cosmology (accessed 12 Oct 2012).

Lee, Khoon Choy. 1995. *Japan: Between Myth and Reality*. Singapore: World Scientific.

Lee, Nam-Beck. 2001. "Protestantismus und Ahnenverehrung in Korea: Entwurf einer Theologie der Erinnerung." Presented as doctoral thesis at the Ruhr-Universität, Bochum, 1999. Berlin, Hamburg and Münster: LIT Verlag.

Leeming, David Adams. 2001. *A Dictionary of Asian Mythology*. Oxford: Oxford University Press.

Leibniz, Gottfried Wilhelm. 2002 (Original 1705). "Discours sur la théologie naturelle des Chinois." In *Discours sur la théologie naturelle des Chinois*, edited by Gottfried Wilhelm Leibniz, Wenchao Li, Nicolò Longobardi, Hans Poser, and Nicolas Malebranche, 15–112. Frankfurt am Main: Vittorio Klostermann.

Leighton, Taigen Daniel. 2001. "Sacred Fools and Monastic Rules: Zen Rule-Bending and the Training for Pure Hearts." In *Purity of Heart and Contemplation: A Monastic Dialogue Between Christian and Asian Traditions*, edited by Bruno Barnhart and Joseph Wong, 151–164. London: Continuum.

Leighton, Taigen Daniel, and Joan Halifax. 2003. *Faces of Compassion: Classic Bodhisattva Archetypes and Their Modern Expression*. Somerville, MA: Wisdom Publications.

Lennan, Richard. 1998. *An Introduction to Catholic Theology*. New York: Paulist Press.

Lenz, Ilse. 1990. "Hausarbeit als Beruf und Berufung." In *Nippons neue Frauen*, edited by Ruth Linhart and Fleur Wöss, 73–92. Reinbeck bei Hamburg: Rowohlt Taschenbuch Verlag GmbH.

LEO Online-Service. 2006. N.p.: LEO GmbH.

Leonard, George. 1999. *The Power of Ki*. Evolutionary Theory, An Esalen Invitational Conference, 14–19 November 1999. http://www.esalenctr.org/display/confpage.cfm?confid=5&pageid=63&pgtype=1 (accessed 10 Oct 2012).

Leroi-Gourhan, Arlette, and André Leroi-Gourhan. 1995. *Eine Reise zu den Ainu: Hokkaido 1938*. Zürich: Amman Verlag & Co.

Levison, John R., and Priscilla Pope-Levison. 1994. "Toward an Ecumenical Christology for Asia." *Missiology* 22 (1): 3–17.

Lewis, C. S. 1946. *The Great Divorce*. N.p.: Macmillan.

———. 1986a (1942).[9] *The Screwtape Letters: Letters from a Senior to a Junior Devil*. Fourth edition. London: Collins, Fount Paperbacks.

———. 1986b (1950). *The Lion, the Witch and the Wardrobe*, 21st edition. London: Fontana Lions (Collins Publishing Group).

———. 1986c (1954). *The Horse and His Boy*, 16th edition. London: Fontana Lions (Collins Publishing Group).

———. 1986d (1947). "On Forgiveness." In *Fern-Seed and Elephants*, edited by Walter Hooper, 39–44. London: Fontana Lions (Collins Publishing Group).

Lewis, David C. 1993. *The Unseen Face of Japan*. Tunbridge Wells, Kent: Monarch.

Lienhart, Elfriede. n.d. *Was ist Reiki?* http://www.elflien.at/Angebote/Was%20ist%20 Reiki.htm (accessed 12 Oct 2012).

Lightner, Robert P. 1998. *The God of the Bible and Other Gods: Is the Christian God Unique among World Religions?* Grand Rapids, MI: Kregel.

Lim, David, and Steve Spaulding. 2003. *Sharing Jesus in the Buddhist World*. South Pasadena, CA: William Carey Library.

Lindblad, Bengt. 2000. *Secrets of Aikido – Volume One – A New Jersey Ki Society Manual*. New Jersey: New Jersey Ki Society. http://www.reocities.com/Tokyo/dojo/1804/soa1/soa1.html (accessed 13 Oct 2012).

Linhart, Sepp. 1984a. "Arbeit und Betrieb." In *Japan-Handbuch*, edited by Horst Hammitzsch, 531–546. Second edition. Stuttgart: Franz Steiner Verlag Wiesbaden GmbH.

———. 1984b. "Macht über Küche, Kasse, Kinder: Die Frau in der Familie." In *Die Frau in Japan* (OAG-Reihe Japan modern, volume 1, 2), edited by Gebhard Hielscher, 87–105. N.p.: Erich Schmidt Verlag.

Link-Wieczorek, Ulrike. 1991. "Reden von Gott in Afrika und Asien: Darstellung und Interpretation afrikanischer Theologie im Vergleich mit der koreanischen Minjung-Theologie." Presented as doctoral thesis at the Universität Erlangen-Nürnberg, 1989, Göttingen: Vandenhoeck & Ruprecht.

Linrothe, Rob. 1999. *Ruthless Compassion: Wrathful Deities in Early Indo-Tibetan Esoteric Buddhist Art*. Chicago, IL: Serindia Publications.

---

9. A dictionary for old proverbs.

Locher, Gottfried Wilhelm, and Ulrich Zwingli. 1981. *Zwingli's Thought: New Perspectives.* Leiden: Brill.

Lochman, Jan Milič. 1975. *Marx begegnen: Was Christen und Marxisten eint und trennt.* Volume 104 of Gütersloher Taschenbücher; GTB; 104. Second edition. Gütersloh: Gütersloher Verlagshaus Mohn.

Loewen, Jacob A. 1986. "Which God Do Missionaries Preach." *Missiology* 14 (1): 3–19.

———. 1991. "Which God Do Missionaries Preach." In *Engaging the Enemy: How to Fight and Defeat Territorial Spirits,* edited by C. Peter Wagner, 165–175. Ventura, CA: Regal Books, a division of Gospel Light.

Lohse, Bernhard. 1994. *Epochen der Dogmengeschichte.* Berlin, Hamburg and Münster: LIT Verlag.

———. 1995. *Luthers Theologie in ihrer historischen Entwicklung und in ihrem systematischen Zusammenhang.* Göttingen: Vandenhoeck & Ruprecht.

Long, Bruce J. 1981. "Astrology." In *Abingdon Dictionary of Living Religions,* edited by Keith Crim, 71–75. Nashville, TN: Abingdon.

Lopez, Donald S. Jr. 2007. "Introduction." In *Buddhism in Practice: Abridged Edition,* edited by Donal S. Lopez Jr., 3–38. Princeton, NJ: Princeton University Press.

Loretz, Oswald. 1984. *Habiru-hebräer: Eine Sozio-linguistische Studie über die Herkunft des Gentiliziums íbrî vom Appellativum Habiru.* Berlin and New York: Walter de Gruyter.

Lose, David. J. 2003. *Confessing Jesus Christ: Preaching in a Postmodern World.* Grand Rapids, MI: Eerdmans.

Lössl, Josef. 1997. *Intellectus Gratia: Die erkenntnistheoretische & hermeneutische Dimension der Gnadenlehre Augustins von Hippo.* Leiden: Brill.

Low, Douglas. 2000. "Corporate Personality." In *Eerdmans Dictionary of the Bible,* edited by David Noel Freedman, Allen C. Myers, and Astrid B. Beck, 285–287. Grand Rapids, MI: Eerdmans.

Lüddeckens, Dorothea. 2002. *Das Weltparlament der Religionen von 1893: Strukturen interreligiöser Begegnung im 19. Jahrhundert.* Berlin and New York: Walter de Gruyter.

Lundell, Peter N. 1995. "Behind Japan's Resistant Web: Understanding the Problem of Nihonkyo." *Missiology* 23 (4): 401–412.

Luther, Martin. 1862. *Dr. Martin Luthers doppelte Hauspostille.* Edited by Ernst Ludwig Enders. Volume 1, second edition. Frankfurt am Main und Erlangen: Verlag von Heyder und Zimmer.

———. 1983. *Tischreden: Die Werke Martin Luthers in neuer Auswahl für die Gegenwart.* Edited by Kurt Aland. Göttingen: Vandenhoeck & Ruprecht.

———. 1987 (1531). *Der Galaterbrief* (Epistelauslegung). Second edition. Edited by Hermann Kleinknecht. Göttingen: Vandenhoeck & Ruprecht.

———. 1891. *Dr. Martin Luthers Werke: Kritische Gesamtausgabe.* Volume 12. Wien, Köln and Weimar: H. Böhlau.

Lutherjohann, Martin. 1998. *Kulturschock Japan*. Fourth, updated edition. Bielefeld/Brackwede: Reise Know-How Verlag Peter Rump GmbH.

Lutum, Peter. 2005. *Das Denken von Minakata Kumagusu und Yanagita Kunio*. Berlin, Hamburg and Münster: LIT Verlag.

Lwamba, Enos. 2013. *Safari Based Theology: Context, Methodology, & Application of a Motif to Theology and Mission in Africa*. Bloomington, IN: AuthorHouse (eBook).

Lyons, John. 1971. *Einführung in die moderne Linguistik*. Munich: C. H. Beck'sche Verlagsbuchhandlung [Oscar Beck].

Ma, Julie C. 2007. "Pentecostalism and Asian Mission." *Missiology* 35 (1): 23–37.

Ma'ax, K'ayum, and Christian Rätsch. 1984. *Ein Kosmos im Regenwald: Mythen und Visionen der Lakandonen-Indianer*. Köln: Eugen Diederichs Verlag (Diederichs Gelbe Reihe).

Mabuchi, Touichi (馬淵東一). 1976 "A Note on Ancestor Worship in 'Cognatic' Societies" In *Ancestors*, edited by William Hare Newell, 105–118. Prepared as paper for the Ninth International Congress of Anthropological and Ethnological Sciences in Chicago, 1973. Berlin and New York: Walter de Gruyter.

Mace, François. 1993. "Japanese Conceptions of the Afterlife." In *Asian Mythologies*, edited by Yves Bonnefoy and Wendy Doniger, 270–274. London and Chicago: University of Chicago Press.

MacFarlane, Alan. 1997. *The Savage Wars of Peace: England, Japan and the Malthusian Trap*. Oxford: Wiley-Blackwell.

Mae, Michiko (前みち子), and Julia Schmitz. 2007. "Zwischen Öffentlichkeit und Privatheit: Die moderne Familie in Japan und Deutschland bis 1945." In *Japanstudien: Jahrbuch des Deutschen Instituts für Japanstudien: Familienangelegenheiten*, volume 19, edited by Peter Backhaus, 49–80. Munich: Iudicum Verlag.

Maier, Gerhard. 1981. *Die Johannesoffenbarung und die Kirche* (Wissenschaftliche Untersuchungen zum Neuen Testament, 25). Tübingen: Mohr Siebeck.

———. 1982. *Der Prophet Daniel*. Wuppertaler Studienbibel. Wuppertal: R. Brockhaus Verlag.

———. 1990. *Biblische Hermeneutik*. Wuppertal: TVG.

Makimoto, Yuugo (槇本有吾). 2006. 「人間」をめぐる「幽霊」の話 (*"ningen"-o meguru "yuurei"-no hanashi*) [On "ghosts" that surround "humans"]. Tokyo: Bungeisha (文芸社).

Malek, Roman. 1992. "Ahnenkult: In Ostasien." In *Lexikon der Religionen: Phänomene, Geschichte, Ideen*, founded by Franz Kardinal König, edited by Hans Waldenfels, 17–18. Second edition. Freiburg, Basel, Wien: Herder.

Malley, Brian. 2004. *How the Bible Works: An Anthropological Study of Evangelical Biblicism*. Lanham, MD: Rowman Altamira.

Ma Mpolo, Masamba. 1986. *Les personnes Âgées et leurs Familles dans une Société Rural Changeante: Le Cas de la République du Zaïre*. Kinshasa, Zaire: EDICVA.

Mann, A. T. 1995. *Prophezeiungen zur Jahrtausendwende: Eine Gesamtschau der Voraussagen von Propheten, Weisen, Sehern, Schamanen und Astrologen für das neue Jahrtausend*. Translated by Hans Freundl. Bern, Munich, Wien: Scherz.

Manzanera, Miguel. 1974. "Theologie der Befreiung: Ansatzpunkte – Ziel – Methode." In *Theologie und Befreiung*, edited by Heribert Bettscheider, 39–73. N.p.: Steyler Verlag.

Maraldo, John C. 1995. "Questioning Nationalism Now and Then: A Critical Approach to Zen and the Kyoto School." In *Rude Awakenings: Zen, the Kyoto School, and the Question of Nationalism*, edited by James W. Heisig, and John C. Maraldo, 333–364. Honolulu: University of Hawaii Press.

Marran, Christine L. 2007. *Poison Woman: Figuring Female Transgression in Modern Japanese Culture*. Minneapolis, MN: University of Minnesota Press.

Marsden, George M. 2006. *Fundamentalism and American Culture*. Oxford: Oxford University Press.

Marttila, Marko. 2006. *Collective Reinterpretation in the Psalms: A Study of the Redaction History of the Psalter* (Forschungen zum Alten Testament 2. Reihe). Tübingen: Mohr Siebeck.

Maruyama, Masao (丸山眞男). 1988 (1946 in Sekai). "Logik und Psyche des Ultranationalsozialismus." In *Japan ohne Mythos: Zehn kritische Essays aus japanischer Feder, 1946–1963*, edited and translated Karl Friedrich Zahl, 37–59. Munich: Iudicium Verlag GmbH.

Masaki, Akira (正木晃), and Isako Nakao (中尾伊早子). 2007. よくわかる！神社神宮 (*yoku wakaru! Jinja jinguu*) [Prefect knowledge! Shrines and main shrines]. Kyoto: PHP Kenkyuujo (PHP研究所).

Mase-Hasegawa, Emi (間瀬・長谷川恵美). 2008. *Christ in Japanese Culture: Theological Themes in Shusaku Endo's Literary Works*. Volume 28 of Brill's Japanese Studies Library. Leiden: Brill.

Mason, J. W. T. 2002. *The Meaning of Shinto*. Victoria, BC: Trafford Publishing.

Matson, Alesia. 2004. *7 Mysteries: Contemplative Arts for the Modern Mystic*. Second edition. Jyväskylä: Metaphor Publications.

Matsubara, Hisako (松原久子). 1983. *Weg zu Japan: West-östliche Erfahrungen*. Munich: A. Knaus.

Matsubara, Taidou (松本泰道). 1994. 仏教をひらく言葉 (*bukkyou-o hiraku kotoba*) [Words that open buddhism]. Tokyo: Mizushobou (水書房).

Matsuda, Kaoru (松田薫). 1994. 血液型と性格の社会史：血液人類学の起源と展開 (*ketsuekigata-to seikaku-no shakaishi: ketsugatajinruigaku-no kigen-to tenkai*) [Social history of blood type and personality: Origin and development of blood type anthropology]. Tokyo: Kawade Shoboushinsha (河出書房新社).

Matsuda, Shigezou. 2002. "慢性疲労症候群：加味逍遥散などの柴胡剤が効果免疫力がしっかり元気に (*Manseihiroushou kougun: kamishouyousan nado-no saikosai-ga kouka menekiryoku-ga shikkari genki-ni*) [The vast group of candidates of the chronic fatigue syndrome: On a strong health of the effective immune-system using Seiko-medication such as *kami-shouyousen*]." In 漢方辞典：名医と治す (*kanpoujiten: meii-to naosu*) [Encyclopedia of chinese traditional medicine: Healing together with the physician], edited by weekly journal Shuukan Asahi (週刊朝日), 327–330. Tokyo: Asahi Shinbunsha (朝日新聞社).

Matsumoto, David Ricky. 1996. *Unmasking Japan: Myths and Realities about the Emotions of the Japanese*. Palo Alto, CA: Stanford University Press.

Matsumoto, Shigeru (松本茂). 1972. "Introduction." In *Japanese Religion: A Survey by the Agency of Cultural Affairs*, edited by Ichiro Hori, Fuji Ikado, Tsuneya Wakimoto and Keiichi Yanagawa, 11–27. First edition, second print. Tokyo: Koudansha International. New York und San Francisco, CA: Kondansha International/USA.

Matsumoto, Yukiko. 2001. "Japan's 'parasite singles.'" *BBC News*. http://news.bbc.co.uk/2/hi/asia-pacific/1362106.stm (accessed 16 May 2016).

Matsunaga, Yuukei (松長有慶). 2008. こだわらない (*kodawaranai*) [Easygoing]. Kyoto: PHP Kenkyuujo (PHP研究所).

Matsuoka, Fumitaka. 1971. "Christianity in Japan: An Observation." *International Review of Mission* 60 (239): 373–381.

Maurer, Chr. 1976. "Die Einheit der Menschheit in biblischer Sicht." In *Um Einheit und Heil der Menschheit*, edited by J. Robert Nelson and Wolfhart Pannenberg, 49–74. Second edition. Frankfurt am Main: Verlag Otto Lembeck.

Mayer, Hans-Jürgen. 1994. "Minderheiten: Probleme und Perspektiven." In *Länderbericht Japan: Geographie, Geschichte, Politik, Wirtschaft, Gesellschaft, Kultur*, edited by Hans-Jürgen Mayer and Manfred Pohl, 119–124. Bonn: Bundeszentrale für politische Bildung.

Mayr, Hans, and Helmuth Uhrig. 2002. *Tu dich auf* (Ergänzung zum Evangelischen Tagzeitenbuch im Auftrag des Rats der Evangelischen Michaelsbruderschaft). Göttingen: Vandenhoeck & Ruprecht.

McDowell, Bart. 1974. "Those Successful Japanese." *National Geographic* 145 (3): 322–359.

McFaul, Thomas R., and United States Congress (Joint Economic Committee). 2006. *The Future of Peace and Justice in the Global Village: The Role of the World Religions in the Twenty-first Century*. Westport, Connecticut and London: Praeger.

McGrath, Alister Edgar. 2006. *Christian Theology: An Introduction*. Fourth edition. Oxford: Blackwell.

McGrath, Alister Edgar, and Duncan Forrester. 1995. *The Blackwell Encyclopedia of Modern Christian Thought*. Oxford: Wiley-Blackwell.

McGrath, Alister Edgar, and Darren C. Marks. 2004. *The Blackwell Companion to Protestantism*. Oxford: Wiley-Blackwell.

McKinney, Carol V. 2000. "Shaman, Shamanism." In *Evangelical Dictionary of World Missions*, edited by A. Scott Moreau, Harold Netland and Charles Van Engen, 869–870. Grand Rapids, MI: Baker; and Carlisle, Cumbria: Paternoster.

McLelland, Mark J. 2000. *Male Homosexuality in Modern Japan: Cultural Myths and Social Realities*. Oxford: Routledge.

McLeod, Hugh. 2006. *World Christianities c. 1914–c. 2000*. Cambridge: Cambridge University Press.

McNabb, David E. 2016. *A Comparative History of Commerce and Industry: Converging Trends and the Future of the Global Market*. New York, NY: Palgrave MacMillian (eBook).

McVeigh, Brian. 1992. "The Vitalistic Conception of Salvation as Expressed in Sukyo Mahikari." *Japanese Journal of Religious Studies* 19 (1): 41–68. http://nirc.nanzan-u.ac.jp/publications/jjrs/pdf/358.pdf (accessed 13 Oct 2012).

Medd, Iola Lyttle. 2003. *Sunshine and Shadows: Remembering Nagasaki*. Bloomington, IN: iUniverse.

Melanchthon, Philipp. 1988. *Das Augsburger Bekenntnis Deutsch: 1530–1980*. Revised text, edited by Günther Gassmann and Niels Hasselmann. Göttingen: Vandenhoeck & Ruprecht.

Melton, Gordon J., ed. 2011. *Religious Celebrations: An Encyclopedia of Holidays, Festivals, Solemn Observances, and Spiritual Commemorations*. Volume 1. Santa Barbara, CA; Denver, CO; Oxford: ABC-Clio.

Mendenhall, George E., and Gary A. Herion. 2001. *Ancient Israel's Faith and History: An Introduction to the Bible in Context*. Louisville, KY: Westminster John Knox Press.

Menge, Hermann. 1981. *Langenscheidts Großwörterbuch Griechisch-Deutsch: Unter Berücksichtigung der Etymologie*. 24th edition. Berlin, Munich, Wien, Zürich: Langenscheidt.

Mette, Norbert. 2007. *Praktisch-theologische Erkundungen 2*. Theologie und Praxis, volume 32. Münster, Hamburg and London: LIT Verlag.

Metzger, Gilbert. 2006. *Liang Qichao, China und der Westen nach dem ersten Weltkrieg: Ein Viertel der Menschheit hat gegenüber der gesamten Menschheit die Verpflichtung für ein Viertel ihres Glücks*. Berlin, Hamburg and Münster: LIT Verlag.

Meuthtrath, Annette. 2006. "Theologie aus der Sicht asiatischer Frauen." *Stimmen der Zeit* 4: 253–265. http://www.con-spiration.de/texte/2006/asiawomen.html (accessed 13 Oct 2012).

Michel, Otto. 1978. *Der Brief an die Römer* (Meyers kritisch-exegetischer Kommentar über das Neue Testament). Last edition by Otto Michel, 1966. Göttingen: Vandenhoeck & Ruprecht.

Melanowicz, Mikolaj. 1981. "The Cry of a Moralist: On Ôe Kannzaburô's World of Ideas." In *Transcultural Understanding and Modern Japan: Fourth Symposium by Toukai University, held at the Ruhr University, Bochum, West Germany, October 1981*, edited by Klaus Kracht and Helmuth Morsbach, 88–102. Bochum: Studienverlag Dr. Norbert Brockmeyer.

Michalson, Carl. 1962. *Japanische Theologie der Gegenwart*. Gütersloh: Gütersloher Verlagshaus Gerd Mohn.

Miller, Roy Andrew. 1993. *Die japanische Sprache: Geschichte und Struktur.* Volume 4 of Reihe: Monographien aus dem Deutschen Institut für Japanstudien der Philipp-Franz-Seibold-Stiftung. Munich: Iudicum Verlag.

Min, Anselm Kyongsuk. 1989. *Dialectic of Salvation: Issues in Theology of Liberation.* Albany, NY: SUNY Press.

Minamoto, Ryoen (源了圓). 1986. "Giri und Ninjo in der japanischen Gesellschaft." In *Gewissen und soziale Kontrolle in Japan und Deutschland*, edited by Anke Wiegand-Kanzaki, and Shin'ichi Minamioji, 57–68. Würzburg: Königshausen and Neumann.

Mitsuhashi, Takeshi (三橋健). 1995. "神道とその歴史 (*shintou-to sono rekishi*) [Shintosim and its history]" In 神道：わが家の宗教 (*shintou: waga ie-no shuukyou*) [Shintoism: Religion of our house], edited by Takeshi Mitsuhashi, 10–43. Tokyo: Ouhouronkaku (大法論閣).

———. 2007. 神道の常識がわかる小事典 (*shintou-no joushiki-ga wakaru shoujiten*) [Small dictionary for general knowledge of shintoism]. Kyoto: PHP Kenkyuujo (PHP研究所).

Miura, Oto (三浦於菟). 2005. こころと体に効く漢方学 (*kokoro-to karada-ni kiku kanpougaku*) [Chinese medicine working for heart and body]. Tokyo: Shinchousensho (新湖選書).

Miyahira, Nozomu (宮平臨). 2008. "Christian Theology under Feudalism, Nationalism, and Democracy in Japan." In *Christian Theology in Asia*, edited by Sebastian C. H. Kim, 109–129. Cambridge: Cambridge University Press.

Miyamoto, Arata. 2010. *Embodied Cross: Intercontextual Reading of Theologia Crucis.* Eugene, OR: Wipf & Stock.

Miyata, Mitsuo (宮田光雄). 1984. *Mündigkeit und Solidarität: Christliche Verantwortung in der heutigen japanischen Gesellschaft.* Gütersloh: Gütersloher Verlagshaus Gerd Mohn.

———. 2009. *Authority and Obedience: Romans 13:1–7 in Modern Japan.* Volume 294 of American University Studies: Theology and Religion, translated by Gregory Vanderbilt. New York: Peter Lang.

Miyata, Noboru (宮田登). 1998. 七福神信仰事典 (*Shichifukuijin Shinkou Jiten*) [Dictionary for the faith in the Seven Auspicious Deities]. Tokyo: Ebisu Koushou Publication (戎光祥出版株式会社).

Moisio, Olli-Pekka. n.d. *Human Beings Do Not Eat in Order to Live, but Because They Live: Ernst Bloch on Wishful Imagination, Hope and Hunger.* https://www.academia.edu/4362605/Human_Beings_Do_not_Eat_in_Order_to_Live_but_because_they_Live_Ernst_Bloch_on_Wishful_Imagination_Hope_and_Hunger (accessed 14 Mar 2016).

Moltmann, Jürgen. 1966. *Theologie der Hoffnung: Untersuchungen zur Begründung und zu den Konsequenzen einer christlichen Eschatologie.* Sixth revised edition. Munich: Chr. Kaiser Verlag.

———. 1971. *Mensch: Christliche Anthropologie in den Konflikten der Gegenwart*. Themen der Theologie, volume 11, edited by Hans Jürgen Schultz. Stuttgart and Berlin: Kreuz-Verlag.

———. 1976. "Die Einheit des Menschengeschlechts in der Perspektive des christlichen Glaubens." In *Um Einheit und Heil der Menschheit*, edited by J. Robert Nelson and Wolfhart Pannenberg, 213–234. Second edition. Frankfurt am Main: Verlag Otto Lembeck.

———. 1987. *Der gekreuzigte Gott: Das Kreuz Christi als Grund und Kritik christlicher Theologie*. Fifth edition. Munich: Chr. Kaiser Verlag.

———. 1988. *Was ist heute Theologie?: Zwei Beiträge ihrer Vergegenwärtigung*. Freiburg, Basel und Wien: Herder.

———. 2002. *Theology of Hope*. Translation of *Theologie der Hoffnung*, fifth edition, 1965. Translated by James W. Leitch. Second English edition. London: SCM.

Monnet, Livia. 2007. "Invasion of the Women Snatchers: The Problem of A-Live and the Uncanny in Final Fantasy: The Spirits Within." In *Robot Ghosts and Wired Dreams: Japanese Science Fiction from Origins to Anime*, edited by Christopher Bolton, Istvan Csicsery-Ronay, and Takayuki Tatsumi, 193–221. Minneapolis, MN: University of Minnesota Press.

Morean, Brian. 1986. "Individual, Group and Seishin: Japan's Internal Cultural Debate." In *Japanese Culture and Behavior: Selected Readings*, edited by Takie Sugiyama-Lebra, and William P. Lebra, 62–79. Revised edition. Honolulu: University of Hawaii Press.

Moreau, A. Scott. 2000. "Occultist; Occultism." In *Evangelical Dictionary of World Missions*, edited by A. Scott Moreau, Harold Netland and Charles Van Engen, 703. Grand Rapids, MI: Baker; and Carlisle, Cumbria: Paternoster.

———. 2012. *Contextualization in World Missions: Mapping and Assessing Evangelical Models*. Grand Rapids, MI: Kregel.

Mori, Sakutarou (森作太郎). 1927. 心靈研究と新宗教 (*shinreikenkyuu-to shinshuukyou*) [Parapsychological Research and the New Religions]. Tokyo: Shinreikagakukenkyuukai (心霊科学研究会).

Mori, Takeo, and Dragan Milenkovic. 1995. *Die Geheimnisse der japanischen Astrologie: Ein einführendes Handbuch zur Persönlichkeitsanalyse; Fünf Elemente, neun Sterne und zwölf Tierkreiszeichen weisen den Weg zur richtigen Entscheidung*. Aitrang: Windpferd Verlagsgesellschaft mbH; Reihe: Schangrila.

Morisaki, Seiichi (守﨑誠一), and William B. Gudykunst. 1994. "Face in Japan and the United States." In *The Challenge of Facework: Cross-Cultural and Interpersonal Issues*, edited by Stella Ting-Toomey, 47–94. Albany, NY: SUNY Press.

Moriguchi, Katsu (森口豁). 2005. 子乞い: 沖縄孤島の歳月 (*kogoi: Okinawa-kotou-no saigetsu*; *Child Beggary*) [Days on Lonesome Okinawa]. Yokohama: Shunpusha (春風社).

Morita, Shouma (森田正馬). 1998. *Morita Therapy and The True Nature of Anxiety-Based Disorders (Shinkeishitsu)*. Translated by Akihisa Kondou. Albany, NY: SUNY Press.

Morita, Takashi. 2001. "Der Naturbegriff der japanischen Kultur." In 11. Deutschsprachiger Japanologentag in Trier 1999: Sprache, Literatur, Kunst, Populärkultur, Medien, Informationstechnik, edited by Hilaria Gössmann and Andreas Mrugalla, 251–260. Berlin, Hamburg and Münster: LIT Verlag.

Morris, Ivan. 1994. *The World of the Shining Prince: Court Life in Ancient Japan*. Tokyo: Koudansha Globe.

Morsbach, Helmut. 1983. "Report on Critiques of the Oversimplified Nakane-Doi Model of Japanese Social Interaction." Transcultural Understanding and Modern Japan: Fourth Symposium by Toukai University, held at the Ruhr University, Bochum, West Germany, October 1981, edited by Klaus Kracht and Helmuth Morsbach, 45–52. Bochum: Studienverlag Dr. Norbert Brockmeyer.

Morton, Jeff. 2012. *Insider Movements: Biblically Incredible or Incredibly Brilliant?* Eugene, OR: Wipf & Stock.

Mughal, Humayun A. 2001. イスラムは日本を変えるか?: 国際結婚はグローバル化の切り札 (*Isuramu-wa Nihon-o kaeruno-ka?: kokusaikekkon-wa guroobaruka-no kirifuda*) [Will Islam change Japan?: International marriages as trump card of globalization]. Tokyo: Bungeisha (文芸社).

Muirhead, Enid L. 2005. "Spirituality and Holistic Healing Modalities: Creating a Place in Wellness Promotion." Lecture at the University of British Columbia School of Nursing. http://www.spirit.nursing.ubc.ca/Downloads/Modalities_Muirhead.pdf.

Müller, Karl. 1985. "Das Ziel der Mission." In *Missionstheologie: Eine Einführung von Karl Müller mit Beiträgen von Hans-Werner Gensichen und Horst Rzepkowski*, edited by Karl Müller, 61–85. Frankfurt am Main: Dietrich Reimer Verlag.

Müller-Fahrenholz, Geiko. 1974. *Heilsgeschichte zwischen Ideologie und Prophetie: Profile und Kritik heilsgeschichtlicher Theorien in der ökumenischen Bewegung zwischen 1948 und 1968*. Freiburg, Basel und Wien: Herder.

Müller-Karpe, Hermann. 2009. *Religionsarchäologie: Archäologische Beiträge zur Religionsgeschichte*. Frankfurt am Main: Verlag Otto Lembeck.

Mulligan, John. 1857. *Exposition of the Grammatical Structure of the English Language: Being an Attempt to Furnish an Improved Method of Teaching Grammar. For the Use of Schools and Colleges*. New York: D. Appleton & Co.

Mullins, Mark R. 1998. *Christianity Made in Japan: A Study of Indigenous Movements*. Honolulu: University of Hawaii Press.

Murakami, Haruki (村上春樹). 1990. "Ein Elefant verschwindet." In *Zeit der Zikaden: Japanisches Lesebuch: Erzählungen der Gegenwart*, edited by Tadao Araki and Ekkehard May, 104–127. Munich and Zürich: Piper.

———. 1994. *The Elephant Vanishes: Stories*. New York: Vintage Books.

———. 2002. *Untergrundkrieg: Der Anschlag von Tokyo*. Köln: DuMont Literatur und Kunst Verlag.

———. 2005. 象の消滅 (*Zou-no shoumetsu*) [The vanishing of an elephant]. Tokyo: Shinchousha (新潮社).

Nadin, Mihai. 1997. *The Civilization of Illiteracy*. N.p.: Dresden University Press.

Naka, Uryuu (中瓜生). 2006. 仏像鑑賞が10倍楽しくなる (*butsuzou kanshou-ga juubai tanoshiku naru*) [The appreciation of buddha statues becomes ten times more fun]. Kyoto: PHP Kenkyuujo (PHP研究所).

Nakae, Katsumi (中江克己). 1998. 日本史怖くて不思議な出来事 (*Nihonshi kowakute fushigi-na dekigoto*) [Scary and strange incidences in Japanese history]. Kyoto: PHP Kenkyuujo (PHP研究所).

Nakajima, Ryouichi (中島亮一). 2003. 日本人の信仰思想のすがた: 古代・中世篇 (*Nihonjin-no shinkoushisou-no sugata: kodai, chuuseihen*) [The form of the religious thoughts of the Japanese: Antiquity and middle ages]. Tokyo: Bungeisha (文芸社).

Nakajou, Setsuko (中条節子). 1999. 救いの切符 (*sukui-no kippu*) [Ticket of salvation]. Tokyo: Bungeisha (文芸社).

Nakamaki, Hirochika (中牧弘允). 2003. *Japanese Religions at Home and Abroad: Anthropological Perspectives*. London: Routledge.

Nakamura, Hajime (中村元). 1967. "Basic Features of the Legal, Political, and Economic Thought of Japan." In *The Japanese Mind: Essentials of Japanese Philosophy and Culture*, edited by Charles A. Moore, 143–163. Eighth edition. Honolulu: University of Hawaii Press.

———. 1998. *A Comparative History of Ideas*. Delhi: Motilal Banarsidass.

Nakamura, Hajime (中村元), and Philip P. Wiener. 1964. *Ways of Thinking of Eastern Peoples: India, China, Tibet, Japan*. Honolulu: University of Hawaii Press.

Nakane, Chie (中根千枝). 1970. *Japanese Society*. Berkeley and Los Angeles, CA: University of California Press.

———. 1978. タテ社会に力学 (*Tateshakai-no Rikigaku*) [Mechanics of a vertical society], third edition. Tokyo: Koudansha (講談社).

———. 1984. "Criteria of Group Formation." In *Japan-Handbuch*, edited by Horst Hammitzsch, 171–185. Second edition. Stuttgart: Franz Steiner Verlag Wiesbaden GmbH.

Nash, Ronald H. 1992. *Worldviews in Conflict: Choosing Christianity in a World of Ideas*. Grand Rapids, MI: Zondervan; Academic and Professional Books (a division of Harper Collins).

Naturalists: Webster's Quotations, Facts and Phrases, edited by ICON Group International. 2008. San Diego, CA: ICON Group International.

Naumann, Nelly. 1984a. "Ahnenkult." In *Japan-Handbuch*, edited by Horst Hammitzsch, 1541–1544. Second edition. Stuttgart: Franz Steiner Verlag Wiesbaden GmbH.

———. 1984b. "Seelenglaube." In *Japan-Handbuch*, edited by Horst Hammitzsch, 1630–1632. Second edition. Stuttgart: Franz Steiner Verlag Wiesbaden GmbH.

———. 1996. *Die Mythen des alten Japan*. Munich. C. H. Beck'sche Verlagsbuchhandlung (Oscar Beck).

Naumann, Nelly, Jan G. P. Best, and Fred Woudhuizen. 1988. *Die einheimische Religion Japans: Teil 1: Bis zum Ende der Heian-Zeit* (Handbuch der Orientalistik). Edited by B. Spuler. Leiden: E. J. Brill.

Naumann, Nelly, and Wolfram Naumann. 1990. *Die Zauberschale: Erzählungen vom Leben japanischer Damen, Mönche, Herren und Knechte*. Munich: Deutscher Taschenbuch Verlag GmbH & Co. KG.

Naumann, Nelly, Makio Takemura, (竹村牧男), and Yoshiro Tamura (田村芳朗). 1984. "Gottheiten." In *Japan-Handbuch*, edited by Horst Hammitzsch, 1578–1588. Second edition. Stuttgart: Franz Steiner Verlag Wiesbaden GmbH.

Nauwald, Nana. 2012. *Der Flug des Schamanen: Schamanische Märchen und Mythen*. Norderstedt: BoD – Books on Demand.

Nawrocki, Johann. "1998 Inoue Tetsujirô (1855–1944) und die Ideologie des Götterlandes: Eine vergleichende Studie zur politischen Theologie des modernen Japan." Presented as dissertation at the Universität Hamburg, 1997, Berlin, Hamburg and Münster: LIT Verlag.

———. 2001. "Zur Ideengeschichte des Shintō im Nachkriegs-Japan: Hori Ichirō 堀一郎 (1910–1974) und das *saisei bunri* 祭政分離." In *11. Deutschsprachiger Japanologentag in Trier 1999: Sprache, Literatur, Kunst, Populärkultur, Medien, Informationstechnik*, edited by Hilaria Gössmann und Andreas Mrugalla, 207–212. Berlin, Hamburg and Münster: LIT Verlag.

Ndabiseruye, Alphonse. 2002. "Burundische und biblische Sprichwörter über den Frieden: Ihr Beitrag und ihre Verwendung im Religionsunterricht in Burundi." Presented as inaugural doctoral (Catholic theology) thesis at the Albert-Ludwigs-Universität Freiburg im Breisgau. http://www.freidok.uni-freiburg.de/volltexte/446 (accessed 13 Oct 2012).

Nelle-Rublack, Ursula. 1999. *Der modernisierte Strafprozess: Zur Soziologie konsensorientierter Wirtschaftsverfahren*. Berlin, Hamburg and Münster: LIT Verlag.

Nelson, Andrew Nathanael. 1992. *The Modern Reader's Japanese-English Character Dictionary:* 最新漢英辞典 (*saishin kan-ei jiten*) [Latest Chinese-English Dicitionary]. Second revised edition. 36th edition. Rutland, VT, and Tokyo: Charles E. Tuttle Company.

Nelson, John K. 1996. *A Year in the Life of a Shinto Shrine*. Seattle, WA: University of Washington Press.

———. 1997. "Warden + Virtuoso + Salaryman = Priest: Paradigms within Japanese Shinto for Religious Specialists and Institutions." *The Journal of Asian Studies* 56 (3): 678–707. Edited by the Association for Asian Studies.

Nemeto, Misako. 2002. "Mondernité Fictive." In *La modernité après le post-moderne*, edited by Henri Meschonnic, and Shigehiko Hasumi, 51–60. Paris: Maisonneuve & Larose.

Nesbitt, Mariana. 2007. "Japanese Ancestral Practices: A Contextualized Teaching Tool in the Afterlife in the Local Church (Hibachi Theology)." Presented as Master of theology thesis at the South African Theological Seminary. https://www.sats.edu.za/userfiles/Nesbitt%20MTh%20Thesis%2012%20Jul%202007.pdf (accessed 7 Apr 2017).

Neuhold, Leopold. 2000 "Religion und katholische Soziallehre im Wandel vor allem der Werte: Erscheinungsbilder und Chancen." Presented as habilitation treatise at the Universität Graz, 1999. Berlin, Hamburg and Münster: LIT Verlag.

Neuss, Margret. 1984. "Von der Hausmutter zur Kriegshelferin: Zwischen Meiji-Restauration und 2. Weltkrieg." In *Die Frau in Japan* (OAG-Reihe Japan modern, volume 1), edited by Gebhard Hielscher, 41–63. Second edition. N.p.: Erich Schmidt Verlag.

Nickel, Joachim. 2002. "Reiki – Die universelle Lebensenergie: Was ist Reiki? – Eine Kurzeinleitun." http://www.lichtinfo.net/reiki/was-ist.shtml (accessed 13 Oct 2012).

Niebuhr, Reinhold. 1958. "Sin." In *A Handbook of Christian Theology: Definition Essays on Concepts and Movements of Thought in Contemporary Protestantism*, edited by Marvin Halverson and Arthur A. Cohen, 348–351. Third edition. New York: Meridian Books (Living Age Books).

Nientiedt, Susa. 2007. *Mahakala, der große Schwarze, Shri Devi und Ekajata*. Second revised edition. Bochum: Verrückter Yogi Verlag.

Nihon Minzoku Gakkai (日本民族学会). 1999. *Bulletin of the Folklore Society of Japan*. Editions, 217–220.

Niles, D. Preman. 1982. "Christian Mission and the Peoples of Asia." *Missiology* 10 (3): 279–300.

Nishioka, Yoshiyuki Billy. 1997. *Rice and Bread: Metaphorical Construction of Reality: Toward a New Approach to World View*. Pasadena, CA: Fuller Theological Seminary.

———. 1998. "Worldview Methodology in Mission Theology: A Comparison between Kraft's and Hiebert's Approaches." *Missiology* 26 (4): 457–476.

Nishiyama, Takahiro. 2006. "Betriebliche Weiterbildung für industrielle Arbeiter in Japan: Produktionsmanagement und Qualifikationsformen in der japanischen verarbeitenden Industrie." In *Japanstudien: Jahrbuch des Deutschen Institutes für Japanstudien: Arbeitswelten in Japan*, volume 18, edited by René Haak, 181–220. Munich: IUDICUM Verlag.

Nitobe, Inazou (新渡戸稲造). 2001. *Bushido: The Soul of Japan*. Edited by William Elliot Griffis. Herts, England: IBC Publishing.

———. 2007. 武士道がよくわかる本 (*bushidou-ga yoku wakaru hon*) [A Book for a Good Understanding of Bushidou]. Kyoto: PHP-Kenkyuujo (PHP研究所).

Nnamani, Amuluche Gregory. 1995. *The Paradox of a Suffering God: On the Classical, Modern-Western and Third World Struggles to Harmonize the Incompatible Attributes of the Humanitarian God*. Volume 95 of Studies in the Intercultural History of Christianity (Études d'histoire interculturelle du christianisme.) Bern, Berlin, Bruxelles, Frankfurt am Main, New York and Wien: Peter Lang Verlagsgruppe.

Noble, Lowell L. 1975. *Naked and Not Ashamed: An Anthropological, Biblical, and Psychological Study of Shame*. Jackson, MI: Jackson Printing.

Noble, Thomas A. 1996. "The Spirit World: A Theological Approach." In *The Unseen World: Christian Reflections on Angels, Demons, and the Heavenly Realm*, edited by Anthony N. S. Lane, 185–223. Grand Rapids, MI: Tyndale House; Carlisle, Cumbria: Paternoster.

Nolte-Hamilton, Sharon. 1984. "Individualism in *Taishou* Japan." *The Journal of Asian Studies* 43 (43): 667–684. Edited by the Association for Asian Studies.

Nomura, Genryou (野村玄良). 2001. 日本語の意味の構造 (*nihongo-no imi-no kozou*) [The structure of meaning of the Japanese language]. Tokyo: Bungeisha (文芸社).

Norton, James. 1993. "Is Shintoism a Real Religion?" *Japan Journal* (Christmas 1992 and New Year 1993): 13–17.

Numazawa, Kiichi (沼澤喜一), S.V.D. 1970. "Das Menschenbild im Schintoismus." *Studia Missionalia: Man, Culture and Religion: Homme, Culture et Religion* 19: 193–214. Rome: Gregorian Biblical BookShop.

Nürnberger, Klaus. 2003. *Zuspruch des Seinsrechts: Verstellt die Lehre die Sache?* (Studien zur systematischen Theologie und Ethik). Berlin, Hamburg and Münster: LIT Verlag.

Obara (first name unknown). 1976. "Der Novize und der Fuchs." In *Japanische Märchen*, edited and translated by Toshio Ozawa, 40–41. Third edition. Frankfurt am Main: Fischer Taschenbuch Verlag GmbH.

Obeyesekere, Gananath. 1984. *The Cult of the Goddess Pattini*. Chicago: University of Chicago Press.

Odagaki, Masaya (小田垣雅也). 1992. ロマンティシズムと現代神学 (*romantishizumu-to gendai shingaku*) [Romanticism and the theology in the presence]. Tokyo: Soubunsha (創文社).

———. 1997. "Theology after 1970." In *A History of Japanese Theology*, edited by Yasuo Furuya, 113–140. Grand Rapids, MI: Eerdmans.

Oden, Robert A. 1999. *The Bible without Theology: The Theological Tradition and Alternatives to It*. Champaign, IL: University of Illinois Press.

Odin, Steve. 2001. *Artistic Detachment in Japan and the West: Psychic Distance in Comparative Aesthetics*. Honolulu: University of Hawaii Press.Ogasawara, Kinzo. 1976. "Gobudschiroh." In *Japanische Märchen*, edited and translated by

Toshio Ozawa, 62–64. Third edition. Frankfurt am Main: Fischer Taschenbuch Verlag GmbH.

Ogasawara, Kouji (小笠原孝次). 2001 (1959). "大祓祝詞の話 (*ooharae norito-no hanashi*) [On the incantation of the Great Purification]." In 会報 (*kaihou*) [Circle news]. Reprint, n.p.: *kototama & 100 deities* (言霊百神). https://sites.google.com/site/ametutinokagami/wi (accessed 16 May 2016).

Ogata, Mamoru. 1993. "The New Religion Boom." *Japan Harvest* 8.

Ogawa, Akihiro. 2015. *Lifelong Learning in Neoliberal Japan: Risk, Community, and Knowledge*. Albany: State University of New York Press.

Ogawa, Keiji (小川圭治). 1965. *Die Aufgabe der neueren evangelischen Theologie in Japan*. Basel: Verlag Friedrich Reinhardt.

Ogihara-Schuck, Eriko. 2014. *Miyazaki's Animism Abroad: The reception of Japanese Religious Themes by American and German Audiences*. Jefferson, NC: McFarland & Company.

Oguro, Tatsuo. 1982. *Die rätselhafte Nation: Mentalität und Denkweise der Japaner*. Stuttgart: Horst Poller Verlag.

Ok, Chin Chae. 2004. "Integrity of Mission in the Light of the Gospel: Bearing Witness of the Spirit: An Asian Perspective." Paper presented at the 11th International Conference of The International Association for Mission Studies, Port Dickson, Malaysia. http://missionstudies.org/archive/conference/0plenary_papers/CHUN_Chae_Ok.pdf (accessed 13 Oct 2012).

Okada, Takashi (岡田尊司). 2005. 子どもの「心の病」を知る: 児童期・青年期とどう向き合うか (*kodomo-no "kokoro-no yamai"-o shiru: youjiki, seinenki-to dou mukiau-ka*) [Knowing about children's "heart grieves": How to encounter children and youths?]. Kyoto: PHP Kenkyuujo (PHP研究所).

Okakura, Kakuzo (岡倉覚三). 2006 (1904). 東洋の理想 (*touyou-no risou*) [Ideals of the east and the west]: *Ideal of the East with Special Reference to the Art of Japan*. Herts, UK: IBC Publishing.

Okano, Haruko (岡野治子). 1976. *Die Stellung der Frau im Shinto: Eine religionsphänomenologische und -soziologische Untersuchung*. Studies in Oriental Religions, volume 1. Wiesbaden: Otto Harrassowitz.

———. 2002. *Christliche Theologie im japanischen Kontext*. Frankfurt am Main: IKO – Verlag für interkulturelle Kommunikation.

Okonogi, Keigo (小此木啓吾). 1990. "Der Ajase-Komplex des Japaners." In *Die kühle Seele: Selbstinterpretation der japanischen Kultur*, edited by Jens Heise, 30–69. Frankfurt am Main: Fischer Taschenbuch Verlag; Abteilung Sozialwissenschaft.

Ölschleger, Hans Dieter. 1993. "John Batchelor's Contribution to Ainu Ethnography." In *European Studies on Ainu Language and Culture* (Monographien aus dem Deutschen Institut für Japanstudien der Philipp-Franz-von-Siebold-Stiftung, volume 7), edited by Josef Kreiner, 137–150. Munich: Iudicum Verlag.

Ölschleger, Hans Dieter, Helmut Demes, Heinrich Menkhaus, Ulrich Möhwald, Annelie Ortmanns, and Bettina Post-Kobayashi. 1994. *Individualität und Egalität im gegenwärtigen Japan: Untersuchung zu Wertmustern in Bezug auf Familie und Arbeitswelt* (Monographien aus dem Deutschen Institut für Japanstudien der Philipp-Franz-von-Siebold-Stiftung, volume 7). Munich: Iudicium Verlag GmbH.

Olsson, Herbert. n.d. "Die Lehre Luthers vom Gesetz." In *Luther und Melanchthon: Referate des Zweiten Internationalen Lutherforscherkongresses*, no editor, 49–62. Göttingen: Vandenhoeck & Ruprecht.

Omran, El-Sayed Ewis, Arnold Bregt, and Ian P. Williamson. 2007. "Spatial Data Sharing: A Cross-Cultural Conceptual Model." In *Research and Theory in Advancing Spatial Data Infrastructure Concepts*, edited by Harlan Onsrud, 75–92. Redlands, CA: ESRI Press.

Ono, Yasuhiro (小野泰博), Sekiyo Shimode (下出積與), Shigetsugu Sugiyama (椙山林継), Norihisa Suzuki (鈴木範久), Minoru Sonoda (薗田稔), Yasuaki Nara (奈良康明), Masao Butou (尾藤正英), Hitoshi Miyake (宮家準), and Noboru Miyata (宮田登). 1985. 日本宗教辞典 (*nihon shuukyou jiten*) [Encyclopedia of Japanese religion]. Tokyo: Hirofumidou (弘文堂).

Onoyama, Harumi (斧山春水). 2004. 自分とはなんだろう―新しい人間像を求めて (*jibun-to-wa nan darou: atarashii ningenzou-o motomete*) [What could that possibly be, "I"?: In search for a new concept of man]. Tokyo: Bungeisha (文芸社).

Ooguri, Douei (大栗道榮). 2000. 図説密教入門 (*Zusetsu mikkyou nyuumon*) [Introduction into visual Buddhist esoteric]. Tokyo: Suzuki Shuppan (鈴木出版).

Ooiwa, Keibou (大岩圭之), and Masato Ogata (緒方正人). 2001. *Rowing the Eternal Sea: The Story of a Minamata Fisherman*. Translated by Karen Colligan-Taylor. Lanham, MD: Rowman & Littlefield.

Ooms, Herman. 1976. "A Structural Analysis of Japanese Ancestral Rites and Beliefs." In *Ancestors*, edited by William Hare Newell, 61–90. Prepared as paper for the Ninth International Congress of Anthropological and Ethnological Sciences in Chicago, 1973. Berlin and New York: Walter de Gruyter.

Oono, Ken (大野健). 2001. 伝説の日本: *The Legend Says that Japanese* (*densetsu-no Nippon*) [The Traditional Japan]. Tokyo: Bungeisha (文芸社).

Oonuki-Tierney, Emiko (大貫恵美子). 1984. *Illness and Culture in Contemporary Japan: An Anthropological View*. Cambridge: Cambridge University Press.

Ootsu, Makoto (大津誠), Tomio Imanari, and Solomon B. Levine. 2002. *Inside Japanese Business: A Narrative History, 1960–2000*. Armonk, NY: M. E. Sharpe.

Oppenheimer, A'haron, and I. H. Levine. 1977. *The 'am ha-aretz: A Study in the Social History of the Jewish People in the Hellenistic-Roman Period*. Leiden: Brill Archive.

Oshige, Koutarou. 2003. "Arbeitsmarktstruktur und industrielle Entwicklung in Japan: Eine Bestandsaufnahme mit Thesen zur Zukunftsentwicklung." Duisburger Arbeitspapiere Ostasienwissenschaften; Duisburg Working Papers on East Asian Studies, no. 50. Duisburg: Institut für Ostasienwissenschaften (Institute for East

Asian Studies) at the Gerhard-Mercator-Universität Duisburg. https://www.uni-due.de/in-east/fileadmin/publications/gruen/paper50.pdf (accessed 30 Jan 2016).

Osho, Bhagwan Shree Rajneesh. 1997. *Vedanta: Seven Steps to Samadhi: Talks on Indian Mysticism*. Pune, India: Rebel Publishing.

Otto, Eckart. 2002. *Max Webers Studien des antiken Judentums*. Tübingen: Mohr Siebeck.

Ouhira, Saku. 1976. "Der Schlangenbräutigam." In *Japanische Märchen*, edited and translated by Toshio Ozawa, 45–46. Third edition. Frankfurt am Main: Fischer Taschenbuch Verlag GmbH.

Ootsu, Makoto (大津誠), Tomio Imanari, and Solomon B. Levine. 2002. *Inside Japanese Business: A Narrative History, 1960–2000*. Armonk, NY: M. E. Sharpe.

Oyama, Reiji (尾山令仁). 1995. 日本人とキリスト教の受容 (*Nihonjin-to kirisuto-kyou-no juyou*) [The Japanese and their acceptance of Christianity]. Tokyo: Yougunsha (羊群社).

Oyibo, Innocent. 2004. *Aspekte afrikanischer Eschatologie aufgezeigt am Beispiel des Ahnenkults bei den Igala von Nigeria: Ein Kernelement afrikanischer Religiosität als Anfrage an den christlichen Glauben*. Berlin, Hamburg and Münster: LIT Verlag.

Ozu, Yasujirou (小津安二郎); Noda, Kougo (野田高梧). 2003. *Tokyo Story: The Ozu/Noda Screenplay*. Translated by Donald Richie. Berkeley, CA: Stone Bridge Press.

Pachuau, Lalsangkima. 2006. "Mizo 'Sakhua' in Transition: Change and Continuity from Primal Religion to Christianity." *Missiology* 34 (1): 41–57.

Packer, James Innell. 1973. *Knowing God*. London, Sydney, Auckland and Toronto: Hodder & Stoughton.

Paley, Maggie. 2000. *The Book of the Penis*. N.p.: Grove/Atlantic.

Palu, Ma'afu. 2012. *Jesus and Time: An Interpretation of Mark 1:15*. London: T & T Clark.

Pannenberg, Wolfhart. 1976. "Einheit der Kirche und Einheit der Menschheit." In *Um Einheit und Heil der Menschheit*, edited by J. Robert Nelson and Wolfhart Pannenberg, 7–22. Second edition. Frankfurt am Main: Verlag Otto Lembeck.

———. 1993. *Systematische Theologie*. Volume 1. Göttingen: Vandenhoeck & Ruprecht.

Parachini, John V., and Katsuhisa Furukawa (古川勝久). 2007. "Japan and Aum Shinrikyo." In *Democracy and Counterterrorism: Lessons from the Past*, edited by Robert J. Art and Louise Richardson, 531–562. Washington, DC: United States Institute of Peace Press.

Park, Andrew Sung. 2000. "The God Who Needs Our Salvation." In *The Changing Face of God*, edited by Karen Armstrong, Andrew Sung Park, and Frederick W. Schmidt, 81–94. Harrisburg, PA: Morehouse Publishing.

———. 2001. "The Bible and *Han*." In *The Other Side of Sin: Woundedness from the Perspective of the Sinned-against*, edited by Andrew Sung Park and Susan L. Nelson, 45–60. Albany, NY: SUNY Press.

———. 2003. "Forgiveness". Lecture on 2003/7/24, United Theological Seminary, Center for Process Theology. http://www.ctr4process.org/publications/SeminarPapers/26_3%20Forgivingness%20by%20Park.pdf (accessed 22 Oct 2012).

———. 2009. *Triune Atonement: Christ's Healing for Sinners, Victims, and the Whole Creation*. Richmond, VA: Westminster John Knox Press.

Park, Bradley. "Buddhism and Japanese Aesthetics." Department of Philosophy and Religious Studies, St. Mary's College of Maryland. http://www.columbia.edu/cu/weai/exeas/resources/pdf/buddhism-japanese-aesthetics.pdf (accessed 13 Oct 2012).

Parusel, Peter. 1992. "Unterwelt." In *Lexikon der Religionen: Phänomene, Geschichte, Ideen*, edited by Hans Waldenfels, 687–690. Second edition. Freiburg, Basel, Wien: Verlag Herder Freiburg im Breisgau.

Patočka, Jan, and Lugder Hagedorn. 2005. *Andere Wege in die Moderne: Studien zur europäischen Ideengeschichte von der Renaissance bis zur Romantik*. Würzburg: Königshausen & Neumann.

Pattison, Stephen. 2000. *Shame: Theory, Therapy, Theology*. Cambridge: Cambridge University Press.

Paul, Gregor. 2001. "Comparative Philosophy, Japanese." In *Encyclopedia of Asian Philosophy*, edited by Oliver Leaman, 130–132. London: Taylor & Francis.

Pelletier, Philippe. 1992. *L'insularité dans la Mer Intérieure japonaise*. Pessac Cedex: Presses Université de Bordeaux.

Peres, Imre. 2003 "Griechische Grabinschriften und neutestamentliche Eschatologie." Habilitation treatise at the Reformed Károli Gáspár University, Budapest, 2002. Tübingen: Mohr Siebeck.

Peters, George W. 1972. *A Biblical Theology of Missions*. Chicago: Moody Press.

Petersen, Uwe. 2005. *Das Böse in uns: Phänomenologie und Genealogie des Bösen*. Horitschon, Wien and Munich: Novum Verlag GmbH.

Peterson, Eugene H. 1997. *Leap Over a Wall: Earthy Spirituality for Everyday Christians*. San Francisco: Harper San Francisco.

Petit, Jean Claude. 1993. "Von der Schwierigkeit und den Grenzen einer Theologie der Natur heute: Einige Bemerkungen im Blick auf Paul Tillich." In *Natural Theology versus Theology of Nature?: Tillich's Thinking as Impetus for a Discourse Among Theology, Philosophy and Natural Sciences* (*Proceedings of the IV. International Paul Tillich Symposium held in Frankfurt/Main 1992*) / *Natürliche Theologie versus Theologie der Natur: Tillichs Denken als Anstoß zum Gespräch zwischen Theologie, Philosophie und Naturwissenschaft* (*Beiträge des IV Internationalen Paul-Tillich-Symposiums in Frankfurt/Main 1992*), edited by Gert Hummel, 3–14. Berlin and New York: Walter de Gryuter.

Petroschkat, Katrin. 2008. *Osôshiki- die Etikette der japanischen Bestattung anhand des Filmes "osôshiki" von Itami JÛZÔ (1984)* (*Akademische Schriftenreihe*). Munich: GRIN-Verlag.

Petter, Frank Arjava. 1997. *Reiki Fire: New Information about the Origin of the Reiki Power: A Complete Method*. Lohne: Lotus Press.

Pflugfelder, Gregory M. 1999. *Cartographies of Desire: Male-male Sexuality in Japanese Discourse, 1600–1950*. Berkeley and Los Angeles: University of California Press.
Philippi, Donald L. 1959. *Norito: A New Translation of the Ancient Japanese Ritual Prayers*. Tokyo: Institute for Japanese Culture and Classics, Kokogakuin University.
Phillipps, Susanne. 2004. *Schnellkurs Japan*. Köln: DuMont Literatur und Kunst Verlag.
Picken, Stuart D. B. 1994. *Essentials of Shinto: An Analytical Guide to Principal Teachings*. Westport, CT: Greenwood Publishing.
———. 2004. *Sourcebook in Shinto: Selected Documents*. Westport CT: Greenwood Publishing.
Pienisch, Markus. 2000. *Lecture in Dogmatics*. Akademie für Weltmission, Korntal.
Pieris, Aloysius. 1988. *An Asian Theology of Liberation*. Edinburgh: T & T Clark.
Piers, Gerhart, and Milton B. Singer. 1953. *Shame and Guilt: A Psychoanalytic and a Cultural Study*. Edition 171 of American Lecture Series (American Lectures in Psychiatry). N.p.: Thomas.
Pike, Paul. 1992. "The Japanese Calendar." *Japan Harvest* (Fall): 8.
Pironio, Eduardo F. 1984. "Die Spiritualität des neuen Menschen in Lateinamerika: Welche Aspekte sind grundlegend für eine echte Spiritualität des Menschen?" In *Spiritualität und Befreiung in Lateinamerika*, edited by Eduardo Bonnín, 33–39. Translated by Antonio Reiser. Würzburg: Echter Verlag.
Plutschow, Herbert. 1996. *Matsuri: The Festivals of Japan*. Richmond, Surrey (Japan Library (Curzon Press).
Plutschow, Herbert E., and Patrick Geoffrey O'Neill. 1996. *Matsuri: The Festivals of Japan*. London: Routledge.
Poewe, Karla O. 1994. *Charismatic Christianity as a Global Culture*. Columbia, SC: University of South Carolina Press.
Pohlmann, Karl-Friedrich, and Thilo Alexander Rudnig. 2001. *Der Prophet Hesekiel/Ezechiel: Kapitel 1–19* (Altes Testament Deutsch, ATD 22, 1). Göttingen: Vandenhoeck & Ruprecht.
Pöhlmann, Horst Georg. 1980. *Abriß der Dogmatik*. Third improved and enlarged edition. Gütersloh: Gütersloher Verlagshaus Gerd Mohn.
Pontifical Council for Culture (Päpstlicher Rat für die Kultur). 2005. "Jesus Christus, der Spender lebendigen Wassers: Überlegungen zu New Age aus christlicher Sicht" (Jesus Christ: The Bearer of the Water of Life: A Christian Reflection on the "New Age"). Päpstlicher Rat für den Interreligiösen Dialog. http://www.kath.ch/infosekten/pdf/new_age.pdf (accessed 13 Oct 2012).
Pope-Levison, Priscilla, and John R. Levison. 1992. *Jesus in Global Context*. Louisville, KY: Westminster John Knox Press.
Pörtner, Peter. 2002. *Japan: Von Buddhas Lächeln zum Design – Eine Reise durch 2500 Jahre japanischer Kunst und Kultur*. Second updated edition. Köln: DuMont Reiseverlag.

Priest, Robert J. 2000. "Animism." In *Evangelical Dictionary of World Missions*, edited by A. Scott Moreau, Harold Netland and Charles Van Engen, 63. Grand Rapids, MI: Baker; and Carlisle, Cumbria: Paternoster.

———. 1993. "Cultural Anthropologie, Sin, And the Missionary." In *God and Culture: Essays in Honor of Carl F. H. Henry*, edited by D. A. Carson and John D. Woodbridge, 85–105. Grand Rapids, MI: Eerdmans.

Proksch, Otto. 1933. "ἅγιος – ἁγιάζω – ἁγιασμός – ἁγιότης – ἁγιωσύνη." In *Theologisches Wörterbuch zum Neuen Testament*, volume 1, edited by Gerhard Kittel. Stuttgart: Verlag von W. Kohlhammer.

Pye, Michael. 1996. "Shinto, Primal Religion and International Identity." In *Marburg Journal of Religion* 1 (1) (April). https://www.uni-marburg.de/fb03/ivk/mjr/pdfs/1996/articles/shinto1996.pdf (accessed 16 May 2016)

———. 2001. "Religion und Recht in Japan: Pluralismus, Toleranz und Konkurrenz" In *Marburg Journal of Religion* 6 (1): 1–17. http://www.uni-marburg.de/fb03/ivk/mjr/pdfs/2001/articles/pye2001.pdf?searchterm=japan (accessed 13 Oct 2012).

Pye, Michael, Katja Triplett, Monika Schrimpf. 2007. *Streben nach Glück: Schicksalsdeutung und Lebensgestaltung in japanischen Religionen: Mit Beiträgen von Monika Schrimpf* (Religiöse Gegenwart Asiens: Studies in Modern Asian Religions, volume 1). Berlin, Hamburg and Münster: LIT Verlag.

Quack, Anton, SVD. 1992. "Magie." In *Lexikon der Religionen: Phänomene, Geschichte, Ideen*, edited by Hans Waldenfels, 382–383. Second edition. Freiburg, Basel, Wien: Verlag Herder Freiburg im Breisgau.

Ramm, Bernard. 1976. "The Fortunes of Theology from Schleiermacher to Barth and Bultmann." In *Tensions in Contemporary Theology*, edited by Stanley N. Gundry and Alan F. Johnson, 15–41. Chicago: Moody Press.

Ratschow, Carl Heinz. 1986. "Rechtfertigung: Diakritisches Prinzip des Christentums im Verhältnis zu anderen Religionen." In *Von den Wandlungen Gottes: Beiträge zur systematischen Theologie: zum 75. Geburtstag Carl Heinz Ratschow*[s], edited by Christel Keller-Wentorf and Martin Repp, 336–375. Presented in abridged form at the occasion of the celebration of 25 years of the Evangelischen Zentralstelle für Weltanschauungsfragen gehalten, 1985. Berlin and New York: Walter de Gruyter.

Reader, Ian. 1995. "Cleaning Floors and Sweeping the Mind: Cleaning as a Ritual Process." In *Ceremony and Ritual in Japan: Religious Practices in an Industrialized Society*, edited by Jan van Bremen, and Dolores P. Martinez, 227–245. London: Nissan Institute/Routledge Japanese Studies.

———. 1996. *A Poisonous Cocktail?: Aum Shinrikyō's Path to Violence*. Copenhagen: Nordic Institute of Asian Studies (NIAS).

Reader, Ian, and George J. Tanabe Jr. 1998. *Practically Religious: Worldly Benefits and the Common Religion of Japan*. Honolulu: University of Hawaii Press.

Redeker, Mirjam-Christina. 2011. *Wahrnehmung und Glaube: Zum Verhältnis von Theologie und Ästhetik in gegenwärtiger Zeit.* Berlin and New York: Walter de Gruyter.

Rehfeld, Emmanuel R. 2012. *Relationale Ontologie bei Paulus: Die ontische Wirksamkeit der Christusbezogenheit im Denken des Heidenapostels* (Wissenschaftliche Untersuchungen zum Neuen Testament, second series, 326). Tübingen: Mohr Siebeck.

Reichart, Eugen. 1964. *Hände weg von Wahrsagerei und Zauberei.* Volume 2 of Schriftenreihe "Evangelisation und Zeugnis." Second edition. Gießen and Basel: Brunnen-Verlag.

Reid, David. 1991. *New Wine: The Cultural Shaping of Japanese Christianity.* Volume 2 of Nanzan Studies in Asian Religions. Fremont, CA: Jain Publishing.

Reinhardt, Wolfgang. 1995. "Das Wachstum des Gottesvolkes: Biblische Theologie des Gemeindewachstums." Presented as doctoral thesis at the Universität Wuppertal, 1992. Göttingen: Vandenhoeck & Ruprecht.

Reinhuber, Thomas. 2000. "Kämpfender Glaube: Studien zu Luthers Bekenntnis am Ende von De servo arbitrio." Presented as thesis at the Universität Tübingen, 1999. Berlin and New York: Walter de Gruyter.

Renard, John. 2002. *101 Questions and Answers on Confucianism, Daoism, and Shinto.* New York: Paulist Press.

Repp, Martin. 1997. *Aum Shinrikyō: Ein Kapitel krimineller Religionsgeschichte.* Marburg: Diagonal-Verlag.

———. 2004. "Aum Shinrikyou and the Aum Incident: A Critical Introduction." In *Controversial New Religions*, edited by James R. Lewis, and Jesper Aagaard Petersen, 153–194. Oxford: Oxford University Press.

———. 2014. "Aum Shinrikyou and the Aum Incident: A Critical Introduction." In *Controversial New Religions*, edited by James R. Lewis and Jesper A. Petersen, 195–140. Second edition. Oxford and New York: Oxford University Press.

Reps, Paul, and Nyogen Senzaki (千崎如幻). 1998. *Zen Flesh, Zen Bones: A Collection of Zen and Pre-Zen Writings.* North Clarendon, VT, and Tokyo: Tuttle Publishing.

Resch, Andreas. 1992. "Seele." In *Lexikon der Religionen: Phänomene, Geschichte, Ideen*, edited by Hans Waldenfels, 597–601. Second edition. Freiburg, Basel, Wien: Verlag Herder Freiburg im Breisgau.

Reynolds, David K. 1993. "Yoshimoto Ishin: The Life of the Founder of Naikan." In *Plunging through the Clouds: Constructive Living Currents*, edited by David K. Reynolds, 173–182. Albany, NY: SUNY Press.

Richie, Donald, and Edwin O. Reischauer. 1994. *Introducing Japan.* Revised and illustrated edition. Tokyo: Koudansha International.

Riemann, Fritz. 1995. *Grundformen der Angst: Eine tiefenpsychologische Studie.* Second edition. Munich and Basel: Ernst Reinhardt Verlag.

Rimer, Thomas J., and Van C. Gessel. 2007. *The Columbia Anthology of Modern Japanese Literature: From 1945 to the Present.* Modern Asian Literature, volume 2 of The Columbia Anthology of Modern Japanese Literature. New York and Chichester, West Sussex: Columbia University Press.

Ritchie, Mark Andrew. 1996. *Spirit of the Rainforest: A Yanomamö Shaman's Story.* Chicago: Island Lake Press.

Rochedieu, Edmond. 1973. *Der Shintoismus und die neuen Religionen Japans* (Große Religionen der Welt). Genf: Edito-Service S.A.

Röhl, Wilhelm. 2005. *History of Law in Japan since 1868.* Handbook of Oriental Studies; volume 12 of Handbuch der Orientalistik, edited by M. Blum. Leiden: Brill.

Rohls, Jan. 1997. *Protestantische Theologie der Neuzeit.* Volume 2. Tübingen: Mohr Siebeck.

———. 2002. *Philosophie und Theologie in Geschichte und Gegenwart.* Tübingen: Mohr Siebeck.

Rohrbach, Hans. 1985. *Unsichtbare Mächte und die Macht Jesu.* Wuppertal: R. Brockhaus Verlag.

Roman, David W. "Lordship and Missions: Conversion in Japan." In *Missions in a New Millennium: Change and Challenges in World Missions*, edited by Edward W. Glenny and William H. Smallman, 172–197. Grand Rapids, MI: Kregel Academic.

Rooker, Mark F. 2010. *The Ten Commandments: Ethics for the Twenty-First Century.* Nashville, TN: B & H.

Rosenkranz, Gerhard. 1959. "Yamato-Damashii – vor 1945." In *Christus kommt nach Japan,* edited by Gerhard Rosenkranz, 20–23. Bad Salzuflen: MBK-Verlag, Verlag für Missions - und Bibelkunde.

———. 1962. "Shintoismus." In *RGG*, volume 6, 8–13. Third revised edition. Tübingen: Mohr Siebeck.

Rotermund, Hartmut O. 1993. "Buddhism and Archaic Beliefs in the Shinto-Buddhist Syncretism of Japan." In *Asian Mythologies*, edited by Yves Bonnefoy and Wendy Doniger, 275–276. London and Chicago: University of Chicago Press.

Rothlauf, Jürgen. 2009. *Interkulturelles Management: Mit Beispielen aus Vietnam, China, Japan, Russland und den Golfstaaten.* Third edition. Munich: Oldenburg Verlag.

Rowe, Eriko. 2007. アメリカ・インディアン笑って生きる知恵 (*Amerika-indian waratte ikiru chie*) [The laughing wisdom of American Indians]. Kyoto: PHP Kenkyuujo (PHP研究所).

Rowe, Mark Michael. 2011. *Bonds of the Dead: Temples, Burial, and the Transformation of Contemporary Japanese Buddhism.* Buddhism and Modernity. Chicago and London: University of Chicago Press.

Rowthorn, Chris, John Ashburne, Andrew Bender, David Atkinson, and Craig McLachlan. 2003. *Japan.* N.p.: Lonely Planet.

Roy, Christian. 2005. *Traditional Festivals: A Multicultural Encyclopedia.* Volume 1. Santa Barbara, CA; Denver, CO; Oxford: ABC-Clio.

Rudert, Erwin. 1985. *Ich will von Blumhardt lernen, daß Jesus Sieger ist: Leben und Werk von Pfarrer Johann Christoph Blumhardt*. Second edition. Metzingen: Verlag Ernst Franz.

Ruppert, Brian Douglas. 2000. *Jewel in the Ashes: Buddha Relics and Power in Early Medieval Japan*. Cambridge, MA: Harvard University Asia Center.

Rushdoony, Rousas John. 1972. *The Institutes of Biblical Law*. Harmony, PA: P & R.

Sachsse, Hans. 1976. "Der Mensch als Partner der Natur: Überlegungen zu einer nachcartesischen Naturphilosophie und ökologischen Ethik." In *Überleben und Ethik: Die Notwendigkeit, bescheiden zu werden*, edited by Gerd-Klaus Kaltenbrunner, 27–54. Munich: Herder.

Saeki, Ariyoshi (佐伯有義). 1935. 垂加神道 (*suika shintou*) [Suika-Shintoism]. Volume 2. Tokyo: Shunyoudoushoten (春陽堂書店).

Sailhamer, John H. 2010. *Introduction to Old Testament Theology: A Canonical Approach*. New York, NY: Harper Collins (eBook).

Sakade, Florence. 1971. *Japanese Children's Favorite Stories*. 17th edition. Rutland, VT and Tokyo: Charles E. Tuttle.

Sakade, Yoshinobu (坂出祥伸). 2003. 今でも使われている運勢暦と大雑書のなかの占い: その仕組みを知っていますか (*Ima-de-mo tsukawarete-iru unsei-koyomi-to Oogissho-no naka-no uranai: sono shikumi-o shitte imasuka*) [Fate-almanacs used in the presence and the fortune-telling of the Oogissho: Do you know the structure?]. Memorial lecture at the occasion of the special exhibition "Fortune-Telling Literature of the Edo and Early Meiji-Period: Fortune-Telling in the Life of Ordinary People," given on 28 November 2003. http://ci.nii.ac.jp/naid/110000966630 (accessed 16 May 2016).

Sakaguchi, Ango (坂口安吾). 1990. "Unter der vollen Blüte im Kirschbaumwald." In *Das große Japanlesebuch*, edited by Siegfried Schaarschmidt, 139–161. Munich: Wilhem Goldmann Verlag.

———. 1997. "In the Forest, under Cherries in Full Bloom." In *The Oxford Book of Japanese Short Stories*, edited by Theodore W. Goossen. Translated by Jay Rubin. Oxford: Oxford University Press.

Sakamaki, Shunzou. 1987. "Shinto: Japanese Ethnocentrism." In *The Japanese Mind: Essentials of Japanese Philosophy and Culture*, edited by Charles A. Moore, 24–32. Eighth edition. Honolulu: University of Hawaii Press.

Sakuta, Keiichi (作田啓一). 1986. "Soziale Kontrolle und Selbstkontrolle." In *Gewissen und soziale Kontrolle in Japan und Deutschland*, edited by Anke Wiegand-Kanzaki and Shin'ichi Minamioji, 12–23. Würzburg: Königshausen und Neumann.

Saler, Benson. 1997. "E. B. Tylor and the Anthropology of Religion." Paper for the 95th Annual Meeting of the American Anthropological Association in San Francisco, 21 Nov 1996. In *Marburg Journal of Religion* 2 (1). http://www.uni-marburg.de/fb03/ivk/mjr/pdfs/1997/articles/saler1997.pdf (accessed 13 Oct 2012).

Salomon, Gerhard. 1980. *Was bald geschehen wird*. Fourth edition. Lahr-Dinglingen: Kommissionsverlag der St.-Johannis-Druckerei C. Schweickhardt.

Salomon, Richard, and Andrew Glass. 2000. *A Gāndhārī Version of the Rhinoceros Sūtra: British Library Kharoṣṭhī Fragment 5B*. Seattle, WA: University of Washington Press.

Sanders, Anne. 2005. "Einführung in das japanische Recht." In *HFR 2005*, contribution no. 6. http://www.humboldt-forum-recht.de/druckansicht/druckansicht.php?artikelid=114 (accessed 13 Oct 2012).

Sanders, J. Oswald. 1967. *Spiritual Leadership*. Chicago, IL: Moody Press.

Sano, Yoko. 2003. "Changes and Continued Stability in Japanese HRM Systems: Choice in the Share Economy." In *Human Resource Management: Critical Perspectives on Business and Management*, volume 2 of Comperative, International and Strategic Human Resource Management, edited by Michael Poole, 135–150. London and New York: Routledge.

Sansom, George Bailey. 1978 (1931). *Japan: A Short Cultural History*. Stanford, CA: Stanford University Press.

———. 1987 (1931). *Japan: A Short Cultural History*. London, Melbourne, Sydney, Auckland, Johannesburg: Cresset Library.

Saruta, Yuu (猿田悠). 恐い話怖い話 (*kowai hanashi kowai hanashi*) [Scary stories, scary stories]. Tokyo: Bungeisha (文芸者).

Sasaki, Koukan (佐々木宏幹). 1980. シャーマニズム：エクスタシーと漂霊の文化 (*shaamanizumu: ekusutashii-to pyourei-no bunka*) [Shamanism: The culture of ecstacy and obsession]. Tokyo: Chuuoukouronsha (中央公論社).

Sasaki, Mitsurou (佐々木光郎), Fujiwara Masanori (藤原正範). 2000. 戦前感化・教護実践史 (*senzenkanka: kyougojissenreki*) [Impacts of the pre-war era: A history of the actual prexis in reformatories]. Yokohama: Shunpusha (春風社).

Sasaki, Sanmi (佐々木三味). 2002. *Chado: The Way of Tea: A Japanese Tea Master's Almanac*. Translated by Shawn McCabe. Rutland, VT: Tuttle Publishing.

Saso, Michael R. 1991. *Tantric Art and Meditation*. Honolulu: University of Hawaii Press.

Satou, Hiroshi. 2002. "やさしい基礎解説：漢方治療の特徴と処方選択の目安 (*yasashii kisokaisetsu: kanpouchiryou-no tokuchou-to shohousentaku-no meyasu*) [An essay to understand explanation of the basics: Characteristics of Chinese traditional medicine and criteria of the choice of recipe]." In 漢方辞典：名医と治す (*kanpoujiten: meii-to naosu*) [Encyclopedia of Chinese traditional medicine: Healing together with the physician], edited by weekly journal Shuukan Asahi (週刊朝日), 12–30. Tokyo: Asahi Shinbunsha (朝日新聞社).

Satou, Toshio (佐藤敏夫). 1997. "The Second Generation." In *A History of Japanese Theology*, edited by Yasuo Furuya, 43–82. Grand Rapids, MI: Eerdmans.

Sauer, Erich. 1983. *Der Triumph des Gekreuzigten: Ein Gang durch die neutestamentliche Offenbarungsgeschichte (mit 90 Predigtentwürfen)*. Wuppertal: R. Brockhaus Verlag; Basel: Brunnen-Verlag.

Sauma, Rabban. 2002. "Ancestor Practices in the Muslim World: A Problem of Contextualization from Central Asia." *Missiology* 30 (3): 323–345.

Schaack, Thomas. 1998. "Die Ungeduld des Papiers: Studien zum Alttestamentlichen Verständnis des Schreibens anhand des Verbums katab im Kontext administrativer Vorgänge." Presented as doctoral thesis at the Universität Kiel, 1996/1997. Berlin & New York: Walter de Gruyter.

Schad-Seifert, Annette. 2007. "Japans Abschied von der Mittelschichtgesellschaft: Auflösung des Familienhaushalts oder Pluralisierung der Lebensformen?" In *Japanstudien: Jahrbuch des Deutschen Instituts für Japanstudien: Familienangelegenheiten*, volume 19, edited by Peter Backhaus, 105–128. Munich: Iudicum Verlag.

Schaeffer, Francis. 2006. *Escape From Reason: A Penetrating Analysis of Trends in Modern Thought*. Downers Grove, IL: InterVarsity Press.

Schäfer, Klaus. 2005. "Thematischer Teil." In *Bericht des evangelischen Missionswerkes in Deutschland: Mission als Dienst der Versöhnung*, edited by Herbert Meißner and Maren von der Heide, 5–37. Fourth convention of the 4. Tagung der 10th synod of the Evangelischen Kirche in Deutschland, Berlin, 6–10 November 2005, n.p.: Evangelisches Missionswerk (EMW). http://www.ekd.de/download/bericht_emw_2005_kpl.pdf (accessed 13 Oct 2012).

Schäfer-Lichtenberger, Christa. 1983. "Stadt und Eidgenossenschaft im Alten Testament: Eine Auseinandersetzung mit Max Webers Studie 'Das antike Judentum.'" Revised version of the doctoral thesis presented at the Universität Heidelberg, 1979/1980. Berlin and New York: Walter de Gruyter.

Schedler, Claude. 2004. *Shōninki: Historische Geheimschrift der Ninja*. Norderstedt: Books on Demand (BoD).

Schenck, Paul-Christian. 1997. *Der deutsche Anteil an der Gestaltung des modernen japanischen Rechts- und Verfassungswesens: Deutsche Rechtsberater im Japan der Meiji-Zeit*. Volume 68 of Beiträge zur Kolonial- und Überseegeschichte. Stuttgart: Franz Steiner Verlag.

Schiller, Manfred. 2007. "Impulsseminar zum Thema Animismus." Held at the board meeting of DMG interpersonal, 17 November 2007.

Schilling, S. Paul. 1986. "Albert Cornelius Knudson: Person and Theologian." In *The Boston Personalist Tradition in Philosophy, Social Ethics, and Theology*, edited by Paul Deats and Carol Robb, 81–104. Macon, GA: Mercer University Press.

Schinzinger, Robert. 1983. *Japanisches Denken: Der weltanschauliche Hintergrund des heutigen Japan*. OAG-Reihe Japan Modern, volume 5. Berlin: Erich Schmidt Verlag.

Schlatter, Adolf. 1905. *Glaube im Neuen Testament*. Third revision. Calw: Verlag der Vereinsbuchhandlung.

———. 1911. *Das christliche Dogma*. Calw: Verlag der Vereinsbuchhandlung.

———. 1952 (1935). *Gottes Gerechtigkeit: Ein Kommentar zum Römerbrief.* Second edition, memorial edition on the occasion of Adolf Schlatter's 100th birthday. Stuttgart: Calwer Verlag.

———. 1961a. *Die christliche Ethik.* Fourth edition. Stuttgart: Calwer Verlag.

———. 1961b. *Jesus und Paulus: Eine Vorlesung und einige Aufsätze.* Third edition. Stuttgart: Calwer Verlag.

———. 1961c. *Das Evangelium nach Matthäus.* Volume 1 of Erläuterungen zum Neuen Testament. Stuttgart: Calwer Verlag.

———. 1977 (1961). *Das Evangelium nach Matthäus.* Volume 1 of Erläuterungen zum Neuen Testament. Stuttgart: Calwer Verlag.

———. 1982. *Der Evangelist Matthäus: Seine Sprache, sein Ziel, seine Selbständigkeit: Ein Kommentar zum ersten Evangelium.* Seventh edition. Stuttgart: Calwer Verlag.

———. 1983. *Die Kirche der Griechen im Urteil des Paulus: Eine Auslegung seiner Briefe an Timotheus und Titus.* Third edition. Stuttgart: Calwer Verlag.

Schlaudraff, Karl-Heinz. 1988. "Heil als Geschichte"?: Die Frage nach dem heilsgeschichtlichen Denken anhand der Konzeption Oscar Cullmanns. Tübingen: Mohr Siebeck.

Schlieper, Andreas. 1997. *Die Nähe fremder Kulturen: Parallelen zwischen Japan und Deutschland.* Frankfurt am Main and New York: Campus Fachbuch.

Schlusslicht. ARD-Tagesschau (8. 9. 2008). 2008. http://www.tagesschau.de/schlusslicht/compu terschrein100.html (The ARD had to delete this resource.); new source: http://www.oldieboard.de/German/print.php?threadid=426&page=11&sid=e0a4b3e92ab6c98057aafb8562677b67 (accessed 12 Oct 2012).

Schmidt, Brian B. 1994. *Israel's Beneficent Dead.* Volume 11 of Forschungen zum Alten Testament. Tübingen: Mohr Siebeck.

Schmidt, Helmut, and Richard von Weizsäcker. 2007. *Innenansichten aus Europa.* Munich: C. H. Beck oHG.

Schmidt, Klaus. 1998. *Christi Sinn.* Crailsheim: Selbstverlag.

Schmidt, Thomas E. 1995. *Straight & Narrow?: Compassion & Clarity in the Homosexuality Debate.* Downers Grove, IL: InterVarsity Press.

Schnabel, Eckhard J. 2002. *Urchristliche Mission.* Wuppertal: R. Brockhaus Verlag.

Schnackenburg, Rudolf. 1982. *Der Brief an die Epheser.* Volume 10 of EKK. Second edition. Zürich/Einsiedeln: Benziger Verlag.

Schnell, Scott. 1999. *The Rousing Drum: Ritual Practice in a Japanese Community.* Honolulu: University of Hawaii Press.

Schoenhals, Martin. 1993. *The Paradox of Power in a People's Republic of China Middle School.* Armonk, NY: M. E. Sharpe.

Schopenhauer, Arthur. 1854. *Über den Willen der Natur: Eine Erörterung der Bestätigung, welche die Philosophie des Verfassers, seit ihrem Auftreten, auch die empirischen Wissenschaften erhalten hat.* Second enhanced and enlarged edition. Frankfurt am Main: Joh. Christ. Hermann'sche Buchhandlung.

―――. 1859. *Die Welt als Wille und Vorstellung,* volume 1. Third enhanced and enlarged edition. Leipzig: F. A. Brockhaus.
Schott, Heinz, and Rainer Tölle. 2006. *Geschichte der Psychiatrie: Krankheitslehren, Irrwege, Behandlungsformen.* Munich: C. H. Beck.
Schreiter, Robert J. 2004a (1985). *Constructing Local Theologies.* Twelfth edition. Maryknoll, NY: Orbis Books.
―――. 2004b (1997).[10] *The New Catholicity: Theology between the Global and the Local.* Seventh edition. Maryknoll, NY: Orbis Books.
Schrimpf, Monika. 2001. "Zum buddhistischen Blick auf das Christentum in der *Meiji-Zeit*." In *11. Deutschsprachiger Japanologentag in Trier 1999: Sprache, Literatur, Kunst, Populärkultur, Medien, Informationstechnik,* edited by Hilaria Gössmann, and Andreas Mrugalla, 167–180. Berlin, Hamburg and Münster: LIT Verlag.
―――. 2008. "Nationale Selbstbehauptung in neuen religiösen Bewegungen: Das Beispiel Kōfuku no Kagaku." *Marburg Journal of Religion* 13 (1): 1–12. http://www.uni-marburg.de/fb03/ivk/mjr/pdfs/2008/articles/schrimpf2008.pdf?searchterm=japan (accessed 13 Oct 2012).
Schröder, Jan, and Morinaga, Yoshiko. 2005. "Zum Einfluß des BGB auf das japanische Zivilrecht." In *Rechtstransfer durch Zivilgesetzbücher: Beiträge 29/2005,* edited by Elisabeth Berger, 38–44. Bendern, Fürstentum Liechtenstein: Liechtenstein-Institut Forschung und Lehre.
Schröer, Henning. 1977. "Reue: Systematisch-theologisch." In *Theologische Realenzyklopädie,* TRE, volume 29, edited by Horst Robert Balz, Gerhard Krause, Siegfried M. Schwertner, Gerhard Müller, Claus-Jürgen Thornton, Michael Glatter, Albrecht Döhnert, Matthias Glockner, and Stephan Schwerdtfeger, 105–107. Berlin and New York: Walter de Gruyter.
Schroeter, Kai-Uwe. 2006. *Zur Mitte des Universums: Von der Größe Gottes und der Schönheit des Weltalls.* Norderstedt: Books on Demand (BoD).
Schründer-Lenzen, Agi. 1996. "Sozialisation im 'Reich der Zeichen.'" In *Harmonie und Konformität: Tradition und Krise japanischer Sozialisationsmuster,* edited by Agi Schründer-Lenzen, 7–29. Munich: Iudicum Verlag.
Schüler, Alfred. 1948. *Verantwortung vom Sein und Ethos der Person.* Krailing vor Munich and Freiburg/Br.: Erich Wewel Verlag.
Schüßler, Werner. 1993. "Protestantisches Prinzip versus Natürliche Theologie?: Zu Paul Tillichs Problem mit einer natürlichen Theologie." In *Natural Theology versus Theology of Nature?: Tillich's Thinking as Impetus for a Discourse Among Theology, Philosophy and Natural Sciences* (*Proceedings of the IV. International Paul Tillich Symposium held in Frankfurt/Main 1992)/Natürliche Theologie versus Theologie der Natur: Tillichs Denken als Anstoß zum Gespräch zwischen Theologie, Philosophie*

---

10. The books *Constructing Local Theologies* and *New Catholicity* are listed according to the date of their first edition.

und Naturwissenschaft (Beiträge des IV Internationalen Paul-Tillich-Symposiums in Frankfurt/Main 1992), edited by Gert Hummel, 14–30. Berlin and New York: Walter de Gryuter.

Schuster, Jürgen. 2002. "Karl Hartenstein: Mission with a Focus on the End." *Mission Studies* 19 (1): 53–81.

———. 2003. "Schamanismus und die christliche Kirche in Japan." In *Mission in fremden Kulturen: Beiträge zur Missionsethnologie: Festschrift für Lothar Käser zu seinem 65. Geburtstag*, edited by Klaus Müller, 243–252. Nürnberg: Verlag für Theologie und Religionswissenschaft: Edition afem.

Schütz, Eduard. 1973. *Gottes Heil in einer säkularen Welt*. Wuppertal: Oncken Verlag.

Schwade, Arcadio. 1984. "Christentum." In *Japan-Handbuch*, edited by Horst Hammitzsch, 1569–1577. Second edition. Stuttgart: Franz Steiner Verlag Wiesbaden GmbH.

Schwalbe, Hans. 1970. *Acht Gesichter Japans: Im Spiegel der Gegenwart*. Volume 52 of Mitteilungen der Deutschen Gesellschaft für Natur- und Völkerkunde Ostasiens. Tokyo: Deutsche Gesellschaft für Natur- und Völkerkunde Ostasiens.

Schwambach, Claus. 2006. "'Siehe, ich mache alles neu' – Schöpfung und Neuschöpfung." In *Wahrheit und Erfahrung: Themenbuch zur systematischen Theologie*, volume 3: Heiliger Geist, Kirche, Sakramente, Neuschöpfung, edited by Christian Herrmann, 290–361. Wuppertal: R. Brockhaus Verlag; Gießen: Brunnen Verlag (Theologische Verlagsgemeinschaft, TVG).

Schwarz, Gabriele. 1989. *Allgemeine Siedlungsgeographie: Die ländlichen Siedlungen. Die zwischen Land und Stadt stehenden Siedlungen*. Berlin and New York: Walter de Gruyter.

Schwarzwäller, Klaus. 2000. *Fülle des Lebens: Luthers Kleiner Katechismus: Ein Kommentar*. Hamburg: LIT-Verlag.

Schweitzer, Albert. 1995. *Reich Gottes und Christentum: Werke aus dem Nachlaß im Verlag C. H. Beck*. Munich: C. H. Beck.

———. 1998. *Straßburger Vorlesungen: Werke aus dem Nachlaß im Verlag C. H. Beck*. Munich: C. H. Beck.

Schwentker, Wolfgang. 1998. *Max Weber in Japan: eine Untersuchung zur Wirkungsgeschichte 1905–1995*. Tübingen: Mohr Siebeck.

Schwienhorst-Schönberger, Ludger. 2003. "Vertritt Kohelet die Lehre vom absoluten Tod?: Zum Argumentationsgang von Koh 9, 1–6." In *Auf den Spuren der schriftgelehrten Weisen: Festschrift für Johannes Marböck anlässlich seiner Emeritierung*, edited by Johannes Marböck, Irmtraud Fischer, Ursula Rapp, and Johannes Schiller, 207–220. Berlin and New York: Walter de Gruyter.

Schwindt, Rainer. 2002. *Das Weltbild des Epheserbriefes: Eine religionsgeschichtlich-exegetische Studie*. Volume 148 of Wissenschaftliche Untersuchungen Zum Neuen Testament. Tübingen: Mohr Siebeck.

Sears, Robert T. *Discernment of Energy Healing.* http://www.earthhealing.info/Discernment%20of%20Energy%20Healing.pdf (accessed 13 Oct 2012).

Seats, Michael. 2006. *Murakami Haruki:*[11] *The Simulacrum in Contemporary Japanese Culture.* Lexington, MA: Lexington Books.

Seidel, Helmut. 2001. "Ernst Bloch zu Marxens Thesen über Feuerbach." In *Ernst Blochs Leipziger Jahre: Beiträge des Fünften Walter-Markov-Kolloquiums*, edited by Manfred Neuhaus and Helmut Seidel, 77–81. Schkeuditz: GNN Verlag. http://www.praxisphilosophie.de/seidelfth.pdf (accessed 13 Oct 2012).

Seiyaku.com. 2006. *Shichifukujin: The Seven Gods of Japan.* http://www.seiyaku.com/reference/seven/shichifukujin.html (accessed 9 Oct 2012).

Seki, Yuuji (関裕二). 2004. 「古代史」:秘められた謎と真相:封印された歴史のカギを握る人 (*"kodaishi": himerareta nazo-to shinsou: fuinsareta rekishi-no kagi-o nigiru hito*) ["Prehistory": Secluded secrets and facts: The one who holds the key to the sealed history]. Kyoto: PHP研究所 (PHP Kenkyuusho).

Sered, Susan Starr. 1999. *Women of the Sacred Groves: Divine Priestesses of Okinawa.* New York, NY: Oxford University Press US.

Sharma, Kamal Prashad. 2004. *Folk Dances of Chambā: Where Every Talk Is a "Song" and Every Step Is a "Dance."* New Delhi: Indus Publishing.

Sharrock, Russell. 2007. *Spiritual Warfare: A Struggle for Truth.* Morrisville, NC: Lulu Enterprises.

Shawver, Lois. 2008. "Postmodern Pedagogy." In *The Praeger Handbook of Education and Psychology*, edited by Joe L. Kincheloe, and Raymond A. Horn, 454–462. Westport, CT: Greenwood Publishing.

Shenouda III, Pope. 1997. *Contemplations on the Ten Commandments, volume 2: The Fifth Commandment* (*Honour Your Father and Mother*). Second revised edition. Cairo: Dar El Tebaa El Kawmia.

Shew, Paul Tsuchido. 2005. "Pentecostals in Japan." In *Asian and Pentecostal: The Charismatic Face of Christianity in Asia*, edited by Allan Anderson and Edmond Tang, 487–508. Baguio City, Philippines: APTS Press.

Shibata, Chizuo (柴田千頭男). 1985. "Some Problematic Aspects of Japanese Ancestor Worship." In *Christian Alternatives to Ancestor Worship: 祖先崇拝問題* (*sosen suuhai mondai*) [Problems of ancestor veneration], edited by Bong Rin Ro, 247–260. Taichung, Taiwan: Asia Theological Association.

Shillony, Ben Ami (ベン=アミー・シロニー). 2004. ユダヤ人と日本人の不思議な関係 (*Yudayajin-to Nihonjin-no fushigi-na kankei*) [The unique relationship between the Jews and the Japanese]. Translated by Masaru Taki (立木勝). Tokyo: Seikoushobou (成甲書房). (Original title: 1991. *The Jews & the Japanese: Successful Outsiders.*) Tokyo: Charles E. Tuttle.

---

11. 村上春樹.

Shimada, Shingo (島田真吾). 1993. "Das Phänomen der Geburt in der japanischen Kultur." In *Japan: Selbstbild und Fremdbild*, edited by Gerhard Baer et al., 22–28. Strauhof Zürich: Offizin.

Shimazaki, Touzon (島崎藤村). 1989 (1906). *Ausgestoßen (hakkai (破戒))*. Translated by Jürgen Berndt. Frankfurt am Main: Insel Verlag.

Shimazono, Susumu (島薗進). 1999. "イノチと救い：二元的宗教構造の理論枠組を超えて (*inochi-to sukui: nigenteki shuukyoukouzou-no rironwakugumi-o koete*) [Life and salvation: Beyond the theory formation of a two-dimensional religious structure]." In 民俗宗教を学ぶ人のために (*minzokushuukyou-o manabu hito-no tame-ni*) [For people who learn folk religion], edited by Tetsuo Yamaori (山折哲雄) and Nimitsu Kawamura (川村邦光), 88–108. Kyoto: Sekaishisousha (世界思想社).

———. 2011. "New Religions: The Concept of Salvation." In *Establishing the Revolutionary: An Introduction to New Religions in Japan*, edited by Birgit Steammler and Ulrich Dehn, 69-88. Münster: LIT Verlag.

Shinmura, Izuru (新村出), ed. 1995. 広辞苑 (*koujien*). Tokyo: Iwanami Shoten (岩波書店). (This is one of the most comprehensive Japanese Dictionaries.)

Shintani, Takanori (新谷尚紀). 2006. なるほど!民俗学 (*naruhodo! minyougaku*) [Of Course! Folklore]. Kyoto: PHP Kenkyuujo (PHP研究所).

Shiraev, Eric B., and David A. Levy. 2015. *Cross-Cultural Psychology: Critical Thinking and Contemporary Applications*. Fifth edition. London and New York: Routledge (Taylor & Francis Group).

Shirohara, Mari (城原真理). 2000. 神人 (*Kaminch*) [God-People]. Tokyo: Bungeisha (文芸社).

Shively, Donald H., and William H. McCullough. 1999. *Heian Japan*. Cambridge: Cambridge University Press.

Singe, Georg. 2006. *Theologische Grundlagen für eine postmoderne Soziale Arbeit*. Berlin, Hamburg and Münster: LIT Verlag.

Singh, Nigel. 2005. *Compliance Analysis of a Fundamental Aikido Technique*. San Diego: University of California.

Skoglund, Herb. 1975. "St Francis Xavier's Encounter with Japan." *Missiology* 3 (4): 451–467.

Sleeper, Charles Freeman. 1992. *The Bible and the Moral Life*. Louisville, KY: Westminster John Knox Press.

Smend, Rudolf. 2002. "Die Mitte des Alten Testaments." In *Die Mitte des Alten Testaments: Exegetische Aufsätze*, edited by Rudolf Smend, 30–74. Tübingen: Mohr Siebeck.

Smith, Robert J. 1974. *Ancestor Worship in Contemporary Japan*. Stanford: Stanford University Press.

———. 1976. "Who Are the 'Ancestors' in Japan? A 1963 Census of Memorial Tablets." In *Ancestors*, edited by William Hare Newell, 33–60. Prepared as paper for the

Ninth International Congress of Anthropological and Ethnological Sciences in Chicago, 1973. Berlin and New York: Walter de Gruyter.

Snyder, T. Richard. 2000. *The Protestant Ethic and the Spirit of Punishment*. Grand Rapids, MI: Eerdmans.

Sobrino, Jon. 1985. *Christology at the Crossroads: A Latin American Approach*. Eighth edition. Maryknoll: NY: Orbis Books.

Soete, Annette. 1992. "Schuldaufhebung." In *Lexikon der Religionen: Phänomene, Geschichte, Ideen*, edited by Hans Waldenfels, 594–596. Second edition. Freiburg, Basel, Wien: Verlag Herder Freiburg im Breisgau.

Soga, Masanosuke (曽我政之助). 2001. 神の国と人の子: イエスの教えの正しい解釈 (*kami-no kuni-to hito-no ko: Iesu-no oshie-no tadashii kaishaku*) [Kingdom of God and Son of Man: The correct interpretation of the teaching of Jesus]. Tokyo: Bungeisha (文芸社).

Solheim, Dagfinn. 1984. "Japanese Culture and the Christian Church." *Missiology* 12 (2): 213–221.

Soothill, William Edward, and Lewis Hodous. 1987 (1937). *A Dictionary of Chinese Buddhist Terms: With Sanskrit and English Equivalents and a Sanskrit-Pali Index*. South Delhi: Motilal Banarsidass Publishers.

Spahn, Mark, Wolfgang Hadamitzky, and Kimiko Fujie-Winter. 1996. *The Kanji Dictionary*. Rutland, VT: Tuttle Publishing.

Spickard, Paul R. 1991. *Mixed Blood: Intermarriage and Ethnic Identity in Twentieth-Century America*. Madison, WI and London: University of Wisconsin Press.

Spina, Frank A. 2005. *The Faith of the Outsider: Exclusion and Inclusion in the Biblical Story*. Grand Rapids, MI: Eerdmans.

Spiro, Melford E., and Audrey G. Spiro. 1975. *Children of the Kibbutz: A Study in Child Training and Personality*. Cambridge, MA and London: Harvard University Press.

Sprinkle, Randy. 2001. *Follow Me: Becoming a Lifestyle Prayerwalker*. Birmingham, AL: New Hope Publishers.

Spychinger, Maria. 2007. "Zur Rolle der Scham beim Lernen aus Fehlern und beim Aufbau von Normen und Fehlerkultur." In *Scham – Beschämung – Anerkennung*, volume 3 of Erinnern und Lernen, Texte zur Menschenrechtspädagogik, edited by Wilhelm Schwendermann and Stephan Marks, 71–88. Berlin, Hamburg and Münster: LIT Verlag.

Stark, Rodney. 2003. *For the Glory of God: How Monotheism Led to the Reformations, Science, Witch-Hunts, and the End of Slavery*. Princeton, NJ: Princeton University Press.

Steffánsson, Finn. 1993. "Japan – The Pure Land: The Impressions of a Visitor." In *Japanese Religions: Past and Present*, edited by Ian Reader, Esben Andreasen, and Finn Stefánnson, 14–20. Honolulu: University of Hawaii Press.

Steffánsson, Halldór. 2002 (1995). "On Structural Duality of Japanese Conceptions of Death: Collective Forms of Death Rituals in Morimachi." In *Ceremony and*

Ritual in Japan: Religious Practices in an Industrialized Society, edited by Jan Van Bremen and D. P. Martinez, 83–107. Nissan Institute/Routledge Japanese Studies. New York, NY: Routledge.

Steineck, Christian. 2007. *Der Leib in der japanischen Bioethik: mit einer Diskussion der Leibtheorie von Merleau-Ponty im Licht bioethischer Probleme.* Würzburg: Königshausen & Neumann.

Steyne, Philip M. 1993 (English original 1990). *Machtvolle Götter: Eine Untersuchung über Glaube und Gebräuche des Animismus, wie er von Naturvölkern praktiziert wird und wie er heute in allen religiösen Bewegungen vorkommt.* Bad Liebenzell: Verlag der Liebenzeller Mission.

Stiebert, Johanna. 2002. *The Construction of Shame in the Hebrew Bible: The Prophetic Contribution.* London and New York: Continuum.

Stier, Rudolf. 1837. *Epistelpredigten für das christliche Volk: Ein vollständiger Jahrgang, besonders zum Vorlesen in Landkirchen eingerichtet.* Halle: Schwetschke und Sohn.

Stimac, Miroslav. 2004. *Arbeit, Freizeit und Konsum im modernen Japan.* Berlin: Tenea Verlag.

Störig, Hans Joachim. 1976. *Kleine Weltgeschichte der Philosophie in zwei Bänden*, volume 1. Eleventh revised and supplemented edition. Frankfurt am Main: Fischer Taschenbuch Verlag GmbH.

Storm, Rachel. 2000. *Die Enzyklopädie östlicher Mythologie.* Translated by Elisabeth Liebl. Reichelsheim: Edition XXL, GmbH.

Strack, Hermann L., and Paul Billerbeck. 1982. *Kommentar zum Neuen Testament aus Talmud und Midrasch*, volume 1. Das Evangelium nach Matthäus, eighth edition. Munich: C. H. Beck.

Strecker, Georg. 2000 (1996). *Theology of the New Testament.* New York and Berlin: Walter de Gruyter; Louisville, KY: Westminster John Knox Press.

Stucki, Lorenz. 1978. *Japans Herzen denken anders.* Bergisch Gladbach: Gustav Lübbe Verlag GmbH (originally Bern and Munich: Scherz Verlag).

Stuhlmacher, Peter. 1989. *Der Brief an die Römer.* Göttingen: Vandenhoeck & Ruprecht.

Sugimoto, Yoshio (杉本良夫). 2003. *An Introduction to Japanese Society.* Second edition. Cambridge: Cambridge University Press.

Sugitani, Kiyotoki (杉渓一言), Jirou Nakazawa (中澤次郎), Tatsuya Matsubara, (松原達哉), and Mitsugi Niregi (楡木満生). 2007. 産業カウンセリング入門: 産業カウンセラーになりたい人のために (*sangyou kaunseringu nyuumon: sangyou kaunseraa-ni naritai hito-no tame-ni*) [Introduction into industrial counselling: For people who want to become counselors in industry]. Tokyo: Nihon Bunka Kagakusha (日本文化科学社).

Sugiyama-Lebra, Takie. 1976. *Japanese Patterns of Behavior.* Honolulu: University of Hawaii Press.

———. 1982. "Self-Reconstruction in Japanese Religious Psychotherapy." In *Cultural Conceptions of Mental Health and Therapy*, volume 4 of Culture, Illness, and Healing, edited by Anthony J. Marsella and Geoffrey M. White, 269–284. Dortrecht, Holland: D. Reidel Publishing.

———. 2004. *The Japanese Self in Cultural Logic*. Honolulu: University of Hawaii Press.

Sugiyama-Lebra, Takie, and William P. Lebra. 1986. *Japanese Culture and Behavior: Selected Readings*. Honolulu: University of Hawaii Press.

Sun, Lixin. 2002. *Das Chinabild der deutschen protestantischen Missionare des 19. Jahrhunderts: Eine Fallstudie zum Problem interkultureller Begegnung und Wahrnehmung*. Marburg: Tectum Verlag.

Sunohara, Yoshi. 2009. 神学文献大調査 (*shingaku bunken daichousa*) [Great Review of Theological Literature]; http://home.interlink.or.jp/~suno/yoshi/references/ref_41.htm (accessed 15 May 2009).

Suwa, Yumiko (諏訪裕美子), and Yuu Irobe (色部祐). 2008. 過労死の労災申請: 過労死？と思ったら読む本 (*karoushi-no rousaishinsei: karoushi?-to omottara yomu hon*) [Claiming compensation in the case of death from overwork: A book to read if you think of death from overwork]. Tokyo: Jiyuukokuminsha A.G. (株式会社自由国民社).

Suzuki, Daisetsu Teitarou (鈴木大拙貞太郎). 1973. *Erfülltes Leben aus Zen: Mit einer Einführung in die Texte von Wei-Lang (Hui-neng)*. Munich and Bern: Otto Wilhelm Barth Verlag.

———. 1986. *Die grosse Befreiung: Einführung in den Zen-Buddhismus*. Translated by Felix Schottlaender. Twelfth edition. Munich and Wien: O. W. Barth Verlag.

———. 2007 (1935). *Manual of Zen Buddhism*. N.p.: Forgotten Books.

Suzuki, Hikaru (鈴木光). 2003. "The Japanese Way of Death." In *Handbook of Death and Dying*, volume 1, 656–672. Thousand Oaks, CA: SAGE.

Suzuki, Kansan (鈴木寛山). 1999. 日本語解体新書: 倭語原語学提要 (*Nihongo kaitai shinsho: yamatokotoba gengogaku teiyou*) [A new paper on the anatomy of the Japanese language: Compendium of the linguistic of Yamatokotoba]. Tokyo: Bungeisha (文芸社).

Suzuki, Takao (鈴木孝夫). 1990 (Original Japanese title 1975). *Eine verschlossene Sprache: Die Welt des Japanischen*. Introduced and translated from Japanese by Irmela Hijiya-Kirschnereit. Munich: Iudicum Verlag.

Taber, Charles R. 1981. "Animism." In *Abingdon Dictionary of Living Religions*, edited by Keith Crim, 37–38. Nashville, TN: Abingdon.

Tadokoro, Nazu. 1976. "Der Pferdetreiber und die Onibaba." In *Japanische Märchen*, edited and translated by Toshio Ozawa, 28–29. Third edition. Frankfurt am Main: Fischer Taschenbuch Verlag GmbH.

Tai, Yukiko (田井友季子). N.d. 対馬物語 (*Taibamonogatari; Taiba-Story*). Tokyo: Kougensha (光言社).

Taira, Masayuki (平雅行). 1990. "Religion before the Modern Age." In *Historical Studies in Japan (VII): 1983–1987: Japan at the XVIIth International Congress of Historical Sciences in Madrid*, edited by the National Committee of Japanese Historians, 189–209. Leiden: Brill.

Takariki, Masashiro. 1976. "Der goldene Kessel." In *Japanische Märchen*, edited and translated by Toshio Ozawa, 43–45. Third edition. Frankfurt am Main: Fischer Taschenbuch Verlag GmbH.

Takayanagi, Noriaki (高柳憲昭). 2001. みんなの弓道 (*Minna-no kyuudou*) [Archery for everybody]. Tokyo: Gakushuukenkyuusha (学習研究社).

Takeda, Choushuu (竹田聴洲). 1976a. "'Family Religion' in Japan: *Ie* and Its Religious Faith." In *Ancestors*, edited by William Hare Newell, 119–128. Prepared as paper for the Ninth International Congress of Anthropological and Ethnological Sciences in Chicago, 1973. Berlin and New York: Walter de Gruyter.

―――. 1976b. "Recent Trends in Studies of Ancestor Worship in Japan." In *Ancestors*, edited by William Hare Newell, 129–138. Prepared as paper for the Ninth International Congress of Anthropological and Ethnological Sciences in Chicago, 1973. Berlin and New York: Walter de Gruyter.

Takemitsu, Makoto (武光誠). 2006. 「古代日本」誕生の謎: 大和朝廷から統一国家へ (*"kodai Nippon" tanjou-no nazo: yamatochoutei-kara touitsu kokka-e*) [The riddle of the birth of "Old Japan": From Yamatochoutei to the united nation]. Kyoto: PHP Kenkyuujo (PHP研究所).

Takemura, Makio (竹村牧男), and Yoshiro Tamura, (田村芳朗). 1984a. "Jenseitsvorstellungen: Jenseitsvorstellungen, buddhistische." In *Japan-Handbuch*, edited by Horst Hammitzsch, 1588–1590. Second edition. Stuttgart: Franz Steiner Verlag Wiesbaden GmbH.

―――. 1984b. "Opfer: Opfer, buddhistische." In *Japan-Handbuch*, edited by Horst Hammitzsch, 1611–1612. Second edition. Stuttgart: Franz Steiner Verlag Wiesbaden GmbH.

Takenaka, Masao (竹中正夫). 1972. "Salvation in the Japanese Context (Japanese title: 現代における救い (*gendai-ni okeru sukui*) [Salvation in the Presence])." *International Review of Mission* 61 (241): 79–89.

―――. 1986. *God Is Rice: Asian Culture and Christian Faith*. Geneva: World Council of Churches.

Takikawa, Masajirou (瀧川政次郎). 1984. 神道史論叢: 瀧川政次郎先生米寿記念論文集 (*shintoushi ronsou: Takakawa Masajirou-sensei beiju kinen ronbunshuu*) [An essay collection on the history of Shintoism: A collection of papers commemorating the 88th birthday of Masajirou Takikawa]. Tokyo: Kokushokankoukai (国書刊行会).

Takiya, Yoshikazu. 1992. "Japan and the Domestic Scene." In *A World in Shambles in an Ordered Universe: Renewing Mission Engagement*, edited by Robert Lee, 71–79. Hayama Seminar Annual Report, Tokyo: Tokyo Mission Research Institute.

Takizawa, Katsumi (滝沢克己). 1988. 純粋神人学序説: 物と人と (*junsui shinjingaku josetsu: mono-to hito-to*) [Introduction into pure The-Anthropology: Thing and man]. Fukuoka: Sougensha (創言社).
Talmon, Shemaryahu. 1997. "The Signification of שלום and Its Semantic Field in the Hebrew Bible." In *The Quest for Context & Meaning: Studies in Biblical Intertextuality in Honor of James A. Sanders*, edited by Craig A. Evans and Shemaryahu Talmon, 75–116. Leiden: Brill.
Tan, Jonathan Y. 2004. "Missio Inter Gentes: Towards a New Paradigm in the Mission Theology of the Federation of Asian Bishops' Conference (FABC)." *Mission Studies* 21 (1): 65–95.
Tang, Edmond. 2004. "East Asia." In *An Introduction to Third World Theologies*, edited by John Parratt, 74–104. Cambridge: Cambridge University Press.
Tanigawa, Kenichi (谷川健一). 1999. 日本の神々 (*nihon-no kamigami*) [The gods of Japan]. Tokyo: Iwanami Shoten (岩波書店).
Tanno, Tamotsu. 1976. "Die drei Talismane." In *Japanische Märchen*, edited and translated by Toshio Ozawa, 27–28. Third edition. Frankfurt am Main: Fischer Taschenbuch Verlag GmbH.
Tateishi, Atsuko. 2009. "Allegations of Abuse Reported in AERA-Magazine." *Japan Harvest*: 22–24.
Tateishi, Keiji (立石恵司). 2005. 聖徳太子のほほえみ (*Shoutoku-Taishi-no hohoemi*) [The smile of Prince Shoutoku]. Tokyo: Bungeisha (文芸社).
Teeuwen, Mark. 1993. "Attaining Union with the Gods. The Secret Books of Watarai Shinto." *Monumenta Nipponica* 48 (2): 225–245. Edited by Sophia University.
Teichler, Ulrich. 1994. "Erziehung und Ausbildung." In *Länderbericht Japan: Geographie, Geschichte, Politik, Wirtschaft, Gesellschaft, Kultur*, edited by Hans-Jürgen Mayer and Manfred Pohl, 401–407. Bonn: Bundeszentrale für politische Bildung.
Terazono, Yoshiki (寺園喜基). 1987. "Japanische Theologie." In *Lexikon missiologischer Grundbegriffe*, edited by Karl Müller and Theo Sundermeier, 185–193. Wuppertal: Hammer-Verlag.
———. 1988. *Brennpunkte in Kirche und Theologie Japans: Beiträge und Dokumente*. Edited by Heyo E. Hamer. Neukirchen-Vluyn: Neukirchener Verlag des Erziehungsvereins GmbH.
———. 2006. "Japanese Theology." In *Dictionary of Mission: Theology, History, Perspectives*, edited by Karl Müller, Theo Sundermeier, Stephen B. Bevans, and Richard H. Bliese, 223–230. Eugene, OR: Wipf & Stock.
The Japan Times. 2005. "Pastor Balks at Sexual Abuse Plea." *The Japan Times*, 25 June 2005. http://www.japantimes.co.jp/news/2005/06/22/national/pastor-balks-at-sexual-abuse-plea/#.VfHkgUrQKrX (accessed 29 Dec 2015).
Thelle, Notto R. 1987. *Buddhism and Christianity in Japan: From Conflict to Dialogue, 1854–1899*. Honolulu: University of Hawaii Press.

Theologische Realenzyklopädie (*TRE*), volume 8, edited by Claus-Jürgen Thornton, Gerhard Krause, Gerhard Müller, Siegfried M. Schwertner, Matthias Glockner. 1981. Berlin and New York: Walter de Gruyter.

Thiel, Josef Franz. 1983. *Grundbegriffe der Ethnologie*. Volume 16 of Collectanea Instituti Anthropos. Fourth enlarged and revised edition. Berlin: Dietrich Reimer Verlag.

Thielicke, Helmuth. 1978. *Theologie des Geistes: Der dritte Glaubensartikel. Die Manifestation des heiligen Geistes im Wort, in der Kirche, in den Religionen und in den letzten Dingen*. Volume 3 of Dogmatik: Der Evangelische Glaube: Grundzüge der Dogmatik. Tübingen: Mohr Siebeck.

———. 1979. *Das Schweigen Gottes: Fragen aus der Bedrängnis*. Wuppertal: R. Brockhaus Verlag.

———. 1981. *Theologische Ethik: Prinzipienlehre: Dogmatische, philosophische und kontrovers theologische Grundlegung*, volume 1. Fifth edition. Tübingen: Mohr Siebeck.

Thomas, William, and Kaste Pavian. 1994. *Book of Talismans, Amulets and Zodiacal Gems*. Whitefish, MT: Kessinger Publishing.

Thomsen, Harry. 1963. *The New Religions of Japan: A Spotlight on the Most Significant Development in Postwar Japan*. Rutland, VT and Tokyo: Charles E. Tuttle Company.

Thornton, Sharon G. 2003. "America of the Broken Heart." In *Realizing the America of Our Hearts: Theological Voices of Asian Americans*, edited by Fumitaka Matsuoka and Eleazar S. Fernandez, 200–213. St Louis, MI: Chalice Press.

Thränhardt, Anna Maria. 1994. "Soziale Sicherung in Japan." In *Länderbericht Japan: Geographie, Geschichte, Politik, Wirtschaft, Gesellschaft, Kultur*, edited by Hans-Jürgen Mayer and Manfred Pohl, 426–441. Bonn: Bundeszentrale für politische Bildung.

Tillich, Paul. 1959. *Gesammelte Werke: Offenbarung und Glaube*. Trebbin: Evangelisches Verlagswerk.

Tobe, Tamio (戸部民夫). 2007. 「頼れる神様」大事典: 縁結び、商売繁盛だけじゃない! (*"tayoreru kamisama" daijiten: enmusubi, shoubaihanjou dake-janai!*) [Encyclopedia of the "gods that can be trusted": Matchmaking and economic affluence is not everything!]. Kyoto: PHP Kenkyuujo (PHP研究所).

Tokuzen, Yoshikazu (徳善義和). 1981. "Kultur der Scham – Kultur der Schuld: Reformatorische Theologie japanisch erleben." In *Lutherische Monatshefte* 20 (10): 568–570.

Toujou, Takanobu (東條隆進). 1992. "Salvation in a Secularistic, Urban Society." In *Salvation: Some Asian Perspectives*, edited by Ken Gnanakan, 177–182. Bangalore, India: Asia Theological Association.

Toya, Manabu (戸矢学). 2006. 陰陽道とは何か: 日本史を呪縛する神秘の原理 (*onnyoudou to-wa nani-ka: Nipponshi-o jubaku-suru shinpi-no genri*) [What is Onnyoudou?: Mystical principle disenchant the history of Japan]. Kyoto: PHP Kenkyuujo (PHP研究所).

Toyozaki, Youko; Varnam-Atkin, Stuart. 2008. ニッポン風物詩: *Are Japanese Cats Left-handed?* (*Nippon fuubutsu shi*) [The seasonal poetry of Nippon]. Herts, England: IBC Publishing.

Treichlinger, W. M. 1954. *Japanische Spruchweisheiten: Dreihundertdreißig Japanische Sprichwörter*. Fifth edition. Zürich: Verlag der Arche.

Triandis, Harry C. 1995. *Individualism & Collectivism*. Boulder, CO, San Francisco, CA, and Oxford: Westview Press.

Triebel, Johannes. 1988. "Leiden als Thema der Missionstheologie: Der Beitrag Georg Vicedoms zum Thema im Kontext gegenwärtiger Stimmen." In *Jahrbuch Mission*. Hamburg: Missionshilfe-Verlag.

———. 1998. "The Paradox of a Suffering God: On the Classical, Modern-Western and Third World Struggles to Harmonise the Incompatible Attributes of the Trinitarian God." Book review of the eponymous book by Gregory Nnamani; Frankfurt am Main, Bern and New York: Peter Lang. *Missiology* 26 (3): 366.

Triplett, Katja. 2004. *Menschenopfer und Selbstopfer in den japanischen Legenden: Das Frankfurter Manuskript der Matsura Sayohime-Legende*. Volume 2 of Religiöse Gegenwart Asiens. Berlin, Hamburg, Münster: LIT Verlag.

———. 2006a. "Das Pluralismusmodell 'Religionsfreiheit' und die religiöse Vielfalt Japans." In *Religionen nebeneinander: Modelle religiöser Vielfalt in Ost- und Südostasien: Proceedings of a meeting held Sept. 28–Oct. 1, 2003 in Erfurt, Germany*, edited by Edith Franke and Michael Pye, 103–120. Berlin, Hamburg and Münster: LIT Verlag.

———. 2006b. "The Discourse on War or Harmony in Contemporary Japanese Religions and Society." In *Religious Harmony: Problems, Practice, and Education: Proceedings of the Regional Conference of the International Association for the History of Religions, Yogyakarta and Semarang, Indonesia, September 27th – October 3rd, 2004*, edited by Michael Pye, Edith Franke, Alef Theria Wasim and Abdurrahman Ma'sud, 179–188. The International Association for the History of Religions Regional Conference. Berlin and New York: Walter de Gruyter.

Tsan, Tsong-Sheng. 1997. "Ahnenkult und Christentum in Taiwan heute: Eine asiatische Fallstudie." *Zeitschrift für Mission* 23 (3): 184–204.

Tsuchiya, Haruhito (土屋晴仁). 2008. ニッポンのしきたり: *Customs of Japan* (*Nippon-no shikitari*) [Customs of Japan]. Tokyo: IBC Publishing.

Tsugita, Uruu (次田潤). 2008. 祝詞新講 (*norito shinkou*) [New lecture on norito]. Tokyo: Ebisu Koushou Publication (戎光祥出版株式会).

Tsunoda, Ryusaku (角田柳作), Wm. Theodore de Bary, and Donald Keene. 1964. "Sources of Japanese Tradition." In *Introduction to Oriental Civilizations*, edited by Wm. Theodore de Bary. New York: Columbia University Press.

Tsunogawa, Shunju (角川春樹). 1982. 角川古語大辞典 (*tsunogawa kogo daijiten*) [Tsunogawa encyclopedia of classic Japanese]. Tokyo: Tsunogawa Shoten (角川書店).

Tsushima, Michihito (対馬路人), Shigeru Nishiyama (西山茂), Susumu Shimazono (島薗進), and Hiroko Shiramizu (白水寛子). 1979. "The Vitalistic Conception of Salvation in Japanese New Religions: An Aspect of Modern Religious Consciousness." In *Japanese Journal of Religious Studies* 6 (1/2): 139–161. Proceedings of the 1978 Tokyo Meeting of the Conference Internationale de Sociologie Religieuse. Nanzan Institute for Religion and Culture. http://www.jstor.org/stable/30233195 (accessed 13 Oct 2012).

Tsushima, Yuuko (津島佑子). 1990. "Im Bad." In *Zeit der Zikaden: Japanisches Lesebuch: Erzählungen der Gegenwart*, edited by Tadao Araki and Ekkehard May, 232–248. Munich and Zürich: Piper.

———. 1993. "The Bath." In *The Company of Animals*, edited by Martin Holman and Michael J. Rosen, 133–157. New York: Doubleday.

Turaki, Yusufu. 2000. "African Traditional Religious System as Basis of Understanding Christian Spiritual Warfare." http://www.lausanne.org/en/documents/all/nairobi-2000/194-west-african-case-study.html (accessed 13 Oct 2012).

Turnbull, Stephen R. 1998. *The Kakure Kirishitan of Japan: A Study of Their Development, Beliefs and Rituals to the Present Day*. London: Routledge.

———. 2006. *The Samurai and the Sacred: The Path of the Warrior*. Botley, Oxford: Osprey Publishing.

———. 2008. *The Samurai Swordsman: Master of War*. Rutland, VT and Tokyo, Japan: Charles E. Tuttle Company.

Turner, Patricia, and Charles Russell Coulter. 2001. *Dictionary of Ancient Deities*. New York, NY: Oxford University Press.

Turner, Victor Witter. 1995. *The Ritual Process: Structure and Anti-Structure*. The Lewis Henry Morgan Lectures; Foundations of Human Behavior. Hawthorne, New York: Aldine Transaction (Aldine de Gruyter; A Division of Walter de Gruyter).

Tutu, Desmond. 1987 (1982). *Desmond Tutu: Ausgewählte Texte*. Munich: Wilhelm Goldmann Verlag.

Uchima, Chokujin (内間直仁). 2006. 沖縄語辞典：那覇方言を中心に (*okinawago jiten: nahahougen-o chuushin-ni*) [Dictionary of the Okinawan language: With particular regard to the Naha-dialect]. Tokyo: Kenkyuusha (研究社).

Uda, Kiyoko (宇多喜代子). 2007. 古季語と遊ぶ：古い季語・珍しい季語の実作体験記 (*Kokigo-to asobu: Furui kigo, mezurashii kigo, jissakutaikenki*) [Playing with Old Seasonal (Haiku) Key Words: A Chronicle of the Actual Experience of Old and Rare Seasonal (Haiku) Key Words.] Tokyo: Kadokawagakukei Shuppan (角川学芸出版).

Umezawa, Emiko (梅沢恵美子). 2003. 額田王の謎:「あかねさす」に秘められた衝撃のメッセージ (*Nukada-Oo-no nazo: "akanesasu"-ni himerasareta shougeki-no messeeji*) [The riddle of King Nukada: The shocking secret message of the "Akasasu"]. Kyoto: PHP Kenkyuujo (PHP研究所).

Underwood, A. C. 2007 (1934). *Shintoism: The Indigenous Religion of Japan*. Alcester, Warwickshire: Read Books.
Underwood, Horace G. 1994. "Christianity in Korea." *Missiology* 22 (1): 65–76.
Usui, Ryuuichirou (臼井隆一郎). 2009. "Die Minamata-Krankheit und die Sprache jenseits des ius talionis: Auf der Suche nach der Sprache der Anima im *Paradies im Meer der Qualen* von Michiko Ishimure." In *Grenzen des Lebens – Grenzen der Verständigung*, edited by Heinz-Dieter Assmann, Karl-Josef Kuschen and Karin Moser v. Filseck, 57–66. Würzburg: Königshausen & Neumann.
Van Bragt, Jan. 1992. "Inculturation in Japan." In *A Universal Faith?: Peoples, Cultures, Religions, and the Christ: Essays in Honor of Frank de Graeve*, edited by Catherine Cornille, V. Neckebrouck, and Frank De Graeve, 49–72. Louvain: Peeters Publishers; Grand Rapids, MI: Eerdmans.
Vance, Timothy J. 1984. "The Etymology of Kami." *Japanese Journal of Religious Studies* 10 (4): 277–288.
Van der Horst, Pieter. 2003. "Das Zölibat im Frühjudentum." In *Frühjudentum und Neues Testament im Horizont Biblischer Theologie* (mit einem Anhang zum Corpus Judaeo-Hellenisticum Novi Testamenti), edited by Wolfgang Kraus and Karl-Wilhelm Niebuhr, 3–15. Tübingen: Mohr Siebeck.
Van der Veere, H. 2003. *Boeddha's en Kami: de ontwikkeling van de Japanse religie*. Amsterdam: Amsterdam University Press.
Van Dijk, Lutz. 2007. *Die Geschichte von Liebe und Sex*. Frankfurt and New York: Campus Verlag.
Van Ess, Hans. 2008. *Die 101 wichtigsten Fragen: China*. Munich: C. H. Beck.
Van Gennep, Arnold. 2005 (1909). *Übergangsriten: (Les Rites de Passage)*. Translated by Klaus Schomburg and Sylvia M. Schomburg-Scherff. Frankfurt and New York: Campus Verlag; Paris: Édition de la Maison des Sciences de l'Homme.
Van Lin, Jan. 2002. *Shaking the Fundamentals: Religious Plurality and Ecumenical Movement*. Amsterdam and New York: Editions Rodopi B.V.
Van Rheenen, Gailyn. 1993. "Animism, Secularism and Theism: Developing a Tripartite Model for Understanding World Cultures." *International Journal of Frontier Missions* (IJFM) 10 (4): 169–171. http://www.ijfm.org/PDFs_IJFM/10_4_PDFs/04_Van_Rheenen.pdf (accessed 13 Oct 2012).
———. 1996. *Communicating Christ in Animistic Contexts*. South Pasadena, CA: William Carey Library.
———. 2002. *Shaking the Fundamentals: Religious Plurality and Ecumenical Movement*. Amsterdam and New York, NY: Editions Rodopi B.V.
———. 2003a. *Defining an Animistic Worldview*. http://globalchristiancenter.com/academic-research/defining-an-animistic-worldview.html (accessed 13 Oct 2012).
———. 2003b. *Proclaiming the Kingdom of God among Animists and Secularists*. http://www.missiology.org/?p=491 (accessed 13 Oct 2012).

Veldhuis, Henri, and Renate Drewes-Siebel. 1994. "Ein versiegeltes Buch: Der Naturbegriff in der Theologie J. G. Hamanns (1730–1788)." Presented as doctoral thesis by Henri Veldhuis in Utrecht, 1990, Berlin and New York: Walter de Gruyter.

Veltri, Guiseppe. 1997. "Magie und Halakha: Ansätze zu einem empirischen Wissenschaftsbegriff im spätantiken und frühmittelalterlichen Judentum." In *Texte und Studien zum Antiken Judentum* 62. Presented as inaugural dissertation at the Freie Universität Berlin, 1996. Tübingen: Mohr Siebeck.

Vicedom, Georg Friedrich. 1963. *Das Geheimnis des Leidens der Kirche*. 111 of Theologische Existenz heute, eine Schriftenreihe, edited by K. G. Steck and G. Einholz. Munich: Chr. Kaiser Verlag.

———. 1965. *Gebet für die Welt: Das Vater-Unser als Missionsgebet*. Munich: Chr. Kaiser Verlag.

Victoria, Brian. 1999. *Zen, Nationalismus und Krieg: Eine unheimliche Allianz*. (English original *Zen at War*, 1997). N.p.: Theseus Verlag.

Villiers, Elizabeth. 1996. *The Mascot Book: The Book That Brings Good Luck*. Pomeroy, WA: Health Research Books.

Vivelo, Frank Robert. 1988 (1978). *Handbuch der Kulturanthropologie: Eine grundlegende Einführung*. Munich: Deutscher Taschenbuchverlag GmbH & Co. KG.

Volker, T. 1975 (1950*). The Animal in Far Eastern Art and Especially in the Art of the Japanese Netsuke, with References to Chinese Origins, Traditions, Legends, and Art*. Leiden: Brill.

Vollmer, Klaus. 2011. "Reinheit und gesllschaftliche Ordnung in Japan: Dimensionen des sogenannten *buraku*-Problems in historischer und zeitgenössischer Perpsektive." In *Reinheit*, edited by Peter Burschel and Christoph Marx, 325–348. Wien, Köln, and Weimar: Böhlau Verlag.

Von Balthasar, Hans Urs. 1962. *Karl Barth: Darstellung und Deutung seiner Theologie*. Second edition. Köln: Jakob Hegner.

Von Brandt, Ahasver. 2007. *Werkzeug des Historikers: Eine Einführung in die historischen Hilfswissenschaften*. Volume 33 of Kohlhammer Urban-Taschenbücher. Stuttgart, Berlin, Köln: Verlag W. Kohlhammer.

Von Brück, Michael, and Whalen Lai. 2000. *Buddhismus und Christentum: Geschichte, Konfrontation, Dialog*. Second edition. Munich: C. H. Beck.

Von Bülow, Vicco. 1999. "Otto Weber (1902–1966): Reformierter Theologe und Kirchenpolitiker." Presented as doctoral thesis in Bonn, 1997/1998. Göttingen: Vandenhoeck & Ruprecht.

Von Klemperer, Klemens. 1995. "Über Luther hinaus?: Dietrich Bonhoeffer und der Widerstand gegen den Nationalsozialismus." In *Politischer Wandel, organisierte Gewalt und nationale Sicherheit: Beiträge zur neueren Geschichte Deutschlands und Frankreichs: Festschrift für Klaus-Jürgen Müller*, edited by Klaus Jürgen Müller,

Ernst Willi Hansen, Gerhard Schreiber and Bernd Wegner, 403–416. Munich: Oldenbourg Wissenschaftsverlag GmbH.
Von Rad, Gerhard. 1987. *Das 1.Buch Mose, Genesis*. Altes Testament Deutsch, ATD 2–4. Göttingen: Vandenhoeck & Ruprecht.
Von Siebold, Philipp Franz. 2001. *Nippon: Archiv zur Beschreibung von Japan und dessen Neben- und Schutzländern Jezo mit den südlichen Kurilen, Sachalin, Korea und den Liukiu-Inseln*, volume 2. Chestnut Hill, MA: Adamant Media Corporation.
Waddell, Laurence Austine. 1972. *Tibetan Buddhism: With Its Mystic Cults, Symbolism and Mythology, and in Its Relation to Indian Buddhism*. N.p.: Courier Dover Publications.
Wagner, C. Peter. 1991. "Territorial Spirits." In *Engaging the Enemy: How to Fight and Defeat Territorial Spirits*, edited by C. Peter Wagner, 43–50. Ventura, CA: Regal Books, a division of Gospel Light.
———. 1992. *Warfare Prayer: How to Seek God's Power and Protection in the Battle to Build His Kingdom*. Ventura, CA: Regal Books, a division of Gospel Light.
Wahl, Harald-Martin. 1997. "Die Jakobserzählungen." Presented as habilitation treatise at the Universität Marburg, 1995, Berlin and New York: Walter de Gruyter.
Wahlen, Clinton. 2004. *Jesus and the Impurity of Spirits in the Synoptic Gospels*. Wissenschaftliche Untersuchungen zum Neuen Testament, second series, 185. Tübingen: Mohr Siebeck.
Waldenfels, Hans. 1974. "Befreiung und Erlösung: Systematisch-theologische Überlegungen." In *Theologie und Befreiung*, edited by Heribert Bettscheider, 104–122. N.p.: Steyler Verlag.
———. 1995. "Nordostasien." In *Einleitung in die Missionsgeschichte: Tradition, Situation und Dynamik des Christentums*, edited by Karl Müller and Werner Ustorf, 131–142. Stuttgart, Berlin, Köln: Verlag W. Kohlhammer.
Wallace, B. Allan. 2006. "Energy Dynamics." *Life Positive*: 63–66. http://www.alanwallace.org/Energydynamics.pdf (accessed 13 Oct 2012).
Walldorf, Friedemann. 1996. "Mission in Partnerschaft: Zum Aufbruch der evangelikalen Missionsbewegung in Afrika, Asien und Lateinamerika." In *Werdet meine Zeugen: Weltmission im Horizont von Theologie und Geschichte*, edited by Hans Kasdorf and Friedemann Walldorf, 221–247. Stuttgart: Hänssler.
Waltke, Bruce K. 1995. *Finding the Will of God: A Pagan Notion?* Grand Rapids, MI, Cambridge, UK: Eerdmans; Vancouver, BC: Regent College Publishing.
Walton, John H., Victor H. Matthews, and Mark W. Chavalas. 2000. *The IVP Bible Background Commentary: Old Testament*. Downers Grove, IL: InterVarsity Press.
Warneck, Johannes. 1913. *Lebenskräfte des Evangeliums: Missionserfahrungen innerhalb des animistischen Heidentums*. Fifth edition. Berlin: Verlag von Martin Warneck.
Wartofsky, Marx W. 1982. *Feuerbach*. London, New York, New Rocelle, Melbourne, and Sydney: Cambridge University Press.

Watanabe, Baiyu (渡辺楳雄). 1957. "Modern Japanese Religions: Their Success Explained." In *Monumenta Nipponica* 13 (1/2): 153–162. Edited by Sophia University.

Watanabe, Rikizou (渡辺力蔵). 2002. 日本人のアイデンティティー: 日本文化の構造と日本文明の盛衰 (*Nihonjin-no aidentitii: Nihonbunka-no kouzou-to Nihonbunmei-no seisui*) [Japanese identity: The structure of the Japanese culture and rise and fall of the Japanese civilization]. Tokyo: Bungeisha (文芸社).

Watanabe, Shouichi (渡部昇一). 2005. 私の家庭教育再生論:鍵は「お母さんの知恵」にある (*watakushi-no katei kyouiku saiseiron: kagi-wa "okaasan-no chie"-ni aru*) [A doctrine of the revival of parenting in my home: The key is the "wisdom of mother"]. Tokyo: Kairyuusha (海竜社).

Watsky, Andrew Mark. 2004. *Chikubushima: Deploying the Sacred Arts in Momoyama Japan*. Seattle, WA: University of Washington Press.

Watsuji, Tetsurou (和辻哲郎). 1988. "The Family as an Ethical System." In *Inside the Japanese System: Readings on Contemporary Society and Political Economy*, edited by Daniel I. Okimoto and Thomas P. Rohlen, 3–5. Stanford, CA: Stanford University Press.

Watts, Alan. 1999. *Buddhism the Religion of No-Religion: The Edited Transcripts*. North Clarendon, VT and Tokyo: Tuttle Publishing.

Watts, Rikke E. 2002. "The New Exodus/New Creational Restoration of the Image of God: A Biblical-Theological Perspective on Salvation." In *What Does It Mean to Be Saved?: Broadening Evangelical Horizons of Salvation*, edited by John G. Stackhouse, Jr., 15–41. Grand Rapids, MI: Baker Academic.

Weber, Otto. 1955. *Grundlagen der Dogmatik*, volume 1. Neukirchen and Moers: Verlag der Buchhandlung des Erziehungsvereins.

Weggel, Oskar. 1997. *Die Asiaten: Gesellschaftsordnungen, Wirtschaftssysteme, Denkformen, Glaubensweisen, Alltagsleben, Verhaltensstile*. Second edition. Munich: Deutscher Taschenbuch Verlag.

Weiming, Tu (杜維明). 2006. "Beyond the 'Enlightenment Mentality': An Anthropocosmic Perspective." In *Asian New Humanities Net Third Annual Meeting: The Fine Line in the Between: Humanities and Sciences in the 21st Century*; 第三屆亞洲新人文聯網會議 分合之際: 二十一世紀的人文與科學. Hosted by 國立中央大學人文中心; The Humanities Center at National Central University; 中央研究院明清研究會; The Ming-Ch'ing Studies Group, Academia Sinica. Sponsoren: 教育部顧問室、行政院文化建設委員會、國家高速網路與計算中心、誠藝建設公司; Ministry of Education Advisory Office, Council for Cultural Affairs, National Center for High-Performance Computing, Cheng-Yi Construction Corporation, 13–14 June 2006: 3–13. http://mingching.sinica.edu.tw/text/Artike_papers.pdf.

Weiss, Gabriele. 1987. *Elementarreligionen: Eine Einführung in die Religionsethnologie*. Wien and New York: Springer Verlag.

Wellhausen, Julius. 2004. *Israelitische und jüdische Geschichte*, tenth edition. Berlin and New York: Walter de Gruyter.
Wendt, Ingeborg Y. 1970. *Die "unheimlichen" Japaner*. Stuttgart, Berlin, Köln, Mainz: Verlag W. Kohlhammer.
Wernhart, Karl R. 2002. "Ethnische Seelenkonzepte." In *Der Begriff der Seele in der Religionswissenschaft*, edited by Johann Figl, and Hans-Dieter Klein, 45–60. Würzburg: Verlag Königshausen & Neumann.
Werthmüller, Lucius. o. J. *Lebensenergie – zwischen Mysterium und Forschungsobjekt*. http://www.psizentrumbasel.ch/index.php?lebensenergie (accessed 12 Oct 2012).
West, Donald James, and Richard Green. 1997. *Sociolegal Control of Homosexuality: A Multi-Nation Comparison*. Berlin: Springer.
Westermann, Claus. 1978. *Theologie des Alten Testaments in Grundzügen*. Grundrisse zum Alten Testament; ATD Ergänzungsreihe 6. Göttingen: Vandenhoeck & Ruprecht.
———. 1985. *Theologie des Alten Testaments in Grundzügen*. Grundrisse zum Alten Testament; ATD Ergänzungsreihe 6. Second edition. Göttingen: Vandenhoeck & Ruprecht.
Westhelle, Vítor. 1998. "Befreiungsbewegung, systematisch." In *Religion in Geschichte und Gegenwart: Handwörterbuch für Theologie und Religionswissenschaft* (RGG), edited by Hans Dieter Betz, Don S. Browning, Bernd Janowsky and Eberhard Jüngel, 1210–1211. Fourth completely revised edition. Tübingen: Mohr Siebeck.
Wetzel, Klaus. 1995. *Kirchengeschichte Asiens*. Wuppertal and Zürich: R. Brockhaus Verlag.
Wetzel, Patricia J. 2004. *Keigo in Modern Japan: Polite Language from Meiji to the Present*. Honolulu: University of Hawaii Press.
Wheeler, Gordon. 2000. *Beyond Individualism: Toward a New Understanding of Self, Relationship, & Experience*. London and Philadelphia: Routledge.
Whelan, Christal. 1996. *The Beginning of Heaven and Earth: The Sacred Book of Japan's Hidden Christians*. Honolulu: University of Hawaii Press.
———. 2000. "Religion Concealed: The *Kakure Kirishitan* on Narushima." In *Japan's Hidden Christians, 1549–1999*, edited by Stephen R. Turnbull. London: Routledge.[12] (First published in *Monumenta Nipponica* 47, no. 3 (1992): 369–387.)
White, James Wilson. 1970. *Sokagakkai and Mass Society*. Stanford Studies in Comparative Politics, 4. Palo Alto, CA: Stanford University Press.
White, Stanley. 2016 "A Record Number of People in Japan Are Dying from Overwork." *Business Insider (Finance)*, 2 April 2016. http://www.businessinsider.com/a-record-number-of-people-in-japan-are-dying-from-overwork-2016-4?r=UK&IR=T (accessed 6 Apr 2016).

---

12. Page numbers are according to the print in *Monumenta Nipponica*.

Whiteman, Darrell L. 2003. "Anthropology and Mission: The Incarnational Connection." *Missiology* 31 (4): 397–415.

Whorf, Benjamin Lee. 1965. *Sprache – Denken – Wirklichkeit: Beiträge zur Metalinguistik und Sprachphilosophie*. Third edition. Reinbeck bei Hamburg: Rowohlt Taschenbuch Verlag GmbH.

Wiegand-Kanzaki, Anke. 1986. *Gewissen und soziale Kontrolle in Japan und Deutschland*. Würzburg: Königshausen und Neumann.

Wierzbicka, Anna. 1996. *Semantics: Primes and Universals*. Oxford: Oxford University Press.

———. 1997. *Understanding Cultures through Their Key Words: English, Russian, Polish, German, and Japanese*. New York, NY: Oxford University Press US.

Wiher, Hannes. 2003. "Der Animismus als schamorientiertes System." In *Mission in fremden Kulturen: Beiträge zur Missionsethnologie: Festschrift für Lothar Käser zu seinem 65. Geburtstag*, edited by Klaus Müller, 291–305. Nürnberg: Verlag für Theologie und Religionswissenschaft: Edition afem.

Wiley, H. Orton. 1940. *Christian Theology*, volumes 1–3. Kansas City, MO: Beacon Hill Press.

Wilkins, William Joseph. 2004 (1882). *Hindu Mythology, Vedic and Puranic*. Whitefish, MT: Kessinger Publishing.

———. 2001 (1882). *Hindu Mythology, Vedic and Puranic*. Boston: Elibron Classics, Adamant Media Corporation.Williams, E. Lesslie. 2007. *Spirit Tree: Origins of Cosmology in Shintô Ritual at Hakozaki*. Lanham, Boulder, New York, Toronto, and Oxford: University Press of America.

Williams, Yoko. 2003. *Tsumi: Offence and Retribution in Early Japan*. London and New York: Routledge.

Wiltshire, Martin G. 1990. *Ascetic Figures Before and in Early Buddhism: The Emergence of Gautama as the Buddha*. Berlin and New York: Walter de Gruyter.

Wingren, Gustaf. 1962. *Evangelium und Kirche*. Göttingen: Vandenhoeck und Ruprecht.

Wippermann, Carsten. 2000. *Zwischen den Kulturen: Das Christentum in Südkorea*. Religion und Theologie im Asien-Pazifik-Kontext. Berlin, Hamburg and Münster: LIT Verlag.

Wippich, Rolf-Harald. 2001. "Christliche Mission und Kulturimperialismus: Aufbau und Entwicklung der deutschen Protestantischen Missionsräte in der *Meiji*-Zeit." In *11. Deutschsprachiger Japanologentag in Trier 1999: Sprache, Literatur, Kunst, Populärkultur, Medien, Informationstechnik*, edited by Hilaria Gössmann and Andreas Mrugalla, 51–62. Berlin, Hamburg and Münster: LIT Verlag.

Wolff, Hans Walter. 1983. 旧約聖書の人間論 (*kyuuyaku seisho-no ningenron*) [Anthropology of the Old Testament]. Translated by Motosuke Oogushi (大串元亮). Tokyo: Nihon Kirisuto Kyoudan Shuppankyoku (日本基督教団出版局).

———. 1984 (1973). *Anthropologie des Alten Testaments*. Fourth revised edition. Munich: Chr. Kaiser Verlag.

Wood, William. 2006. "Critical Issues: Challenges for the Church in Japan Today: Distorted Spiritual Authoritarianism." *Japan Harvest* (Summer): 18–19. Tokyo: Japan Evangelical Missionary Association.

Woolfolk, Robert L. 2002. *The Power of Negative Thinking: Truth, Melancholia, and the Tragic Sense of Life.* http://psycnet.apa.org/psycinfo/2002-01803-003 (accessed 17 May 2016).

Worm, Herbert. 1994. "Japanologie im Nationalsozialismus: Ein Zwischenbericht." In *Formierung und Fall der Achse Berlin-Tokyo* (Monographien 8), edited by Gerhard Krebs and Bernd Martin, 153–186. Deutsches Institut für Japanstudien. Munich: Iudicum Verlag.

Wright, J. Stafford. 1974. *Der Christ und das Okkulte.* English original *Christianity and the Occult*, 1971. N.p.: Bibellesebund für Deutschland und die Schweiz; Wuppertal: R. Brockhaus Verlag.

Wright, Christopher J. H. 2006. *The Mission of God: Unlocking the Bible's Grand Narrative.* Downers Grove, IL: InterVarsity Press.

Wright, Nigel G. 1996. "Charismatic Interpretations of the Demonic." In *The Unseen World: Christian Reflections on Angels, Demons, and the Heavenly Realm*, edited by Anthony N. S. Lane, 149–163. Grand Rapids, MI: Tyndale House; Carlisle, Cumbria: Paternoster.

Wrogemann, Henning. 1995. *Mission und Religion in der Systematischen Theologie der Gegenwart: Das Missionsverständnis deutschsprachiger protestantischer Dogmatiker im 20. Jahrhundert.* Volume 79 of Forschungen zur systematischen und ökumenischen Theologie. Göttingen: Vandenhoeck & Ruprecht.

———. 2012. *Interkulturelle Theologie und Hermeneutik: Grundlagen, aktuelle Beispiele, theoretishe Perspektiven.* Gütersloh: Gütersloher Verlagshaus (eBook).

Würthwein, Ernst. 1938. *Wort und Existenz: Studien zum Alten Testament.* Göttingen: Vandenhoeck & Ruprecht.

Yaegashi, Minoru. 2002. "月経前症候群：当帰芍薬散＋補中益気湯で改善：気・血・水のバランスを調整 (*gekkeizenshoukougun: toukishakuyakusan + hotchuu ekikitou-de kaizen: ki, chi, sui-no baransu-o chousei*) [The vast growd of candidates for PMS: Improvment through (medication with) *Toukishakuyakusan + Hotyuu Ekikitou*: Balancing *ki*, blood and water]." In 漢方辞典：名医と治す (*kanpoujiten: meii-to naosu*) [Encyclopedia of Chinese traditional medicine: Healing together with the physician], edited by weekly journal Shuukan Asahi (週刊朝日), 91–93. Tokyo: Asahi Shinbunsha (朝日新聞社).

Yagi, Seiichi (八木誠一). 1967. "Geschichte und Gegenwart der neutestamentlichen Forschung in Japan." In *Theologische Stimmen aus Asien, Afrika, Lateinamerika*, volume 2, edited by Hans-Werner Gensichen, Gerhard Rosenkranz and Georg F. Vicedom, 29–39. Munich: Chr. Kaiser Verlag.

———. 2002. "Ego And Self in the New Testament and in Zen." In *The Bible in a World Context: An Experiment in Contextual Hermeneutics*, edited by Walter Dietrich and Ulrich Luz, 33–53. Grand Rapids, MI: Eerdmans.

Yagi, Seiichi (八木誠一), and Leonardo J. Swidler. 1990. *A Bridge to Buddhist-Christian Dialogue*. New York: Paulist Press.

Yahata, You (矢幡洋). 2007. 心理療法 (*shinri ryouhou*) [Psychotherapy]. Kyoto: PHP Kenkyuujo (PHP研究所).

Yamaguchi, Ichirou (山口一郎). 1997. *Ki als leibhaftige Vernunft: Beitrag zur interkulturellen Phänomenologie der Leiblichkeit*. Volume 31 of Übergänge: Text und Studien zu Handlung, Sprache und Lebenswelt. Edited by Richard Grathoff and Bernhard Waldenfels. Munich: Wilhelm Fink Verlag.

Yamaguchi, Momoo (山口百々男), and Steven Bates. 2014. 和英日本の文化・観光・歴史辞典 (*waei nihon-no bunka, kankou, rekishijiten*) [A Japanese-English dictionary of culture, tourism and history of Japan]. Tokyo: Sanshuusha (三修社).

Yamakage, Motohisa (山陰基久), Paul de Leeuw, and Aidan Rankin. 2006. *The Essence of Shinto: Japan's Spiritual Heart* (Eastern Philosophy and Taoism Series). Tokyo, New York, London: Koudansha International.

Yamamori, Tetsunao (山森鉄直). 1974. *Church Growth in Japan: A Study in the Development of Eight Denominations 1859–1939*. South Pasadena, CA: William Carey Library.

Yamaori, Tetsuo (山折哲雄). 1999. 宗教の力：日本人の心はどこへ行くのか (*shuukyou-no chikara: Nihonjin-no kokoro-wa doko-e ikuno-ka*) [The power of religion: Where do the hearts of the Japanese go?]. Kyoto: PHP Kenkyuujo (PHP研究所).

Yamashita, Hisako. 1976. "Te-te Koboschi." In *Japanische Märchen*, edited and translated by Toshio Ozawa, 38–39. Third edition. Frankfurt am Main: Fischer Taschenbuch Verlag GmbH.

Yamashita, Kouichi (山下孝一). 2003. 人を育てる人が社会を伸ばす *(hito-o sodateru hito-ga shakai-o nobasu)* [People who raise people further society]. Tokyo: Bungeisha (文芸社).

Yancey, Philip. 2002. *Warum ich heute nich glaube: Menschen, die mir halfen, die Gemeinde zu überleben*. Wuppertal: R. Brockhaus Verlag.

Yasuda, Takuto (安田拓人). 2004. "Schuldfähigkeit des geistesgestörten Täters in japanischem Strafrecht: Zugleich ein Exkurs zum Schuldbegriff in Japan – Marburger Gastvortrag am 30.6.2004." *Osaka University Law Review* 52 (27): 27–36. http://ir.library.osaka-u.ac.jp/dspace/bitstream/11094/3830/1/oulr052-027.pdf (accessed 17 May 2016).

Yato, Sadahiko (谷戸貞彦). 2005. 七福神と聖天さん: 民間信仰の歴史 (*Shichifukujin-to shoutensan: Minkanshinkou-no rekishi*) [The Seven Auspicious Deities and Shoutensan: A history of folk belief]. N.p.: Oomoto Shuppan (大元出版).

Yewangoe, Andreas Anangguru. 1987. *Theologia Crucis in Asia: Asian Christian Views on Suffering in the Face of Overwhelming Poverty and Multifaceted Religiosity in Asia*. Amsterdam and Kenilworth, NJ: Rodopi.

Yonemura, Shouji. 1976. "Dôzoku and Ancestor Worship in Japan." In *Ancestors*, edited by William Hare Newell, 177–204. Prepared as paper for the Ninth International Congress of Anthropological and Ethnological Sciences in Chicago, 1973. Berlin and New York: Walter de Gruyter.

York, Michael. 2005. *Pagan Theology: Paganism as a World Religion*. New York, NY: New York University Press.

Yoshida, Hideaki (吉田秀昭). 2002. "セピアに染まる (*sepia-ni somaru*) [Faded into sepia]." In 香るケ丘 (*kaorugaoka*) [*Kaorugaoka*], 113–132. Tokyo: Bungeisha (文芸者).

Yoshiyama, Mitsuru (吉山満). 2003. 剣道昇段審査合格術：悩める剣士に贈る (*kendoushoudan shinsagoukakujutsu: nayameru kenshi-ni okuru*) [The art one needs to pass a kendou exam: Dedicated to the swordsman that has a hard time]. Tokyo: Sukiijaanaru (スキージャーナル).

Yoshino, Kosaku (吉野耕作). 1997. "The Discourse on Blood and Racial Identity in Contemporary Japan." In *The Construction of Racial Identities in China and Japan: Historical and Contemporary Perspectives*, edited by Frank Dikötter, 199–212. London: Hurst & Company.

Yoshizawa, Noburo. 1996. "Identitätsgenese und japanischer Narzißmus: Anmerkungen der Perspektive der japanischen Bildungsphilosophie." In *Harmonie und Konformität: Tradition und Krise japanischer Sozialisationsmuster*, edited by Agi Schründer-Lenzen, 184–190. Munich: Iudicum Verlag.

"Young People Easily Get Sucked into Aum Shinrikyo Spinoff Aleph." In *Japan Today*, 20th August 2012. http://www.japantoday.com/category/kuchikomi/view/young-people-easily-get-sucked-into-aum-shinrikyo-spinoff-aleph (accessed 2 Mar 2016).

Young, Virgina Heyer. 2005. *Ruth Benedict: Beyond Relativity, Beyond Pattern*. Lincoln, NE: University of Nebraska Press.

Youngblood, Ronald T. 1995. "Peace." In *The International Standard Bible Encyclopedia, illustrated in Four Volumes, Volume Three: K-P*, edited by Geoffrey W. Bromiley, 731–733. Grand Rapids, MI: Eerdmans.

Yusa, Michiko. 1996. "Nishida and Hearn." *Monumenta Nipponica* 51 (3): 309–316. Edited by Sophia University.

Ziemer, Benjamin. 2005. *Abram – Abraham: Kompositionsgeschichtliche Untersuchungen zu Genesis 14, 15 und 17*. Beihefte zur Zeitschrift für die alttestamentliche Wissenschaft, volume 350. Berlin and New York: Walter de Gruyter.

Ziesemer, Bernd. 1995. "Praktisch schon tot." *Wirtschaftswoche* 45 (49): 116–119.

Zimmer, Heinrich Robert, and Joseph Campbell. 1972. *Myths and Symbols in Indian Art and Civilization*. Princeton, NJ: Princeton University Press.

Zimmer, Manfred, Herausgeber. 2006. "Religion und Politik im Zeichen von Krieg und Versöhnung." In *Beiträge und Materialien zur Jahrestagung der Internationalen Erich-Fromm-Gesellschaft, Bad Marienberg/Westerwald, Mai 27–29 2005*. Norderstedt: Books on Demand (BoD).

Zimmerli, Walther. 1982. *Grundriß der Alttestamentlichen Theologie*. Fourth revised and complemented edition. Theologische Wissenschaft. Stuttgart, Berlin, Köln, Mainz: Verlag W. Kohlhammer.

Zobel, Hans-Jürgen. 1993. "Altes Testament: Literatursammlung und Heilige Schrift?" In *Altes Testament: Literatursammlung und Heilige Schrift*. Festschrift edited by Julia Männchen, Thomas Neumann, Ernst-Joachim Waschke, and Konstantin Zobel, 1–18. Berlin and New York: Walter de Gruyter.

Zoccatelli, PierLuigi. 2005. "Notes in the Aumist Religion." In *Controversial New Religions*, edited by James R. Lewis, and Jesper Aagaard Petersen, 215–226. Oxford: Oxford University Press.

Zöllner, Reinhard. 2009. *Geschichte Japans: Von 1800 bis zur Gegenwart*. Second edition. Paderborn: Schöningh.

Zukeran, Pat. 2008. "The World of Animism." In *World Religions through a Christian Worldview: A Handbook to Analyzing the World's Religions from a Christian Worldview Perspective*, edited by Pat Zukeran, 43–63. Maitland, FL: Xulonpress.

Zur Mühlen, Karl-Heinz. 1995. *Reformatorisches Profil: Studien zum Weg Martin Luthers und der Reformation*. Göttingen: Vandenhoeck & Ruprecht.

Zwerenz, Ingrid, and Gerhard Zwerenz. 2003. "Die zwölf Bloch-Thesen." In *Ossietzky* 18. http://www.sopos.org/aufsaetze/3f6b695b432f9/1.phtml (accessed 13 Oct 2012).

Zysk, Kenneth G. 1992. *Religious Medicine: The History and Evolution of Indian Medicine*. Piscataway, NY: Transaction Publishers.

Person Index

A

Abegg, Lily 80
Abe, Masamichi (阿部正路) 22
Aketatsu, Prince 298
Albertz, Rainer 194
Althaus, Paul 281
Arakida, Hisaoyu (荒木田久老) 59
Asahara, Shoukou (麻原彰晃) 439
Augustin 463, 468

B

Bacote, Vincent 430
Barth, Karl 83, 96, 288, 423, 452
Ben-Dasan, Isaiah 86
Benedict, Ruth 334, 335
Bernard of Clairvaux 412
Bloch, Ernst 448
Blumhardt, Johann Christoph 324
Boff, Clodovis 429
Boissonade, Gustave Emile 172
Boman, Thorleif 456
Bonhoeffer, Dietrich 196, 473
Bosch, David Jacobus 431
Bourdin, Gilbert 441
Bowne, Bordon Parker 194
Bradshaw, Bruce 15, 148
Braithwaite, John 343
Budai 406
Bulatao, Jaime 20

C

Carus, Friedrich August 140
Cho, David (Paul) Yonggi 422
Chung, Hyun Kyung 54, 427
Cox, Ralph 102
Cullmann, Oscar 454, 457

D

Darwin, Charles 105

Deguchi, Nao (出口なお) 313
De Vos, George 334
Doi, Takeo (土居健郎) 155, 216
Durkheim, Émile 198

E

Endou, Shuusaku (遠藤周作) 54, 79, 152, 383
Etzioni, Amitai 208

F

Fasching, Gerhard 14, 19
Feuerbach, Ludwig 464, 472
Forsyth, Peter Taylor 422
Freud, Sigmund 75
Freytag, Walter 461

G

Gunkel, Hermann 193

H

Hall, Edward Twitchell 112
Hamsananda Sarasvati 442
Harnack, Adolf von 431
Hartenstein, Karl 461
Hattori, Yuuichi (服部雄一) 246
Hayashi, Ryoushou (林亮勝) 280
Hepburn, James Curtis xvii, 71, 422
Heuvers, Hermann 74
Hick, John 477
Hiebert, Paul G. 9, 16
Hirata, Atsutane (平田篤胤) 42, 81, 245
Hiratsuka, Raichou (平塚雷鳥) 159
Hofmann, J. Chr. K. von 454
Hofstede, Geert 409
Hölldobler, Bert 162
Homujiwake, Prince 298
Hori, Ichirou (堀一郎) 173
Hoshino, Tomihiro (星野富弘) xvi, 485

615

I

Ishibashi, Tanzan (石橋湛山) 159
Iwano, Houmei (岩野泡鳴) 159

K

Kajiwara, Kazuyoshi (梶原和義) 286
Kamono, Mabuchi (賀茂真淵) 81
Käser, Lothar 10, 134
Katou, Genchi 72
Kawanabe, Kyousai (河鍋暁斎) 404
Kawashima, Takeyoshi (川島武宜) 155, 170
Keyßer, Christian 224
Kierkegaard, Søren 345
Kitabatake, Chikafusa (北畠親房) 63
Kitamori, Kazou (北森嘉蔵) 350
Kitamura, Sayo (北村サヨ) 313
Knudson, Cornelius 194
Koda, Shousei (香田証生) 332
Kopfermann, Wolfram 323
Koushirou (幸四郎) 238
Kozawa, Heisaku (小沢平作) 75
Künneth, Walter 191, 197, 206
Kuuya, Shounin (空也上人) 219
Kuyper, Abraham 432

L

Le Bon, Gustave. 207
Lévy-Bruehl, Lucien 198
Löwith, Karl 455
Luther, Martin 97, 99, 321, 415, 433, 480

M

Mackintosh, H. R. 422
Mansei (満誓) 46
Martin, William 172
Marx, Karl 467
Matsumoto, Chizuo (松本智津夫) 440
McGrath, Alister 101
Miyata, Mitsuo (宮田光雄) 429
Moltmann, Jürgen 428, 451, 464
Morita, Shouma (森田正馬) 317
Motoori, Norinaga (本居宣長) 45, 59, 81
Mulford, Prentice 51

N

Nakane, Chie (中根千枝) 155, 203
Ninshou, Ryoukan (忍性良観) 409
Nishi, Amane (西周) 41
Nishida, Kitarou (西田幾多郎) 83, 286
Nitobe, Inazou (新渡戸稲造) 134
Noble, Lowell L. 334
Nomi, Masahiko (能見正比古) 301

O

Oogushi, Motosuke (大串元亮) 141
Oouchi, Seiran (大内青巒) 72

P

Panikkar, Raimondo 477
Park, Andrew Sung 427
Paterson, W. 422
Pelagius 278
Petitjean, Bernard-Thadée 237
Pfenninger 244
Pieris, Aloysius 278, 425, 438
Pusa 406
Pu-Tai 406
Pu-Tai Ho-schang 406

R

Ratzinger, Joseph 428
Robinson, H. Wheeler 198

S

Sauer, Erich 456
Schlatter, Adolf 97, 329
Schweitzer, Albert 446
Sears, Robert 51
Shaku, Souen (釈宗演) 263
Shimazono, Susumu (島薗進) 14
Shoutoku Taishi (聖徳太子) 250
Singer, Milton B. 334
Song, C. S. 79
Stott, John 430
Suzuki, Daisetsu Teitarou (鈴木大拙貞太郎) 64, 245, 263
Suzuki, Yoshimasa (鈴木芳正) 301
Swami, Sivananda 442

T

Takakura, Tokutarou (高倉徳太郎) 422
Takenaka, Masao (竹中正夫) 424
Takizawa, Katsumi (滝沢克己) 83
Talmon, Shemaryahu 267
Tanabe, Hajime (田辺元) 286
Tanaka, Oudou (田中王堂) 159
Thomas Aquinas 192
Tokugawa, Ieyasu ((徳川家康) 236
Triebel, Johannes 415
Troeltsch, Ernst 422
Turner, Victor Witter 469

U

Ueda, Akinari (上田秋成) 67
Uemura, Masahisa (植村正久) 422

V

Van Gennep, Arnold 469
Van Rheenen, Gailyn 190
Van Rheenen, Gaiylin 321
Vicedom, Georg Friedrich 415

W

Wagner, C. Peter 323
Watanabe, Zenta (渡辺善太) 455
Watsuji, Tetsurou (和辻哲郎) 73, 250
Weaton, Henry 172
Wellhausen, Julius 18, 192, 198
Wierzbicka, Anna 166, 250
Wilson, Edward O. 162
Wolff, Hans Walter 139

X

Xavier, Francis 71, 209

Y

Yamaguchi, Ichirou (山口一郎) 136
Yamaori, Tetsuo (山折哲雄) 134
Yanagida, Kunio (柳田國男) 183
Yoshimoto, Ishin (吉本伊信) 343

Subject Index

Symbols
7, meaning of the number 395
33, as unlucky number 378
42, as unlucky number 378
108 chimes 373
800 strong salt-water currents 29

A
abdomen, soul concept (נֶפֶשׁ) 497
Abel, and han 427
abolition of God 465
abolition of religion, Marx 464
abomination, and moral impurity 382
abomination, as sin 289, 359
abortion, and ancestor veneration 218
abortion, and survivor guilt 217
Abram 269
absent-mindedness 130, 135
Absicht, soul concept (לֵבָב) 514
accommodation, as missiological approach 71
accountability
 before God 88
 in society 332
actions of will, soul concept (רוּחַ) 506
addressing language, groupism 157
adolescence 132
aeons, two 459
AEPM 224
Affirmation of Suffering Vow. Aum 442
affluence for others 523
after-life 449
agape, Nygren 414
agenda for Christian action, not to be written by the world 425
agents of socialization 339
aging of society 354
agitation, soul concept (רוּחַ) 505
Agon-Shuu 440

agriculture
 agricultural cultures, and groupism 156
 agricultural rites, and phallus worship 404
 agriculture, and familial structures 173
 agriculture, Seven Auspicious Deities 523
agronomy, as divine gift 399
aikidou 49
Ainu
 Ainu-Pantheon 66
 discriminated 351
 Ebisu 396
 mythology 87
 shamanism 311
 soul concept 30
 worldview 30
air, soul concept (רוּחַ) 502, 503
Ajase-complex 75, 341
Aleph, successor organization of Aum 440
alienating the gospel 420
alienation 466
alienation, from God 467
alienation, shame 349
alien, God 320
alien righteousness 196
A Life of Jesus, Endou 243
All-embracing 417
all-embracing motherly love 419
Allgemeinsünde 282
All-Souls-Day, Buddhist 187
All Soul's Day, Japanese version 238
almanacs 301
amae
 amae-mentality, overcoming of 243
 ancestor veneration 181
 as key-concept 250
 as need and as emotion 167
 Bible 240
 defined positively and negatively 168

definition 167
faith 242
formation of conscience 340
groupism 155
Jesus 243
roots of 169
samurai nobility 173
technical term for the mother-child-relationship and for many other relationship 169
technical term in sociology and used in spoken Japanese 169
universal concept 163
word-field 164
Amaterasu 70
Amaterasu-Ookami 409
Amaterasu-Oomikami 244, 397
amazement, soul concept (רוּחַ) 505
Amida 391
Amida-cult 236
Amida Nyorai 52
Amnon, *amae* 241
Amos, as Old Testament apocalyptic 446
amulets 126, 314
analogia entis 95
ancestor veneration 64, 70, 122, 295, 389
   ancestor altar 186
   ancestor religion 173
   ancestors and apotropaic magic 314
   ancestors and divinity 226
   ancestors, and parenting 338
   ancestors, as significant others 338
   ancestor worship 403
   ancestral spirits 125, 188, 225, 240
   apostasy 153
   Bible 208
   Buddhism 185
   changes today 185
   collectivism 173
   first ancestral deity 245
   history of law 222
   psychological dimension 215
   shamanism 313
   sociological dimension 222
   theological dimension 226

anger, calmed 253
anger, soul concept (רוּחַ) 505
Angst 325, 345
anima 140
animal divination 306
animatism 40
animism
   characteristics of animistic worldviews 11
   Christian faith 15
   Hebrew religion 18
   science 301
   working-definiton 10
annihilation, of sin 367
annoyance, soul concept (רוּחַ) 505
anonymity, massification 206
anthropocentrism 472
Anthropologie des Alten Testaments, Wolff 139
anthropology, and peace 247
anthropology, Biblical 495
anthropology, of the Old Testament 283
anthropophobia 333
Antichrist 450
anticipation, of the eschaton 447
Antou-sama 238
an (安) 257
apathia, of God 79, 485
apathy 79
apocalyptic vigilance 272
apocalyptism, Aum 443
apokatastasis 414
apology 342
Apostles' Creed, forgiveness of sins 76
apotropaic magic
   allegiance to God 330
   ambivalence 315
   apotropaic rites, and purification rites 373
   gense riyaku (現世利益) 393
   in Japan 313
   in superstitions 377
   origin of *hadaka mattsuri* 370
   purification 369, 375
   rituals 376

Subject Index

terminology 356
appeasement 262
appeasement, of the soul 116
appetite, excessive, soul concept (נֶפֶשׁ) 498
appetite, soul concept (נֶפֶשׁ) 498
arbitration 261
architecture, traditional 265
arctic hysteria 313
Armageddon, Aum 444, 471
art, and mana 44
ashes, shattering of 364
Ashura 29, 187
Asian religiosity 278
asset management, unlucky days for 304
assimilation 80
assimilation, criterion for 388
astrology 301, 389
Atemgeruch, soul concept (רוּחַ) 503
Atemluft, soul concept (רוּחַ) 503
Atem, soul concept (נֶפֶשׁ) 496
Atem, soul concept (רוּחַ) 502
atmosphere of man, soul concept (לֵבָב) 510
Atmung, soul concept (נֶפֶשׁ) 497
atomic bomb vicitms, discriminated 352
atomization, massification 206
atonement, Japanese terminology 356
atonement payment 367
atonement rituals 368
atonment, after death 373
attitude 118
attribute, Nakane 156
Aum
   as referential framework 438
   Aumism 441
   Aum Shinsen-no-kai 440
   groupism 34
   meaning 441
   New New Religions 393
   overview 439
   politics 445
   subject of salvation 471
aura-channels 43
authoritarianism, church 328
authority, Confucian family constitution 171

authority, soul concept (רוּחַ) 504
autonomy 339
Avalokiteshvara 52
awareness 132
awareness, reduction, massification 207
awareness, soul concept (לֵבָב) 513
awe 59, 319
Axis, Age of 262
Ayurvedic sleep therapy 318

B
Babylonia, ancestor cult 228
badgers, as gods 67
bad mood, soul concept (רוּחַ) 505
balance, Confucianism 257
baptismal names 379
baptism for the dead 421
baraka 239
bars, purification of 376
Bastian-sama 238
bathing, as cult 379
Bauch 497
beans, apotropaic magic 377
bear, as Ainu-deity 311
bears, as gods 68
beauty 44
beauty, goddess of 401
Bedürftigkeit, soul concept (נֶפֶשׁ) 497
Begabung, soul concept (רוּחַ) 504
Begehren 496
Begehren, soul concept (לֵבָב) 510
Begehren, soul concept (נֶפֶשׁ) 498
beginnings, lucky days for 304
being, soul-concept 141
belittled, deities 410
Bell on New Year's Eve 373
belly sash 316
benevolence, Confucianism 260
Benten 400, 410
Benzaiten 391, 400, 406, 409, 523
Bewußtsein, soul concept (לֵבָב) 513
Bible, infallibility of 456
Bible translations, anthropological terminology 495
biblicism 193, 422, 454

biomass, groupism 162
birds, as gods 68
birds of prey, and defilement 363, 517
birth, as defilement 364
birth, dedication rituals after 316
birthing spirit 42
birth preparation practices 32
Bishamon 401
Bishamonten 401, 523
Biwa 400
black defilement 362, 363, 364
blemished animals, abomination 289
blessing 370, 393, 405, 422
blindness, shamanism 311
bliss 405
bliss, and contentment 407
bliss, Seven Auspicious Deities 523
blood defilement 362
bloodshed, impurity 382
blood-taboo 363
blood-type divination 301
Bluestocking Society 159
boat people, discriminated 352
Bodhisattva 52, 408
body
  body-soul-unity 47
  controlled by tamashii (魂), soul 115
  defilement in connection with the body 362
  soul 116
bonsai 70
Boston Personalism 194
bottom to top salvation 461
Brahma 401
breaking down ridges 516
breath of life, soul concept (רוּחַ) 503
breath, soul-concept 141
breath, soul concept (נֶפֶשׁ) 496
breath, soul concept (רוּחַ) 502, 503
breeze, soul concept (רוּחַ) 502
brine 518
bubble economy, end of 179, 259, 353
Buddhism
  and women 308
  Buddhification of Shintoism 82

immanentized 390
importance in Japan 22
National Socialism 263
Ten Worlds of 29
the world of Buddhas 29
violence 441
bullying 150
Buraku-Liberation League 352
Burakumin 352
Bureau of Thought Control 250
burial rituals, ancient 363
bushidou 70
business ethics, Confucianism 260
butsumetsu 302

C

calamities 517
calamities, and defilement 363
calamities, and sin 293
calamities, protection from 523
calamities, seven 396
calamus, apotropaic magic 377
calm 260
Canberra, 1991 54, 427
cancellation of punishment 289
candor 396
Canopus 404
capitalism 178
capital punishment, soul concept (נֶפֶשׁ) 500
Cardinal Principles of the National Polity, 1937 250
caricatural help 435
Carina, constellation of 404
carnal 123
carnality, deity of 406
carnality, Seven Auspicious Deities 523
carp 398
cars, protection for 316
Cartesian-dualistic thinking 323
Catholic Church 71, 95, 152, 236, 245, 383, 422, 475
causality 13
cause and effect, Buddhist law of 412
caution, soul concept (לֵבָב) 513
Cell-Group-Church 158

ceremonies, minimal, New New Religions 390
change of heart 128
Ch'an-tradition 406
cheerfulness, Seven Auspicious Deities 523
Ch'i 48
Chiba, phallus worship 404
childlessness 185
children, Confucian family constitution 171
children of God 86
child sacrifice, abomination 289
chimes, 108 373
China, ancestor veneration 239
Chinese characters, and Japanese language 111
Chinese medicine 44
Chokurei 52
chopsticks, death-taboos 364
christhood, of the poor 426
Christian community, and collectivism 196
Christian humanism 473
Christianity in Japan
  ancestor veneration 209
  Aum 445
  Imperialism 72
  weakness 463
Christianization, all of culture brought under Christ 322
Christianization of Japan
  ancestor veneration 208, 225
  failure 74
Christianization, through supplementation 426
Christ, in the womb of humanity 463
Christocentrism, versus theocentrism 478
church, groupism 158
church struggle, and ancestor veneration 208
Civil Code, 1898 172, 222
clan-societies, and Japan 200
clapping, of one hand 132
classless society 466
cleansing 122
clothing, traditional 264

cod 398
co-dependence 166, 177
codification debate 172
Cogito ergo sum 151
Cognatus ergo sum 151
cognitio naturalis 94, 97
cognitio supernaturalis 94, 97
cognitive faculty, soul-concept 143
collective penal law 195
collectivism
  and individualism 190
  as promiment feature of the Japanese society 412
  concpets 427
  ethics 280
  extreme 205
  family 170
  individualism 159
  Japanese terminology 160
  New Testament 196
  Old Testament 194
  preference for 194
  socio-anthropological background 198
  soteriology 190
  synthesis with individualism 199
colonial insects, and groupism 162
comfort, and the peace-concept 268
Coming of Age Day 301, 317
coming world 411
commemoration services 223
Commentary on Romans, Barth 453
commission, sins of 288
communial feelings, ancestor veneration 216
Communitarian Platform 208
community, ethics 332
community of communities 208
compassion 413, 431
compassion, divine 388
compensation 367
competition, versus cooperation 179
conceit, soul concept (רוּחַ) 506
Condescendencia 471
conduit, pain as 413
conduits of God's will, Takenaka 480

confession of sins, in shame-cultures 348
confidence, versus confidentiality 320
confidentiality 166
confidentiality, versus confidence 320
conflagration 396
conformity 262
confrontation, versus dialogue 425
Confucianism
   business ethics 260
   classical Chinese 253
   family ideal 170
   harmony 256
confusion 127
Congregation for the Doctrine of the Faith 428
conscience 133
   formation 334
   guilty 152
   internal peace 289
   Japanese terminology 133
   mothers 336
   primary conscience 339
   resting position 348
   shame 133
   soul concept (לֵבָב) 514
consciousness 132, 135
consciousness, heart 132
consciousness, soul concept (לֵב) 507
consequent eschatology 446
consideration, organ of, soul concept (לֵבָב) 513
constitution, demanded by General McArthur 170
contentment, patron of 407
contentment, Seven Auspicious Deities 523
contextualization 71
continuity, passing through discontinuity 460
control, expectations of other 337
conversion, and rehabilitation 342
conversion, of individuals 322
conversions, not to be desired 478
conversion theology 322
cooperation, in salvation 472
cooperation, versus competition 179
coquettish behavior 166
coram Deo 351
coram hominibus 351
corporate personality 198
corporate punishment 195
corpse, soul concept (נֶפֶשׁ) 501
corpulence, sign of prosperity 399
cosmic peace 271
cosmic religion 438
cosmic religion, meta-cosmic religion 426
cosmological principle 39
costly discipleship 431
costly identification 431
co-suffering, of Christ 244, 419
courage, soul concept (רוּחַ) 506
covenant faithfulness, peace-concept 269
Covenant Theology 456
covering up the ditches 516
crane 405
craving, soul-concept 140, 143
craving, soul concept (נֶפֶשׁ) 498, 499, 500
craw populations, Japanese society compared to 157
craw, superstitions 377
created world, and fallen world 460
creation, and eschatology 457
creation, lord of 398
creative life-force, soul concept (רוּחַ) 503
credibility, Confuciamism 257
cross
   according to Bloch 451
   as solidarity with the suffering 479
   crucifixion, as shaming 349
   culture 423
   joy 437
   love 414
   meaning in a shame-culture 348
   reduplication of the crucifixion in the messengers of Christ 416
   salvation-historic interpretation 451
   solidarity 419
   solidarity with the weak 425
   suffering of the poor 428
cruelty 258
Crypto-Christians, ancestor veneration 236

CSER-structure 457
cultivated 255
cultural identity, ancestor veneration 224
cultural liberation, according to Moltmann 466
cultural studies, biased 484
culture, and gospel 423
culture, Seven Auspicious Deities 523
curse 187, 370
curse spirits 296
cutting dead flesh 516
cutting living flesh 516
cycle of rebirth, and salvation 442
cyclic sense of time 453

D

Dacca 1977, hijacking of 75
Daianji 395
Daikokuten 397, 398, 409, 523
Dai Komio 52
Daiseishi Bosatsu 52
Daiwa Securities 259
Dalai Lama 440
dance, goddess of 400
dance, Seven Auspicious Deities 523
dancing religion 307, 313
Danichi Nyorai 52
Daniel 321, 449
Das Prinzip Hoffnung, Bloch 448
Day of the Dog 32, 316
Day of the Lord 446
dead, dependent on the living 186
dead, newly dead and settled dead 187
deafness, and good luck 397
death
  as defilement 362
  as purification 373
  death-god 66
  death of Jesus, according to Schweitzer 447
  defilement in connection with 363
  eternal 347
  in isolation 185
  shame 364
  soul after 119

deceased souls 295
deceases, caused by evil spirits 125
deceit, sins of 288
deception, soul concept (לֵבָב) 512
decision 131
Declaring Myself the Christ, Asahara 444, 471
dedication, Confucianism 260
dedication date, for girls 378
dedication rituals 316
de-eschatologizing of religion 448
defecation 516
defilement
  shame 349
  Unheil experienced as 356
  with guilt 362
  without guilt 362
deformations, sin 293
deified ancestors 227
De ira Dei, Lactantius 79
delay of Parousia 447
demigods 29
democracy 174
demons
  apotropaic magic 377
  demon-gates 376
  in fairytales 120
  Japanese 120
  the world of 29
  witches 373
dependence 166
dependence on God, divination 326
dependency, feeling of and religion 472
depressionc, caused by overwork 258
depression, suicide and death caused by 258
desire, *amae* 168
desires, Buddhist 373
desire, soul-concept 140, 143
desire, soul concept (לֵבָב) 510
desire, soul concept (נֶפֶשׁ) 496, 498, 499
desire, unfulfilled, soul concept (נֶפֶשׁ) 499
destruction, lord of 398
Deutsche Christen 72
Deva of Bliss 392

development, does not bring the kingdom 462
devil 294
dialectic materialism 464
dialogue, and mission 476
dialogue, versus confrontation 425
dignity 396
dignity, shame 335
directive leadership styles 329
dirtiness, terminology 356
discontinuity, eschatological 460
discouragement, soul concept (לֵבָב) 511
discrimination 351
diseases, as defilement 362
diseases, as sin 293, 359
diseases, gods causing 377
disfigurements, gods depicted with 397
disgrace 196
disgrace, and hell 449
disobedience to parents, sin 289
disorder, outside group 158
disposition 136
Disposition, *seelische*, soul concept (רוּחַ) 506
disposition, viewed as irrational 142
dispossession 371
ditches, covering up of 516
divination 127, 297
divination, and the Bible 325
divination, with wounds 362
Divine Life Society 442
doctor appointments, lucky days for 304
doctrines, simplified, New New Religions 390
domesticated, deities 410
domiciled shamans 312
dominion, spirits of 294
donum, of Christ 418
Doshisha University 424
double planting 516
double, spirit-like (Käser) 117
double, spiritual 8, 11
dreams, divination 306
dream world 411
drive of his throat, man determined by 498

dualism, versus holism 15
dwarf-deity 397
dying, in peace 269

E

earthly deities 517
earthly gospel 429
earthly sins 516
Easter, and salvation 437
Ebisu 316, 396, 410, 523
Ebisuten 396
ecclesiology, and collectivism 196
ecological liberation, according to Moltmann 466
economical liberation, according to Moltmann 465
economic help 435
economic sciences, as divine gift 399
ecstasy, shamanism 310
Edo 391
education, goddess of 400
education system 440
effectivity, determining exegesis 323
ego, reduction 317
Einheit, versus Vereinerleiung 255
Einsicht, soul concept (לֵבָב) 512
elan vital 135
election of Israel, amae 242
Elijah 321
Elisha's permission 240
eloquence, goddess of 400
emanation 245
Emotionalität, soul concept (לֵבָב) 509
emotions
  heart 132
  place of 115, 118
  soul-concept 142
  viewed as irrational 142
emotion, soul concept (נֶפֶשׁ) 499
Emperor
  Emperor-veneration 70
  groupism 159
  loyalty 250
  the private life and the Emperor 161
empiricism 388

enchantment 127
Encounter of the Third Kind 320
encounter, spiritual 324
Endou, and Kitamori 417
enlightenment 51, 132, 279, 407, 442
Enlightenment 16, 29, 30, 49, 90, 191, 319, 344, 430, 473
enlightenment, soul concept (לֵבָב) 511, 513
entertainers, goddess of 400
enthusiasm 135
enveloping 414
environmental questions, and peace 262
Epaphroditus, amae 241
Epicureans 79
epidemic demons/gods 371
epidemics 396
epileptic seizure 117
equality, of the truthfulness of pain 413
Erbsünde, history of the term 282
erotic art 403
Erregung, soul concept (רוּחַ) 505
error, sin 287
erythrophobia 333
eschatology
    according to Barth and Moltmann 452
    and protology 457
    as history 454
    as principle 445
    consequent 446
    eschatological tension 448, 457
    inaugurated 322
    Kitamori 414
    social justice 479
esteem 196
Eta 352, 362
eternal life 45
eternal life, versus human immortality 149
eternity, man's desire 464
ethics
    collectivism 280
    ethical liberation 422
    ethical values, ancestor veneration 224
    ethic of Jesus 459
    ethic of love, Moltmann 454
    ethic of love, Schweitzer 446

    Japanese terminology 332
    pain 412
    social justice 479
etiquette 257
Evangelicalism 430
Evangelicalism, Japanese 421
Evangelicalism, North American 194
evangelism 75
evening oracle 298
evil, criminal law 343
evil inclination 283
evil spirits 125, 126, 370
evocation 127
evolution, as redemption 474
evolutionism 198, 462
excellence 124
excessive appetite, soul concept (נֶפֶשׁ) 498
excluded middle 16, 19
exemplum, Christ as 418
existence of God, as predisposition 92
existence, soul concept (נֶפֶשׁ) 500
Exodus-event 465
exorcism 322, 371, 377
exorcism, and purification 518
expectation, not met 342
experience, determining exegesis 323
experience of infants, and animism 162
exploitation of life, Christian action called for 424
extended family 174
external control, conscience 340
external responsibility 340
external sins 288
extraordinary, the 123

F
factories, protection for 316
fad religion 390
faint, soul concept (לֵבָב) 507
faith, and *amae* 242
faithful to the earth, Feuerbach 464
faith in God, versus ancestor veneration 226
fallen world, and created world 460
fallen world, and redeemed world 460

Fall, the, guilt and shame 345
falsa opinio de Deo 96
False Prophet 450
false self 246
fame, deity of 406
fame, Seven Auspicious Deities 523
family
  ancestor veneration 222
  familial structures, peasant families 173
  familism 250
  family constitution 177
  family deities, apotropaic magic 314
  family head, Confucian family constitution 171
  family law 170
  family love 175
  family religion 228
  family structures, of the Japanese 170
  family structures today 174
  modern 176
famined ghosts 29
farmers, patron deity of 398
fascination 127
fascination of evil 19
fatalism 47
fate 300
fate, soul concept (נֶפֶשׁ) 500
father, Confucian family constitution 171
fatherhood, of God 86
fear
  animism 292
  fear of God 319
  love for God and fear of God 321
  object-defined 345
  spirits 293
  spirits of living persons 295
  spirits of the dead 295
female power, fear of 308
feminisms 76
Feng-hwang 68
Feng-Shui 376
Ferraira 245
fertility
  deity of 406
  fertility cult 401

Seven Auspicious Deities 409
fertility, Seven Auspicious Deities 523
festival for the dead 122, 223
festivities, lucky days for 304
fetishism 314
fighting spirit 118
filthiness, as sin 359
fine arts, goddess of 400
fines, as purification 368
fire, as defilement 363
fire, for purification 375
first truth, existence of God 93
fisher, patron deity of 396
fishers, patron deity of 398
fishery, Seven Auspicious Deities 523
five Yen, apotropaic magic 378
flattery 166
flaying 516
flesh 123
flesh, sin 282
floods 396
flower arrangement 70
focus 128
folk-Christianity, in Japan? 226
folk religion, criticized by Buddhism 389
folk-religious salvation 410
folktales, reform versus punishment 342
foreign laborers, discriminated 352
forgiveness, and ancestor veneration 222
forgiveness, and purification 375
forgiveness, and repentance 75
forgiveness, Japanese 244
forgiveness of sins, and rehabilitation 289
forgiveness of sins, as principal part of salvation 433
forgiving, versus excusing 349
fornication, with a woman and her child 362
fortune, lucky tickets 300
Forum for World Evangelization, 2004 247
four, as unlucky number 378
Four Horsemen, Aum 444
fox-deity 64
foxes, as gods 67
frame, Nakane 156

freedom 153, 193
freedom of speech 157
freedom, versus harmony 251
freemasonry 172
free self 208
freeter 353
French law 172
friendship, between nations 261
friendship, Seven Auspicious Deities 523
frog, as talisman 378
fruitfulness, suffering 415
fruit of the Spirit, peace-concept 272
Fudou 391, 403
Fukujima, shamanism 311
Fukurokuju 404, 405, 523
fulfillment of life, as salvation 436
funeral, purification after 375
funeral rites 375
funerals, unlucky days for 305
furoshiki-theology 414
future, knowledge about, salvation 297

G

Gagouji 395
gall 129
Gandharvas 401
gay-discos 403
Gedatsukai 188
Geduld 500
Geheimnis, soul concept (לֵבָב) 509
geisha 70, 400
geishas, goddess of 400
Geist, soul concept (רוּחַ) 506
Gemütsverfassung, soul concept (לֵבָב) 510
genealogies 195
general sin 282
genitals, openness towards 403
Genji-Monogatari 263, 295
Genji, Tales of 263
gense riyaku 388
geographical character, of salvation 432
geomantic rules 376
German Christians 263
German individualism 192
Geschmackssinn, soul concept (נֶפֶשׁ) 497

Gewissen, soul concept (לֵבָב) 514
ghastly, God being 319
ghost, and spirit 127
Gideon, divination 326
Gideons International in Japan 495
Gier, soul concept (נֶפֶשׁ) 496
giri 250
glory of God, as purpose of salvation 469
Gochinza Denki 409
God
  according to Moltmann 451
  categorically different 18, 79
  female characteristica 74
  God-centeredness of salvation 425
  God Creator, versus Japanese god-concept 279
  God's crucifixion 428
  God's preferential option for the poor 478
god-concept *kami* (神)
  heart 130
  mind 60
  soul 135
God Is, God Spoke, God Came, 1998 102
God Is Rice, Takenaka 77
gods
  as demons 66
  gods making diseases 377
  not almighty 73
  not personal beings 73
  not transcendent 73
  the God of the Bible 90
god-shelf 227, 376
good age, dying 269
Good and Evil 19
good fate, harbinger of 401
good luck, goddess of 400
Good Shepherd 76
good spirits 370
Goryoue 296
Goryou-Society 296
gospel of prosperity 422
Gott, der liebe 74
go with the flow 259
grace

and sin 434
　Catholic understanding 472
　Confucianism 260
　grace of God and pain 413
　Takakura 423
grave-visiting 221
Great and Shining Buddha 52
Great Bear, in divination 303
Great Black, the 398
Great-Japan 263
Great Origin 61
Great Purification 29, 368
Great Purification, text 515
Great Reverse 430
Great Sun-Deity 71
Greek words
　ἄγνοιά 287
　ἀδικία 288
　αἰδείσθαι 196
　αἴδος 196
　ἁμαρτάνω 288
　ἀνομία 288
　ἀνόμως 288
　ἀπείθεία 289
　ἀποστασία 289
　ἀποτροπιάζομαι 316
　ἀσεβέω 288
　ἀφίστημι 289
　ἐπὶ τὸ αὐτό 196
　ὁμόνοια 271
　παραβαίνω 288
　παράβασις 288
　παρακοή 287
　παρακούω 287
　παρανομέω 288
　παραπίπτω 289
　παράπτωμα 289
　πλανάω 287
　πνεῦμα 149
　προσκαρτερεῖν 196
　σάρξ 282
　σέβω 288
　φιλεῖν 196
　φρόνημα 282
　φύσις 41

ψυχή 140
greeting, peace-concept 269
grief work, ancestor veneration 216
group-climate 259
groupism 154
groupism, mechanisms of 154
grudge, spirits holding a 295
gruelty 133
Grundprobleme der Ethik, Troeltsch 422
guilt
　change of guilt-concept 368
　dialectical unity of guilt and shame 344
　guilt-feelings and ancestor veneration 217
　guilt-feelings and thankfulness 221
　interaction with 339
　internalized 340
　internalized guilt-feelings 335
　Old Testament 345
　shame 334
gullet, soul-concept 140
gullet, soul concept (נֶפֶשׁ) 496
gullibility of masses, New New Religions 390
guts 135
Gyouganji 395

H

hadaka matsuri 370, 403
Hades 518
hagoita 377
hair, and defilement 372
hair, apotropaic magic 314
Hals, soul concept (נֶפֶשׁ) 497
hamartiology, superficial 429
han 427
hanami 70
handicaps, gods depicted with 397
happiness
　contentment 407
　goddess of 400
　salvation 410, 436
　Seven Auspicious Deities 409
　symbols 405

happiness, interpersonal, Seven Auspicious
    Deities 523
happiness, marital, Seven Auspicious
    Deities 523
happiness, psychological, Seven Auspicious
    Deities 523
harae 367
haragei 155
harakiri, soul 134
harbinger of death 66
hare, as god 68
harmony
    Confucianism 256, 257, 260
    groupism 157
    honne, tatemae 246
    Japan 250
    Japanese peace-concept 253, 267
    maintained at any cost? 255
    of the family 178
    parenting 338
    pleasure 254
    purification 374
    salvation 297, 387
harvest-deity 64
hasty, soul concept (רוּחַ) 505
haughty person, soul concept (רוּחַ) 506
Haupt 329
healing
    healing deity 405
    peace-concept 268
    shamans as healers 312
health 135
    as salvation, Bloch 465
    peace-concept 268
    psychological 135
heart
    as organ 146
    as organ, soul concept (לֵבָב) 507
    as synonym for ki (気) 138
    change of 128
    god 130
    heart attack, soul concept (לֵבָב) 507
    Hebrew soul concept 142
    lexical field 128
    soften the 254

soul 128
soul concept 115
soul concept (לֵבָב) 508, 510, 513
soul concept (נֶפֶשׁ) 499
word-field 129
heart, as organ, soul concept (לֵבָב) 507
heart, condition of, soul concept (רוּחַ) 506
heaven and earth, not completely separated
    263
heavenly kings, four 402
heavenly rock-seat 516
heavenly sins 516
heaven on earth 480
heaven, soteriological focus on 467
Hebrew-holistic worldview 17
Hebrew religion, viewed as animistic 18
Hebrew words
    אָדָם 150
    אֲדָמָה 150
    ארך 268
    בגד 289
    בוש 344
    בטח 270
    הֶבֶל 90
    הטוב 269
    המה 413
    חטא 288
    חסד 269
    חָקוֹת 90
    יבול הארץ 269
    ידה 329
    ישע 430
    ישעו 269
    כבוד 269
    כלם 344
    לא-אל 90
    לְבָב/לֵב 142
    לִפְנֵי 351
    מורה 329
    מעל 289
    מרד 289
    מרה 289
    מת 269
    נֶפֶשׁ 140
    סרר 289

עבר 288
עוה 289
עול 288
עַל־פְּנֵי 351
פשע 289
צדק 196, 269
צרר 430
רוּחַ 141, 145
רחם 74
רפא 268
שׁאנן 270
שׁגג 287
שׁגה 287
שׁכן 269
שׁלום 268
שׁלם 267
שִׁקּוּץ 289
שׁקט 270
תוֹעֵבָה 289
תעה 287
hedonism, individualism 199
Heiland 419
Heil, and *Heilung* 421
Heilsein, peace-concept 268
Heilsgeschichte 416, 454
Heilung, and *Heil* 421
hell 29, 347
hell, Buddhist 373
helplessness, sin 427
Henoch, according to Schweitzer 446
hereditary sin 282
hermaphroditism, and good luck 397
hermeneutical keys, concerning the religions 461
Herzanfall, soul concept (לֵבָב) 507
Herz, soul concept (לֵבָב) 507
hesitation 131
heterodoxy, Crypto-Christians 237
he (平) 257
hidden God, Luther 418
hierarchy 262
hierarchy, and groupism 154
hierarchy, Confucianism 260
high-context communication 112
highest bliss 523

High-God 14
high seas, soul concept (לֵבָב) 508
hikikomori 246
Hilkiah 269
Hiroshima 412
Hiruko 397
Historia gravida Christi 463
historical Christ 476
historical Jesus 84, 451
historical realism, peace-concept 270
history, God as Lord of 463
history of production, Marx 466
history, pregnant with Christ 463
Hochmut, soul concept (רוּחַ) 506
holiness code 380
holiness, Japanese concept 124
holism
   ancestor veneration 216
   animistic worldviews 12
   holistic salvation 322
   in early childhood 163
   versus dualism 15
Holy Spirit
   caution with Japanese church-terminology 295
   eschatology 458
   Japanese words for 127
   mana 149
Holy Spirit, soul concept (רוּחַ) 503
Holy War, and divination 326
homeland, patriotism 424
homeless 354
Homer's moral vocabulary, relational 196
homoerotic culture 403
homogeneity 258
Homo homini deus est 472
homosexuality 289
homosexuality, male 402
honne 246
honor
   as salvation 387
   groupism 154
   shame 335
Hon Sha Ze Sho Nen 52
hope

according to Bloch 448
according to Moltmann 451
hopelessness as sin 481
society with hope-disparity 353
hope, according to Moltmann 481
hope, soul concept (נֶפֶשׁ) 498
hope, suffering and persecution for the sake of 446
horizontal mandate of the church 435
horizontal salvation, versus vertical salvation 480
horror, and fear of God 319
horror films 320
Hotei 406, 410
Hotei Oshou 406, 523
Houryouji 395
house altar, parenting 338
house, and shame 338
Houzanji-Temple 392
hubris, Feuerbach 472
human immortality, versus eternal life 149
humanism, and liberal Christianity 423
humanism, Christian 473
humanity, Confuciamism 257
humanity in Christ 425
humanization, of theology 425
humanization, of the world 480
humbleness 132
humility, and divination 325
humpback, and good luck 397
hunger, according to Bloch 465
hunger, biblical 467
hunger, soul concept (נֶפֶשׁ) 497, 498
Hunger, soul concept (נֶפֶשׁ) 498
hungry ghosts 29
Hungry Spirits 187
husband, Confucian family constitution 171
husband-wife-relationship 255
husband-wife-relationship, ambivalent 254
hygiene, and ritual purity 379
hyper-individual economic power, massification 206
hypersensitivity, shame 334
hysteria, shamanism 313

I

identification, with poor 350
idolatry, impurity 382
ignorance, sin 287
ikebana 70
imago-Dei 86
Imamiya-Ebisu-Shrine 397
imitatio, of the suffering of Christ 416
immanence of God 427
immanence, veiling holiness 408
immanentized Buddhism 390
immanent orientation, collectivism/individualism 205
Immanuel, in Barth's theology 83
Immanuel, salvation principle 424
immaterial world 13
imminent expectation 447
immortality 449
immortality of the soul, not biblical 458
immortality, speaking against 149
impatient person, soul concept (רוּחַ) 505
imperialism 72
Imperial Rescript on Education 26, 171, 250
Imperial University, Sendai 455
impermanency 46
impurity
    as sin 359
    in the Bible 380
    rebellion 383
    shame 349
    Unheil experienced as 356
inadequacy, feeling before God 320
Inari 391
inattention, sin 287
inaugurated eschatology 322
incarnation, reduplication in the messengers of Christ 416
incest 362, 516
incorruptibility of the soul 150
incurvatus in se ipsum 288
India, groupism, compared to Japan 160
indigenized churches 421
indigenous Japanese 262
indignation, soul concept (רוּחַ) 505

indirective leadership styles 330
individualism
  collectivism 190
  dangers of 208
  extreme 208
  family 170
  German 192
  individualistic movements, *Taishou-Japan* 159
  in the Japanese context 159
  Japanese terminology 160
  North American 193
  preference for 192
  soteriology 190
  synthesis with collectivism 199
individualistic narrowness, Evangelicalism 430
individual rights 171
individuals, no autonomy 176
individuals of reference 337
individual, soul-concept 141
individuation, absence of 178
individuum, soul concept (נֶפֶשׁ) 500
indulgence, criminal law 343
indulgence, parental 165
indulgence, versus restraint 339
Industrialization Age, eschatological hope of 461
inertia, as sin 481
infallibility of the Bible 456
infanticide, for safeguarding prosperity 149
infant mortality 317, 364
infertility, shamanism 313
inheritance law 184
iniquity, sin 288
initiation, of shamans 312
injustice, Christian action called for 424
inner tension, conscience 340
inner voice of authority, conscience 346
insight, soul concept (לֵבָב) 512
insight, taken away, soul concept (לֵבָב) 512
inspiration 127
instincts, massification 207
Instruction on certain aspects of the "Theology of Liberation" 428

intactness, and the peace-concept 267
integrity, and the peace-concept 267
integrity, shame 335
intellect 117
intellect, massification 207
intellectuals, Japanese, and the Bible 206
intention, soul-concept 144
intention, soul concept (לֵבָב) 514
interest 130
interim period 457
interim period, as hermeneutical key 462
intermission, salvation historical 457
internal control, conscience 340
internalized guilt 340
internal peace 289
internal responsibility 340
internal sins 288
internals of the body, soul concept (לֵבָב) 507
interpersonal happiness, Seven Auspicious Deities 409, 523
introspection, method of 343
Iomante-festival 311
irreligion, sin 288
irresponsibility, massification 207
irrigation sluices, releasing of 516
Isaac, and *amae* 241
Isaiah, missionary prophet 271
Isaiah, recognizing sinfulness 321
Islam, ancestor veneration 239
Islam, and shame 345
Israel, and ancestor cult 228
Italian method, groupism 157
Izanagi 245, 306, 363, 367, 397
Izanami 245, 306, 363, 397

J

Jacob, awe 319
Jambhala 401
Japan, and war 262
Japanese Bible translations, and Wolff 145
Japanese companies, familial structures 179
Japanese, God, the Bible, and Christ, 1998 102
Japanese language

amalgamation of written Japanese and Chinese 58
Hepburn-System xvii
Pronunciation xviii
transcription of xvii
Japanese spirit 118
Japanization, of Buddhism 2, 82
Japan, old names 262
jealousy, divine 400
Jesuanic Principle 476
Jesus, and amae 243
Jesus, and the peace-concept 271
jewel, as symbol for prosperity 523
Jibeta-Matsuri-Festival 403
Jizou 391
Joab 269
Job 427, 449
John the Baptist, according to Schweitzer 446
Jonathan, divination 326
Joseph, and *amae* 241
Joudo Shinshuu 344
Joudoshuu 219
joy, amidst pain 413
joy, and salvation 437
Judaism 432
Judaist-eschatological world-view 446
judgment, ripening unto 461
jun (均) 257
Juroujin 404, 410, 523
justice
  Confuciamism 257
  peace 347
  salvation as 347
  social justice in Japan 351
  thirst for 449
just language 262
juta 311

K
Kadavergehorsam 197
kakure kirishitan 236
kami (神)
  as animals 67
  as gods 65
  as humans 63
  as spirits 64
  as syncretistic term 80
  as the Absolute 61
  secular usage 60
kamu 59
kamui 59, 311
kamui-oroshi 311
kankakariya 117
Kannon 52, 391, 395
Kannouji 395
Kardinalfrage 92
karma, salvation as freedom from 442
karoushi 258, 352
Kawasaki, *Jibeta-Matsuri* 403
Kawasaki Seiwain 395
Kehle, soul concept (נֶפֶשׁ) 496
Kichidenji 395
Kichijouten 405
killing animals 517
kindergartens, shame-oriented education 339
kindness 396
kingdom-centeredness 476
kingdom of evil, versus the kingdom of God 459
kingdom of God, to be established between people 428
kingdom of God, versus kingdom of Christ 477
kingdom-theology 321
kingdom theology, in New New Religions 390
Kinnaras 401
Kirchenkampf, and ancestor veneration 208
Kirin 68
Kirisuto Sengen, Asahara 444, 471
Kisshouten 401
Kitamori, Asian context 417
Kitamori, departing from orthodoxy 419
kitchen deity 399
kitchen, protection for 316, 523
Kiyomizudera 395
ki (気)
  as emotion 136

as interpersonal factor 136
as mana-energy of humans outside of
  humans 39
as substance 38
as temperament 136
as will 136
in Japanese art 44
in the Japanese view of nature 40
in traditional medicine 42
knowledge, Confuciamism 257
knowledge, heart 130
knowledge, soul concept (לֵבָב) 512, 513
Kojiki 397
Kokkurisan 299
Kokumin Seishin Bunka Kenkyuujo (国民精
  神文化研究所) 263
Kokumin Seishin Soudouin (国民精神総動
  員) 263
Kokutai-no Hongi 250
Korea, Japanese settlements in 262
Korean shamanism 313
Korean shamanism, in Japan 308
Koreans, third-generation, discriminated
  352
Korean temples 313
Koudou(革堂)-District 395
Koufukuji 395
Koufuku-no Kagaku 393
Kounomiya Shrine (国府宮神社) 370
Koyama, and Kitamori 417
Kraft, soul concept (רוּחַ) 504
Kuan-yin 239
Kubera 401
Kuruma Shrine 402
Kuvera 401
Kwan In 427
Kwei 69
Kyoto School of Philosophy 83, 211

L

Lactantius 79
lady shamans 311
Lake of Fire 450
Land of Roots 518
Land of Roots, deepest land of the 518
Land of the Fresh Ears of Grain 515
Land of the Plentiful Reed Plains 515
Langmut, soul concept (רוּחַ) 506
language, as owing mana-power 370
language games 439
language systems, two 111
Lao-Tze 404
Lao-Tze, avatar of 405
larynx, soul concept (נֶפֶשׁ)496
laughter, Zen-Buddhism 407
Lausanne Covenant, 1974 430
leadership change, church, dangers 158
leadership, New New Religions 390
leadership principles, biblical 329
Leben 500
Lebenskraft, soul concept (רוּחַ) 503
Lebensodem, soul concept (רוּחַ) 503
lefthandedness, and good luck 397
lenience 165, 339
leniency, criminal law 343
leprosy 516
leprosy, impurity 381
lethargy, sins of 288
lexical translation 139
liberalism 174
liberalism, Japanese 421
Liberal Protestantism 431
liberation, from God 472
liberation theology
  Asia 425
  atheism 473
  collectivism 429
  orientation on this world 463
life-force
  elan vital 135
  fertility 403
  sexuality 403
  soul-concept 141
life-force, soul concept (רוּחַ) 503
lifelong learning, Confucianism 260
life, soul-concept 141
life, soul concept (נֶפֶשׁ) 497, 500
lightning 517
lightning, as defilement 363
liminality, of Christians 469

Subject Index

lineage-groups 65
linguistic determinism 164
literature, goddess of 400
literature, Seven Auspicious Deities 523
little flock 461
Little Red Riding Hood, Japanese version 343
liver 129
living being, soul concept (נֶפֶשׁ) 496
Living Bible 495
living dead
   ethical values 186
   incorruptible soul 120
living, dependent on the dead 188
living ghosts 295
li (理) 257
lo-determinatives 225
longevity
   apotropaic magic 316
   as salvation 387
   deity of 406
   ju 405
   Juroujin 405
   peace-concept 268
   seven virtues of Confucius 396
longevity, Seven Auspicious Deities 523
longing, soul-concept 140
longing, soul concept (נֶפֶשׁ) 496, 498
longsuffering, soul concept (נֶפֶשׁ) 500
longsuffering, soul concept (רוּחַ) 506
lose consciousness 507
losing face 333
lost souls 295
Lotus-Sutra 308
love
   Confucianism 257
   feminine terminology for God's love 74
   goddess of 400
   kokoro (心) as emotions 132
   orders of, Kitamori 417
   romantic love 174
   the Cross, Kitamori 414
low-context communication 112
loyalty, Confucianism 260
luck 396

lucky days 302
Luftröhre, soul concept (נֶפֶשׁ) 497
Lung, as mythological animal 69
lust, sexual, soul concept (נֶפֶשׁ) 497
lust, soul concept (לֵבָב) 510
Lutheran Church of Japan, ancestor veneration 235
Luther, and Feuerbach 472

M

mabui 117
Machpela 232
macro-cosmos, and divination 298
Mafia, Japanese 171
magic
   Crypto Christians 237
   divination 326
   magic hammer 400
   magicians 311
   prayer 51
   using names of deities 87
magnanimity 396
Mahakala 398
Mahayana-Buddhismus 239
Maitreya-faith, Chinese 408
majority decisions, avoided 180
male-male erotic 402
male-male love, patron deities of 403
malevolent sorcery 517
malevolent spirits 296
malice, demons 120
mana 116
   as human life-force 135
   as part of humans 43
   as spirit of God 149
   blood 44
   Christian belief 49
   emotions 136
   gods considered as 62
   heart 44, 138
   in mythology 27
   interpersonal factor 136
   its power in words 370
   ki (気) and the originally Japanese *ke* (気) 35

ki (気) in Japanese art 44
ki (気) in the Japanese view of nature 40
ki (気) in traditional medicine 42
mana-concept 34
medicine 39
meteorology 38
pneumatics 38
reason 135
Takenaka 77
talent 136
temperament 136
will 136
man, as subject of salvation 424
Manchester School of Anthropology 469
mandalas 400
manipulation, massification 206
man, non-material aspects of 115
Manoah 321
Manyoushuu 314
mappo 444
Marian devotion, and *amae* 245
marital happiness, Seven Auspicious Deities 523
marriage, postponed 185
martial arts 47
Marx, and libeartion theology 466
Marxism, influence on Moltmann 464
massage-saloons, purification of 376
massification 206
massification, groupism 162
mass-media, massification 206
mass-organizations, massification 207
matchmaking, Seven Auspicious Deities 394
material benefits 405
materialism 123
materialism, and animism 388
materialism, and individualism 199
materialization of Christianity 465
material riches, Seven Auspicious Deities 523
material world 411
maternal principle 180
Matsuomaru, hero of *Terakoya* 419
Matthias, divination 326

maturity, freedom to 473
MBB-churches, ancestor veneration 239
means-oriented values, versus purpose-oriented values 160
means to an end, salvation as 410
Medellín, 1968 427
mediatory rituals 186
medicine, as divine gift 399
mediums 125
Meiji
   crystallization point of national thinking 263
   Imperial Rescript on Education 171
   its Constitution 178
   its constitution and ancestor veneration 222
   public religion 30
melancholy, as sin 481
memorial ceremonies 186
memorial service 125
memorial tablets 125
memory, and heart 130
menstrual blood 363
mentality 131
mericelessness, *ebisugokokoro* (夷心) 133
meta-cosmic religion 438
meta-cosmic religion, and cosmic religion 426
meta story 439
Micah, missionary prophet 271
Michikai 285
micro-cosmos, and divination 298
middle class, consciousness of 353
Mikado system 263
mild 254
millenialism 444
mind
   Gemüt 115
   heart 130
   loss of 130
   pacified 253
mind-god 39, 61
Minjung 429
miracles 124, 126
miracles, New New Religions 390

Subject Index

miraculous power 122
Miscanthus sinensis, apotropaic magic 315
misfortune, lucky tickets 300
misogi 367
missing the mark, sin 288
missio Dei 247
missional church 416
missionary prophets 271
mission as dialogue, Knitter 476, 477
mistresses, shamans 311
Mitgefühl, soul concept (נֶפֶשׁ) 499
modern family 176
Modernity 31
modernization, after WW II, family law 170
modern mission movement 430
monasteries, and homoerotic culture 403
monasteries, patron deity of 398
monasteries, protection of 523
money, Seven Auspicious Deities 523
monkeys, as gods 68
monocular vision, and good luck 397
mood 136
mood, bad, soul concept (רוּחַ) 505
mood, soul concept (לֵבָב) 510
moon, as deity 397
moral 133
morality, Confuciamism 257
morals, collectivism 280
moral terminology, Japanese 332
moriko 311
Morita-therapy 317
mortal sins 288
mortuary tablets 186
Mosaic Law, purity 381
mother
    as primary reference person 344
    as significant other 336
    God as 74
    mother-child relationship 337
    motherly principle, not merciful 246
    mother-son relationship 75
motivation, soul concept (לֵבָב) 514
mountain capital 263
mountain habitat 263

mouse populations, Japanese society compared to 157
mouth, soul-concept 140
Mt Adagosan 395
Mt Fuji 70
Mt Hieizan 395
Mt Hirasan 395
Mt Ibukiyama 395
Mt Ikoma 312
Mt Katsuragisan 395
Mt Kinbusan 395
Mt Kouyasan 395
Mt Kuruma 52
Mt Osore 312
Mt Shinbousan 395
Mt Sumeru 402
mugwort, apotropaic magic 377
Mukyoukai 421
multicultural societies 262
multiple faith 80
mündig man 473
murder, as meritious deed 442
music, goddess of 400
music, Seven Auspicious Deities 523
music, traditional 264
Mutlosigkeit, soul concept (לֵבָב) 511
muzzle, soul-concept 140
myriad currents of the brine 518
myriad layers of heavenly clouds 516
mysteriousness, New New Religions 390
mysticism of suffering 412
mysticism, of the pain of God 412

N

Nacken, soul concept (נֶפֶשׁ) 497
Nagasaki 412
Naikan-method 317, 343
Nakatomi, the Great 517
Naked and Not Ashamed, 1975 334
Naked Festivals 403
naming 379
naming, and controlling 87
nanten-bush 377
narcissism, and individualism 199

national identity, and ancestor veneration 223
nationalism, Japanese 63, 118, 132
National Socialism, and Buddhism 263
national soul, of Japan 118
natives, Japanese 123
natural burial 364
naturalism 423
naturalism, and salvation 436
natural theology 93
nature
   as source of religion 472
   defilement through 363
   nature-concept, Japanese terminology 41
   nature drawings 77
   nature force, deified 314
   nature-*kami* 279
   Nature-*Kami*, the Great 61
   nature religion 387
   nature religion, and sexuality 403
   nature worship 25
   Naturkraft 141
   obedience to 317
   of a person 136
   the Biblical peace-concept 268
Nazi propaganda 250
nearness of the kingdom 447
neck, soul-concept 140
neck, soul concept (נֶפֶשׁ) 497
necromancers, shamans 312
necromancy 216
needs, soul concept (נֶפֶשׁ) 499
needy human, soul concept (נֶפֶשׁ) 497
NEET 353
neighbor, unbelieving 414
nervosity, Morita 317
Nether-Land 29
neurosis, shamanism 313
neurosis-theory, Morita 317
Nevius method 211
New-Age Movement 34
new humanity 445, 463
New New Religions, and shamanism 313
New New Religions, influenced by Christianity 390

New Religions 33, 327, 392, 443, 444
New Religions, and shamanism 311
new world, correlated to the old 462
new world order 476
New Year lucky tickets 300
New Year's Eve 394
next world 294
Nihonjin-to kami, seisho, Kirisuto (日本人と神、聖書、キリスト), 1998 102
nikkeijin, discriminated 352
Nippon 63
non-Christian soteriologies, instrumentalized 426
non-marital partnerships 174
non-war 258, 261
norito 370
North American individualism 193
North-South-division 262
Nostradamus, and Aum 444
not-yet, salvation 460
nuclear family 171, 174
numbering system, groupism 158
numinous, fear of 320
nursing period, protection during 316

O

obedience, unconditional 171
obesity, as sign of *Hotei's* importance 406
objective sin, and guilt 346
obligation
   ancestor veneration 189
   conscience 341
   etiquette 257
   in Hebrews 469
   Naikan-treatment 344
occultism 14
occultism, caution needed 19
ocean, soul concept (לֵבָב) 508
October, mythology 397
odor, soul concept (רוּחַ) 503
Oedipus-complex 75
offerings, for the dead 125
offices, protection for 316
Ohnmacht, soul concept (רוּחַ) 505

Okinawa, discriminated 352
Okinawa shamanism 117
old self, dying 413
Old Testament, salvation concept of 432
omission, sins of 288
one heart and soul 118
Onesimus, *amae* 241
on (恩) 189
Oomisoka 373
Oomoto-Religion 313
openness to others, kenosis 477
optimism, versus man as sinful 423
oracle
 divination 297
 sumou as 375
 terminology 124
oracles, safe 523
order, and purity 380
order, and the peace-concept 272
Original Gospel Tabernacle 383
original sin
 according to Kajiwara 286
 in the Japanese context 286
 original guilt 191
 pre-existence of souls 284
 systematic 282
Osaka, shamanism 313
ostracism 342
other world 294
other-worldliness, in Judaism 432
Oulanem 467
overwork, death due to 352
overwork, suicide and death caused by 258
oyabun-kobun-relationships 158

P

Paburou-sama 238
pacifism 262
paganism, Christianized 20
pain, eased 253
pain, of the heart, soul concept (לֵבָב) 509
painting, goddess of 400
painting, Seven Auspicious Deities 523
palmistry 301
Panaitios 94, 95
pan-animation of nature 11
pan-generational solidarity 195
pangs of conscience 348
pantheon, Japanese 73
Papua New Guinea, ancestor veneration 224
paralogy 439
parapsychology 17, 123
parasite singles 353
parental deities, of the clan 64
parental indulgence 165
parent-child relationship 327
parenting
 protection for 316
 role of ancestors 338
 shame and guilt 335
Park, and Kitamori 417
Parousia, delay of 447
participation, in Christ's suffering 416
participation, in the suffering of others 431
participatory unity, ancestor worship 239
partnering leadership styles 329
passivism, not Christian 480
pastors, and shamanism 327
patience, soul concept (נֶפֶשׁ) 500
patriarchy
 modern 179
 paternal principle 180
 patriarchal house-concept 184
 patrilinear house-concept 184
 patrilocal house-concept 184
patriotism 72, 250, 424
patron deities
 amulets as patrons 314
 classes of gods 65
 ujigami 65
patron-deity, for the teaching of Buddha 523
Paul
 according to Bloch 451
 amae 241
 leadership style 329
 missionary 109
pax Salomonica 271
peace

apotropaic magic 315
as central concept of soteriology 247
as non-war 261
Christian peace-concept 271
Confucianism 257
internalized 351
Japanese peace-concept 249
justice 347
negative peace 269
Old Testament peace-concept 267
peace of mind 253, 260
peace-science 262
purification 374
peach, apotropaic magic 377
peccatum hereditarium 282
penal law, collective 195
Pentecostalism, Japanese 421
perception, reduction, massification 207
performance society, end of 353
persecution, for the sake of hope 446
persecution of Christians, in Japan 236
persecution of Christians, reason 224
perseverance, soul concept (נֶפֶשׁ) 500
personality, soul concept (נֶפֶשׁ) 496
personal pronouns, absence of 161
personal pronoun, soul-concept 141
personal pronoun, soul concept (נֶפֶשׁ) 501
person, soul-concept 141
person, soul concept (נֶפֶשׁ) 500, 501
perversion, sin 289
Peter 321
phallicism
    phallus cults 403
    phallus worship 406
    shamanism 403
phallus-symbolism 523
phantom 411
Pharisees, leadership styles 329
pharynx, soul-concept 140
pharynx, soul concept (נֶפֶשׁ) 496
Philippians, amae 241
piblokto 313
Pietism 430, 455
P'ing ho (和平) 253
placidity 260

planets, change of 396
plantatio ecclesia, as purpose of mission 476
plants, for purification 369
Platonism, ressurection 453
pleasure, sexual, Seven Auspicious Deities 523
pluralism 425
pneuma 35
pneumatological character, of salvation 431
pneumatology, and salvation 437
poa 442
poetry 264
politics
    political character of salvation 431
    political liberation according to Moltmann 466
    political order 253
    Takakura 423
polytheism, and the Catholic Church 238
pondering, soul concept (לֵבָב) 513
Pontifical Council for Culture, 2005 149
pop culture, and erotic art 403
popularity 396
population, soul concept (נֶפֶשׁ) 497
possession 123
possession, and shamanism 309
Post-Modernity 31, 421, 438
postmortem name, Buddhist 239, 379
postmortem salvation 186
postmortem section 516
post-theistic 473
potion, shamanism 312
potted flowers, as bad omen 378
poverty, and sin 428
poverty, and this-worldliness 391
poverty, new 353
power, as salvation 387
power encounter 321
practitioners, shamans 311
pragmatism 388
pranks, as sin 367
praxis, salvation centered on 476
prayer
    for the dead 125

Subject Index 643

in order to change fate 301
Japanese and Christian 216
magic 51, 237, 327
prayer march 324
pre-birth experience, and animism 162
pre-existence of souls 284
preference, God's 415
preferential option for the poor 478
pregnancy, fifth month 316
pregnancy, protection during 316
pre-logic psychology 198
pre-marital partnerships 174
present world 411
pride, sins of 288
primal emotions 320
primary reference person 344
Primitive Communism 464
primogenitual house-concept 184
primordial revelation 281
Princess *Yamato* 409
principal part, of salvation 433
prison sentences, as purification 368
private life, serving the publich life 161
private person, soul concept (נֶפֶשׁ) 500
probation-period, missing in Japan 343
process theology 463
process, towards grace 475
proclamation of the gospel to the heathen, and the second coming of Christ 458
Prodigal Son 76
profane history, and salvation history 463
progress, belief in 474
prophesies, deity of 408
prophetic shamanism 309
Pro Rabirio, Cicero 349
prosperity
    as salvation 387
    bringer of prosperity 398, 402
    goddess of prosperity 400
    gospel of prosperity 422
    Seven Auspicious Deities 409
prosperity, independence from 523
prosperity, Seven Auspicious Deities 523
prostitution, and shamanism 311

protection 409
protection, and salvation 297
protection of monasteries and the kitchen 523
protectors, amulets 314
Protestantism, Japanese 421
protology, and eschatology 457
protology, and soteriology 99
psyche 115, 128
psychic power 116, 135
psychic shamanism 309
psycho-analysis 317
psychokinesis 136
psychological disposition, soul concept (רוּחַ) 506
psychological happiness, Seven Auspicious Deities 409, 523
psychological interaction effect 317
psycho-therapy 317
pubic hair, apotropaic magic 314
public character, of salvation 431
public sins 288
Pulastya 401
punishment 289
punishment, for sin 367
Pure Land School 219
purification
    and exorcism 518
    as apotropaic magic 369
    death as purification 373
    heart and body 374
    Heil as purification 356
    hygiene 379
    Japanese terminology 356
    rituals 368
purpose-oriented values, versus means-oriented values 160

Q

quadrupeds, as gods 68
quasi-religion 389
quietness, peace-concept 270
quietude 260

R

Rachen, soul concept (נֶפֶשׁ) 496
rain magic 124, 126
ramat 8, 30
ransom payment 367
rationalism 423
reason 135, 512
reason, soul concept (לֵבָב) 513
rebellion, sin as 289
receptive reason, soul concept (לֵבָב) 512
reconciliation 261, 416
reconciliation, with God 289
reconciliation, with God and man 435, 475
recovery 135
recruitment, New New Religions 390
red defilement 362, 364
redemption
   as worldly concept 430
   Kitamori 414
   redeemed world and fallen world 460
   through evolution 474
refined, peace-concept 255
Reformation, and individualism 194
refugee problems 262
regret, and ancestor veneration 189
regret, soul concept (לֵבָב) 514
rehabilitation
   conversion 342
   salvation as 342, 347
   shalom 346
reiki
   discernment 51
   initiation rituals 52
   medicine 42
   surrender 53
reiki, initiation rituals, incantations for 491
reintegration, into nature 317
rei (霊), versus flesh 123
rei (霊), versus material 123
relativism, individualism 199
relaxation 254
releasing of irrigation sluices 516
religious fidelity 80
religious pluralism, in Asia 91
remember, soul concept (לֵבָב) 513
remorse
   ancestor veneration 188
   evangelism 75
   versus shame 345
Rengeouin 395
repentance, and forgiveness 75
reponsibility, before God 281
reptiles, as gods 68
reputation 333
requiem masses 296
Research Institute for Human Happiness 393
residence-change, lucky days for 304
resignation, as sin 481
respect 196
respiration 47
respiratory organ, soul concept (נֶפֶשׁ) 497
responsibility
   absent 177
   humanity 89
   in society 332
restaurants, purification of 376
restoration, and the peace-concept 270
restoration, of a relationship 255
resurrection
   according to Bloch 449
   according to Moltmann 452
   eschatology 458
revelation, as hermeneutical key 462
revelation, New New Religions 390
Revelation of John, Aum 443
revelation theology 93
reverence 59
rhinoceros, horn of 401
Rhinoceros Sutra 401
riches, material, Seven Auspicious Deities 523
ridges, breaking down of 516
righteous and holy state 424
righteousness, as relational term 196
righteousness, patron deity of 402
right faith, patron deity of 398
rinsing, for purification 374
ripening unto judgement 461
Rishikesh 442

Subject Index

rites de passage 469
rites of passage 316
River *Sai* 219
River *Sanzu* 373
robbery 396
Rokkakudou 395
rokkan-Gebete 238
Rokuharamizuji 395
romantic love 174
roofs, damage to 517
rootlessness, religious, massification 207
rover goddess 400
Russia, Aum 440
Ryuukyuu-Archipel (琉球列島) 63

S

Sabbath-keeping 354
sacral, and secular 12
sadness 46, 128
SAD (social anxiety disorder) 333
safe oracles 523
safety
   divination 325
   massification 207
   Seven Auspicious Deities 409
   the peace-concept 268
safety, Seven Auspicious Deities 523
sages, as gods 63
Saidaiji 395
saints, Japanese 238
sakkoku 250
salt, for purification 375
salvation
   antropological aspect 355
   as collectivistic concept 429
   as dynamic event 424
   as worldly concept 430
   changes in Buddhism 390
   comprehensive 424
   cosmological aspect 291
   folk-religious 410
   glory of God as purpose 469
   gods as means to the end of 410
   holistic 387
   horizontal and vertical 480
   individualism/collectivism 190
   peace-concept 267, 271
   postmortem 186
   Salvation in the Japanese Context, Takenaka 422
   sociological aspect 331
   subject of 471
   suffering 412
   theological aspect 277
   this-worldly 387
   two-dimensional 410
samurai
   converted to Christianity 423
   family ideal 170
   samurai nobility, and *amae* 173
sanctification, Kitamori 414
sanctification, purity 381
San Juan-sama 238
sannyasin 442
Sanzu-river 373
Sapir-Whorf-hypothesis 10
Sarasvati 400, 410
sarin 439
Satan, rule of 322
satori 132
Scandal, Endou 383
scapegoat 370, 372
schizoid personality disorder 246
Schlund, soul concept (נֶפֶשׁ) 496
schools, shame-oriented education 339
science fiction films 320
science, in Post-Modernity 33
scraping, for purification 374
sculpture, goddess of 400
sculpture, Seven Auspicious Deities 523
sea bass 398
sea bream 379, 398
seafarers, patron deity of 398
seafaring, Seven Auspicious Deities 523
sea goddess 400
sea serpent 400
seclusion, of Japan 154, 250
second Adam 151
second coming of Christ 457
second death 347

Second Vatican Council 463
secret sins 288
secrets of the hearts, soul concept (לֵבָב) 509
section, postmortem 516
sect leaders, as gods 64
Sect of the Pure Land 52
Sect-*Shinto* 72
secular, and sacral 12
secularism 17, 18, 411
secularization 473
secularization, of God 93
seduction 127
Seele, ethymology 11
Sehnen, soul concept (נֶפֶשׁ) 498
SEIC, Käser 134
Seiheiki 52
Seiwain 395
self, dependent on others 344
self-destruction, conscience 340
Self-Identity of Absolute Contradiction. Nishida 85
self-image, I and you 337
selfishness, versus freedom 153
self-reflection 343
self-sacrifice 263
self, soul concept (לֵבָב) 513
self, soul concept (נֶפֶשׁ) 500
sengachi 303
seniority principle 179
senmake 303
Sensibilität, soul concept (לֵבָב) 509
sensitivity 509
sentiment 136
separation of religion and government 173
serenity 260
serfdom, massification 206
serpent 400
SER-structure 456
servanthood 431
setsubun 371, 377
setting up stakes 516
Seven Auspicious Deities 393, 439, 522
Seventeen-Article Constitution, 604 250
sexuality
   openness towards sexual intercourse 403

sexism 254
sexual intercourse as defilement 364
sexual intercourse as magic 404
sexual lust, soul concept (נֶפֶשׁ) 497
sexual pleasure, Seven Auspicious Deities 523
sexual sins, as impurity 362, 382
shakkou 303
shalom
   dimensions 247
   freedom 473
   missiology 247
   shalom-concept 267
   word-field 270
shamanism
   Cho 422
   Christianity 73
   church leadership 327
   institutionalized 312
   phallicism 403
   popular among women 308
   roles of shamans today 117
   Shintoism 25
   soul-concept 11, 13, 126
   spiritism 188
shame
   as derived emotion 320
   as root of virtue 335
   before God 350
   death 364
   defilement 349
   guilt 334
   hell 449
   interaction with 339
   in the Old Testament 344
   negative feelings 133
   shame and guilt, dialectical unity 344
   shame-guilt-dualism, speaking against 334
   shame-orientation, superimposed 339
   shaming, in the Church 346
   Unheil as 333
   Unheil experienced as shaming 342
   versus remorse 345
Shasekishuu 364, 390

shepherd, leadership styles 329
Shichifukujin 416, 439, 522
shichigosan 316
Shingon-Sect 52, 71
Shinmin-no Michi 161
Shinritou, Aum 445
Shinsenen 296
Shinshinshuukyou 392
Shinshuukyou 392
Shintoism
   animism 24
   as indigenous religion of Japan 24
   changed by Buddhism 390
   definitions 5
   divination 297
   even today? 30
   festivals and defilement 364
   folk moral 25
   nationalism 263
   Shintoist theology, modern 368
Shiva 398, 410, 441
Shogunate 485
short-tempered, soul concept (רוּחַ) 505
Shotoku, Emperor 370
Shrine-*Shinto* 72
sickness 135
sickness demons 377
sickness, soul departed 117
significant others 336, 341
significant others, shame 333
Silence, Endou 55
sin
   an Asian concept 427
   annihilation of 367
   as collectivistic concept 427
   as misdeed 282
   biblical anthropology 423
   causes 287
   impurity, in the Bible 381
   nature of 288
   punishment 367
   sinfulness as feeling before God 320
   sinned-against, and sinners 428
   sins committed unknowingly 369
   sins concealed 348

sins, sexual 362
   terminology 356
   tsumi according to Norinaga 359
skin excrescences 516
skinning alive 516
skinning backwards 516
sky-people 30
sleep therapy, Ayurvedic 318
snake bites, defilement 362
social anxiety disorder 333
Social Gospel 423
social groups, familial structures of 178
social harmonization 332
social harmony 262
socializing agents 339
social justice, in Japan 351
social order 256
social phobia 333
social shame 345
social transformation 248
sociology, and animism 151
sodomy 362, 517
Sogo, farmer 258
sola gratia 480
Solomon, peace 271
Song, and Kitamori 417
sorcery, as defilement 364
sorcery, malevolent 517
soteriology
   as hermeneutical key 462
   intrinsically eschatological 486
   protology 99
   two-dimensional 426
Soukagakkai 388
soul 499
   after death 115
   body 116
   cleansing of 122
   closeness to spirit 122
   detachable 116
   during sickness departed 117
   emotionality, soul concept (לֵבָב) 509
   incorruptible 120
   location of 122, 128, 134
   of Japan 118

of the dead 122, 129
postmortem 119
soul concept (נֶפֶשׁ) 499, 500
souls going astray 186
South Pacific, religious influence 396
South Pole Star 404
Sovereign Grandchild 515, 518
sovereignty, of God 322
sowing, lucky days for 304
spatial categories, purity 380
Speiseröhre, soul concept (נֶפֶשׁ) 496
spirit
   as god 126
   as spirits 126
   as spirits of the dead 125
   demarcation of the world-field *rei* (霊) (spirit) 123
   during pregancy 316
   ghost 127
   indwelling in all things 35
   of the dead 129
   the extraordinary 123
   vengeful spirits 126
Spirited Away (motion picture) 87
spiritism 125, 127, 188
spirit of God, *mana* as 149
Spirit of Jesus Church 421
spirit, soul concept (רוּחַ) 502, 506
spiritual double 30
spirituality 123
spiritual mapping 324
spiritual power, apotropaic magic 314
spiritual, versus carnal 123
spiritual world 411
split-level Christianity 20
spoiled children 165
stability of society, ancestor veneration 223
stag, and *Juroujin* (寿老人) 405
State *Shinto* 71
Stoics 79
stopgap solution, Schweitzer 447
store openings, lucky days for 304
storm-god 397
Strasbourg lectures, Schweitzer 446
strength 135

strength, soul concept (רוּחַ) 504
stress, released 253
striving, soul-concept 140
striving, soul concept (נֶפֶשׁ)498
stubbornness 131
subjection, and peace 262
subjective rights 172
subjectivism, liberal 423
subject of salvation, man as 424
submission, unconditional 177
subordination, Confucianism 260
suffering
   Christian action called for 424
   emotional 133
   for the sake of hope 446
   of the heart, soul concept (לֵבָב)509
   of victims, and sin 427
   salvation 412
   the suffering God, and shame 350
   the suffering God, Bonhoeffer 473
   vicarious 416, 442
   Vicedom 415
   with God 473
suggestibility, massification 208
suicide
   bullying 150
   caused by overwork 258
   collectivism 156
   conscience 340
   juvenile 353
   taking responsibility 340
summum bonum 469
sumou 375
Sun-Goddess 29, 63
superego 75
superiority, god 64
super-natural 13
supernatural skill 297
superorganism 162
superstition 330
supplementation, Christianization 426
suppression, cross as symbol of protest against 431
suppression, social 352
supreme 59

Subject Index

survivor guilt 189, 217
Susanoo 367
Suwa-Shrine 370
swamp, Endou 245
symbolic anthropology 469
sympathetic human, organ of, soul concept (נֶפֶשׁ) 499
sympathy 132
sympathy, organ of, soul concept (נֶפֶשׁ) 499
syncretism
    Crypto-Christians 236
    Old Testament 20
    overcoming motherly religion 246
    plurality of Japanese religion 80
    Yonggi Cho 422
Syria, ancestor cult 228

T

taboo-concept 363
taboos, connected with death 364
tabula rasa, as missiological approach 71
taian 303
Taichi-ch'uan 48
talent 136
talent, extraordinary, soul concept (רוּחַ) 504
talents, Seven Auspicious Deities 523
talismans 314
Tantra-Buddhism 441
Taoism 47
taste, locality of, soul concept (נֶפֶשׁ) 497
tatemae 246
tateshakai 155
Tatsünden 288
tea ceremony 70, 257
Teaching of the Absolute Truth 440
telos, of all existing things 77
Tennou 70, 71
Tenrikyou 313
Tenshoukoutaijinguukyou 313
Ten Worlds, Buddhism 29
Terakoya 419
territorial deities 376
territorial spirits 323
thankfulness, and ancestor veneration 188, 221

thankfulness, and guilt-feelings 221
thanksgiving 317
theft 396
theism, Moltmann opposed to 451
theistic dualism 17
theocentric focus 323
theocentrism, versus Christocentrism 478
theogonic continuity 87
theogonism 279
theogony 244
theologia crucis, Bonhoeffer 473
theological embarrassment, of the delay of Parousia 447
theology of freedom 473
theology of nature 76
theology of the cross, Endou 417
Theology of the Pain of God, 1965 412
Theology of the Pain of God, Kitamori 79
theopathy 127
The Powerless Savior, 1979 244
The Principle of Hope, 1982 448
The Samurai, 1997 152
The Sea and Poison, 1984 383
Thessalonians, *amae* 241
The Wounded Heart of God, 1993 427
thinking, heart 118, 130
thinning of seedlings, infanticide 149
Third World War, Aum 445
thirst for justice 449
this-worldliness, in Judaism 432
this-worldly benefits 387
this-worldly orientation 227
this-worldly salvation 387
Thomas Aquinas 94
three-selves, South Korea 211
throat, soul-concept 140
throat, soul concept (נֶפֶשׁ) 496, 497, 498
Thummim 326
thunder-god 69
Tibetan Tantra-Buddhism 441
t'ien chu 84
tiger, as god 68
time-concept, Hebrew 456
time, cyclic and linear 456
TKS (taijin kyoufushou (对人恐怖症)) 333

Todeskult 118
Tokugawa-Shogunate 236
Tokyo Story, 1953 174
Tokyo subway sarin attack 439
Tokyo Theological Seminary 422
tolerance 89
tomobiki 302
top to bottom, salvation 461
torii 45
totalitarian atmosphere, family 176
totaliter aliter 82, 320, 423
totaliter aliter, fear 293
totemism 198
Toudaiji 395
Touhoku University, Sendai 455
tower of many treasures 402
tower of riches 523
Trachten, soul concept (נֶפֶשׁ) 498
traders, patron deity of 398
trade, Seven Auspicious Deities 523
traffic safety amulets 316
tranquility 260
transcendence of God 91
transcendent orientation, , collectivism/
 individualism 205
transcendent orientation, dangers 208
transcendent relationship with God, and
 salvation 434
transgression, sin 288
transience 47
transition, apotropaic magic 316
transition, created, fallen, and redeemed
 world 460
travels, unlucky days for 304
travesty 289
treachery, sin 289
treasure-ship, Seven Auspicious Deities 394
Treaty Revision, 1889 224
tribal societies, and Japan 200
true heart 128, 133, 134
True Jesus Church 421
true self 246, 343
trustworthiness, Confuciamism 257
trustworthiness, peace-concept 269
truthfulness 133

truthfulness, of love 413
tsusemkul 311
Tulana Research Center (Dialogue Center)
 425
Turkey, ancestor veneration 239
two-dimensional salvation 410
two-dimensional soteriology 426
Tylor's soul-concept 140
typhoon 396

U

Überlegen, soul concept (לֵבָב) 513
ujigami(氏神)-system 64
ullam-bana 187
uncertainty avoidance 409
unclean professions 352
unclean spirits 382
unconsciousness 132
unconsciousness, soul concept (לֵבָב) 507
understanding, power of, soul concept
 (לֵבָב) 513
understanding, soul concept (לֵבָב) 511
under-world 518
unequal opportunity. society with 353
unexporable, the, soul concept (לֵבָב) 508
unfaithfulness, sin 289
Ungeduld, soul concept (רוּחַ) 505
Unheil
 cosmological aspect 291
 origin of 278
 under the anthropological aspect 380
 under the sociological aspect 331, 344
 under the theological aspect 280
unification with God 413
unified human race 477
uniformity, linguistic 154
United Church of Christ 213
universal priesthood, and shamanism 327
universal priesthood, in New New Religions
 390
universe, pacified 270
unlucky ages 305
unlucky ages, protection during 316
unlucky days 302
Unmut, soul concept (רוּחַ) 505

Subject Index

unruly deities 515
uprightness, as basis for protection 409
uprightness, Confuciamism 257
urban centers, massification 206
urbanization, impact on the family 176
Urfaktum Immanuel 84
urge of will, soul concept (לֵבָב) 514
Urgeschichte, guilt and shame 345
Urim 326
Uroffenbarung 281
Ursünde, history of the term 282
utilitarianism 423
utopian peace 270

V

Vaisravana 396, 401
value, massification 207
vanity, Budhism 391
Vasuki 402
vengeful spirits 295
venial sins 288
Verantwortung 207
Vereinerleiung 255
Verlangen, soul concept (לֵבָב) 510
Verlangen, soul concept (נֶפֶשׁ) 498
Vermassung 162
Vernunft, soul concept (לֵבָב) 512
Verstand, soul concept (לֵבָב) 513
Verstehen, soul concept (לֵבָב) 511
vertically structured groups, dangers 158
vertical salvation, over horizontal salvation 437
vertical salvation, versus horizontal salvation 480
vertical society 155
vexation, and ancestor veneration 189
vicariousness, apotropaic magic 314
vicarious suffering, Aum 442
victor quia victima 419
virility, deity of 406
virility, Seven Auspicious Deities 523
virtue, and shame 133
visana (毘沙拏) 401
Volcano, Endou 383
Volk Gottes, Keyser 225

Volkschristentum Keyser 226
Vollmacht, soul concept (רוּחַ) 504
voluntarism 193
voracity that cannot be stilled, soul concept (נֶפֶשׁ) 496
vox populi vox dei 57

W

Wahrheit, and *Wirklichkeit* 484
wand, purification 369
warfare prayer, not biblical 324
war, helping deity 402
warrior class, and homoerotic culture 403
warrior deity 399
washing of feet 421
washing, terminology 356
Watarai-Clan 244
Watarai-Shintou 61
water, for purification 375
water, purification 374
wa (和), word-field 249
weddings, lucky days for 304
weddings, unlucky days for 304, 305
welfare, as salvation 436
well-being, and the peace-concept 268
well-being, as salvation 387
wellness, as salvation 436
Wesen, soul concept (נֶפֶשׁ) 500
Western thinking, recognized in Japan 83
whale, as divine manifestation 398
white leprosy 516
wholeness, and the peace-concept 267
wholeness, peace-concept 267
Whorf, linguistic relativity principle 164
Wie kriege ich einen gnädigen Gott? 433
wife, Confucian family constitution 171
wild boars, as gods 68
wild brine 518
wild-gods 376
will 513, 514
  heart 131
  Japanese terminology 136
  soul-concept 142
  strong will 131
  will of God 131

will-power 136
Wille, soul concept (לֵבָב) 514
Wille, soul concept (רוּחַ) 506
will, soul concept (רוּחַ) 506
wind, for purification 375
windpipe 145, 497
wind, soul-concept 141
wind, soul concept (רוּחַ) 502
Wind, soul concept (רוּחַ) 502
Wirklichkeit, and *Wahrheit* 484
wisdom 523
wisdom, Confuciamism 257
wisdom, deity of 405, 406
wisdom, goddess of 400
wish-granting jewel 402
wishing jewel 523
witchcraft 517
    abomination 289
    Buddhism and witches 373
    Japanese terminology 127
    means against witches 121
    using God's name 88
withdrawal of affection 337
wolves, as gods 68
women, and Buddhism 308
word games, magic 377
words, divine power of 379
work process, Marx 466
worldly desires, Buddhism 373
world of the dead 294
worldview, biblical 17
worldview, Christian 17
World War II 119
worship-songs, Buddhist 264
wounds, and divination 362
wounds, as defilement 362
wrath of God 418, 436
wrath, soul concept (רוּחַ) 505
Wunsch, soul concept (נֶפֶשׁ) 499

X

xin (信) 257
xùndào (殉道) 238

Y

Yakshas 401
Yakushi 391, 403
Yakushiji 395
Yakuza 171
Yamasachi and *Umisachi* 29
Yamato 65, 70, 262
Yamato-hime 409
Yamato-hime-no Mikoto Seiki 409
Yamato, Japan at war 262
Yamato, Spirit of 263
Yanomamö 327
Yawata-scandal 328
yearning 498
yearning, soul concept (לֵבָב) 510
yearn, soul-concept 140
Yi-King, divination 297
Yin and *Yang* 255
yi (義) 257
yonder, meta-cosmic 426
yonder world 420
Yoshida-Shintou 62
yuta 117

Z

Zedekiah 269
Zen-Buddhism 64, 132, 257, 407
Zen, Buddhism 21
Zen-Buddhism, nationalism 263
zhi (知) 257
zodiac 303

Scripture Index

Old Testament

Genesis
1:2 502
1:3 147
2:7 .... 150, 496
2:25–3:21 345
3 283
4:10 427
6:3 282
6:5 282
6:6 78
6:12 283
8:21 .... 144, 282
15:15 269
24:67 241
28:21 268
31:20 512
41:38 .... 145, 504

Exodus
2:12 465
3:7 88
3:14 88
10:19 502
14:31 453
20:3 90
20:4 90
20:12 .... 239, 321
21:23 500
23:9 499
33:19 88
34:6 198
35:21 514

Leviticus
12:6, 8 382
14:19, 31 382
17:11 500

18:17 362
18:22 289
20:13 289
26:40 289

Numbers
5:12, 27 289
6:6 501
12 382

Deuteronomy
4:11 508
4:29 92
5:6 283
6:4 90
7:25–26 289
12:31 289
16:26 90
17:1 289
18:9–12 289
21:18 289
22:5 289
23:25 499
25:5–10 346
29:3 511
32:8 457
32:21 90

Joshua
7:1 289
9:6 269
22:20 289

Judges
3:11 270
4:17 269
5:31 270

8:28 270
13:22 321
16:18 513
16:30 501
19:20 269
20:16 288
21:13 269

1 Samuel
16:4–5 269
16:7 508
17:32 511
20:21 268
24:6 .... 144, 514
25:37 507

2 Samuel
7:3 514
19:31 268

1 Kings
2:6, 33 269
2:13 269
5:5 271
8:46 282
10:5 505
16:26 90
17:18 321
21:7 507
22:22–23 19

2 Kings
5:21–22 269
17:15 90
19:7 504
22:20 269

2 Chronicles
18:21–22 19
23:28 269
26:21 382

Ezra
1:5 .... 145, 506

Job
5:23 268
5:23–24 268
6:11 500
12:3 513
15:13 505
16:4 501
19:17 503
30:25 .... 145, 499
31:7 .... 146, 510
33:9 382
34:14 503

Psalms
4:9 268
14:2–3 282
21:3 .... 146, 510
22:10 242
25:17 509
27 .... 169, 242
31:7 90
32 348
32:3–5 244
32:4 348
32:8 289
32:39 502
32:57 289
33:6 503
35:25 498
36:10 278
37:11 268
44:22 509
51 .... 382, 384
53:3–4 282
63:2 282
83:16 348
85:10 273
90:3, 7–9 150
104:27 76
105:18 497
119:65 268
119:165 268
130:3 282
131 76
131:2 242
143:2 282
145:12 150
146:4 .... 150, 502

Proverbs
3:2 268
3:22 .... 145, 500
7:23 500
8:35–36 500
10:3 497
14:26 320
14:29 .... 145, 505
14:30 .... 146, 510
15:14 512
16:9 513
16:26 498
18:14 506
18:15 512
19:2 288
20:9 382
23:2 498
27:7 497
28:26 513

Ecclesiastes
3:11 150
6:9 496
7:8 .... 145, 506

Isaiah
1:2 289
1:20 289
5:14 .... 145, 496
6:1–6 321
8:17–20 322
9:5–6 271
11:1–5, 10 271
11:2 .... 145, 151, 504
13:19 457
27:5 271
29:24 506
31:3 283
32:15–18 270
40:6 .... 282, 283
42:5 502
45:7 273
53:5 .... 273, 348
54:10 273
54:10–13 273
57:18–19 269
57:18f 272
57:19 273
60:17 273
63:9 78
65 271
65:1 92
65:17 513
66:12 273
66:24 .... 347, 449

Jeremiah
2:5 90
2:20 90
2:24 .... 497, 503
2:27 20
3:3 348
3:10 289
4:10 .... 145, 497
4:19 507
6:15 348
7:1–11 321
8:12 348
8:19 90
10:3 90
10:8–14 90
13:27 90
14:19 269
14:22 90
16:19 90
17:5 282
29:7 273
31:20 78

33:6 269
34:5 269
49:13 457
51:17–18 90

Ezekiel
1:20 147
2:3 289
16 90
18:2 198
33:10–11 192
34:25 273
37:6 502
37:26 273

Daniel
7:11–12 457
9 431

9:27 449
10:12, 19 268
10:16 321
11:44 449
12:2f 449

Hosea
2:20 268
6:1 269
11:1 86

Joel
3:1 283

Micah
3 431
4:4–5 271
5:1–5 271

6:8 88

Jonah
2:4 508
2:9 90

Haggai
2:9 .... 271, 273

Zechariah
6:13 271
8:12 273
8:16 271

Malachi
2:11 289
3:20 269
3:23–24 271

New Testament

Matthew
5:3–10 460
5:44f 459
6:12–15 289
6:25–34 468
6:33 464
7:7 92
7:11 243
7:16 51
7:21–23 460
8:11–12 460
9:2 76
10:23 447
11:5 448
11:25–30 .... 243, 450
12:32 459
13:24–30 459
13:44–46 .... 459, 460
13:47–50 460
15:18–20 382
16:24 417
16:26 437
17:6–7 321
18:8–9 347

18:17 287
18:20 330
18:23–35 289
22:1–14 460
22:37–40 290
23:8–10 329
24:31 450
25:1–13 460
25:14–30 460
25:31–46 478

Mark
2:7 76
5:36 287
8:34 417
8:36 437
9:43–48 347
9:48 347

Luke
1:52 457
3:33 150
5:8–9 321
6:32–34 414

6:36 459
9:23 431
12:1–3 350
12:32 461
14:28–33 460
15:3–7 287
15:4–7 76
15:19 76
15:20–21 76
16:1–9 433
17:21 450
17:25 414
18:30 459
20:35 459

John
1:12 150
1:33 151
3:6 282
5:14 76
5:29 450
6:63 147
8:11 76
10:10 416

10:11, 15 76	14:17 460	3:10 412
10:15 416		3:12 414
11:25b..................................151	**1 Corinthians**	4:5 437
14:1–3 .... 470, 478	4:20 460	
18:36 450	6:9 460	**Colossians**
	8:10 239	1:16 90
Acts	10:21 240	1:19f....................................272
3:17 287	10:23 77	4:11 460
8:9–13..................................51	15:23ff.................................450	
14:22 416	15:30–31.............................416	**1 Thessalonians**
17:26 457	15:50 460	2:7–8..................................241
17:30 287		4:14ff..................................450
23:3 288	**2 Corinthians**	
	1:5 412	**2 Thessalonians**
Romans	4:7 150	1:5 460
1 94	4:8–12................................416	2:3 289
1:13 287	5:20 475	2:3–12................................461
1:16–17..............................196	6:9 287	2:6–7..................................458
1:18–32..............................109	10:6 287	
1:18ff..................................100		**1 Timothy**
1:20 .... 86, 90, 97,	**Galatians**	4:1 .... 287, 289
100, 104, 109	1:22 287	
1:21–22................................89	2:19 412	**2 Timothy**
1:23 100	3:1 85	3:2 289
1:24 19	3:15ff..................................433	3:13 287
1:28 93	3:22 282	4:18 460
1:30 289	5:16 282	
2:4 76	5:17 282	**Hebrews**
3:9ff....................................282	5:21 460	1:2 90
5:10 414	5:24 412	1:3 382
5:12 283		2:2–3..................................287
5:19 287	**Ephesians**	3:12 289
6:3 412	1:4 469	4:12–13..............................348
6:19–23..............................345	2:2 ....53, 289	4:13 320
8:3 282	2:3 282	4:16 470
8:6 282	2:7 459	6:5 459
8:7 282	2:14 272	6:6 289
8:11 437	4:14 287	9:7 287
8:12 282	4:15 469	11:1f....................................468
8:15 243	5:6 289	11:6 92
8:38 90		12:1 470
11:32 282	**Philippians**	12:28 470
12:15 413	1:12–14..............................416	13:10 470
13:1–7................................424	2:25–28..............................241	13:11–14............................470
13:11 453	3:9 351	13:13–15............................469

13:20 269

James
2:26 147
4:5 325

1 Peter
1:14 287
2:21, 24 412
4:13 412
5:5 325
5:6 222

2 Peter
2:10 282
3:5 147

1 John
1:5–10 244
1:8 287
1:8–10 282
1:9 .... 381, 382
2:16 282
4:1 50
4:4 322
4:6 287

3 John
2 422

Revelation
11:1 147
12:7–12 346
13 461
19:20 450
19:29 450
20:6, 14 347
20:10, 14f 450
21:1 389
21:8 347

Japanese Words

A

Aarephu (アーレフ) 440
Adagosan (愛宕山) 395
aemaze (和交 or 甕交) 255
aemono (和物) 255
aeru (合える or 和える or 甕える or 齋える) 256
aesagasu (和えさがす) 256
aganai (購い) 367
Agon-Shuu (阿含宗) 440
ahanachi (畦放ち) 516
aikidou (合気道) 49
aka fujou (赤不浄) 362, 364
akaki kokoro (明き心) 133
akami (明見) 60
aki-no kehai (秋の気配) 40
akogareru あこがれる) 496
akogare (あこがれ) 498
akueki taisan-no tou (悪疫退散の祈) 371
akuma (悪魔) 294
akuryoutachi (悪霊たち) 294
akuryou (悪霊) 29, 120, 126, 370
amaenbou (甘えん坊) 165
amaeru (甘える) 165, 242, 254
amaetai (甘えたい) 167
amaetaku naru (甘えたくなる) 242
amae (甘え) 155, 162, 173, 177, 181, 216, 240, 250, 254
amai (甘い) 164, 165
amanau (和う or 甘なう) 254, 255
ama-no ukihashi (天の浮橋) 306
amanzuru (甘んずる) 166, 254
amashi (甘し) 169
amatareru (甘たれる) 166
Amaterasu-Ookami (天照大神) 409
Amaterasu-Oomikami (天照大御神) 244, 397
Amaterasu (天照) 70
amatsugami (天津神) 66

amatsu norito (天津祝詞) 517
amatsutsumi (天津罪) 371
amattareru (甘ったれる) 165
amayakasu (甘やかす) 166
ama (尼) 61
Ame-no Minakanu-shi-no Mikami (天之御中主神) 42
Ame-no Minakanushi-no Mikami (天之御中主神) 244, 245
Ame-no Minakanushi (天の御中主) 244
Amida Nyorai (阿弥陀如来) 52
Amida (阿弥陀) 391
anshinkan (安心感) 315
anshin (安心) 315, 389
anshin (安心 or 安神) 60
Antou-sama (殉道様) 238
araarashii (荒荒しい) 255
arahanigoto (顕明事) 84
arahitogami (現人神) 64
arahitogami (荒人神) 227
aramitama (荒御魂) 27
arashine (荒稲) 255
aria (洗い) 356
asanagi (朝和凪) 261
Ashiharashikoo-no-kami (葦原色許男神) 399
ashiwara-no nakatsu kuni (葦原の中つ国) 28
ashura (阿修羅) 29, 187
atoyaku (後厄) 305
Aum-Shinrikyou (オウム真理教) 393, 439
Aum Shinsen-no-kai (オウム神仙の会) 440
aware-to omou hito (哀れと思う人) 46
awaseru kao-ga nai (合わせる顔がない) 333
awaseru (合わせる) 254
ayabu (危) 304

B

bakasu (化かす or 魅かす) 113, 127
bakemono (化け物) 127
bakufu (幕府) 485
bambutsu-no reiki (万物の霊気) 39
Bastian-sama (バスティアン様) 238
batsu (罰) 368
ba (場) 156, 203
Benten (弁天) 400
Benzaiten (弁財天) 391, 406, 409, 523
Benzaiten (弁財天 or 弁才天) 400
be (邊 or 部) 65
Bishamonten (毘沙門天) 401, 523
Bishamon (毘沙門) 401
bodai (菩提) 401
bonnou (煩悩) 373
bonsai (盆栽) 70
bosatsu (菩薩) 29
boukon (亡魂) 295
bourei (亡霊) 122, 125, 129, 187
bunke (分家) 184
bunrei (分霊) 314
bunshin (分神) 314
bun (分) 160
Buraku Kaihou Doumei (部落開放同盟) 352
bushidou (武士道) 70
busshin (物心) 129
busshou (仏性) 87
butsujin (仏神) 81
butsumetsu (仏滅) 302
butsu (仏), Welt der 29
byoudouheiwa (平等平和) 304
byouki (病気) 135

C

cha-no yu (茶の湯) 70
chifujou (血不浄) 362
Chiihoaki Mizuho-no Kuni (五百秋瑞穂の国) 262
chiimi (血忌) 363
chikushoudou (畜生道) 29
Chimata-no-kami (巷神 or 岐神 or 衢神) 404
chimimouryou (魑魅魍魎) 127

chimi (魑魅) 127
chinju kami (鎮守神) 64
chinkon-no girei (鎮魂の儀礼) 296
chinkonsai (鎮魂際) 188
chi-no wa (茅の輪) 315
chishiki (知識) 512, 513
chiyorozu-no kami (千万の神) 65
Choku-Rei (直霊) 491
chounan (長男) 184
choushi-ga au (調子が合う) 255
choushi-o awaseru (調子を合わせる) 255
chouzu-no gi (手水の義) 375
chuudanjuunichoku (中段十二直) 303

D

Daianji (大安寺) 395
daian (大安) 303
daikichi (大吉) 300
Daikokuten (大黒天) 397, 398, 409, 523
daimeishi (代名詞) 501
dainakou (大儺公) 371
daina-no kimi (大儺公) 371
daina (大儺) 371
dai-Nippon (大日本) 263
Daiseishi Bosatsu (大勢至菩薩) 52
Daishou-Kangiten (大聖歓喜天) 392
dai uso (大うす) 71
dai-wa (大和) 263
dai (大) 316
Danichi Nyorai (大日如来) 52
dansonjohi (男尊女卑) 308
Datsueba (奪衣婆 or 脱衣婆) 373
Deusu-sama (デウス様) 237
deusu-sama (天主様) 71
dohi (奴婢) 372
dokufu (毒婦) 342
Doshisha Daigaku (同志社大学) 424
doubutsu uranai (動物占い) 306
douchou suru (同調する) 255
douhou-no seishin (同胞の精神) 424
doui suru (同意する) 255
douji (童子 or 童児) 403
Doukai (道会) 285
douki (動機) 514
doukyou (道教) 47

dousatsu (洞察) 512
doutokushin (道徳心) 133
douzoku (同族) 184
dou (道) 47

E

ebisugokokoro (夷心) 133
Ebisu-mai (恵比須舞 or 戎舞) 398
Ebisuten (恵比寿天) 396
Ebisu (恵比寿) 316, 396, 410, 523
Edo (江戸) 391
eiki (英気) 44
eirei (英霊) 125
ekibyou (疫病) 315, 396
ekiki (疫鬼) 371, 377
ekikyou (易経) 297
engaku (縁覚) 29
engimono (縁起物) 313
Enjerusan (エンジェルさん) 299
enryo (遠慮) 250
Eryouju (衣領樹) 373
eta (穢多) 352, 362

F

Fudou-Myou-Ou (不動明王) 403
Fudou (不動) 391, 403
fukabun-no tan-i (不可分の単位) 157
fukigen (不機嫌) 505
Fukuinteki Kirisutokyou (福音的基督教) 423
Fukurokuju-no ichidachi (福禄寿の市立ち) 406
Fukurokuju (福禄寿) 404, 405, 523
fukutoku (福徳) 401
fuku (福) 377, 394, 405
funadama (船魂 or 船霊 or 船玉) 122
fungeki (憤激) 505
funiki (雰囲気) 40, 142, 510
furiitaa (フリーター) 353
furoshiki-shingaku (風呂敷神学) 414
futonorito-no mikoto (太祝詞の命) 297
fuuchou (風潮) 259
fuufu aiwasu (夫婦相和す) 255
fuufu-no wagou (夫婦の和合) 254

G

Gagouji (元興寺) 395
gakidou (餓鬼道) 29
gaki (餓鬼) 29, 187
gaman suru (我慢する) 500
ganbou (願望) 499
garigari mouja (我利我利亡者) 186
gasshou (合掌) 208
Gedatsukai (解脱会) 188
geisha (芸者) 70
gendai-ni okeru sukui (現代における救い) 422
Genji-Monogatari (源氏物語) 263, 295
genki-o dasu (元気を出す) 507
genki (元気) 135, 511
Genroku (玄鹿) 405
gensechuushinshugi-no shuukyou (現世中心主義の宗教) 387
gense riyaku (現世利益) 387, 388, 405, 411, 422, 436, 443, 446, 484
genseshugi (現世主義) 411
gense (現世) 388, 411
genshou (現象) 286
genzai (原罪) 284
genzai (現在) 411
Gochinza Denki (鎮座伝記) 409
goen (五円 or 御縁) 378
gofu (護符) 315
go-on (呉音) 264
Goryoue (御霊会) 296
goryoushin (御霊神) 227
goryou (御霊) 227, 294, 295
gosenzosama (ご先祖さま) 222
gose (後世) 388, 390
guntai (群体) 161
guruupumenbaa (グループメンバー) 162
Gyouganji (行願寺) 395
gyousha (行者) 311

H

haatobureeku (ハートブレーク) 132
haatofuru (ハートフル) 133
haato-uoomingu (ハートウォーミング) 132
haato (ハート) 132

hadaka matsuri (裸祭) 370
hadamamori (肌守り) 315
hagoita (羽子板) 377
haha-to ko-to okasu tsumi (母と子と犯す罪) 362
haiki (排気) 39
haji-nai (恥じない) 133
haji-o haji-to omowanu mono-wa yaku-ni tatanu (恥を恥と思わぬ者は役に立たぬ) 335
haji-o koraeru (恥をこらえる) 333
haji-o shinobu (恥をしのぶ) 333
haji (恥) 133
hakamairi (墓参) 221
hakige (吐き気) 136
hakujin (白人) 516
hakurei (魄霊) 115, 316
hakuryoku (魄力) 116
hanabusa (英) 44
hangyaku (反逆) 289
hankichi (半吉) 300
happouyokeshugo (八方除け守護) 316
haraeyareru na (祓えやられる儺) 372
harae (祓え) 356, 367, 368, 373
haragei (腹芸) 155
haraigushi (祓い串) 369
harainusa (祓い幣) 369
harai (祓い) 356
harakiri (腹切り) 134
hara-no naka (腹の中) 134
hara-no soko-kara (腹の底から) 134
haraobi (腹帯) 32, 316
hara (腹) 134
harigata (張形) 406
hasshinden (八神殿) 42
hate (果て) 411
Hatsu-Ebisu (初恵比寿) 398
hatsu-miyamairi (初宮参り) 316
hatsuyume (初夢) 306
hau mushi-no wazawai (昆虫の災) 363
hau mushi-no wazawai (昆虫災) 517
Hayaakitsu-hime (速開津姫) 518
Hayasaura-hime (速佐須良姫) 518
heiankyou (平安京) 296
heika (兵火) 396
heion (平穏) 260
heiwagaku (平和学) 262
heiwa kaigi (平和会議) 261
heiwa kousaku (平和工作) 261
heiwa koushou (平和交渉) 261
heiwa-ni suru (平和にする) 262
heiwa (平和) 253, 261
he-i (平易) 260
Hida (飛騨) 82
Hieizan (比叡山) 395
higyou-no shi (非業の死) 296
hihanachi (樋放ち) 516
himitsu (秘密) 509
Hinshuu (飛州) 82
hiraku (開) 305
Hirasan (比良山) 395
Hiruko (蛭子) 397
hitogami (人神) 64, 82
hitogata (人型) 369
hitokatamari-no kumo (一塊の雲) 160
hito-no wa (人の和) 261
hiwatari (火渡り) 383
hoke (火気) 38
Hokutoshichisei (北斗七星) 303
Homujiwake (誉牟治別) 298
honji suijaku (本地垂迹) 81
honke (本家) 184
honkyochi (本拠地) 294
honne (本音) 246
honshin (本心) 134
honyaku (本厄) 305
Hotei Oshou (布袋和尚) 406, 523
Hotei (布袋) 406, 410
hoten ronsou (法典論争) 172
hotoke (仏) 122, 182
houji (法事) 186
houjutsu (方術) 297
Houryouji (法隆寺) 395
houshin (放心) 130
housoushi (方相氏) 371
hyuuman sukeepugooto (ヒューマン・スケープゴート) 372

I

iba shinen (意馬心猿) 131

Japanese Words

Ibukiyama (伊吹山) 395
Iesu-no Mitama Kyoukai (イエス之御霊教会) 421
Iezo Kirisuto-sama (イエズ・キリスト様) 237
ie (家) 156, 222
ihai (位牌) 239
ijime (苛め) 150
ikebana (生花) 70
ikigami (生神) 64, 82
ikihadatachi (生膚断) 516
ikihagi (生き剥ぎ) 516
ikimono (生きもの) 496
ikiru chikara (生きる力)) 500
ikiru mono (生きる者) 496
ikiryou (生霊) 120, 126, 293, 295
ikisudama (生魑魅 or 生霊) 295
ikita mono (生きた者) 496
iki (意気) 136
iki (息) 496, 502
ikka wagou (一家和合) 254
ikki (一気) 39
Iku-Musubi-no-Kami (生産霊) 42
Imamiya-Ebisu-Jinja (今宮戎神社) 397
imi (忌 or 斎) 363
inadama (稲魂 or 稲霊 or 稲玉) 122
inari kami (稲荷神) 64
Inari (稲荷) 391
ina (稲) 401
inga (因果) 411
inochi (命) 410, 497, 500
inochi (命 or いのち) 500
intou (咽頭) 496
inu-no hi (戌の日) 32
inyou aiwasu (陰陽相和す) 255
irei (慰霊) 122, 125
irodama (色魂 or 色霊) 122
ishikifumei (意識不明) 507
ishiki (意識) 259, 507
ishi (意志) 136
ishi (意思) 513
issaijouju-no harae (一切成就祓) 369
issho-ni suru (一緒にする) 255
itako (巫子) 311
itaria-shiki (イタリア式) 157

ito (意図) 514
ittaika-no kyouchou (一体化の強調) 156
ittai (一体) 242
Izanagi (伊弉諾神 or 伊邪那岐命 or 伊耶那岐命) 66, 245, 306, 363, 367, 397
Izanami (伊弉冉 or 伊邪那美 or 伊耶那美 or 伊弉弥) 245, 306, 397
Izumo (出雲) 397

J

jibun-no sukikatte-ni (自分の好き勝手に) 153
jibun-to iu zettai ishiki (自分という絶対意識) 286
jibun (自分) 343, 500, 513
jigashin (自我心) 294
jigokudou (地獄道) 29
jigoku-kara mukae-no fune (地獄から迎えの船) 373
jigoku (地獄) 29
Jikkinshou (十訓抄) 408
jikkon (入魂) 118
Jikkunshou (十訓抄) 408
Jikokuten (持国天) 402
jikoshudougata (自己主導型) 91
jinbutsu (人物) 500
jinguu hiki (神宮秘記) 244
jinjashintou (神社神道) 72
jinkaku (人格) 496
jinrei 人霊 (人霊) 294
jinrin-no michi (人倫の道) 250
jinseiun (人生運) 379
jin (仁) 258
jiseishin (自制心) 133
Jizou Bosatsu (地蔵菩薩) 219
Jizou (地蔵) 391
jorei (除霊) 122
joretsu (序列) 156
joubutsu (成仏) 87, 122, 186
Joudo Shinshuu (浄土真宗) 344
Joudoshuu (浄土宗) 219
jourei (浄霊) 122
joutei (上帝) 71
joya-no kane (除夜の鐘) 373
jubutsusuuhai (呪物崇拝) 314

jukuryo (熟慮) 513
jumon (呪文) 299
Juroujin (寿老人) 410, 523
Jusei (寿星) 404
juujuu goen (重々御縁) 378
juumin (住民) 497
juunichoku (十二直) 303
Juunishi (十二支) 303
ju (寿) 405

K

kabi (彼靈) 60
kachou fuugetsu (花鳥風月) 41
kachouken (家長権) 184
kachou (家長) 184
kaeru (蛙) 378
kafuu (家風) 184
kagamimochi (鏡餅) 372
kagayakimiru (照覽) 60
Kagayaku Ake-no Myoujou-to Eien-no Seimei-o Manabu-Kai (輝く明けの明星と永遠の生命を学ぶ会) 286
kago (加護) 301
kaiki (快気) 135
kaimyou (戒名) 239, 379
kakki (活気) 135
kakomirai (過去未来) 411
kakure kirishitan (隠れキリシタン) 236
kakure-nembutsu (隠れ念仏) 236
kakure-no kami (幽神) 84
kami-ai-sai (神会い際) 397
kamiarizuki (神在月) 397
kamidana (神棚) 227, 239, 376
kamidanomi (神頼み) 91
kamigakari (神懸り or 神憑り) 310
kamige (神気) 310
kamigoto (幽冥) 84
kamigoto (幽冥事) 84
kamikakushi (神隠し) 66
kamimamori (神守り) 372
Kami-musubi-no-kami (神皇産霊神) 42, 245
Kami-Musubi-no-Kami (神皇産霊神) 42
Kamimusubi-no-kami (神皇産霊神 or 神産巣日神) 397

kaminari (雷) 69
kaminazuki (神無月) 397
kaminchu (神人) 63
kami-no ko (神の子) 149, 279
kamisama (神様) 206, 351
kami-sane (神さね) 69
kamisan (上さん) 311
kamiteki (神的) 59
kamiwaza (神業) 59
kami-zane (神ざね) 69
kami (上) 59
kami (神) 54, 182, 216, 226, 237, 279, 314, 374, 390, 403
kamu-goto (神言) 370
kamu-kaze (神風) 69
kamunagara-no michi (随神ノ道) 26
kanashibari (金縛) 293
kangae (考え) 514
kangen (甘言) 165, 254
Kangiten-sama (歓喜天様) 392
Kangiten (歓喜天) 392
kan-goto ((神言) 370
kanjusei (感受性) 509
kanju suru (甘受する) 166, 254
kan-kaze (神風) 69
Kankiten (歓喜天) 392
kanki (寒気) 38
kanki (勘気) 136
kanki (換気) 38
kanku (甘苦) 165
kannagara-no michi (神ながらの道) 26
kannazuki (神無月) 397
Kannon (観音) 52, 391
Kannouji (感応寺) 395
kansan (甘酸) 165
kansei (感性) 509
kansha (感謝) 469
kansha (感謝) 188
kanshin (感心) 133
kanshin (関心) 130
kanshoujutsu (観掌術) 301
kanwa kea byoutou (緩和ケア病棟) 260
kanwa (緩和) 260
kao-ga hiroi (顔が広い) 333
ka-on (和音) 264

kao-o dasu (顔を出す) 333
kao-o kashite kudasai (顔を貸してください) 333
karada-no naibu (体の内部) 507
karaku (和楽) 254
karoujisatsu (過労自殺) 258
karoushi (過労死) 258
kashikoki kami (賢き神) 68
kashikomu (畏) 60
kasu (和す) 253
katamari (かたまり or 塊 or 固まり) 160
Katsuragisan (葛城山) 395
Kawasaki Seiwain (河崎清和院) 395
kazeori eboshi (風折烏帽子) 398
kaze (風) 502
kazudama (数魂 or 数霊 or 数玉) 122
kegare (穢れ) 356, 362
kega (怪我) 362
kehai (気配) 36, 40
kei (敬) 257
kemono okaseru tsumi (畜犯せる罪) 362
kemonotaoshi (畜仆し) 517
kendou (剣道) 48
Ken-e-ou (懸衣翁) 373
kenkiseiseibutsu (嫌気性生物) 39
kenkou (健康) 300
kenri (権利) 172
ken (権) 172
kessai (潔斎) 368
kesshin (決心) 131
ketsuen-no oyako (血縁の親子) 87
ke (気) 116
kiai (気合) 48
kiatsu (気圧) 38
kiboku (亀卜) 124
kiboukakusashakai (希望格差社会) 353
kibou (欲望) 496
kibun (気分) 136, 142, 260, 510
Kichidenji (吉田寺) 395
Kichijouten (吉祥天) 405
kichi (吉) 300
ki-ga kawaru (気が変わる) 136
kigaku (気学) 38, 302
ki-ga sumanai (気がすまない) 189
kigi (気々) 138

kigokoro-no shireta yuujin (気心の知れた友人) 138
kihaku (気魄) 116
kihin (気品) 44
kihou (気泡) 39
kijin (鬼神) 66
kijun saseru (帰順させる) 262
kikaki (気化器) 39
kikan (気管) 39, 145
kika (気化) 39
kikentaiitchi (気剣体一致) 48
kikkyoukafuku (吉凶禍福) 370
kikou (気候) 38
kikou (気孔) 39
kikubari (気配り) 138
kikuyu (気球) 38
kimitsu (気密) 38
kimochi (気持) 136, 499
Kinbusan (金峰山) 395
kin-un (金運) 300
kion (気温) 38
ki-o sumasu (気をすます) 189
kirin (麒麟) 68
Kirisuto Sengen (キリスト宣言) 444, 471
kiryoku (気力) 44, 135
kiryuu (気流) 38
kisei (気勢) 135
kishitsu (気質) 136
kishitsu (気性) 136
kishou (気象) 38
kisoku (気息) 39
kisoukan (気送管) 39
Kisshouten (吉祥天) 401
kitai (気体) 39
kiun (気運) 40
kiyasume (気休め) 315
kiyoharae (清祓) 368
kiyoki kokoro (清き心) 133
kiyome (清め) 356, 373
Kiyomizudera (清水寺) 395
kiyuu (帰幽) 294
kizetsu (気絶) 43
ki (気) 34, 77, 135, 141, 143, 145, 310, 315, 507, 511
kodama (木魂 or 木霊 or 木玉) 122

kodou (蠱道) 517
koi (鯉) 398
Kojiki (古事記) 397
kojinshugi (個人主義) 160
kojin-wa saibunka sareru (個人は細分化される) 156
kojin (個人) 500
Kokkurisan (狐狗狸さん) 299
kokochi (心地) 36, 128, 132, 133
kokoroari (心あり) 132
kokoroatari (心当たり) 130
kokorodamashii (心魂) 128
kokorodama (心魂 or 心玉) 128
kokorodate (心立て) 131
kokoroeru (心得る) 130
kokorogaeri (心帰り) 128
kokorogake (心掛け or 心懸) 131
kokorogamae (心構え) 132
kokoro-ga uzuku (心が疼く) 133
kokorogawari (心変わり) 118
kokoro-ga yawaragu (心が和らぐ) 253
kokorogimo (心肝 or 心胆) 129
kokorogokoro (心心) 138
kokorogumi (心組み) 132
kokorogurushii (心苦しい) 133
kokorojitaku (心支度 or 心仕度) 132
kokorokubari (心配) 130
kokoromayoi (心迷い) 132
kokoromochi (心持) 131
kokoronarazu (心ならず) 131
kokoronikui (心憎い) 133
kokoro-ni ukabu (心に浮かぶ) 143
kokoronodoka-ni (心のどかに) 260
kokoro-no hataraki (心の働き) 242
kokoro-no kate (心の糧) 130
kokoro-no kurushimi (心の苦しみ) 509
kokoro-no kusa (心の草) 130
kokoro-no nayami (心の悩み) 509
kokoro-no oni (心の鬼) 133
kokoro-no uma (心の馬) 131, 142
kokoro-o itasu (心を致す) 132
kokoro-o yawarageru (心を和らげる) 254
kokorowasure (心忘れ) 130
kokoroyoui (心用意) 132
kokorozashi (志 or 心指し) 131

kokorozashi (志し or 心指し) 144
kokoro (心) 44, 60, 115, 118, 128, 138, 142, 145, 146, 373, 499, 506, 507, 508, 510, 513
kokugaku (国学) 67
kokumin (国民) 257
kokumi (久美) 516
Kokutai-no Hongi (国体の本義) 250
kokutai (国体) 1
kokyuuki (呼吸器) 497
kokyuu (呼吸) 502
konbaku (魂魄) 115
Konjin (金神) 66
konki (根気) 44
konkyuu (困窮) 497
konpon-no michi (根本の道) 250
kontan (魂胆) 117
kororosasu (志す or 心指す) 131
korosu kami (殺す神) 63
kotai (個体) 161
kotodama (言霊) 370, 379
kotodama (言霊 or 言魂) 122
kotonakare-shugi (事なかれ主義) 259
Koto-Shiro-Nushi-no-Kami (事代主神) 42
Kotoshironushi-no-mikoto (事代主命) 397
koto (琴) 264
Koufukuji (興福寺) 395
Koufuku-no Kagaku (幸福の科学) 393
koufuku (幸福) 257
kougoushii (神々しい) 59
Kougoyaku Seisho (口語訳聖書) 495
koukai (後悔) 514
koukiseibutsu (好気性生物) 39
kouman (高慢) 506
Koumokuten (広目天) 402
Kounomiya Jinja (国府宮神社) 370
koureijutsu (降霊術) 127
kourei (皇霊) 125
kouryo (考慮) 513
koushin (降心) 132
koushin (降神) 127
koutsuuanzenomamori (交通安全お守り) 316
Kouyasan (高野山) 395
Kuan-in (観音) 239

kubi (首 or くび) 497
kuchi-wa wazawai-no kado (口は災いの門) 379
kuchi-yose (口寄せ) 311
kudoku (功徳) 388
Kuni-no Tokotachi (国常立) 244
kunitsugami suuhai (国津神崇拝) 227
kunitsugami (国津神) 66
kunitsukami (国津神) 399
kuro fujou (黒不浄) 362, 363, 364
Kurumajinja (車神社) 402
kusai mono-ni futa-o suru (臭い物に蓋をする) 259
kushizashi (串刺) 516
kusodo (糞戸 or 屎戸) 516
kutsukarada (屈体) 53
kutsurogi amanjiru (寛ぎ安んじる or 寛ぎ甘んじる) 254
kuukirikigaku (空気力学) 38
kuuki (空気) 38, 259, 503
kuyami (悔やみ) 189
kuyashii (悔しい) 189
kuyou (供養) 188, 223
kyakkon (客魂) 129
kyoriyan wakan (草梁倭館) 262
kyoudoutai (共同体) 374
Kyougi-ni Kansuru Chokugo (教育ニ関スル勅語) 250
kyouten (教典) 93
kyouyoku (強欲) 496
kyou (凶) 300
kyuudou (弓道) 53
kyuusai-no dekigoto (救済の出来事) 455
kyuusaishi (救済史) 455
kyuusai (救済) 389
kyuushin (休心) 133
kyuushin (休心 or 休神) 60, 135

M

maboroshi (幻) 411
mabuigume (マブイ籠め) 117
mabuiotoshi (マブイ落とし) 117
machibito (待ち人) 300
maeyaku (前厄) 305
magagoto (凶言) 370

ma-ga sashita (魔が差した) 294
magokoro (真心) 133
majimono (蠱物) 517
majiriau (混じり合う) 255
Makai (魔界) 294
makimono (巻物) 405
Makyaraten (摩訶迦羅天) 399
mamemaki (豆撒き) 377
mandara (曼荼羅 or 曼陀羅) 400
mansoku suru (満足する) 254
Manyoushuu (万葉集) 314
manzoku (満足) 499
marebito (客 or 賓 or 稀人) 398
marehito (客 or 賓) 398
maremono (稀者) 398
maroudo (客 or 賓) 398
marouto (客 or 賓) 398
Matsuomaru (松尾丸) 419
mayoke (魔除け) 314, 356, 376
mazeawaseru (混ぜ合わせる) 255
ma (間) 155
meido (冥土 or 冥途) 294
meikon (冥婚) 218
meikon (迷魂) 186
meishin (迷信) 330
meiwaku (迷惑) 344
memeshii (女々しい) 254
menboku maru tsubure (面目まるつぶれ) 333
menboku-mo nai (面目もない) 333
menboku-o ushinau (面目を失う) 333
messhi houkou (滅私奉公) 161
mi-agamono (身購物) 367
mi-ga narisagaru (実が生り下がる or 身が成り下がる) 378
migawari omamori (身代わりお守り) 314
miiru (魅入る) 127
mikaku (味覚) 497
Miketsu-no-Kami (御膳神) 42
mikokoro (御心) 131
miko (神子) 309
mikuji (御籤 or 神籤) 300
mi-ni tomaru akuji (身に泊まる悪事) 383
minpouten ronsou (民法典論争) 172
minzoku-no shuukyou (民俗の宗教) 25

miroku-no shosa (弥勒の所作) 408
miryoku (魅力) 128
miryousuru (魅了する) 127
misaseru (魅させる) 127
mishirabe (身調べ) 343
misogi-harae (禊祓え) 368
misogi-no ooharai (禊ぎの大祓い) 368
misogi (身削ぎ) 374
misogi (禊ぎ) 356, 367, 373
misuru (魅する) 127
misusugi (身滌ぎ or 身濯ぎ) 374
misu (魅す) 127
mitama (ミタマ) 296
mitama (御魂 or 御霊 or 御玉) 122
mitama (御霊) 126, 127
Mitama (御霊) 503
mitomeru (認める) 93
mitsu (満) 304
miwakusuru (魅惑する) 127
mizoume (溝埋め) 516
mizu-ni nagasu (水に流す) 375
monogokoro 287
monogokoro-ga tsuku (物心が付く) 168
monogokoro (物心) 130, 132
mono-no aware (ものの哀れ) 44
mono-no ke (ものの気) 44, 369
mono-no ke (物の怪) 295
mono-no ke (物の気) 35, 116
mono-no kokoro (ものの心) 44
mono (もの) 45
moriko (もりこ) 311
Morita ryouhou (森田療法) 317
mouja (亡者) 186, 373
mouryou (魍魎) 127
mujou (無常) 47
mukuimatsuru (報い祀る) 219
Mukyoukai (無教会) 421
mune-ga itamu (胸が痛む) 133
mura ujigami (村氏神) 64
mushin (無心) 48
mushi (虫) 343
musubi, musuhi (産霊) 42
muteiken (無定見) 255
muzukashii mono (難しいもの) 260

N

nagitaru (なぎたる) 261
nagi (和凪) 261
nagomu (和む) 254, 260
nagoyaka (和やか) 255
nagusame (慰め) 241
nagushi (和し) 260
nagu (和ぐ or 凪ぐ) 261
naikanhou (内観法) 343
Nakatomi (中臣) 517
nakatsukuni (中津国) 28
namame (雛豆) 371
Nangyoku-Juroujin (南極寿老人) 404
nanten (ナンテン) 314, 377
nanten (ナンテン or 難点) 377
naoinin (儺負人) 371
naoki kokoro (直き心) 133
naru (成) 305
nasake (情け) 143
natsugoshi-no harae (夏越の祓え) 368
natsuishinji (難追神事) 371
nayameru (悩める) 499
na (儺) 371
negai (願い) 510
ne-no kuni soko-no kuni (根国底国) 518
ne-no kuni (根国) 28
nenriki (念力) 136
neseru kami (寝せる神) 63
netsubou (熱望) 498
netsuku (寝付く) 378
nezuku (根付く) 378
nicchuu (日中) 264
nichibei (日米) 264
nichidoku (日独) 264
nichifutsu (日仏) 264
nichiro (日露) 264
Nigihayami Kohaku Nushi (饒速水琥珀主) 87
nigimitama (和御魂) 27, 254, 255
nihonjinron (日本人論) 81
Nihon Kokusai Gideon Kyoukai (日本国際ギデオン協会) 495
nihonkyou (日本教) 81, 244
Nihon seishin (日本精神) 263
nijuushiki (二十四気 or 二十四季) 38

nikibu (和ぶ) 254
nikimu (和む) 254
nikishine (和稲) 255
nikitama (和魂) 254, 255
nikkeijin (日系人) 352
nikoge (和柔毛 or 和毛 or 毳) 253
nikomu (和む) 260
nikoshi (和し or 柔し) 255
nikosumi (和柔炭) 253
nikote (和手 or 柔手) 254
nikutai (肉体) 295
nikutai (肉体) 115
nikuteki (肉的) 123
ningen (人間) 29, 332
ninjou (人情) 143
ninki (人気) 40
nintai (忍耐) 500, 506
nioi (臭い) 503
nippondamashii (日本魂) 118
nisou (尼僧) 61
nodobue (のど笛) 497
nodobue (喉笛) 146
nodoka (閑) 260
nodomaru (和まる) 260
nodomeku (長閑めく or 和めく) 260
nodomu (和む) 260
nodo (閑和) 260
nodo (喉 or のど) 496, 497
nokori-fuku (残り福) 398
nono (のの) 311
nozokisaru (除き去る) 373
nozomi (望み) 498
nuhi (奴婢) 65, 372
nyuukon (入魂) 118
nyuushin (入神) 59

O

obi (帯) 315
obon (御盆) 223, 238
ohara (お腹) 497
okaeshi (お返し) 344, 469
okamin (おかみん) 311
okotoba-ni amaete (おことばに甘えて) 166
oku-no oku (奥の奥) 509
omoidasu (思い出す) 513
omoiokosu (思い起こす) 513
omoiyari (思いやり) 241, 250
omoi (思い) 115
omote kimon (表鬼門) 376
onibaba (鬼婆) 373
onigami (鬼神) 66
oni (鬼) 63, 120, 377
Onmakyara (御摩訶迦羅) 399
onmyoushi (陰陽師) 376
ono-ga ko okasu tsumi (おのが子犯す罪) 362
onryou (怨霊) 126, 295, 296
onwa n (温和) 255
onwa (温和) 254
on (恩) 189, 250, 257, 344, 469
Ooanamuchi-no-mikoto (大己貴命) 399
ooguchi-magami (大口真神) 68
ooharae (大祓) 368
ookami (狼) 68
Ookuninushi-no-Mikoto (大国主命) 397, 399
Ookuninushi (大国主) 397
Oo-Maga-tsu-Bi-no-Kami (大禍津日神 or 大枉津日神) 66
oomisogi (大禊) 383
Oomisoka (大晦日) 373
oomitama (大御魂 or 大御霊 or 大御玉) 122
Oomiya-Me-no-Kami (大宮売神) 42
Oomononushi-no-kami (大物主神) 399
Oomoto-kyou (大元教) 313
oomoto (大元) 61
Oonakatomi (大中臣) 517
Ooshima-no Kuni (大八洲の国 or 大八島の国) 262
ootomurai (大弔い) 238
oroshi (卸し or 下ろし or 降ろし) 311
osan (収) 305
oshichiya (お七夜) 395
oshie (教え) 93
otentousama (お天道様) 71
otoborai (大弔い) 238
otodama (音魂 or 音霊 or 音玉) 122
otogaborai (大弔い) 238

ouben (オーベン) 59
ougi (扇) 407
oyabun-kobun (親分子分) 158, 171
oyagami (祖神) 64
oya-koukou (親孝行) 221
oyayubi (親指) 362, 377

P
Paburou-sama (パブロウ様) 238
pan-no katamari (パンの塊) 160
parasaito shinguru (パラサイトシングル) 353

R
raise (来世) 388
reianshitsu (霊安室) 125
reibaijutsu (霊媒術 *or* 冷媒術) 125
reibai (霊媒 *or* 冷媒) 125
reiboku (霊木) 124
reibutsu (霊物) 125, 126
reibyou (霊廟) 125
reichigaku (霊智学) 127
reichi (霊知 *or* 霊智) 124
reichi (霊地) 124
reichi (霊池) 127
reichourui (霊長類) 124
reichou (霊長) 124
reichou (霊鳥) 124
reidai (霊代) 125
reidai (霊台) 122
reidan (霊壇) 126
reiden (霊殿) 125
reidou (霊動) 123
reidou (霊堂) 126
reieki (霊液) 124
reien (霊園) 125
reifu (霊府) 122
reifu (霊符) 126
reigen (霊験) 126
reihai (霊牌) 125
reihou (霊宝) 124
reihou (霊峰) 124, 127
reii (霊位) 125
reii (霊威) 126
reii (霊異) 123

reiji (霊寺) 124
reijou (霊場) 124
reijuu (霊獣) 123
reikai (霊怪) 123
reikai (霊界) 123
reikan (霊感) 127
reika (霊化) 123
reika (霊歌) 123
reiken (霊剣) 124
reiken (霊見) 127
reikin (霊禽) 123
reiki (霊域) 124
reiki (霊気) 40, 42
reiki (霊亀) 124
reikoku (霊告) 127
reikon fumetsu (霊魂不滅) 120
reikon (霊魂) 115, 122, 123, 134
reikoujutsu 霊交術) 125
reikou (霊交) 125
reikou (霊光) 126
reikyou (霊境) 124
reikyou (霊香) 123
reikyuusha (霊柩車) 125
reikyuu (霊柩) 125
reimu (霊夢) 127
reimyou-naru michi (霊妙なる道) 297
reimyou (霊妙) 123
reiniku (霊肉) 123
reiou (霊応) 126
reiryoku-o appu suru (霊力がアップする) 295
reiryoku (霊力) 42, 122, 124, 314
reisatsu (霊刹) 124, 126
reisei (霊性) 45, 126
reisei (霊生) 123
reiseki (霊石) 124
reiseki (霊跡 *or* 霊迹) 126
reisen (霊泉) 124
reisha (霊舎 or 霊社) 125
reisha (霊社) 126
reisha (霊車) 125
reishi (霊祀) 125
reishou (霊障) 295
reisou (霊草) 124
reisui (霊水) 124

reitai (霊体) 294, 295
reitaku (霊託) 127
reiteki seibutsurei (霊的生物霊) 294
reiteki (霊的) 123
reiteki (霊笛) 123
reitoku (霊徳) 124
reitou (霊灯) 126
reiun (霊雲) 125
reiu (霊雨) 124, 126
reiyaku (霊薬) 124
reizan (霊山) 124, 127
reiza (霊座) 125
reizen (霊前) 126
reizou (霊像) 126
reizui (霊瑞) 124
rei (霊) 42, 121, 128, 141, 143, 145, 491, 502, 506
Rengeouin (蓮花王院) 395
Ribingu Baiburu (リビングバイブル) 495
rikairyoku (理解力) 513
rikai (理解) 511
rinri (倫理) 332
risei (理性) 512
Rokkakudou (六角堂) 395
Rokuharamizuji (六波羅蜜寺) 395
rokuyou (六曜) 302
roku (禄) 405
Roujinsei (老人星) 404
Roushi (老子) 404
ruiji shuukyou (類似宗教) 389
rusugami (留守神) 397
ryoubo (霊簿) 125
ryoubyou (霊病) 125
ryouge (霊気) 124
ryougu (霊供) 125, 126
ryoukokukan-no wa (両国間の和) 261
ryoushin (良心) 133, 514
Ryuu-ou (竜王) 400

S

sagashimono (探し物) 300
sahou (作法) 257
Saidaiji (西大寺) 395
saikikappatsu (才気活発) 136
saiki (才気) 135

Sai-no kawara Jizou wasan (賽の河原地蔵和讃) 219
sakahagi (逆剥ぎ) 516
sakki (殺気) 40
sakkoku (鎖国) 250
sakoku (鎖国) 154
sakubyougami (作病神) 377
San Juan-sama (サンフアン様) 238
sansen soumoku (山川草木) 41
Santa Mariya-sama (サンタマリヤ様) 237
sanzan (三三 or 産山 or 散々) 378
sanzan (散々) 378
Sanzugawa (三途河) 373
satori (悟り) 21, 279, 513
satoru kokoro (悟る心) 511
segakie (施餓鬼会) 187
seibutsurei (生物霊) 294
seichoku (正直) 374
seichouun (成長運) 379
seidou (聖堂) 45
seifuu (西風) 502
seigi (kokka, 正義国家) 424
seiheiki (青碧) 52
Sei-Heki (青碧) 491
seijin-no-hi (成人の日) 301, 317
seikatsu (生活) 300
seiki (正気) 135
seiki (生気) 39
seiki (精気) 39
seikon (精魂) 116
seimeihandan (姓名判断) 379
seimei-no ibuki (生命のいぶき) 503
seimeiryoku (生命力) 503
sei-naru (聖なる) 395
seirei (生霊) 295
seirei (精霊) 122
seirei (聖霊) 127, 295
seiryoku (精霊) 370
seishin kougo sayou (精神交互作用) 317
seishin (精神) 115, 250
Seitou-sha (青鞜社) 159
seizensetsu (性善説) 285
sekensama (世間様) 351
sekentai (世間体) 205
sekimenkyoufushou (赤面恐怖症) 333

sekinin (責任) 207
sekkachi (せっかち) 505
semei seichoku (清明正直) 374
semeru (責める) 207
semushi (傴 or 僂) 516
senbu (先負) 303
sengachi (先勝) 303
senjutsu (仙術) 297
senkachi (先勝) 303
senmake (先負) 303
senryo (占拠) 294
senshou (先勝) 303
senzodana (先祖棚) 227
senzosuuhai (先祖崇拝) 227
senzo, 先祖 187
Seoritsu-hime (瀬織津姫) 518
seppuku (切腹) 134
setsubou (切望) 498, 499, 510
setsubun (節分) 371, 377
setsuri (摂理) 242
setsuwa (説話) 390
sewa (世話) 344
shakaikyoufu (社会恐怖) 333
shakaiun (社会運) 379
shakkou (赤口) 303
shichidaiji (七大寺) 395
shichifukujin (七福神) 522
Shichifukujin (七福神) 387, 416
shichi-go-san (七五三) 316
shichikanon (七観音) 395
shichikousan (七高山) 395
shichinansokumetsu (七難即滅) 396
shifuku (至福) 408
shigo-no seizon (死後の生存) 393
shihairei (支配霊) 294
shikei (死刑) 500
shikimaki (重播き or 頻蒔き) 516
Shikishima-no Kuni (敷島の国 or 磯城島の国) 262
shiki (志気) 136
shikke, shikki (湿気) 38
shimo (下) 59
Shinbousan (神峰山) 395
shinbutsu bunri-no rei (神仏分離の令) 82
shinbutsu shuugou (神仏集合) 82

shingan (心眼) 130
shingi (神技) 59
shingonshuu (真言宗) 71
shinhadatachi (死膚断) 516
shinigami (死神) 66
shi-ni (死に) 378
shini (心意) 131
shinjin gouitsu (神人合一) 87
shinji (心耳) 132, 143
shinji (神事) 130, 368
shinjou (心情) 133
Shinkaiyaku Seisho (新改訳聖書) 495
shinkeikei (神経系) 61
shinkeishitsu (神経質) 317
shinkei (神経) 61
shinki (心気 or 神気) 135
shinki (心気 or 神気) 60
shinki (神気) 61, 310
shinkon (心魂) 128
shinkon (心魂 or 神魂) 60, 135
shinkon (身魂) 128
shinkou shuukyou (新興宗教) 390
shinkou (信仰) 93, 389
Shinkyoudouyaku (新共同訳) 495
Shinnmin-no Michi (臣民の道) 161
shi-no jittai (死の実体) 286
shin otoko (紳男) 370
shinpai (心配) 130, 138, 344, 511
shinpai (神拝) 53
shinpenka (神変化) 69
shinrai (信頼) 93
shinrai (神来) 127
shinrei (神霊) 121, 126
Shinritou (真理党) 445
shinri (真理) 512
shinsei (心性) 131
Shinsenen (神泉苑) 296
shinsen (心洗) 374
shinshinshuukyou (新新宗教) 313
Shinshinshuukyou (新新宗教) 392
shinshin (心神) 39, 61
shinshin (心身) 128
shinshoku jijaku (神色自若) 61
shinshoku (神色) 61
shinshudougata (神主導型) 90

shinshutsu kibotsu (神出鬼没) 66
Shinshuukyou (新宗教) 392
shinsoku (神速) 61
shintai (神体) 69
shinteki (心的) 129
shintou (神道) 297
shintsuu (心痛) 133
shinwa (神話) 66
shinzouhossa (心臓発作) 507
shinzou (心像) 130
shinzou (心臓) 146, 507
shinzui (真髄 or 神髄) 61
shirahito (白人) 516
shiranu hotoke (知らぬ仏) 63
shiranu kami (知らぬ神) 63
shirei (死霊) 125, 186, 293, 295
shiryou kekkon (死霊結婚) 218
shisha (死者) 296
shisshin (失心) 132
shisshin (失心 or 失神) 60
shisshin (失心 or 失神) 135
shitai (死体) 501
shiten-ou (四天王) 402
shizenryoku (自然力) 141
shizen shuukyou (自然宗教) 387
shi (死 or 四) 378
shogun (将軍) 485
shoki (暑気) 38
shokudou (食道) 496
shokuyoku (飲食) 498
shokuyoku (食欲) 498
shonanoka (初七日) 395
shosa (所作) 408
shoubu-un (勝負運) 300
shoujiki (正直) 375
shoujou (猩猩) 410
shoukon (商魂) 118
shoumon (唱門 or 唱聞) 29
shounakou (小儺公) 371
shouna-no kimi (小儺公) 371
shouna (小儺) 371
shourai (将来) 411
shouran (照覽) 60
shouryou (精霊) 125
Shouten (聖天) 392

shou (小) 316
shujou (衆生) 401
shuudanshugi (集団主義) 160
shuudan (集団) 156
shuuhashintou (宗派神道) 72
shuukyou (宗教) 25
sonzai (存在) 500
soreishinkou (祖霊信仰) 210
sorei (祖霊) 125, 186
soroban (算盤) 265
sosengami (祖先神) 64
sosenkyou (祖先教) 173
sosensuuhai (祖先崇拝) 210
soshin (祖神) 64
Soukagakkai (創価学会) 388
soushin (送心) 130
soushin (送心 or 送神) 60, 135
souun (総運) 379
souwa (総和) 253
soyokaze (微風) 502
sudama (魅) 115, 121, 127
sue-kichi (末吉) 300
sue-shoukichi (末小吉) 300
suijouki (水蒸気) 38
sukui (救い) 410
Sukunahikona-no-kami (少名毘古那神) 399
Sumemima-no Mikoto (皇美麻命) 84
sumimasen (すみません) 342
sumou (相撲) 375
sunao (素直) 318
Susanoo-no-Mikoto (素戔嗚尊 or 須佐之男命) 397
Susanoo (素戔嗚尊 or 須佐之男命) 367
suteru kami (捨てる神) 63
suuhai (崇拝) 189
Suwa-Jinja (諏訪神社) 370
suzuki (鱸) 398

T

tadashiki kokoro (正しき心) 133
taeshinobu (耐え忍ぶ) 500
tahira (平) 304
tahoutou (多宝塔) 402
taian (大安) 303

taifuu (大風) 396
taigen kousoshin (大元高祖神) 42
Taigen Kousoshin (大元高祖神) 245
taijin kyoufushou (対人恐怖症) 333
taijin kyoufu (対人恐怖) 333
taika (大火) 396
taiki (大気) 38
tairyou (大量) 409
taisui (大水) 396
tai (鯛) 379, 398
takaburu kokoro (高ぶる心) 506
takagami (高神) 64
takamagahara (高天原) 28
Takamimusubi-no-kami (高御産巣日神 or 高皇産霊神) 397
Takami-musubi-no-kami (高皇産霊神) 42, 244
Takami-Musubi-no-Kami (高皇産霊神) 42
takarabune (宝船) 394
takatsukami-no wazawai (高つ神の災) 363
takatsukami-no wazawai (高津神の災) 517
takatsutori-no wazawai (高つ鳥の災) 363
takatsutori-no wazawai (高津鳥の災) 517
Take-Maka-Zuchi-no-Oo-no-kami (建御雷之男神) 69
takiabi (滝浴び) 383
tamagaeri (魂帰り) 118, 128
tamakiharu (魂極る or 霊極る or 玉極る) 122
tamamatsuri (魂祭 or 霊祭 or 玉祭) 122
tamamukae (魂迎 or 霊迎 or 玉迎) 122
tama-no o (玉の緒 or 魂の緒) 119
tamaokuri (魂送 or 霊送 or 玉送) 122
tamashii (たましい) 145
tamashii (魂) 119, 127, 140, 145, 286, 499, 500
tamashii (魂 or 魄) 115
tamashiro (霊代) 125
tamashizume-no matsuri (魂鎮めの祭) 116
Tama-Tsume-Musubi-no-Kami (魂留産霊) 42
tamaya (魂屋 or 霊室 or 玉屋) 122

tamaya (霊室) 125
tama (魂) 69, 140
Tamonten (多聞天) 402
Tamon (多聞) 402
tanki-na mono (短気な者) 505
ta-no kami (田の神) 399
taosu kami (倒す神) 63
tara (鱈) 398
Taru-Musubi-no-Kami (足産霊) 42
tatarirei (祟霊) 296
tatari (祟り) 187, 293, 296
tatemae (建前) 246
tateshakai (タテ社会) 155
tatsudou (達道) 256
tatsu (建) 304
tawayame (手弱女) 254, 255
tengu (天狗) 120
tenjin chigi (天神地祇) 66
tenjou-no takamagahara (天上の高天原) 28
tenjou (天上) 29
tenki (天気) 38
Tennou (天皇) 70, 161
Tenrikyou (天理教) 313
Tenshoukoutaijinguukyou (天照皇大神宮教) 313
tenshu (天主) 71, 84
tentai-no ihen (天体の異変) 396
ten (天) 71
Terakoya (寺子屋) 419
tessekishin (鉄石心) 131, 144
tesshin (鉄心) 131
tobu tori-no wazawai (飛ぶ鳥の災) 517
tokeau (溶け合う) 255
tokoshieteki seimei (永久的な生命) 45
tomoe (巴 or 鞆絵) 400
tomo (友) 65
Tooka-Ebisu (十日恵比寿) 398
torii (鳥居) 45
torimono (執物 or 取物) 369
toriuranai (鳥占い) 229
toshikoshi-no harae (年越の祓) 368
Toudaiji (東大寺) 395
toufuu (東風) 502
toukon (闘魂) 118

Japanese Words 675

Toukyou Monogatari (東京物語) 174
touyou-no doutoku, seiyou-no gijutsu (東洋の道徳、西洋の技術) 224
touzoku (盗賊) 396
Toyo Ashihara-no Chiaki Nagaioaki-no Mizuyoguni (豊葦原之千秋長五百秋之水穂国) 263
toyoashihara-no mizuho-no kuni (豊葦原の瑞穂の国) 28
Toyo Ashihara-no Nakatsu-Kuni (豊葦原中つ国) 262
toyoko-no kuni (常世の国) 28
Toyouke (豊受) 244
tozu (閉) 305
tsuchi-no katamari (土の塊) 160
tsuina (追儺) 371
Tsukiyomi-no-Mikoto (月読尊) 397
tsumi (罪) 293, 367, 369
tsumi (罰) 368
tsuradamashii (面魂) 118
tsurasa (辛さ) 419
tsura (面 or 頬) 333

U

ubusuna kami (産土神 or 生土神 or 産社神) 64
uchide-no-kozuchi (打ち出の小槌) 400
uchitokeru (打ち解ける) 254
ue (飢え) 497, 498
ujibito (氏人) 65
ujigami (氏神) 64
uji-no kami (氏の神) 65
uji (氏) 65
ukajin (宇賀神) 401
uka (食) 401
uke (食) 401
umashisa (うましさ) 242
umashi (美味し) 169
uma-uma (うまうま) 169
uma (うま) 169
umi-no ki (海の気) 38
unasaka (海境 or 海坂 or 海界) 29
unmei (運命) 500
unubare (うぬばれ) 506
un (運) 301

urabon (盂蘭盆) 187
ura kimon (裏鬼門) 376
urami (怨み) 295
uranaiwa-no kami (卜庭神) 297
uranaki (心泣き) 129
ura (心) 129
usagi-kami (兎神) 68
utagokoro (歌心) 129

W

wabei (和米) 264
waboku koushou (和睦交渉) 261
waboku (和睦) 261
wabun (和文) 264
wadoku (和独) 264
wado (倭奴) 262
waei (和英) 264
wafutsu (和仏) 264
wafuu kenchiku (和風建築) 265
wafuu-no tatemono (和風の建物) 265
wafuu ryokan (和風旅館) 265
wafuu (和風) 265
wagaku (和学) 264
wagaku (和楽) 264
wagashi (和菓子) 265
wage (和解) 264
wagin (和琴) 264
wagi (和議) 261
wagotoshi (和事師) 255
wagoto (和事) 255
wagou (和合) 254
wago (倭語) 262
wago (和語) 265
wagura (和鞍) 265
wain (和韻) 256
wai (和裁) 264
wajin (倭人) 262
wakai suru (和解する) 255
wakai (和解) 261
wakai (和諧) 261
waka miko (若巫女) 311
waka-no miya (若の宮) 311
wakan (和姦) 256
wakan (和漢) 264
waka (若) 311

waka (和歌) 264
wakeiseijaku (和敬清寂) 257
waki aiai (和気靄靄 or 和気藹藹) 261
waki (和気) 261
wakonkansai (和魂漢才) 119
wakonyousai (和魂洋才) 119
wakon (和魂) 254, 255
wakun (和訓 or 倭訓) 264
wakyou (和協) 254
wamono (和物) 265
wa-o midasu (和を乱す) 280
wa-o musubu (和を結ぶ) 261
wa-on (和音) 264
waon (和音) 256
waraku (和楽) 264
waro (和露) 264
wasai (和裁) 264
wasan (和産 or 倭産) 264
wasan (和算) 265
wasan (和讃) 264
waseigaku (和声学) 256
waseihou (和声法) 256
wasei (和製) 264
wasen jouyaku (和戦条約) 261
wasen (和戦) 261
washiki benjo (和式便所) 265
washiki eihou (和式泳法) 265
washiki (和式) 265
washin jouyaku (和親条約) 261
washin (和親) 261
washitsu (和室) 265
washi (和紙) 265
washi (和詩 or 倭詩) 264
washuu (和習) 265
waso (和装) 264
wasuru (和する) 255, 261
watakushi (私) 501
watashi (わたし) 501
wateki uta (和的歌) 264
wayaku (和訳) 264
wayou kenchiku (和様建築) 265
wayou (和様) 265
wazawai (災) 363
wa (和) 249, 374

Y

yaburu (破) 304
Yachioko-no-kami (八千矛神) 399
Yaekotoshironushi-no-kami (八重言代主神) 397
yaki (夜気) 38
yakubyougami (疫病神) 371
yakubyouki (疫病鬼) 121
yakudoshi-no hito (厄年の人) 371
yakudoshi (厄年) 305, 371
Yakushiji (薬師寺) 395
Yakushi-Nyorai (薬師如来) 403
Yakushi (薬師) 391, 403
yaku (厄) 371
yama-no ki (山の気) 38
yamato-damashii (大和魂) 263
yamatodamashii (大和魂) 118, 132
yamato-e (大和絵) 264
yamato-goe (和音 or 倭音) 264
yamatogokoro (大和心) 118, 132
Yamato-hime-no Mikoto Seiki (倭姫命世記) 409
Yamato-hime (倭姫) 409
yamatokotoba (倭語) 262
yamato-nadeshiko (大和撫子) 264
Yamato (大和) 65, 70
Yamato (大和 or 山跡 or 山迹) 263
Yamato (倭) 262
yashiki ujigami (屋敷氏神) 64
Yaso-Maga-tsu-Bi-no-Kami (八十禍津日神 or 八十枉津日神) 66
yasuragi (安らぎ) 242
Yatsu-no Kami (谷津の神 or 夜刀神) 68
yawarageru (和らげる) 254
yawarage (和) 260
yawaragu (和らぐ) 253
yawaraida (やわらいだ) 257
yawarakai (和らかい) 254
yawarakai (和らかい or らかい or 軟らかい) 253
yawaraka (和らか or 柔らか or 軟らか) 254
yawasu (和す) 262
yogore (汚れ) 356
yogoto (吉言) 370

Yoi-Ebisu (宵恵比寿) 398
yokeru (除ける) 316
yokkyuu (欲求) 498
yokubou (欲望) 496, 498, 500, 510
yokujou (欲情) 497, 510
yomi-no kuni (黄泉の国) 28
yomi-no kuni (夜見の国) 28
yomotsukami (黄泉神) 29
yoru-no kehai (夜の気配) 40
youjin (用心) 132
yousha (容赦) 301
yume (夢) 411
yunagi (夕和凪) 261
yurumeru (緩める) 260
yurushi (容赦) 301
yuukai (幽界) 294
yuuke (夕占) 298
yuuki (勇気) 506
yuumeikai (幽冥界) 84
yuurei (幽霊) 122, 125, 126

Z

zange (懺悔) 188
zatokata (ざとたか) 311
zazen (座禅) 21
zeninashi-no ichidachi (銭無しの市立ち) 406
zenken (全権) 504
zenrei (善霊) 370
zense (前世) 286
zenshin (善心) 133
zentaiun (全体運) 300
Zoujouten (増長天) 402
zouka (造化) 41

Langham Literature and its imprints are a ministry of Langham Partnership.

Langham Partnership is a global fellowship working in pursuit of the vision God entrusted to its founder John Stott –

> *to facilitate the growth of the church in maturity and Christ-likeness through raising the standards of biblical preaching and teaching.*

Our vision is to see churches in the majority world equipped for mission and growing to maturity in Christ through the ministry of pastors and leaders who believe, teach and live by the Word of God.

Our mission is to strengthen the ministry of the Word of God through:
- nurturing national movements for biblical preaching
- fostering the creation and distribution of evangelical literature
- enhancing evangelical theological education

especially in countries where churches are under-resourced.

Our ministry

Langham Preaching partners with national leaders to nurture indigenous biblical preaching movements for pastors and lay preachers all around the world. With the support of a team of trainers from many countries, a multi-level programme of seminars provides practical training, and is followed by a programme for training local facilitators. Local preachers' groups and national and regional networks ensure continuity and ongoing development, seeking to build vigorous movements committed to Bible exposition.

Langham Literature provides majority world preachers, scholars and seminary libraries with evangelical books and electronic resources through publishing and distribution, grants and discounts. The programme also fosters the creation of indigenous evangelical books in many languages, through writer's grants, strengthening local evangelical publishing houses, and investment in major regional literature projects, such as one volume Bible commentaries like *The Africa Bible Commentary* and *The South Asia Bible Commentary*.

Langham Scholars provides financial support for evangelical doctoral students from the majority world so that, when they return home, they may train pastors and other Christian leaders with sound, biblical and theological teaching. This programme equips those who equip others. Langham Scholars also works in partnership with majority world seminaries in strengthening evangelical theological education. A growing number of Langham Scholars study in high quality doctoral programmes in the majority world itself. As well as teaching the next generation of pastors, graduated Langham Scholars exercise significant influence through their writing and leadership.

To learn more about Langham Partnership and the work we do visit **langham.org**

www.ingramcontent.com/pod-product-compliance
Lightning Source LLC
Chambersburg PA
CBHW050514020526
44111CB00052B/1553